CHINA'S FOREIGN PLACES

CHINA'S FOREIGN PLACES

*The Foreign Presence in China in the Treaty Port Era,
1840–1943*

ROBERT NIELD

Hong Kong University Press
The University of Hong Kong
Pokfulam Road
Hong Kong
www.hkupress.org

© 2015 Hong Kong University Press

ISBN 978-988-8139-28-6 (*Hardback*)

All rights reserved. No portion of this publication may be reproduced or transmitted in any form or by any means, electronic or mechanical, including photocopy, recording, or any information storage or retrieval system, without prior permission in writing from the publisher.

British Library Cataloguing-in-Publication Data
A catalogue record for this book is available from the British Library.

10 9 8 7 6 5 4 3 2 1

Printed and bound by Paramount Printing Co., Ltd., Hong Kong, China

In presenting to the public the following pages, the [writer has] had but one object in view—that of producing a book of general use for intending visitors to, and residents in, the [country] of which it treats. As the first attempt to embody in a comprehensive and accessible form the various important particulars scattered over the many works upon China ... hitherto published, a certain amount of consideration will doubtless be accorded by the public. To have entered fully into the historical details respecting each port which would be necessary to form a work of sufficient completeness to satisfy a student of Eastern policy in these countries, would be obviously beyond the scope of a single volume, nor has such been its object. While not pretending to these claims, there is, it may be hoped, much which will be found new and unknown to the general mass of readers.

— From the preface to *The Treaty Ports of China and Japan*
by Mayers, Dennys and King, published in 1867

Contents

Preface ... ix
Acknowledgements ... xiii
Timeline ... xv
Maps ... xx
Treaty Ports and Other Foreign Stations ... xxxi
Principal Characters ... xxxvii
Introduction ... 1

Aigun	23	Kiukiang	137
Amoy	24	Kiungchow	141
Antung	37	Kongmoon	146
Baku	39	Kowloon	147
Canton	39	Kuling	150
Changsha	49	Kwangchowwan	151
Chefoo	51	Kweilin	153
Chengtu	66	Lappa	153
Chimmo Bay	67	Lintin Island	154
Chinchew Bay	68	Lungchow	155
Chinkiang	68	Lungkow	156
Chinwangtao	73	Macao	157
Chungking	75	Mengtse	158
Chusan	80	Mokanshan	159
Cumsingmoon	82	Mukden	160
Dalny/Dairen	82	Nanking	162
Foochow	85	Nanning	164
Haichow	95	Newchwang	166
Hangchow	95	Ningpo	173
Hankow	97	Pakhoi	181
Harbin	118	Peitaiho	184
Hokow	121	Peking	186
Hong Kong	121	Port Arthur	188
Ichang	133	Port Hamilton	191
Kashkar	136	Saddle Islands	192

Samshui	192	Tsingtao	252
Sanmun Bay	195	Wanhsien	258
Santuao	195	Weihaiwei	259
Shanghai	196	Wenchow	271
Shanhaikwan	209	Whampoa	277
Shasi	210	Woosung	279
Soochow	211	Wuchow	281
Swatow	213	Wuhu	283
Szemao	224	Yochow	286
Tachienlu	225	Yunnan-fu	288
Taiwan-fu	225	Russian Frontier Stations	288
Taku	229	Japanese Stations in the North-East	289
Tamsui	230	Yangtze River Ports-of-Call	291
Tengyueh	234	West River Ports-of-Call	292
Tientsin	235	Tibetan Ports	292
Tsinan	250		

Appendix	295
Notes	297
Glossary of Terms	329
Bibliography	331
Index	347

Preface

This book grew from an interest in the treaty ports of China, an interest that developed into a fascination—and then an obsession. On moving to Hong Kong from England in 1980 I became aware of the very special nature of the city. While being difficult to find on a map of the globe, this tiny place boasted the world's tenth-largest trading economy. It was an anachronism with little right to such economic status, and yet . . . In addition to spending all hours of the day contributing to the continuing prosperity of Hong Kong through my work as a public accountant, I started to take an interest in why it was that Hong Kong enjoyed such success; indeed, why it was there at all. Nor was Hong Kong alone in terms of European settlements tacked on to the side of China. All of these are now Chinese towns or cities of varying size but many of them retain a trace, or rather more, of their former foreign occupation.

My initial research focused on the European commercial approaches to China, starting with the Portuguese in the 16th century, then the Dutch in the 17th. The British became dominant in the 18th and 19th centuries, and that dominance led to a conflict that gave rise to not only the colony of Hong Kong but also the first five treaty ports—Amoy (Xiamen), Canton (Guangzhou), Foochow (Fuzhou), Ningpo (Ningbo) and Shanghai. I described these six cities, and the historical background to the treaty port system, in my book *The China Coast: Trade and the First Treaty Ports*, published in 2010. My next step was obvious—to describe each of the former treaty ports of China individually in a new book. This was last done in 1867, when Mayers, Dennys and King produced their monumental *The Treaty Ports of China and Japan*. My update would include not only treaty ports, but the many other foreign commercial settlements in China, large and small.

It has been said that, as they are by definition on the periphery, 'most written history has treated port cities rather shabbily'.[*] Indeed, surprisingly little has been written about a great many of China's treaty ports as individual places. Frances Wood's *No Dogs and Not Many Chinese: Treaty Port Life in China 1843–1943*, published in 1997, provides an admirable, accessible overview. One or two ports have been the subject of comprehensive histories, although some of these are now not easy to find. Examples include O. D. Rasmussen's *Tientsin: An Illustrated Outline History* (1925) and William T. Rowe's *Hankow: Commerce and Society in a Chinese City, 1796–1889* (1984). There are excellent volumes on the history and development of Hong Kong and Shanghai. Some books cover one particular issue in the majority of treaty ports without describing many of them in detail, such as P. D. Coates's *The China Consuls* (1988). References to some of the more obscure ports may be found in the indexes of even more obscure books. My mission was to bring each place to life by providing interesting and concise information not readily available elsewhere. I also wanted to make my entries as complete as possible, using all the sources my detection skills could identify. Only the entries on Hong Kong and Shanghai have been given a different treatment. Their inclusion in the same manner as the others would have created a volume many times the size of this one. Instead, I have provided a concise history of these two cities over the relevant period without attempting to make those histories complete.

Places that served solely as missionary stations have been excluded, firstly because they have been extensively documented elsewhere (for examples, see Cohen's *China and Christianity* [1963] and Carlson's

---
[*] Osterhammel, 277.

The Foochow Missionaries [1974]); and, secondly, because my chief interest is in commercial activity. What is left is a comprehensive summary of the many Chinese places that at one stage came under foreign administration to a greater or lesser degree during the Treaty Port Era, roughly 1840 to 1943. Most entries start with a brief background history, in order to put the place in context. Similarly, I have assumed some knowledge of events happening on the Chinese and world stages on the part of my readers, so as to concentrate on matters at the local level in each of the places covered. For example, the individual stages of the Second Opium War are not explicated, but the entry on Canton describes that conflict to the extent it had a direct bearing on the city.

Each entry is intended to stand alone (although the option to read the book cover to cover is, of course, available). This requires some degree of repetition, although I have ensured that where this happens—the story of tea, for example—there is a different yet relevant and complete treatment in each of the entries affected. Continuing the example, I have not attempted to research and write about the subject of tea per se, but I have included the material I found while researching, in this case, Hankow (Hankou) and Foochow. Although there is very little to be said about some of the smallest places covered, the length of each entry does not necessarily reflect its subject's relative importance. Rather, length has tended to be determined by the amount of interesting source material available.

In most cases a separate entry for each of the ports and other places covered has been given. Taku (Dagu), for example, had a history and existence that was independent of Tientsin (Tianjin), its much bigger neighbour. Similarly Hong Kong and Kowloon are treated separately; Kowloon was an extremely important customs station that operated independently of Hong Kong. However, where two or more places were so closely related that separate entries would have been pedantic, I have combined them—Swatow (Shantou) and Namoa (Nanao), for example, and Tamsui (Danshui) and Keelung (Jilong). Where there are books that add further information about specific ports I have listed these in a 'Further reading' note at the end of the relevant entry. Furthermore, the Bibliography at the end of the book has been made as comprehensive as possible, to encourage further reading and research and be of use to other scholars.

Initially, my goal was to visit all the places that merited an entry in this book. These good intentions faltered in the face of harsh realities, for instance the inadvisability of poking about areas close to the North Korean border, and logistical difficulties such as tramping through Manchuria looking for remote former Japanese and Russian outposts. Nor would visiting a place that only existed for one or two years as a treaty port a hundred years ago necessarily add value to a written description of its brief role. Nevertheless I have travelled extensively in China gathering information and impressions. The 69 places I visited are listed in the Appendix. Effort was required to overcome significant difficulties in establishing exact locations and present place names for each place included in the book. Landing stages on the West River and Russian trading posts in Manchuria presented special challenges. A combination of Google Earth satellite imagery and as many maps, new and old, as could be found allowed most location puzzles to be solved.

During my travels I was frequently impressed by the interest ordinary Chinese people took in what I was doing. Taxi drivers happily took over the responsibility for finding some of the more remote places, and then accompanied me round them. Security men asked for copies of my old photographs of the buildings they were guarding. People in the street asked why I was examining what appeared, to them, a crumbling old building. Many of the old Treaty Port-Era buildings are, however, far from crumbling. Chinese provincial and city governments have undertaken many first-class renovation projects. Furthermore, buildings in Pakhoi (Beihai), Kongmoon (Jiangmen) and Foochow have been relocated to make way for a development or a road-widening, when demolition would have been much cheaper and easier. This is both impressive and encouraging.

To help the reader visualize the world of the treaty ports I have illustrated the book with over 130 photographs, postcards and maps from the relevant period, many of which have rarely been seen elsewhere. Almost all are specifically related to something mentioned in the text and come from over 50 different sources.

This narrative has been constructed from a myriad of sources, most of them in English. This does not reflect a desire to portray one particular viewpoint, and if the same story were told using primarily Chinese sources, interpretations, emphases and narrative structure would be very different. The same could be said of books based on Japanese, Russian or German documents dating from this period. There are other books on the treaty ports waiting to be written; their various 'truths' will further illuminate a deeply complex subject.

Much of the content of this book is based on primary sources largely previously unused in the context of the British treaty ports. In particular I have drawn extensively on the National Archives in London, old newspapers published in Hong Kong and elsewhere and my own extensive collection of British government consular and other reports. These items are listed individually in the Bibliography. To supplement this material I have drawn on the work of authors who have written on the Japanese, Russian, French and German treaty ports for purposes of comparison and explication. Of particular value have been the works of Chinese and Western scholars who have accessed Chinese-language archives and other primary sources.

Every author who writes about 19th- and 20th-century China has to make decisions about how to transliterate Chinese words into English in the certain knowledge that reviewers and readers will disagree with those decisions. The difficulty lies in which system is used (if, indeed, any formal system is). Pinyin superseded Wade-Giles in the mid-20th century so that Peking became Beijing and the familiar Chiang Kai-shek and Sun Yat-sen became unrecognized strangers—Jiang Jieshi and Sun Zhongshan. With the exception of Chiang and Sun and one or two others, all Chinese personal names are written in pinyin. Regarding place names, my decision was to use the names by which they were known at the time, but have included for reference the name by which each place is currently known where it is first mentioned in the text of each entry. Modern writers of history refer happily to Hong Kong instead of Xianggang, but then go to great pains to also refer to places such as Nanjing and Xiamen. There never was a Treaty of Nanjing—it was the Treaty of Nanking. Xiamen was never mentioned in any treaty—Amoy was. However, when referring to a place in a present-day context I have used present-day spelling.

Robert Nield
Hong Kong
January 2015

Acknowledgements

For any publication to reach the bookshelves, the efforts of an army of people need to be acknowledged. And for one that has been eight years in the making, such as this one, that army is very large. Let me try to do them justice here.

First, there is my long-time friend and travelling companion Nick Kitto. Throughout the period this book has been coming together, he and I have been rooting out some of China's more remote Foreign Places, as well as those that will be more familiar to readers. Nick's sleuthing skills and general support were invaluable. Together we would walk for miles, working hard, but always sparing time at the end of the day for a bottle or two of Tsing Tao.

Next, I would like to acknowledge all the encouragement, help and advice given to this newcomer by people far more experienced in this field than I: Peter Cunich, Elizabeth Sinn, Fei Chengkang, John Carroll, Carol Tan, Frances Wood and, not least, May Holdsworth for first suggesting it was possible.

Once the project got under way, many people came forward to share their knowledge and to give on-the-ground help. My late friend Phillip Bruce started bombarding me years ago with useful information for my shoebox, all of which I still have. David Oakley got me into places in Taiwan that otherwise would not have been possible. Butterfield & Swire used to have a presence in many of the places I visited in China; those visits were made much more rewarding by having in my hand detailed historical records generously shared by Rob Jennings and Charlotte Bleasdale from the Archives of John Swire and Sons. Li Shuqin, Director of the Beihai Archives Bureau, and Zhang Jianguo, former Director of the Weihai Municipal Archive, were also generous in allowing me access to their material.

To provide adequate and appropriate illustrations for a book of this nature was always going to be a challenge. My work here was made very much easier thanks to Peter Crush, Chester Cheng, David Mahoney and Duncan Clark, each of whom gave me unlimited access to their valuable collections. I am also indebted to Tim Ko, Jonathan Wattis, Martyn Gregory, Patrick Conner, Peter Hibbard and Robert Bickers.

Just when I thought my work as author was finished, it was made very clear to me that this was not the case. Veronica Pearson, as my editor, demonstrated to me skills I had not seen before. With her magic wand she reduced my number of words by around ten percent (significantly more in some entries)—without removing any of the content. How she did that I will never know. But being cut so seriously was a very pleasant experience.

The final stage of this long process was getting all the words and pictures into the printed book that you are now holding. Here I must record my thanks to Chris Munn of Hong Kong University Press and Michael Duckworth, the Press's former publisher, for having faith in me. In the production process I benefitted tremendously from the other members of the Press team: Clara Ho, Yuet Sang Leung and designer Jennifer Flint. The concept of 'attention to detail' was taken to a whole new level by copyeditor Vicki Low. Any errors and inaccuracies that have stubbornly resisted the efforts of Veronica and Vicki are entirely my own.

This list would be incomplete if I did not thank my adored wife Janet. She remains my biggest fan, most loyal supporter and chief inspiration for anything that I try to do.

Timeline

1644 Accession of Qing dynasty to throne of China
1685 Kangxi Emperor declares all his ports open to foreign trade
1689 Treaty of Nerchinsk (Russia)—attempts to agree border with Russia, establishes reciprocal trading rights; authoritative version was in Latin
1724 Yongzheng Emperor prohibits the practice and propagation of Christianity in China
1727 21 October—Treaty of Kiakhta (Russia)—further attempt to agree border with Russia
1757 Qianlong Emperor issues edict closing to foreign trade all ports except Canton
1792 to 1793—Lord Macartney's embassy to Peking, fails to obtain easing of trading restrictions
1816 to 1817—Lord Amherst's embassy to Peking, tries to establish commercial relations, also fails
1832 East India Company official Hugh Hamilton Lindsay sails up China Coast from Canton in *Lord Amherst*, looking for possible trading sites
1832 William Jardine sends opium ships up the coast
1833 British Slavery Abolition Act outlaws slavery in British Empire
1838 December to October 1842—First Anglo-Afghan War, extremely expensive in terms of money and reputation for Britain
1839 19 March to 29 August 1842—First Opium War
1840 5 July—British troops occupy Chusan for first time
1841 20 January—Convention of Chuenpi (Britain)—brings temporary halt to First Opium War
1842 29 August—Treaty of Nanking (Britain)—creates first five treaty ports, cedes Hong Kong to Britain in perpetuity
1843 8 October—Supplementary Treaty of the Bogue (Britain)—details trading regulations, introduces concept of Most Favoured Nation
1844 3 July—Treaty of Wanghia (America)—based on British treaties, introduces concept of extraterritoriality, provides for right of revision after twelve years
1844 24 October—Treaty of Whampoa (France)—based on British treaties
1844 14 December—Imperial Edict confirms that Chinese will not be punished for adopting Christianity
1846 February—under French pressure, Daoguang Emperor legalizes practice of Christianity, allows missionaries to reclaim former buildings
1846 4 April—Convention of Bocca Tigris (Britain)—allows admission of foreigners to Canton 'when the time is right', evacuation of Chusan
1847 2 April—British forces under d'Aguilar sail up Pearl River and threaten Canton
1847 6 April—Commissioner Qiying agrees to entry to Canton and trade at Honam
1849 Britain repeals Navigation Acts, set of laws allowing only British ships into British ports
1849 1 April—Daoguang Emperor issues edict, is powerless to oppose people of Canton regarding foreign entry
1851 11 January—Hong Xiuquan announces founding of Taiping Heavenly Kingdom, Taiping Rebellion begins, lasts until 1864
1851 25 July—Treaty of Kuldja (Russia)—opens border towns to trade

Timeline

1854 11 July—Shanghai Municipal Council formed
1854 12 July—Foreign Customs Board of Inspectors established in Shanghai, beginning of foreign-managed Chinese Maritime Customs
1855 14 August—Chinese Passengers Act (Britain)—regulates conditions for carriage by sea of Chinese emigrants
1856 8 October—Chinese officials board the *Arrow* in Canton, provoking Second Opium War, lasts until 18 October 1860
1857 10 May—commencement of Indian Mutiny, delays sending of British troops to Second Opium War
1858 28 May—Treaty of Aigun (Russia)—extends Russian territory into China
1858 June—treaties of Tientsin (America, Britain, France, Russia)—open eleven more treaty ports, establish foreign legations in Peking, introduce transit passes, lead to legalizing opium
1858 8 November—opium legalized
1859 October—foreign-managed Custom House established in Canton, soon followed in all treaty ports
1860 24 October—Convention of Peking (Britain)—brings Second Opium War to an end, cedes Kowloon to Britain, opens Tientsin as treaty port, legalizes Chinese emigration
1860 14 November—Treaty of Peking (Russia)—extends Russia's gains of Chinese territory as far as the Pacific at Vladivostok
1861 12 April to 9 May 1865—American Civil War, restricts American cotton supplies, boosts Chinese production
1862 Foreign forces join war against the Taipings
1862 13 August—Treaty of Tientsin (Portugal)—attempts to achieve recognition of sovereignty over Macao, not ratified by Peking
1863 21 September—merger of British and American settlements in Shanghai to form International Settlement
1863 15 November—Robert Hart appointed Inspector-General of Chinese Maritime Customs
1864 25 September—Protocol of Chuguchak (Tahcheng)—cedes to Russia 430,000 square kilometres of territory around Lake Balkhash
1865 Muslim rebellion in north-west gathers momentum
1865 Kiangnan Arsenal established in Shanghai
1866 30 May—five sailing ships leave Foochow on what comes to be known as The Great Tea Race, 99 days later *Taeping* and *Ariel* arrive in London within 20 minutes of each other
1866 August—construction of Foochow Imperial Arsenal commences
1867 to 1886—Imperial Maritime Customs imposes a virtual blockade of Hong Kong
1868 Establishment of Chinese customs stations on border with Hong Kong to suppress smuggling, effectively blockades the colony
1869 23 October—'Alcock Convention' (British)—would have introduced radical reforms to Sino-British relations, not ratified in London
1869 17 November—Suez Canal opens, reducing significantly journey times to Europe
1870 21 June—massacre of foreign and Chinese Catholics in Tientsin
1871 13 September—first treaty between China and Japan grants commercial privileges and extraterritoriality
1872 Li Hongzhang establishes China Merchants Steam Navigation Co., China's first modern commercial enterprise
1873 Muslim rebellions suppressed
1874 7 May—Japan lands troops on Formosa to punish aboriginals for murdering Japanese shipwreck survivors
1875 21 February—murder of British official Raymond Margary, gives rise to more British claims for compensation from China
1876 21 August—Chefoo Agreement (Britain)—resolves Margary affair, opens more treaty ports and ports-of-call, extends concept of

extraterritoriality, exempts foreign areas of treaty ports from *likin*
1878 Catastrophic famine in the north
1880 31 March—Supplementary Convention of Peking (Germany)—gives numerous concessions to German shipping, opens Woosung for taking on and discharging cargo
1881 24 February—Treaty of St Petersburg (Russia)—settles border issue in China's north-west, opens more treaty ports, cedes more territory
1883 France annexes present-day Vietnam
1884 23 August—French bombardment of Foochow Imperial Arsenal, start of Sino-French War, lasts until 4 April 1885
1885 9 June—Treaty of Tientsin (France)—concludes Sino-French War, agrees to set the Tonkin border, opens treaty ports
1885 18 July—Additional Article to 1876 Chefoo Agreement places opium imports under Maritime Customs
1885 Foochow tea banned in London market owing to poor quality
1886 25 April—Treaty of Tientsin (France)—opens border stations to trade, to be defined later
1886 24 July—Burmah Convention (Britain)—agrees to define borders
1886 11 September—Opium Agreement signed in Hong Kong, ends blockade, establishes foreign-managed Custom House in Kowloon
1887 23 June—Additional Commercial Convention (France)—opens Lungchow, Manhao and Mengtse
1887 26 June—Convention Concerning the Tonkin Border (France)—defines the border
1887 1 December—Treaty of Peking (Portugal)—recognizes Macao as Portuguese territory
1890 17 March—Convention Relating to Sikkim and Tibet (Britain)—settles the boundary
1890 31 March—further Additional Article to 1876 Chefoo Agreement permits British steamers to navigate to Chungking provided Chinese steamers have already done so ('Chungking Agreement')
1890 4 December—Hanyang Iron and Steel Works inaugurated
1891 Work starts at both ends of the Trans-Siberian Railway
1891 Wave of anti-foreign riots, especially in Yangtze River ports
1893 5 December—Supplement to Sikkim Convention (Britain)—opens Yatung for trade
1894 1 March—Burmah Convention (Britain)—attempts to define boundary and regularize trade between Burma and China
1894 1 August to 17 April 1895—Sino-Japanese War
1894 24 November—Sun Yat-sen organizes Revive China Society in Honolulu
1895 17 April—Treaty of Shimonoseki (Japan)—brings war to an end, cedes Formosa to Japan, opens more treaty ports
1895 20 June—Complementary Convention (France)—opens Szemao as treaty port
1895 8 November—Japan agrees to sell back to China the Liaodong Peninsula, seized in recent war
1896 8 September—Russia awarded contract for Chinese Eastern Railway
1896 30 September—secret 'Cassini Convention' between China and Russia gives railway concessions in Manchuria, promises Russia the use of Kiaochow Bay (existence of convention still disputed)
1897 4 February—British agreement modifies 1894 Burmah Convention, opens West River to trade, opens more treaty ports
1897 14 November—Germany occupies Kiaochow Bay
1898 6 March—Germany leases Kiaochow Bay
1898 8 March—Archibald Little first to reach Chungking by steamer
1898 27 March—Russia leases Port Arthur and Talienwan
1898 5 April—Imperial Decree opens Chinwangtao, Funing (Santuao) and Yochow to foreign trade

Timeline

1898 22 April—France leases Kwangchowwan
1898 24 May—Britain leases Weihaiwei
1898 9 June—Britain leases Hong Kong's New Territory
1898 28 July—Inland Steam Navigation Regulations—open Chinese inland waters to all registered steam vessels
1898 August—Yangtze Regulations—open more ports-of-call
1899 11 August—Dalny created as Free Port
1900 14 August—Boxer siege of the foreign legations in Peking broken after 55 days
1901 Work on Trans-Siberian Railway substantially complete
1901 7 September—Boxer Peace Protocol (multinational)—replaces Tsungli Yamen with Foreign Office, brings native customs collections near treaty ports under foreign-managed inspectorate, mandates improvements to Peiho and Whangpu rivers
1901 November—Imperial Maritime Customs given responsibility for collecting *likin* to better facilitate payment of Boxer indemnities
1902 5 September—Commercial Treaty (Britain)—introduces uniform national coinage, cleans Canton River, makes Kulangsu an International Settlement, attempts to eradicate *likin*
1903 8 October—separate American and Japanese treaties for the opening of Mukden, counter to Russian advances in the north-east, Japanese treaty requires 'voluntary' opening of ports by China
1903 December—Col. Francis Younghusband leads armed British mission to Lhasa
1904 8 February to 5 September 1905—Russo-Japanese War
1904 7 September—Convention Respecting Tibet (Britain)—opens Gartok and Gyantse as last treaty ports
1905 5 September—Treaty of Portsmouth (Russia, Japan)—brings Russo-Japanese War to an end
1905 24 April—'death of one thousand cuts' banned as a punishment
1905 22 December—Treaty Relating to Manchuria (Japan)—opens Aigun and 15 other towns and cities in Manchuria
1906 Chinese Regiment (Weihaiwei) disbanded
1907 Anglo-Chinese agreement to eliminate export of Indian opium to China over ten-year period
1909 4 September—Gando Convention identifies border between China and Korea
1911 5 October—Kowloon-Canton Railway opens
1911 10 October—uprising in Wuchang leads to revolution and overthrow of imperial system
1913 November—so-called Second Revolution instigated by Sun Yat-sen against Yuan Shikai
1914 Conference in Simla between Britain, Tibet and China aims at clarifying borders and Tibetan sovereignty, China refuses to sign resulting accord
1914 23 August—Japan declares war on Germany
1914 7 November—Japan occupies Tsingtao
1915 18 January—Japan issues the 'Twenty-One Demands' to China
1915 25 May—Treaty Respecting Shandong (Japan)—gives railway and other rights to Japan
1915 25 May—Treaty Respecting South Manchuria and Eastern Inner Mongolia (Japan)—extends lease of Port Arthur and Dairen, extends railway and other privileges
1917 14 August—China declares war on Central Powers
1919 18 January—Paris Peace Conference opens, denies China the return of former German-occupied territory
1919 4 May—anti-Japanese student demonstration in Peking, gives rise to May Fourth Movement
1921 22–31 July—First Congress of Chinese Communist Party held in Shanghai
1921 12 November—Washington Conference opens, former German-occupied territory returned to China
1922 4 February—Japan restores Shandong to Chinese control

1922	12 November to 6 February 1923—Washington Disarmament Conference
1923	August—Presidential Mandate—the last to open a city for foreign trade (Pengpu)
1924	30 May—Sino-Soviet agreement establishes diplomatic relations
1925	30 May—Shanghai municipal police shoot Chinese demonstrators, gives rise to massive protests and boycotts across the country
1927	19 February—Chen-O'Malley Agreement (Britain)—gives back British Hankow Concession to China
1927	20 February—similar agreement gives back British Kiukiang Concession
1929	15 November—British Concession at Chinkiang handed back to China
1930	17 September—Britain relinquishes Amoy Concession
1930	1 October—Weihaiwei handed back to China by Britain
1931	1 January—*likin* abolished
1931	18 September—Mukden Incident, a Japanese-engineered trigger for the invasion of Manchuria
1932	9 March—puppet state of Manchukuo created
1937	7 July—Marco Polo Bridge Incident, prompts commencement of full hostilities between China and Japan
1937	1 December—Central government established at Chungking 'on a temporary basis'
1941	8 December—commencement of Pacific War
1941	9 December—China declares war on Japan
1943	11 January—Treaty for the Relinquishment of Extra-Territorial Rights in China (British)—formally brings treaty ports to an end

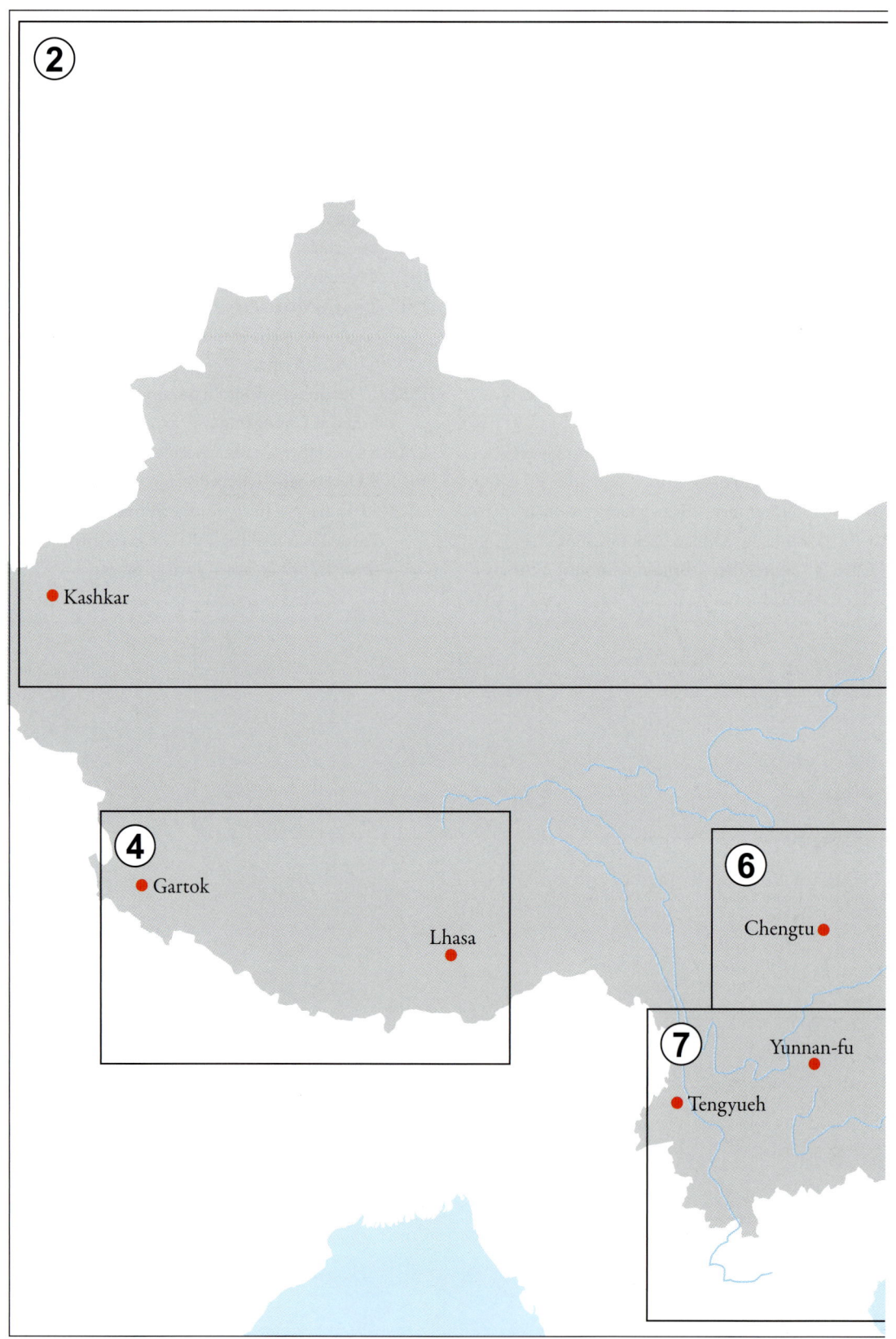

Map 1 China, showing the main areas in which treaty ports and other foreign settlements were found

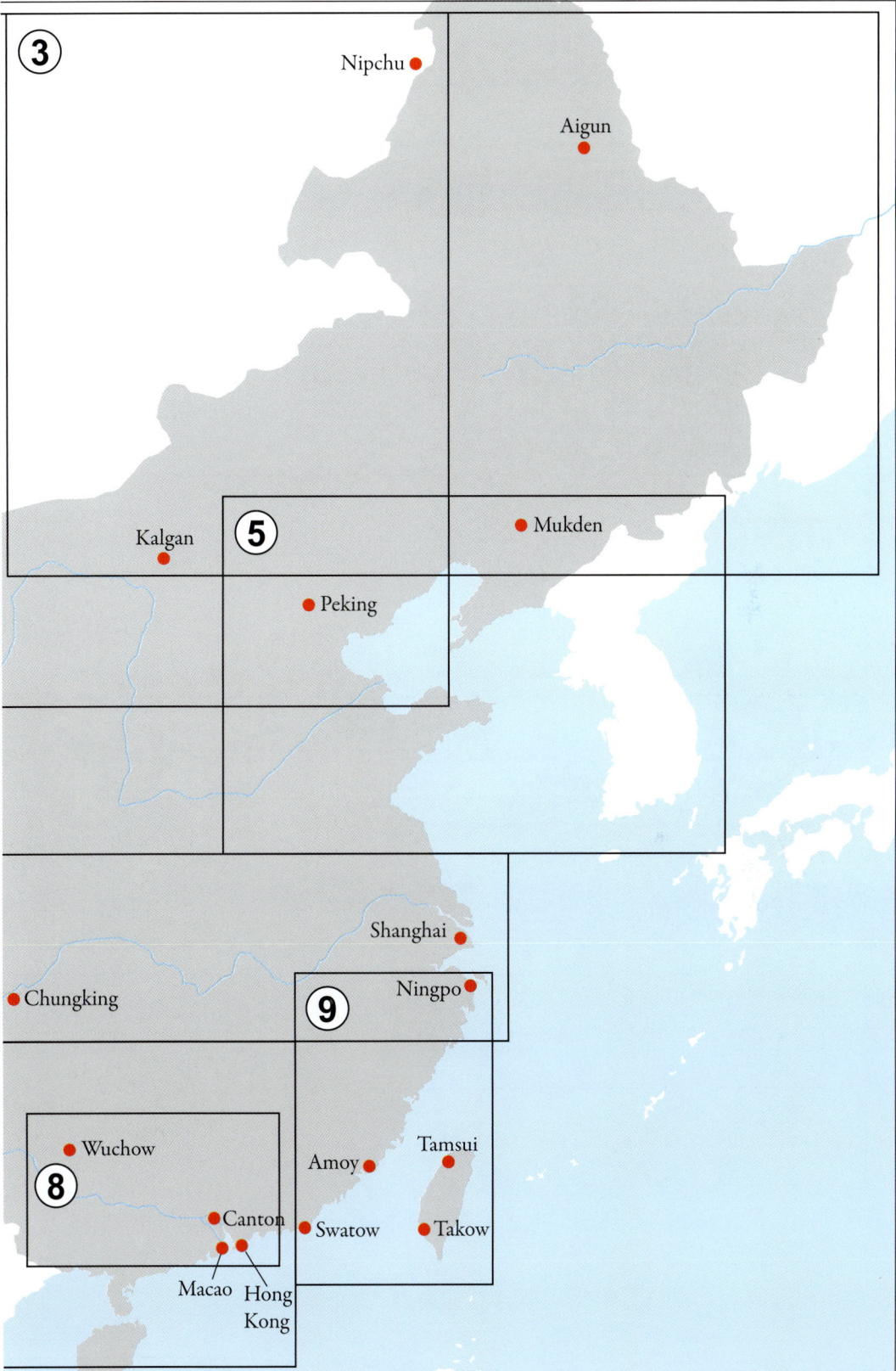

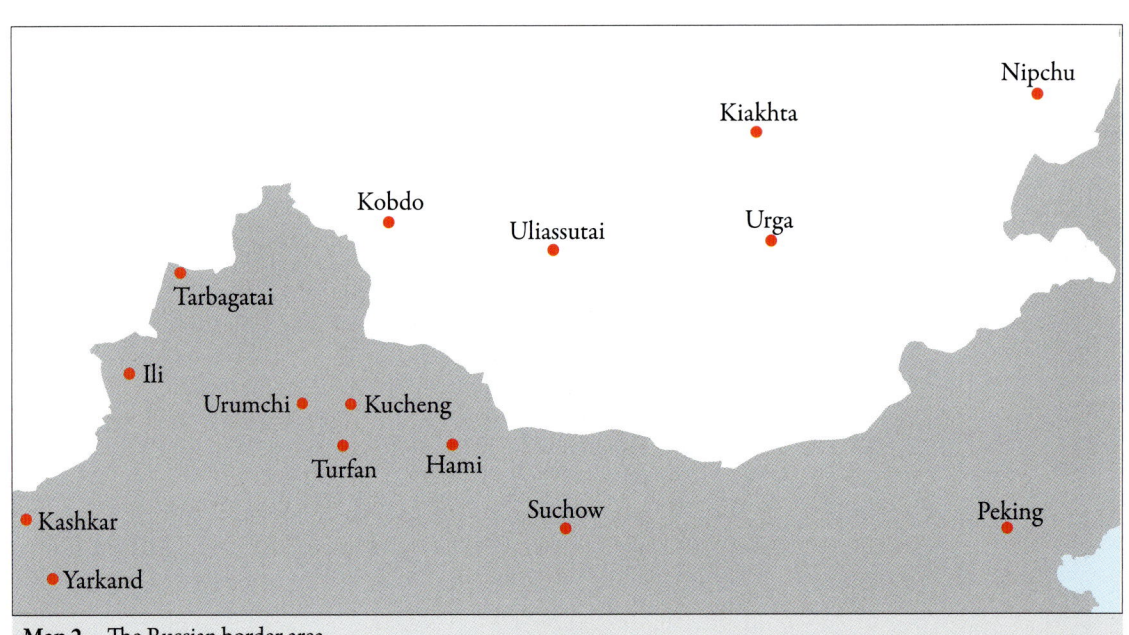

Map 2 The Russian border area

Map 3 Manchuria

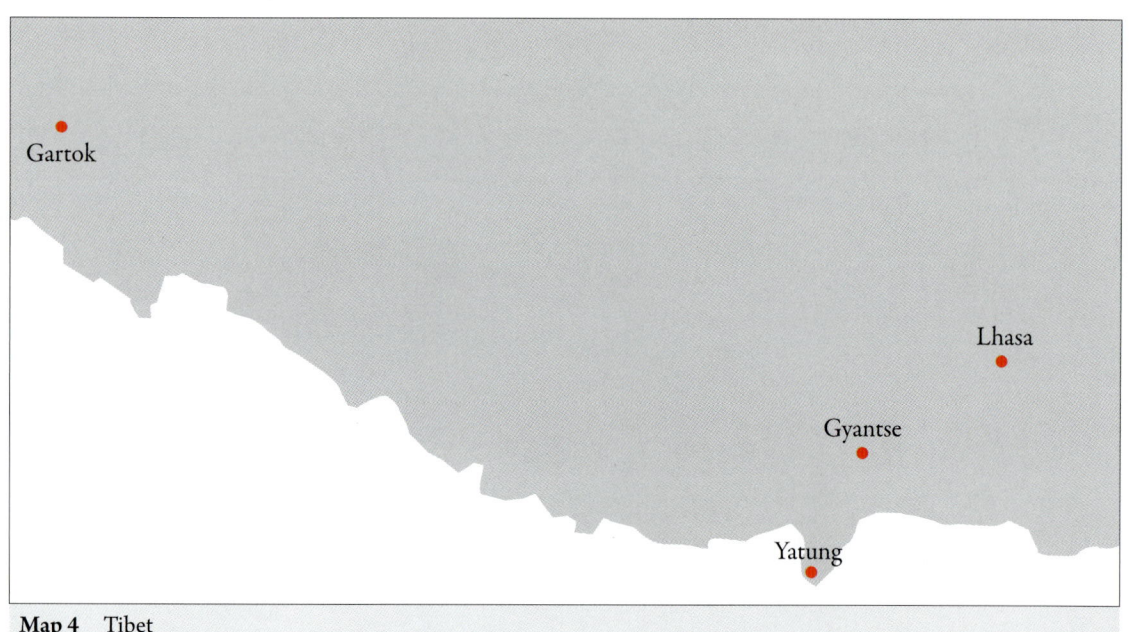

Map 4 Tibet

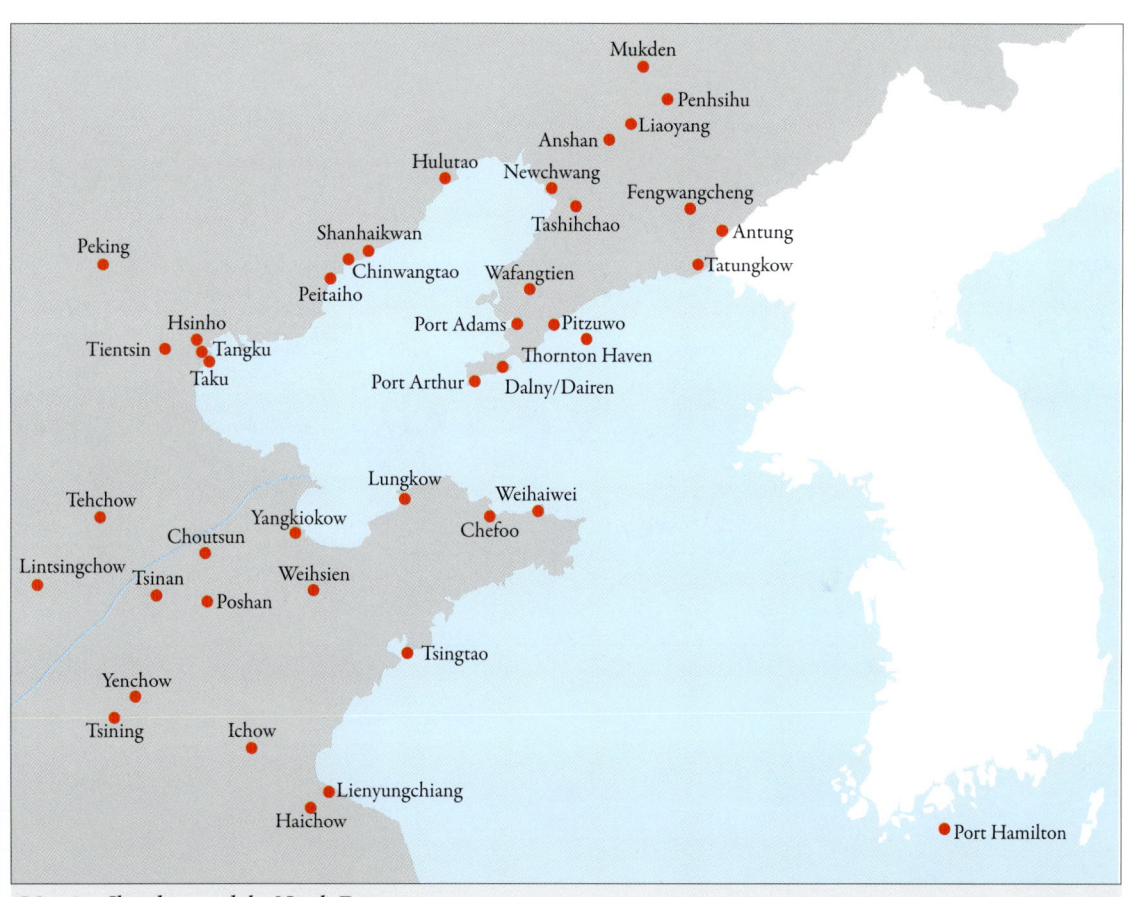

Map 5   Shandong and the North-East

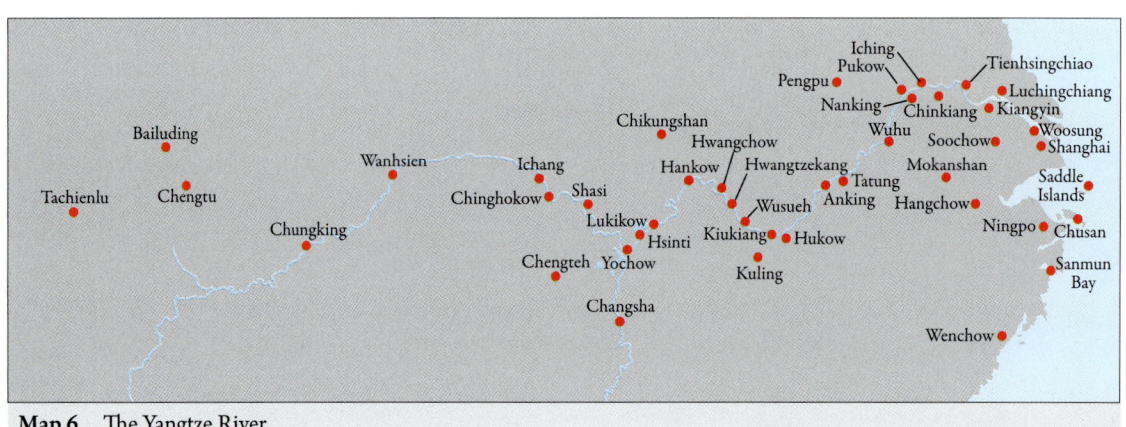

Map 6 The Yangtze River

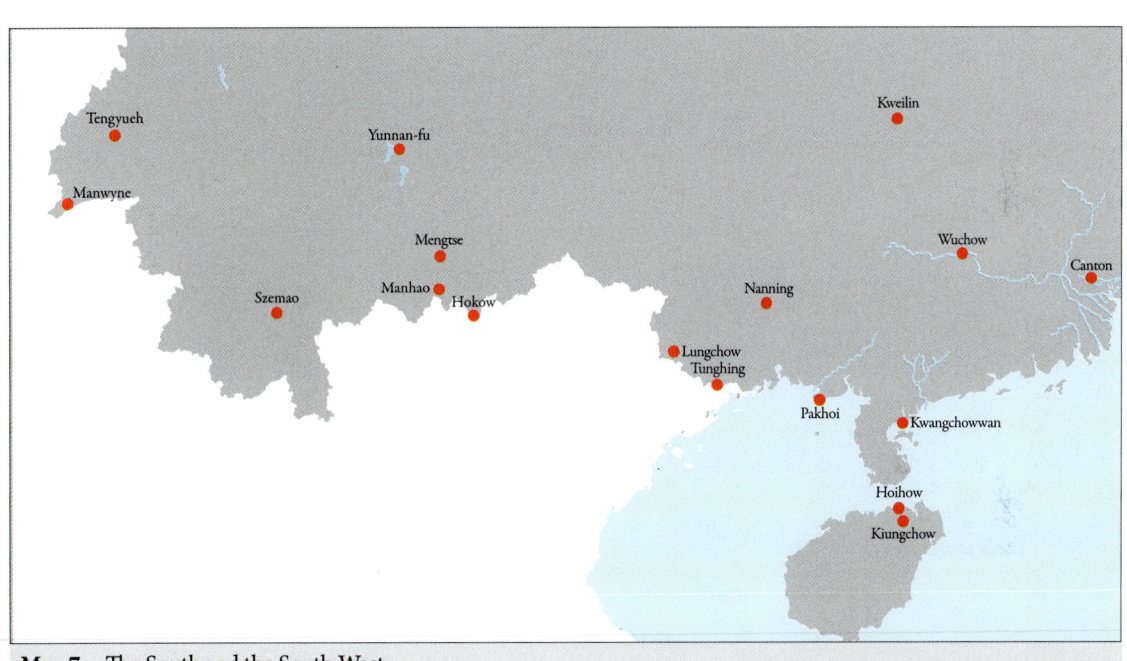

Map 7   The South and the South-West

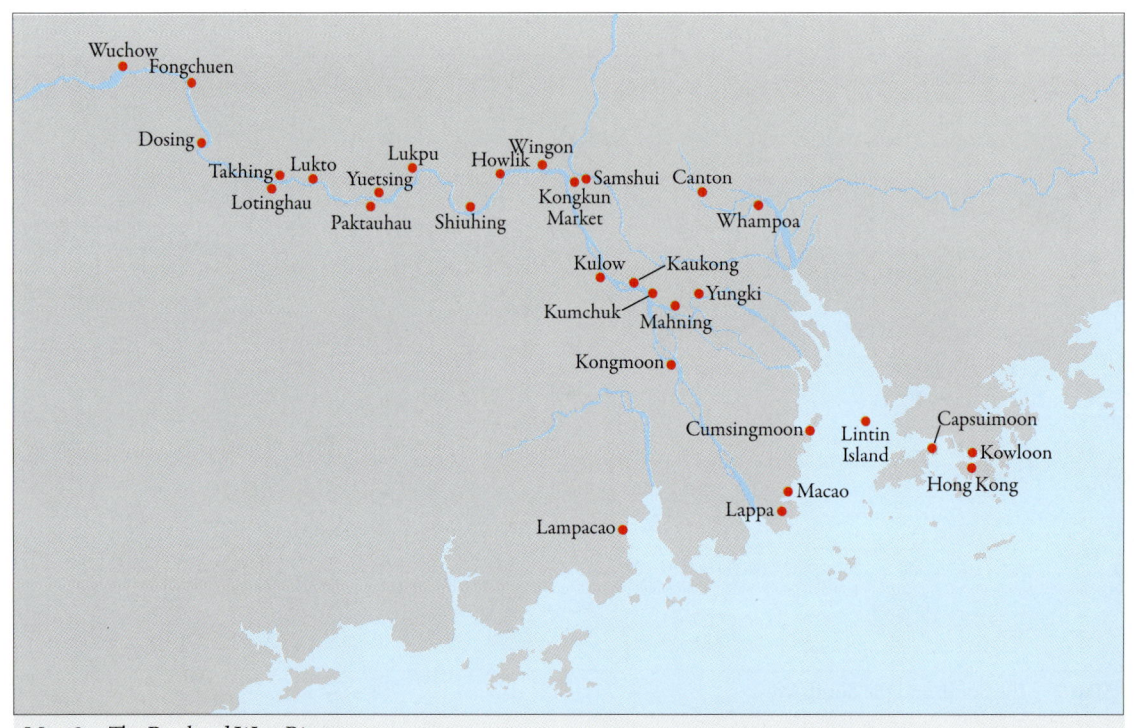

Map 8 The Pearl and West Rivers

Map 9 The East Coast and Formosa (Taiwan)

Treaty Ports and Other Foreign Stations

(*in alphabetical order*)

	Status	Nationality	Year
Aigun (Aihun)	Open City	China	1905
Amoy (Xiamen)	Treaty Port	Britain	1842
Anking (Anqing)	Port-of-Call	Britain	1876
Anping	Customs Station	China	1865
Anshan	Industrial Centre	Japan	1918
Antung (Dandong)	Open City	China	1903
Bailuding (Bailu)	Hill Station for Chengtu		1915
Baku (Magong)	Military Station	France	1885
Banka (Wanhua)	Port for Tamsui		1862
Canton (Guangzhou)	Treaty Port	Britain	1842
Capsuimoon (Jishuimen/Ma Wan)	Opium Receiving Station		1820s
Changchun	Open City	China	1905
Changsha	Treaty Port	Japan	1903
Chefoo (Yantai)	Treaty Port	Britain	1858
Chengteh (Changde)	Open City	China	1908
Chengtu (Chengdu)	Consular Station	Britain	1902
Chihfeng (Chifeng)	Open City	China	1914
Chikungshan (Jigongshan)	Hill Station for Hankow		1908
Chimmo Bay (Shenhu Wan)	Opium Receiving Station		1820s
Chinchew Bay (Quanzhou Wan)	Opium Receiving Station		1820s
Chinghokow (Yidu)	Port-of-Call	Britain	1898
Chinkiang (Zhenjiang)	Treaty Port	Britain	1858
Chinpeng (Jinpeng)	Open City	China	1915
Chinwangtao (Qinhuangdao)	Open City	China	1898
Choutsun (Zhoucun)	Open City	China	1904
Chuitzuchien (Yanji)	Open City	China	1909
Chungking (Chongqing)	Treaty Port	Britain	1890
Chusan (Zhoushan)	Occupied Territory	Britain	1840
Cumsingmoon (Jinxingmen)	Opium Receiving Station		1820s
Dalny/Dairen (Dalian)	Leased Territory	Russia/Japan	1898
Dolonor (Duolun)	Open City	China	1914
Dosing (Yunan)	Port-of-Call	Britain	1902
Double Island (Mayu)	Customs Station	China	1860
Fakumen (Faku)	Open City	China	1905
Fengwangcheng (Fengcheng)	Open City	China	1905
Fongchuen (Fengkai)	Landing Stage	Britain	1902
Foochow (Fuzhou)	Treaty Port	Britain	1842
Fushun	Industrial Centre	Japan	1918
Gartok (Gar Yasha)	Treaty Port	Britain	1904
Gyantse (Gyangze)	Treaty Port	Britain	1904
Haichow (Haizhou)	Open City	China	1905

Treaty Ports and Other Foreign Stations

	Status	Nationality	Year
Hailar (Hulunber)	Open City	China	1905
Hami (Kumul)	Treaty Port	Russia	1881
Hangchow (Hangzhou)	Treaty Port	Japan	1895
Hankow (Hankou)	Treaty Port	Britain	1858
Harbin	Open City	China	1905
Hoihow (Haikou)	Port for Kiungchow		1876
Hokow (Hekou) (Red River)	Treaty Port	France	1896
Hokow (Hekou) (West River)	Port for Samshui		1897
Hong Kong (Xianggang)	Colony	Britain	1842
Howlik (Dinghu)	Landing Stage	Britain	1902
Hsiao Kulun (Kulun)	Open City	China	1915
Hsin Hsu (Xinxu)	Port for Kongkun Market		1897
Hsinho (Xinhu)	Port for Tientsin		1890s
Hsinmintun (Xinmin)	Open City	China	1905
Hsinti (Xindi)	Port-of-Call	Britain	1898
Hukow (Hukou)	Port-of-Call	Britain	1876
Hulutao (Huludao)	Open City	China	1914
Hunchun	Open City	China	1905
Hwangchow (Huangzhou)	Port-of-Call	Britain	1898
Hwangtzekang (Huangshigang)	Port-of-Call	Britain	1898
Ichang (Yichang)	Treaty Port	Britain	1876
Iching (Yizheng)	Port-of-Call	Britain	1898
Ichow (Linyi)	Open City	China	1915
Ili (Yining)	Treaty Port	Russia	1851
Jehol (Chengde)	Open City	China	1914
Kailuhsien (Kailu)	Open City	China	1915
Kaiyuan	Industrial Centre	Japan	1918
Kalgan (Zhangjiakou)	Treaty Port	Russia	1860
Kalgan (Zhangjiakou)	Open City	China	1914
Kashkar (Kashgar)	Treaty Port	Russia	1860
Kaukong (Jiujiang)	Landing Stage	Britain	1902
Keelung (Jilong)	Dependent Port of Tamsui		1861
Kiakhta	Treaty Port	Russia	1727
Kiangyin (Jiangyin)	Port-of-Call	Britain	1898
Kirin (Jilin)	Open City	China	1905
Kiukiang (Jiujiang)	Treaty Port	Britain	1858
Kiungchow (Qiongzhou)	Treaty Port	Britain	1858
Kobdo (Khovd)	Treaty Port	Russia	1881
Kongkun Market (Jianggen)	Treaty Port	Britain	1897
Kongmoon (Jiangmen)	Port-of-Call	Britain	1897
Kongmoon (Jiangmen)	Treaty Port	Britain	1902
Kowloon (Jiulong)	Customs Station	China	1886
Kucheng (Qitai)	Treaty Port	Russia	1881
Kueihuacheng (Hohot)	Open City	China	1914
Kulangsu (Gulangyu)	International Settlement		1903
Kuliang (Guling)	Hill Station for Foochow		1886
Kuling (Lushan)	Hill Station for Kiukiang		1895
Kulow (Gulao)	Landing Stage	Britain	1902
Kumchuk (Ganzhu)	Port-of-Call	Britain	1897
Kungchulin (Gongzhulin)	Industrial Centre	Japan	1918
Kwangchowwan (Zhanjiang)	Leased Territory	France	1898

	Status	Nationality	Year
Kweilin (Guilin)	Consular Station	Britain	1942
Lampacao (Langbaigang)	Trading Station	Portugal	1500s
Lappa (Hengqin Dao)	Customs Station	China	1886
Liampo (Zhenhai)	Trading Station	Portugal	1533
Liaoyang	Open City	China	1905
Lichuan (Fuli)	Open City	China	1915
Lienyungchiang (Lianyungang)	Port for Haichow		1905
Linsi (Linxi)	Open City	China	1915
Lintin Island (Neilingding Dao)	Opium Receiving Station		1820s
Lintsingchow (Linqing)	Open City	China	1915
Lookong (Ligang)	Opium Receiving Station		1840s
Lotinghau (Nandukou)	Port-of-Call	Britain	1902
Luchingchiang (Lujinggang)	Port-of-Call	Britain	1898
Lukikow (Luxi)	Port-of-Call	Britain	1876
Lukpu (Lubu)	Landing Stage	Britain	1902
Lukto (Dahe)	Landing Stage	Britain	1902
Lungchingtsun (Longjing)	Open City	China	1909
Lungchow (Longzhou)	Treaty Port	France	1887
Lungkow (Longkou)	Open City	China	1914
Macao (Aomen)	Occupied Territory	Portugal	1557
Macao (Aomen)	Colony	Portugal	1887
Mahning (Maningwei)	Landing Stage	Britain	1902
Manchouli (Manzhouli)	Open City	China	1905
Manhao	Treaty Port	France	1887
Manwyne (Manghuan)	Treaty Port	Britain	1894
Mengtse (Mengzi)	Treaty Port	France	1887
Mokanshan (Moganshan)	Hill Station for Hangchow		1890
Mukden (Shenyang)	Open City	China	1903
Namoa (Nanao)	Opium Receiving Station		1820s
Nanking (Nanjing)	Treaty Port	France	1858
Nanning	Open City	China	1899
Nantai	Port for Foochow		1842
Newchwang (Yingkou)	Treaty Port	Britain	1858
Ningpo (Ningbo)	Treaty Port	Britain	1842
Ninguta (Ning'an)	Open City	China	1905
Nipchu	Treaty Port	Russia	1689
Pagoda Island (Mawei)	Consular Station	Britain	1868
Paitsaokou (Baicaogou)	Open City	China	1909
Pakhoi (Beihai)	Treaty Port	Britain	1876
Paktauhau (Jiangshui)	Port-of-Call	Britain	1902
Peitaiho (Beidaihe)	Seaside Resort		1890s
Peking (Beijing)	Diplomatic Station	Britain	1858
Pengpu (Bengbu)	Open City	China	1923
Penhsihu (Benxi)	Industrial Centre	Japan	1918
Pingchuan (Pingquan)	Open City	China	1915
Pitzuwo (Pikou)	Customs Station	China	1915
Port Adams (Pulandian)	Customs Station	China	1910s
Port Arthur (Lüshun)	Leased Territory	Russia	1898
Port Hamilton (Geomun-do)	Occupied Territory	Britain	1885
Poshan (Boshan)	Open City	China	1915
Pukow (Pukou)	Customs Station	China	1915

	Status	Nationality	Year
Quemoy (Kinmen)	Trading Station	Portugal	1516
Saddle Islands (Shengsi)	Holiday Resort for Shanghai		1900s
Samshui (Sanshui)	Treaty Port	Britain	1897
Sanhsing (Yilan)	Open City	China	1905
Sanmun Bay (Sanmen Wan)	Naval Base (attempted)	Italy	1899
Santuao (Sandu)	Open City	China	1898
Shanghai	Treaty Port	Britain	1842
Shanhaikwan (Shanhaiguan)	Military Base	Japan	1894
Sharp Peak (Chuanshi)	Seaside Resort for Foochow		1880s
Shasi (Shashi)	Port-of-Call	Britain	1876
Shasi (Shashi)	Treaty Port	Japan	1895
Shiuhing (Zhaoqing)	Port-of-Call	Britain	1897
Soochow (Suzhou)	Treaty Port	Japan	1895
Ssupingkai (Siping)	Industrial Centre	Japan	1918
Suchow (Jiuquan)	Treaty Port	Russia	1881
Suifenho (Suifenhe)	Treaty Port	Japan	1895
Swatow (Shantou)	Treaty Port	Britain	1858
Szemao (Simao)	Treaty Port	France	1895
Tachienlu (Kangding)	Consular Station	Britain	1913
Taheiho (Heihe)	Port for Aigun		1900
Taiwan-fu (Tainan)	Treaty Port	Britain	1858
Takhing (Deqing)	Port-of-Call	Britain	1897
Takow (Kaohsiung)	Dependent Port of Taiwan-fu		1864
Taku (Dagu)	Consular Station	Britain	1862
Talai (Dalai Nuori)	Open City	China	1915
Tamsui (Danshui)	Treaty Port	France	1858
Tangku (Tanggu)	Port for Tientsin		1865
Taonan	Open City	China	1914
Tarbagatai (Qoqek)	Treaty Port	Russia	1851
Tashihchao (Dashiqiao)	Industrial Centre	Japan	1918
Tatung (Datong)	Port-of-Call	Britain	1876
Tatungkow (Dadonggou)	Open City	China	1903
Tehchow (Dezhou)	Open City	China	1915
Tengyueh (Tengchong)	Treaty Port	Britain	1897
Thornton Haven (Haiyang Dao)	Naval Base	Russia	1899
Tiehling (Tieling)	Open City	China	1905
Tienhsingchiao (Tianxingqiao)	Port-of-Call	Britain	1898
Tientsin (Tianjin)	Treaty Port	Britain	1860
Tinghai (Dinghai)	Port for Chusan		1840
Toutaokou (Toudaogou)	Open City	China	1909
Tsinan (Jinan)	Open City	China	1904
Tsingtao (Qingdao)	Leased Territory	Germany	1898
Tsining (Jining)	Open City	China	1915
Tsitsihar (Qiqihar)	Open City	China	1905
Tunghing (Dongxing)	Consular Station	France	1895
Tungkiangtzu (Tongjiangkou)	Open City	China	1905
Turfan (Turpan)	Consular Station	Russia	1881
Twatutia (Dadaocheng)	Port for Tamsui		1862
Uliassutai (Uliastai)	Treaty Port	Russia	1881
Urga (Ulaanbaatar)	Treaty Port	Russia	1860
Urumchi (Urumqi)	Treaty Port	Russia	1881

	Status	Nationality	Year
Wafangtien (Wafangdian)	Industrial Centre	Japan	1918
Wanhsien (Wanxian)	Open City	China	1917
Weihaiwei (Weihai)	Leased Territory	Britain	1898
Weihsien (Weifang)	Open City	China	1904
Wenchow (Wenzhou)	Treaty Port	Britain	1876
Whampoa (Huangpu)	Port for Canton		1600s
Whampoa (Huangpu)	Consular Station	Britain	1843
Wingon (Yong'an)	Landing Stage	Britain	1902
Woosung (Wusong)	Port-of-Call	Germany	1880
Woosung (Wusong)	Open City	China	1899
Wuchanghsien (Wuchang)	Open City	China	1915
Wuchow (Wuzhou)	Treaty Port	Britain	1897
Wuhu	Treaty Port	Britain	1876
Wusueh (Wuxue)	Port-of-Call	Britain	1876
Yangkiokow (Yangkou)	Open City	China	1915
Yarkand (Yarkant)	Consular Station	Britain	1870
Yatung (Yadong)	Treaty Port	Britain	1893
Yenchow (Yanzhou)	Open City	China	1915
Yochow (Yueyang)	Open City	China	1898
Yuetsing (Yuecheng)	Landing Stage	Britain	1902
Yungki (Suixiang)	Landing Stage	Britain	1902
Yunnan-fu (Kunming)	Consular Station	Britain	1902
Zakow (Zhakou)	Port for Hangchow		1907

Principal Characters

Aberdeen, Earl of (1784–1860): British Foreign Secretary at outbreak of First Opium War, later Prime Minister 1852–55

Alcock, Sir Rutherford (1809–97): British Consul in Foochow 1844, British Minister in Peking 1865–69

Amherst, Earl (1773–1857): led an unsuccessful mission to Peking in 1816 aimed at improving trade relations with Britain

Asiatic Petroleum Company: founded 1903 as a joint venture between the Shell and Royal Dutch oil companies, had a presence in many treaty ports

Beresford, Lord Charles (1846–1919): British admiral and politician, led a commercial fact-finding mission to China 1898–99

Bonham, Sir Samuel (1803–63): colonial administrator, Governor of Hong Kong 1848–54

Bowring, Sir John (1792–1872): political economist, Governor of Hong Kong 1854–59

Bruce, Sir Frederick (1814–67): British diplomat, Hong Kong Colonial Secretary 1844–46, Minister to China 1857–65, brother of Earl of Elgin

Butterfield & Swire: established 1866 in Shanghai, became one of the leaders in the shipping industry in China

Chen Yujen (a.k.a. Eugene Chen) (1878–1944): born in Trinidad, qualified as a lawyer, became Sun Yat-sen's Foreign Minister in the 1920s

Chiang Kai-shek (1887–1975): political and military leader, ally of Sun Yat-sen, China's de facto President 1928–48, President of Taiwan 1949–75

Cixi, Empress Dowager (a.k.a. Tzu-hsi) (1835–1908): imperial concubine, rose to absolute power, successfully deflected the Boxer rebels against the foreign powers

Crossman, Major William (1830–1901): officer in the Royal Engineers, in charge of British diplomatic and consular buildings in China 1866–69

Davis, Sir John (1795–1890): joined East India Company in Canton 1813, became diplomat and noted Sinologist, Governor of Hong Kong 1844–48

Deng Tingzhen, Admiral (a.k.a. Teng Ting-chen) (1776–1846): Viceroy of Guangdong and Guangxi 1836–40, hero of First Opium War

East India Company: founded 1600 to promote English trade in the East, dominant supplier of Indian opium for China market, dissolved 1874

Elgin, Earl of (1811–63): colonial administrator and diplomat, Commissioner to China 1857–59, ordered destruction of Summer Palace 1860

Elliot, Captain Charles (1801–75): British naval officer, appointed to Napier's staff in Canton 1833, first administrator of Hong Kong 1841

Feng Zicai (a.k.a. Feng Tse-choy) (1818–1903): bandit-turned-imperial-general at time of Sino-French War

Fortune, Robert (1812–80): Scottish botanist, travelled extensively in China, introduced Chinese tea plants to India

Gordon, Charles (1833–85): British army officer, served in China in 1860s, commanded Ever-Victorious Army 1863–64

Guo Songtao (a.k.a. Kuo Sung-tao) (1818–91): diplomat and statesman, Minister to Britain and France 1877–79, supporter of railways in China

Hart, Sir Robert (1835–1911): British consular official in China 1854–63, Inspector-General of Maritime Customs 1863–1911, knighted 1882

Hennessy, Sir John Pope (1834–91): Governor of Hong Kong 1877–82, appointed first Chinese member of Legislative Council

Jardine, William (1784–1843): Scottish physician, merchant and politician, traded in Canton 1820–39, co-founder of Jardine, Matheson & Co. 1832

Koxinga (a.k.a. Zheng Chenggong) (1624–62): Ming loyalist, military leader, defeated Dutch in Formosa 1661, proclaimed himself King of Taiwan 1662

Lay, George Tradescant (1800–1845): British missionary, diplomat, consul in Canton, Foochow, Amoy, first of many in his family to serve in China

Li Hongzhang (a.k.a. Li Hung-chang) (1823–1901): military leader and statesman, promoter of modernization and industrialization

Li Liejun (a.k.a. Li Lieh-chun) (1882–1946): military leader and anti-Qing revolutionary, opposed Yuan Shikai

Lin Zexu (a.k.a. Lin Tse-hsu) (1785–1850): Qing official and scholar, sent to Canton 1839 to suppress opium, actions prompted First Opium War

Lindsay, Hugh Hamilton (1802–81): official in East India Company in Canton, led a voyage up the China Coast 1832 looking for likely places of trade

Little, Archibald (1838–1907): merchant and pioneer, came to China 1859, first to reach Chungking by steamer 1898

Liu Mingchuan (a.k.a. Liu Ming-chuan) (1836–96): Qing official, resisted French attacks on Formosa 1884, Governor of Province of Taiwan 1885

Macartney, Lord (1737–1806): colonial administrator and diplomat, led unsuccessful mission to Peking aimed at opening China to trade 1792–93

MacDonald, Sir Claude (1852–1915): diplomat, British Minister to Peking 1896–1900, obtained leases of Weihaiwei and Hong Kong's New Territory

Mao Zedong (a.k.a. Mao Tse-tung) (1893–1976): Communist revolutionary, founder of The People's Republic of China 1949

Martin, Montgomery (1801–68): Hong Kong Colonial Treasurer 1844–45, famously reported in 1844 that Hong Kong had no prospects

Matheson, James (1796–1878): Scottish merchant in India and Canton, co-founder of Jardine, Matheson & Co. 1832

Napier, Lord (1786–1834): first Chief Superintendent of British Trade in China, lacked experience to be successful, died in post

Palmerston, Lord (1784–1865): British politician and statesman, at various times Foreign Secretary and Prime Minister 1830–65

Parkes, Sir Harry (1828–85): British diplomat, came to China 1841, his protests regarding the *Arrow* affair 1856 led to Second Opium War

Plant, Cornell (1866–1921): mariner and river cartographer, came to China 1900, pioneered successful use of steamships on Upper Yangtze

Pottinger, Sir Henry (1789–1856): soldier and colonial administrator, first Governor of Hong Kong 1841–44

Qishan (a.k.a. Keyshen) (1786–1854): Manchu Qing official, replaced Lin Zexu 1840, negotiated abortive end to First Opium War

Qiying (a.k.a. Keying) (1787–1858): Qing statesman, negotiated Treaty of Nanking 1842, not so successful in seeking end to Second Opium War

Salisbury, Lord (1830–1903): four times British Foreign Secretary between 1878 and 1900, three times Prime Minister between 1885 and 1902

Shen Baozhen (a.k.a. Shen Pao-chen) (1820–79): in Self-Strengthening Movement, Director of Foochow Arsenal 1866, Lin Zexu's brother-in-law

Stanley, Lord (1799–1869): statesman, politician, British Colonial Secretary 1841–44, three times Prime Minister between 1852 and 1868

Sun Yat-sen (1866–1925): Chinese revolutionary and first President of the Republic of China, co-founder of Kuomintang

Tang Jingxing (a.k.a. Tong King-sing) (1832–92): Jardines' comprador 1863–73, manager of China Merchants and Kaiping Mines 1873–84

Tower, Sir Reginald (1860–1939): Secretary to British Legation in Peking 1900–1901, conducted review of British consular requirements in China

Wade, Sir Thomas (1818–95): diplomat, Sinologist, produced Chinese dictionary 1859 that became basis of Wade-Giles system of romanization

Walton, Sir Joseph (1849–1923): politician and industrialist, travelled widely in China 1899–1900 to report on commercial and political situation

Wu Peifu (a.k.a. Wu Pei-fu) (1874–1939): Wuhan warlord 1916–27, referred to as 'one of the few better despots'

Ye Mingchen (a.k.a. Yeh Ming-chen) (1807–59): refused to allow British to enter Canton after First Opium War, Viceroy of Two Guangs 1852–58

Yuan Shikai (a.k.a. Yuan Shi-kai) (1859–1916): general and politician, President of China 1912–16, failed in attempt to become emperor 1915

Zhou Enlai (a.k.a. Chou En-lai) (1898–1976): close supporter of Mao Zedong, first Premier of The People's Republic of China 1949–76

Zuo Zongtang (a.k.a. Tso Tsung-tang) (1812–85): statesman and soldier, leader of the Self-Strengthening Movement and rival of Li Hongzhang

Emperors of China who feature in the text, with their years of reign:

Ming Dynasty
- Hongwu (1368–98): first Ming emperor
- Yongle (1402–24): took throne by force from teenaged nephew
- Jiaqing (1521–66): evicted Portuguese from Ningbo

Qing Dynasty
- Kangxi (1661–1722): longest-ruling emperor, brought stability, wealth
- Yongzheng (1722–35): hard-working, despotic but efficient ruler
- Qianlong (1735–96): period of gathering storm from within and without
- Jiaqing (1796–1820): attempted to eradicate opium smuggling
- Daoguang (1820–50): First Opium War and Taiping Rebellion
- Xianfeng (1850–61): Second Opium War and more rebellions
- Tongzhi (1861–75): ruled by his mother, Empress Dowager Cixi
- Guangxu (1875–1908): attempted reforms, but overruled by Cixi
- Xuantong (1908–11): last emperor, became a puppet of Japan

Introduction

History matters in modern China. Not only is the past a different country, it is also replete with unfinished business. From the perspective of the Chinese, the period 1842 to 1943 was a century of humiliation so severe that it is charted in a Dictionary of National Humiliation, four centimetres thick.[1] But this sense of humiliation goes back much further. For much of the previous thousand years, China was ruled by people who originated from outside its borders: the Jin (from present-day Russia), Yuan (Mongol) and Qing (Manchu) dynasties.[2] In the story told in this volume the major actors are nation-states, and the themes interwoven over the 101 years of the treaty ports' existence are complex, volatile and continue to colour China's relationship with the rest of the world.

For example, one of many defining moments in the history of this period was China's defeat by Japan (a former tributary) in the Sino-Japanese War of 1894–95. This was concluded by the Treaty of Shimonoseki and the payment of 230 million *taels* of silver in reparation, and the cession of Taiwan to Japan; the victorious Japanese also annexed the Diaoyu Islands, known by them as the Senkaku Islands. These territorial losses continue to resonate in China's 'foreign' (or, as China sees it, 'domestic') policy. China marked the 120th anniversary of this defeat by a campaign of exoneration fronted by *The People's Daily* and *The PLA Daily* firmly relocating blame from the military forces, especially the Northern (Beiyang) Fleet, to the antiquated Qing government and their unwillingness to invest in sufficient firepower.[3] These are old wounds but they are still open and consequently powerfully affect relations between today's nation-states. This book provides comprehensive coverage of the interaction between China and a multiplicity of foreign powers within the global context of 101 years of radical change in political structures, power sources, technology, industry, communication, transport, agriculture and population size.

First encounters

When two powerful nations initially confront each other, both equally convinced of their own moral, cultural and national superiority, the chances of it ending in tears are very high. When one, but not the other, of those nations has been the cradle of the Industrial Revolution and has an active colonial track record then the outcome, while not desirable, is inevitable.[4] Thus it was with China and Britain. It was the expansion of trade and commerce internationally that was a key factor in the economic dynamism of the 19th century. What made it different from the 18th century, also notable for global commerce, was that it expanded to include not only luxury goods but everyday items; in China's case, not only silk and fine porcelain but pig bristles and wax.

The Western powers tended to believe that trading was as natural a human function as breathing and assumed the right to trade with whomsoever they pleased. China did not share this view. Traditionally, the mandarins who ruled China perceived commerce as an activity undertaken by people of a lower, unrefined kind—be they Chinese or foreign.[5] Indeed, they could cite evidence to support their view. The behaviour of at least some merchants—their unreasonable demands and their involvement in the illegal opium trade—was a source of frequent 'headaches' for consular staff.[6] There were most certainly successful Chinese merchants but it was the ranking bureaucrats who held the keys that would open the doors to trade with foreigners. Consequently, engaging in international commercial activity with China was never going to be straightforward.

The first Europeans to establish a commercial presence in China were the Portuguese. They visited several places along the coast in the early 16th century, including Ningpo (Ningbo), before settling on Macao in 1557. The Chinese considered them no better than pirates, but tolerated them, believing they would deter other foreign predators. By the 17th century the Dutch were easing Portugal out of its colonial possessions. The Portuguese retained Macao, forcing the Dutch to go along the coast to Amoy (Xiamen), before briefly colonizing the island of Formosa (Taiwan). The Portuguese and Dutch transported China's most prized products—tea, porcelain and silk—to Europe, to be sold at great profit. In the 18th century the British followed suit.

By the early 19th century a wealthy, resurgent Britain was championing free trade. British merchants in Canton (Guangzhou) were unhappy with the system of Chinese customs duties, the corruption of the tax-collecting mandarins, and the rule that all foreign merchants leave Canton at the end of the trading season. Furthermore, the British government became concerned at the outflow of silver needed to pay for its imports from China. The Chinese wanted nothing the West had to offer and accepted only silver in payment for their exports. During the late 1700s opium was identified as something that the Chinese might take instead of silver, and foreign merchants started to import it in increasing quantities. The drug, already popular, became much more so, and immensely profitable for those who dealt in it. Dozens of Imperial Edicts were issued banning its import—yet volume soared. In turn, British chambers of commerce increased their pressure for free trade in all commodities, including that which the Chinese government had declared to be contraband. The Daoguang Emperor was occupied with uprisings, rebellions and natural disasters, leaving little time for complaints emanating from Canton. Britain's newfound world dominance meant it was not accustomed to having its demands ignored. Its default reaction to China was confrontation.

The British were not seeking increased territory. Britain's administrative capacity was already stretched by India and the other parts of the world where the Union Jack flew. Avoiding the enormous expense of imperial administration,[7] Britain's primary goal was an open, predictable and stable trading system, which it considered a natural right. A military victory was a means to that end. When the British fleet threatened Nanking (Nanjing) in 1842, the resulting treaty settled a number of issues, in British eyes, and ceded to Britain the island of Hong Kong in perpetuity, at the time not considered much of a prize.

Regarding his country's aims in China, Lord Aberdeen, British Foreign Secretary, said in 1841: 'We seek no exclusive advantages, and demand nothing that we shall not willingly see enjoyed by the subjects of other nations.'[8] However, having opened China to their merchants, at some cost to themselves, the British feared that other nations would now form their own, more advantageous agreements with China and usurp Britain's position. Accordingly, the 1843 Supplementary Treaty of the Bogue—the agreement that added practical details to the 1842 Treaty of Nanking—included a safeguard. 'Should the Emperor', stated the agreement, 'be pleased to grant additional privileges or immunities' to any other foreign countries, the same would automatically be extended to and enjoyed by British subjects.[9] This simple and convenient (for the foreign parties) device, known as the Most Favoured

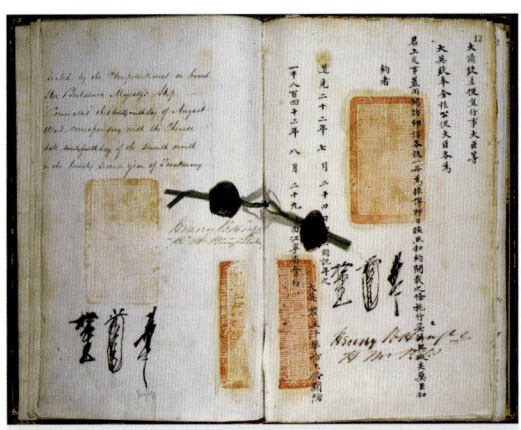

The 1842 Treaty of Nanking (Nanjing), showing the signatures of Sir Henry Pottinger and Chinese Imperial Commissioner Qiying. Reprinted with permission by the National Archives.

Nation principle, shaped all treaties, both British and otherwise, for the next hundred years. More than 20 nations would have treaties with China, and thereby become 'Treaty Powers', in a list that was ultimately to include Peru and the Congo Free State.

For our purposes, the most important outcome of the Treaty of Nanking was the opening of five cities as places for British merchants to live and conduct business: Amoy, Canton, Foochow (Fuzhou), Ningpo and Shanghai. Many more 'treaty ports' would be created by later treaties.

Britain felt its initial aims had been achieved by the establishment of the five treaty ports, plus the colony of Hong Kong, from where it could manage trade with China. The treaty allowed British subjects and their families to reside at the five places, to pursue mercantile interests, 'without molestation or restraint'. Britain was also permitted to install consular officers at each port. They were the conduits between the Chinese authorities and the merchants, responsible for seeing that the duties and other dues of the Chinese government were paid. However, what followed can hardly be said to have measured up to British expectations. The colony of Hong Kong was ridiculed in the British Parliament. Of the five open ports, one (Canton) remained closed, ultimately giving rise to a second war, and two (Foochow and Ningpo) were so disappointing that Britain tried exchanging them for somewhere better, like unsuitable birthday gifts. (The Chinese refused, explaining it would make a complete mockery of the treaty.) Amoy had a slow start and Shanghai, in time becoming bigger than all the others combined, was far smaller than many nearby cities.

The treaty's focus was not on the government of the nascent foreign settlements. Little was anticipated beyond a small gathering of merchants and their godowns at each place. In time, municipal councils would be established at the major ports, but initially each was left to develop individually. Two forms of foreign area came to be recognized—the concession and the settlement. A concession arose where the foreign government identified an area of land for its nationals and leased it in its own name. The area was cleared, roads were laid out and individual lots auctioned off, each purchaser taking a lease from the foreign government concerned. A settlement was also a discrete area for foreign occupation, but the title remained with the individual Chinese owners; the foreign merchants had to negotiate their own leases or purchases. Many of the smaller treaty ports had neither a concession nor a settlement. Even where one did exist, it was neither intended nor required that all foreigners live there. That they generally did so was more for reasons of mutual protection and support.

A MATTER OF INTERPRETATION

Chinese people felt a certain ambivalence about foreigners living permanently in China. Foreigners embodied the country's political and military weakness. Yet, on the other hand, they created trading and employment opportunities and later on a certain freedom in the areas they controlled. Article II of the English version of the Treaty of Nanking stated that British merchants were 'allowed to reside' at the five places named. In the Chinese version the relevant clause translates as permitting British subjects 'to dwell temporarily at the river's mouth of the five coastal cities'.[10] With the exception of Amoy, all the cities listed in the treaty were indeed on a river and each had a recognized port that was some way downstream from the city. The British claim that the treaty gave them unrestricted city access in each case appalled the Chinese. A second war had to be fought before the matter of entry to Canton was finally resolved.

The other four cities grudgingly allowed foreign residence within their walls. In Amoy and Foochow the British Consuls took up residence inside the city despite the inconvenience, mostly to demonstrate they could. More sympathetic elements of British society could understand Chinese reluctance, given colonial conduct in other parts of the world.[11] Beneath it all there were major differences in understanding about the commercial aspects of the treaty, exacerbated by China's unwilling engagement and profound mistrust. The primary purpose for the British was removing impediments to developing trade. For the Chinese, the treaty simply gave certain defined rights and immunities to foreign merchants, the 'least worst' view. What happened to imported goods, for example, once they left the hands of the British merchant the Chinese considered to be their business alone. This conflict of principles, and the imbalance in power, was to underlie many of the future trade-related difficulties.

The opening of the first five treaty ports resulted in increased prosperity locally. Despite this, the foreign powers were aware they were unwelcome. Nothing fundamental had changed. China was too big to be influenced by 'a marginal sea-frontier contact with foreign ideas'.[12] Soon the war of 1839–42 seemed too brief and the battles too localized to have impressed Peking (Beijing).[13] A major unspoken factor was opium. Banned by China, opium was the most profitable import for foreign merchants on the China Coast. Chinese officials also amassed enormous fortunes by averting their eyes instead of implementing Imperial proclamations. The Imperial government was also a beneficiary of 'squeeze'. British India needed the revenue from opium, China's tea exports could not be bought without it, it was illegal to import it, the treaty did not mention it—and the opium trade went from strength to strength. Banned yet endemic, this curious state of affairs could not continue. The peace generated by the Treaty of Nanking increasingly seemed but an armistice.[14]

Thus there was an inevitability to the Second Opium War of 1856–60, but now there was another factor. The Americans' 1844 Treaty of Wanghia (Wangxia) included a clause allowing for automatic revision after twelve years—in 1856. Applying the Most Favoured Nation principle, Britain started preparing for a revision of its treaty, in 1854. Negotiations over such matters as clarifying inland duty arrangements and opening China further took place with senior mandarins, none of whom believed that increased foreign trade was beneficial to China. Trade and merchants were despised in the traditional Chinese hierarchy, colouring the negotiators' attitudes towards a state that raised the activity to a national priority.[15] It was not helped by the tendency of every foreigner in China 'to wrap themselves in their national flag'.[16]

The 1858 treaties of Tientsin (Tianjin) listed a further ten towns and cities to be opened as treaty ports, and the 1860 Treaty of Peking added Tientsin itself to the list. The new coastal ports were Kiungchow (Qiongzhou), Swatow (Shantou), Chefoo (Yantai) and Newchwang (Yingkou). In addition more were added along the Yangtze River: Chinkiang (Zhenjiang), Nanking, Kiukiang (Jiujiang) and Hankow (Hankou); the foreign powers now understood that access to the empire's principal river was essential to increasing foreign trade. On Formosa, Taiwan-fu (Tainan) and Tamsui (Danshui) were opened. However, as with the initial five ports, many of the hopes that attended the next eleven were to be dashed.

Most of the new treaty ports saw an influx of foreign merchants, including the major China Coast firms of Jardines, Dents and Russells, as well as independent traders. They were all hoping to amass fortunes by exporting tea, silk and porcelain, and importing opium and cotton and woollen goods. Some succeeded, becoming very wealthy before returning home to comfortable retirement. However, it soon became apparent that the needs of the perceived hundreds of millions of customers were being well served by Chinese merchants and there was no commercial vacuum that the foreigners could fill. Besides, the Chinese thought their own products were superior to imports; in most cases they were cheaper.

It was only in the early years of the 20th century the foreign powers realized continually opening treaty ports and installing a consul in each was unnecessary. The considerable expense was one factor. More importantly, the existing Chinese commercial networks could facilitate the import and distribution of foreign goods. Although the treaty port system was to last another 40 years, the last to be opened in China proper by a foreign power other than Japan was Kongmoon (Jiangmen), by Britain in 1902. As we shall see, the Japanese increased the number significantly in the next few years.

1858　　　　　　　　　　　　　　1900

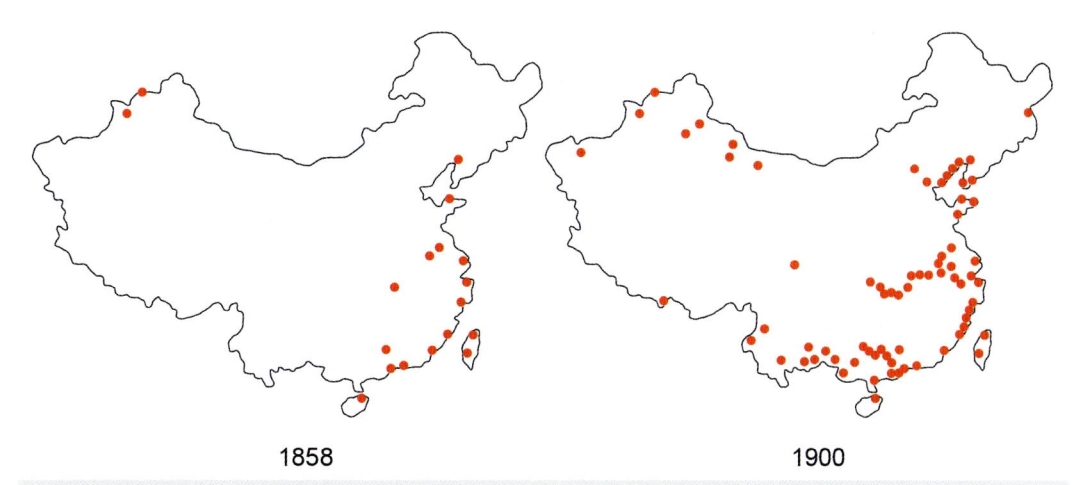

Two maps showing the proliferation of treaty ports and other open cities between 1858 and 1900

Unequal treaties?

The various agreements giving rise to the Treaty Port Era are often described, by Chinese and Western writers alike, as 'unequal treaties'. The primary objective of Western powers in China was not colonization but trade, a goal possible to achieve through negotiation. In Chinese eyes negotiations could only proceed if the foreigners first acknowledged China as the superior party. China was forced, through armed conflict, to abandon this position (although never the belief). The Chinese perceived the resulting treaties, with their territorial losses, indemnities and erosion of sovereignty, as the cause of their misfortunes. Having repeatedly stated that they had no use for foreigners or their products, they were forced to accept them by overwhelming military force. In the face of a population deeply hostile to foreigners, damage containment became the only alternative for the Chinese government. Foreigners 'could best be held at bay by giving them clearly defined areas of residence and negotiating only through their community leaders'.[17]

Content with their initial gains Britain and France were focused on ensuring the agreed treaties were upheld, not on increasing territory. Indeed, following the Second Opium War the first military act by the Allies after withdrawing from Peking was to assist the empire's defeat of its internal enemies, the Taiping rebels.[18] Britain knew ensuring China's peace and stability was the most productive way of protecting British commercial interests, meanwhile encouraging China to enforce British treaty rights.[19]

It is not within the scope of this volume to describe the foreign missionary experience in China. Missionaries were often unwelcome, particularly in the interior, and in times of crisis such feelings were extended to foreign merchants.[20] One of the merchants' chief concerns was taxation. Later treaties attempted to clarify further the impact of domestic duties (*likin*) on foreign trade, and to extend exemptions from Chinese laws to activities in the interior; both are discussed further below. The most radical treaty was one that was never ratified. In the context of the allowed-for review of the 1858 Treaty of Tientsin, British Minister in Peking Sir Rutherford Alcock drafted what became known as the Alcock Convention. Both China and Britain saw the revision as an opportunity to address existing problems, generating huge amounts of correspondence and memorials. The new treaty, signed on 23 October 1869, was the first welcomed by China.[21] Alcock had drafted it as an agreement between equals. For example, the convention stated British subjects would no longer claim privileges under the Most Favoured Nation principle without honouring conditions imposed on the other nation.[22] However, British merchants in Hong Kong and Britain claimed that too much was being given to China and the British government refused to ratify the treaty.

Having itself been forced to ratify treaties in the past, the Chinese government was dumbfounded that one so mutually beneficial could be turned down in London.[23] China was forced to conclude that, ultimately, its interests would always be secondary to those of the foreigner. The effect on relations was disastrous. Within a year there were many anti-foreign riots, particularly in Tientsin.[24] These affected all foreign powers, particularly the French as the leading champion of missionary activities.

Lacking significant commercial interests, France's ambition in China involved extending its colonial influence beyond the French Indo-China border. Victory in a war with China in 1884–85 consolidated France's position in what is today Vietnam, and raised British anxieties concerning Britain's interests in Burma. Britain wanted to promote trade over the Burma–China border, and consequently in south-west China itself. France, on the other hand, made repeated threats to seize Chinese territory. The opening, at British insistence, of the West River to foreign trade in 1897 stemmed French ambitions.

The other principal foreign powers that were active in China in the latter part of the 19th century were America and Russia—and they also had very different aims. The Americans, adopting the mantle of reluctant colonialists, distanced themselves from anything resembling territorial gain. The short-lived American Concessions in Shanghai and Tientsin were the only real exceptions. Instead, American merchants contented themselves with participating as a major force in the treaty ports' commercial activity. Territorial expansion certainly topped Russia's Chinese agenda. When necessary, Russia presented itself to China as a fellow Asiatic nation, distinct from the individualistic Western powers, and empathetic to the Asian way of thinking.[25] Whether or not the Chinese were deceived, they lost more land to Russia than to any other power. While China was distracted by the concurrent Second Opium War and Taiping Rebellion, Russia took all the Chinese territory north of the Amur (Heilong) River in the 1858 Treaty of Aigun (Aihun). Further Russian gains are dealt with elsewhere in this volume.* It is puzzling that China should have felt the cession of Hong Kong and Kowloon so deeply over the decades, yet complained so little about the loss of almost two million square kilometres of territory to Russia. The present size of China is approximately ten million square kilometres.

Britain started the treaty port system and was initially the dominant foreign power in China. In the following century the baton passed to Japan, which reversed the British position, being more interested in territory than trade. As early as 1843, before any other Western nation concluded a treaty with China, Britain recognized that France and America would insist on equal footing. 'History teaches us', said the *Colonial Gazette*, 'that interference in the domestic affairs of other nations is usually done out of dread at what a neighbour might do if we fail to interfere. For the French and American diplomats, our mere presence in China will be an irresistible inducement to involve themselves in the intrigues of the country and while they are busy in the south, we may be sure Russia will not be idle in the north.'[26] This prediction was correct, although Britain's dominance was to last well into the 20th century.

Open cities numbered 16 in 1858, growing to 58 by the turn of the century and doubling before the end of the Treaty Port Era in 1943. China's internal disturbances and inability to adapt to changing circumstances meant foreign powers continued their semi-colonial practices.

Partitioning the empire

A succession of wars had left China with its fleet annihilated, its army defeated and crippling war indemnities to be paid. Yet the country's leaders lacked the knowledge and resolve to cure its ills. Any changes taking place were characterized more 'by the movement . . . of the hour-hand than of the minute-hand of a watch'.[27] In 1841, only Britain had been able to impose its will on China. Half a century later, Britain had been joined by France, Germany, Japan and Russia. All five, and to some extent America,

---

*   See entry on Aigun.

Foreign spheres of influence in China by 1912

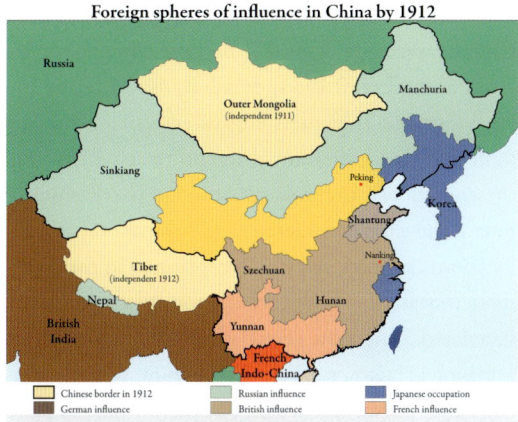

China in 1912, showing how almost the whole country came within the foreign powers' spheres of influence

were planning spheres of influence or domination of large areas of China. They and others acted together in 1900 when the Boxers besieged their nationals in Peking. However, there were such differences of aim, opinion and culture between them they were unable to use their dominance to further impinge on Chinese territory.

In 1900 only Japan and Russia seemed capable of taking over all of China. The Western powers trusted neither to do so without damaging wider international interests. Without its problems in South Africa and India, Britain might have been interested, but only with American assistance.[28] And American action was constrained by its 'Monroe Doctrine', which forbade participation in the oppression of a foreign government. The outcome which seemed certain to outsiders was the implosion and partition of the Chinese Empire.[29]

All this came to nothing, but seen through the eyes of contemporary observers things could only end badly. Ten years after the French defeat of China in 1885, a heavier blow was inflicted by Japan. Attempts at modernization, described below, did not produce a militarily stronger China. Money was spent on new warships, guns and fortifications, but the nation lacked the ability to use them effectively. The Japanese victory made the imminent collapse of the empire even more likely. Between 1895 and 1901 eight nations claimed concessions in Hankow

and Tientsin. However, Germany had more ambitious plans. Having occupied Kiaochow (Jiaozhou) Bay on a spurious pretext in late 1897, the Germans demanded and received a lease of 500 square kilometres of adjacent territory the following March. This prompted Russia to follow three weeks later by leasing Port Arthur (Lüshun) and Talienwan (Dalianwan). Not to be left out France forced a lease of Kwangchowwan (Zhanjiang) in April, and Britain took over Weihaiwei (Weihai) from the Japanese in May. The rapid chain reaction culminated in Britain leasing the New Territory in June 1898, thus adding to its colony in Hong Kong.

In just over three months, half a dozen physically small but psychologically enormous pieces of China had been taken into foreign ownership. The first grab, by Germany, prompted largely congratulatory press

A very graphic contemporary image of the foreign powers preparing to tear up China: 'Dissection of the Chinese monster. The Cossack to John Bull: You can look, but don't touch!' Courtesy of Chester Cheng.

coverage, cheering others on to do likewise instead of wasting time on fruitless diplomacy. The apparent inevitability of the collapse of the empire also encouraged Chinese rebels. The Boxers emerged as the most powerful, in 1900 looking as though they would overthrow the Qing dynasty. A brilliant sleight of hand by Cixi, the Empress Dowager, redirected the rebels' fury against the foreigners, away from herself and her family. The foreign powers buried their differences and ensured the Boxers' defeat; in the final analysis, the ruling dynasty was seen as the least of the available evils.

By 1900 there was a new class of foreign-controlled entity—the leased territory. The lessee exercised sovereignty for the duration of the lease, and governed according to its own laws. Rent was paid, usually nominal, and the area was outside the Chinese customs net. It would be well at this stage to review the other classes of foreign presence. First was the colony, a piece of China ceded in perpetuity to a foreign power. There was initially only one—Hong Kong, created in 1842. Macao, settled by Portugal in 1557, was only formally recognized as Portuguese territory in 1887. Colonies were under the total control and jurisdiction of the foreign power.

Next were the treaty ports, numbering around 50 by 1900. These were centred on, or near, Chinese towns and cities agreed to be opened to foreign trade and residence by individual treaties between China and foreign powers. A clear and understood set of rules, developed in successive treaties, was applied to facilitate and control foreign trade. In each case the boundary of the treaty port was defined, and within that limit the rules of the Imperial Maritime Customs determined the amount of import and export duty to be paid. The Treaty Powers could install consuls at each treaty port with jurisdiction over their respective citizens. Although a requirement since the 1876 Chefoo Agreement, not all treaty ports had a defined area for foreign settlement; some were too insignificant. In others, ironically including Chefoo itself, it proved too difficult to establish a discrete foreign area. Where this was done it was either a concession or a settlement. Within concessions, where the land had been acquired en bloc by the foreign government, Chinese were not allowed to become tenants.

In a number of cases, detailed inspection by the newly arrived foreigners suggested that the wrong place had been mentioned in the treaty. Reflecting the attitudes of the time, the foreign parties moved into what they considered to be the more suitable location, assuming the place mentioned in the treaty was a mistake. Examples are Chefoo, where the treaty stipulated Tangchow (Penglai), 70 kilometres away; Hoihow (Haikou), where Kiungchow was the official treaty port; Newchwang, where the named place was impossible to reach; and Swatow, chosen as more suitable than the official Chaochow-fu (Chaozhou). The territorial limits of some treaty ports were never resolved satisfactorily, despite strenuous diplomatic efforts.

In Shanghai a different sort of entity emerged—the international settlement, created in 1863 when the former British and American settlements combined. Although predominantly British, no single nation controlled the Shanghai International Settlement. Its governing body, the Shanghai Municipal Council, formed its own set of regulations and its members were drawn from the foreign community at large. It remained unique until 1902 when another was created on Kulangsu (Gulangyu), the residential island off Amoy.

The treaty port concept had become formulaic, the first few having set a pattern and structure and created expectations. This was then replicated, but starting in 1898 a quasi–treaty port started to appear. In an attempt to halt the foreign powers' acquisitive tendencies, by then running rampant, the Imperial government declared certain towns and cities open for foreign trade and residence on much the same lines as treaty ports. The absence of a treaty per se meant they could not be described as treaty ports; 'open city' was used instead. These 'voluntary' openings fell into two broad categories. First were cases where the government—Imperial and later Republican—opened ports to prevent a foreign power doing so, which would have made Chinese control impossible. Woosung (Wusong) was an example, opened by

Imperial Decree in 1898 albeit coerced by Britain, which feared a rival establishing itself at the gateway to Shanghai. Tsinan (Jinan) was another, its opening in 1904 prompted by Japan as a counter to German encroachment. A foreign residential quarter was usually provided in these quasi-treaty ports, where Chinese people also resided, but the municipal governments that developed were strictly in the hands of the Chinese.

The second type of 'voluntary' opening was based on treaties, and makes precision about the total number of treaty ports difficult. The 1842 Treaty of Nanking permitted British subjects to reside at the five places listed. Later treaties permitted foreign subjects to enjoy the same privileges and immunities as at previously opened ports. Different wording was used in the Japanese 1903 Treaty of Commerce and Navigation. Under this treaty Changsha was opened as a treaty port, just like all the others, but the same clause added that Mukden (Shenyang) and Tatungkow (Dadonggou) 'will be opened by China itself' as places of international residence and trade. The parallel American treaty used the same wording regarding Mukden and Antung (Dandong). Too much should not be read into this subtle change in terminology, but I have taken 1903 as a watershed—from this point onwards no new treaty ports were created, in the classic sense of the term, in China proper.† Instead Japan was forcing China to open new ports unilaterally; Chinese refusal to do so was never an option. Japan opened more than 50 cities, towns and even villages in China's north-east, mainly Manchuria, changing the concept of a treaty port from a commercial entity to a purely political one. Clearly these were steps towards the ultimate goal of colonial control.

Foreign expansion away from the coast and into China's great river systems produced other types of presence—'ports-of-call' and 'landing stages'. The first ports-of-call were created by the 1876 Chefoo Agreement. Six intermediate towns along the Yangtze were identified, allowing foreign steamers to pick up and set down passengers and cargo. The need arose because foreign steamers were only allowed to sail from one treaty port to another. On China's long rivers this was not only an inconvenience, but restricted rather than promoted trade. Further treaties in 1897, 1898 and 1902 created 15 more ports-of-call on the Yangtze and West rivers as well as 10 landing stages on the latter, for passengers only. Foreign merchant establishments were not permitted at any of these places. Nonetheless, the regular appearance of their steamers made the foreign presence obvious.

Apart from missionary stations, not within the scope of this book, there was another entity partly within foreign jurisdiction. Hot and humid summers in the southern and Yangtze treaty ports prompted Westerners to take to the hills and northern beaches to cool off. A number of hill stations and resorts developed, such as Kuling (Lushan) and Peitaiho (Beidaihe). Many of them were governed by municipal councils, like the larger treaty ports.

In total, more than 250 places, including consular, diplomatic and customs stations, can be identified in China as having had foreign non-missionary presence or jurisdiction before the end of the Treaty Port Era in 1943.

Treaty ports and China's modernization

One of the principal and longest-lasting agents of modernization derived from the treaty port system was the complete reorganization of the collection of duty on imports and exports. The foreign-managed Imperial Maritime Customs service appeared almost by accident in 1854, thanks to the Taiping rebels. When the Shanghai Custom House fell into rebel hands, the foreign merchants toyed momentarily with the happy prospect of paying no duty. Cooler heads prevailed. The British, French and American consuls agreed that the dues would be collected by one of their representatives and passed to Peking. It had been the previous practice that deductions were made by each official through whose hands the revenue passed. Thus amounts eventually submitted

---

† An Anglo-Tibetan convention in 1904 opened two places in Tibet as the last treaty ports.

were but a small percentage of those collected. Never before had the full amount been passed on with the underlying records fully auditable. The service is described in more detail below.

Foreign merchants repeatedly found they could not compete with existing trading patterns. What they did introduce, from their bases in the treaty ports, were different ways of facilitating that trade, although some early examples were spectacular failures. Attempts to erect a telegraph line in 1875 from Foochow to Amoy were thwarted when the poles were dug up by angry locals claiming an interference with their *fengshui*. A foreign company built China's first railway in 1876 at Woosung, against the direct orders of the local *taotai*. Accordingly, it was closed at the first available opportunity.

China repeatedly demonstrated it had fallen behind in engineering and technology, particularly regarding its military capability. Britain's active role in the suppression of piracy had removed some of the urgency for naval development.[30] The generous budget awarded in 1885 to rebuilding the navy, following the destruction of half of it by France, was diverted to rebuild the Summer Palace.[31] The challenge for forward-thinking Chinese leaders was how to balance the need to modernize against the desire to preserve national integrity and identity. Chinese officials opposed innovations likely to upset the time-honoured social balance of the country.[32] Confucianism exercised a very strong hold on how Chinese people, particularly the powerful scholar-officials, considered their country should be run—and telegraphs, railways and steamships were not part of it. In recent years, precisely these elements have been identified as facilitating the revolution in communications that made the development and diversification of global capitalism possible.[33]

China's early efforts at industrialization have been described as 'isolated cases rather than an epidemic'.[34] The foreign occupation of the capital in 1860 prompted the creation of modern dockyards and armament factories to prepare for future attacks: the Kiangnan (Jiangnan) Arsenal in Shanghai in 1865 and the Foochow Arsenal in 1866. These initiatives owed more to the ability and foresight of provincial governors than to the Imperial Court.[35] Military industries were seen as the first priority to try to ensure the long-term security of the state. Only then could attention and resources be devoted to other areas.[36]

The first of these was shipping. Long used to junks as the only means of transporting their goods along coasts and rivers, local traders could see advantages in the size, speed, efficiency and economy of foreign steamships serving the treaty ports. Chinese merchants started investing in steamers in the 1860s; about one-third of the capital of the first three foreign operators formed in Shanghai, between 1862 and 1868, was subscribed by Chinese.[37] By 1872 China had its own, very successful, steamship company, the China Merchants Steam Navigation Co., with Chinese crew and largely British officers. Its founding was partly precipitated by the actions of the Taiping rebels. The Grand Canal was the traditional route for the shipment of tribute rice to the capital. When this was blocked by rebel activity, a number of senior Chinese officials, notably Li Hongzhang, investigated using steamers to take the rice along the coast.[38] Within a few years the new ship operator was born.[39] The vessels of American firm Russell & Co. enjoyed a leading role in the coast and river trade, but faced with increasing competition from China Merchants, and British newcomer Butterfield & Swire, Russells sold their entire fleet to the Chinese company in December 1876. China Merchants emerged as the biggest ship operator in China.

The new company was promoted and supervised by the Chinese government but funded and managed by merchants, under a system known as *kuan-tu shang-pan* (government-supervised merchant enterprise). More companies were formed along similar lines. The government examined the relative merits of each proposal, controlled the central planning and left the merchants both to bear the bulk of the financial risk and keep the majority of the profits. The Kaiping Mining Co. (1877) and the Shanghai Cotton Cloth Mill (1878) are other early examples. These enterprises can be linked to the Self-Strengthening

Li Hongzhang in 1896. Source: Mrs Archibald Little, *Li Hung-chang, His Life and Times* (London: Cassell & Co., 1903), frontispiece.

Movement, of which Li Hongzhang, Zuo Zongtang, Zeng Guofan and Sheng Xuanhuai were among the principal proponents. It was Li who memorialized the throne in 1872 in support of *kuan-tu shang-pan*.[40] Li had risen through the ranks as a provincial government official and military leader, becoming one of the major forces for reform in his country. He is recorded as saying: 'If one is stationed in Shanghai for some time and yet unable to learn from the foreigners' strengths, there will be many regrets.'[41] ‡

Chinese commercial ideas and trade practices would have developed without Western input, although perhaps on different lines, but the presence of an alien culture accelerated change. Indeed, the emergence of the major foreign concessions, 'from skyscrapers and department stores down to pavement slabs and sash windows', has been described as 'the largest cultural transfer in human history'.[42] The

shipyards, public utilities and factories that developed in the concessions were 'training grounds for workers, managers and entrepreneurs alike'.[43] Three types of Chinese businessman came to drive this process. From early days in Canton the role of the Chinese comprador had grown to be one that was indispensable to the foreign merchants. Skilled businessmen themselves, these intermediaries quickly became familiar with the foreigners' methods and, to an extent, their language. Some used this foundation to set up and prosper by themselves in the treaty ports.

In the latter half of the 19th century a new breed of Chinese entrepreneur appeared—the returning migrant. When they started to return, either having made their fortunes or forced back by discriminatory legislation in the United States or Australia, they revitalized their home towns. Swatow is a case in point. Having learnt different ways of living, they tended to be more forthright in their dealings with what they now saw as a backward home regime.

The third class of Chinese entrepreneur comprised wealthy or aspiring officials, landowners and merchants, who saw in the treaty ports an environment that would allow them to invest their money in relative safety. Some projects have already been mentioned. The later decades of the century saw a number of others: steelworks in Hankow; coal mines centred on Tientsin; and more cotton mills in Shanghai. From a small beginning in 1879 in Tientsin, telegraph lines began to proliferate: Chinese realized how unsatisfactory it was for foreigners in their home countries to know sooner about happenings in China than the Chinese themselves. It was the foreigners' introduction of railways that left the biggest physical impression on the development of China. These lumbering, noisy contraptions were seen as totally unnecessary by the majority of the people, and as a violent transgression of *fengshui*. Li Hongzhang contravened the weight of traditional thinking when in 1881 he publicly supported building railways in China. He was dismayed when the small but successful Woosung Railway was torn up in 1877, but others appeared. First, in 1881, was an eleven-kilometre line from the Kaiping mines to the nearest navigable water. This was

---

‡ See the entry on Tientsin for more on Li Hongzhang.

extended to Tientsin in 1889 and to Shanhaikwan (Shanhaiguan) a few years later. Defeat at the hands of the Japanese in 1895 prompted a massive increase in railway investment, both foreign and Chinese. In a little over ten years there were almost 10,000 kilometres of track, with more being planned, connecting all the major cities in the country.

Another outcome of the Sino-Japanese War was the clear statement, in the 1895 Treaty of Shimonoseki, that Japanese (and therefore all the Treaty Powers) were permitted to manufacture in the treaty ports. This prompted industrial growth on a scale hitherto unseen. In the larger ports, such as Shanghai, Hankow and Tientsin, the emergence of foreign factories forced local industries to be competitive, especially in the field of textiles. By 1913 of all the cotton spindles operating in factories in China 60 percent were Chinese-owned, 27 percent European and 13 percent Japanese. Between 1912 and 1920 Chinese industry had one of the highest growth rates in the world.[44] Due to warlordism, a lack of vigorous development goals and Japanese imperialist aggression this early promise was not to be realized.

The foreign merchants were never happy to have their ideas and plans quashed by what they saw as superstition and Chinese fatalism. An example was the deteriorating state of the river at Tientsin, by 1900 the sixth-largest of the open cities. To improve navigation to the city from the coast was a major undertaking, not least dredging the infamous Taku (Dagu) Bar. However, the same Chinese merchants making money out of trade were saying that as the sand bar had been put there by the gods, who were they to interfere?[45] In this case the foreign powers took the opportunity of the 1901 Boxer Peace Protocol, an agreement ostensibly nothing to do with shipping and navigation, to impose a system of river conservation and improvement. The following year, Britain's Commercial Treaty placed a requirement upon China to introduce a national coinage, a step that benefited the entire country.

The aftermath of the Boxer troubles, that anti-dynastic rebellion cleverly diverted to be a fight with the foreigners, was to produce two more notable foreign-inspired results. The first was the abolition of the Tsungli Yamen. Founded in 1861 following the Second Opium War as the government agency dealing with foreign affairs, it was later described as 'an invertebrate, gelatinous body' that acted more to curtail than extend China's foreign relations.[46] It was replaced in July 1902 by a more modern Foreign Office, the Wai-wu Pu. By no means perfect, this was a step towards enabling China to communicate effectively with other nations.

Also inspired by the Boxer rising was the Provisional Government that ruled Tientsin from 1900 to 1902. As the Chinese authorities had absconded, the foreign powers took up governing the city. They introduced many improvements—more, in the opinion of one commentator, than the Chinese authorities had done in the previous few centuries.[47] Furthermore, they ran the city at a profit and handed over the surplus, together with full accounts, to the very surprised incoming Chinese government.

There was one more aspect of the treaty port system of practical use to a large number of Chinese. Despite the hated presence of foreigners, the Western enclaves proved on many occasions to be places of refuge, both for individuals and for the masses. Hong Kong was a case in point, once word spread that it was a safe and fair place in which to do business. When troubles beset the rest of the country large numbers of refugees found security within the boundaries of the treaty ports. Many a commercial boom and bust in Shanghai can be attributed to the sudden influx and then exodus of people taking shelter. Chinese reformers were able to benefit from the pockets of protection provided by Hong Kong and the treaty ports. Sun Yat-sen received some of his high school education and gained his medical qualification in Hong Kong. Even in the turbulent 1920s, described below, when anti-foreign sentiments were running high, the foreign enclaves remained places of refuge.

Law and extraterritoriality

The principle of taking 'an eye for an eye' was well known in the West, stemming as it does from the Old Testament. The early European visitors to China were surprised to find that a similar concept existed, and that it was taken literally, applying equally to foreigners and Chinese. A case in 1784 became infamous. A British vessel, the *Lady Hughes*, arrived at Whampoa (Huangpu) and fired the customary salute. Unfortunately a live round was used and two nearby Chinese spectators were killed. The authorities demanded that the British surrender for punishment either the sailor who fired the shot or somebody else—it did not matter whom. After a stand-off, when all trade was suspended, the British sacrificed the oldest and weakest member of their community for public strangulation.[48] In a similar case in 1821, American seaman Francis Terranova had to be surrendered after inadvertently killing a Chinese woman.[49] There were many other such cases.

It was not only the consequences to themselves that foreigners feared but to those Chinese who assisted them. There was a case of a Chinese man who had been found guilty of helping foreigners to explore the interior, something which was strictly forbidden. Not only was he condemned to the 'death of one thousand cuts' (the very worst of all punishments, combining pain with unfiliality) but his entire family was beheaded, his native village destroyed and the countryside for 30 kilometres around laid waste.[50] An extreme case, but the feeling among foreigners was that the Chinese legal system was something better avoided. The Qing legal code was systematic and, on its own terms, logical; actions had consequences.[51] In late imperial China 'the majority of criminals found guilty by county magistrates were sentenced to fines, beatings, penal servitude, exile or death. Imprisonment was not used as a legal penalty'.[52] This began to change only after 1895, with the defeat of China in the Sino-Japanese War and the greater interest in 'strengthening China' that this engendered among intellectuals and reformers.

To put matters into perspective, let us compare some Chinese penalties with those prevailing in England. In China in the 1840s wilful and premeditated murder was punishable by public beheading or worse. For homicide without an express desire to kill, the penalty was strangulation. Penalties also depended on the relationship between victim and perpetrator; killing a parent was punished more severely than a neighbour. Accidental killing could be redeemed by compensation to the victim's family, and killing in self-defence was not punishable at all.[53] Meanwhile in England, attempted murder, even without resulting in injury, was a capital offence, as, until 1830, was stealing a horse.[54] In some respects the two systems were not far apart, although the foreigners 'avoided looking themselves in the mirror . . . eliding their own legacy of violence and autocracy'.[55] For them the logic of Chinese law was opaque, making them feel vulnerable and a long way from the security and predictability of home.

In the context of the Terranova case, the Americans made a declaration that they would submit to Chinese laws, 'be they ever so unjust'.[56] The British were more circumspect, knowing the requirement of Chinese law that the accused must confess, under torture if required. Given the defeat of the Chinese in the 1839–42 war the British feared that retribution might be exacted on individuals via the legal system. Yet the 1842 Treaty of Nanking included no safeguards of a legal nature. In the months following his signing of the treaty, Sir Henry Pottinger was pressured to provide for greater protection for British subjects from the alien legal regime in which they would be living and working.[57] Accordingly, the 1843 Supplementary Treaty of the Bogue provided for the repatriation of fleeing British or Chinese criminals for punishment according to the laws of their respective countries and at the hands of their respective officials.

The British wanted a form of extraterritoriality, often shortened to 'extrality'. Now best described as diplomatic immunity, extrality was extended to all foreigners, putting them outside the reach of the domestic laws of their country of residence. It was a concept already operating in other parts of the world. British Consuls in the Turkish Empire, for instance, were given the power to punish British offenders; if the consul thought the crime too serious or outside his experience he then had the power to send the culprit back to Britain for full trial.[58] Nor was this concept unknown to the Chinese. The first recorded treaty between China and a foreign power, the 1689 Treaty of Nerchinsk with Russia, included a provision whereby people crossing the border in either direction without authority were to be returned 'without delay' to their own side for punishment.[59]

In Hong Kong the legal situation was much clearer. As a British colony, English law applied, in theory, to all residents. Many of Hong Kong's early laws discriminated against the Chinese, justified by the argument that nobody had invited them to live there and they were free to leave.[60] Naturally, this logic was never applied in reverse; China had not invited foreign merchants to live in the treaty ports, yet was obliged to agree to privileged measures that would ensure their legal protection.

It was the Americans who took the step of codifying the principle of extrality for the benefit of all. In their 1844 Treaty of Wanghia they reversed the position they had taken after the Terranova affair. Article XXI of that agreement spelt out that Chinese subjects suspected of a crime against an American citizen would be arrested and punished by the Chinese authorities according to the laws of China. Similarly, and more importantly for the foreign population, subjects of the United States who committed any crime in China were to be tried and punished by an American Consul. Under the existing Most Favoured Nation principle, citizens of all current and subsequent Treaty Powers enjoyed similar protection. Later treaties confirmed and amplified the principle, which stood for almost the next hundred years.

Extrality put foreign consuls in the powerful position of hearing criminal and civil cases involving their nationals. Many were unprepared, and most were unqualified for the role. The Chinese system at the time was similar, in that cases were heard by magistrates who were seen as administrators rather than judges; they made their decisions based on the particular circumstances of the case.[61] The main differences were the nature of punishments and the lack of safeguards for the accused that generally applied in Western jurisdictions.[62] Nevertheless, a British commentator later in the century noted that there was far greater security for life and property in the majority of Chinese towns than in London.[63] The same is true today.

Appeals from British consular courts, as well as cases that exceeded consuls' jurisdiction, were heard in the Supreme Court of Hong Kong. In 1865, after Shanghai emerged as the senior treaty port, Britain established a Supreme Court for China there under a full-time judge. In 1871 a courthouse was constructed in the grounds of the British Consulate, where it still stands.[64]

Britain's Supreme Court for China, after renovation in 1913. Reprinted with permission by the National Archives.

Successive British judges demonstrated that the privilege of extraterritoriality did not include breaking Chinese laws with impunity. British violators were tried by British judges in a British court, but on behalf of the Chinese state,[65] giving public recognition to China's legal sovereignty. But problems persisted; missionaries claimed the right to live anywhere in the empire and still be protected from Chinese laws they disliked.[66] Foreign merchants' repeated demands to be allowed to trade with the interior were met with the Chinese response that, provided they submitted to Chinese law and taxation, they could go anywhere. Peking's view was that the point of the treaty ports was that foreigners could enjoy the exemptions they demanded in those specific areas; the rest of China was sovereign Chinese territory.[67] It was not just the Chinese who were expressing dissatisfaction. Writing in 1868 Rutherford Alcock was indignant that foreigners expected carte blanche exemption from Chinese laws: 'Such unequal and incompatible conditions might possibly be imposed by force upon a conquered nation, but can never be the result of negotiations.'[68]

In 1863 another institution had been created, also in Shanghai, aimed at redressing some of the problems of extrality. The 'Mixed Court' was a response to the unacceptable alternative of having a full Chinese court in the foreign settlement. A Chinese magistrate would hear cases where both parties were Chinese, and would be joined by a foreign consular official for Chinese cases involving a foreigner. Questions of land ownership, for example, were to keep lawyers very busy. As early as 1856 Sir John Bowring wrote to the British Consul in Amoy regarding legal arrangements for Chinese renting property to foreigners. He recorded the British law officers' opinion: '…the law and custom of China, if they can be ascertained, must govern the decision.'[69] The operative words here are 'if they can be ascertained'. There were genuine efforts to ascertain what the Chinese system was in order that it could be improved (at least in foreign eyes), and to make life easier for foreigners. The British 1902 Commercial Treaty tried to encourage Chinese legal reform. Even the carrot of surrender of all extraterritorial rights was dangled, provided China improved matters to Britain's satisfaction.[70] The cynic would say this was an empty gesture as there was no chance of satisfactory reforms being introduced. I believe the intention and spirit were genuine. The ill-fated Alcock Convention of 1869 would have introduced a commercial code to China, seen as the first of three steps towards scrapping extrality; the next two would have been a civil code and a criminal code.[71] As it was, laws for companies and bankruptcy were not introduced until 1903.[72]

In the early decades of the 20th century China embraced a number of international initiatives for legal and fiscal change.[73] Despite this progress, foreigners' contempt for China's legal system remained a continuing source of irritation for the Chinese. The Chinese might not have defended some of the laws with which they had to comply, but the disrespect and the principle mattered. Some Chinese objections to extrality raised in the early part of the 20th century were quite valid. The China of the 1920s was very different from that on which the concept was forced in 1844. There was a proliferation of foreign courts with sometimes conflicting rules and practices. If there was no official from an offending foreign party's country to try him, he would probably escape punishment altogether. Furthermore, foreign judges at times protected their own nationals, even against just claims by Chinese. The concept was open to abuse, both by foreigners trying to evade legitimate restrictions, on smuggling for example and by Chinese claiming spurious foreign protection.[74] Extrality was not abandoned until 1943 when, as an encouragement to the Nationalists in their war against Japan, Britain relinquished 'all existing treaty rights relating to the system of treaty ports in China'.[75] Under the Most Favoured Nation principle, Britain's action effectively applied to almost all other Treaty Powers. Remaining were the French presence in Hankow, Kwangchowwan and Tientsin; the Italian Concession in Tientsin; Hong Kong; and the Portuguese colony of Macao, relinquished in 1946, 1947, 1997 and 1999 respectively.

Treaty port business

Apart from those prompted by political rather than commercial motives, treaty ports were selected as places of potential profitable activity for foreign merchants. It is thus remarkable how few of them were commercially successful. Indeed, most of them were downright disappointing. Shanghai was the biggest success story. Then, in no particular order, came Tientsin, Hankow, Canton, Dairen (Dalian) and Harbin. But the sum of the trade conducted and customs revenue collected at all the others would hardly amount to that of any one of the six just mentioned. Thus their description as 'vacuum pumps for the extraction of resources'[76] seems somewhat overstated. Shanghai's success is attributable to its unique location both on the coast and at the mouth of China's greatest river. Tientsin grew largely through being the port for Peking. Hankow was the collection point for much of the huge Chinese interior. Canton's success came about through the 300 years' start it had on all the others. Dairen and Harbin were positioned to cash in on the development of the hitherto untapped resources of Manchuria.

Into these larger ports were taken cotton and woollen goods, opium and latterly the whole array of industrial and consumer products that the West manufactured. Out of them came the traditional tea, silk and porcelain, as well as grain, raw cotton and minerals. At the other end of the scale Chungking (Chongqing), after its much heralded and long-awaited opening as a treaty port in 1890, proudly recorded as its major exports pig bristles, fungus, rhubarb and wax.[77] Looked at from today's perspective, the business operations in the lesser treaty ports were tiny, but each had behind it a businessman—Chinese or foreign—determined to turn a profit on whatever could be bought or sold. A 1000-tonne steamer was considered to be a large vessel; these water-borne workhorses would carry whatever was available from one treaty port to another.

Many foreign merchants at the treaty ports acted as 'commission agents', sourcing exports for overseas principals and earning a commission on the value of the contract. Imports were similarly handled. There were exceptions, of course, but typically British agents would deal in what was seen as the higher end of the market—tea, silk and porcelain. Germans, and later Japanese, were noted for getting their hands dirty in the 'muck and truck' trade, meaning lower-end and perhaps unattractive commodities such as pig bristles, used for making particularly abrasive brushes. Agency business required minimal capital outlay and offered reduced risk.

The major foreign firms in the early days, such as Jardines, Dents and Russells, had the resources and the volume of business to be able to afford large godowns and fine residences for their senior men. Smaller firms found it hard to compete, but did. All of them faced stiff competition from indigenous Chinese merchants. The quality of life expected by the treaty ports' foreigners meant much had to be

A small steamer loading up at Wuchow (Wuzhou), typical of the remote outposts, under the watchful eye of a gunboat. © Peter Lockhart Smith. Image courtesy of Historical Photographs of China, University of Bristol.

spent on housing and the provision of essential supplies, for the merchant and often his family, before business could start. The Chinese had no such concerns; they lived as they had always lived and required no additional investment. As early as the mid-1860s most foreign trade in the treaty ports was handled by Chinese merchants. The foreigners depended on their Chinese compradors, but the compradors no longer needed the foreigners.[78]

Until the end of the 19th century it was believed that the more treaty ports there were, the more business could be done. Each port would need a consul, together with his household, to protect his countrymen's interests. From about 1900 the realization gradually dawned that there were extensive and efficient Chinese networks the foreigner could use, rather than compete with. After that there were few new treaty ports, and consuls were withdrawn from others. In the case of Britain, by far the largest investor in a consular network in China, economies were also forced by a series of government reviews. The most influential was conducted by Reginald Tower, a secretary in the British Legation in Peking. Tower's recommendations reinforced the merchants' realization that they need not reside somewhere to benefit from business done there. Chinese agents were increasingly appointed to replace expensive foreign staff.

The posting of a consul to each treaty port was permitted in the 1842 Treaty of Nanking, then a necessary presence. The rules of foreign trade were still fluid and individual foreign merchants could not negotiate easily with Chinese officials. In the main, British Consuls performed well, and their numerical dominance meant the Chinese expected them to maintain order over the entire foreign population, a view not shared by non-British residents. Nevertheless, British Consuls' prestige was a deciding factor in the establishment of foreign customs inspectors.[79] Not all consuls were paragons, even less so some of the merchants acting as vice-consul for countries having no formal consular presence. Smaller nations were happy to be associated with more influential states through the device of appointing a merchant as their representative. In many cases these were fictitious arrangements enabling appointees to circumvent regulations applied by their own national consul. James Tait in Amoy, for example, used his appointment as Spanish Vice-Consul to avoid British restrictions on coolie emigration.

Taxation was inevitable in the treaty ports, impinging on merchants of all nationalities. Collecting customs duties was a Chinese practice long before the Europeans arrived. Arbitrary, unpredictable duties were one cause of the war of 1839. The 1842 Treaty of Nanking introduced a clear and all-embracing rate of five percent that was to be levied on the value of all items imported to or exported from treaty ports. What happened before outgoing goods arrived at the port or once incoming items left was a Chinese matter and not within the scope of the treaty. This seemed fair at the time, but problems arose as foreign merchants became more familiar with the sources of their exports and the ultimate destination of their imports.

Goods changed hands freely within the boundaries of each treaty port. Imported 'duty paid' goods heading off into the interior then faced barrier after barrier, sometimes only a few kilometres apart, at each one of which the goods were examined and levies made by local officials. The farther the goods travelled, the more the duty paid. In 1853 a new all-pervading local duty was introduced to help fund the fight against the Taiping rebels. This applied in addition to existing taxes, and the whole package became known collectively as *likin*.

Likin was levied on everything that moved in the empire outside the treaty ports. Naturally, the definition of the boundary of a treaty port was constantly challenged. The foreign merchants became increasingly frustrated that their goods, imported at a price agreed with the customer, were far more expensive by the time they reached him. They had no control over this increase, nor was it predictable. The 1858 Treaty of Tientsin tried to circumvent this problem by agreeing a fixed rate of 2.5 percent to be levied on all goods transiting from the point of purchase to the treaty port, or from the treaty port to the customer, in lieu of local taxes that would otherwise be levied. The carriers of such goods would theoretically be able to avoid any *likin* levies en route by showing a duly authorized 'transit pass'.

Yet problems remained. Whereas customs revenue was paid to the central government in Peking, *likin* accrued to the province. Provincial authorities therefore suffered a real loss of income, not to mention the 'squeeze' typically withdrawn. Local people were afraid to accept transit passes as they feared retribution for depriving provincial officials of their 'squeeze'. As a result, these were not always honoured, or goods were detained until a 'handling fee' was paid. When it worked, the reduction in price of foreign imports, even if small, made them more competitive with local equivalents, producing more resentment. Foreign merchants' complaints about *likin* would typically be met with the argument that it was levied on Chinese, not foreigners, and so was not a matter for the Treaty Powers. Such a view was not without justification. There must come a point when imported goods cease to be foreign for the purposes of duty collection. Similarly exported items must have started life as local goods as opposed to foreign. Despite claims by angry foreign merchants that their goods should be free of inland charges, practicality and economics made it impossible.[80]

Likin began in 1853 as a temporary measure, but by 1867 was fundamental to the economies of every province and the central government that demanded its share.[81] With the inefficiency and corruption in the collection system, estimates suggest only 30 percent of the collected amount was reported. Additionally, no records were kept, making the system unauditable. Furthermore, collection was 'farmed'; collectors were required to provide a fixed total amount of revenue. At some collection stations money was thrown into a basket until it looked enough, after which it went straight into the collector's pocket.[82] Removing *likin* would mean re-engineering the whole Chinese economy. Yet this is what was needed. The foreign powers used the opportunity presented by their part in the suppression of the Boxer Rebellion to exert their influence with the ruling dynasty. The 1901 Boxer Peace Protocol went far beyond simply sealing the peace after the rebels' defeat. One necessary measure placed the collection of *likin* under the much respected Imperial Maritime Customs (IMC). This body was so successful in collecting and accounting for the maritime customs duties that it was given this additional role, enabling the country to finance a new set of indemnity payments. Although the IMC's *likin* brief extended only to a radius of 50 *li* (about 25 kilometres) from the treaty ports, the transfer of authority symbolically recognized the existing system was inefficient. Instances arose of IMC commissioners reducing by 75 percent the number of people engaged in *likin* collection, while still producing more revenue.[83]

With the IMC in partial control, proposals were made to abolish *likin*. The first serious attempt was contained in the 1902 British Commercial Treaty, in which the Chinese government recognized *likin* was an impediment to trade and agreed to 'undertake to discard [it] completely'. In return the British government agreed to a compensating increase in the long-standing tariff rates. The new arrangements were to take effect from 1 January 1904. However, the changes were only agreed between China and Britain, and were conditional on all 15 of the other Treaty Powers entering into similar agreements—an unlikely outcome.[84] The American and Japanese commercial treaties of 1903 complied, but the other powers were not sufficiently interested to act. *Likin* was abolished on 1 January 1931, in return for the restoration to China of the tariff autonomy it had lost in the 1842 Treaty of Nanking.

Native customs station at Hoihow (Haikou), 1898. © SOAS. Image courtesy of Historical Photographs of China, University of Bristol.

The Imperial Maritime Customs service is central to our story,§ so further description of its role is necessary. In essence, the IMC collected duty on goods arriving in China or leaving the country for overseas destinations. When the service was first introduced in 1854, all such movements were by sea. Apart from some junk trade to neighbouring countries, all imports and exports were handled by foreigners. Whether a ship was Chinese- or foreign-owned could instantly be determined by its appearance: foreign schooners, barques and brigs bore no resemblance to Chinese junks. Furthermore, until the late 1860s Chinese were not allowed to own steamers. Every such vessel was therefore, by definition, foreign and foreign vessels were only permitted to enter the treaty ports. Regulations were therefore confidently drafted requiring the IMC to collect duty from foreign-style vessels entering or leaving the treaty ports. At first, this distinction worked well. The waters became muddied in the 1860s when Chinese started to own and operate steam-driven vessels. Regulations were therefore introduced in 1867 whereby all Chinese vessels of the foreign type were placed under IMC control.[85] Distinctions again became blurred in the 1890s when foreigners started to operate junks on the Upper Yangtze, requiring regulations of increasing complexity.

With increasing volumes of trade, the demands on the IMC were heavy; more so once the service, under Sir Robert Hart's direction, started to take on responsibility for matters other than duty collection, such as lighthouses, river maintenance and postal services. In 1907 the IMC employed almost 1400 foreign staff—Europeans, Americans and Japanese—and over 12,000 Chinese.[86] The senior customs person in a treaty port was the commissioner. Until more Chinese staff rose through the ranks in the 1920s this person was always a foreigner, and he often had the distinction of being the port's most senior Chinese government official.

In most treaty ports the customs staff formed the largest group within the foreign population. Social distinctions were strong. High expectations were placed on customs staff at all levels, and in return they enjoyed considerable job security.[87] The 'outdoor staff' watched and waited for vessels to arrive, then boarded them to examine the goods carried. These men were often rough and considered to be 'of the lower orders'. The senior staff—supervisors, surveyors and clerks, as well as commissioners and their assistants—were referred to as the 'indoor staff'. In terms of social standing, the Commissioner of Customs and the British Consul would vie for seniority, keenly aware of the other's housing and benefits. This leads us to look at the life the foreigners typically led in the treaty ports.

A LIFE OF PRIVILEGE

A number of writers and filmmakers have depicted treaty port life for the foreign population as one of affluence and privilege. This is partially accurate. A number of foreign merchants became seriously wealthy as a result of their involvement in the China trade, but they were in the minority. Furthermore the foreign customs officials could only look forward to retiring on a pension after a lifetime of hard work. Among them the 'indoor staff' lived well compared with the local population, but whatever benefits they and other foreigners had were seen as compensation for the often primitive conditions in which they worked and lived.

Treaty ports varied considerably in terms of size and what they offered the foreign resident. Some, like Shanghai, Harbin and Tientsin, were very large and cosmopolitan, functioning in some respects just like similar-sized European cities. They had clubs, restaurants, shops, sporting facilities and theatres. From these glittering centres 'the China coasters saw themselves and the semi-colonial ports whose affairs they dominated as the wave of the future which must sooner or later engulf the whole of the country.'[88] For them the process seemed unstoppable, the vastness of the country that lay outside their immediate boundary forgotten or ignored. 'Engulfing' was and always would be impossible.

---

§ See entry on Shanghai for details about how the service came into being.

Other ports remained 'attractively provincial',[89] such as Swatow, Amoy and Foochow. In these places social groupings were more pronounced, with particular reference to where and how one lived. Yet other ports were so small as to be claustrophobic for the handful of foreign residents, endlessly having the same conversations with the same people.[90] Most treaty ports were referred to as 'outports'—'practically all the Treaty Ports except Shanghai',[91] according to Byron Brenan in 1897, after 35 years in China with the British consular service. Slightly exaggerated, perhaps, but only slightly, especially when applied to the smallest ports.

The first British Consuls to Pakhoi (Beihai) and Kiungchow struggled to find anywhere to live. Their presence was resented and no assistance was offered. British Prime Minister Lord Salisbury, writing in 1895, acknowledged that China postings were not favoured by potential high-flyers. The prospect was so unpopular 'that no-one will go who has a chance of anything else'.[92] A few years earlier an official review of Britain's consular establishments in China noted that reports received about 'the unhealthiness of Formosa, the unfriendliness of the natives of the Upper Yangtze, or the rough life in Hainan ... [were] not in the least exaggerated'. The writer also reported that in the Formosan ports of Tamsui, Keelung (Jilong) and Anping he found one foreigner in two suffering from fever, and that he had stayed in the 'miserable hovels' in which the consuls at Hoihow and Ichang (Yichang) were forced to live.[93]

Most foreigners, even junior police officers, would have had at least one Chinese servant—in some cases many more. At an individual level both parties usually worked and lived amicably with each other. Yet none of the treaty ports was big enough to shield the

A group of foreign 'sportsmen' returning from a successful shooting expedition. Source: Trea Wiltshire, *Encounters with China* (Hong Kong: FormAsia, 1995), 142. Reprinted with permission by FormAsia Books Limited.

foreign residents from the fear of being surrounded by an alien and often hostile race. Sheer bluff, supported by gunboat diplomacy, was enough in the early years to suppress local hostility. Missionaries in the remoteness of the Chinese interior were most at risk. When threatened, or as was often the case actually attacked, they would flock to the treaty ports for protection. But there came a time when even those bastions of foreign confidence were no longer safe.

THE 1920s: THE BEGINNING OF THE END

In the aftermath of the Boxer troubles of 1900, a new breed of Chinese nationalism took root. There was an increasing desire to retrieve and defend full sovereignty, rather than continue preserving the traditional Confucian status quo.[94] However, the revolution of 1911 put in place a regime that was no more competent than its Imperial forerunner. The Republican government wanted to correct the many wrongs done to China, both by the Manchu dynasty and the foreign powers, but became enmired in internal divisions and warlordism. The outrage China felt about foreign incursions into its territory increased further in 1914 when Japan took advantage of the Great War by invading Shandong Province. Japan claimed to be ousting the Germans, against whom they had made a tactical declaration of war. China remained neutral for the first three years of the conflict, but also declared war on Germany in August 1917, making the Chinese and Japanese uneasy allies. With, therefore, a seat at the post-war peace-negotiating table, China hoped for much in the bargaining that followed the conclusion of the war. It was severely disappointed.

The Versailles Peace Conference in 1919 supported Japan's claim to the parts of China that it had sequestrated, enraging the Chinese. A major anti-Japanese demonstration on 4 May that year gave rise to the May Fourth Movement of students and others, intent on redressing their government's perceived weakness at Versailles and fomenting a spiritual revival of Chinese nationalism. However, the Japanese remained in place until obliged to withdraw by the treaties concluding the Washington Conference of 1921. But by that time the damage was done. As their country descended into chaos, the Chinese pressed their case against all foreigners, again seeing the 'unequal treaties' as the root of their misfortunes. Any positive aspects of the foreign presence were ignored, not least the fact that the only reliable source of government revenue was the still foreign-managed customs service.

An incident in May 1925 in Shanghai ignited protest. An industrial dispute at a Japanese-owned cotton factory prompted a street demonstration, then a riot. A number of demonstrators were killed by the foreign-controlled police force that included British officers and Chinese and Sikh constables. This incident gave rise to yet another movement—the May Thirtieth Movement. Riots and disturbances in all the major treaty ports followed. Particularly targeted were the British Concessions in Hankow and Kiukiang. These were formally returned to China in February 1927 as an attempt to defuse the situation.

The Japanese felt cheated of the territorial gains they had made in 1895. Partial revenge had come with the occupation of Shandong in 1914 and Japan's issuing in 1915 of the infamous 'Twenty-One Demands'. These included formal recognition of Japanese possession of what territory it held in Shandong and Manchuria as well as the granting of railway and mineral rights. Most demands were acceded to in the form of two treaties in 1915, concerning Shandong and Manchuria respectively. However, as part of the preliminaries to the Washington Disarmament Conference in 1921 Japan agreed to return Shandong to Chinese control as the price for keeping its Manchurian possessions. It was there the Japanese decided to consolidate their position and renew their ambitions against China.

A Japanese-engineered small explosion in Mukden in September 1931 provided an excuse to mount a full-scale invasion of Manchuria, achieved with great rapidity. In March 1932 Japan created the puppet state of Manchukuo, with China's last emperor lending cosmetic legitimacy to the regime. Intermittent fighting between Chinese and Japanese forces continued without a formal declaration of

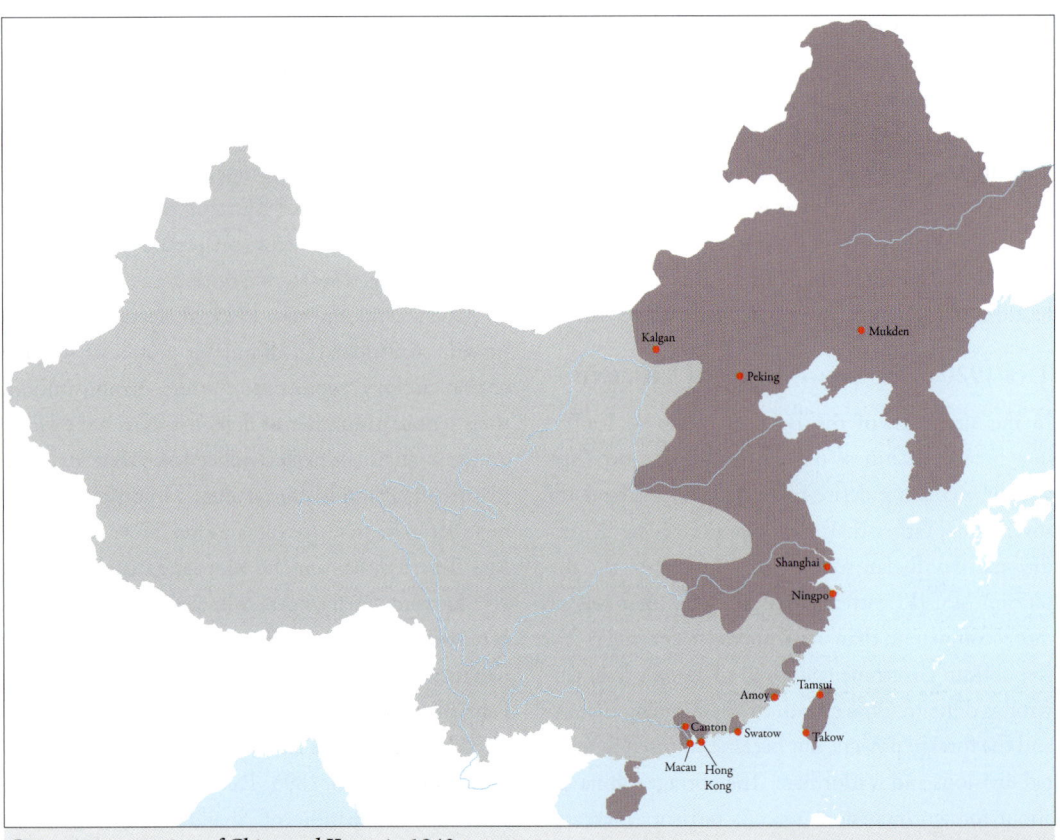

Japanese occupation of China and Korea in 1943

war. However, on 7 July 1937 a panicked response by a nervous Chinese guard to an imagined Japanese invasion gave Japan the excuse it wanted. This day is generally seen as the day on which full hostilities commenced. The Japanese army's advance was swift, with Nanking and other major cities taken later in the year. Shanghai's position was precarious—surrounded by Japanese troops, yet still functioning almost normally. Restaurants and nightclubs were full, races were well attended, money was made and spent, and people carried on as if nothing untoward was happening elsewhere. The outbreak of the Pacific War on 8 December 1941 removed all pretence and Shanghai was occupied by the Japanese army, with all the misery that entailed.

Japan advanced along China's coast and up the Yangtze River as far as Ichang. Most treaty ports ceased to function as places of international trade. China fought back, with the help of the Allies. In January 1943 the treaty by which Britain surrendered all its extraterritorial rights in China was signed. The era of the hated 'unequal treaties' had ended. China was released from foreign oppression, but continued fighting between Nationalists and Communists meant a continuing absence of political stability.

After 1949 attempts were made to revive some treaty port communities. Port Arthur and Dairen were occupied by Soviet forces until the mid-1950s. Hong Kong and Macao, now anachronisms, were foreign colonies until the end of the century. For the remainder, the revolution of 1949 closed the door on foreign occupation for ever.

Aigun (Aihun) 瑷珲

Heilongjiang, 49.58° N, 127.29° E
Open City, 1905 Japanese Treaty

For many years Russia had been trying to extend its empire to the Pacific seaboard. In 1858, distracted by the Taiping Rebellion and the Anglo-French invasion, China signed the Treaty of Aigun, ceding the entire left bank of the Amur (Heilong) River to Russia, land equivalent to the size of France. In 1860, with China weakened by conflict, the Treaty of Peking (Beijing) transferred the remaining territory as far as the ocean to Russia; the meaning of Vladivostok in Russian is 'Ruler of the East'.

Imperial Russia was still not satisfied. Instead of agreeing that the new border with China was a line down the middle of the Amur, it claimed the entire waterway, denying access to Chinese shipping.[1] Furthermore, Russian Cossacks and bandits made regular incursions into the Chinese side. The old town of Aigun was destroyed in one such raid in August 1900,[2] and was never to recover its importance. Chinese merchants moved 30 kilometres upstream to Taheiho (Heihe), immediately opposite the Russian settlement of Blagovestchensk.[3] Therefore when, in the aftermath of the Russo-Japanese War, it was made an open city in 1905 by the Japanese Treaty Relating to Manchuria, Aigun existed in name only; all the commercial activity was at Taheiho.

At just under 50° of latitude, Aigun was the northernmost of China's open cities, 3500 kilometres from Pakhoi (Beihai), the southernmost. The port was formally opened on 28 June 1907 but, given Russian control of the river, the establishment of a Custom House proved difficult. When the customs

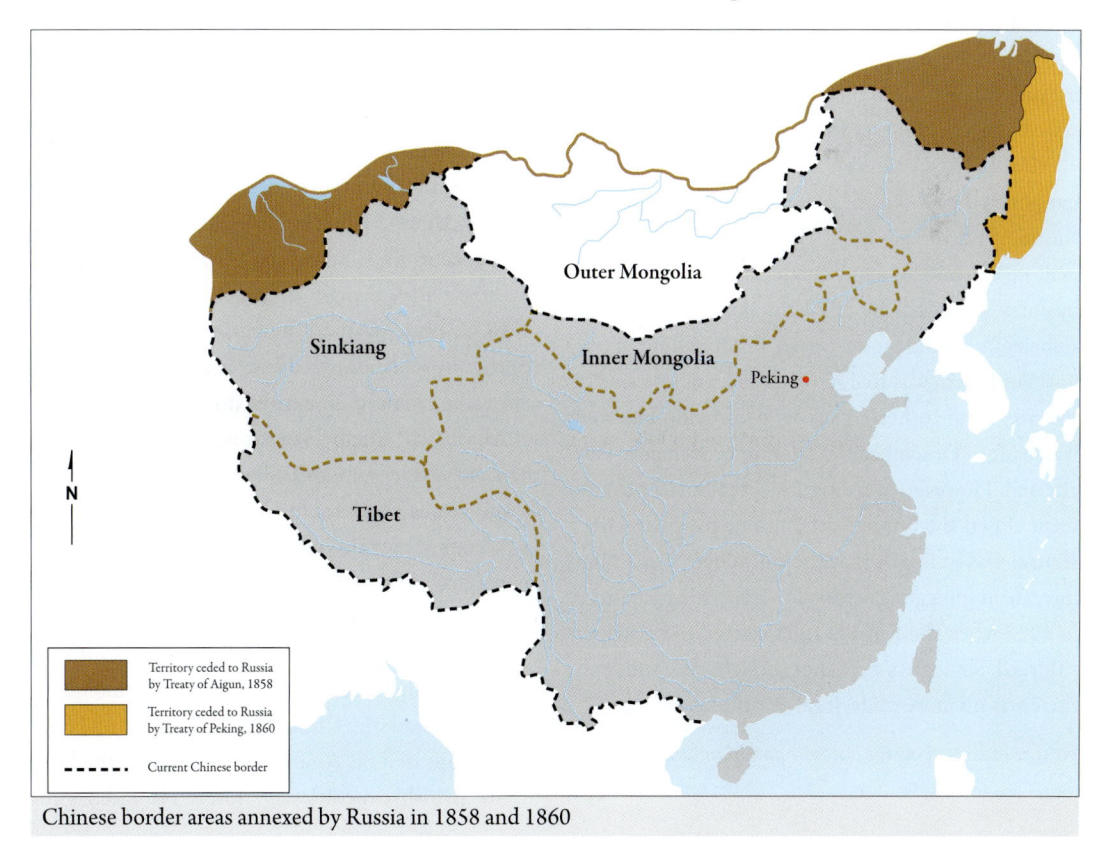

Chinese border areas annexed by Russia in 1858 and 1860

established a presence in July 1909, they found that the only vessels in the harbour were Russian, and their officers were not permitted to board them.[4]

During this tense situation, it was rumoured in late 1909 that Britain and America had won a contract to build a railway to Aigun from Chinchow (Jinzhou), 1000 kilometres to the south-west, where it would link to Tientsin (Tianjin) and Peking.[5] Russia expressed immediate strong objections; the line would be an arrow pointing at Russia's eastern belly bringing who knows what problems to the Russians' back door. The Japanese were also outraged, having their own plans for Manchuria. Awareness of these plans had prompted active American interest. The press said that if Japan's protest prevailed, then 'the pretence of China's retention of sovereign rights over Manchuria had better be frankly abandoned'.[6]

Japan did prevail, whereupon America suggested that all Manchurian railway projects, existing and proposed, become internationalized—a suggestion that 'ignored in a surprising way the realities of the situation'.[7] This idea was no more successful than the Chinchow-Aigun Railway. Rumour and counter-rumour continued. Even in 1924 it was still being referred to as a 'projected scheme'.[8]

The 1917 revolution in Russia gave Aigun a temporary boost. Chinese merchants began buying Russian vessels and using them for river trade. A pent-up demand for many products in Siberia ensured business was good. By 1920 the customs staff were sufficiently confident to board boats calling at the port, and there was free movement from one side of the river to the other.[9] A survey of Taheiho Harbour was made in December 1922 and improvements were effected. However, in spring 1923 the Soviet government closed the border, although faraway Moscow's control was so fragile that the only effect was a huge increase in smuggling across the river. Things changed in 1926 when the Russian rules started to be strictly enforced. Smugglers were shot on sight, and suddenly there was no more trade, legal or otherwise.[10]

Further reading: Foust, *Muscovite and Mandarin*.

AMOY (XIAMEN) 廈門

Fujian, 24.27° N, 118.04° E
Treaty Port, 1842 British Treaty

Amoy's rare direct access to the sea attracted a succession of European adventurers. The Portuguese arrived in 1516, and from 1575 the Spanish made Amoy the terminus of their trans-Pacific trade to Mexico.[1] In the 17th century the Dutch tried, unsuccessfully, to trade at Amoy. The English East India Company made an exploratory visit in 1670, setting up a factory in 1676;[2] trade continued until 1681, when the factory closed.[3] A lingering Spanish commercial presence remained in Amoy until the early 19th century, long after all other foreign nations had been confined to Canton (Guangzhou).[4]

In 1806 the Canton firm of Magniac took a shipment of Bengal cotton to Amoy;[5] some years later William Jardine was admitted as a partner. In 1823 another Canton firm, Yrissari & Co., sent a cargo of opium;[6] James Matheson was already a partner in this concern. Thus, when the newly formed Jardine, Matheson & Co. sent another shipload of opium in 1832, both partners were already familiar with Amoy.[7] In addition, the East India Company was expressing renewed interest in the port as a potential source of tea.[8] Hugh Hamilton Lindsay, visiting in the *Lord Amherst* in 1832, concluded that no place in the empire had more wealthy and enterprising merchants. Amoy was clearly on the foreigners' list of 'must have' ports in China and the chance to have it was not long in coming.

In 1841 Sir Henry Pottinger, two weeks into his post as Plenipotentiary and Chief Superintendent of British Trade in China (and Governor of Hong Kong) appeared off Amoy on 25 August at the head of the British expeditionary force. He faced guns

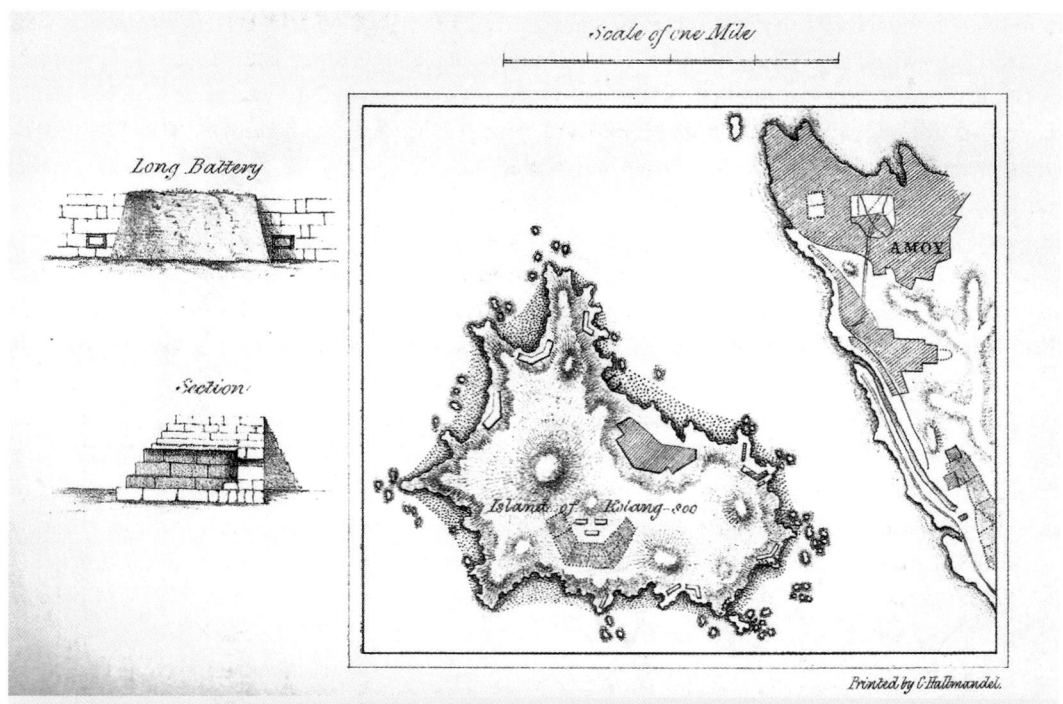

Ouchterlony's 1842 map of Amoy (Xiamen) and Kulangsu (Gulangyu); a cross-section of the Long Battery shows its 'solid mass of masonry'. Source: Ouchterlony, *The Chinese War*, 175.

bristling from the Long Battery, a defensive structure that ran for over a kilometre to the east of the city, and more on the island of Kulangsu (Gulangyu), on the opposite side of the inner harbour from the city.[9] These proved to be no match. The British captured Amoy, and on 5 September the bulk of the expeditionary force departed for Chusan (Zhoushan).

Left behind were three ships and about 500 soldiers, garrisoned at the north end of Kulangsu.[10] The Treaty of Nanking (Nanjing) in 1842 listed Amoy as a treaty port and contained a stipulation that Kulangsu would continue to be held until the indemnities had been paid. Kulangsu had already been used as a place of residence by Amoy's wealthy.[11] It was, and still is, a pleasant, quiet retreat from the bustling city. Jardines' agent, Captain Duncan Forbes, built a house there in 1841 while conducting business Amoy-side, and other merchants followed.[12] As a place of European residence the island had advantages that the walled city of Amoy did not. In the summer of 1843 Robert Fortune was appalled by the filth in the city's tiny streets, 'even worse than Shanghae [*sic*], and that is bad enough'. (Some quarters of the city still have tiny streets but these are very clean and a delightful reminder of earlier times.) He was also struck by the relative peace and quiet of Kulangsu.[13] It is not surprising, therefore, that it proved difficult for the British to leave.

GREAT HOPES

The new treaty port of Amoy was opened on 2 November 1843. Hopes were high given that its sea approach was an infinite improvement on Canton. Furthermore, despite the pounding that their defences had received, the population appeared friendly. Amoy merchants already traded with Singapore and Penang, and so were familiar with the British and their ways.[14] The man appointed by Pottinger as the first British Consul, Captain Henry Gribble, ex–East India Company, was a private merchant in Macao.[15] Gribble had been told to rent a house as a consulate, and advise whether a new building was needed.[16] Being shown five or six hongs,[17] he chose one next to the Custom House on the harbour front. Here he established the British presence and erected a flagpole to prove it.[18]

Gribble elected to place himself in the most crowded and noisy part of the bustling port. The arrangement was far from satisfactory. After only a few days Gribble reported to Pottinger that 'in order to place the Officers of the Consulate in habitable houses' he had started to repair some of the now-ransacked buildings that had been used by the military on Kulangsu.[19] Welcoming the feeling of security that a stretch of water gave them, the authorities encouraged the foreigners to live on the island, adding that they were sure the emperor would grant this right officially once the troops left.[20] Pottinger gave his approval.[21] Besides, as Gribble reported, British occupation of Kulangsu would serve the higher purpose of keeping out the French.[22]

However, this happy understanding was short-lived. Once Imperial Commissioner Qiying became aware that foreigners were settling on Kulangsu he complained to Pottinger. The treaty, he said, stated that the island would be occupied only until the indemnity had been paid. Pottinger passed these concerns to Gribble, adding that he should stay until alternative arrangements were made.

When another East India Company man, Sir John Davis, became the British chief in China, he replaced Gribble with somebody in whom he had more confidence, Rutherford Alcock. Evacuation of the British forces was imminent and Davis needed a capable consul on site to oversee matters. Qiying was still insisting that when the British forces left Kulangsu, all other foreigners should leave with them.

Alcock arrived on 2 November 1844.[23] As he was later to do in Foochow (Fuzhou), he wanted to raise his flag inside the walled city, simply to prove that he could. Having therefore rejected a house halfway up the Long Battery hill, he agreed with the *taotai* that a consulate and residence would be built on the site of the latter's *yamen*, which had been sacked by local residents in the recent hostilities. This was but a 20-minute walk from the office, and contained enough ground to house all the consular staff.[24] Meanwhile he occupied Gribble's house on Kulangsu.

Alcock agreed the design of a new consulate, with the help of the Royal Engineers. His interpreter, Harry Parkes, found a Chinese builder who could transfer the plan into a reality, and building commenced.[25] Qiying again wrote to Davis, on 6 May 1845, insisting that once the new consular residence was complete the consul and all British merchants should remove themselves Amoy-side, in accordance with the treaty.[26] But Davis had already moved Alcock to Foochow, exchanging his post with George Tradescant Lay.

On 12 August Lay took over the new consulate,[27] the first in China that had been purpose-built.[28] The buildings were erected by the Chinese and rented to the British on a 14-year lease.[29] Almost immediately Lay started complaining about the inconvenience—Alcock's 20-minute walk to the office had become half-an-hour for his less energetic successor—and so Lay moved as many of the office functions as he could to the residential compound.[30] Fever claimed him on 6 November.[31]

When Lay's successor, Temple Layton, made his introductory visit to the *taotai*, the military commandant was present. He had been rewarded by the emperor with a peacock feather for shooting Robert Thom through the heart with an arrow while Thom had been trying to deliver a letter from Pottinger in 1840. Layton was proudly told that Thom's head was currently on display in the provincial capital, Foochow, preserved in oil. Thom was actually at that time British Consul at Ningpo (Ningbo), where in his office hung a picture of his 'death'. Layton's powers of self-control must have been severely tested when the *taotai* calmly asked after the health of his Ningpo colleague.[32]

We must not lose sight of the fact that the consuls were there to serve the British mercantile community. As soon as the port was opened, merchants came to trade in sugar, tea, cotton and woollens; ten vessels called in the first month.[33] In the first year the total volume of trade, £72,000, was more than three times all the other open ports combined.[34] In 1846 the number of ships entering and clearing the port was 87, over half of them British,[35] and the foreign population was 23.[36]

James Tait and the 'pig trade'

The countryside surrounding Amoy was impoverished; the port would not become a major market for British goods. However, this poverty was to give much business to certain British merchants, leading to an unanticipated degree of prosperity for the people of Amoy. Britain abolished slavery in 1833 but plantation colonies in Africa, America and the Far East increased. Then in the 1850s gold was discovered in Australia and California. Both activities needed cheap labour and demand met supply in Amoy. For centuries Chinese from Fujian had been leaving to settle in what became Malaya and the Dutch East Indies. As American clippers began to dominate the tea trade, British ships found that they were looking for work. They did not have to look far.[37] The first recorded export of coolies from Amoy on a British vessel took place on 7 March 1847, when the *Duke of Argyll* took between 450 and 500 to the Havana sugar plantations. Described as 'free labourers', the records do not indicate how many of them actually arrived.[38] Conditions on the vessels engaged in what became known as the 'pig trade' were appalling and many passengers died en route.

The lure of profits overrode human decency; recruits were herded into barracoons (a word borrowed from the African slave trade, which the Amoy operations increasingly resembled). Here they were stripped and either stamped or painted with a letter 'C' if they were intended for California, 'P' if bound for Peru, 'S' if for the Sandwich Islands, etc. This process was observed by Dr. John Bowring in August 1852, when he was Acting Chief Superintendent. He was deeply uncomfortable that in Amoy one of the main British trading activities was this one.

Bowring recorded: 'The principal shipper of coolies is Mr. Tait, a British subject, who has all the advantages and influence which his being Spanish, Dutch, and Portuguese Consul gives him.'[39] Arriving in 1845, James Tait was one of the first and most successful British merchants in Amoy. All the six to eight European members of his firm spoke the local dialect, obviating the need for a comprador.[40] Taits

A mass of faces on a crowded 'pig trade' ship leaving Amoy (Xiamen). Source: Pitcher, *In and About Amoy*, 105.

were to hold a number of prestigious agencies, but this respectability was to come later.

In the early years of the treaty port evidence suggests that Tait was an irritant to the British community. The concept of British citizens holding consulships for other countries had become common in the old Canton days. There the device was a means of enabling trade; in Amoy, Tait was using it as a means of avoiding inconvenient interference. In December 1846 Consul Layton questioned Davis about Tait acting as a consul for a foreign power, although he assured him of Tait's respectability.[41] Three months later Layton was giving Tait a grilling over the *Duke of Argyll* case; Tait had said the coolies were only going as far as Manila, not Havana.[42] Twelve months after that Layton sent an 18-page letter to Davis, detailing Tait's sharp practices and ability to upset both Chinese and British authorities, regretting his earlier praise of Tait.[43]

Taits were not the only firm engaged in this sordid business. Rivals Syme, Muir & Co. erected a barracoon in front of their hong on the harbour,[44] and another on Kulangsu.[45] Taits' equivalent was a receiving ship—the *Emigrant*.[46] Bowring's official interest had been prompted by reports of high mortality on the coolie ships once they left Amoy. While the demise of numerous Chinese was accepted as collateral damage, the death of foreign crew members made headline news. On 5 August 1852 *The New York*

Times reported that an American ship, the *Robert Bowne*, had left Amoy on 21 March with 400 coolies bound for San Francisco. Eight days into the voyage they managed to break out of the hold in which they were being kept, seize weapons and kill the captain and a number of his men. The remainder of the crew, spared so they could sail the vessel, managed to escape with their ship when the coolies, seeking freedom, disembarked on an island.[47] This 'outrage' directed official attention to what was going on at Amoy. A high-level review in London[48] concluded that while British Consuls in China must not aid in the shipment of coolies, they were not required to prevent shipment of willing emigrants.[49]

The British government tried to eliminate the more unpleasant aspects of the trade. James White was appointed as Emigration Officer in China, with a brief to establish a workable system that could operate under British control.[50] He arrived in Amoy in October 1852 and immediately set about his work, trying to ensure that a contract was given to the emigrants and was understood by them, and that the ships had sufficient space, provisions and medical and other facilities.[51] White's efforts were reinforced by the 1855 Chinese Passengers Act, which laid down minimum conditions of space and facilities for all British ships carrying Chinese emigrants. White's own conclusion was more practical, although controversial. He said that there were other ports besides treaty ports, and so Taits moved the *Emigrant* to Swatow (Shantou) and carried on as before.[52] As for Amoy, coolie departures continued but the conditions of passage gradually improved, especially after emigration was officially sanctioned by the 1860 Peking (Beijing) Convention.

THE BRITISH CONCESSION

As Amoy approached the beginning of its second decade as a treaty port, the initial burst of mercantile enthusiasm was waning. The foreign population barely grew—from 29 in 1850 to 34 in 1855, including not only merchants but consular and customs staff and missionaries.[53] Although foreign residence on Kulangsu had been more or less accepted by the Chinese authorities, Amoy-side was still the place of business. The main export was sugar. Foreign imports were limited by the ability of the local people to buy them, which, apart from opium, was low. Yet Chinese business was flourishing. It is remarkable how many of the business names listed in the early trade directories were Chinese—many more than at other treaty ports.

In addition to local competition, the foreign merchants suffered from the absence of a dedicated place to build their offices and godowns. Various British Consuls had tried to secure land from the *taotai*, but each attempt was met with prevarication and obfuscation. When Harry Parkes returned briefly to the consulate in November 1851 he focused his energies on this issue. He pointed out to the *taotai* that the British had been waiting years for a land allocation, suggesting that if they had to wait any longer the customs duties might go unpaid. A deal was struck.[54] An exchange of notes between the *taotai* and Consul George Sullivan, dated 9 February 1852, served as the sole basis for what became the British Concession. An annual rental of just over a thousand *tael*s was agreed for an area 189 metres long that stretched 69 metres back from the water.[55] A formal lease was requested to give legal standing to the sub-leases to be granted by the consul, but the Chinese denied it was necessary.[56]

The concession is not discernible today, but the area is approximately bound on the north-west by Datong Road and the south-east by Zhongshan Road. Indeed, as it had no clearly marked boundary or security perimeter, most of the local population were unaware of its existence as a piece of foreign property. There were, however, some visible differences between the British area and the neighbouring parts of the city. George Wingrove Cooke, China correspondent for *The Times*, saw in 1857 four houses of European style, but '[t]he rest of the place...looks like a small slice of Wapping* in very bad repair, and grotesquely painted.'[57]

The small concession served Britain's purpose. Sullivan formulated regulations, announcing them on 20 February 1852. He granted 99-year leases on

---

* Wapping was at that time an insalubrious dock area of London.

five lots that stretched from the rear boundary to the beach. Despite being more a mud flat than a beach, this piece of foreshore was reclaimed, becoming known as the Beach Ground, and was added pro rata to the existing lessees' lots.[58] A sixth lot was reserved for the British government. Each lot-holder was obliged to create a wharf about eight metres wide, and these combined to form a nascent bund.[59]

Bandits and other undesirables

No sooner had the British gained their concession than the Chinese lost their city. On 14 May 1853 the city authorities warned that an army of 3500 insurgents was approaching Amoy, having already captured two nearby towns.[60] These were the so-called Small Swords, a secret society devoted to the overthrow of the Manchu government. They had had followers in Amoy since about 1848.[61] In anticipation of problems, British Consul Daniel Robertson ordered the opium-receiving ships into the harbour. The resident gunboat, HMS *Rattler*, was at sea chasing pirates so the opium vessels' guns could prove useful. Dents' receiving ship was none other than the venerable *Lord Amherst*, now in somewhat reduced circumstances. To this safe repository Robertson removed the consular records and archives.[62]

On 18 May the rebels entered the city unopposed.[63] The foreign community was very surprised to see how orderly was the whole process. The rebels took over all government offices, including the Custom House next to the new British Concession, and posted guards to ensure the foreigners were not molested.[64] Thus protected from harm, and with *Rattler* now back alongside the British hongs, the foreign community adopted a stance of strict impartiality: James Tait and Francis Syme made profitable business out of supplying gunpowder to both sides.[65]

The occupation of the city ended on 11 November when the rebels simply left. Having given only token resistance back in May, the Imperial troops celebrated this windfall with mayhem and murder. Far more people than could ever have been complicit in the capture of the city were rounded up and beheaded in the streets. The harbour was littered with the bodies of hundreds of dead and dying Chinese. Impartiality abandoned, the British brought their guns to bear on the blood-lusting Imperial soldiers and ordered them to stop.[66] They did, but carried on the next day away from interfering foreign eyes.[67]

Large numbers of Chinese from Singapore and Malaya lived in Amoy, many having British citizenship. Being informed that some of their citizens were not Chinese at all but British became a source of irritation to the Chinese government. Imperial Commissioner Xu Guangjin, at the request of British Plenipotentiary Sir Samuel Bonham, provided on 18 April 1851 a list of 60 Singapore British Chinese then residing in Amoy. But Xu suggested that a person's dress and hairstyle should be the gauge of whether or not they were Chinese, not some accident of residence.[68] Bonham replied that they were born in a British colony and so they were entitled to British protection.[69] Xu then asked if, by the same reasoning, all English babies born in China were in fact Chinese.[70] Xu had a valid point.

For the foreign merchants sugar and coolies continued to be the chief exports, together with small amounts of tea; imports were opium, cotton and beancake. Despite the increasing volume of shipping that visited Amoy, there were no scheduled services linking the port with others along the coast. In the early 1860s two companies started operating routes on a regular basis between Amoy, Hong Kong, Swatow and Foochow—P&O and Douglas Lapraik; vessels bound for Shanghai only called in if there was a profitable cargo for them. In 1864 it was the turn of the Taiping rebels to plunge the surrounding countryside into a state of anarchy. The city was under serious threat again, business was paralysed and all commercial activity stopped. When the prefectural capital Changchow (Zhangzhou) was regained in April 1865 business began to recover.[71] But one aspect of the Taiping troubles refused to go away—the 'temporary' war tax *likin*.

Erratic local taxes were nothing new; there was one tax collection office for each type of product—opium, cotton piece-goods, etc. Revenue collection was outsourced to people connected with the mandarins, and the proceeds shared. Transit passes were practically inoperative at Amoy; if a Chinese merchant applied for one he would be followed and there would be 'consequences'.[72] The Maritime Customs' Trade Report for 1867 opined that the people of Amoy were not so rebellious as those down the coast at Swatow and Canton, where there had been major objections to *likin*, and so in Amoy it continued.[73] Any foreign objections were met with the response that *likin* was a tax on Chinese, and so outsiders had no right to interfere.[74]

Throughout China, tea exports began to diminish at this time, although the business was never as great in Amoy as in some other ports. The year 1867 saw the highest volume on record, but at about 3500 tonnes it was only one-tenth of what was being shipped from Foochow.[75] The following year tea exports fell by half.[76] But all was not lost. James Tait, who had done so much to bring his native country into disrepute, had an idea that was to give a major boost to Amoy. In 1867 he imported a shipment of tea from Formosa (Taiwan). Tamsui (Danshui) had been opened as a treaty port in 1858 and John Dodd of that port had been promoting a local tea-growing industry. The absence of proper port facilities in Tamsui, and the presence of them and the required expertise and contacts in Amoy, proved to be a good match. It was not long before all the other British firms in Amoy followed Tait's lead, setting up operations of their own in Formosa.[77] The comment in the 1867 guide to the treaty ports that Amoy was a 'formerly important centre of commerce' was looking to be premature.[78]

New customs and a new consulate

On 1 April 1862 the foreign-managed Maritime Customs service opened an Amoy office.[79] Robert Hart himself came to supervise,[80] which was perhaps as well; the local customs mandarins said that with all their experience of collecting taxes the new system was superfluous.[81] Hart prevailed. In August 1867 the customs took a lot in the concession.[82] The present-day multi-storey concrete and glass Xiamen Customs Building is very close to this site, if not actually on it.

Long before this the buildings housing the British Consul and his staff had once again become a problem. The purpose-built city premises started to show signs that the builder had followed Harry Parkes's design, but not the intended quality of construction. As early as 1848 money was required to repair a leaking roof.[83] By 1858 rain was pouring in again, doors and windows were falling off and there were holes in the floor.[84] Doing the majority of the consular work in the residential compound had become inconvenient[85] and the lease would expire in 1859. The matter had become urgent, but it was not until 1861 that Consul William Pedder made it a priority. In a flurry of letters to Frederick Bruce, British Minister in Peking, he stated his case very clearly. On 6 August he said that 'rags and rottenness' best described his residence.[86] In a separate letter on the same day he stated there was an urgent need for a new gaol.[87] Keeping the pressure on, four days later he reported that his chief assistant was gravely ill owing to the poor state of his housing.[88] Two days later he wrote again (while his first letter was still in transit) pointing out that Kulangsu was the only place where foreigners would think of building their houses. Indeed, so many were living there (he provided a list of 17) or were about to do so (another list of 7) that most of the best sites had gone already.[89]

Waiting a respectful month for his concerns to reach their target, on 20 September he wrote again to say that the old nemesis of the early British Consuls in Amoy, James Tait, was willing to sell his two-storey house on Kulangsu for use as the consul's residence. Sounding rather like a present-day property agent, Pedder describes the house as 'in every respect so excellent and so peculiarly adapted for a consulate that I feel it to be my duty to recommend in the strongest terms that it be purchased'. From its private jetty one could reach the office 'in about four minutes'.[90] The building commanded a good view over the entrance to the harbour, enjoyed constant sea breezes and stood in grounds big enough for the erection of a gaol and other necessary buildings. It remains a beautiful building, and one can understand

Pedder's enthusiasm. With a provisional green light, Pedder then negotiated a deal with Tait.[91]

A China-wide review of British consular properties in 1867 by Major Crossman prompted plans in 1870 for an office building to be constructed on a compound near the ferry pier on Kulangsu, thereby leaving no consular functions at all Amoy-side. A handsome brick building, apparently a skilful recent rebuild, today occupies the site of the former British consular offices. As for the residences, one penalty the consul and his staff paid for their glorious view was exposure to the elements. A new roof was needed for the consul's residence in about 1868.[92] Then, not many years later, the whole upper floor was lost in a typhoon. An elaborate plan was devised to convert what was left into the attractive and apparently purpose-built single-storey structure that stands today.[93]

THE DOCK AND OTHER DEVELOPMENTS

The import of Formosan tea for processing and re-export brought a new lease of life to Amoy. By the mid-1860s the foreign population was over 100.[94] The Amoy Dock Company, founded in 1858 and already with three docks next to the British Concession, opened another on Kulangsu in 1867.[95] There was also by this time a hotel, the Oriental, as well as billiard rooms and a bowling alley.[96]

The Hongkong & Shanghai Bank appointed Tait & Co. as their agent in 1865. In view of the increase in the tea business, the bank upgraded its presence in 1873 to a branch manned by its own staff, its first outside Hong Kong and Shanghai.[97] Although the bank's premises have long gone, the residence used by its staff can still be seen on Kulangsu, a bit neglected but proudly standing beside a stone gatepost announcing 'WEI FOONG' in English and Chinese. In November 1886 the bank issued its own paper currency in Amoy, based on the still-circulating Spanish silver dollar. Even as late as 1913, the Maritime Customs reported that the Spanish unit had been retained by the bank in Amoy as a bookkeeping standard against which all other forms of currency were measured for reporting purposes.[98]

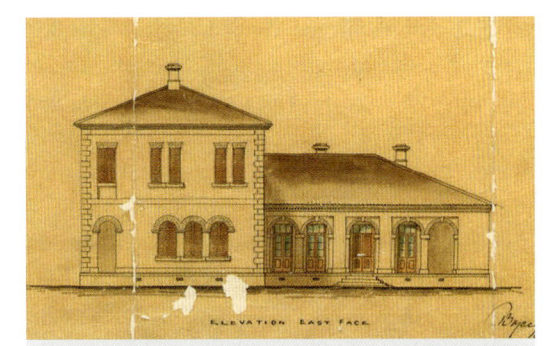

East elevation of the new consular office, 1872. Reprinted with permission by the National Archives.

Another important new business venture was the electric telegraph. In April 1873 the Danish company Great Northern Telegraph erected a short line from its office on Kulangsu to the American Consulate. The purpose was to demonstrate the revolutionary new technology to the Chinese, but none of the invited officials turned up. Furthermore, the *taotai* protested that the installation was against the treaties. The press reported that, as Chinese were very superstitious about long poles pointing to the sky, they would pull the whole system down as soon as the resident British gunboat, HMS *Elk*, left port for one of its regular cruises.[99] Notwithstanding this initial resistance, permission was granted the following year for a line to run from Amoy to Foochow.[100] This was eventually built, but for the first year or so as soon as a few poles had been erected, armed bands appeared, as foretold, to tear them down again.[101]

In 1871 a municipal council was created for the British Concession. Comprising five members elected from the ratepayers, this body was given responsibility for the usual functions, including law and order. A foreign police inspector was appointed to oversee two Chinese constables.[102] The council had only been in existence a few years when, in May 1879, almost half the poorly built new bund collapsed into the sea. All the major foreign firms in Amoy suffered damage as 100 metres of their sea frontage disappeared. It was not fully rebuilt until 1885.[103]

As usual, things on Kulangsu were not nearly so dramatic. A foreign-run Roads Committee served as a nascent municipal council for the island.[104] Sporting activities were popular, especially cricket and tennis.[105] There was a local daily paper, the *Amoy Gazette*, and shops selling European goods, as well as locally made ice and aerated water. Milk was supplied from a dairy herd imported from Australia.[106] The island even had a professional piano-tuner.[107] A new, improved Amoy Club came into being in 1875, replacing an earlier version.[108] This had the usual complement of bar, billiards and books. The club also boasted a small theatre for the staging of balls and amateur theatricals, although the acting was described as 'rather tame and self-conscious'.[109] Balls were also held at the 'beautiful and spacious bungalow of the Customs Commissioner'.[110] Not so highly thought of was the island's one hotel. This was 'run as the servants please' and, when it was full, guests had to sleep on tables and couches.[111]

In 1882 a serious international incident was created out of some cooking utensils. A German company had for a while been manufacturing iron pans, for which there was a good market in Amoy. There were official objections from the Chinese, not least over whether foreigners were allowed to manufacture in a treaty port. Furthermore, as anything iron could easily be melted down for other purposes, the pans in question were classified as munitions of war. On 20 November the company's products were seized by the *likin* authorities. On 29 December two German frigates arrived, and 300 armed sailors and marines were landed. They marched to the *likin* office and took back the pans, returning them to their manufacturer. A guard was left behind to make sure the pans were not taken again.[112] The question of the right to manufacture was raised with the Tsungli Yamen by the foreign ministers in Peking, but the answer was negative.[113] The compromise solution was a rule forbidding the export from Chinese ports of iron pans manufactured by foreigners.[114]

Other business was less exciting but satisfactory. Paper and tobacco joined sugar as principal exports. Amoy tea continued to diminish. The French blockade of Formosa in 1884 prompted a sudden demand for the local product, but this was short-lived.

The German Consulate in Amoy (Xiamen), 1880s. © SOAS. Image courtesy of Historical Photographs of China, University of Bristol.

Formosan re-exports, on the other hand, continued to grow—from 5500 tonnes in 1882 to over 9000 tonnes in 1891. All the foreign tea business at Tamsui and Twatutia (Dadaocheng) was done by branches of Amoy firms.[115]

Amoy's import trade continued to be dominated by Chinese. Even so, by the mid-1880s the foreign population was 300, treble what it had been 20 years previously and now higher than that of Canton. Half of them were British, as were two-thirds of the foreign firms.[116] The majority of foreigners lived on the island and commuted across to their offices and hongs in Amoy. And now some of the wealthier Chinese were also buying properties there,[117] many of them returning emigrants. The horror stories of the pig trade had, by the 1890s, been replaced by a more civilized process of emigration, sometimes permanent but usually for a period of years. Malaya was the most popular destination; almost 50,000 workers left Amoy in 1888 for its tin mines.[118] Hawaii was also taking people in large numbers for the sugar plantations; in 1896 Amoy merchant Robert Bruce won the rare distinction of being created consul for the Hawaiian Republic.[119] The majority of the very attractive 'European' houses that presently adorn Kulangsu were in fact built by returning emigrants in a style that was to a greater or lesser degree foreign.

THE APPEARANCE OF THE JAPANESE

In the closing years of the century there appeared in Amoy a new class of immigrant. Following the

Japanese annexation of Formosa in 1895, Japanese citizenship was given to large numbers of Fujian people on that island, as well as to many living on the mainland. For their own purposes, the Japanese wanted to have Han subjects. The Chinese favoured the idea as it conferred status, and possibly extraterritoriality benefits. The Amoy authorities had previous experience with the Straits Chinese, but not on the scale that now happened with these proto-Japanese. Whereas Britain required two generations of residence in order for its colonial subjects to qualify for consular protection, with Japan it was instant.[120] One reason for the early expansion of the Japanese consular presence was because so much of their staff's time was absorbed by nationality issues;[121] the large Japanese Consulate, built on Kulangsu in 1898, still stands, along with some later additions to the compound.

For the foreign merchants in Amoy a more significant aspect of the Japanese colonization of Formosa was that the tea grown there started to be sent to Japan. There was still a good market for the product in America, and the Japanese were determined to get the benefit of it.[122] As Japan developed its new possession, installing railways and port facilities, there was less need to use Amoy. Japanese infrastructure development was backed by a differential tax system that favoured exports to Japanese ports.[123] Efforts to revitalize the local tea industry came too late. Other commercial ventures were equally unsuccessful. Amoy merchant Francis Cass started a flour mill, but could not make it pay. There being good clay around Amoy, Cass also planned a modern brick factory, but he could not break into the market for the traditional handmade product. A Captain Fleming of the Royal Engineers surveyed the nearby hills and found good deposits of coal and iron ore at Anxi, 60 kilometres from the city. Plans to develop these resources were frustrated by the lack of roads.[124]

By the dawn of the 20th century the foreign merchants of Amoy had experienced a number of vicissitudes. The only bright spot was the carrying trade, which was mostly in British hands, even though almost all business being carried was Chinese.[125] Furthermore, as passenger fares were so low, locals would go to Hong Kong to buy cotton and woollen goods and smuggle them back as 'personal baggage'.[126] British merchants could not adapt to the changing circumstances. They considered trading in tea and silk (both now effectively dead) to be genteel, and therefore appealing to their sensibilities. The lesser, but profitable, business lines were disparagingly referred to as 'muck and truck'. German and Chinese merchants were keen to take up the slack, happily booking orders for very small margins. British Consuls tried to encourage home manufacturers to make things like cotton goods, soap and biscuits specifically for the Chinese market, but to no avail.[127] British Consul Pierre O'Brien-Butler put it best in his report for 1906, referring to the uselessness of the many trade catalogues that he received: '... nine persons out of ten live in pretty much the same way ... as their ancestors 1,000 or 2,000 years ago'. There was therefore no market, he pleaded, for things such as motorcars.[128]

It was the Japanese who were to make their mark on Amoy in the new century. In 1895, shortly after the Sino-Japanese War, there was already a community of some 60 ethnic Japanese in Amoy.[129] A Japanese Settlement was marked out on Kulangsu in 1899, but nothing more done about it.[130] Then, ten days after the relief of the foreign legations in Peking, on 24 August 1900 a Japanese cruiser landed a party of marines who proceeded to take possession of the port area, also taking up positions on Kulangsu. A Japanese Buddhist temple had been burnt down the day before,[131] and this was taken to be the pretext for a mini-invasion, the planning for which must have been done beforehand.[132] Forty thousand Chinese fled the city and all trade stopped.[133] The British cruiser HMS *Isis* arrived on 29 August[134] and landed a contingent of armed sailors 'to assist the Chinese police to maintain order'.[135] On 5 September both Japanese and British withdrew.[136]

Although the matter was resolved without violence, Kulangsu suddenly looked very vulnerable. The next move by Japan was formally to demand recognition of its previously marked-out settlement, which amounted to about one-third of the island.

America responded by demanding the remaining two-thirds.[137] A 'Scheme for the Better Management of the Municipal Affairs of the Island of Kulangsu' had in 1897 been put to the powers that be in Peking by the island's residents. The Americans blocked it[138] and the Chinese had been against it too,[139] but the latest action by Japan focused foreign minds. The Roads Committee had been instituted in 1870, with annual election of its members. A set of municipal regulations had been drawn up in 1876,[140] but the committee had little real power.[141] Something more substantial was now needed.

An international settlement

The outcome was the recognition of Kulangsu as an international settlement in the British Commercial Treaty of 1902. Using the infinitely larger Shanghai as a model, the new entity came into being on 1 May 1903. Regulations and by-laws were drafted and approved by the foreign consuls in Amoy in consultation with Chinese officials, and they were confirmed in Peking. A municipal council, comprising six foreign members elected by the ratepayers and one Chinese, appointed by the *taotai*,[142] had the usual powers of revenue collection and policing. Separate from the force in the British Concession over the water in Amoy, the Kulangsu municipal police comprised a European superintendent, 3 Sikh sergeants, 25 Sikh and 4 Chinese constables.[143] The force was later to recruit members of the Chinese Regiment of Weihaiwei (Weihai) when that body was disbanded in 1906.[144] Roads were improved and the Chinese villages on the north of the island, home to 5000 people, were cleaned and drained. More than 200 old foreign graves were relocated to an enlarged foreign cemetery,[145] and stayed there until it was destroyed in 1958;[146] the site is now occupied by the Gulangyu Music Hall.[147] Other facilities on the island included a decent hotel (at last), run by a retired German seaman and considered to be 'one of the best little establishments of its kind'.[148] There were also two hospitals financed by the Dutch community in America—the Hope for men (which is still there, although not used as such), and the Wilhelmina for women.

Within the confines of this tiny island, barely two kilometres long and one wide at its broadest, the foreign community wanted for nothing. There were 15 consulates, although all but 5 were represented either by other countries or by merchants. An increasing number of wealthy Chinese were building houses in the foreign area; land prices rose 100 percent in the settlement's first decade of existence.[149] In partial recognition of their growing influence, the ratepayers agreed in 1922 that an Advisory Committee of Chinese residents be elected to 'assist the members of the Municipal Council'.[150] A further and more meaningful change was made in 1929 when the composition of the council itself was changed to five foreigners and three Chinese.[151] To put these changes into context we must cross the harbour and see what was happening Amoy-side.

Fujian had never been a rich province, and this gave rise to two factors that were to cast a shadow over the whole existence of Amoy as a treaty port. First was the desperate need of the local government to raise revenue, and second was the willingness of large numbers of men to go overseas to find work. These two fed upon each other: the strangulation of the tea industry by over-taxation led to an even greater number of unemployed potential emigrants. Much of the revenue that was collected was siphoned off before it got to where it should go. It was not unknown for foreign businessmen, commuting across the harbour to their place of work, to have

The men of the trimmed-down Amoy (Xiamen) Custom House, early 1900s. Source: Trea Wiltshire, *Encounters with China* (Hong Kong: FormAsia, 1995), 49. Reprinted with permission by FormAsia Books Limited.

The untidy waterfront in the 1920s, prior to reclamation. Photograph by Warren Swire. © Image courtesy of John Swire and Sons and Historical Photographs of China, University of Bristol.

their briefcases opened by zealous *likin* agents and duty charged on any 'imports' that they might be carrying.[152] Things were made worse owing to the heavy indemnities payable following the Boxer Rebellion. When the Imperial Maritime Customs took over the work of the 'Native Customs' in November 1901, they found 200 people doing the work of 50 and costing half the recorded revenue.[153] There were in addition some 600 *likin* runners and watchers, estimated to be the same number as the smugglers they were employed to catch, with individuals moving between the two groups as it suited them.[154] Against this depressing background emigration proceeded apace; 102,000 left in 1902, three-quarters of them to Singapore for the Malayan plantations.[155]

The money these people provided ensured the continued growth and prosperity of Amoy. Although a combination of permanent settlement and changing markets caused a drop in departures, 52,000 left in 1909,[156] enough to maintain the flow of remittances. New industries were founded with the emigrants' money. A number of sugar mills were built, employing the latest foreign machinery. An electric light plant was created in 1913.[157] A new waterworks supplied the city from its massive reservoirs. The Amoy Tinning Factory was established in 1908 with a capital of $40,000. This produced canned fruit, soy and beancurd and proved to be very successful.[158]

Later becoming Amoy Canning, the company moved its head office to Hong Kong in 1938 and remains a major regional manufacturer of foodstuffs and seasonings. In 1921 a university was founded and a new city-wide telephone system installed, all financed by the wealth of returning emigrants.[159] A new bund was built and the old city walls torn down. So while foreign businessmen were moaning that the port had no hope unless coal could be developed, or a railway built,[160] the Chinese were doing very well.

BRIDGE OVER TROUBLED WATER

Confidence and wealth encouraged the expression of xenophobia across China. Objections to the foreign-run customs system, that had removed opportunities for job and wealth creation, led to a riot on 31 August 1905. A crowd threatened to burn down the Custom House but dispersed when British marines were landed armed with machine guns.[161] Xenophobic concerns, however, continued to fester. The next major manifestation was prompted by a most unlikely source. The conservative firm of Butterfield & Swire had operated in Amoy since 1884; the company's China Navigation Co. had taken a lease that year in the British Concession[162] and built large godowns.[163] The line developed a successful niche in the coastal trade, particularly taking sugar up to Newchwang (Yingkou) and bringing beancake back south.[164] Its vessels moored alongside the company's hulk, the *Shanghai*, at the concession. In April 1899 the company built a wooden bridge from the bund to their hulk, replacing the rickety planks used for loading and unloading their ships.[165]

On 6 November 1921 work started to replace the wooden bridge with one of reinforced concrete. However, some elements in the local population managed to construe this action as an infringement on China's sovereignty and fomented outrage. There was an immediate boycott of the Swire steamers and work on the bridge was suspended.[166] It is claimed that 52 organizations in Amoy came together to form a 'Citizens' Association to Safeguard the Haihou Bund' and representatives were sent to gather support in Shanghai and Peking.[167] The matter was resolved after a few months and the bridge was finished, but the underlying jealousies and concerns remained.

The de facto ruler of Amoy during the confusing and turbulent 1920s was General Tsang Chih-ping. A man of no fixed loyalties, his energies focused on levying 69 separate taxes on the local population.[168] Some of the Chinese banks and other businesses responded by removing themselves across the narrow stretch of water to the safety of Kulangsu.[169]

At the time of the Shanghai Incident in May 1925† Amoy had become a major educational centre and was home to a large number of students keen to help organize anti-foreign demonstrations. More came down from Shanghai. There was here as elsewhere a boycott of British shipping but no general strike. Cooler heads prevailed. British Consul Meyrick Hewlett brought about the end of the boycott by persuading Jardines to organize a shipment of coolies, something that was clearly to the benefit of all parties. Indeed, in the period 1925 to 1927 Amoy was the sole major Chinese port not only to maintain its volume of trade, but significantly increase it.[170]

Despite this relatively happy outcome, there can have been no illusions among the British and the other foreigners about the precariousness of their possessions of Amoy and Kulangsu. Consideration had been given in 1922 to giving up the two places as both had become inconvenient targets for anti-foreign activities[171] and trade could carry on without these two provocative bases. The problem was Shanghai. Notwithstanding the enormous difference in their respective sizes, if one international settlement were given up there would soon develop a Chinese expectation that the other should follow suit. For the British Concession, precedents had already been set. The concessions in Hankow (Hankou) and Kiukiang (Jiujiang) had been handed back in 1927, and the leased territory of Weihaiwei was about to be returned. With little viable alternative and with much relief, on 17 September 1930 the British gave up their concession in Amoy, their oldest in China, in the same way as they had gained it—by way of an informal exchange of notes.[172] The accumulated surplus of $11,000 was given to the Chinese police in recognition of the help they had given in the recent troubles.[173]

The international settlement was able to carry on a lonely existence for another eleven years. We have seen how the Japanese laid claim to one-third of the island in 1899. The demand was repulsed then, but a sizeable Japanese population grew. In 1916 they established a police station to protect their interests. Against strong Chinese objections, it remained.[174] Relations between Japan and China were increasingly tense. In Amoy the situation was not helped when in the 1920s General Tsang rejected any suggestion of treaty protection and refused to recognize the Japanese Formosans as anything other than Chinese. Tokyo sent warships to Amoy and threatened to land troops, but they were dissuaded by the Japanese mercantile community who did not want their business to be disrupted.[175]

By 1938 the Japanese did not have to be so coy. As part of their grand design for China they landed troops in Amoy in May, quickly taking control.[176] Practically the entire Chinese population evacuated—most to the mainland but some to the international settlement.[177] In the following year, the death of the pro-Japanese Chairman of the Chamber of Commerce was used as a pretext for Japan to land troops on Kulangsu and make a number of demands.

---

† For further details see entry on Shanghai.

When Britain, America and France also landed armed men there was a stand-off. An agreement was reached between the municipal council and the Japanese Consul-General for Japanese officers to be added to the island's police force. All parties withdrew but shortly after the start of the Pacific War, the Japanese returned. This time they were not opposed. Although occupied, Kulangsu retained its international status until 11 January 1943, when the British and Americans, on behalf of the international community, handed the island back, via the treaties relinquishing extraterritorial rights in China.[178]

Further reading: Brown, *Discover Gulangyu*; Campbell, *Chinese Coolie Emigration*; Chen, 'The Making of a Bund in China'; Haffner, *Amoy: The Port and the Lodge*; Hughes, *Amoy and the Surrounding Districts*; Johnston and Erh, *The Last Colonies;* Nield, *The China Coast*; Pitcher, *In and About Amoy*.

ANTUNG (DANDONG) 丹東

Liaoning, 40.07° N, 124.23° E
Open City, 1903 American Treaty

As Russia consolidated its position in Manchuria in the early 20th century, two powers were sufficiently concerned to take action. Japan saw Russia's advance as a threat to its own borders. America was motivated by the apparent trampling on its 'open door' policy, aimed at safeguarding the Chinese state's integrity. For different reasons, each signed a treaty with China on 8 October 1903. Both treaties provided for the opening of Mukden (Shenyang), but the Japanese added Tatungkow* (Dadonggou) and the Americans, Antung. Tatungkow was at the mouth of the Yalu River, the border between Manchuria and Korea, while Antung was 30 kilometres upstream.

The Russo-Japanese War of 1904–5 prevented Antung from being opened until March 1907, when the Custom House was established. The victorious Japanese had already moved in, and had been very busy.[1] A visitor in April 1904 had seen nothing but 'a miserable collection of hovels'.[2] Three years later there was a Japanese population of 6000 living in a well laid-out settlement[3] of over two square kilometres, with extensive wharves that monopolized the waterfront.[4] A general foreign residential area was to be established on rising ground to the west of the town.[5] A foreign house in the Danish style is today the sole survivor. (Danish missionaries were a major presence.)[6] A formal international settlement was discussed, between the Japanese enclave and the Chinese town; broad streets were laid out in 1907 and 1908,[7] then activity ceased. Britain and America established consulates, although they only lasted until 1910 and the late 1920s respectively.

In terms of trade Antung grew to be one of the larger open cities for two reasons.[8] First was the railway. During the war, Japan built a 300-kilometre line from Antung to Mukden. The Japanese retained the right to run it for 15 years,[9] joining it to their South Manchuria Railway (SMR) network. A steel bridge was built across the Yalu, opening in 1911.[10] Antung therefore found itself on the main line between Manchuria and metropolitan Japan, via Japanese Korea.

The second reason for Antung's growth was the commodity that had initially attracted Russia and Japan—timber. The hinterland along the flanks of the Yalu was rich in forests. Logs were strapped together to form large rafts, which then floated downstream to be cut into planks for shipment. Enabled by modern Japanese machinery,[11] within 15 years Antung became one of the world's largest timber ports.[12] However, insatiable demand was not matched by limitless supply. By the 1920s hills in the immediate area had been stripped bare. The SMR started a programme of reforestation but the damage had been done. Between 1921 and 1930 the number of logs sent down the river fell by 75 percent.[13]

---

* See entry on Japanese Stations in the North-East.

Other industries developed. Beans, a Manchurian staple, were brought to Antung for export. Again, the Japanese introduced modern methods to replace the old mule-driven crushing mills.[14] This trade, along with timber, attracted Butterfield & Swire to make Antung a regular port for their vessels[15] although the majority of trade used the railway line. Volumes were boosted during the years of the Great War. As exports to China from Europe and America lessened, Japanese industry filled the gap. The rail network was strained to capacity. By 1921 70 percent of Antung's customs revenue came from rail traffic.[16]

Nearly all the non-Chinese merchants in Antung were Japanese. One notable exception was Irishman George Shaw. Arriving in about 1909, Shaw won a number of lucrative agencies, including Asiatic Petroleum, many insurance companies and Jardines' and Swires' shipping lines. He became a shipowner himself. Just beating the Japanese, the port's first modern sawmill was a Shaw venture. By 1910 he had a staff of four Europeans.[17] Although his wife was Japanese, Shaw was sympathetic towards the Koreans' struggle to expel the Japanese. When a Korean Provisional Government was established in Shanghai in 1919,[18] Shaw allowed part of his house to be used as a communications centre.[19] The Japanese suspected him of shipping arms for Antung's Korean population. He rarely left his house but in July 1920 he crossed into Korea to meet his wife returning from Japan and was arrested by the Japanese authorities.[20] He was deported,[21] but bounced back. In 1929 he was speaking to the London Chamber of Commerce about the attractions of doing business in Antung[22] and was still listed as being resident in the port in 1940.[23]

The construction of the bridge across the Yalu in 1911 not only enabled Japan to speed up its programme of colonial expansion into Manchuria. It also allowed Japanese goods to enjoy a customs discount. Following the precedent of a similar concession granted to Russia for cross-border trade with China, Japan successfully claimed a two-thirds reduction in the rates of duty formerly applied to its exports;[24] as goods were coming in by rail, the maritime rates no longer applied. This infuriated the Americans, being the only major power without a direct or colonial land border with China, especially as Japanese vessels unloaded on the Korean side of the river and sent their cargoes on by rail.[25]

Over-felling of the timber in the interior led to soil and mud being washed into the river in increasing amounts. Much of this was deposited near the river's mouth, resulting in the port becoming navigable only for ships with a shallow draught. Dredging was attempted in 1912 and 1914, then abandoned.[26] Instead the port limits were extended so as to include Santalantu (Langtou), ten kilometres downstream.[27] Incoming ships had to moor there and transfer their cargo onto lighters for the remainder of the journey. Other ports facing similar problems created a conservancy board but not Antung. The Maritime Customs, the SMR and the Yalu Timber Co. all tried, but as the Korean border ran down the middle of the waterway possibilities were limited.[28]

But there seemed to be no limit to Japanese achievements. By the 1920s their population had doubled to almost 12,000.[29] New buildings were springing up, and the number of Japanese businesses grew; Shaw's was the only non-Japanese firm still there.[30] There was, however, the foreign-managed Maritime Customs service. In July 1932 plain-clothes police of the new puppet state, Manchukuo, entered the house of the Customs Commissioner, R. M. Talbot, an American, and forced him at gunpoint to hand over the office archives. The Japanese Consul lived next door, but was deaf to appeals for help.[31]

Lumber rafts passing the new South Manchuria Railway bridge over the Yalu River, 1910s. Source: *Manchuria: Land of Opportunities*, 28.

The police returned in September and for three hours tried to bully Talbot into handing over the customs revenue which by then had been deposited in the Bank of Chosen. No doubt the Japanese got hold of it eventually.[32]

Baku (Magong) 馬公

Taiwan, 23.33° N, 119.34° E
Military Station, 1885 France

Baku is the principal town in the Pescadores (Penghu) Islands. The Dutch sheltered in Baku's harbour in 1622 after attempting to capture Macao; deterred by Chinese forces, they colonized Formosa (Taiwan) instead.[1] In March 1885, towards the end of the Sino-French War, the islands were captured by the French, who held them until July.[2] The 1895 Treaty of Shimonoseki ceded the Pescadores to Japan. France, Germany and Russia pressured Japan to agree not to cede them to any other power.[3] A few foreign tea-traders established themselves at Baku.[4] Japan opened the port to foreign shipping in 1913, but its business volume was insignificant.[5]

Canton (Guangzhou) 廣州

Guangdong, 23.06° N, 113.14° E
Treaty Port, 1842 British Treaty

At the beginning of our period, Canton was alone among Chinese cities in having extensive experience of foreign trade. British merchants, although successful, claimed the rules were one-sided. Their frustrations erupted with the First Opium War of 1839–42. One of the outcomes of this conflict was that Canton became a treaty port, under the Treaty of Nanking (Nanjing), and a more liberal set of regulations was drawn up. But in reality, life in Canton for foreigners changed very little.

Canton continued to be a major centre of trade: tea, silk and porcelain were coming out, and cotton, wool and opium going in. The continuance of this lucrative business came at a price. Only four months after the signing of the treaty in 1842 the foreign factories were burned down by an angry mob, resentful of the foreign presence.[1] For years such arson attacks had been a regular occurrence. Far from driving the foreigners out they allowed for rebuilding on an increasingly elaborate scale, always in the same place—the Thirteen Factories site, just outside the city walls.

For centuries, the port for Canton had been Whampoa (Huangpu), foreign occupancy of the Thirteen Factories being allowed only during the trading season. The British believed that the new treaty allowed their merchants to live in the city of Canton. The Chinese thought otherwise, seeing no reason why the practice of centuries should change. Until this important and controversial question was resolved, Canton could not become a true treaty port; that is where we start our story.

The question of entry

In order to keep the after-effects of the war as far from the palace as possible, the Daoguang Emperor commissioned Qiying to 'soothe and control the barbarians'.[2] It is with this charming yet wily official that the British had to deal regarding post-war practicalities. Much correspondence remains in which first Sir Henry Pottinger and then Sir John Davis, as the senior British officials in China, press Qiying to allow entry to the city. Qiying maintained consistently that the treaty did not permit it. A stalemate ensued. Explaining why Canton should be different when the other four cities allowed foreigners access, Qiying explained that the people of the other provinces had 'good breeding' and followed orders.

Conversely, the people of Canton 'are of a ferocious disposition . . . and if the laws are contrary to their inclination, then they do not regard them'.[3]

Strong principles were held by both sides: the Cantonese saw their walled city as a bastion of independence and self-respect, whereas the British regarded it as a symbol of defiance.[4] They needed the extra space because business was booming. Pottinger's efforts in 1843 to seek permission to rent warehouses to the east of the factory area were met with prevarication.[5] However, in 1846 Davis secured a formal convention from Qiying that foreigners would be admitted to the city when the time was 'safe and right'.[6] Qiying's assessment of the people of Canton was proving accurate. 'Ferocious' riots and bodily attacks on foreigners continued throughout 1846. British merchants at home and in China were saying that the only solution was the old gunboat ploy.[7] They suspected Davis of being an appeaser, so they put their faith in Lord Palmerston. Back in office as Foreign Secretary, in July 1846 Palmerston ordered Davis to do something to redress the constant stream of insults to British prestige. Davis's first step was to demand punishment of those who had attacked his countrymen, but he received no response. Without further warning, on 2 April 1847 Davis accompanied a force of 900 men and three steamers up the river, under the command of Major-General George d'Aguilar,[8] capturing all the forts along the way and spiking their guns. It was an arrival that was intended to be noticed. British troops occupied the factories and Davis demanded to see Qiying, otherwise the city would be attacked. Just before the deadline for the commencement of hostilities on 6 April, Qiying sent a note to Davis agreeing that British subjects would have free entrance to the city—in two years' time.[9]

However, Qiying did recognize Honam (Honan) as a place where British merchants could live and do business.[10] Honam, the large island that lies opposite the city on the south bank of the river, was a garden suburb for Canton, home to a number of rich Chinese. Severely pressed for space, foreign merchants had already been establishing themselves along Honam's riverfront, and now their presence was officially sanctioned.

The news of the two-year delay was both unwelcome to the British and enraging to the Canton populace, making it more difficult for Qiying to do his job. In 1848 he was replaced by Xu Guangjin as Imperial Commissioner, and Davis was succeeded by Sir Samuel Bonham as British Plenipotentiary. With Qiying's deadline only months away, Bonham asked Xu about arrangements regarding British entry to the city and was disappointed (if not surprised); entry was impossible as there had been no improvement in the attitude of the Cantonese people. The impasse was becoming intractable. Both parties began to assess the advantages and disadvantages of Britons gaining access to the city proper when trade continued satisfactorily from the factories area and Honam. However, in the general confusion and uncertainty trade came to a virtual standstill. On 1 April 1849, Xu passed to Bonham an edict from the emperor (although many believe it was written by Xu himself) in which Daoguang proclaimed himself powerless to oppose the unanimous will of the people of one of his largest cities.[11] There were celebrations in Canton, and anger in Hong Kong and London.[12] At least clarification meant trade resumed.

Renewed hostilities

The early 1850s saw the start of the Taiping Rebellion to overthrow the ruling dynasty. There were skirmishes within a few kilometres of Canton. For foreigners, even travel on the river in armed boats was risky.[13] Naturally, trade suffered once more.

In 1852 Ye Mingchen was appointed as the new Viceroy and Imperial Commissioner at Canton. Whereas Qiying had been briefed to 'soothe and control', it seemed that Ye's mission was to make things as uncomfortable as possible for the barbarians. The (temporary) withdrawal of British demands to enter the city three years previously was perceived by the Cantonese as a major victory. Ye sat in splendour in his extensive city *yamen*, refusing audience to all foreigners. He was more concerned with trying to control the rebels. A British consular report noted 70,000 public executions.[14]

The year 1854 would see the twelfth anniversary of the Treaty of Nanking, a time when renegotiation of its terms had been scheduled. As Foreign Secretary, Palmerston had been unwilling to resort to war again. Twelve years later, as incoming Prime Minister and faced with what was perceived as Chinese obduracy, he was more willing to force the issue. An unexpected opportunity arose on 8 October 1856. A small boat, the *Arrow*, supposedly British-registered in Hong Kong, was boarded in the river at Canton by Chinese soldiers. They were looking for suspected pirates and arrested the Chinese crew of twelve, tearing down the British flag. This incident can be related in many ways but rightly or not the perceived insult to the flag, which probably the vessel had no right to be flying, provided sufficient excuse for a hostile British response.

Once more a British fleet sailed up the river, and the Second Opium War began. Destroying, again, the forts along the estuary, by 23 October Admiral Seymour was at Canton. The following day he captured the forts in the immediate vicinity of the city, including two at Shameen (Shamian). On 28 October British forces breached the city walls and attacked Ye's mansion.[15] A few weeks later, in retaliation, the foreign factories were up in flames—again. All trade ceased and the foreign merchants fled, although some only across the river to Honam.

Seymour's punitive mission had been contained and achievable, but Britain was not militarily prepared for a more substantial campaign, particularly when the 'Indian Mutiny' rocked the British Empire six months later in May 1857. The French, specifically Napoleon III, wanted to raise their profile within China. The murder of one of their missionaries in February 1856 provided an excuse. Thus it was a combined Anglo-French fleet that arrived in the river in December 1857 and proceeded to bombard the city. Once more under the command of Seymour, the fleet also established a blockade of the river. By the following day Canton was in foreign hands. There was no formal surrender, but a city of over a million resentful inhabitants had fallen with surprisingly little resistance to General Sir Charles van Straubenzee's land forces.[16] That then raised the issue of what to do with it.

It was out of the question to attempt the direct administration of such a large metropolis—only three of the occupying force could speak and read Chinese[17]—but some form of government was imperative. Accordingly, Ye was arrested at the beginning of January 1858 and Bai Gui, Governor of Guangdong, appointed in his place. Although installed with full ceremony, Bai was under no illusions. It was made clear to him that he was to be supervised by a three-man Allied Commission, comprising the senior British and French military officers and British Consul Harry Parkes. As Parkes was the only member who knew anything about Chinese language and culture, he found himself de facto governor of the city and in his element. A police force of 100 British and 30 French soldiers was created, assisted by 700 Chinese to patrol the city and 600 more for the suburbs.[18] The British and French soldiers occupied the Five-Storey Pagoda, which still commands a panoramic view over the city from the former north wall.[19]

The lifting of the blockade of the river in February 1858 allowed trade slowly to recommence. Despite the state of war that still existed, Elgin required that customs duty be paid at Whampoa, the Canton Custom House having been closed by Ye. Then, on 29 April, the boat that had housed the Custom House at Whampoa was towed up the river to Honam.[20]

Although a campaign of civil disobedience started almost immediately the foreigners took over the city, there was initially good cooperation between the Chinese administrators and their foreign overlords. For one thing, the Chinese hoped that the foreign presence would prevent the city falling to the Taipings.[21] The local population were particularly impressed when foreign soldiers who were found guilty of looting were flogged in public, but the deep-rooted resentment was still there. As 1858 progressed, attacks on foreigners increased. All junk traffic near the city was forbidden. The British, French and American consuls withdrew. In July the new viceroy raised the stakes by issuing a proclamation calling for death to all foreigners. Posters appeared offering rewards for foreign heads. The decision to have the Chinese run the city was now seen by the Allies as a mistake (although there had been no real alternative) and by the Chinese as a sign of foreign weakness. In the summer of 1858 the Allies had at Canton 5000–6000 men and over 30 vessels, but their position was still precarious.[22] In June Straubenzee placed the city under martial law.[23]

Relative calm did not return until September, when news arrived of the signing of the treaties of Tientsin (Tianjin).[24] However, given the false hopes engendered by that event, the occupying forces were not able to withdraw until October 1861, almost four years after they arrived. Canton could now function as a treaty port, having been one in name for 19 years.

Shameen

Despite continuing uncertainties, in March 1858 the Royal Navy surveyed three possible areas where a British Concession could be established. The first was just downstream from the old factory site, between the river and the city wall. The second was on the island of Fati (Huadi), a garden suburb upstream and on the opposite bank. The third was hardly a place at all. 'Shameen' translates as 'Sandy Surface', although 'muddy' would have been a more appropriate description for the parts that actually broke the surface of the river. The survey chart shows details such as 'hovels on piles', 'large rafts of bambu', 'mud' and 'ruins'. Among the latter were the small forts that had once stood sentinel.[25] Demonstrating enormous confidence, this was the site that Parkes chose.

When the British and other foreign merchants started to return to Canton in late 1858, they found the factory area in ruins. It was to remain so, becoming a public park years later. There are, however, still some reminders today: the street that used to run along the landward side, Shisanhang (Thirteen Factory) Road; the labyrinth of tiny, stone-flagged lanes just to the north, which cannot have changed much over the years; the occasional hong dealing in bulk cloth; and the unmistakable buzz of business being done. When the returning merchants saw the muddy stretch of riverbed where their new homes were to be, they questioned the wisdom of the man who had chosen it. Besides, site preparation would be a lengthy process, and mercantile premises were needed immediately,[26] whereas Honam was available straight away and with no need for time-consuming and costly preparations.

Parkes was adamant, and his choice proved wise. The project of creating a solid 16-hectare site took two years. A surrounding wall was constructed of large blocks of granite, some taken from the ruined forts. Within the wall, the area was drained and then filled with material suitable for foundations. On the southern edge of the new site was the river. To the north a small canal was left, thereby isolating the area and making it more easily defendable. Two bridges connected Shameen with the mainland. Although a British endeavour, one-fifth of the cost was shared with France in return for a grant of one-fifth of the resulting concession. In fact both countries' expenses were met ultimately by war indemnity payments from China.

The finished site was well laid out, with one central avenue crossed by five small streets. A total of 82 lots were identified in the British section. A block of six was retained for the consulate, and one at the west end for an Anglican church. The remaining 75 were auctioned on 3 September 1861. Bidding was 'fast and furious' and some of the riverfront lots went for twice the asking price.[27] All but 20 lots were sold at the first attempt, realizing almost as much as the cost of creating the site.[28] The French were not to show any interest in developing their section for many years.

Shameen had an advantageous location compared to Honam: it was closer to the western suburbs, home of the huge Chinese business community.[29] Despite this, there was still some reluctance to uproot from Honam[30] but the beauty and tranquillity of Shameen won the day. Its position at the end of the Macao Passage meant that welcome cooling breezes sometimes blew in the summer. Thus the new site became the favoured place of residence, with godowns remaining on the other side of the river. There are

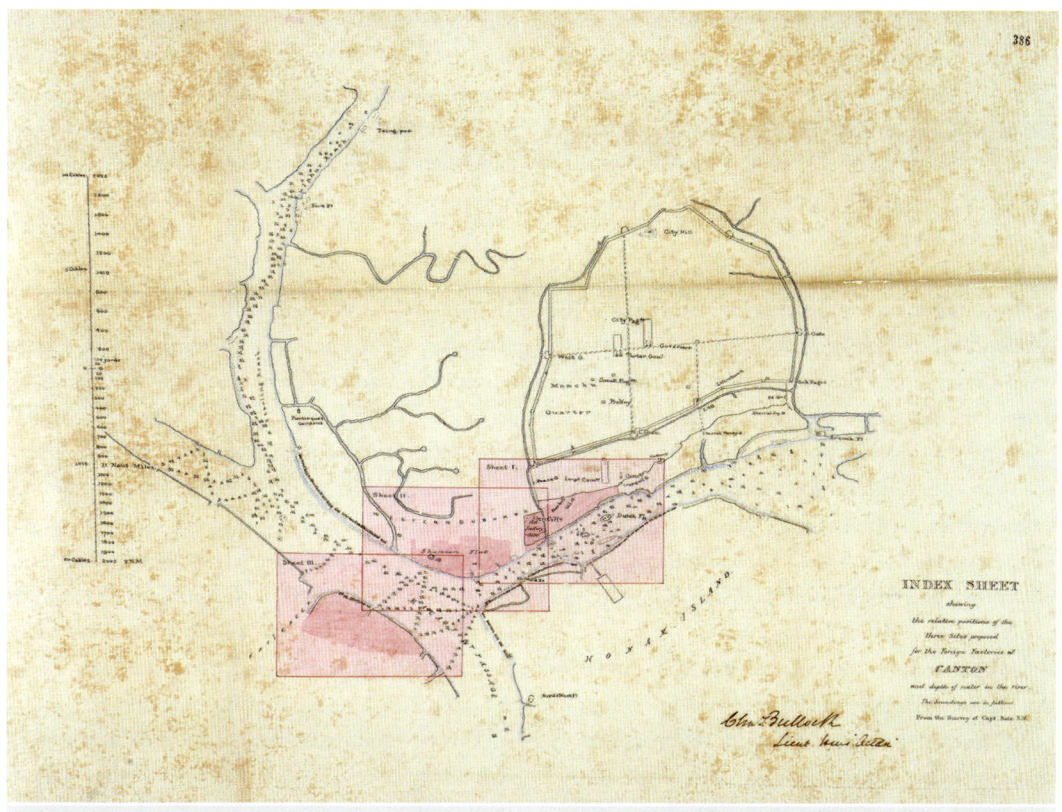

1858 plan of the three sites considered for the British Concession. Reprinted with permission by the National Archives.

still a number of late 19th- or early 20th-century tiny streets in Honam, but I have been able to find but one warehouse from the early days.

Today, Shameen contains, for its size, the most impressive collection of European architecture in the whole of China. However, in the initial years progress was slow. A visitor in 1866, five years after the auction, describes staying in a matshed, albeit a palatial one.[31] The new British Consulate was completed in 1865. The junior staff moved over from Honam but the consul stayed on in his residence in the city. He occupied a two-storey house in the grounds of the Tartar General's former *yamen* and was determined to continue to do so, given how difficult it had been for any foreigner to even set foot within the city walls.[32] The French Consul kept a similar official residence nearby, for the same reason.[33] In retaliation for this difficulty, no Chinese were allowed to own lots on Shameen. All treaty nations were free to come, although the Americans were at first reluctant to do so. The two largest American firms preferred to build on the former factories site. Photographs from the 1870s show an elegant two-storey building standing there in splendid isolation.[34]

On 22 June 1871 a municipal council was formed for British Shameen, with responsibility for law and order and public works, funded by a property tax.[35] Formal land regulations were approved three months later.[36]

Getting back to business

Witness to much of the turbulence of the late 1850s was someone who was to have a pivotal role in the development of China's Maritime Customs. Robert Hart had joined the British consular service in 1854 in Ningpo (Ningbo) as a student interpreter. By 1858 he was with the Canton consulate and in March was seconded to the Allied Commission as its secretary.[37]

In May 1859 he resigned from the consular service to take up a post with the Imperial Maritime Customs (IMC) in Shanghai. From there he was asked to return to Canton and establish a foreign-managed Custom House on the Shanghai model. The new facility was opened in October, with Hart as its Deputy Commissioner.[38]

British victory in the war of 1856–60 was to be a hollow one for Canton's status as a treaty port. The development of the new concession on Shameen was a boon, as was the more liberal access to other parts of the city where foreigners could establish and grow their businesses. But the treaties that brought about an end to the conflict opened up eleven more Chinese ports to foreign trade—along the coast and up the Yangtze River. The city of Canton was perhaps bigger than all of these combined, but its importance as a port of foreign commerce was being eclipsed. Tea still dominated the export trade, but from the 1870s this was to suffer the twin blows of other treaty ports being closer to the source of supply, and market share declining in the face of the Indian product. Canton's continuing strength lay in its wealth, size and longevity as a business centre. For example, even at the beginning of the Treaty Port Era the city had 17,000 people employed in silk weaving, and a further 50,000 engaged in manufacturing cloth.[39] These figures could not be matched by any other city, and there were new manufacturing businesses. Preserved ginger became a major industry in the mid-19th century, with factories opening on Honam.[40] Fans and wooden and ivory carvings also featured heavily in the export figures.

All of this growth was firmly in the hands of the Chinese. The role of the foreign merchant was becoming that of a shipper only. The 362 foreigners living in the city in 1850 had more than halved by the mid-1860s.[41] A business posting to Canton was coming to be seen as mundane compared with the larger and more exciting foreign centres of Hong Kong and Shanghai. Yet, despite the new ministries in Peking (Beijing), Canton maintained its importance as a point of contact between foreign nations and China. At the beginning of the 1870s nine countries had a consular presence in Canton, although the majority of these engaged the services of merchants in a vice-consular capacity. Britain's was the largest of the consulates, with a British staff of six supported by more than 20 Chinese,[42] operating from a compound of six or more residential and office buildings.[43]

An insular existence

The importance of Canton as a treaty port declined yet, as expected, the small foreign population lived quite well. Two travellers visited in 1879 and left accounts of their impressions. Constance Gordon Cumming wrote about Shameen: 'Here is transported an English social life so completely fulfilling all English requirements, that the majority of the inhabitants rarely enter the city!'[44] Perhaps the desire to stay alive was a reason for such lack of adventurous spirit. According to Isabella Bird: 'The settlement, insular and exclusive, hears little and knows less of the crowded Chinese city at its gates.'[45]

This tranquil oasis was in for a rude shock when xenophobia erupted again. On 10 September 1883 an angry mob gathered on the city's bund. True or not, rumour had it that a Chinese passenger on a steamer inbound from Hong Kong had been kicked overboard by a Portuguese ticket collector.[46] The rioters crossed over into Shameen and burned down nine houses and five bungalows before dispersing.[47] This invasion prompted the tiny community to organize a volunteer self-defence force, a gesture that could only ever have been token.[48]

Given the frenzy caused by this one incident, it was widely expected that worse would follow when hostilities broke out between France and China in 1884.[49] The Macao Passage, the deepest river approach to Canton, was closed and the rest of the city—the French Consul and residents had wisely departed in August—braced itself for the inevitable attack. Remarkably, however, the remaining foreign community was unmolested. Once normal relations were resumed trade picked up fast.[50]

In the aftermath of the troubles of 1883 and the concerns of 1884, an 1889 report on Britain's consular establishments recommended upgrading its official presence in Canton to a consulate-general. The report stated that 'no consulate in the whole of China is more important from a political point of view'. The British Consul in Canton had direct intercourse with the Viceroy and with the Governor of Hong Kong, a line of communication that was invaluable when 'grave and delicate situations' arose.[51]

The French end of Shameen, still undeveloped, was put to good use as a cricket pitch.[52] No other interest was expressed until 1889, when a number of the lots were sold and buildings started to appear, in anticipation of which a French municipal council was created.[53] Among the new buildings was the charming little Roman Catholic church that is still in use. In 1863 the French had secured possession of the site of Commissioner Ye's *yamen* inside the city and had started to build the Cathedral of the Sacred Heart of Jesus, completed in 1888. This massive stone building with its twin spires, known locally as 'The Stone House', is today the largest place of Christian worship in China.

In the same year as the cathedral's completion, the first hotel on Shameen opened, occupying the site of Concordia Hall, a theatre that was among the buildings destroyed in 1883.[54] Becoming the Victoria Hotel in 1895, and today the Victory, it is my favourite place to stay in the city. By the 1880s Shameen had taken on more or less the shape and appearance that it still has in the 2010s. Much remains in this small, peaceful and almost traffic-free area, including the Anglican church and the striking building that was erected in 1881 by Butterfield & Swire. Others include the former office building of Sassoons, built in 1862; the former premises of the Banque de l'Indo-Chine, dating from 1890; and the former Canton Club building, built in 1868. Perhaps the most impressive is the splendidly renovated former mess or club building of the Imperial Maritime Customs. Today, very appropriately, it is used by the Chinese customs authority as a staff recreation facility. This glorious building of three generous storeys dominates the east end of the island, as it has done since it was built in 1907. At that time the customs employed over 100 Europeans at Canton, although the junior,

The French Cathedral in 1900, towering above the neighbouring buildings. Source: Browne, *China: The Country and its People*, 112.

or 'outdoor', staff would have been required to use the only slightly less grand building that was founded one year later at Honam Point. This is also still there, although these days used as public housing.

A very good sense of the atmosphere of old Shameen can still be enjoyed. Happily for us, however, is that although the sense of peace and tranquillity stops when one crosses the bridges to the mainland, one's personal safety is still assured. Following the 1883 riot, Chinese guards were stationed at the English and French bridges. At nine o'clock in the evening a long horn was blown, drums were beaten and cannon fired to announce that the bridges were being closed for the night.[55] Protection was also provided by Chinese gunboats of the IMC, under British commanders, stationed in the river.[56] Yet in 1886 British Consul Chaloner Alabaster complained that much remained to be done in the area of personal security, when one 'cannot venture a few miles only away without an armoury of swords and muskets'.[57]

THE WORLD OUTSIDE

Canton was a huge, wealthy city long before the first Europeans arrived, and this continued. While the foreigners' share of total trade went from small to smaller, the volume of local business continued to grow, although trade was shrinking as a contributor to Canton's prosperity. Tea was still being processed on Honam, although in much smaller quantities. Preserving ginger continued and silk still accounted for half of total exports.[58] These traditional industries were joined in the early years of the 20th century, in Canton's suburbs, by such diverse activities as bell-founding, paper-dyeing and the manufacture of underwear, rubber tyres and matches.[59]

The city-side of the riverfront, just across the French Bridge, was also an area of intense activity and bustle. In the 1850s there had been an estimated 200,000 people living on small boats that stretched some six or seven kilometres along the river.[60] No serious attempt was made to clean up the area until the early 20th century. Extensive bunding was undertaken in 1906 on both sides of the river and continued for the next ten years.[61] European-style buildings started to appear, including a new Custom House, replacing the old structure. A major fire in 1912 destroyed it, along with the post office, steamer wharves and a number of other new buildings, but by 1916 they had been rebuilt.[62] The foundation stone for the new Custom House was laid in March 1914. The building has been restored in recent years and looked startlingly new as it approached its hundredth birthday. The nearby post office building dates from the same time and is currently used as a retail establishment. A number of other structures from the 1920s and 1930s stretch eastwards along Yanjiang Road, including hotels and department stores.

The other necessary trappings of modern living began to appear also. In 1887 a ship, the SS *Fuchan*, was chartered at some considerable risk to bring from Hong Kong a very large balloon full of gas, to provide Shameen with street lighting. Five years later the Canton Electric Light Co. had taken over the job, the new invention quickly spreading to the rest of the city. A telephone service started in 1906.[63] In the late 1920s the creek that had marked the eastern boundary of the factories site was filled in, eventually becoming today's Renmin Road.[64] The ancient walls, symbol of Canton's defiance for so many years, were demolished by the city government in 1920–21 and replaced by wide streets, on which a public bus system was introduced.[65]

After a long period of waiting, the Canton-Kowloon Railway opened for business in 1911, greatly reducing the travelling time to Hong Kong; people started to come to the Victoria Hotel for weekend breaks.[66] Soon Canton was linked to the growing national network of railway lines although shipping remained the more important means of commercial transport. Coastal steamers anchored alongside the concessions, as did the daily ferries to Hong Kong and Macao. Businessmen could book space on vessels going regularly to the other treaty ports in China. The Inland Steam Navigation Regulations of 1898 prompted the registration of hundreds of smaller craft that developed very popular passenger services, particularly to the West River.[67]

Over the years, with Canton threatened if not attacked so many times, the river approaches from the sea had become littered with wreckage and barriers, some placed there deliberately as a means of defence. All complaints by foreign ship operators to have them removed were futile, and met with the response that they were being kept there 'just in case'.[68] Nothing was done until a clause in the British Commercial Treaty of 1902 secured China's undertaking to tidy up the river.[69] A deadline of two years was given, but it took slightly longer.[70] Extensive new wharf and godown facilities started to appear along the Macao Passage.[71]

In 1906, of the nearly five million tonnes of shipping that visited Canton, 70 percent was British.[72] It is not surprising, therefore, that among the largest of the new port handling facilities were those of Butterfield & Swire and Jardines. Although access is somewhat restricted, by continuing use as private cargo wharves, or by construction sites and military installations, there is much to be seen from treaty port days along both banks of the Macao Passage. Most majestic of all, on the left bank, are the ten godowns of the former Butterfield & Swire site dating from 1904. Now known as Taigucang Wharf and given over to design studios and upmarket retailers, they have been restored to a high standard and are totally accessible. On the opposite bank things are a bit more difficult to access, but still recognizable are the former handling and storage facilities of Jardines, Asiatic Petroleum and the Japanese NKK Line. A few other red-brick godowns and office buildings can

The first train at Tai Sha Tou Station, Canton (Guangzhou), 1911. Courtesy of P. A. Crush Chinese Railway Collection.

be found along Changdi Street, the right-bank riverside road.

All this was happening at the time when foreigners still held a virtual monopoly on shipping and its related services of banking and insurance. Having been static for a few decades, at the end of the 19th century the foreign population started to grow. Concerns were even being expressed that Shameen was not big enough and another concession area should be found.[73] By 1909 the foreign population of the tiny island had grown to 1350, and more were living elsewhere in the city.[74] No new concession was forthcoming, but the foreigners soon found themselves living in a very different environment.

REVOLUTION AND DANGEROUS TIMES

The early years of the new century saw a rebellion in neighbouring Guangxi. Not only did this interrupt Canton's West River trade, but also the general lawlessness it engendered spread into Guangdong. No sooner had order been restored than something much more far-reaching took place. Canton had long been a point of emigration for Chinese seeking opportunities abroad. They brought back not just money but ideas as well. One of them, Sun Yat-sen, had since the mid-1890s been planning to overthrow the ancient imperial system and make the country a republic. As he was a Guangdong man, it was inevitable that Canton would feature heavily in his plans. In May 1911, sensing trouble to come, the Shameen Defence Corps of volunteers boosted their number to 44 as a gesture. More significantly, Britain deployed one of its Indian regiments from Hong Kong to safeguard the foreign concessions. With guns of various sizes, barbed wire and sandbags, Shameen looked like an island under siege. Indian troops were to stay until August 1913.[75]

There had been severe fighting in the city, which four consecutive provincial governors had tried to control. When a fifth took over, General Long Jiguang, his ruthless methods ensured order and the continuance of trade. Exports in 1913 increased 21 percent over the previous year, two-thirds of the value being represented by silk. Long maintained stability for the next two years. But he was unable to prevent the turmoil of the Yunnan revolution of 1916 spilling over into Guangdong. There was heavy fighting between the forces of Long and his challenger Li Liejun. However, both recognized the importance of the foreign presence and Shameen became a safe haven. A short-lived provincial declaration of independence in April hardly improved matters, but continuing shortages in war-torn Europe kept manufacturers and exporters busy.[76]

The year 1917 was another eventful one for Canton. After the death of would-be emperor Yuan

Shikai the previous year, Sun Yat-sen returned in relative triumph, accompanied by ships of the Chinese navy, and formed a new national government. There was violence against Japanese interests, following Japan's activities in Shandong. Students took to the streets in large numbers—the smart new bund was a favourite gathering place—invading customs examination sheds and damaging department stores. Most inland steamers and launches were put under foreign flags for protection, mainly British.[77] But despite all this, commercial activities remained more or less unaffected, sometimes advancing, sometimes retreating.

Sun's government did not last for long, overwhelmed by the activities of warlords. However, he came back in 1920 and declared a new Constitutional Government, and was elected President of China.[78] This time he was in a stronger position, although his job was far from easy, particularly because of lack of funds. In 1921 he attempted to seize the Custom House but was dissuaded by foreign pressure.[79] In 1923 he made a formal application to the diplomatic body for a share of the customs revenue of the southwest provinces, over which he held a precarious hold. The response was the appearance in December of 15 gunboats, representing America, Britain, France, Italy and Portugal. As with the Indian troops a few years earlier, their presence was enough and no force was used. Nevertheless, Sun was thwarted and anti-foreign feelings grew as a consequence.[80]

Tensions increased further in 1924 when, on 19 May, there was an assassination attempt on the visiting French Governor of Indo-China. This prompted stricter controls over Chinese entering Shameen, which in turn fuelled further anti-foreign sentiment,[81] and there was no shortage of foreigners against whom to express such feelings—more than 2000 of them, mainly Americans, British and Japanese, with large numbers of Germans, Portuguese and French.[82] It was not long before an opportunity presented itself for pent-up emotions to be released. When the news reached Canton that some Chinese had been shot by foreign-controlled police in Shanghai, the 'Shanghai Incident' of 30 May 1925, mass demonstrations were organized. A general strike was declared on 20 June. The Custom House closed and all customs work was transferred to the relative safety of the mess building on Shameen.[83]

On 23 June a large crowd was seen marching along the opposite side of the canal on Shameen's north side. British and French marines had been landed from their gunboats to prevent access to the island. At the end of the procession were a few hundred proud cadets from Chiang Kai-shek's new naval academy at Whampoa. Shots rang out near the English Bridge, where the new police barracks stood. There was pandemonium. It was never established who fired first, but a French merchant was killed and the Customs Commissioner injured. More importantly, at least 50 Chinese demonstrators lost their lives and hundreds more were wounded. A boycott of foreign trade followed and lasted for 16 months. Britain brought up another Indian regiment from Hong Kong, and this time Shameen really was under siege.[84]

The Chinese government demanded the rendition of the concessions, punishment of the naval officers responsible for the shootings and the dismissal of the British Consul-General but their thoughts were on bigger issues and they soon lost interest. In mid-1926 a new 'Nationalist' government was established, with Russian help, and it started to concentrate on unifying the country. Shameen's bridges were partially opened and Chinese staff returned to work. Both sides had been suffering, and the Kuomintang formally declared the boycott terminated in October 1926.[85]

But the drama was by no means over. Strikes, Communist insurrections, boycotts and crippling taxation continued for the remainder of the decade. Most remarkably, the overall volume of trade more than doubled between 1922 and 1931.[86] A severe flood in 1915 prompted steps towards flood control and general improvements to the river. A conservancy board was created and some progress was made. Envious of Hong Kong's position as a far larger port, Sun had declared that Canton would become 'The Great Southern Port'. Major dredging works in the river approaches were completed just in time to

Aerial photograph from 1937, showing the huge difference between tranquil Shameen (Shamian) and the surrounding bustle. Reprinted with permission by the National Archives.

'welcome' the Japanese in 1938.[87] After a prolonged period of aerial bombing, Canton fell to Japan in October. Shameen, on which there was already a sizeable Japanese community, remained unmolested until the outbreak of the Pacific War in December 1941.

Further reading: Bard, *Traders of Hong Kong*; Conner, *The Hongs of Canton*; Garrett, *Heaven is High*; Gilbert, *The Unequal Treaties*; Hutcheon, *The Merchants of Shameen*; Johnston and Erh, *The Last Colonies*; Nield, *The China Coast*; Staples-Smith, *Diary of Events*.

Changsha (Changsha) 長沙

Hunan, 28.12° N, 112.57° E
Treaty Port, 1903 Japanese Treaty

At the time of its opening as a treaty port, Changsha was important, but not as a commercial city. With its clean, paved and lighted streets, prosperous shops[1] and handsome public and private buildings,[2] it was the capital of Hunan Province and a residential and scholastic centre.[3] A number of home-grown modern innovations sprang up in Changsha, including steam launches on the river and a modern police system.[4] Its position at the geographical centre of China was seen as a potential advantage by the foreign mercantile powers. Yet Changsha was for many years an active centre of anti-foreign feeling. The citizens prided themselves that their city was the last to succumb to the unwanted attentions of foreigners.

The British Commercial Treaty of 1902 included Changsha as one of five ports to be opened. The relevant clause was included in an article that was more concerned with the abolition of *likin*, and so lapsed when that task proved too difficult. The Japanese Commercial Treaty of 1903 was much clearer—Changsha was to become a treaty port. The Custom House opened on 1 July 1904,[5] and the Japanese Consulate soon afterwards.[6] For a number of years the only other consulate was that of Britain, established in December 1905. The timing was unfortunate; this was the age of rising Chinese nationalism, following the threat implied by Japan's shock defeat of Russia. Successive British Consuls faced hardships and indignities not seen since the early treaty port days.[7] After using a large disused *yamen* in the city[8] and a succession of other sites, Britain decided to follow the lead of Japan, and indeed the Customs Commissioner, and build a new consulate on Shuiluchow (Ju Zhou), the long sandy island that gives Changsha its name.[9] An optimistically grand consulate of classic Edwardian design was erected in 1910.[10]

The island was eventually where all foreigners lived, apart from missionaries who preferred to live in the city. At one time there would have been a row of large residences facing east to the river, as well as consulates and the Changsha Club. In about 2004, just about everything was razed with the exception of the former residence of the Customs Commissioner. Today Ju Zhou is an immaculately kept public park.

The first foreign businesses to make an impression on Changsha were the steamship companies—the Japanese line NKK as well as those of Butterfield & Swire and Jardines. Their mooring pontoons and hulks stood in a line along the riverbank, with regular services to Hankow (Hankou), 400 kilometres away. Between the river and the city's west wall could be found the offices and hongs of the three shipping companies as well as the Custom House. Hidden in a tiny lane still stands the former residential block of the customs' outdoor staff, built of red brick on solid stone foundations.

It was the Germans and Japanese who became dominant in the foreign mercantile community, although it was a Briton who was first to test the water. Henry Bennertz went to Changsha in 1905, expecting to find a city that had been opened to foreign trade. He was disappointed. Forcibly restrained from doing any business in the city proper, and faced with endless obstructions,[11] Bennertz became an unwilling celebrity. The foreign merchants gave him their full support—from the safe distance of Hankow and Shanghai. He received no practical assistance from the Changsha British Consul, for which that official received a lashing in the press.[12] Bennertz stubbornly maintained his position but faced financial ruin. After an 18-month stand-off, the city authorities paid him $25,000 to go away. Even in 1907 the Governor of Hunan was still claiming the newly opened city was in fact closed.[13] The matter was resolved only when the Chinese authorities reluctantly issued a proclamation declaring the city open.[14]

An area had been identified for a foreign settlement outside the North Gate. It was no surprise given past experience when nothing materialized. The import trade in the early years was virtually nil. It was the export potential that was first identified, with the Germans and Japanese leading the way. Hunan Province is rich in many kinds of minerals, the most important being coal and antimony, a substance with many uses in the metallurgical industry. Carlowitz & Co. already had an antimony smelting plant at Hankow, and in Changsha the Germans soon dominated the market for exporting locally mined ores, including lead and zinc.[15] The Japanese did even better. There were already 100 Japanese in Changsha by the end of 1905, engaged in activities as diverse as retail and, in the case of the giant firm Mitsui, coal export.[16] Foreign trade was growing impressively. The advent of steamers, coupled with periodic flooding, had necessitated the bunding of the river outside the city walls.

Then, on 16 April 1910,[17] a sudden rise in the price of rice brought an angry mob onto the streets. Foreigners could hardly be blamed, but were a visible focus for people's frustrations. Nearly all the foreign establishments in Changsha were destroyed. Hulks lying in the river were torched, along with all the Chinese merchants' goods stored inside.[18] Neither did missionary buildings escape. The standard British response of 'sending a gunboat' did not work; HMS *Thistle*'s attempts to get to Changsha were frustrated by low water in the river and an unexpectedly long journey time.[19] Nevertheless, almost the entire European community managed to get away and wait downstream.[20] Not only the foreigners suffered: the governor's *yamen* and many government schools were destroyed.[21] Alarming as these events were, they put only a temporary stop to trade.

It was realized at the outset that the commerce of Changsha would always be at risk if the river was too low to admit steamers all year round. A solution came in the form of the railway, which in the early 20th century was proliferating in China. The local work required was good news for the Germans, with their strong engineering capabilities; four new German firms opened in Changsha in 1910.[22] When the line to Hankow opened in 1918,[23] the port was no longer dependent on an unreliable river for its transport needs. Furthermore it was becoming less reliant on foreigners for new ideas and capital. In 1908 a Hunan

The parlous state of the 'bund' at low water, 1906. Photograph by Warren Swire. © Image courtesy of John Swire and Sons and Historical Photographs of China, University of Bristol.

student in Paris bought new plant and machinery for an antimony smelting works, and engaged two French engineers to come back with him and set it up.[24] The following year a Chinese student who had just completed his education in America established a new lead smelting works with two of his classmates.[25] These led the way for more local industries.

The foreigners maintained their lead in shipping, and Western tobacco and oil companies became major presences in Changsha. Members of the foreign community were leading the usual treaty port life. There was the Changsha Club, and similar institutions for the Japanese and the Germans. Any visiting gunboat provided an excuse for a party.[26] The once-proud city walls were being torn down and the area outside the North Gate, originally intended as a foreign settlement, was being developed as a business area for foreigners and Chinese.[27] The approximate position of the north wall can be placed thanks to three churches that remain from a hundred years ago. The 'North Church' of the American Presbyterians and the Roman Catholic Church were both outside the wall, and the former Trinity Church was within. All three continue to be used by the Chinese Christian community.

Changsha's end as a treaty port was brought about by the same factor that gave rise to its beginning—its geographical location. The city is a natural focus for the passage of any army wishing to invade the south from the north or, as happened in 1930, the north from the south. Communist forces captured Changsha in July and did much damage, before being ousted nine days later.[28] Changsha was to change hands a number of times during the long and bitter conflict.[29] In November 1938, in the face of an unstoppable Japanese advance the Chinese military commander set fire to the city and completely destroyed it. Over 30 square kilometres were reduced to ashes.[30] When they eventually captured the city a few years later, the Japanese closed the port that they had opened 40 years before.

CHEFOO (YANTAI) 煙台

Shandong, 37.32° N, 121.23° E
Treaty Port, 1858 British Treaty

As a treaty port, Chefoo never really existed. The 1858 British Treaty of Tientsin (Tianjin) refers to Tengchow, now known as Penglai. The place chosen by the merchants was just outside the walled city of Yantai, 70 kilometres to the south-east. Chefoo (Zhifu) was the name of a small fishing village north of Yantai, of no interest to the early foreign merchants. But this is the name that the British and French

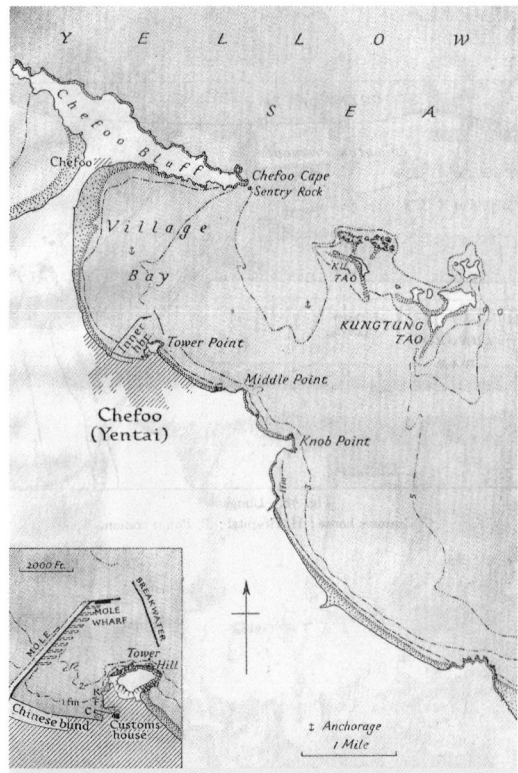

Map showing the city, the bay, Chefoo (Yantai) Bluff, Tower Point and Kungtung (Kongtong) Island. Source: *China Proper*, Vol. 3, 402.

remembered from earlier visits, and so the village found itself thrust into international prominence.

On their way to Taku (Dagu) to press for the ratification of their respective Tientsin treaties, the British and French had gathered their fleets in the vicinity of Chefoo in July 1859. Some Shanghai merchants, including Alexander Michie of Lindsay & Co., were already there scouting out business prospects in anticipation of the port's opening.[1] The British fleet anchored in the channel between Tengchow and the Miao Islands. The French sheltered in the lee of the Chefoo Bluff, before joining up with the British.[2]

Michie had 'pegged out mentally the site of the future settlement'[3] but the French were the first to establish themselves ashore. In July 1860 a small number of French troops were left to garrison the place when the main force returned to Taku.[4] British Lt. Col. George Fisher left an account of a visit he made at this time, finding the walled town had a population of 10,000 but the appearance of a small village.[5] He had expected it to be larger, judging by the number of ships in the harbour, but noticed that all goods coming in were immediately carried into the country, obviating the need for storage facilities.[6] The outline of the walled town can still be seen, as can some of the tiny streets and houses inside. A plaque in Shengli Road records that it dates from 1398. The walls had gone when Fisher visited, but the gates remained. These too have now disappeared, although the ends of the central street, Suochengli Main Street, are still signposted as East Gate and West Gate.

Although Tengchow was a coastal town, it had no harbour. Fisher reports seeing a small dock,[7] but nothing that could be of any use for commercial or military purposes. Hence, after the signing of the Convention of Peking (Beijing) in 1860 and having left troops in Tientsin, the returning British force wintered once more in the Miao Islands. They held the largest of the islands, Nanchangshan, as security for war reparations;[8] it was generally presumed that this large island with its sheltered bay would become the commercial port, not the less convenient Tengchow.[9] The French spent the winter in Chefoo, holding it as security for their share of the damages.

Tengchow is opened—as Chefoo

Martin Morrison, the son of prominent missionary Robert Morrison, was responsible for opening the port of Tengchow-fu to British trade. He arrived on 28 February 1861. However, suspecting that he was in the wrong place, he moved to Chefoo where, on 18 March, he gave official notification of the establishment of the Tengchow-fu British Consulate. (Tengchow-fu remained the official title of the British Consulate in Chefoo until 1884,[10] after which the name no longer features in the history of the treaty port.) Morrison commandeered fellow passenger Robert Douglas to help in the general business of the consulate pending further instructions. Douglas was a good choice; he later became Keeper of Oriental Books at the British Museum and Professor of Chinese at King's College London.[11]

The attraction of Chefoo to the British was twofold. First, it was seen to have strategic importance, being, with Talienwan (Dalianwan), one of the two guardians at the entrance to the Gulf of Chihli. Second, it was believed that Chefoo would become the major port for the populous province of Shandong. Both hopes were to prove overly optimistic. Certainly the large harbour appeared to be well sheltered; to the west and north there was a bluff, and to the east were the Kungtung (Kongtong) Islands.

Inside the former walled city of Yantai in 2010. Little must have changed in the last 100 years or more. Photograph by author, 2010.

However, these were not very effective in blocking the gales blowing from that direction, leaving the harbour not only exposed but also sometimes inaccessible. Besides, the shoreline was a gently sloping beach; vessels had to drop anchor and wait to be served by lighters.

Chefoo's major exports were dates, dried fruit, peas, beans and beancake.[12] So important were the latter two that the rules of trade attached to the Treaty of Tientsin prohibited British ships from carrying them. This seemingly odd condition had been inserted out of a fear that the foreigners would take away the livelihoods of thousands of Chinese junk operators. However they, in turn, were quick to see that foreign steamers could transport their goods faster and more efficiently than their own sailing craft. Chinese junks would therefore take the beans to foreign ships waiting just outside the port limits; alternatively, the foreigners would bring their vessels to nearby small ports and so the 'protection measures' became farcical.[13] The British merchants in Chefoo, led by T. T. Fergusson, one of the first to arrive, appealed to Lord Elgin to have the prohibition reversed. They claimed that imports were more expensive than necessary as vessels were being forced to leave empty. Besides, as the foreigners were not allowed to share in the single most important export, what they brought in was being paid for in silver. This was an even greater concern for the Chinese, whose fear of silver draining from the empire was well known. Elgin's initial response was to insist that all treaty terms be observed,[14] but he soon relented. The offending clause was abrogated,[15] creating a positive effect on trading prospects for the young treaty port.

An Imperial Maritime Customs office was opened in March 1863, and trade statistics started to become available. The major imports around this time were opium, sugar and cotton goods.[16] A number of Shanghai and Hong Kong firms set up branches, and some intrepid merchants followed Fergusson and established their own businesses. However, even though the foreign merchants could now share in the beancake export business, they found they were hampered by a shortage of available steamers. As for imports, they encountered a general reluctance to buy foreign products, particularly cotton goods; the Chinese preferred their own, which were cheaper and more durable.[17] The American Civil War meant the quantities of British cotton goods were significantly curtailed and more expensive. Chinese merchants still wishing to buy British cloth and other imported products bypassed their foreign competitors and went direct to Shanghai, the market through which Chefoo was being served.[18] This caused many of the Shanghai firms and their agents to close their Chefoo branches; the number of foreign firms listed in the directories fell from 14 in 1865 to 9 the following year.[19]

The gradual passing of trade to the Chinese was a major concern to the British. The Shanghai-based businesses could afford simply to retreat but British firms such as Fergusson & Co. and fellow new arrival Wilson, Cornabé & Co. had more to lose. When Consul Morrison was moved on in February 1865, the treaty port's future looked so dismal that the British presence was downgraded to a vice-consulate. By the end of that year, trade in British goods had almost ceased to be in the hands of British merchants. It was even being rumoured that the Chinese government wanted to close the northern treaty ports, there being few foreign interests remaining to be hurt by doing so. If it had pressed its case, this might well have happened.[20]

What was needed was for vessels to come to Chefoo direct from England, bypassing Shanghai. But this needed capital that the fledgling merchant community did not have. Help came from an unexpected quarter via a French bank in Shanghai that provided financial help to the British in Chefoo, allowing them to take business away from Shanghai. In 1867, ships started to arrive direct from England with cotton piece-goods, iron and coal. The landed prices were higher than in Shanghai, but overall costs were lower when transshipment was taken into account. The credit for this coup was Fergusson's.

With the main problems affecting exports and imports overcome, the foreign merchants in Chefoo could concentrate on growing their businesses. Beancake became one of their principal interests.

Beans, particularly soya beans, were grown extensively in Shandong and over the gulf in Manchuria. Once harvested, the beans were crushed. The resulting oil was used for cooking, and the remaining mush was pressed into flat cakes. There was a huge market for these beancakes all over the south, where they were used as fertilizer for sugar and other crops. A number of foreign merchants, along with many Chinese, set up crushing plants and warehouses, and the business grew.[21]

Britain in danger of losing its grip

There was a great deal of interest among the major powers in northern China's potential. Before 1860 foreign commerce had been confined to the south and south-east coasts. Chefoo, as the only northern port that did not freeze in winter, was seen as a seasonal entrepôt for Tientsin. The British took an early lead but they were not alone. Of the 178 vessels that arrived in 1862, only 69 were British.[22] There was competition from Germans and others, so much so that in 1865 Vice-Consul James Middleton complained that Britain was losing its 'fair share' of the shipping market.[23] But there were problems in other quarters.

Within three months of arriving Consul Morrison had mapped out a site for a British Concession and agreed its boundaries with the *taotai*. At the same time he suggested to Fergusson, who had been appointed as vice-consul for France, that he do the same for a French Concession. Fergusson secretly made an application for the very same site, even using the plan that Morrison had lent him. Reverting to type, a period of intense bickering between these two rival nations began. The French claimed that as they were there first, they should have first choice. In 1860 France had, indeed, occupied much of the area that was now being claimed by both nations. But French troops withdrew in February 1861, leaving a ruined wooden hut and a dilapidated jetty, visited occasionally by sailors from the French warship anchored in the bay. This they described as the 'French Establishment'. Furthermore, on behalf of his adopted masters Fergusson was claiming the French government had rented the site, deterring the British from buying land there. The British merchants therefore occupied the opposite shore of the isthmus, along with the British Consulate.[24]

The French, ably abetted by Fergusson, remained intransigent, maintaining the principle that irritating the British was a national duty, if not an actual sport. Apart from one storekeeper and boarding-house proprietor, there would be no French commercial interests in Chefoo for many years. The British still needed land set aside so that their merchants, coming to Chefoo in increasing numbers, could establish themselves properly. In 1862 Morrison wrote to Sir Frederick Bruce, British Minister in Peking, advising that it would be 'a mistake to defer the selection of [a settlement] until speculators and the parasites of trade had an opportunity of forestalling the legitimate merchant'.[25] Bruce rejected the idea, saying that the treaty port had little chance of growing.[26]

When Morrison arrived he had been obliged to rent rooms for his consulate and residence. In April 1862 he managed to secure an entire building that was sufficient for all his needs.[27] This was in a commanding position on the north-east corner of Yantai Hill, therefore a long way inside the area being claimed by France. When Bruce found out where his consul was living, he ordered him to move immediately.[28] However, the French were soon to lose interest. The first sign came in October 1863 when Bruce managed to secure the appointment of the British Consulate to represent France in Chefoo, not wanting Fergusson to keep the job.[29] Furthermore, much of the land France claimed as its concession had been sold by its individual Chinese owners to foreigners, only five percent going to French interests. In addition, the *taotai* claimed that as the area included a fort it could not be granted to France, adding that the French had paid nothing for the right they were claiming.[30]

Nevertheless, in the summer of 1864, the French naval officer in charge of his country's military affairs at Chefoo was in imminent expectation of receiving confirmation that a French Concession had been granted. He publically declared that he would land a party of armed men immediately the good news arrived, to exert French authority.[31] He waited long and in vain. In May 1866, Rutherford Alcock reported to Vice-Consul Middleton that the French had formally withdrawn their claim to a concession. Alcock added that in Middleton's additional capacity as French Vice-Consul, he would be receiving instructions to remove the French boundary stones from the site.[32] With this obstacle finally overcome, Britain could now go ahead with its plans for building a consulate. The British government had been the largest purchaser of land in the defunct French Concession and now had the right to some 25 percent of Yantai Hill,[33] an area that was increasingly assumed to have China's tacit approval as a reservation for foreigners.[34] Plans were immediately drawn up for a new residence, which was ready for occupation in October 1866.[35] A gaol and constable's quarters were added as well as a consular office,[36] which still stands.

With the reinstatement of the British presence to a full consulate in 1868, a new and grander residence was needed. This too is still there. Having waited for years, the British were at last well placed in terms of their consular needs—four fine buildings sitting on a compound roughly 300 metres by 150. However, pressure for ground on which others could build was such that the northern part of the British lot was sold. In 1874, therefore, instructions were issued for a new gaol and constable's quarters to be built within the redefined boundary. Of the land given up, the Americans took the north-eastern part for their consulate, and the Germans the south-western for theirs.[37] Of the latter, nothing remains except the outline of the footing of the building and the steps that used to lead up to the front door. The colonial-style building on the former American plot still occupies the best location on the promontory and retains its lovely 'wraparound' verandah.

An international community

A total of 15 nations were to have consular representations in Chefoo but only the British had a fully established consulate throughout the treaty port's life. In response to the massacre in Tientsin in 1870, France established a naval command centre at Chefoo, and for two years its chief officer also acted as vice-consul. France did not open a full consulate of its own until 1896. This closed in 1924. The impressive

c. 1910 view of the British consular compound, looking north-west from the bund. Courtesy of David Mahoney.

but unmarked building still stands on Yantai Hill. Another beautiful building close by is described as the former Danish Consulate; to prove it the front garden contains a replica of Copenhagen's Little Mermaid. However, Denmark never had a consulate in Chefoo. The building is most likely the residence of Percy Lavers, Danish Vice-Consul from 1891.

Russia opened a consulate in 1918. Perhaps there was no more room on Consulate Hill, or maybe the new Bolshevik government preferred to keep its people away from the pernicious influence of the imperialists' consuls. The Russians occupied rather forbidding premises at the far eastern end of the foreign settled area, now used as a police station.

Apart from 1875, when Consul Eli Sheppard was installed on the new lot acquired from Britain, the Americans used the services of successive merchant vice-consuls until 1896. In that year the United States opened the consulate that was to be one of the few that remained in 1941. A consulate and adjacent consul's residence were built in the early 1900s on the southern part of the hill. Both still stand and are in excellent repair. The latter houses an impressive museum that describes Yantai in the Treaty Port Era.

Germans had been among the first foreign merchants to come to Chefoo. With the creation of the modern state of Germany in 1871, German merchants acted as vice-consuls until a full German Consulate was established in 1890. This remained until 1915.

Japan had the largest foreign presence in Chefoo, consular or otherwise, although initially they appointed British merchant George Maclean as their representative in 1876. For many years Maclean had the agency of the Mitsubishi Mail Co., until the Japanese Imperial Post Office established a Chefoo branch. Japan opened a consulate in 1883, occupying a large building near the French Consulate,[38] and the Japanese presence in Chefoo began to increase: Nippon Yusen Kaisha, the steamship line, in 1886; conglomerate Mitsui in 1887; and the Yokohama Specie Bank in 1895. Although there were Japanese merchants in Chefoo, all these were initially represented by non-Japanese. The full effect of the Japanese interest in China was not to be felt until the 1930s. By this time they had replaced their original consulate with the imposing art deco-style building that still stands on the western side of Yantai Hill. The front of the building bears traces of large Chinese characters that probably told the former occupants exactly what the locals thought of them—presumably after they left.

Yantai Hill was not only occupied by consulates. The Maritime Customs also had residences there. The commissioner was granted a large house, complete with terraced garden and two tennis courts. In the grounds was a separate bungalow that was reserved for the use of the Inspector-General when he visited.[39] These two buildings are still there, although somewhat altered. A little to the west, and overlooking the old harbour, is a line of five Victorian terraced houses that would grace any English town today, with their half-timbered gable ends. These provided accommodation for some of the less senior officers, of whom there were many.

THE FOREIGNERS HELP THEMSELVES

In the absence of a defined settlement, foreign occupation developed in a haphazard manner, but concentrated in two areas: north of the walled city, clustered around the harbour and Consulate Hill; and later along the seafront to the east. In the early days a Roads Committee was formed which, with voluntary contributions from the foreign community, ensured that the thoroughfares were kept clean and in good repair. Such conditions immediately made the foreign part of town very different from the rest, with its tiny, dirty streets. The more wealthy Chinese started to move into the Foreign Quarter and enjoy the better facilities that prevailed there. The absence of a boundary made security a potential problem, but the *taotai* was sensitive to the foreigners' concerns. As early as 1872 he was paying for a force of three Chinese policemen under a British constable, whose salary he also paid.[40] For a number of years this post was filled by James Husden, who was also the proprietor of a billiard hall;[41] presumably he was chosen for his skill with a big stick.

By 1892 the registered foreign population had grown to 370, although 200 of these were missionaries living in the interior.[42] Still, this added up to a sizeable community. The Roads Committee was doing its job well enough, but the growing population wanted more. In particular, there was no public street lighting.[43] In 1893 a General Purposes Committee was formed, with a wider brief than its predecessor. The new body took on the municipal lighting of the roads, for which it needed money. Help came in the unexpected form of the Local Post Office (LPO). Originating in Shanghai, LPOs arranged for the mutual delivery of each other's stamped letters. Managed by missionary-cum-businessman James McMullan, the Chefoo branch made a profit of $1200 in its first six months, in no small part thanks to stamp dealers and collectors (Chefoo issued its own stamps at that time), all of which went towards funding the activities of the committee.[44] Although a Chinese Imperial Post Office was established under the highly respected Maritime Customs service, there were doubts as to its ability to deliver. The Japanese established their own post office in 1896, and were quickly followed by the British, French, Russians and Germans. The building occupied by the last can be seen in Hai'an Street, as can the decorative carved stone name board: 'Kaiserlich Deutsches Post Amt' (Imperial German Post Office).

The Foreign Quarter was proving too small by the turn of the century. Given the harbour to the west and the Chinese city to the south, the only direction for expansion was east. Private houses and small hotels appeared along the seafront. The bund was narrow and the beach sloped down to the sea. Just inland was the East Boulevard, now known as Guangren Road. The buildings along almost the whole length of this street have been preserved—rather like a dowager in full make-up, with a touch of Disney. Municipal plaques are plentiful and informative, marking the ex-premises of the Chefoo Electric Co., Chefoo Straw Braid & Hair Net Export Co. and the YMCA, among others.

By 1908 the General Purposes Committee was levying a $10 annual poll tax on every male person living within its area.[45] Again, this was voluntary and there was no means of enforcing payment. Consequently there was never enough to pay for a better water supply, something that was badly needed. One improvement the committee was able to make was naming the roads using carved stone plaques. Surprisingly, a number of them survive: 'Eckford Road' at the north end of Haiguan Street; 'Old Telegraph Street' (parallel to and inland from Hai'an Street); 'Broadway' (Daima Road); and 'Gipperich Street' (Chaoyang Street). Those from Morrison Road and Cross Street can be seen in the museum in the former US Consul's residence.

In late 1899 the Japanese led negotiations for the establishment of the Foreign Quarter as a formal foreign settlement.[46] It was a pleasant area and well managed but it lacked the security of formal status. Although the consular body was generally in favour of the idea, objections were raised by the Germans.[47] Hopes were boosted with the creation in 1903 of Kulangsu (Gulangyu) as an international settlement. On 7 January 1905 a meeting of the foreign community proposed Chefoo should follow suit. A set of land regulations and by-laws was drawn up, taking those of Shanghai as a model. The ministers of the major foreign powers even petitioned

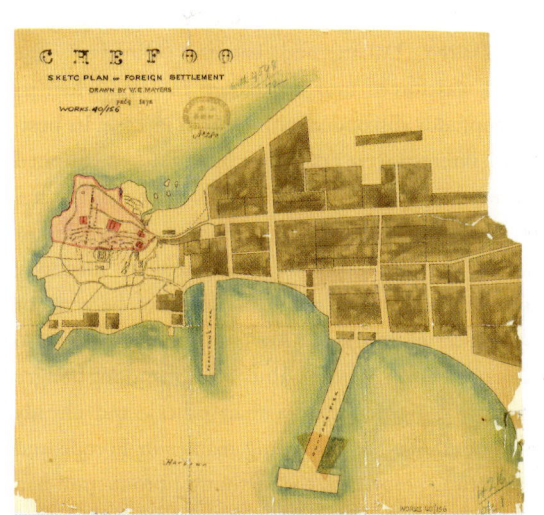

1872 map of the foreign settled area, extending south (right) of Consulate Hill. The British government property is marked in red. Reprinted with permission by the National Archives.

the Chinese government at the highest level, but this was a particularly delicate time for foreigners in China to talk about special privileges. The imperial government, with real fears about its own future, was anxious to exercise more control over the many and increasing foreign-occupied areas. The news broke in October 1906 that the Chefoo Chinese Chamber of Commerce had submitted a counter-petition to establish a municipal council covering the Foreign Quarter. The *Chefoo Daily News* reported the *taotai* as saying 'that the Peking government will never repeat former mistakes by granting municipal powers to foreign residents at any of the Treaty Ports'.[48] What eventually came about at the end of 1909 was the prosaic sounding 'International Committee of Section Six'.[49]

The new body comprised six foreigners, representing the (still voluntary) foreign ratepayers, and six Chinese, representing the local taxpayers. The twelve enjoyed 'harmonious cooperation unhampered by official interference'.[50] The former Foreign Quarter later became known as Section One (a promotion from Section Six), under the overall municipality of Yantai, and began to see a number of improvements. More roads were laid, there was better sanitation[51] and improved policing arrangements. The extra expense was funded in part by local taxes on theatres and brothels, with the balance paid for by the province.[52] Also, in 1911, the city government took over responsibility for the telephone system. Chefoo had been linked to Shanghai and Tientsin by telegraph since 1885.[53] Within the town there had been a telephone line in 1894, but this only connected the Chinese military commander's house to the camps where his troops were.[54] A larger network was established and was operated by the German Post Office.[55]

Getting on with business

In 1867 there was a foreign population of 25 to 30, half of them British and the rest German, French and American.[56] The two major firms were Fergusson & Co. and Wilson, Cornabé & Co.[57] Fergussons remained in business as general merchants until 1900. Wilson, Cornabé & Co. lasted longer, remaining for many years the most influential foreign firm in the port. Initially buying produce locally and shipping it to the southern ports, the company soon became a shipowner itself and agent for a number of other lines. William Cornabé was also instrumental in the formation of the Chefoo Club, providing it with its first seafront premises in the 1860s. The firm later gained the agency of nearly all the foreign banks represented in Chefoo; only the Hongkong & Shanghai Bank remained in the hands of chief rivals Fergusson & Co.

Successful ventures for Cornabés in the 1880s were the export of straw braid and the manufacture of hairnets, the latter principally for the New York market. The firm moved into silk manufacture, becoming agents for the Chefoo Filanda silk-spinning mill in 1896. In terms of shipping, one of Cornabés' most important agencies was that of Butterfield & Swire's China Navigation. They held this until Swires established themselves in Chefoo in 1900. By then senior partner Andrew Eckford had changed the business name to Cornabé, Eckford & Co. It continued to grow, expanding into lighterage and port services. The firm managed the Chefoo Lighter Co., the Bluff Water Co. and the Hokee Lighter Co. and had a virtual monopoly on the business of loading and unloading ships in the harbour. In 1898 Cornabés opened a branch in Weihaiwei (Weihai), and later in Dairen (Dalian) and Tsingtao (Qingdao). The firm was forced into liquidation in 1932 when its comprador absconded with most of its cash. Its business interests were taken over by the aforementioned James McMullan,[58] whom we shall meet again later.

Silk was for a time one of Chefoo's leading industries. Silkworms had been cultivated in Shandong for centuries and Chefoo had risen to be a major producer of pongee, or woven silk cloth. Using also cocoons brought from Manchuria, Shandong pongee was of a lighter texture than others, and already in the 1860s had a thriving market in Europe and America.[59] However, the method of production had remained virtually unchanged for centuries, and the foreign merchants in Chefoo saw an opportunity to make improvements. In 1874 the German firm Crasemann & Hagen built the Chefoo Filanda (already mentioned) west of the city on the Tung Shen River. This was the first steam-operated silk weaving factory in China and its state-of-the-art methods were looked on with suspicion by the traditional Chinese producers. After all, they had made silk for millennia and were reluctant to be told how it should be done. The new venture was unsuccessful and had to be wound up in 1885. The operation was bought the following year by local interests[60] and was in operation again a few years later with Cornabé Eckford as agents.

The idea of weaving silk using modern machines in specially designed factories caught on, though that of using steam to operate them did not. By 1905 almost 9000 people were employed in a total of 28 filatures in Chefoo, only 3 of which used steam power.[61] The number had grown to 43 by 1911, but still only 3 were steam-powered.[62] This growth was clearly a good thing for the economy; 14,000 people had jobs. But as is often the case, the producers developed more of an eye for quantity (which, hopefully, meant profit) rather than quality. Already in 1890 there had been complaints from customers in London. An inquiry revealed that there was no opportunity for inspection prior to shipping the product.[63] The following year it was being reported that Chefoo's silk exports were so coarse that they could only be used for making umbrellas and coat linings.[64] Increase in demand, as happened in 1908–9, immediately led to a decrease in quality. A Silk Improvement Commission was established in 1920 but its efforts were resisted by the predominantly peasant-controlled silk industry.[65] The Japanese, on the other hand, had no problem with using modern methods and they relished the chance to remove the silk business from Chefoo. Once they gained control of the cocoon-producing areas of Manchuria they had an even greater advantage. By 1931, Chefoo's once-thriving industry had waned to a mere eight filatures and the export business was moribund.[66]

The straw braid industry had been insignificant when the treaty port opened, but it grew steadily to provide one of Chefoo's principal exports. Unlike silk, the main use for straw braid was a Western one—making hats. Two-thirds of the braid went to Europe and one-third to America,[67] and much of the export business was controlled by foreign firms.[68] Much like silk, the production was in the hands of local Chinese, many of whom were not averse to sacrificing quality when demand was high. After all, the growers' main interest was in the grain produced by their wheat crops; the straw was simply a by-product.[69] Things came to a head in 1888 when there was an almost total boycott by the foreign buyers.[70] For a while, improvements were made and the ever-present Japanese competition was fended off, but only temporarily. By 1907, cheating on a massive scale had crept back: poor-quality braid was wrapped around with good-quality; and braid was packed before it was dry, hence it had shrunk by the time it was received by the customer. Objections were raised at the highest levels in Peking, but it was not long before a change in fashion killed demand.[71]

There is one industry from the 19th century that still thrives in modern Yantai. In 1897 three Chinese from the Straits Settlements founded the Pioneer Wine Company. They engaged the technical assistance of an Austrian expert in viticulture, Baron von Babo, and proceeded to plant 80 hectares with Austrian vines.[72] This company started big (with a cellarage capacity of 20,000 hectolitres)[73] and stayed that way. It is now listed on the Shenzhen Stock Exchange with a market capitalization of almost RMB 19 billion.*

One grand little building that still stands in the old Foreign Quarter is the former Chefoo branch of the Hongkong & Shanghai Bank, near the junction of Hai'an and Haiguan streets. The bank first appeared in Chefoo in 1875 as an agency, represented by Fergussons. In 1900 the agency was taken up by Butterfield & Swire. The bank itself opened an office in 1921 and in 1922 began issuing its own banknotes;[74] any found today are highly valued by collectors. Another beautiful building standing on the same street is the former office of Brunner Mond, the predecessor of Britain's Imperial Chemical Industries.

---

* In November 2014.

Business-minded missionaries

Two missionaries feature in the commercial history of Chefoo. The first is the Rev. Dr. John Livingston Nevius. A member of the American Presbyterian Mission, Nevius believed in showing non-believers that Christian people thrived in self-supporting communities.[75] One of his self-help projects in Chefoo was demonstrating the cultivation of Western fruit by grafting cuttings onto hardy Chinese plants.[76] In this way he introduced a whole new industry. By 1902 there was a buoyant export trade.[77]

The leading mercenary missionary was Irishman James McMullan, already mentioned, a member of the China Inland Mission (CIM). McMullan and his wife Eliza came to China with the CIM in 1884. They first appear in Chefoo's records in 1890, when a daughter's birth was registered at the British Consulate.[78] Two more daughters and two sons followed in the next ten years. The McMullans entered the Chefoo business scene in 1895, when James became manager of the Local Post Office. He also started the Chefoo Book Depot & Printing Office, which printed and published mainly religious books. At the same time, Eliza established and managed the Seamen's Haven, one of the many hotels that were to open in Chefoo.

The couple's main contribution was the Shantung Industrial Scheme, founded in 1896. Later changing its name to the Chefoo Industrial Mission, the project was inspired by a lady member of the American Presbyterians who had started to teach pillow lace-making to Chinese women. Eliza McMullan converted what sounded like a fireside activity into an industrial enterprise. She took on the training of workers, while her husband formed a company to market the output. The business was so successful that sales produced enough money to fund the training of the workers, who were largely village-based, and other missionary work the couple undertook. In 1902 the McMullans built a church, and in 1912 they opened two orphanages, one for boys and one for girls. They founded four girls' schools, the pupils devoting some of their time to earning their keep through lace-making. James also opened a jam and preserved fruit

The sign that still marks the entrance to the former Brunner Mond building. Photograph by author, 2010.

factory in 1897, presumably using fruit grown by Dr Nevius's followers.[79] He manufactured silk, woollen underwear, bristle brushes and furniture.[80] In 1915 the company added the manufacture of hairnets to its activities.[81] By 1917 the couple were estimated to be providing work for 10,000 people.[82] In 1918 McMullan started publishing the *Chefoo Daily News*, and in 1922 he added the *Morning Star*, a Chinese-language Christian monthly.

McMullan's two sons followed him, as did a daughter-in-law, into what had become a very substantial business empire. In 1937 McMullans put up a new office building in the foreign business centre, on a lot between Beach Road and Morrison Road, purchased from Butterfield & Swire. Although somewhat defaced on its lower floor, this striking art deco building is still there, but sadly with no acknowledgement of its former owners. Another lovely building can be found nearby at the corner of Chaoyang Street, the former premises of H.E. Railton & Co., pongee and lace merchants and exporters; Railton had worked for McMullan before setting up his own business in 1912.

No roads, and not much of a harbour

One continuing problem faced by all businessmen plying their trade in Chefoo was the lack of infrastructure outside the city. Chefoo had never been a trading centre as such—more of a landing stage from which goods were transported into the interior. In the 1870s, entering or leaving Chefoo every day were at least 3000 beasts of burden—horses, mules and donkeys.[83] By the 1890s the situation was still the same. Animals had to do all the carrying as none of the tracks leading out of Chefoo could take a cart of any description. There were even camels sharing the work, although these had to travel at night as the mules were frightened by them.[84] Ten years later still nothing had changed; even the road to the new British territory of Weihaiwei was only a rough track. But by this time most talk was of a railway connection rather than roads. Railways had been spreading over much of China, spurred on by foreign capital and expertise. The business community of Chefoo could only look on in envy when a ship docked in 1893 carrying 4000 tonnes of railway tracks bound for Port Arthur (Lüshun).[85]

Envy turned to concern when in 1904 the Germans completed a railway line from Tsingtao to the provincial capital Tsinan (Jinan). Soon straw braid, a staple of Chefoo's economy, was being diverted south to Tsingtao. Germany was keen to derive maximum advantage from its new base. Although the British consular map of 1909 still marked a rail link to Chefoo as 'proposed',[86] the Germans would hardly be likely to assist a competitor port in this manner. Neither was there sufficient capital in Chefoo to finance such an expensive undertaking. Despite repeated appeals from the foreign businessmen, who saw the German sphere of influence engulfing the entire province, no railway came. Chefoo's commerce dwindled as Tsingtao's grew. By 1907 a general air of depression was setting over the foreign business community, but for the Chinese it was much worse. The Tsingtao-Tsinan railway was taking business from the south of Chefoo's catchment area, and the Japanese were taking it from the north, by way of Dairen. Five hundred local merchants went out of business in 1907.[87] When motor roads eventually started to appear in the 1920s and 1930s they led towards the railhead at Tsinan.

One of the attractions of Chefoo as a port was that it did not freeze in winter. However, when Tientsin and Newchwang (Yingkou) were closed for this reason, Chefoo also had to hibernate. Strong gales meant that no port activity could be undertaken, sometimes for weeks at a time. In some years almost two months were lost owing to the inability of lighters to serve ships waiting at anchor.[88] A harbour improvement and bunding scheme was undertaken in 1896–97, the outline of which can still be seen, but what was needed was a breakwater to protect the harbour from the weather. This would cost a great deal of money, and the local government said that they had none to spare. If anything was to be done, it would be up to the foreign merchants to do it. A funding plan was formulated whereby a voluntary contribution would be levied at a rate of one-tenth of one percent of the value of all goods passing through the Custom House. This was small enough not to be felt by the importers and exporters, but it also meant that it would be a long while before there was enough to start work.

The Chinese government had far greater problems than these and when, in 1900, the Chefoo Chamber of Commerce tried to exert pressure on the government for a start to be made there was no response.[89] Reclamation work commenced in 1902 to extend the bund west of the small stone harbour. Compared with the need for a protective breakwater this was the cheaper end of the project, and clearly inappropriate as the first step. The shallow, sloping sea floor meant steamers had to lie up to a kilometre offshore. When lighters moored against the new reclamation they found the sea so rough during gales that they risked being battered against the stone wall. All work was stopped.[90] By this time some 30 to 40 steamers were entering and clearing the port every day and the need was becoming acute.

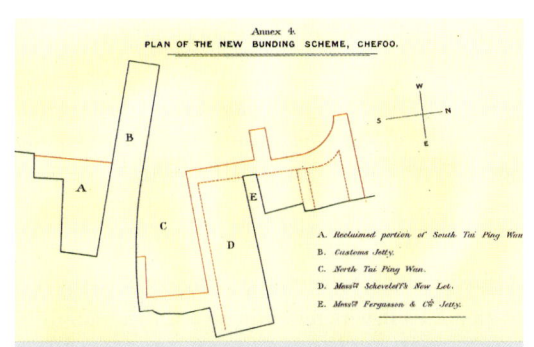

Plan of the new harbour scheme, the results of which can still be seen today. Source: *Foreign Office Report for Chefoo*, 1896.

In 1905 the mercantile community finally committed to the voluntary levy. A proposal was put to Peking together with an application for a loan to finance the initial capital. But again, there was no progress. A revised plan, on a larger scale, was sent in 1910 and a deal was on the verge of being agreed when the worst fears of the Qing government were realized and they were ousted from power by the revolution.[91] Flush with reforming zeal the new administration acted quickly. By May 1913 a Chefoo Harbour Improvement Commission had been formed, with a determined, high-powered board. The Dutch, for centuries masters of holding back the sea, provided the design and the Netherlands Harbour Works Co. was commissioned to undertake the work.

An army of 20 Dutch engineers descended on Chefoo and established a works site out on the bluff; this was to be the source of the vast amounts of stone that would be needed.[92] At their head was the suitably grand-sounding Chief Engineer, Mr. O. C. A. van Lidth de Jeude, who had been lent by the Dutch government. Work on the breakwater began in August 1915, but the total plan was for much more than that. The defence wall was to be 800 metres long and 8 metres wide, with an opening at each end. The harbour's western boundary was to be marked by a mole extending 1800 metres into the sea. This was to be served by a narrow-gauge railway along its length to a 200-metre quay on its northern arm, which provided accommodation for two or three coasters to tie up alongside. A large part of the 100 hectares of water that was now enclosed would be dredged to a depth of six to eight metres.[93] The huge project, for which Chefoo had waited for so long, was completed in May 1922,[94] some 30 years after it was first proposed. The finished product undoubtedly benefited from the advances in engineering taking place during those three decades. Mr. Fergusson especially would have been pleased; one of the new piers was named after him, albeit the smallest of the three. The others were those of the Kaiping Coal Co., with a 90-metre frontage, and the Maritime Customs wharf, with a capacity for 60 lighters.[95] The very smart customs inspection house, which dates from 1866, was accommodated in the new plan and it still stands at the seaward end of the wharf.

A SEASIDE SANATORIUM

One aspect of Chefoo seemed to thrive independently of the merchants and their machinations and tribulations. Some of the earliest foreign visitors found the weather to be 'thoroughly bracing'.[96] In many ways the climate was, and still is, ideal from a European perspective. The autumn months are perfect, with warm days and chilly nights. In all seasons sea breezes bring dry air to this part of the Shandong coast. It was not long before these benefits were widely known and Chefoo became a popular destination for escaping from the sweaty heat of the southern ports. Americans were comparing the climate with that of Boston, the Scots with that of Edinburgh, while the English referred to Chefoo as 'the Brighton of China'.

An early recreational activity for residents and holidaymakers alike was horse racing. A Chefoo Race Club was formed in 1864. The course, which only came together for the May season, was a couple of kilometres along the beach to the east. The races held in the early days had 'an atmosphere entirely their own'.[97] A picture of early treaty port life can be had from the description of the other events that followed the pony racing: 'donkey races, foot races, running in sacks, leaping, throwing the hammer, chasing a greased pig etc.'[98]

Reports such as this could only have added to the attractiveness of Chefoo as a holiday destination. Among the first hotels to appear were the Beach Hotel, just to the east of Consulate Hill, and the Family Hotel, much further east. These grew to be the largest and lasted longest, but by the early 1870s they had a dozen or more competitors. There were boarding houses, holiday cottages and inns. Indeed, the presence of so many bars, coupled with regular visits by ships of the world's navies, was to prove a major problem (or depending on viewpoint, business opportunity). Into the 1920s visiting sailors were creating havoc with their drinking, whoring and violence; at that time, during the summer, there were seldom fewer than 20 or 30 warships in the outer harbour.[99] A meeting of foreign and Chinese officials agreed that an area should be set aside for the recreation of the seamen. However, Chinese parties immediately bought land there, such that the prices went up to a level that the bar operators could not afford. They therefore went elsewhere without Chinese 'assistance'.[100] Today there is a very pleasant line of bars and small restaurants along Chaoyang Street, and all is peace and quiet.

The hospitality industry of Chefoo was more responsive to holidaymakers who wished to come and enjoy a healthy seaside vacation. In the latter part of the 19th century a number of steamer lines made regular stops, linking Chefoo to most major ports on the China Coast. The journey time from Shanghai was two days. All hotels and boarding houses were full in the summer months, and more were being opened all the time. Some were owned by people who had lived in Chefoo and decided to retire there. All levels of the market were being catered for, but it was the top end that had to work hardest. The Family Hotel was so successful that it added a second storey to its original building.[101] The centrally located Beach Hotel was the biggest and the best, but even this establishment could not afford to be complacent. After a major renovation in the early 1900s it emerged with 60 well-furnished rooms, lighted throughout by electricity, and advertised itself as 'the only first class hotel in Chefoo'; a brave statement as only the year before the Astor House, the epitome of hotel modernity and luxury in Shanghai, had opened a Chefoo branch. Competition was intense between these two magnificent hotels, each vying for first place. A winner emerged by 1914, when the Beach was being described as an annex to its former rival.[102]

For many years these two were the centre of Chefoo's social life. Between them was St. Andrew's Church, the main Anglican place of worship. Beyond the Beach to the west was the Roman Catholic Church of St. Mary. Neither survived. However, the ghost of the Chefoo Club can still be seen. William Cornabé's original building was enlarged in 1907 to accommodate the activities of its 50-odd members, but there was soon talk of the need for a total rebuild.[103] The early 1930s replacement stands at the western end of Hai'an Street, many of its internal features still intact.

In the early Treaty Port Era the only alternatives Westerners had for educating their children were to risk exposing them to heat and disease in the cities in which they lived or to send them back to their home countries, perhaps not seeing them again for years. The idea of a boarding school in a place as pleasant as Chefoo had great appeal. In 1881 the Protestant Collegiate School for Boys opened, with a total roll of three pupils. The school was the brainchild of the Rev. Dr. James Hudson Taylor, founder of the China Inland Mission, and was an instant success. By 1908 it had become the China Inland Mission Schools, comprising separate boys' and girls' schools and a preparatory school. Most pupils were boarders. Initially intended for the children of missionaries, the schools started accepting applications from foreign mercantile families from all over China. The institution enjoyed a high reputation for academic achievement and pastoral care. By the early 1930s there were 100 children in each of the three schools. Boarders spent the summer at school as well, making the long journey home only in the winter when the school was closed for two months.[104]

A SAFE HAVEN

Chefoo had an uncanny ability to avoid most of the troubles that beset the rest of the country. The name of the treaty port is most often associated with the Chefoo Agreement of 1876, something that otherwise had nothing to do with Chefoo at all. The murder in 1875 of A. R. Margary, one-time member of the British Consulate in Chefoo, while exploring the China–Burma border gave Great Britain another opportunity to press for the opening of treaty ports, and a few other things besides. Robert Hart arranged for the chief negotiators, Li Hongzhang and Sir Thomas Wade, to meet in the pleasant atmosphere of Chefoo. The document was signed on 13 September 1876 at a temple on Temple Hill to the south of the walled city.[105] This hill grew into a Western religious centre as well, with a church, a cemetery and other facilities run by the American Presbyterian Mission.[106] Nothing remains now except for the original Chinese temple.

In 1894 the Sino-Japanese War was being fought all around Chefoo, not least at the end of the peninsula at Weihaiwei. In December the foreign residents started planning for their defence.[107] A well-attended meeting at the Chefoo Club resulted in 32 men and boys volunteering to be drilled on military lines. Then foreign warships started landing men to protect the foreign community.[108] It was believed that Chefoo was not attractive to the Japanese in view of its poor facilities.[109] Nevertheless, the commander-in-chief of the nearby Japanese forces wrote to all the foreign consuls in Chefoo saying that 'in case our army should find it necessary to occupy Chefoo' the foreigners would be protected.[110] The meaning was clear to the Chinese population, who fled in large numbers.[111] When, on 19 January 1895, Japanese warships bombarded Tengchow HMS *Daphne* and USS *Yorktown* sped along the coast from Chefoo to observe and take notes.[112] In addition to these two, there were eleven warships in the harbour, including some from France, Germany and Russia.[113] In the end, far from suffering from the hostilities Chefoo's trade increased, with the following year's level of business being the highest then on record.[114] The Treaty of Shimonoseki brought an end to the fighting and the ratifications were exchanged in Chefoo at the Beach Hotel.[115]

The Boxer Rebellion was only marginally harder to sidestep. Shandong was the starting point for the unrest, but Governor Yuan Shikai went to great lengths to keep order[116] to the benefit of the foreign population and Chinese Christians wishing to escape persecution.[117] Trade in 1900 suffered, but surprisingly little.[118] When war broke out between Japan and Russia in 1904, once more Chefoo had a grandstand seat. Thanks to junks from the port supplying both sides, 1905 was the most prosperous year so far in its commercial history.[119]

The events of 1911 and their immediate aftermath were to see the treaty port's luck finally run out, although there was no loss of blood in Chefoo.[120] A revolutionary Provisional Government was established for the city; the provincial capital, Tsinan, remained for a while in Qing hands.[121] Normal business was impossible: imports had to be paid for in advance, credit being unavailable. Chefoo's had become a cash economy. Banknotes issued by local Chinese banks ceased to have any value, and even some foreign banknotes circulated only at a considerable discount. However, by the end of the year the Provisional Government had largely restored order and normality.[122] The revolutionaries appointed a new governor, but he was opposed by the Chamber of Commerce (which was backed by the police and the troops stationed in the city) as he was trying to squeeze the local business community by holding their stocks to ransom. He was forced to resign.[123]

Tensions continued to flare. In 1912 the American Consul ordered a warship to come and land US Marines as he feared for the safety of the port's foreign residents.[124] Ultimately, it was only trade that suffered. The opening in 1914 of Lungkow (Longkou) to foreign trade, 100 kilometres to the west, added to Chefoo's concerns. A steamer service had already started from Lungkow to Newchwang, transporting 80,000 coolies who would have otherwise gone via Chefoo.[125] Realistically, any threat that this tiny new port posed to the prosperity of Chefoo had already been overshadowed by German progress further south.

THE 1920S AND THE 1930S

At the 1919 Paris Peace Conference, China was told that it was not going to be given back the parts of the country formerly occupied by Germany. The announcement that these were to be handed over to Japan instead gave birth to the May Fourth Movement and an anti-Japanese boycott. The movement was particularly strong in Chefoo, which was already smarting from Japanese competition in the silk and other leading industries.[126] There were some new factories, all Chinese concerns: an aerated water and beer plant in 1921, a soap factory in 1922, a match factory in 1924, and one assembling clocks, using movements imported from Germany. There were also new fruit, vegetable and meat canneries and a flour mill.[127] From 1925 to 1927, Chefoo played its part in the national boycott of British and Japanese goods and shipping, stemming from the Shanghai Incident. Local trade should have benefited from this exclusion of the two biggest foreign competitors, but there were more troubles of a home-grown nature that interfered with this.

Large parts of the country collapsed into warlordism, and bandits and small private armies were operating right up to the outskirts of the town. In 1929 there were battles between General Liu Zhennian and General Zhang Zongchang in the area surrounding Chefoo. Liu claimed to be an adherent of the Central Government, whose campaign colour was blue. All the houses in the area in which his troops might be active were therefore painted blue when Liu was in the ascendancy and repainted white when he was not. This happened three times, and must have given some welcome business to paint suppliers and decorators.[128] But in true style, Chefoo enjoyed for a few years a period of relative stability 'despite the charade-like campaigns constantly conducted in the hinterland'.[129] There was even a surge in property development during this period. Houses in the foreign style 'sprung up like mushrooms'. Prices doubled in the space of two years, making them for a time more expensive than Shanghai.[130] Thanks to the municipal arrangements, the city's affairs were being well managed and the electric light system was unrivalled in China.[131]

For most of the foreign population it seemed in many ways that nothing had changed, so often the case in those days of pampering and privilege. Mary Campbell, wife of Butterfield & Swire's man Gordon Campbell, recalled that in the 1930s food was good and plentiful, and that they grew their own vegetables and fruit out at the company house on East Beach: asparagus, strawberries, grapes, apples, pears. They had ponies, and it was possible to ride through the countryside quite safely. There were about 750 Europeans at Chefoo,[132] including a number of permanent residents who ran silk businesses and embroidery factories. Trade was very bad—'just about limping along'—but it did not seem to matter. There were some Germans, who had escaped from Tsingtao after the Japanese took over, and a few White Russians. Mrs. Campbell remembered the Chefoo Club, with its terraces overlooking the sea, where there were dancing and bridge nights during the season.[133] A visitor in early 1937, after arriving on a small steamer, wrote that it was 'wonderful to be at the Chefoo Club with real heat, lights, plumbing,

c. 1896 view of the Family Hotel and East Beach. Consular Hill is in the distance on the right. Courtesy of Duncan Clark.

good food and a proper bed'.[134] There were two other clubs as well: the Beach Club, east of the town, near the CIM Schools, and the Customs Club for junior customs officers. Cabarets moved up from Shanghai for the summer and criminals were still being executed on Second Beach, way out to the east and discreetly away from the town.[135] To the west of the town, on the banks of Freshwater River, pupils from the CIM Schools went for camping trips.[136]

When the Japanese Army entered Chefoo in the summer of 1937, it put the European population in an odd position. The Japanese were not at that time enemies of the other foreigners, and would not be so until the attack on British and American possessions in December 1941. But it was clear that the stationing of troops by any authority other than the Chinese did not bode well. The Japanese soldiers were polite enough, and they lived up to the promise made 40 years previously that the British and other nationalities would not be disturbed.[137] However, when Weihaiwei was attacked in 1938, a number of Chinese wounded were accommodated at the CIM Schools,[138] and the position of the Europeans started to look precarious. Then a 10:00 p.m. to 7:00 a.m. curfew was imposed.[139] Even though it was still only China and Japan that were at war, conditions for the non-belligerents became more untenable, with frequent requests by Japanese soldiers for proof of identity and other inconveniences. Worse, there were threats of bombing raids by the Japanese aircraft that were based nearby. British businessmen painted Union Jacks on the roofs of their buildings, believing this would spare them from aerial attack. Even the Chinese Maritime Customs station flew the British flag, probably without permission.[140] The position of the foreign residents was finally clarified at the end of 1941 when they were herded into the Astor House on the bund and told that they were being interned.[141]

Further reading: Johnston and Erh, *Far from Home*; Martin, *Chefoo School*; Nield, 'Bits of Broken China'; Osborne, *Lilla's Feast*.

CHENGTU (CHENGDU) 成都

Sichuan, 30.39° N, 104.03° E
Consular Station, 1902 Britain

The fertile plain on which Chengtu sits enabled it to prosper even though, due to the surrounding mountains and inhospitable terrain, its prosperity grew in isolation from the rest of China. The ancient Sichuan provincial capital contained three separate walled cities, similar to Peking (Beijing): the Tartar city, the Imperial and the Chinese.[1] For this reason, coupled with the city's remoteness, it was an easy decision for the Empress Dowager to remove the Imperial Court there in 1901 when things became too uncomfortable in the capital.

Chengtu became a focus of foreign missionary activities in the latter years of the 19th century, and they were not popular. A riot in 1895 destroyed all missionary establishments in and around the city. Many of the occupants were killed. The foreign powers, deciding that the offer of indemnity payments was inadequate, procured the dismissal of the provincial governor. *The New York Times* hailed this move as resolving such difficulties forevermore,[2] an overly optimistic claim. As late as 1926 a missionary's wife was stabbed to death in one of the city's streets.[3]

There was another source of foreign interest. The French were eyeing Sichuan as the next step in their designs on neighbouring Yunnan, and this sparked British interest. In addition to being on the border with British India, Sichuan provided the passageway between China and Tibet, where Britain was also developing a presence. A 1901 review of British consular requirements prompted the opening of consulates in Chengtu and Yunnan-fu (Kunming) the following year. These were the first to be established in cities that had not been opened as treaty ports. The

Chengtu consulate remained a diplomatic and political station, with trade matters handled in Chungking (Chongqing).

Foreign trading interest in Chengtu was hampered by its inaccessibility. The city was on the Min River, but almost 250 kilometres from where this joined the Yangtze at Chungking. For most of this distance the Min was only deep enough for steamers of the shallowest draught. When these vessels could not get through, the overland journey took two weeks.[4] Of the 120 foreign (non-Japanese) residents of Chengtu in 1907, only one was a businessman; apart from a few consular people the rest were missionaries.[5]

From 1911 the dangers for foreigners in Chengtu steadily increased. The announcement that year of a new Hankow-Chengtu railway, to be built by a foreign syndicate, prompted a riot and the rapid departure of all foreigners;[6] recovery of railway rights was a rallying cry for the expression of Chinese grievances.

Many of these foreigners had been involved in establishing the West China Union College in 1910. This had to close, although it reopened in 1913.[7] The impressive gate to the campus, now part of Sichuan University, can be seen on Renmin South Road, as can campus buildings from the 1920s and 1930s.

In 1906, because of Chengtu's status as a provincial capital, Britain built a consulate-general.[8] This stood in the south-west corner of the city on Wangjiaguai Street, but nothing remains today. For the first 20 years of the Republican period Chengtu was surrounded by violence, latterly between Nationalist and Communist forces. Some missionaries could escape to the hill station at Bailuding (Bailu). An American, Robert Service, leased an entire hilltop there in 1915 and built a holiday bungalow.[9]

The nationwide anti-British boycott in 1927 was felt in Chengtu. No reassuring gunboat could be sent, and so the British Consulate-General was closed 'temporarily' in January; permanent closure followed in 1933.[10] The consul and vice-consul had to vacate their 'stately English house'[11] and all British residents left with them.

The Japanese had both a large presence and a consulate in Chengtu. When this was attacked by a mob in 1926, Japan pressed, unsuccessfully, for Chengtu to be opened as a treaty port so that protection could be given to foreigners.[12] Their consulate lasted slightly longer than Britain's but closed as a result of resentment at Japanese encroachments in Manchuria in 1931. In 1942 the city became home temporarily to a number of universities escaping the Japanese in the east. The British Consulate reopened in November that year, but closed permanently in 1947.[13]

CHIMMO BAY (SHENHU WAN)
深滬灣

Fujian, 24.39° N, 118.40° E
Opium Receiving Station, 1820s

Opium was traded illegally at the first treaty ports long before their official opening. To avoid consular attention, principal dealers Jardines and Dents moved their illegal activities to sheltered bays along Fujian's coast, like Chimmo. As it would have been equally unlawful for cotton to be brought to Chimmo as for opium to be shipped direct to Amoy (Xiamen), 60 kilometres south-east, the two businesses developed separately.[1] Opium was paid for in silver, and the

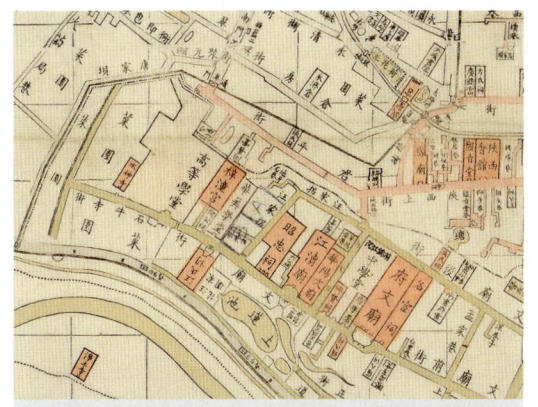

Extract of a 1906 map, showing the site of the British Consulate-General. Reprinted with permission by the National Archives.

quantities held by the dealers at Chimmo proved irresistible to pirates. They overran the receiving ships in 1847, forcing the business to move 20 kilometres north to Chinchew (Quanzhou) Bay.²

Chinchew Bay (Quanzhou Wan) 泉州灣

Fujian, 24.49° N, 118.40° E
Opium Receiving Station, 1820s

Known to 13th-century Arab traders as Zaiton, Chinchew was with Canton (Guangzhou) one of the two Chinese ports open to foreign trade. Japanese pirates forced Chinchew's Superintendency of Trade to close in 1522,¹ although Portuguese and Spanish business continued for some years.² In 1832 the sheltered bay attracted first Jardines'³ then Dents' opium ships.⁴ In 1843 Hong Kong Governor Sir Henry Pottinger suggested to Imperial Commissioner Qiying that Chinchew become officially recognized as an opium depot, thereby keeping the trade out of Hong Kong and the treaty ports. Qiying's rent demands were too high. The idea lapsed,⁵ but the trade continued.

Chinkiang (Zhenjiang) 鎮江

Jiangsu, 32.13° N, 119.26° E
Treaty Port, 1858 British Treaty

The British were already convinced of the potential of Chinkiang long before it was opened as a treaty port by the 1858 Treaty of Tientsin (Tianjin). The First Opium War dragged on in a desultory manner from 1839 to 1842, with very little actual fighting. Most action took the form of one-sided naval demonstrations by the British. Chinkiang was the site of one of the conflict's few military engagements.¹ The Chinese had expected, and planned for, a British assault on the Peiho (Hai) River, the nearest waterway to Peking (Beijing).² The appearance in the Yangtze of General Sir Henry Gough* and Admiral Sir William Parker in July 1842, with their force of 12,000, was therefore unexpected. Nonetheless, the Chinese garrison at Chinkiang conducted a strong defence. It took the British three days to subdue the city before moving 70 kilometres upstream to Nanking (Nanjing).

Chinkiang is strategically located at the juncture of the Yangtze and the Grand Canal. It occupied an important position, both militarily and economically, as the gateway to the Great River and to the capital. By wresting it from China's control, Britain was able to halt the all-important rice shipments up the canal and gain the emperor's full attention. Imperial Commissioner Qiying was ordered to negotiate terms at any cost,³ and the Treaty of Nanking was signed a few weeks later.

The humiliation of the capture of the city by an outside enemy was quickly followed by its annihilation by a domestic foe. The Taiping rebels swept up from the south, making Nanking their capital and capturing Chinkiang in April 1853. Short of supplies, they abandoned Chinkiang in early 1857, but not before destroying everything. The inhabitants who had not already fled now did so. Returning in 1858 during the Second Opium War, one member of the British army recorded that he imagined himself to be in Pompeii, such was the scene of devastation.⁴

The concession and the consulate

The British waited until the Taipings had been cleared from the environs of the city before formally opening the new treaty port in February 1861. Harry Parkes, then 33, had the job of making the necessary arrangements. He installed Thomas Adkins, aged 27,

---

* On his elevation to the peerage in 1846, Gough took the title Viscount Gough of Ching Kang Foo.

THE FLEET PASSING GOLDEN ISLAND.

The British fleet passing Golden Island, 1842. Source: Ouchterlony, *The Chinese War*, 426.

as British Consul, referring to him as 'a youngster'.[5] Another duty, and one at which Parkes generally excelled, having had much practice, was to identify a site for a British Concession. He marked out an irregular plot of land on the riverfront just upstream of the mouth of the Grand Canal, about 400 metres long and between 80 and 230 metres wide.

The consulate was to be built at the western end of the concession, but there was a need for immediate accommodation. Parkes therefore removed some Chinese soldiers from a partly ruined temple on Silver Island (Jiao Shan), then as now home to a number of significant Buddhist temples and shrines. The chosen building was almost the only one near the water that still had a roof.[6] Not only did the Chinese raise immediate objections to this barbarian invasion of one of their sacred places, but also the few British merchants who started to make an appearance complained that it was too far away—some five kilometres downstream from the concession. Accordingly, another temple was commandeered, this time on Silver Hill (Yuntai Shan), the rise that formed the western boundary of the concession.[7]

There were initially 17 lots, averaging just over 3000 square metres each. Lot No. 1, at the eastern end and double the normal size, was taken by Dent & Co. By July 1864 the next five had also been occupied. The nine lots along the riverfront were separated from the water by a 12-metre bund, and behind them a road of similar width had been marked out.

Beyond this were two blocks of four lots each, separated by a smaller road.[8] It was an ambitious undertaking and represented a huge leap of faith by Parkes, one of the many for which he was to become noted. His confidence was even more remarkable considering that Chinkiang's once-thriving trade was by 1861 at a standstill.[9]

One factor that Parkes overlooked was the fickle nature of the Yangtze. With 250 kilometres to go before reaching the sea, the level of water varied with the seasons, and its flow was rapid and forceful. In addition, the effects of the ocean tides were evident, even this far inland.[10] At the time the treaty port was settled, the current on the south bank was so strong that ships could not anchor safely, nor could the merchants moor the hulks they used as residences. The flow on the north bank was not so fierce, and so in 1863 a number of them moored their floating dwellings there and bought plots of land ashore. Title deeds for 99 years were issued by young Adkins, each bearing his official seal. Naturally, the Chinese authorities objected to this unlawful occupation and denied foreign access. Unable to get either enjoyment of their purchases or refunds of their investments, the angry foreign traders reluctantly started to build on the concession, while initially leaving their hulks on the other side.[11] Also erected at this time was a house and offices for the Imperial Maritime Customs near the entrance to the canal; a floating Custom House under foreign management had been opened in April

1861. By 1867 there was a foreign community of about 20, including 7 customs staff.[12]

At that time a China-wide review of British consular properties noted that because Chinkiang 'appears so desolate, the trade so insignificant, the number of British residents so few' there was no need to build a residence for the British Consul.[13] When Consul Frederick Harvey left in 1868 for sick leave and early retirement, it was decided not to replace him. The British presence was left in the hands of an assistant or an interpreter, sometimes the constable, under the watching brief of the consul in Shanghai.[14] It was only in 1876 that the station was upgraded once more and a purpose-built residence-cum-office was provided for the consul.[15]

Early hopes dashed

Once the Chinese population started to return to the city after the Taiping threat was over, the manufacture of silk piece-goods began to resume its former importance.[16] By 1869 foreign traders handled a quarter of the silk exports.[17] Other local staples were rice to Canton (Guangzhou) and items that appealed solely to the Chinese market: dried lily flowers, sesame seeds, groundnuts and sheep skins. Foreign merchants imported opium, making Chinkiang by 1871 the third-largest centre for the drug,[18] but there was little scope for further involvement by non-Chinese. Robert Hart predicted that Chinkiang would probably overtake Shanghai as a centre of trade, but only a few years into the new treaty port's life this was looking extremely unlikely. There were two reasons for this, both the result of nature. In 1855 the Yellow River changed its course dramatically, flooding much of the northern part of the Grand Canal. This prompted the use of coastal steamers to transport tribute rice to Peking. The canal became sidelined, as did Chinkiang's position as one of its major ports.[19]

The second reason for Chinkiang's early eclipse was the behaviour of the Yangtze. All foreign vessels on this stretch of the river found that the detailed and usually completely reliable British Admiralty charts very soon became useless in terms of what lay beneath the surface of the water. In November 1858, all the vessels in Lord Elgin's mission up the river suffered the humiliation of running aground at one time or another.[20] The new foreign settlement soon came to respect the awesome power of the river. By 1875 the bund was being undermined. Dents' lot was the first to be affected, and the depth of water there grew to 20 metres. Rectification was estimated to require 'a small mountain to fill it'.[21] The physical damage was serious enough, but there was also the inconvenience. It had become difficult and dangerous to moor hulks to handle cargo and passengers. Only Butterfield & Swire and China Merchants were able to place their floating landing stages less than 60 metres from the shore. Even then, goods and people were faced with a rickety journey along the connecting wooden bridges. These two firms had the consolation of being able to charge more for their less inconvenient service, but the situation was far from satisfactory.[22]

Further problems were faced by steamers bringing in goods that required customs inspection and clearance. The state of the river often prevented them from approaching the customs jetty, as they were obliged to do. They were forced instead to offload onto the bund by way of lighters. There was no customs shed and so incoming cargo was left at the mercy of the weather, resulting in much damage.[23] A general feeling evolved that something ought to be done—by the consulate or the customs or both—but nothing was. Perhaps with the technology of the time nothing could have been done to tame the Great River to the extent required.

The strong current brought down huge amounts of sediment, deposited just as the river entered the relatively calm final stretch of its long journey. Chinkiang's name translates into English as 'Guardian of the River'—ironic as the place itself needed so much guarding *from* the river. Golden Island, near the north bank at the time of Marco Polo,[24] became during the first few years of the British presence part of the south bank. Worse was to come. A large sandbank had been seen upstream, to the west of the concession—part of the same activity that had engulfed Golden Island. The more this spit advanced on the concession, the more people worried—but no action was taken. The bund steadily became inaccessible for steamers. The hulks and pontoons had to relocate downstream. Even there things were not safe, as the swift currents had also been displaced downstream by the silting. In 1904 a 200-by-20-metre stretch of the bank fell into the water, taking with it six godowns and creating a tidal wave that travelled up and down the river for several kilometres.[25] The foreshore at the large Standard Oil and Asiatic Petroleum facilities, a kilometre to the east, was the next to go in 1909, when the front half of the Butterfield & Swire property also collapsed into the torrent.[26] Meanwhile the southern entrance to the neglected Grand Canal was becoming 'nothing but an evil smelling drain'.[27]

All this had a devastating effect on the small port and its ability to handle such of the river trade that still called. However, with the hindsight of over a century it has left us a desirable inheritance. Zhengrun Zhou, the former Chengjenchow Spit, so isolated the former concession that it was spared further development. The result is that a surprising number of Treaty Port-Era buildings still remain, including godowns and commercial and residential buildings. Chief among these are the former British and American consulates, now incorporated into the Zhenjiang Museum.

LITTLE SUBSTANCE

As with many of the other minor treaty ports, the operation and servicing of passenger and cargo vessels came to dominate foreign mercantile activity at Chinkiang. By the beginning of the 1880s eight steamer companies provided regular services on the Lower Yangtze, all calling at Chinkiang. The largest were the British firms of Jardines and Butterfield & Swire, and China Merchants. The foreign population had edged up to about 40, including 20 in the customs service, and there were twelve foreign firms with a permanent establishment at Chinkiang.[28]

Despite the small population, a municipal council had been formed in the early years at the prompting of the British Minister in Peking. Its responsibilities were the usual round of road maintenance, drainage, security and the like. When street lighting was introduced in 1881 there was a grand total of two lamps,

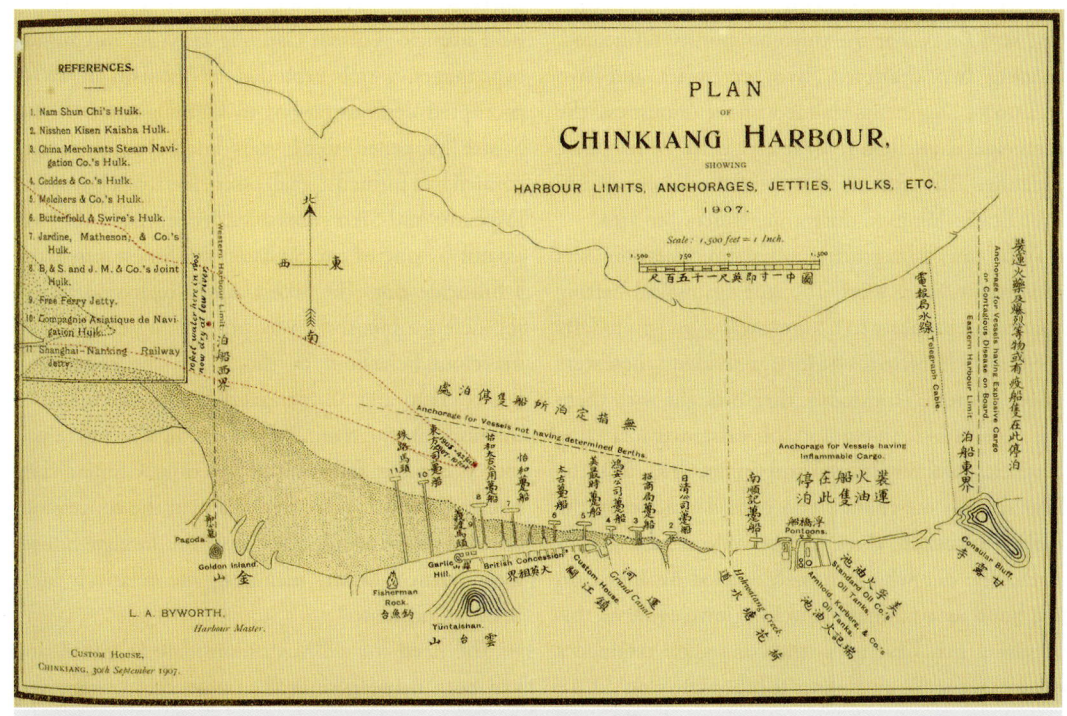

1907 plan of Chinkiang (Zhenjiang) Harbour. The red dotted line shows the encroachment of the spit towards the shipping jetties. Reprinted with permission by the National Archives.

costing $2.00 each. Meetings were often dominated by tedious discussions about procedure with little of actual substance being talked about.[29] The ability of the council to act effectively was also limited by the unwillingness of the constituent land-renters to tax themselves. In a few years the body was as good as bankrupt. When British Consul Herbert Allen asked to see the books and records prior to approving the council's accounts he was physically assaulted.

Allen's assailant was William Bean, British and one of the first foreign merchants established in Chinkiang. Owner of a number of the concession lots, Bean was the council's chairman and treasurer and did not like the idea of being audited. In fact he disliked the idea of anybody encroaching on his territory. Described by a later consul as a 'coarse, cantankerous, uneducated man of low tastes and malignant disposition',[30] Bean had a rival in the form of Thomas Duff. Also British, Duff had arrived a few years after Bean, but both were to stay until the closing years of the 1890s, continually at each other's throats. In 1888 both Bean and Duff called a meeting of the council, neither of them recognizing the other's gathering. The result was that the tiny community bifurcated, creating two chairmen, two secretaries and two treasurers. Despite its claimed impecuniousness, the municipal council built for itself a three-storey office building. This remains as one of the largest Treaty Port-Era buildings in the former concession area.

The lax management of the concession was reflected in other ways. The rule against sub-letting concession property to Chinese was soon ignored. By 1891, in addition to the 44 foreign residents there were 1566 Chinese.[31] Inevitably, they brought with them the necessities for a comfortable existence, including brothels, gambling houses and opium dens.[32] Of the four foreign merchants who owned practically the entire concession, three had become absentee landlords. The one who remained opened his house on the bund as a Chinese 'hotel'.[33] Unwelcome as this intrusion may have been, the concession retained a prosperous air of bustle that it otherwise would have lacked. The bund and the roads were reasonably well kept and there were trees to provide shade.[34] The 1880s saw an influx of missionaries of all persuasions and by 1885 there were two churches in the concession, Protestant and Catholic.[35]

The community's non-spiritual needs were also well catered for. In addition to the essential Chinkiang Club, with a separate Customs Club for the 'outdoor staff', there was a communally managed shooting bungalow at Wu Chow Shan in the hills to the south. Wild boar was the main attraction, although Consul Edward Allen also shot cicadas from his verandah in an attempt at noise abatement.[36] On the far side of the Chinese city a recreation ground had been laid out, Victoria Park, including tennis, football and cricket grounds.[37] Chinkiang's first recorded cricket match was held in 1873, when a customs eleven played a side of seven residents, the most that could be mustered. The score was not mentioned, but the spectacle was watched by one European lady with a small boy, and about 30 curious Chinese.[38]

Riots, railways and general decline

Anti-foreign riots were all too common in the treaty ports, and Chinkiang was no exception. The deeply held suspicions about Catholic activities in Chinese orphanages, which exploded in Tientsin in 1870, prompted demonstrations in Chinkiang in 1872.[39] Worse happened some years later. The municipal council had formed a small police force of a European inspector and Sikh constables. In February 1889 an assault by one of the Sikhs on a Chinese provoked a full-scale riot. The Sikh claimed to have acted in self-defence but there was pre-existing evidence of malicious behaviour by the Sikhs. The concession was overrun and all foreigners fled to the safety of the hulks in the river. The American Consulate was looted but escaped total destruction. Chinese-style houses, of which there were many in the concession, were carefully avoided but half the foreign houses were burned down, including the relatively new British Consulate.[40]

The need for a British Consulate at Chinkiang had been debated since the outset. However, given the prestige that was now at stake, there was no question about rebuilding especially as a suitable indemnity had been paid by the Chinese government. The indemnity must have been a big one; not only is the three-storey consulate building still there, completed in 1890, but also a stables and a residence and gaol for the constable, all of which also still stand. A new Customs Club and police station were also built, replacing those destroyed in the riot.[41] Sikh policemen were dispensed with and some time later 16 Shandong men were recruited when the Chinese Regiment in Weihaiwei (Weihai) was disbanded.[42]

The coming of the railway dealt yet another blow to Chinkiang. The line from Shanghai to Nanking reached the port in October 1907, the link to Nanking being completed a few months later. While popular with passengers it did little for Chinkiang's trade. Rather, it reduced the port's position even further as a distribution centre—goods could now shoot straight through without stopping.[43] Ironically, Chinkiang's railway station was built on almost the exact spot where the British fleet had anchored in 1842.[44]

Many vessels continued to call at Chinkiang but the port was losing business to newer rivals at Wuhu, a treaty port since 1876, and Nanking, opened for trade in 1899. Attempts at establishing modern albumen, silk, glass and paper factories were generally unsuccessful.[45] The import of kerosene and oil products was just about the only profitable new foreign venture in the late 19th and early 20th centuries. Standard Oil became the largest employer of foreign staff, apart from the customs, and in 1909 erected a substantial three-storey building in the concession, thought to be 'the handsomest building in the port'.[46] It is still there, as is the two-storey premises of rival Asiatic Petroleum, both beautifully restored.

Revolution and rendition

The city of Chinkiang declared for the revolution on 6 November 1911 and the new leaders took over two days later. Nevertheless most of the local population fled as the port filled with soldiers preparing to attack Nanking. The foreign community, although not unduly affected,[47] began to dwindle. The 1920s saw the spread along the Yangtze valley of much anti-foreign feeling, particularly after the 'Shanghai Incident' of 1925. In March of that year Chinkiang's British Concession was overrun and it became unsafe for non-Chinese to live there. The few remaining foreigners ended up where their predecessors had started—living on hulks moored in the river.[48]

In 1928 Chinkiang replaced Soochow (Suzhou) as the capital of Jiangsu Province, but by that time the British Consulate, the only one left, had lost whatever importance it may have had and been vacated. The building was leased to the Maritime Customs.[49] On 15 November 1929 the British Concession was formally handed back to the government of China, and the treaty port was no more.

Further reading: Stevens, 'The Yangzi Port of Zhenjiang'.

Chinwangtao (Qinhuangdao)
秦皇島

Hebei, 39.54° N, 119.36° E
Open City, 1898 Imperial Decree

The earliest reference to Chinwangtao comes from the late third century BC, when it won the affections of the third Shi Emperor of the short-lived Qin dynasty. The name 'Qin Emperor's Island' persisted although the island has long since been joined to the mainland. Jumping forward to the late 19th century, Chinwangtao became one of the 'treaty ports' that was opened to foreign trade unilaterally by China, without a treaty, in an attempt to control a situation that was rapidly deteriorating.

The decree was issued on 5 April 1898[1] and, once the Boxer troubles had been dealt with, a Custom House opened in December 1901.[2] Work had already started, in 1899, on a 200-metre jetty, and a pier and protective breakwater in 1901.[3] Both of these are still doing the job for which they were designed, at the

View over the pier to the breakwater. Both are still recognizable today. Courtesy of David Mahoney.

south-western tip of the former island that came to be known to Europeans as 'The Bluff'.

The Chinese government proclaimed in early 1899 that the entire foreshore of the newly opened port had been reserved for the Chinese Engineering & Mining Co. (CE&M), a Chinese concern but with substantial foreign shareholders and numerous British employees, causing comment that the 'open' status would be of no practical value.[4] Such concerns proved groundless. The company pressured Peking (Beijing) to open Chinwangtao so that its coal exports could be handled at an ice-free, deep-water port instead of via Tientsin (Tianjin). Initially the new facility was run as a private affair but the creation of Chinwangtao as a general winter port for Tientsin had already been anticipated; in 1897 P&O steamers were dropping off the mails there once Tientsin froze in.[5]

Chinwangtao was and is dominated by coal; on arriving one is immediately struck by the smell, a very evocative sensation to one brought up in 1950s Britain. The mines of CE&M were at Kaiping, 130 kilometres inland. The product was brought to the port by rail and, a startling innovation at the time, could be loaded direct onto the waiting ships. In time, electric lighting enabled this and other dock-related activities to happen all through the night, greatly increasing the port's efficiency and attraction. In 1912 CE&M merged with rival Lanchow Mining Co., creating the Kailan Mining Administration (KMA). The growth of the newly merged entity knew no bounds.[6]

The bluff had already been laid out as a small township and the KMA took on much of the role of a municipality.[7] Schools were provided for the children of workers as well as staff quarters for the 3000 Chinese employees.[8] Along and behind Dongshan Street there are lines of simple but solid two-storey terraced houses. At the western end of the street is the very smart former management building of the KMA. This is where the eight or so British shipping superintendents, harbour masters, weighbridge officers and accountants oversaw the operation of the port for which they were responsible. The building is in an excellent state of preservation, but appears to have no current use. From there, across a vast expanse of railway track, can be seen the former KMA power station, cathedral-like in its grandeur, well maintained although not used. Between the two are a number of railway buildings of some apparent antiquity. The Custom House that once stood nearby is no longer.

Coal was not the only industry to take root in Chinwangtao. In 1921 the Yao Hua Glass Works was founded next to sand dunes near the railway station. Initially employing 300 Chinese workers and over 20 European managers and technicians, this was a KMA subsidiary and manufactured window-glass.[9] With its state-of-the-art Belgian machinery, the plant was one of the largest of its kind in the world.[10]

The first European visitors to Chinwangtao immediately recognized its potential as a seaside resort. An initial lack of suitable accommodation was given an unexpected boost. In 1904 the port had been selected as one from which coolies would emigrate to work the South African mines.[11] A depot was established, capable of handling 5000–6000 men,[12] but by 1907 had fallen into disuse. In 1913 it was decided to convert the camp into 19 holiday bungalows,[13] speaking volumes about standards of adequate accommodation for the two types of resident. This 'charming little colony of summer cottages'[14] enabled Chinwangtao to become a member of the Chinese Riviera, along with Shanhaikwan (Shanhaiguan) to the north and Peitaiho (Beidaihe) to the south. Indeed, it was considered to be more secluded and restful than its much larger southern neighbour.[15] In

1917 Camp Burrowes was established, on land leased from the KMA, as a summer base for American troops from Peking and Tientsin.[16] It accommodated 2000 people and incorporated its own water supply, telephone service, cinema, hospital, radio station[17] and, in 1929, a golf course.[18]

By 1918 a number of foreign-style buildings had appeared in Chinwangtao, including offices of Japanese shipping companies.[19] Japan had maintained a small military camp at the port since the Boxer revolt, as had other foreign powers, so this was not seen as ominous.[20] However, the presence of their own soldiers proved useful to Japan when fighting broke out nearby between Chinese and Japanese troops. On 3 January 1933 the Japanese occupied the Chinese city, initially respecting the port area as a foreign enclave, perhaps because Japan was the main beneficiary of Chingwangtao's coal exports.[21] In 1937, rather than simply commandeering it, Japan purchased a stake in the glass factory, significantly increasing its production[22] but very soon pretence was abandoned and the port found itself under new management.

CHUNGKING (CHONGQING) 重慶

Chongqing Municipality, 29.33° N, 106.34° E
Treaty Port, 1890 British Treaty

Over many centuries Chungking grew to be the commercial capital of western China. In a commanding position on the Yangtze, where it was joined by the Jialing, Chungking was over 2000 kilometres from the sea. For the first 500 kilometres the river was treacherous—too shallow in the winter to be safe from rapids and submerged rocks, and too fast-flowing in the summer with the melt-water from Tibet. Incoming trade involved an arduous, dangerous and time-consuming journey. Added to the challenges of getting there, the populous city was perched on a high rocky peninsula between the two rivers, whose water levels could rise and fall some 30 metres according to the season. Within the city's walls, all possible space was built upon. The streets were narrow and, in places, precipitous.[1] This is still the case, making Chongqing one of China's most interesting cities in which to walk.

Chungking's story as a treaty port is inseparable from that of steam navigation on the Upper Yangtze. Britain's interest in Chungking was kindled when the 1858 Treaty of Tientsin (Tianjin) allowed access to the lower river. It would be many years before trading at Chungking became possible but there was an earlier priority. British interests in India had spread eastwards to the Chinese frontier. During a British mission to explore trading routes in 1875 its leader, Raymond Margary, was murdered on Chinese territory. Britain took this opportunity to force China, through the 1876 Chefoo Agreement, to accept an official British presence at Chungking to 'watch the conditions of British trade'. In a proviso that was in later years hailed by the Chinese as a successful delaying tactic and scorned by the British as a sign of weakness, the agreement stated that British merchants would not be allowed to live or trade in Chungking 'so long as no steamers have access to the port'.[2]

Chungking was a consular posting like no other in China, and the British agents posted there had little to do in the way of official business. But that is not to say they wasted their time. The first, Colbourne Baber, explored the source of the Yangtze[3] and discovered two new types of tea,[4] earning him the Royal Geographical Society's Gold Medal. But even with the excitement of such extra-curricular activities, Chungking was not a popular posting. Various incumbents complained of 'an unspeakably dreary life of solitude' and 'the most disagreeable city I have ever seen'. Another reported that 'without exception every officer stationed there had made every effort to escape as soon as possible'. William Spence, when sent from Ichang (Yichang), 500 kilometres downstream, as temporary relief, took 58 days to get there by junk,[5] very possibly delighting at the slow pace of his journey.

Archibald Little and Cornell Plant

Two men take the credit for bringing steam navigation to Chungking—Archibald Little and Cornell Plant. Little came to China as a tea taster in 1859. By 1862 he had his own business in Kiukiang (Jiujiang),[6] where his fascination with the river began. He later moved to Shanghai and developed his ideas for taking a steamship to Chungking. In 1884 he started the first winter steamer service from Shanghai to Hankow (Hankou) (winter being the low-water season), a feat soon followed by others.[7] In 1887 he became the first resident foreign merchant at Ichang[8] and began preparations for his main goal. He arranged a passage to Chungking on a junk and throughout the long journey watched carefully how the junk master navigated through the turbulent water—pulled along by trackers on the upstream journey, and buoyed along midstream on the return.[9] He then used his Shanghai connections to form a company to build a steamer capable of the journey.

The *Kuling*, a 500-tonne, stern-wheeled paddle steamer, was built in Scotland and sent out to Shanghai for assembly. In 1889 Little took his new vessel up to Ichang and applied for a permit to sail to Chungking. Peking (Beijing) agreed, provided the provincial authorities along the river could draft appropriate regulations. These appeared, making Little responsible for any damage his steamer might cause. Recognizing this as official permission to extort, he announced that he was going anyway—permit or no permit. This time the response was to start negotiations to buy the *Kuling*, together with the property that Little had purchased at Ichang as a base for his operations. When discussions foundered, the Tsungli Yamen asked Robert Hart to mediate. Although Hart recorded that 'it is immaterial whether we get the steamer and property or not, so long as by purchasing, we get rid of Little's application',[10] a deal was struck and the *Kuling* was sold at a handsome profit, so eager were the Chinese to be rid of this unwelcome interference.

Chungking was opened as a treaty port in 1890 by the Chungking Agreement, an additional article to the 1876 Chefoo Agreement, but this provided that British steamers could navigate to Chungking only once Chinese steamers had already done so.[11] Little saw this restriction as 'fatuous' and was not alone in feeling bitter about the weakness of the British negotiators.[12] The Japanese were more robust. Having just defeated China in war, Japan's 1895 Treaty of Shimonoseki demanded free and unconditional access to Chungking by Japanese steamers; courtesy of the Most Favoured Nation principle, this included British ships.

However, as the Japanese made no move Little set about his task once more. Having exhausted the goodwill of his backers, in 1897 he designed and financed from his own pocket a twin-screw steamer of nine tonnes, the *Leechuen*. Even though this small craft carried nothing but its two engines, it lacked the power to traverse the rapids and had to be pulled across the worst of them. Nevertheless, after eleven days, on 8 March 1898 Little reached Chungking.[13] Among the crowd that turned out to welcome him would have been British Consul John Tratman, who, in 1897, had written: 'I do not think that the scheme will mature in Mr Little's hands ... [it needs] a man younger and with greater determination of character.'[14]

Having now achieved what he had consistently been told was impossible, Little set off for London to raise support for a steamer that could operate on a commercial basis. The result was the *Pioneer*, capable of carrying 50 tonnes of cargo and a number of passengers.[15] While in London Little met Captain Cornell Plant, who had spent a number of years navigating steamers on the Tigris and Euphrates rivers, in what was is now Iraq. The two struck up a friendship and Plant agreed to come out to China and take charge of the *Pioneer*.[16] When he arrived with his new command in Chungking in June 1900, Plant was greeted by the entire foreign community. The *Pioneer* was the commercial lifeline for which it had been waiting. But almost immediately the vessel was commandeered by the Royal Navy for evacuating the foreign community from the impending threat of a Boxer invasion.[17]

Plant quickly became as enamoured of the Yangtze as his employer. He bought a small junk and traded up and down the river between Chungking and Ichang, all the while charting the many hazards, convinced that steamships should be doing the job instead. By 1908 there was still no regular steamer service between the two places, but in that year Plant convinced the Sichuan provincial authorities and leading businessmen to form the Szechuan Steam Navigation Co. to build and operate a commercial steamer of his design. The company's first vessel, the *Shutung*, was built at Southampton and had a draught of less than one metre when fully loaded with its 60 tonnes of cargo and 72 passengers. By 1910 it was providing a regular service, with 15 round trips a year—six days for the upward journey and two days for the return.[18]

In 1910, capitalizing on his matchless knowledge of the river, Plant was appointed Senior Inspector for the Upper Yangtze by the Imperial Maritime Customs Service. In this guise he was responsible for installing almost a hundred navigation aids along the river.[19] His efforts also led to the introduction of licensed pilots.[20] When he retired in 1919 the Chinese government built a retirement cottage for him at Xintang village, overlooking the river. Sadly, Plant and his wife, who had accompanied him on all his adventures, died in 1921 en route to England for a final holiday before returning to Xintang. Apart from his grave in Hong Kong, there are three memorials to Captain Plant. The first is his *Handbook for the Guidance of Shipmasters in the Ichang-Chungking Section of the Yangtze River*, which was carried by steamer captains for decades after Plant's death. The second is his system of navigation aids—black triangles and balls, and red and white marker buoys—still used on the river. The third is a ten-metre-high obelisk that was erected at Xintang in 1923.[21] Although defaced during the Cultural Revolution, it was moved to higher ground when the Yangtze was dammed at the end of the 20th century.[22] Archibald Little continued to live in Chungking until at least 1900, before retiring to England. He died in 1908, without the recognition he deserved.

A TREATY PORT, BUT NOT AN OPEN ONE

Commissioner Hobson was sent from Ichang to establish the customs presence on 12 September 1890[23] but the agreement remained unratified until January, and trade under the new treaty system did

1925 photograph of *Shutung*, battling against the current. © C. A. L. Palmer FRCS. Image courtesy of Historical Photographs of China, University of Bristol.

not commence until June 1891.[24] Meanwhile the customs staff lived a very uncomfortable existence on junks moored in the river.[25] Hobson had been offered a house, but the state of it made the junk preferable.[26]

Despite the perceived victory by the Sichuan officials over the British regarding access by steamers, trade in foreign items had already taken root. Merchants had been bringing cotton piece-goods, yarn and other foreign items from Hankow and Shanghai under transit passes. Locally grown opium was the main export, but there were silk, hides, skins and wood as well which, if for foreign purchasers, went under transit passes also. Naturally, all this business was controlled by the Chinese. By the time the port was open, therefore, the patterns of trade were already well established and there was no reason to change them.[27] Indeed, in the absence of steamers and on Hart's suggestion, the Chungking Agreement provided that British subjects could buy or charter the same 'vessels of the Chinese type' that had been carrying the trade for years.[28]

Now a treaty port in its own right, there was no longer a need for transit passes for foreign imports and exports to and from Chungking. Then the *taotai* announced the introduction of *likin* on all such trade.[29] Furthermore, transit passes for goods sent up river for the interior were ignored by the *likin* collection agents.[30] All this was clearly in contravention of the treaties. An appeal to higher authorities resolved the matter regarding imports and exports. However, the life of any Chinese associated with internal transit passes was made so uncomfortable that they were no longer applied for and *likin* once more ruled. Indeed, the Chinese merchants paid *likin* as a demonstration of their disapproval of the new foreign Custom House.[31] Those that did use that facility had to take their goods across the river to the inspection pontoon on the south bank, come back again to the Custom House and then venture into the city to pay their dues at the designated bank.[32]

Despite all these difficulties the volume of trade increased. It was an unusual situation. For the first time in China foreign merchants were obliged to employ Chinese junks to carry their goods. The 'native' trade continued as before, but the volume of business for foreign principals grew to about 20 percent of the total. Foreigners had the option to own junks, but they chose to charter, believing that a master in charge of his own vessel would treat it with more respect than if it were owned by a foreigner. Insurance was initially not available, being usually associated with steamer transport. But in 1893 Archibald Little's Chungking Transport Co. offered cover to foreign-chartered junks. Even so the major operators—Butterfield & Swire and Jardines—divided their cargoes among each other's junks so as to minimize risk. Although one vessel in ten arrived at its destination with some water damage to its cargo,[33] only 1 percent were totally wrecked on the journey.[34]

Chungking's foreign population

In 1897 there was but one resident French and one British merchant (Archibald Little). Three British firms were represented by Chinese agents. A German firm had just closed and a Japanese had arrived but not yet started business.[35] But there was a large population of foreign missionaries. In 1881 there were 18 stationed in the city.[36] Nine years later there were 88,[37] and 237 by 1897.[38] They ventured far into Sichuan, Guizhou, Yunnan and Gansu provinces, an area the size of France and Germany combined.[39] Their faith must have been strong, for their position was not without a high degree of danger to their safety. Throughout the 1880s there were riots in the city, and these spread into the rest of the province, where Chinese converts were also attacked. In 1886 the Roman Catholics alone suffered the destruction of some 80 buildings, including schools and libraries as well as churches and residences.[40] A riot in 1889 was triggered by the Catholic cathedral being taller than a nearby Chinese temple.[41] Nevertheless, there is still much evidence in the city of the former Christian presence, with at least two churches and a hospital, now given over to the practice of Chinese traditional medicine.

Conditions for the secular foreign residents were also difficult. In addition to the depressing climate and the huge rise and fall in the level of the river depositing mud everywhere (which it still does), the city was also unsafe. In 1887 the British Consul had to take refuge in the house of the *taotai* when his own residence was attacked.[42]

During 1896 three more powers established consulates at Chungking—France, Japan and America—initially renting buildings inside the city walls. Despite official attempts to deny a permanent foreign consular presence France managed to acquire a site, just south of today's Hou Ci Street and also within the walls, on which to build a consulate,[43] prompting Britain to do the same. In December 1896 a 5500-square-metre site was purchased 500 metres north-west of the French ground and on the south side of today's Lingshi Xiang, once known as 'Consulate Alley';[44] an old curved stone wall can still be seen there, marking the site's northern perimeter. The Americans bought land immediately to the north-east and the residence of the Customs Commissioner was at the British lot's southern corner. Over the next few years grand European-style consular structures appeared on all three lots.[45] Only the French one remains today, a large, sorry-looking three-storey building. The French also established a naval base at Chungking in 1902 on the south bank. The very attractive barracks complex still stands, as does an American consular building from the same period, a little way upstream of the former French base.

Although they were all within a stone's throw of each other, a fact confirmed during the frequent anti-foreign riots, the consular compounds did not constitute a foreign settlement. It would have been usual for this to have been situated close to the Custom House, but there was much discussion as to where that facility should be. A site on the right bank of the Yangtze and a little downriver from the city was identified for this purpose in 1890—Wang Chia To (Wangjiatuo), where there was a small sheltered bay.[46] Then in February 1891 the *taotai* announced that it would be at Shih Tzu Shan (Shixishan), also on the right bank but not as far down. The Customs Commissioner countered by saying that it would remain on the city side of the river, near the Chao Tien Gate (Chaotianmen), but that the customs moorings and inspection area would be at Shih Tzu Shan.[47] Even the viceroy's order that the Custom House be moved over to Wang Chia To, which would then become the Foreign Settlement, did not result in any action; merchants preferred Shih Tzu Shan and its lesser inconveniences, so that was that.[48]

The commencement of commercial steamer operations brought an influx of foreign merchants, although not enough to justify a formal settlement. Instead, they gravitated towards the south bank, a short distance away by steam launch and separate from the teeming city. Archibald Little had leased a plot of land there in 1893, but the authorities conspired never to allow him to take possession.[49] By the beginning of the new century things were easier and large residences started to appear on the tops of the small hills along the riverside. Among the grandest were those of Butterfield & Swire, built in 1929, and Asiatic Petroleum. Both of these can still be found, as can the former residence of Brunner Mond's manager, dating from 1915.

The grand house of Butterfield & Swire, nearing completion in 1929. Photograph by Warren Swire. © Image Courtesy of John Swire and Sons and Historical Photographs of China, University of Bristol.

The Japanese were the only power to have a settlement in Chungking. In 1897 they marked out a large tract of land at Wang Chia To,[50] and this became the nucleus of an increasing Japanese population.[51] Using the right won in their 1895 treaty they started manufacturing too, commencing with a match factory in 1903.[52] Cotton cloth, peanut oil and silk factories followed.[53]

Despite Japanese efforts, Chungking was to remain a backwater until industrialization began in earnest in the 1920s. Simultaneously, conditions in the cramped city received overdue attention. Streets were widened—although a large section of the old wall remains—and some of the slums were demolished.[54] Steamers could reach Chungking in eight days from Shanghai.[55] In 1929 ten companies were operating a total of 58 vessels between Ichang and Chungking, and 28 more upstream of the city.[56]

Following the Japanese invasion of eastern China, on 1 December 1937 temporary central government offices were set up in Chungking, becoming permanent at the end of 1938.[57] The city remained as China's wartime capital until the conclusion of the Pacific War. Thus it was that the document bringing an end to the entire treaty port system was signed in Chungking. On 11 January 1943, in a gesture of solidarity with his Chinese allies, it was recorded that 'His Majesty the King [George VI] relinquishes all existing treaty rights relating to the system of treaty ports in China'.[58]

Further reading: Bromfield and Lee, 'Captain Plant'; Little, *Through the Yang-tse Gorges*; Oxford, *At Least We Lived*; Parkinson, 'The First Steam-Powered Ascent'; Simpson, 'Hell and High Water'; Stevens, 'A Tale of Sour Grapes'.

CHUSAN (ZHOUSHAN) 舟山

Zhejiang, 30.01° N, 122.06° E
Occupied Territory, 1840 Britain

Never a treaty port but very nearly a colony, the island of Chusan played a key role at the beginning of our period. Situated 150 kilometres from the mouth of the Yangtze, Chusan's position was of strategic importance. Vessels based in its sheltered harbour could control, or interfere with, depending on your viewpoint, passing shipping. And Chusan was the largest of many sheltered islands in the archipelago. The East India Company had maintained a presence there at the beginning of the 18th century.[1] Ninety years later Lord Macartney was considering taking possession of the island. Lindsay visited in 1832 and Jardines were known to be doing business there in 1833.[2] Chusan was well known to the British by the time of the First Opium War.

As part of a punitive naval raid along the coast, Sir Gordon Bremer captured and occupied Chusan with ease on 5 July 1840—the first part of China to find itself under British rule. John Davis accompanied the fleet and noted that Chusan was 'delightful'.[3] His enthusiasm would later wane.

In January 1841 Charles Elliot and Qishan signed the Convention of Chuenpi (Chuanbi), bringing the war to a close—or so they thought—and Chusan was vacated. When it transpired that China did not intend to abide by this agreement, Elliot was severely censured for having given away his indemnity so readily. The fleet returned to Chusan, and on 1 October it was captured again. The first occupation had been after a brief (less than ten minutes) show of naval strength, insisted upon by the defending military commander even though he knew he was vastly outgunned.[4] The second occupation was easier still.

Although the British created a quasi-colony, complete with a governor, they never extended their hold much beyond the small walled town of Tinghai (Dinghai). One reason was the exceptionally high mortality rate of the British soldiers. No lives had been lost in the taking of the place, but during the following four years of occupation one-third of the troops—numbering many hundreds—died of malaria.

The 1842 Treaty of Nanking (Nanjing)—the agreement that actually ended the conflict—provided that Britain should continue to hold Chusan until the last instalment of the war indemnity was paid, scheduled for December 1845. So the British settled down to make their occupation as pleasant as possible. This was not difficult, provided they avoided catching malaria. The local population seemed well disposed towards the visitors and welcomed the opportunity to trade with them. Robert Fortune, passing through in 1843, observed that one of the many tailors serving the British garrison promoted himself as 'Tailor to Her Most Gracious Majesty Queen Victoria and His Royal Highness Prince Albert, by appointment—Uniformsofalldescriptions [sic].'[5]

Fortune also saw evidence of a 'regret that we had not secured Chusan as a part of the British dominions . . . instead of the barren and unhealthy island of Hong-kong'.[6] Lord Stanley, Colonial Secretary in London, ordered that a report be prepared on the relative merits of the two places. The man tasked with the job was Montgomery Martin, newly appointed Colonial Treasurer in Hong Kong. In July 1844 Martin reported that Hong Kong was 'utterly valueless'.[7] The following month he waxed lyrical about Chusan: 'Were Chusan a British colony, its hills and vales would be adorned by charming villas, rich orchards, and luxuriant pasturages.' He recommended that Britain take possession of Chusan as a trading emporium, especially as most of the treaty ports had shown such a weak performance. Davis, by now Hong Kong's governor and therefore with a vested interest, disagreed strongly with Martin's conclusions, pointing out that Martin lacked experience, having been in Hong Kong for only a few weeks.[8] Nevertheless, Chusan had a better climate, was about five times bigger, and had much more flat and arable land.

Although the last indemnity payment was made on time, in January 1846 Davis was instructed to obtain the cession of the island. His heart was not in it and negotiations failed.[9] Besides, the British troops were needed back in India. The island was formally handed back with full and amicable ceremony in June 1846.[10] A trade in opium had been flourishing just out of sight of the British authorities. Jardines and Dents removed their receiving ships a few kilometres away to Lookong (Ligang).[11]

The British came back in 1858 during the Second Opium War, this time with the French, and occupied the island for a third time, as a gesture.[12] The Earl of Elgin, on his way north with his expeditionary force,

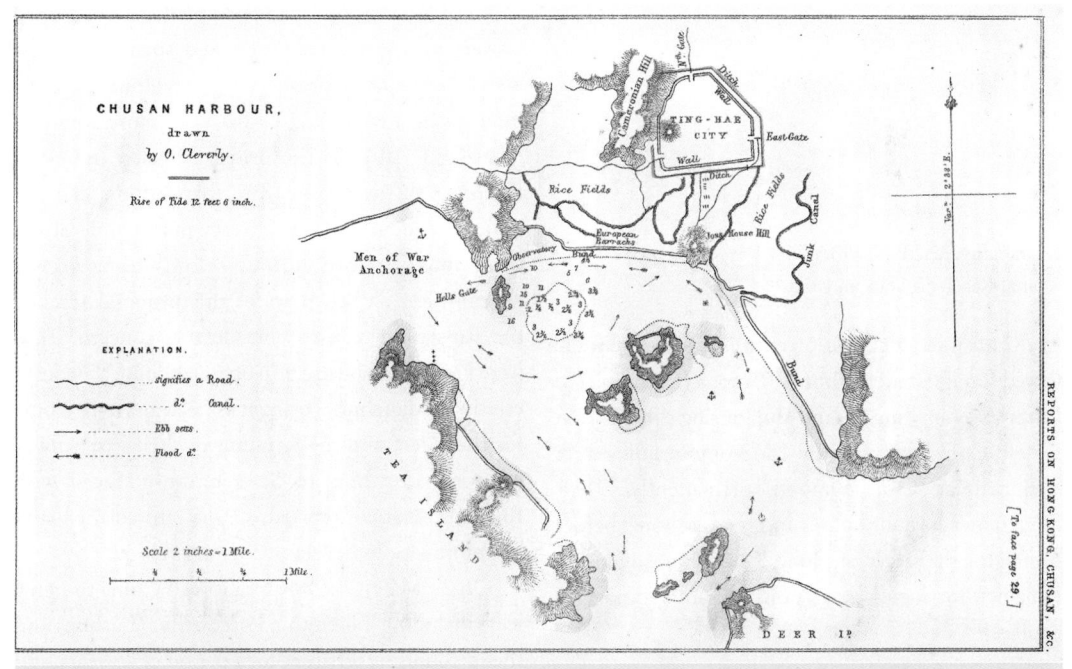

Plan of Chusan (Zhoushan) Harbour c. 1844, drawn by Osmund Cleverly. Source: R. Montgomery Martin's Report on the Island of Chusan, 30 August 1844, in *Papers relating to the Colony of Hong Kong etc. 21 March 1857* (London, 1857), 29.

was as captivated with the place as previous British visitors had been. 'How any people, in their senses,' he said, 'could have preferred Hong Kong . . . seems incredible.'[13] By 1860 the only foreigners left were some missionaries and one or two customs men who were manning a lighthouse.[14] Yet the British still dreamed of Chusan. In 1897 British Minister in Peking (Beijing) Sir Claude MacDonald said that it would be preferable, as a base, to any place further north[15] but the island and its fellows were to remain the haunts of pirates.

Most unusually in today's China, there remains in Dinghai a monument to British army and navy men who lost their lives on Chusan. This very subdued and un-signposted piece of stonework was given official protection in 2002.[16]

Further reading: D'Arcy-Brown, *Chusan*; Munn, 'The Chusan Episode'; Stevens and Welch, 'Monument to the Westmorland Regiment'.

CUMSINGMOON (JINXINGMEN) 金星門

Guangdong, 22.23° N, 113.36° E
Opium Receiving Station, 1820s

In 1821 fear of official action curbing the opium trade forced foreign traders from Whampoa (Huangpu) to Lintin (Neilingding) Island and, during the typhoon season, Cumsingmoon.[1] By 1843 opium hulks were stationed at Cumsingmoon permanently. Their foreign owners built houses and roads ashore,[2] before opting for the safety of Hong Kong. Cumsingmoon remained for some years a point of embarkation for coolies.[3]

DALNY/DAIREN (DALIAN) 大連

Liaoning, 38.55° N, 121.39° E
Leased Territory, 1898 Russia

The British fleet gathered in Talienwan (Dalianwan) in 1860, before moving on to assault the Taku (Dagu) forts.[1] The sheltered harbour clearly made an impression; Sir Thomas Wade threatened to take it by force when his 1876 negotiations with Li Hongzhang in Chefoo (Yantai) were not going to his liking.[2] This was exactly what the Japanese did in 1895, claiming the Guandong Peninsula as part of the spoils of their surprise victory over the Chinese. Combined pressure from Russia, France and Germany forced Japan to retrocede the seized territory later in the year, but it became clear that Russia had plans of its own.

China's defeat by Japan prompted the established powers to assess what they could snaffle from the widely anticipated breakup of the empire. Britain's interests in a collapsing China were more commercial than territorial. The British Minister in Peking (Beijing) suggested in 1897 that Britain demand Talienwan be opened as a treaty port as one of the conditions of a British loan to help China pay its war indemnities.[3] When news of this proposal reached the Russians it caused considerable concern. They were keen to establish a grip on Guandong, the southern tip of Manchuria, using it as both an ice-free port for their fleet and the terminus of their vast railway network, stretching to St. Petersburg. Faced with Russian threats of reprisals China refused the loan,[4] but more serious developments were afoot.

On 27 March 1898 Russia forced China to sign a lease including Talienwan, Port Arthur (Lüshun) and the surrounding territory for a period of 25 years, and announced that their new possession would be open for trade as were the other open ports in China.[5] In

Talienwan's case the world was about to meet a small village, some useless hilly terrain and a few forts built in the 1880s in anticipation of a French attack.[6] Apart from the large bay there seemed to be little attraction to the place. The Russians named their new possession Dalny, meaning 'Far Away', so far away that it soon earned the nickname Lishny, meaning 'Unwanted'.[7]

A large site was chosen on the south-western shore of the bay and the hills were levelled. The man put in charge of the work was V. V. Sakharov, an engineer who had just completed a similar project at Vladivostok. A major inspiration in his work was Paris, and he had a huge map of the French capital on his office wall.[8] On the more or less virgin territory— the few Chinese villages and their occupants were easily cleared by Russian troops—Sakharov laid out a road system with a number of great circular 'squares' connected by wide boulevards. Dalian is today perhaps the most attractive city in China, partly due to professional and thoughtful city management, but also to Sakharov's design, which also featured large parks and other public facilities. The port and its associated wharves were given priority. Work started to create sufficient wharfage for 20 ships of 1000 tonnes to use the port facilities simultaneously, plus a direct link to the railway. A locomotive factory was built in 1901 and the first wharves were completed in 1902.[9] Photographs show a vast area of harbour facilities and railway tracks—but few ships.[10] Nor was there the anticipated population of 30,000,[11] for whom hundreds of houses were built.[12] Apart from the port, development was confined to the area to the north of the main railway line, these days referred to as Russian Town. The large office building of the Russian Governor, sadly neglected, and one or two other iconic buildings of Russian design still stand.

The Russians were forced to flee in May 1904, following the outbreak of the Russo-Japanese War, leaving their new city unfinished. The Japanese found the young town in ruins. Lead pipes and copper wire had been removed, rendering the water and electricity systems useless.[13] What they did discover was a beautifully designed plan for a major city that they were delighted to adopt.

Despite the free-port status conferred by Russia, Dalny held little appeal for non-Russian foreign merchants. Renamed as Dairen by the Japanese, and with its free-port status reconfirmed,[14] a few non-Japanese merchants arrived but far larger were the operations of the *zaibatsu*.[15] Sir Robert Hart had been trying for five years to persuade Russia to have a Chinese Custom House in Dalny to facilitate the collection of duties on goods crossing the border of the leased territory into China. Prevarication by the Russians meant he was not successful.[16] In May 1907 Japan agreed, on the condition that the commissioner was Japanese.[17] The Gothic, turreted building that housed the Maritime Customs from 1915 still stands on Renmin Road, now painted a rather garish red.

Japan was already a major importer of beans and beancakes, products that had traditionally been shipped out of Newchwang (Yingkou). They started to divert this business to their own port. In 1906 Mitsui built the first bean-crushing plant that used modern machinery, taking business away from the traditional hand-operated Chinese factories. Imports were mainly cotton goods, flour and kerosene.[18] By 1909 Dairen had overtaken Newchwang as the largest port in Manchuria.[19]

Railways and further growth

Russia's Chinese Eastern Railway was a huge operation and, under the terms of the 1905 Treaty of Portsmouth, the southern portion passed to Japan as the South Manchuria Railway Co. (SMR).[20] This was no mere operator of trains. In Dairen the company owned the entire five-kilometre foreshore and the wharves. Throughout Manchuria it operated coal mines, steelworks, waterworks and electricity-generating stations. In Dairen the company opened a silk-spinning plant in 1910.[21] In the 1920s it proudly announced that it had created a new breed of sheep, a cross between a Merino and a native Mongolian variant.[22] Owing to the number of staff employed, the company became involved with housing projects, schools and churches. When the SMR opened a new hospital in Dairen in 1927 it was the second-biggest in Asia.[23] The most impressive historical building in

Loading beans and beancake for export, 1922. Source: *Manchuria: Land of Opportunities*, 52.

modern Dalian is the former headquarters complex of the SMR on Lüshun Road. These extraordinarily impressive buildings would not look out of place on London's Whitehall.

The railway company also operated a chain of first-class hotels, under the name Yamato. Every city the line passed through had a Yamato Hotel, and Dairen had three. The former Russian Governor's office building was converted into one, but the biggest was on the Great Square, the showpiece of Sakharov's master plan. Built in 1914 the impressive building operates today as the Dalian Hotel and looks much as it ever did. Now called Zhongshan Square, the Great Square is actually a large circle with ten major roads radiating from it, providing ten sites for iconic buildings, of which six remain. In addition to the hotel there are the 1908 Japanese Police Station; the 1917 Post Office, still functioning as such; the 1909 building formerly occupied by the Yokohama Specie Bank; a 1910 building formerly belonging to the Great Qing Bank; and the Dairen City Hall, erected in 1919. This splendid array of architectural beauties speaks volumes for the importance of their new possession to the Japanese and of their desire to create a model Western city in an eastern location.

In 1905 Japan inherited the 25-year Russian lease. In May 1915 an exchange of notes between the Japanese and Chinese governments extended the term to 99 years from the date of the initial lease.[24] This enabled the Yokohama Specie Bank to grant loans, secured on real estate, to manufacturers.[25] Soon Dairen could boast a full range of heavy industries[26] and the economy soared. Between 1910 and 1921 exports increased sixfold and imports fivefold.[27] The SMR was constantly expanding the capacity of the harbour and wharves,[28] managed from the still-standing large building overlooking the scene of the action. The new lease also enabled a rearrangement of the colony's government from a military administration, headquartered in Port Arthur, to a civil authority based in Dairen as the leased territory's capital.[29]

Russians started to reappear in 1918. These were White Russians, often quite wealthy, fugitives from the 1917 revolution. They gravitated towards Russian Town, where they built houses in their own style. Some of these can still be seen, but many were demolished in the early years of the present century. By 1921 the Japanese population had risen to 30,000, compared with 20,000 Chinese and about 100 of other nationalities.[30] The more wealthy Japanese

The Yokohama Specie Bank, on the far side of the Central Circle from the Yamato Hotel, 1922. Source: *Manchuria: Land of Opportunities*, 92.

built houses in Nanshan, a quiet area south of the city centre. This is still a very attractive area of narrow lanes and large old houses. The 1920s also saw Dairen become a tourist destination, with an estimated 10,000 visitors a year.[31]

During the 1930s Dairen's population rose to 300,000, of whom one-third were Japanese.[32] It was by any measure a major city. The port's volume of trade was only one-third that of Shanghai, but it rivalled second-placed Tientsin (Tianjin). The year 1931 saw the invasion and annexation of Manchuria by Japan, and the puppet state of Manchukuo was born. Dairen was still leased territory, but it was impossible to separate its fortunes from those of Manchukuo. China claimed that the territory was separate, and demanded the continuation of its customs revenues. But when the Japanese commissioner suspended payment in 1932 there was nothing that the Chinese could do.[33] Besides, China had bigger problems than duty collection.

Soviet troops stepped in immediately Japan surrendered at the end of the Pacific War in 1945. Dalian was still in name a free port, but it became a de facto Soviet navy base. China was not to get its city back until 1950.[34]

Further reading: Johnston and Erh, *Far from Home*; Nield, 'Bits of Broken China'.

Foochow (Fuzhou) 福州

Fujian, 26.04° N, 119.18° E
Treaty Port, 1842 British Treaty

The Portuguese are believed to have traded at Foochow in 1517.[1] Japanese pirates temporarily blockaded the mouth of the Min River in 1557,[2] and the city traded with the Spanish Philippines in the late 16th century.[3] The Dutch tried to open commerce in the 1660s but were unsuccessful. The English East India Company (EIC) established a trading factory at Foochow in 1681[4] and company vessels were regular visitors until foreign merchants were confined to Canton (Guangzhou) by Imperial Decree in 1757.[5]

Hugh Hamilton Lindsay called at Foochow in 1832. He found European woollen goods already on sale in the city,[6] which encouraged him in proposing the port be opened. His main interest was in Foochow's proximity to the best tea-growing area of China, the Bohea (Wuyi) Hills. In 1817 another EIC man, Samuel Ball, a long-term resident of China and the company's Tea Inspector, had already noted Foochow's superiority over Canton as a port for exporting tea, observing that Chinese tea merchants in Canton all seemed to come from Foochow anyway.[7]

Although it would grow, the volume of China's tea exports was already very large in the 1840s. Channelling all of it through Canton had made some Cantonese merchants outstandingly wealthy, and with great wealth came great influence. The merchants managed to persuade their emperor to issue an edict forbidding the export of tea from Foochow. On 27 August 1842 Sir Henry Pottinger, chief British negotiator at Nanking (Nanjing), received the emperor's assent to all his demands, except one—Foochow. The British Plenipotentiary stuck to his guns, literally and figuratively. The Chinese side backed down, saying that the edict was withdrawn and allowing the opening of Foochow.[8]

Pottinger had little choice when it came to staffing his five new consulates. Initially the first British Consul to Foochow was to be German, missionary Karl Gutzlaff.[9] Instead, the honour fell to another missionary, George Tradescant Lay. Lay had been proselytizing from Macao since 1836 and his consequent fluency in Chinese won him the job.[10]

Foochow is located on the banks of the River Min, some 50 kilometres from the sea and among beautiful scenery. On entering the river, vessels passed for about 25 kilometres through steep gorges, which many compared with those of the Rhine in Germany. The limit of navigation was marked by where the gorges open out. Upstream from there the river was too shallow for all but the smallest craft. Lay was deposited at this point, to make his way up to his new responsibilities as best he could.[11]

SHOWING THE FLAG

The place that was made available to Lay as a home and office was on the far side of the riverbank, about three kilometres from the city gate. *The Times* described it as 'a miserable house built on piles on a mud flat'.[12] Nevertheless, the consulate was declared open on 1 July 1844. The sensitivities of the new consul were such that when the local population objected when he raised his flag, he responded by raising it 'Chinese-style', which to the average Westerner had the appearance of flying at half-mast.[13] Visitors were prone to ask who, in the tiny community, had already died.[14]

A few months later Sir John Davis, newly appointed Governor of Hong Kong and Superintendent of British Trade in China, visited Lay and was appalled.[15] The place representing British prestige was practically flooded every day at high tide.[16] Davis refused to receive the customary visits from the city's mandarins there, insisting instead that they meet him on a warship in the river.[17] He requested Lay be given a suitable place within the city where he could raise the flag with impunity. Davis even threatened to withdraw his consul,[18] a risky ploy as the Chinese never wanted him in the first place; Lay had nothing to do anyway. After months of wrangling, a site was identified inside the walled city.

Standing on a flat plain Foochow had an attractive aspect, with its walls embracing three small hills. Two of these were crowned by ancient pagodas, both of which still stand. To the east is the White Pagoda, dating from 903. To the west, on Wu Shan, is the Black Pagoda, built in 785. With his new-found confidence, Lay selected the picturesque temple complex at the foot of the latter, which he had inspected with Davis,[19] as his residence and consulate. In December 1844 a lease was agreed with the monks.[20] Other parties in the city's government were less enthusiastic. One of the buildings in the complex, the Kingfisher-Gathering Temple, had been restored in 1821 by Lin Zexu, the official who had commanded the destruction of the opium stores in Canton. British occupation of the site caused deep resentment.[21] Today returned to their former use, these temples still command a view over the city, some 100 metres below, and are still accessible by the small winding path that Lay himself used.

On 7 February 1845, Chinese New Year's day, Lay raised the Union Jack from 'a lofty flag staff'. People came in their thousands to see the foreigner. Lay was 'obliged daily to take a seat in some elevated part of the grounds, to be gazed at by the multitudes'.[22] He had little time to reflect on his changed circumstances as he was replaced in March 1845 by Rutherford Alcock. Joining the new consul as interpreter was Harry Parkes, then 17 years old. Both of these men were to achieve greatness in later years, but their time at Foochow was a tough baptism. Anti-foreign feeling was strong. In October 1845 Parkes was pelted with stones while riding past the Manchu garrison. In making the strongest official complaint about this outrage, Davis bypassed Fujian Viceroy Liu, telling him he had 'sent a steamer to deliver a protest'; possibly a bluff as there was no mention of destination or recipient.[23] Notwithstanding, three of the culprits were flogged and, most surprisingly, three of the Manchu troops placed in the cangue, something the local Chinese had never seen before.[24]

Apart from riding and engaging in whatever other forms of exercise they could, it is difficult to see how the three members of the consular staff filled their days. In 1844 no foreign ships visited the port. Even in 1848 Consul Richard Jackson reported that there had been no official trade. The opium traders, on the other hand, were doing well, operating discreetly outside the port limits.[25] As their fast vessels were the only means of communication with Hong Kong and other treaty ports, British Consuls had no alternative but to entrust them with the official mail.[26]

In late 1848 Sir Samuel Bonham recommended to Foreign Secretary Lord Palmerston that Foochow and Ningpo (Ningbo) be abandoned in favour of Hangchow (Hangzhou) and Soochow (Suzhou), both being near 'the great centres of consumption', and Palmerston agreed.[27] Bonham wrote to Xu Guangjin, the Imperial Commissioner for Barbarian Affairs. Unexpectedly, Xu replied that such an exchange would make a mockery of the treaties agreed between the two nations.[28] Bonham presumably realized that Xu had a point, and the matter was quietly dropped.

In 1850 a recurring Chinese grievance received a very public airing. To honour the accession of the Xianfeng Emperor to the Dragon Throne there were renewed objections to the residence of foreigners within the city walls. Not only was the British Consul installed, but several missionaries and hopeful merchants had followed suit. During the 1844 discussions with Davis,[29] the Chinese authorities at Foochow had stated that the treaty only gave the right of residence at the actual port. In Foochow this meant the landing stage on the river. Even Lin Zexu, who was living near Foochow at the time, joined the fray.[30] The legal position was sufficiently unclear that the British withdrew from the city to the riverside suburb of Nantai.[31]

Nantai

Nantai, where Lay's first residence had been, was and is a pleasant hilly area rising from the point where the ancient Bridge of Ten Thousand Ages touched the river's south bank. This granite bridge, built in 1324,[32] had a span of 500 metres. Some remains can still be seen under its modern replacement. It crossed Middle Island (Zhongzhou Dao), a tiny refuge in the river measuring 350 by 150 metres. Never too concerned with legality, some of the skippers of the opium-receiving ships had already built houses there. The entire foreign population could have fitted round a dinner table. That was about to change.

In 1853 the reason for the foreign trade difficulties became apparent. British Vice-Consul James Walker received a letter from the provincial treasurer in which that official admitted the Imperial Edict of ten years earlier had not been withdrawn, despite confirmation to the contrary. Hence the prohibition on the export of tea from Foochow had continued in place. Walker's correspondent wrote that he was urging his superiors temporarily to suspend the ruling.[33] What helped to tip the balance was the turmoil of the Taiping Rebellion, which disrupted the traditional tea-carrying routes to Shanghai and Canton. First to take advantage of the changing circumstances was the American Russell & Co. Through great energy and not a little expense, their agents travelled 150 kilometres into the tea-growing areas and arranged their purchases.[34] Thus did the long-anticipated tea business take off. In 1854 three ships left Foochow loaded with tea, bound for New York. The following year 55 vessels carried 7,000 tonnes of tea. In 1856 132 left with 18,000 tonnes for Europe, America and Australia.[35]

This sudden burst of activity caused a rise in the foreign population, from 10 in 1850[36] to 28 in 1855.

Nantai c. 1876, looking east towards Middle Island and the Long Bridge. Reprinted with permission by Edward Bangs Drew Collection, Harvard-Yenching Library.

All these people and their associated activities needed space in which to live and operate. Nantai became the main focus of the foreign presence. Stretched out along the riverfront to the east of the old bridge were the hongs of all the firms that were driving the tea industry. They built their residences on the hill behind, among the consulates (initially British and American), the churches and the foreign cemetery.

British and Americans acquired all available lots and still there were not enough. Land prices rocketed. The initial lack of activity, followed by the speed of later development, meant there was neither interest nor time to establish a formal settlement or a concession. But this did not hinder progress in the heady days of the 1850s and 1860s. Voluntary subscriptions were raised to make roads and paths between the new buildings.[37] Lord Elgin visited in 1858, on his way north with the British Expeditionary Force, and described Foochow as a more beautiful place than any other he had seen in China.[38]

Pagoda Island

Being situated some 25 kilometres above the limit of river navigation, ships coming to Foochow for tea had to load at Mawei. The foreigners called this place Pagoda Anchorage or Pagoda Island, after a Song dynasty structure that still stands.[39] The clipper ships used to arrive about mid-April, many of them having come from Shanghai or Hong Kong, where they had unloaded their outbound cargo; there was little or no market for foreign goods in Foochow. As the captains did not know how long it would take the tea merchants to agree a price, they had no alternative but to arrive early and wait. Often the haggling would go on for weeks; a wait of up to 40 days was not uncommon. The Foochow tea men were well aware of the advantage of their city over other ports, and were in no hurry to agree a price if a better one was in sight.

Once a bargain was struck, 'chop boats' would come down the river laden with tea chests that would be hauled into the waiting clippers, a task requiring several days' feverish activity. When fully loaded and with the necessary certificate issued by the marine surveyor, the clippers would race for home.[40] And race they did, as we shall see. The number of ships and their crews that clustered around Pagoda Island meant that a separate community built up to service their needs. There were ships' chandlers and

1868 sketch of Pagoda Island, the limit of navigation. © National Maritime Museum, Greenwich, London.

storekeepers, boarding houses and inns, and a couple of resident doctors. On the southern tip of Mawei was a foreign-owned facility, Foochow Dock, that included a dry dock for major repairs.

There was also a body of experienced pilots. The British Admiralty's *China Sea Directory* advised that the services of a pilot were 'very necessary'.[41] The anchorage at Pagoda may have been the limit of navigation, but reaching it was not without significant hazards. The River Min was narrow, and at its mouth were sandbanks that moved from one season to the next. In 1858 a Pilot Board was established. Both foreigners and the Chinese authorities agreed to issue licences to Chinese and foreign pilots who passed an examination. Once issued, the licence had to be stamped by all seven consuls and vice-consuls. Penalties were imposed on any ship's master who accepted the services of an unlicensed pilot.[42] There were cases of Chinese pilots being in the employ of pirates, and foreign pilots being drunk, but generally the system worked.[43]

When a foreign-style Custom House was opened in Foochow in 1861, this too had a sub-office at Pagoda Island. Located at Chang Le, on the far side of the anchorage from the pagoda, the building remains, smartly restored. Nearby is the former residence of the Pagoda Anchorage Harbour Master.[44] As for the customs staff themselves, they lived on the *Spartan*, a hulk which, despite its name, afforded them safe, hygienic accommodation.[45]

In 1868 Britain established a vice-consulate at Pagoda Island, the most important element of which was the gaol, a facility the consulate at Foochow lacked.[46] This building has also been restored as a small museum. Two or three British consular officials were stationed there, with up to eight Chinese staff.[47] Pagoda Island came to be for Foochow what Whampoa (Huangpu) was for Canton, and Taku (Dagu) for Tientsin (Tianjin)—a necessary appendage but with no official status. The British Vice-Consulate officially closed in 1902, but the constable remained until 1923.[48] Pagoda Island remained for many years a popular holiday destination for the foreign population of Foochow.[49]

Foochow as a tea port

In 1849 Britain repealed its Navigation Acts, a repressive set of laws that prohibited non-British ships from servicing British ports. The immediate effect on the tea trade was to give Britain a rude shock. The first American ship to enter London's West India Dock, the clipper *Oriental*, showed how it should be done. In 1850 this sleek vessel arrived with a full load of tea from Hong Kong, a journey of some 24,000 kilometres, in the then record time of 97 days. The high freight rates, willingly paid for such a speedy delivery, enabled the owners to recoup three-quarters of the vessel's cost on this one voyage.[50] Within a few years, the design of the *Oriental* was being copied and improved upon, both in America and Britain. Tea was now being transported in specially designed vessels.[51] Soon these racing machines were in open competition to be the first to bring each new crop to London, the world's main market.

For Foochow this new development could not have come at a better time. In just three years the tea export trade had expanded exponentially. Suddenly speed was everything. Not only could the fastest ships command the highest freight rates, but commencing in 1856 they would also earn a premium if they were first into London Docks.[52] By 1866, competition had produced what came to be known as The Great Tea Race. Sixteen front-rank clippers were waiting in Foochow for that season's crop. The five favourites left on the same tide on 30 May. Ninety-nine days later three of them docked in London, again on the same tide: *Taeping* was 20 minutes ahead of *Ariel*, with *Serica* just over an hour behind. This astonishing feat received enormous publicity, and people not remotely connected to the sea placed bets on the ship they thought would win. The press coverage and popular excitement was similar to that of a major sporting event today.[53]

In 1867 33,000 tonnes of tea were shipped from Foochow, mainly to London, but with significant amounts going to Australia and America. In the fever of success, however, standards slipped. In 1868 36,000 tonnes were shipped, but concerns about quality began to be heard. Carelessness in picking and packing combined with deliberate additions of stalks, last season's tea and tea-dust (today used for tea-bags) caused alarm. The Chinese authorities posted proclamations around the province, urging the growers and packers to be more careful. Selective myopia left these warnings largely unheeded.[54]

The year 1871 was the watershed in the brief but spectacular era of the tea clippers. In that year 33 sailing ships left Foochow with tea for London, along with 17 steamers. In 1872 there were two more vessels in total, but only 23 under sail compared with 29 steam-powered.[55] Steamers were showing themselves to be more efficient, particularly since 1869 when the journey to Europe was considerably shortened by using the Suez Canal. This was to coincide with a worsening in Foochow's reputation for unreliability. In 1885, a year in which 28 British firms in Foochow were engaged solely in the tea trade,[56] the product was banned in the London market for containing 26 percent dust.[57] In 1890 a consignment of Foochow tea was condemned in Melbourne as being unfit for human consumption.[58] In 1896 a Foochow Tea Improvement Company was formed by a group of foreign tea merchants. They were joined by influential Chinese but the barrier of local prejudice towards novelty was too great.[59]

Two other factors combined to bring about the once vital industry's demise. Thanks to Robert Fortune, Chinese tea plants had been introduced to Ceylon and Assam many years earlier and had become very successful. Their more robust flavours initially provided stiff competition for the Chinese product, and then all but replaced it. The fall in volume of tea shipments from China was initially not great, but as a proportion of all tea being brought into the consuming countries it became dwarfed by the Indian and Ceylonese product.

Another problem was the Chinese taxation system. As early as 1857 the foreign tea men in Foochow had raised concerns about the imposition of excessive *likin*. In 1872 even a group of Chinese merchants petitioned the governor-general for the abolition of *likin*, given that it was initially meant to finance the fight against the defeated Taiping rebels.

They were told that the province needed the revenue as the customs duties it had enjoyed in the past now, under the foreign-managed system, flowed direct to Peking (Beijing).[60]

The once powerful tea industry continued to decline throughout the remainder of the 19th century. A number of Russian firms established brick tea factories in the 1870s and 1880s. They were content to use tea-dust and broken leaves, but by 1908 these too had gone.[61]

Foochow life in the 1860s and 1870s

The opening of the new Custom House in July 1861 introduced a large number of European and American indoor and outdoor staff. Initially around 20, their number grew to 35 by 1877. As usual, a grand house was built for the commissioner with a view overlooking his domain. The Custom House itself, with adjoining inspection yards and accommodation for the junior staff was on the riverfront, towards the eastern end of the line of merchants' hongs.[62] The British Consul had moved his main residence from the city in 1859[63] and was now living among the growing community on Nantai's hill. The grand colonial building lasted for many years although not into our own age.[64]

By the mid-1860s there was a billiards club, a fives court, a bowling alley and a reading room.[65] In 1871 that essential ingredient of colonial life, the Foochow Club, was established, conveniently located next door to the British Consulate. The building still stands, now rejoicing under the name of No. 8 Dongqun Road. Now in poor condition, it still has the same commanding view over the river and beyond from the verandah. In the same year a General Chamber of Commerce was also formed, the committee of which was almost, not surprisingly, identical to that of the Club.[66] There was by now a foreign population of around 100, mainly British, with another 50 at Pagoda Island.[67]

Banking arrangements were undergoing a major change at around this time. The first foreign banks to appear in Foochow were British banks from India. They operated as agencies, each being looked after by a merchant as part of his portfolio of activities. There needed to be several agencies, otherwise one merchant would come to know too much about the operations of his competitors. The Hongkong & Shanghai Bank opened an agency in 1865, upgrading later to a self-staffed branch. The building they erected in the late 1870s has been preserved, just, and now forms the centrepiece to a huge residential tower-block complex.

Shipping thrived as steamers replaced sailing ships, and their reliability and speed made them increasingly attractive both to foreign and Chinese merchants. Butterfield & Swire's China Navigation opened a Foochow branch in 1872. Regular steamer services connected the port to Amoy (Xiamen), Swatow (Shantou) and Hong Kong by the mid-1860s. Links to Ningpo and Shanghai would follow. All passengers were still obliged to take a two-to four-hour trip down to Pagoda Island in order to board ship.[68]

A favourite weekend (or longer) relaxation was excursions along the rivers. Boats could be hired easily, as could the crews to operate them and feed the passengers. Foochow was said at the time to have a 'genteel' air, rather like Shameen (Shamian) Island in Canton, and for the same reason—the common sailors and other rowdy elements were kept elsewhere, in this case at Pagoda Island. Such separation allowed all parties to enjoy themselves without interference or embarrassment.[69]

Against this backdrop was the ever-present fear of anti-foreign feeling. In January 1869 placards appeared all over the city, calling on the native population to rise up and massacre all Europeans. Naturally a gunboat was called up from Pagoda Island.[70]

THE IMPERIAL ARSENAL

With China having been humiliated twice in recent years by military defeat, there was increasing pressure among the more progressive Chinese leaders to strengthen the empire. One such was Zuo Zongtang, Viceroy of Fujian and Zhejiang. Zuo was energetic and had proved himself as a military leader fighting against the Taipings. In 1866 he was Grand Secretary to the Imperial Grand Council and to the Tsungli Yamen.[71] He used his exalted position and reputation to suggest to the throne the building of a modern naval yard. Attached to this, he added, should be a school for instruction in ship construction, engineering, navigation and officer training. The recommendation was accepted immediately by the Tongzhi Emperor.[72] In August 1866 Zuo selected a site at Mawei, alongside the foreign Foochow Dockyard, and construction of one of the first major projects of the Self-Strengthening Movement started.[73]

No sooner had the work started than Zuo was ordered to the north-west to suppress a Muslim revolt.[74] Shen Baozhen, Lin Zexu's son-in-law, was appointed as Director General in Zuo's place, and he was left to work things out with the two Frenchmen Zuo had installed to lead the project—Prosper Giquel and Paul d'Aiguebelle.[75] Both had been officers in the French navy, Giquel later becoming Customs Commissioner at Ningpo.[76] Perhaps influenced by Francophobia, *The China Mail* carried a report from a correspondent ridiculing what he saw at Mawei. He described it as a 'Castle of Indolence', but one which contained some comfortable houses for its well-paid French managers. The report also included scathing comments along the lines of there being a lot of activity but no action.[77] There was indeed an enormous number of people engaged on the project—over 60 Europeans (mainly French but with some British) and around 2600 Chinese workers.[78] Yet progress was slow.

The school opened in 1869, offering five-year courses. Students first had to learn French and English.[79] Naval construction and design was taught by the French, and navigation and officer-training by the British.[80] By 1873 there was a full complement of ironworks, rolling mills, engine factories and building slips—all the plant necessary for a major naval yard, and all of it in full working order.[81] To call the installation an arsenal would not be doing justice to this multi-faceted operation. In its first seven years of operation the facility launched 15 vessels, mainly gunboats and transports, varying in size from 500 to 1400 tonnes,[82] and graduated dozens of students.

When Giquel's contract expired in February 1874, the Chinese had intended to assume full control. Although many activities were under Chinese direction,[83] and the number of European staff was reduced significantly, Giquel was retained as a 'purchasing agent'. This loosely defined title enabled him to visit England and Germany to buy ships for the Chinese navy.[84]

Not many years later, a cruel irony was to be visited upon this proud and successful venture. Arguments over the status of Annam (present-day Vietnam) caused France to resort to military action against China. In August 1884 French Admiral Améedée Courbet brought his fleet into the Min River and dropped anchor at Mawei, a place with which the French navy was already very familiar. Planning their onslaught over the course of a week, on the 23rd the French vessels opened fire, entirely without the element of surprise. Every Chinese vessel was either sunk or disabled, and the arsenal and all its facilities completely destroyed.[85] In 1896 Peking awarded the job of rebuilding the facility. The French Minister in the capital, Auguste Gérard, must have been extraordinarily persuasive because he managed to secure the appointment of a Frenchman to oversee the reconstruction.[86] The yard was soon producing cruisers and other vessels of 2000–3000 tonnes[87] and remains today an important part of the Chinese navy's support systems.

Kuliang

Perhaps still smarting from the actions of the French, the people of Foochow were soon expressing their anger again, although for a very different perceived affront. Since the mid-1860s members of the foreign community had escaped the city's stifling summer heat by renting rooms at a monastery at Kushan, the mountain immediately to the east of Foochow.[88] At about 600–700 metres high the temperatures were noticeably cooler there. The rooms became so popular that they were difficult to get at the height of the season.[89] In 1886 Dr. Thomas Rennie, the leading British medical officer in Foochow, decided to build his own. Unfortunately, his holiday home was visible from the city. Angry crowds gathered in the streets, convinced that their trade and prosperity would suffer and that their *fengshui* would be irreparably damaged. In order to quell what was becoming a major incident, the building was demolished. Once all the excitement had died down, however, Rennie built another one, this time keeping it invisible from the city far below.

Gradually it was tacitly accepted that foreigners could have houses in the mountain retreat. So popular was the idea that by 1910 there were about a hundred small bungalows, with a summer population of 200 to 300—merchants with their families, consular and customs officials and missionaries.[90] The journey was about ten kilometres from the city and could be done in three to four hours by sedan chair. Holidaymakers came from Swatow, Amoy and Hong Kong, and even further afield.[91]

Kuliang was never a sophisticated hill station, such as Mokanshan (Moganshan) or Kuling (Lushan), but its small cottages remained popular right up to the end of the Treaty Port Era.[92] The various residences

French ironclad *Le Bayard*. At 6000 tonnes it was too big to enter the Min River, so guarded Sharp Peak instead. Source: *Western Engravings and Etchings and Sino-French War*, 189.

were linked by stone-flagged paths, constructed by a voluntarily funded Public Improvement Committee, later called the Kuliang Council.[93] Mountain walks were among the most popular activities, along with sports including tennis and swimming. The Imperial Chinese Post Office established a branch in Kuliang for the season, and there was a daily mail service to and from Foochow.[94] The area still retains its serenity as part of the Gu Shan National Park. Some of the stone paths and steps remain, as do a number of retaining walls. Hidden between the newer Spanish-villa style structures there are a handful of bungalows that date from the European period.

Sharp Peak and the electric telegraph

Before returning to Foochow proper, there is another small adjunct to the treaty port that needs to be mentioned. Sharp Peak was the name given to an island (Chuanshi) about five kilometres from the mouth of the river. In the Treaty Port Era it was notable for two reasons. Firstly, Sharp Peak became another popular holiday resort and the site of several sanatoria operated by missionaries.[95] More importantly it was the place where the submarine telegraph cable came ashore to service Foochow.

The traditionally minded Chinese had been sceptical about the benefits of the electric telegraph when Westerners first tried to introduce it. However, the landing of Japanese troops on Formosa (Taiwan) in 1874 convinced Shen Baozhen at the Foochow Arsenal of the benefit of rapid communications across the strait. He obtained sanction to start the process of laying a cable. The Danish Great Northern Telegraph Co. had already been active in China and was commissioned to build a 15-kilometre land line from Foochow to Mawei. This they achieved in the surprisingly short space of twelve days.[96] Their commission to extend the line to Amoy was fraught with problems; each time a new stretch of cable was laid, it was vandalized or destroyed.[97] In order to assuage the people's fear of the new technology, and to take maximum advantage from it, the Chinese authorities established at Foochow a School of Telegraphy, staffed largely by Great Northern employees.[98] But by this time the immediate threat from the Japanese had passed. The link to Formosa was put on hold until 1887, when a cable was laid to Tamsui (Danshui). Another submarine cable was laid from Hong Kong to Shanghai in 1883. As Foochow was roughly the halfway point, a booster station was installed at Sharp Peak. The cluster of buildings that made up this important facility, many of them painted white, became a landmark for vessels approaching the Min River.[99]

A lasting legacy

Foreign vessels still entered the river, and in increasing numbers. Indeed, during the 1880s and 1890s it was the shipping business that was to give the foreign merchants their main reason for being in Foochow. Tea was still exported, although this business was past its peak. Foreign cotton and woollen goods were imported, but almost entirely by Chinese.[100] The import of opium (still, by value, a quarter of all imports)[101] remained in foreign hands until the late 1880s. With effect from 1 February 1887, the Chefoo Agreement made this former staple of smugglers a dutiable item, which had therefore to be stored in customs warehouses. Grateful the government was shielding them from the costs and risks of storage, Chinese merchants started trading in opium, and gradually the foreign firms were eased out.[102]

Later in the 1890s, foreign merchants were to experience a revival. As tea became less significant and the major names pulled out of the market, smaller firms that had been founded in Foochow had to start something new—they had no home base to which they could withdraw. Such people had made their homes in Foochow and turned readily to any new business opportunity. Some Chinese entrepreneurs had established cotton cloth factories and there was thus a demand for yarn. A number of the 'local' foreign merchants decided to compete with the Chinese importers and bring in yarn from India and Japan, accepting low margins, and enjoyed some success.

Despite the challenges for businessmen, Foochow remained a very pleasant place for foreigners to live. As the 19th century came to an end, the foreign

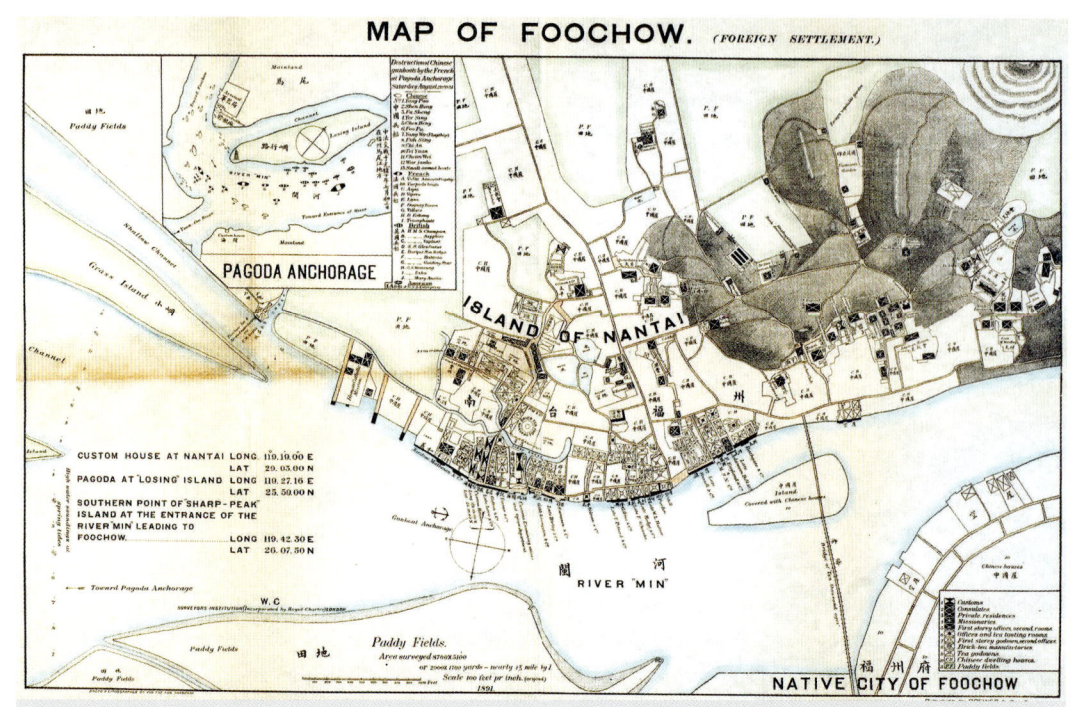

Detailed map of the foreign settlement in Nantai, 1891. Reprinted with permission by Wattis Fine Art.

community was still enjoying the fruits of the treaty port's earlier success. There were some very fine houses available for their occupation, far grander than could have been afforded or justified by later conditions. A number of the British and American owners of these properties had been obliged to sell them to Chinese and then lease them back[103]—but at least they were still there. Nearly all are now long gone, although Nantai remains a peaceful area of small roads, flights of stone steps and little traffic. A church dating from 1905 forms part of a middle-school complex and is in regular use. Next to this is the former British Episcopal Church, St. John's, which dates from 1860 but today is in a state of disrepair. Also nearby is the former French Consulate from 1877 and a former customs residential block.

The foreign population had risen from 200 in 1882 to 350 ten years later, and included more families. An increasing number were missionaries.[104] Since 1881 there had been a hairdresser and a European bakery.[105] The following year a racecourse was inaugurated[106] at the eastern end of the Nantai settlement, on ground rented from the government.[107] Races were held in the spring and autumn, keenly followed by the Hong Kong press, until the 1910s, when the ground was used instead for football and other sports.[108]

The coasting trade was firmly in the hands of foreign shipping companies such as Douglas Steamship Co., Swires and Jardines. By agreement, China Merchants shared the Shanghai traffic, their vessels officered by Europeans. Passenger services linked the port to others along the coast, and in 1891 the Japanese line Nippon Yusen Kaisha started a service to the Philippines and Japan,[109] later linking Foochow to Korea and Vladivostok.[110] Locally, small steamers were running up the river for almost 100 kilometres, as well as providing a regular connection to Pagoda Island.[111]

The occasional new foreign business venture would appear, such as a German sawmill or a British match factory.[112] Chinese factories were also proliferating, initially helped by the import of foreign plant and machinery.[113] As the 20th century progressed, the only major foreign mercantile activity was petroleum, one field where the Chinese had not yet developed their own capability. Both Asiatic Petroleum and Standard Oil had major installations at Pagoda Island.[114]

A lasting legacy from the Treaty Port Era is the work of the missionaries. There are a number of active churches in Foochow and they are regularly attended. One of the most impressive is the Catholic Cathedral of St. Dominic. The present building dates from 1932 but occupies a site on which a church has stood since 1864.[115] Adjacent to the cathedral is a building that dates from those first days. Originally a residence for the Dominican monks who started the institution, this structure, about 30 metres long and 15 wide, became famous for a while in October 2008 when it was moved to make way for a new road. It was undermined, put on rails, shunted 80 metres to the east and rotated through 90 degrees before being set down again. This is an outstanding example of the sort of care that is increasingly being applied by China to old foreign buildings. Less fortunate, however, was the area just to the west of the cathedral complex. When I visited, this was a recently created, vast wasteland that had formerly been small streets and houses. One house of clearly European origin still remained, but its future must be precarious.

Further reading: Giquel, *The Foochow Arsenal*; Johnston and Erh, *Far from Home*; Johnston and Erh, *Near to Heaven*; Lubbock, *The China Clippers*; Nield, *The China Coast*; Otness, *Toiling and Rowing*; Rawlinson, *China's Struggle for Naval Development*; Roche and Cowen, *The French at Foochow*.

Haichow (Haizhou) 海州

Jiangsu, 34.35° N, 119.10° E
Open City, 1905 Imperial Decree

In 1905, by Imperial Decree Haichow was opened to foreign trade as a defensive measure. China feared losing control of this important commercial centre, linked to the interior by railway and the Grand Canal.[1] However, Haichow's port, Lienyungchiang (Lianyungang), was sheltered but with poor prospects; access from the sea was difficult.[2] Besides, the coast was dominated by the larger ports of Tsingtao (Qingdao) and Shanghai. Only in 1933 was a proper harbour constructed at Lienyungchiang.[3]

Hangchow (Hangzhou) 杭州

Zhejiang, 30.19° N, 120.08° E
Treaty Port, 1895 Japanese Treaty

Marco Polo visited Hangchow in the 13th century and described it as 'without doubt the finest and most splendid city in the world',[1] as it may well have been. China's capital in the Southern Song dynasty (1129–1280), Hangchow was enormous and very wealthy. In 1851 Britain formally requested that Hangchow be swapped for the new treaty ports of Foochow (Fuzhou) and Ningpo (Ningbo), neither of which had met expectations.[2] The request was denied[3] and Hangchow remained a tempting possibility for the next half-century.

Japan's 1895 Treaty of Shimonoseki opened Hangchow as a treaty port. Much of the silk that was bought and sold in Shanghai was made there, as was the silk supplied to the imperial household.[4] Having gained the right to manufacture in China, the Japanese saw an opportunity to stem the inroads made by China into their silk market. What they had not taken into account was that the huge output came almost exclusively from small household looms, and the Chinese were unwilling to change methods that had served them well for generations.[5] A mob even attacked and destroyed a silk filature using modern machinery built by Chinese entrepreneurs.[6]

A 70-hectare plot for a foreign settlement was identified on the right bank of the Grand Canal, six kilometres from the city's north-west corner, but the Japanese demanded an exclusive concession. The Zhejiang government attempted to limit the privileges that the unwelcome foreigners were claiming. But the Japanese persisted and were granted a 50-hectare site on the northern boundary of the general settlement, along with the right to govern it.[7] Britain, the only other likely contender, announced that it would not be seeking a concession.[8] The Chinese therefore insisted that foreign merchants could only acquire land within the settlement. The treaties did not permit such restriction so it was not announced formally. However, locals who were found to have leased land elsewhere in the city to foreigners other than missionaries were imprisoned and maltreated.[9] The British Consul-General from Shanghai came to investigate the matter, and the city authorities grudgingly capitulated; this was not announced either.[10]

Thirty-five lots were marked out in August 1896 by Albert Algar, a Canadian surveyor and architect employed by the Chinese government. They were snapped up immediately by British, American and French speculators in Shanghai. The lessees were under no illusions about the possibilities of trading, but they hoped that the requirement for the area to be properly policed would attract Chinese tenants.[11] A British police superintendent was appointed to lead a force of 26 Chinese constables and a few Chinese houses started to appear.[12] For some time the only

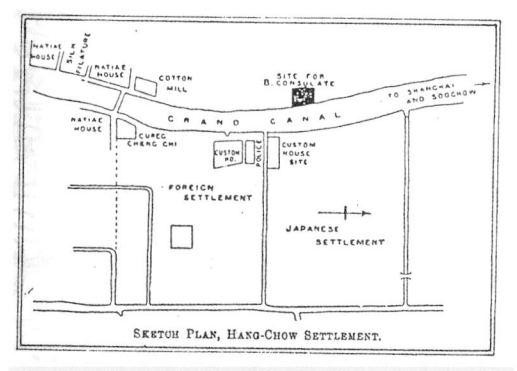

Sketch map of the foreign settlement, c. 1900. Source: Lo and Bryant, *British Diplomatic and Consular Establishments in China*, 142.

foreign-style buildings in the settlement belonged to the Chinese government, designed by Algar before he went back to Shanghai in 1897.[13] Occupying waterfront sites, these comprised the Custom House, the commissioner's residence and quarters for the (by 1899) 14 foreign customs men. All three still stand, within a large hospital compound. The imposing police station[14] is no more. In its day, there were more policemen in the settlement than anybody else. It must have been an extremely safe place, but not without problems.

The purchasers of the various lots started to pressure the Chinese authorities into honouring their side of the deal to build roads, without which the value of their investments would not rise as anticipated. A foreign engineer, Mr. Moller, was engaged to supervise the work, including making a bund and raising the general level of the land to protect it from the occasional overflow from the canal. To achieve this he chose the cheap option, dredging mud that had been filling up the creek that divided his area from the Japanese Concession and piling this on the settlement. The malaria that had been a risk when the area was merely marshy became an epidemic once covered with reeking mud. Moller was one of the first victims and nearly died. He resigned in 1897, leaving a replacement to complete the job in 1901.[15] The settlement remained a notoriously unhealthy place and was quietly forgotten. Even ten years later the Japanese Concession contained only a police station, a post office and a small warehouse.[16] A Japanese Consulate was built about 1908,[17] and only in 1919 was a bridge constructed to connect the two foreign areas.[18]

For reasons of health (or to make a point) Britain chose to build its consulate on the opposite side of the canal. A large and impressive building was completed in 1901,[19] but no full consul was appointed until 1910. Twelve years later the station was closed, absorbed by Ningpo.[20] Apart from Japan, the only other country to install a consul was the United States (in 1904), largely because of the American missionaries operating in and around Hangchow.[21] He was replaced in 1905, but the new incumbent resigned almost immediately, 'complaining of the mode of life of the Chinese, which he cannot stand'.[22] The third and final appointee, Frederick Cloud, did not stay long either, just enough to write a delightful guide to Hangchow and Soochow (Suzhou).*

The treaty port of Hangchow was formally opened on 26 September 1896, almost a year after the deadline stipulated in the Treaty of Shimonoseki. The main exports were tea, the trade having a longer life there than at most other Chinese ports, and silk, firmly in the hands of Chinese merchants. Trade was exclusively with Shanghai and was carried along the Grand Canal and other inland waterways. Hangchow had no prospects as a port for steamers; the nearby Chientang (Qiantang) River was too shallow and its mouth was subject to the notorious Hangchow Bore, a natural tidal phenomenon that periodically produced a three-metre wave. Occasionally a foreign agent would come from Shanghai to buy silk or cocoons,[23] but it was not until 1911 that the first non-Japanese foreign trader came to reside in Hangchow—the agent for Standard Oil.[24]

By then a 20-kilometre railway had been built connecting the settlement to the walled city, and to the river at Zakow (Zhakou). Completed in 1907, this line was the precursor of the Shanghai-Hangchow Railway, which connected the two cities in 1909. The bigger line had a major impact on the movement of goods and people, reducing the journey time from a day to a few hours. The smaller line had the effect of offering Zakow as an alternative, healthier location for the new foreign businesses that started to appear. Standard Oil and Asiatic Petroleum both constructed storage facilities at Zakow and built houses for their foreign staff on the hillside above the river. None remain, but the large goods handling area of Zakow Station is still there, ominously surrounded by a concrete wall, its days presumably numbered.

In 1911 the Republicans took over the city without bloodshed.[25] The city garrison of Manchu bannermen was evicted and the area they occupied flattened by the new government. In its place rose a small model city of wide roads and imposing buildings.[26] The old walls were also demolished, making the West Lake an integral and attractive part of the city, as it remains today. A number of impressive buildings from this period are lined up along Beishan Road at the lake's northern tip.

The missionaries and their facilities were untouched by the revolution. Starting in 1864,[27] there were over 100 living in and around the city by 1913, mostly British and American.[28] The missionary who left the greatest mark was Scotsman Duncan Main. He arrived in November 1881, and when he retired 45 years later he could look back on a legacy of more than a dozen hospitals, training colleges and similar institutions, all thriving.[29] Three buildings dating from 1911, built by American missionaries, now form the nucleus of the attractive, tranquil riverside campus of Zhejiang University, a short distance to the west of Zakow.

Despite the Nationalist government's determination to abolish all foreign privileges in China, the Japanese forced through a renegotiation of the lease on their concession in 1935.[30] One wonders why they bothered when two years later they marched in and took the entire city, which remained in their possession until the end of the Pacific War.

Further reading: Cloud, *The City of Heaven*; Fitch, *Hangchow Itineraries*; Gammie, *Duncan Main of Hangchow*; Schultheis, *Hangchow, My Home*.

HANKOW (HANKOU) 漢口

Hubei, 30.34° N, 114.17° E
Treaty Port, 1858 British Treaty

The official British delegation arriving in Hankow to open the new treaty port hoped to find the great commercial centre of the Chinese Empire—and did.[1] The performance of many of the initial open ports was disappointing but Hankow exceeded that of all the

---
* See Bibliography.

others opened by the 1858 Tientsin (Tianjin) Treaty. Hankow brought the British far more than commercial benefits. Being the furthest that ocean-going vessels could penetrate into the empire's heartland, it enabled Britain to establish a dominant 'sphere of influence' over the thousand navigable kilometres of the Lower Yangtze.

The three cities that constitute modern Wuhan (known as such since 1927) had separate identities in 1858. The conurbation has to face the challenge of being divided by the Han River and the Yangtze, here up to 1500 metres wide even though so far from the sea. Wuchang, on the Yangtze's east bank, was the geographical centre of the empire and provincial capital of Hubei. Surrounded by a double wall and set at the river's edge on a rocky outcrop, Wuchang was the administrative centre, taking its final shape in 1371.[2] On the opposite side of the Yangtze, immediately upstream of where the Han joins it, was Hanyang, a small prefectural town, in steady decline since before the first European traders arrived. Largely laid waste by the Taiping rebels in the mid-1850s, it was left to disintegrate.[3]

The third of the three, Hankow, was the commercial centre. In view of the huge seasonal rise and fall of the Yangtze and its rapid flow, the Chinese city of Hankow developed along the northern bank of the Han rather than down the western shore of the Yangtze. Moorings were easier there, and the river was narrower and less deep.[4] As it was a relatively new commercial creation, there was no city wall. Instead Hankow was bounded by the Yangtze and Han to the east and south, and to the west and north by a drainage canal. The enclosed area was over twice that contained by the other two cities' walls, making it the biggest city in Hubei. Indeed, with an estimated population of one million in 1850, it was one of the largest cities in the world, on a par with London.[5] When the Europeans arrived, up to 10,000 boats were based there, along with some 500,000 people.[6] Hankow was the commercial gateway to China's nine central provinces. The Han was the main route from the centre to the north-west, while the Yangtze itself reached east and west for 6400 kilometres, flowing from Qinghai to the East China Sea.

British interest in Hankow

It was this gateway that Britain wanted. All three cities had been captured by the Taipings in 1851–52 and much damage had been done. What Lord Elgin recognized during his reconnoitre on 6 December 1858[7] was that amid the destruction there was already significant commercial activity, with houses and shops being built or rebuilt.[8] Before 1861 Hankow already possessed a highly differentiated and specialized merchant class, with credit institutions and sophisticated trading networks.[9]

By early 1861 the Taiping threat had receded sufficiently for Hankow to be opened as a treaty port. On 12 February Vice Admiral Hope led a flotilla up the Yangtze from Shanghai, reaching Hankow on 11 March.[10] Lying at anchor was the *Yang-tze*, a steamer owned by British firm Dent & Co. but disguised by flying the American flag, presumably to avoid embarrassing Hope. Dents arrived four days earlier to establish their agent and rent a godown.[11] Laurence Oliphant, Elgin's private secretary, saw posters in the city warning of the foreigners' visit but reassuring the population they were not going to be there for long and their intent was not commercial—wishful thinking.[12] Also in the official British party was Harry Parkes. It was his job to look after the practicalities,

Dents' steamer *Fusiyama* in 1863. Source: Liu, *Anglo-American Steamship Rivalry in China*, 78.

such as locating the area to be settled and a site for the consul's residence.[13]

The new treaty port was declared open on 13 March 1861. As it was located far inland and somewhat isolated, Parkes felt it safer to negotiate for a concession, rather than risk the individual and potentially difficult negotiations that a settlement would entail.[14] The lease was signed on 21 March for an area 840 metres long and 370 metres wide, along the Yangtze and downstream, adjacent to the Chinese city. The plan was for the Chinese to clear the site and the British to lay it out and sell the individual lots by auction. The proceeds would provide compensation to the 2500 families who had been living there.[15] Most of the 108 lots were snapped up. A plot at the northern end was reserved for the British Consulate. An area for a French Concession was also selected, but the French did nothing with it. In 1862 the British Consul reported that many foreigners had acquired plots outside the concession and Hanyang-side, even in the walled city, one of whom was said to be the French Consul. By 1864–65 many had withdrawn to the safer and more salubrious concession.[16]

The river regulations drawn up by Parkes required customs duties to be paid at Shanghai, on entering or leaving the river. This attempt to counter smuggling was interpreted by the Chinese as a device to deprive them of their just revenue. Accordingly, the viceroy announced that a *likin* tax would be levied on all foreign trade,[17] provoking strong objections. Nor were the foreign merchants happy with Parkes's regulations; the British Consulate was already swamped with complaints.[18] Robert Hart, Acting Inspector-General of Customs, arrived to open a Custom House, despite the viceroy's objections to customs being controlled by foreigners.[19] The new facility opened on 2 December 1861 on a riverfront site in the Chinese city. Hart returned the following June and agreed a revised set of river regulations, satisfying everybody.[20]

At year's end there were ten British firms, two American and one Prussian. The foreign population stood at 40,[21] served by two regular steamer services to Shanghai, making two round trips each in a month.[22] A total of 401 vessels visited the port. In the concession, buildings were erected and most lots walled in by their new owners.[23] The land-renters soon organized themselves into a municipal council on the Shanghai model, taking responsibility for roads, drains and policing. A priority was to create a bund to protect against the Yangtze's floods.[24] The seasonal change in the water level could be 15 metres, worsened by prolonged heavy rain. The cost was significant, so wharfage dues were levied. The job was finished in 1863.[25] Despite the new bund, the concession was flooded in 1866.[26] The embankment had to be raised several times, and thousands of tonnes of mud were scooped out of the riverbed and deposited on the building lots in order to raise the ground level. Between 1866 and 1869 the consulate's boundary wall was renewed twice as a result of flooding.[27]

In 1866 an official inspection of all British consular properties in China revealed the Hankow consulate's fittings had 'been provided on a most extravagant scale' and the residence was 'of a size and character out of all proportion to the present or any probable future requirements of the place'. This expense had been unauthorized. The money for this and other consular buildings came from the sale of concession lots; only the net balance had been reported to the Treasury in London.[28]

The original intention of the British in Hankow, as in other new concessions in China, was to rent land only to British tenants. This narrow approach was soon abandoned, and lots were opened to nationals of any Treaty Power. Thus the settlement became, and remained, an international one. By the end of 1863, although most of the foreign population of 150 were British, there were a number of Americans and French,[29] and 44 commercial organizations in addition to two banks. But of the merchant firms, only half remained three years later. Others replaced them, but initial enthusiasm was dampened by the reality that Chinese merchants dominated the import trade, leaving limited scope for foreigners. The Customs Report for 1864 contains numerous descriptions of unfulfilled foreign expectations, confirming that Hankow was not transformed from 'a "national" trading city to a vacuum pump for European and North American capitalism'.[30]

Many of the new residents had moved upriver from Shanghai bringing their lifestyle with them. The Hankow Club was established early on and from the outset was a cosmopolitan affair, with membership open to all nationalities (apart from, of course, Chinese). The club facilities soon had a very high reputation. Elected members of the municipal council and, when it was formed a few years later, the General Chamber of Commerce likewise represented all the foreign business community. A racecourse was laid out in 1864 within the city wall, just to the north of the concession. (The wall had been built in 1863 as a defence against rebel attack.) Racing started in April 1863[31] and a pattern of spring and autumn meets established. Despite there being cash for a flutter on the horses, there were no funds for a permanent church.[32] There was an Ice Club through which, for a monthly subscription of $6.00, ice could be obtained year-round. Welcome though this was, residents found the dues too high and it failed.

THE RISE AND FALL OF THE TEA TRADE

Life was not all clubs, horse racing and cold drinks. There was hard work to be done, most of it involving tea. Hankow's principal attraction to foreign merchants was proximity to the tea-growing areas of Hunan and Hubei. The export trade grew quickly; tea was brought for shipment downriver to Shanghai, then loaded onto ocean-going vessels bound for Europe and America. When it was realized for much of the year ocean-going ships could reach Hankow, shipments started to be made direct.

Tea was a seasonal business. In the slack part of the year the concession had 'the lifeless depressing aspect of a seaside watering-place in the off season'[33] but the coming of the season saw a 'short period of excitement and glory'.[34] In addition to the resident foreign tea merchants, more came from Shanghai to supervise the buying.[35] Larger and more seasoned houses like Jardines and Heards provided some stability, but most foreign tea men were 'commercial adventurers with remarkably little understanding of the market or sense of the risks they ran'. An 1867 report by Jardines' man in Hankow complained: 'I am utterly at a loss to understand how [Mackellar & Co.] are going to pay for all the tea they have bought . . . they have been the utter ruin of this market, which would have been very much lower than this but for the reckless way in which they have been buying.' Mackellar & Co. went bankrupt later that year.[36]

Mackellar was not alone among irresponsible and unscrupulous merchants. Others adopted dishonest practices such as using incorrectly calibrated scales. Most Westerners involved in Hankow's tea trade at this time 'were noteworthy for the shortness of their vision,'[37] sacrificing anything for a quick profit. This cut-throat competition was apparent to Chinese and foreign observers alike. Into the 1880s, some Chinese tea merchants could exploit the disunity to sustain higher prices and obtain better terms.

After the failed attempt to impose *likin* on foreign tea exports, the viceroy established a Black Tea Hong to set prices, from which a three percent tax would be deducted.[38] Sounding rather like the Canton (Guangzhou) co-hong of recent memory, it provoked strong consular protests. The Chinese authorities maintained that it was a tax on their own people, not foreigners, and so the hong remained. It was this body that decided to take collective action regarding the bankrupt Mackellar. The firm owed 300,000 *taels* to Chinese merchants, plus a smaller amount to foreign traders. The Chinese thought British bankruptcy laws were too light, allowing the offender to raise his hands and declare his firm was broke, not himself. The hong, together with the *taotai* and the viceroy, vigorously demanded repayment, but the British Consul insisted that British law must be applied. When the Chinese merchants discovered that two British firms reached a private settlement with Mackellar, they instituted a total boycott of all foreign tea traders.

The Chinese also had bad practices. Some sellers offered a high-quality sample for initial inspection, but would follow up with a low-quality bulk shipment. It was estimated that this affected 30 percent of all transactions after 1870. The tea hong's measures to curb such practices were ineffective,[39] circumvented

Coolies unloading tea on the bund, c. 1935. Source: George Shepherd Library of the Western Development Museum, Saskatoon, Canada. Image courtesy of Western Development Museum.

by the unscrupulous. The Hankow foreign merchants knew they had to clean up the market as, from about 1872, the bulk of the 33,000-tonne tea export business was concluded in Hankow not, as before, in Shanghai. By 1882 matters were serious. The 'sample chest' issue was openly recognized and foreign merchants received large discounts in lieu of good quality tea. The Hankow Customs Commissioner saw fault on both sides, but tended to favour the Chinese especially when, in 1883, the tea hong introduced new regulations. These included the appointment of an independent impartial arbitrator, either Western or Chinese, and standardized and supervised weighing.[40]

The foreign tea men could hardly complain about what was a fair deal but, not being consulted, were reluctant to comply. When the 1883 tea market opened on 12 May there were loud protests, and Dodwells, by now one of the major traders, refused to bid at all. In solidarity all the foreign merchants joined in and a stalemate ensued. Consul Alabaster complained to the *taotai* that the boycott was against the spirit of the treaty and claimed for losses suffered by Dodwells. The hong, reasonably, asked how Dodwells could have lost anything when they did not bid. After that the system seemed to work.[41]

However, a number of factors were combining against Hankow's tea business. First, concern was expressed about quality. Chinese tea was produced by peasant farmers, each keen to maximize his own profit to provide for his family. There was no central means through which strategies to improve quality could be introduced or monitored.[42] Second was the Chinese government's greedy taxation system, which 'milked' tea to an extent that made the product uncompetitive. The final blow came when tastes in the West shifted towards the stronger flavours, and consistent quality, of Indian and Ceylonese teas. Although tea exports from Hankow doubled between 1866 and 1886, those from India and Ceylon increased fourteenfold. By 1887 a problem had become a disaster. That year the Commissioner of Customs observed: 'There was no rush to buy. Though tea poured in, it went out slowly.'[43] This once staple export went into steady decline. In 1900 no tea was shipped direct from Hankow to London.[44] But it was not only the British who had been interested in the tea market. There was another group that kept the business going through other means.

The Russians

An overland tea trade from Hubei to Siberia had existed since the 12th century,[45] conducted mostly through Chinese intermediaries, with camel caravans sometimes taking two years to reach their destination.[46] Even though there had been formal relations between Russia and China for almost 200 years, the existence of Russian traders in China was precarious and of doubtful legality, becoming regularized by the Russian Treaty of Tientsin in 1858.

Russians wanted 'brick tea' and 'tablet tea', products peculiar to the Russian market, which met the logistical complexity of transporting tea over vast distances. Russians were among the first foreigners in Hankow, becoming one of the largest foreign communities. Two Russian vessels called in 1861 and four Russian tea merchants were based there in 1866. By 1873 15 Russians lived and worked in the British Concession. In that year production started at a steam-powered brick-tea plant, the first factory built in Hankow. In 1875 a second opened, with two more in 1878 and 1892, each owned by a different Russian company. They were the largest industry, employing about 100 men[47] and 20 Russian managers.

Making brick tea involved grinding broken leaves and tea dust into fine powder, which was steamed and pressed in a wooden mould. The resulting bricks, about one-sixth of the equivalent bulk of leaf tea, were packed in light bamboo baskets and sent as far as possible up the Han River, where the camels took over.[48] Tablet tea was a higher-end product, wrapped in tin foil and brightly coloured paper, looking rather like a modern chocolate bar.[49] The factories were the most striking buildings in the foreign settled area, with their tall chimneys visible from a long way downriver.[50] With expansion (the factories soon employed thousands rather than hundreds), only two remained inside the British Concession; the two newest factories were built on adjacent land to the north.

By the end of the 19th century almost 50 Russians worked in Hankow's tea business. They also shipped leaf tea to Odessa on the Black Sea for the European Russian market.[51] British merchants still bought 40 percent of the tea brought to Hankow, but this was by now largely shipped to London for Russians to purchase.[52] One of the main players was J. K. Panoff, a relative of Tsar Nicholas I,[53] presumably wealthy even before he made a further fortune in Hankow. Following the visit in 1891 of the Russian Crown Prince (later Tsar Nicholas II) it was decided to stop shipping via the Han. Instead tea would go down the Yangtze by Russian steamer and along the coast to Vladivostok,[54] the prince's next port of call, where he formally opened the construction of the Far East segment of the Trans-Siberian Railway.

Despite the falling quality of local tea, the Russians continued in strength, even importing tea dust from Ceylon, India and Java.[55] The Russian business population peaked at 52 in 1916 as did the output of brick tea, almost 30,000 tonnes. The 1917 turmoil in Russia caused Russian firms to scale down. When the Bolshevik government severed all business connections with China they ceased altogether. Five years later there was only one Russian firm still represented in Hankow, with a skeleton staff headed by Panoff, who was reluctant to abandon his enormous house on the bund. By 1930 he too had gone, after over 50 years in Hankow, thus ending the Russian business presence. Their reputation for free spending and enjoyment, as well as making fortunes, helped make Hankow one of the liveliest cities in the Far East.[56] The Russian Club, opened in 1900, was a favourite place among all nationalities for a convivial evening. Looking rather sad, the building still stands at the corner of Lanling Road and Poyang Street.

A number of other Russian buildings remain: the Russian Orthodox Church on Tianjin Road; and, on Dongting Street, the 1902 Russian Police Station, the grand residence of tea magnate S. W. Litvinoff and, at the corner with Tianjin Road, Bagong House, an imposing four-storey apartment block built by Panoff in 1901. Most impressive is the huge house that he was so reluctant to leave, at No. 170 Yanjiang Avenue, which later became the American Consulate. The 1902 former Russian Consulate stands adjacent at No. 168, looking solid, purposeful and quite beautiful in its current manifestation as a hotel.

Postcard of the house that J. K. Panoff was so reluctant to leave. It later became the American Consulate. Source: Zhe Fu, ed., *Late Qing and Early Republic Wuhan Images*, 147.

Decline and troubles: The 1880s and 1890s

Hankow was the centre of an enormous Chinese mercantile establishment, and Chinese is what it remained. Only in shipping did foreigners have superior technology and operational experience. The mid-1800s saw rapid advances in vessel technology, design and fleet management. In the 1850s the Americans pioneered the clipper ships, and many of these majestic vessels frequented Hankow, including the British icon *Cutty Sark*, up to the late 1870s.[57] The American firm Russells imported a river steamer in 1862 and, with local foreign and Chinese capital, created the Shanghai Steam Navigation Co. They dominated the Yangtze traffic between Shanghai and Hankow, with their white, side-wheeled paddle steamers providing a regular and reliable twice-weekly service. In 1864 there were 16 steamers operating on the river: ten were American, both paddle-and screw-driven, run by three separate companies; and six were British, run by four companies.[58]

By the time the Chefoo Agreement of 1876 opened the Middle Yangtze to foreign trade, Hankow's greatest days as a tea port were over. Clement Allen, returning to Hankow as British Consul in 1888 (having been a student interpreter at the consulate in 1865–66) found that the British population had halved.[59] The number of foreign residents had peaked in 1864 at about 300 and then declined, not to reach that level again until the 1890s.[60] Allen reported that trade had fallen compared with the previous year. Except for the shipping agents, the larger British firms departed, no longer able to make a profit. Jardines and Swires had just one man each to manage their respective affairs. An attempt was made to persuade the Chinese government to contribute towards the cost of maintaining the unnecessarily large concession.[61] The Chinese merchants of Hankow were in much the same position as before the opening of the treaty port, with the convenient additions of a speedy steamer service and predictable, reasonable customs charges.

Opportunities foreign businessmen hoped for were not available to them. Tea continued the main export, and merchants, bankers, tasters and brokers still came to Hankow from Shanghai in the season[62] but it was the Russians who dominated tea-related activity. By 1888 their numbers, about 25, were equal to the British. Including a European customs staff of about 30, the foreign population was around 100. Life would have been pleasant, if uneventful. The bund had long been completed and the concession was generally safe from flooding. Customs Commissioner Moorhead, in his report for 1882–91, described the scene: 'Coming up the Yangtze the traveller observes what looks like a large park, with a row of well-built houses: this is the British Concession.'[63] This hoped-for centre of foreign business had become a quiet but elegant backwater, with the occasional seasonal spurt of activity.

In 1891 a spate of attacks on foreigners, not only missionaries, erupted all along the Yangtze. Hankow was not directly affected, due to the presence of gunboats in the river. A number of missionaries prudently moved to the concession. There was an uneasy feeling among the foreigners, relieved by the knowledge that they could be transported to safety by steamer.

A flurry of new concessions

The sense of humiliation associated with the unwanted presence of foreigners in the country was greatly exacerbated when, in April 1895, Japan won its war with China. The potential threat posed by this newcomer was used by the Treaty Powers to demand additional concessions at the expense of China, not least in Hankow.

The German Concession

The Germans led the way. In October 1895 they obtained a lease for a 420,000-square-metre concession outside the city wall. Initial development was slow, but on 30 May 1899 German Prince Heinrich, the Kaiser's brother, laid the foundation stone for the German Bund, completed in 1903.[64] By 1905 roads had been laid out in the gridiron pattern that is evident today. In 1906 the administration was placed under a municipal council. At the western edge of the concession, lines of *lilong*-style houses (two-storey terraces with a small alley in between) were built for Chinese occupancy. Some are still there.

Many of the German firms in Hankow were engaged in exporting low-end products such as tallow, wax and pig bristles, content to earn small margins on steady, high-volume business. Also considered low-end was the export of animal hides. Their odorous preparation involved hanging skins to be dried and treated. One of the first companies to move into the new German Concession was Meyer & Co., in 1901. They built smart offices on the bund, behind which were their godowns and drying yards. They also had a plant for cleaning sesame seeds, the export of which was becoming big business.[65] Melchers & Co., in Hankow since the mid-1880s, also moved into the new German Concession, expanding as they went. They established a large hide-drying yard[66] with a staff of eight Germans. They also opened an albumen factory. Made from egg-whites, albumen had industrial uses including printing and photography. In 1907 Melchers built a power station that provided electricity to the whole German Concession.[67] A spur line of the new Peking-Hankow Railway (see below) from the main line to the German Bund provided a further boost.[68]

At the southern end of the concession the Germans built the most imposing consulate in the foreign area. However, the 14 October 1905 edition of the *New-York Tribune* took satisfaction in pointing out that the magnificent building had been topped with an American eagle, not a Prussian one.[69] The glorious building still stands, minus eagle, and is home to a branch of the Wuhan Municipal Government. In 1909 the Germans built a combined town hall and police station, also still there on the corner of Eryao Road and Shengli Street, minus its tower and other Germanic features.

A photograph from the early 20th century shows a solid, confident line of North European–looking buildings along the German Bund. However, all impressive German achievements in China halted when China declared war on Germany in 1917. In March that year the German Concession became a Special Administrative District (SAD) under the provincial government. This status was cancelled in January 1929 and the former concession placed under the Hankow city municipality.[70]

The Russian Concession

The Russians already occupied land between the northern end of the British Concession and the city wall. It was easy, therefore, for Russia to identify a specific area and apply for a formal lease as a Russian Concession. At a time when China could not refuse any foreign power's request, the lease was signed in June 1896. The concession was 276,000 square metres, slightly larger than the British area, and the Russian Bund extended along the river for about 700 metres to what is now Hezuo Road. A Russian municipal council was created in 1903, chaired by the consul. Although the Russian Concession was slower to develop than its German counterpart, it was almost as quick to close. Following the Russian Revolution in 1917, and in the midst of the confused relations between the two new republics, the Chinese authorities took temporary charge of the concession on 23 September 1920 under a presidential mandate.[71] The area became SAD No. 2. On 1 July 1924, in fulfilment of the Sino-Soviet Agreement of 30 May, the concession was formally handed back. Its SAD status was cancelled in January 1929 and the area became part of Hankow city.[72]

The French Concession

In June 1896 France leased the remaining 125,000 square metres between the Russian Concession and the city wall, represented at the northern boundary by present-day Yiyuan Road. The French Consul had already lived in this area for some years. A French municipal council was created in 1898 under his chairmanship. A 1902 extension added 50 percent to the French area, taking it almost to the railway line. All three of Hankow's foreign hotels were in the French Concession—the Hankow, the Astor House and the Terminus. The Astor House was the most famous and luxurious. Established in 1902 it had a 40 guest-room building on the French Bund. The only one remaining is the Terminus, on Shengli Street (formerly rue d'Autremer), founded in 1901 to serve customers arriving at the soon-to-be-opened railway station. Its initial 32-room building became inadequate, and was replaced in 1909 with a three-storey,

Bird's-eye view from 1911 showing the five concessions, the new racecourse and the cities of Hanyang and Wuchang. Source: Zhe Fu, ed., *Late Qing and Early Republic Wuhan Images*, 17.

80-room establishment[73] under the prestigious Wagons-Lits franchise. Renamed the Jianghan Hotel in 1954, it is today a joint venture with a Hong Kong company.

The 1865 French Consulate, in the grounds of the racecourse to the north of the British Concession, was replaced by a consulate-cum-residence in the 1880s. This lovely building still stands within its very large walled garden at 81 Dongting Street. The gates have rusted permanently in the open position so access to the site is easy, although the building itself is closed, apparently unused.

During the Second World War the French Concession was nominally administered by the Vichy government, but actually controlled by the Japanese.[74] A complete anachronism, it was the only remaining foreign concession in Hankow when it was handed back in 1946.

The British Extension

Once the Germans, Russians and French had their own concessions, the original British Concession appeared shrunken, as did British prestige. The decision was taken in 1898 to extend the British area to the city wall. This added some 226,000 square metres to the original 243,000. With the imminent arrival of the Peking-Hankow Railway, to be built on an embankment, the city wall was gradually disappearing, encouraging the British to consider extending their enlarged concession further by 50 percent to the railway line; this never happened. The odorous drying of hides was permitted in the extension, despite proximity to sensitive British noses, and it was announced that 'under certain rules and regulations, it is proposed to allow respectable Chinese' to live there as well.[75]

The Japanese Concession

Victory over China in 1895 increased Japanese confidence. In 1898 they leased a plot immediately to the north of the German Concession and established a relatively modest 123,000-square-metre Japanese Concession, extended in 1902 to around 300,000 square metres. When they completed their section of the bund, there was an uninterrupted tree-lined carriageway of over four kilometres, the longest in China.[76]

The growth of Japanese business was rapid; energetic, persistent and more attuned to local business methods than many of the Europeans.[77] The Japanese initially found the similarity of their culture with the Chinese worked to their advantage, and the recent animosity soon turned into keen admiration.[78] The love affair did not last. By 1907 anti-foreign feelings were extended to the Japanese, seen as overtly profiting from efforts to help China modernize.[79] Furthermore, the existing foreign business community realized very serious competition had arrived in their midst.

The largest Japanese concern was the Japan Cotton Trading Co. (predecessor of today's Nichimen Corporation), which opened in 1906 with a staff of 37 Japanese, immediately becoming industry leaders. The company had cotton- and bean-pressing factories in Hanyang and bean oil and cotton seed oil factories in the Japanese Concession. As a clear statement of their intentions, in 1902 the Japanese built a huge consulate, not as architecturally impressive as the Germans' but imposing nonetheless. The Weshun Hotel now stands on this site at 234 Yanjiang Avenue. The development of the entire expanded concession was completed by 1910, containing over 200 buildings and three factories.

Much of the Japanese Concession was destroyed in the late 1930s, but a number of fine buildings remain. In Zhangzizhong Road one can admire a line of terraced houses, three or four storeys high, and a school opposite. Further inland, at the corner of Shengli Street and Sanhaiguan Road, is a long two-storey block, former residences of the Mitsubishi Corporation and built in 1910. On the opposite side of Shengli Street is a smart red-brick police station, which most likely served the same function for the Japanese.

A Belgian Concession?

Belgium, a low-key player in the China market of the late 19th century, suddenly took centre stage on 26 June 1898. A Belgian syndicate was awarded the contract to construct a railway connecting Hankow to Peking (Beijing). Once construction started at the Hankow end in 1903 55 Belgian engineers arrived, increasing to 64. In 1896 there was a team of 24 mostly Belgian engineers at the Hanyang Iron & Steel Works (see below). The railway project was vast, and will be described in more detail later. In addition to the large number of people involved, a significant tract of land was needed to support the project, and to lay out the required sidings and marshalling yards. A plot the same size as the expanded Japanese Concession is marked on maps of the time as 'Pei Han Railway Concession', where the Gare Fluviale (River Station) was located. The Belgians wanted to convert this plot into a formal concession.[80] The question remained unsettled until 1908, when the Belgian claims were formally repudiated.[81]

Beyond the concessions

Beyond the Japanese area the river frontage had been purchased or leased, mainly by Japanese, for about 1000 metres.[82] Then came the railway area, with a bunded frontage of 1100 metres. Next was another kilometre-long area, marked on a 1903 map as 'Foreign Property'. Finally, just before a river inlet known as Seven Mile Creek, came two oil storage depots—Royal Dutch Petroleum and a larger plot belonging to Shell Transport & Trading. Although the formal concessions were the centre of business, in the early 20th century their combined area was only half of the total given over to foreign management.

A concession Wuchang-side

Perhaps impressed by the foreign concessions' well-planned streets and orderly government, the viceroy announced in 1900 that he would establish a general foreign concession Wuchang-side. He realized, despite the vast areas already occupied, that foreigners had difficulty in obtaining land—especially for kerosene and lumber storage and hide-drying. The following year the Wuchang concession opened, complete with its splendid bund, almost as wide as it was long. Foreign residences and offices were allowed there 'under certain rules and conditions',[83] matching the restrictions imposed by the British on Chinese residence in their new extension.

HARMONY AND DISHARMONY IN THE CONCESSIONS

Although the boundaries between each concession were known, the only apparent difference was in policemen's uniforms or an unexpected change in a street name. Borders between concessions were mostly marked by small back alleys; boundaries on wide roads would need international agreements for maintenance and lighting. Each nation built right up to the edge of its concession and to some extent it is still possible to detect where, for example, French buildings stopped and German ones started.

Nationalities were always mixed. In 1897 the British Municipal Council had a Russian member.[84] There was no reason, legal or otherwise, why for example a German should live in the German Concession. Indeed, only about one-third of the 300 Germans in Hankow did live there.[85] Most of them lived in the French Concession; with only 65 French in the whole of Hankow in the late 1890s that concession would have been virtually empty if people had lived along strictly national lines. After the British, Russians were the biggest investors in the

Postcard of the short and stubby Wuchang Bund, 1930s. Source: Zhe Fu, ed., *Late Qing and Early Republic Wuhan Images*, 92.

British Concession even as late as 1913.[86] By 1906, the Hankow Light & Power Co. in the Russian Concession provided electric light to the British and French concessions as well. Melchers' generator extended its services to the Japanese Concession in 1907. By 1911 all concessions were being served by a telephone system managed by the Germans.[87]

This is not to suggest that harmony reigned unchallenged. The Russian Concession included land which had been owned and occupied by British nationals. Their properties were seized and the owners' marker stones removed. In a reversal of the usual benefit, for the foreigner, of extraterritoriality, under Chinese law good title could be claimed after ten years' occupation but not under Russian or British law. Some disgruntled owners fenced off their land, whereupon Russian Cossacks took possession. Britain and Russia only agreed to submit to arbitration when armed British sailors landed from HMS *Woodlark*, creating a stand-off.[88] As for the French, in January 1898 they advertised land in their concession for sale, including lots the ownership of which was claimed by British firms.

Each of the concessions had a different approach to land tenure, even when ownership was undisputed. This became evident at a meeting of British Concession land-renters on 21 July 1920. As in British concessions elsewhere in China, they had been given 99-year leases, due to expire in 1961. The British government considered extending the leases to 999 years, in return for additional rent payable as a percentage of a calculated 1961 valuation. However, French Concession leases were for 999 years automatically, and in the Japanese Concession land grants were freehold. Even in the British Extension leases were for 999 years. Melchers refused a lease in the old British Concession unless it was granted on the same terms as available in the German Concession, namely 999 years. Eventually the British capitulated.[89]

Having parallel yet separate municipal councils encouraged inefficiency, but the system worked well enough, engendering healthy competition among the five nations.

THE PEKING-HANKOW RAILWAY

Every nationality in Hankow celebrated the railway's arrival. Defeat by the Japanese strengthened Chinese realization that they had to take the modernization of their country seriously. On 28 October 1896 an Imperial Edict authorized construction of a railway from Peking to Hankow. German railway engineer Heinrich Hildebrand was commissioned to survey the 1500-kilometre route and a contract was issued on 26 June 1898 for the railway's construction. The principal contractor was a Belgian syndicate, with French backing. Another edict in 1898 authorized raising the necessary finance, and a bond was issued for 112,500,000 French francs via the Banque de Paris et des Pays-Bas.[90] The coupon rate was an attractive five percent and maturity was in 20 years—not the first of China's railway bonds, but the largest so far.

Construction started simultaneously at both ends of the route, at Lukouchiao, outside Peking, and at Hankow; the line was sometimes referred to as the Lu-Han Railway. There was an excited buzz about the prospects for enhanced trade direct with Peking. An army of coolies worked on clearing the land, raising an embankment and laying the track. Progress was about half a kilometre a day, so that by 1902 the Hankow end stretched 550 kilometres north.[91]

When the line opened in 1905 there was a sharp increase in trade in Hankow, which was now connected by rail directly to Europe, although the journey was long and arduous. The Gare Fluviale was the first station to open. Trains started running from there on Christmas Day 1901 to Guangshui, 159 kilometres north on the Henan border.[92] From 1902 there were three trains a week. When the line was fully open the terminus was at the Han River, but the main station for the foreign concessions was just north of the French Concession. The French-designed Hankow Station building of 1903 is still there at the end of Chezhan (Station) Road. It is in beautiful condition and could be mistaken for a church. Adorning its north-east wall is its former French name carved in stone: 'Hank'eou (Ta Tche Men)', with its equivalent in Chinese characters.

The railway was a huge undertaking. A large colonnaded complex housing its administration offices was built in 1920 in the French Concession at 24 rue d'Autremer.[93] Like many of Hankow's old buildings, this has been sensitively restored and current occupants include the local office of China Railways. Initially, the British had the advantage of being next to the Chinese city at the centre of the port's business. Now they feared the railway would draw that centre towards the French Concession. Britain therefore copied Germany and arranged for a spur line to go through its concession to the river's edge, completed in 1920.[94]

In 1906 a line was commissioned to run from Hankow to Canton, the contract awarded to an American syndicate.[95] The turmoil of revolution in 1911 delayed construction for ten years. Completed in stages, this line too had a positive effect on Hankow's trade. Full connection to Canton was not achieved until 1936,[96] just in time to be of great benefit to the Japanese army.[97]

Industrial growth

Early in the 20th century Hankow was described as 'stirring with the certainty of growth'.[98] Two years after the railway was opened the local press listed 84 factories in the three cities,[99] and smoking chimneys were to be seen everywhere; industrialization was being taken seriously.

The foundations of China's first iron and steel plant were laid on 23 December 1890 on a large vacant plot in Hanyang.[100] Supplies of iron ore and coal had been found nearby. Expensive British machinery was acquired,[101] but it took three years for it to be assembled. Then, to their dismay, the plant managers could not get the thing to work. After years of failure and frustration, the viceroy ordered his people to embark on an extensive tour of Europe and North America to see how it should be done. This led to the installation in 1896 of 24 Europeans, mostly Belgians. They found endemic corruption, and inefficiency made worse by a facility partly designed on *fengshui* principles. The Europeans were not allowed to institute the necessary changes.[102] By 1899 there were 16 left and 7 in 1902. The plant may well have been Asia's first, but it was not initially an unalloyed success.

In 1905 it was closed for a complete refit, again at enormous expense.[103] When it reopened the following year, a newly installed team of foreign managers was given the freedom to do their job. Their number grew to 35 by 1911 and they trained local people to take over the running of this huge and, at last, successful facility. Quality was no longer a problem; the plant supplied the rails and iron girders for the new railway's tracks and bridges. Indeed, the plant's new management succeeded in their goal of competing head to head in the American market with the output of Pittsburgh.[104] By 1914 a carriage and wagon works had been added to serve the needs of the railway industry. Five years later the Hanyang Iron & Steel Works was employing 4500 people and was in every sense a triumph.

A major motivation for China's industrializing effort and 70 percent of the capital funding was related to military projects.[105] Thus, closely allied to the iron and steel mill and adjacent to it in Hanyang

The Hanyang Ironworks in 1911, going full pelt. Source: Zhe Fu, ed., *Late Qing and Early Republic Wuhan Images*, 172.

was the Government Arsenal. Construction commenced in 1892. Some of the plant was installed in 1894 after having been stored in an adjacent matshed. The first rifles produced were already obsolete, and could have been purchased cheaper in Germany. However, patriotism was at stake so production went on.[106] But the machinery for making much-needed 50-tonne Krupp cannon had not been installed and was quietly rusting.[107] Other machines that had been set up were lying idle. The German managers were denied authority so were unable to implement required improvements. Furthermore, the products were made with material from next door and so were not initially of sufficient quality. Problems were gradually overcome and the arsenal became an important source of weaponry for China until shortly after the Pacific War.

Cotton goods had become one of the chief imports and China, a major cotton producer, was determined not to rely on foreigners to make the fabric for them. In 1891 cotton mills were built at Wuchang, on flat land immediately upstream from the city. They were designed and fitted out by experts from Britain, at that time the world leader in the industry. Unlike the iron and steel initiative, the cotton mills were an instant success and production started in 1893 under British and Swiss management.

An industry that China was unable for many years to replicate was oil and its related products. American and Russian kerosene was imported in increasing quantities from the early 1880s. Its careless use caused a number of major fires in the crowded Chinese city and the authorities tried to ban it.[108] However, this idea was defeated by the product's sheer convenience. In 1895 the first oil company to establish a presence in Hankow was the Standard Oil Company of New York. They were soon followed by rival Shell, the first to construct a storage facility allowing kerosene to be shipped in bulk. Shell's tanks opened in 1901, well below the concessions, together with a plant to enable kerosene to be tinned on the premises.[109] Standard Oil responded with three large tanks of their own in 1904 at Seven Mile Creek, and still hardly met demand.[110] The Texas Co. joined the market in 1921, ten years later dwarfing all the competition's facilities with a bulk storage facility capable of holding over 15 million litres, and a plant that made its own cans—5000 every day.[111]

Hankow became a major centre of the tobacco industry at the beginning of the 20th century. Although tobacco had long been grown locally, Shanghai-produced American cigarettes were more popular.[112] When the leader in the field, British-American Tobacco (BAT), convinced local farmers to use the better quality American seeds, together with improved methods for curing the leaves, there was nothing to stop cigarettes being made in Hankow.[113] Within a few years, BAT was operating a large factory in the German Concession.[114] Further expansion meant by 1911 the factory was the biggest of its kind in China; the ten million sticks it produced every day were still not enough to meet the demand. An aggressive advertising campaign and an equally enthusiastic sales team kept competitors out of the market. But in 1922 the Nanyang Brothers Tobacco Co. started a rival factory,[115] although they could not catch the leader. BAT's production reached seven billion cigarettes a year in 1931, produced by a workforce of 2800 in two factories.[116]

The Chinese-owned Sui Hua Match Factory was built in the Japanese Concession and by 1908 it was producing half-a-million boxes every day, matching the pace of cigarette production. By 1922 it was the biggest in China, with plans to expand.[117] There were five albumen factories, including the large one operated by Melchers on the German Bund. Ore from nearby mines supplied Hankow's first antimony processing plant in 1899 in Wuchang; the product was an important component in manufacturing matches and small-arms ammunition.[118] China is today by far the largest antimony producer in the world. In the early 20th century, sesame seeds grew to be the second-most important export after tea; in terms of weight it dwarfed tea by a ratio of about nine to one. The Customs Report for 1902–11 stated that sesame-cleaning plants were cropping up 'everywhere' and that the dust they created in the concessions was becoming a problem.[119]

In addition to all these, there were hemp mills, under Japanese management, a number of flour mills, bean-oil crushing plants, paper factories, soap works and a British frozen meat plant.[120] There was also, since 1907, the Yangtze Engineering Works which, from its base at Seven Mile Creek, started to produce steel tugs and lighters, engines and several grades of heavy machinery.[121] During the First World War, the industrial efforts of the sparring nations were almost exclusively focused on the war effort, leaving Wuhan's many factories to benefit even further by supplying the necessities of life that did not involve killing people.

MORE DISTURBANCES AND REVOLUTION

On 23 January 1911 a rickshaw coolie became ill on the street in Hankow's British Concession. The British police took him into the municipal council building, where he died. There were immediate claims by other coolies that the police had kicked him to death, and before long a mob of 3000–4000 attacked the building[122] and the nearby Hongkong & Shanghai Bank. The bank was the British government's chief broker in negotiating the loans China needed for its growing railway network;[123] many of the local population thought the terms of these loans too harsh.[124] The large crowd overwhelmed the municipal police, even when they were supported by the foreign volunteer corps. Urgent help was summoned from British and German gunboats lying in the river.

This mob dispersed, but another twice the size then gathered at the southern edge of the concession. Only when the crowd had grown to an estimated 20,000 to 30,000 and started to attack the Custom House did the *taotai* intervene. His efforts were in vain and he too was attacked. The angry crowd then swept into the British Concession and swarmed the bund. The British officer in charge had hoped fixed bayonets would suffice. When they did not he ordered his troops to fire; 30 to 40 were killed. Order was not restored until 3000 Chinese troops appeared.[125]

The atmosphere remained tense in the months that followed, with anti-foreign feeling extending to the non-Chinese Manchu ruling dynasty. On 10 October 1911 a disturbance inside the military garrison in Wuchang resulted in three soldiers being shot. A number of their sympathizers set fire to the barracks, and fighting broke out between them and imperial loyalists. The British Consul-General sounded the alarm and all able-bodied men in the concessions turned out in response; most were members of the volunteer corps or the fire service. Two British gunboats landed armed sailors, and the senior naval officer present took command. The foreigners built barricades at the entrances to the concessions, using 50-kilogramme bags of sesame seeds and anything else they could find. The imperial troops headed to the railway line, pursued by the rebels, and there was much fighting. The loyalists then managed to confine the rebels to the Chinese city of Hankow. The only way to flush them out was by burning the city, which is what the imperial soldiers did. Almost the entire city was destroyed.

A stalemate ensued, with the imperial troops occupying the left bank of the river, and the rebels the right bank. The foreign concessions were isolated. Telegraph lines had been cut. Only the wireless operators on the gunboats could communicate with the outside world. By 17 October 15 foreign warships were moored opposite the bund, adopting a strict 'observe and report' policy towards unfolding events, even when they themselves were targets. The only reported firing by these ships was when a Russian gunboat arrived and fired a 15-gun salute. This was answered by the British flagship, causing a temporary halt to hostilities while the opposing Chinese factions tried to determine for which side the foreigners had declared.[126] After six weeks 300 soldiers arrived from Hong Kong, later joined by 200 Russians and a regiment of Japanese, whereupon the volunteers were stood down. When it became apparent that this was no longer a local disturbance and the authority of the Manchu emperor had collapsed, there was an armistice between the warring soldiers and the birth of the republic was recognized. Both sides had avoided involving the foreign areas. There was some sniping into the concessions and two foreigners were wounded, but none killed. There had been, of course, an immediate stoppage of all business, but by April 1912 normality was largely restored.[127]

The revolution left the Chinese city of Hankow in ruins. Plans were drawn up to rebuild the city according to a centralized and modern design; Washington was mentioned as a model.[128] Unfortunately, there was insufficient money and gradually new buildings appeared along the same plan as the old city. By 1914, 80 percent of the area had been rebuilt and the 'model city' was quietly forgotten.[129] The city wall, demolished in 1905, was replaced by a wide road.[130] Construction was to be financed by selling adjacent plots of land, but buyers thought the initial prices too high. Gradually land was occupied all the way to the railway embankment half a kilometre away, and the necessary (and expensive) task of raising it above the flood level began. More roads spread westwards beyond the railway.

Meanwhile, the concession area had become an impressive commercial city. Along the riverbank stretched a line of a dozen or more hulks and pontoons. From these in 1914 no fewer than 39 steamers ran regular services to Shanghai.[131] In the 1930s, one of the twelve designated anchorages in the river was reserved for seaplanes.[132] What was happening on land was more impressive still, and much remains. Butterfield & Swire's 1920 four-storey reinforced concrete office building stands at 94 Yanjiang Avenue. Just to the north is the 1922 Custom House, one of the glories of the bund. Built on a spur into the river, this magnificent building enjoys an uninterrupted view along the bund. Clocks face out from all four sides of its 46-metre-high tower, and the chimes of Westminster mark each quarter hour. Further to the north, at No. 139, is the former Yokohama Specie Bank, completed in 1921. No. 140 is the very smart and beautifully preserved four-storey former office building of Alfred Holt & Co. At No. 142 is the five-storey former office of the National City Bank of New York dating from 1920. On the far side of Qingdao Road, at No. 143, is the finest building on the whole bund—the classic structure that was the Hongkong & Shanghai Bank, started in 1917 and finished in 1919. By the 1920s Hankow looked like a version of Shanghai, slightly scaled down.

Tucked in next to the Hongkong & Shanghai Bank building, at No. 144, is the oldest building on the bund. There is no plaque to record its original purpose but it belonged to Panoff, before being acquired by Swires. Beyond the junction with Tianjin Road, the small block now occupied by Nos. 150 and 151 is the site of the British Consulate, which used to mark the northern end of the British Concession. This two-storey statement of British presence stood in a large garden and looked over the bund to the 'Men of War Steps', the official arriving point for distinguished visitors. The main building is long gone, but the former vice-consul's residence, at the western end of the lot, now houses a small club.

The British Bund had become the banking and commercial centre of the foreign concessions, and business was booming. The potentially devastating upheavals of the Sino-Japanese War and the Boxer Rebellion had little effect on Hankow's trade.[133] So it was also to prove with the 1911 revolution; 1912 saw the highest volume of trade on record.[134] The impetus provided by the opening of the railway seemed unstoppable. Living in the concessions were 1350 Europeans and Americans, over 1500 Japanese and almost 28,000 Chinese. Hankow's customs revenue was soon the second-largest of the treaty ports, behind only Shanghai. The combined manufacturing output of the tri-city was also second only to that of Shanghai. Ocean-going ships of 8000–10,000 tonnes

The Butterfield & Swire Building and the Custom House nearing completion, 1923. Photograph by Warren Swire. © Image courtesy of John Swire and Sons Historical Photographs of China, University of Bristol.

The imposing buildings of the National City Bank of New York (left) and the Hongkong & Shanghai Bank (right), taken from HMS *Durban* in 1927. Reprinted with permission by Naval-History.net, courtesy of Chief Yeoman of Signals George Smith, DSM.

could reach Hankow in the high-water season and, apart from being almost 1000 kilometres up a river, the place looked like any other bustling China Coast sea port.

REST AND RECREATION

Alongside the commercial development, social life in early 20th century Hankow was lively. When France claimed the racecourse as part of its new concession, a replacement had to be found. The French offered some compensation and in early 1899 a vast site was acquired to the north-west, beyond the railway line. The Hankow Race Club and Recreation Ground was opened in 1905 and was an instant success. In addition to the race tracks (an inner cinder track and an outer grass one), by the early 1920s it boasted two golf courses, cricket and football fields, twelve tennis courts, a bowling green and a clay-pigeon shooting range.[135] The large swimming pool was not heated, but in the winter it was boarded over and became a sprung-floor ballroom. Within ten years this facility had more than 300 members of all nationalities[136] and was considered to be the best of its kind in China. The extent of the grounds was about 50 percent larger than today's Jiefang Park, the public facility that has taken the old club's place.[137] The only indication of its original activities is a single statue of a horse, standing discreetly near the southern perimeter.

The Race Club enjoyed a loose affiliation with the Hankow Club, referred to as 'the town club', and many were members of both.[138] The town club stood in spacious grounds in Faucheong (Nanjing) Road and was rebuilt at least once after its foundation in 1861, latterly being housed in a splendid two-storey building with open verandahs all round.[139] The club's library deserves a special mention. Rather than simply providing escapism and reminders of home, it grew into one of the most important Far East collections of any library in China, numbering over 3000 volumes. Most of the additions were gifts from members, and some extremely valuable. The University of Hong Kong wisely bought the collection more or less intact in 1932. I have referred to a number of books that used to belong to the Hankow Club when researching my own work, including this volume.

Notwithstanding the international nature of Hankow's main clubs, there were separate clubs for some of the different nationalities. The Russian Club moved into new premises at considerable expense in 1908, and included a hall for presentations by the Russian Amateur Dramatic Club;[140] presumably these were fairly intimate gatherings, being 'all Greek' to the rest of the community. There was from 1899 a Cercle Gaulois for the French and, briefly in the early 1900s, a Cercle Belge. The Japanese had their own club, as did the Germans, but with the demise of the German Concession in 1917 this was converted into a club for officers of the customs service.[141] Golfers were well looked after; in addition to the Race Club courses, there was to the west of the railway station a Hankow Golf Club, founded in 1878 and latterly with a membership of over 100.[142]

POLITICAL TROUBLE

Anti-foreign feelings surfaced again in many parts of China in 1925. There had been strikes in Shanghai in foreign-owned factories and the news travelled swiftly to Hankow. On 23 May there was a strike at the British-American Tobacco factory; three thousand workers walked out, objecting to the introduction of more efficient machines.[143] Another strike broke out the following day at an egg-processing plant, over inadequate wages. Two days later a third strike occurred, at the match factory in the Japanese

Concession. The disputes were soon settled. Then on 3 June there was a report that the 'Wu-Han People's Diplomatic Association' and the 'Association for Hastening the Citizens' Conference' were to mobilize in support of labour agitators and strikers. Over the next few days workers walked out of a number of foreign-owned factories, including the cigarette factory again. This time the strikers were not making any demands of their employers; they were simply following orders. On 6 June, 25,000 students in Wuchang joined in and it became dangerous for foreigners to walk the streets except in the concessions.[144]

Butterfield & Swire (B&S) were to be the focus of the next escalation. In the evening of 10 June there was an argument between two coolies unloading a steamer at the B&S compound, escalating into a mass stone-throwing brawl. The B&S site, south of the British Concession, was beyond British jurisdiction. Chinese police stationed nearby did nothing until an hour had elapsed, by which time restoring order was more challenging. The warring parties patched up their differences, but the following day the mob took control of the extensive B&S facility, as well as the nearby China Navigation Co. vessels. Disconcertingly, like the cigarette workers, they made no demands of B&S—they simply stopped work. Their aims became clearer when they gathered at the southern end of the British Bund, and pelted the Chinese police with stones. When they were about to storm the concession, a contingent of British marines came to the aid of the police, and jointly they forced the crowd back.[145]

In the evening the mob regrouped on the landward boundary of the concession and caused havoc. The police and foreign volunteers combined could not reassert order and a machine gun was turned on the mob, ending the riot and killing four.[146] On 12 June the B&S coolies returned to work as two American destroyers dropped anchor in the river. There were more strikes over the next few days, but slowly things returned to normal. The Chinese police, now anxious to demonstrate their worth, executed a number of Bolsheviks and other undesirables. The British Municipal Council increased the number of Chinese representatives on the council from four to six, and there matters rested temporarily.[147]

However, Hankow was not immune from the turmoil that was sweeping the country. In 1926 the combined Nationalist and Communist forces of Chiang Kai-shek occupied Hanyang and the Chinese city of Hankow. Wuchang held out for another month, thanks to its ancient but still excellent walls.[148] Refugees flooded into the concessions, and sailors from the foreign gunboats had to ensure order. Men with machine guns were posted outside the Hongkong & Shanghai Bank and a sandbagged redoubt was erected at the entrance to the Custom House.[149] Chiang's forces consolidated their position by declaring Hankow to be their capital in November, in place of remote Canton, where their struggle had begun.[150]

Everyone knew that the Nationalists were determined to abolish the treaty port system and take back the concessions. Their chief advisers, the Russians, were paragons in this regard, having already relinquished their Hankow and Tientsin concessions. Inevitably, commercial activity almost came to a standstill as railway rolling stock was commandeered for troop movements. Emboldened by their success, the Nationalist government sought unilaterally to impose on what little foreign trade was continuing rates of duty higher than those provided for by treaty, demonstrating that the treaties already meant nothing to them. It looked as though open conflict between China and the Treaty Powers was inevitable. Wishing to avoid this, on 18 December Britain issued

British landing party, prepared to protect the concession, 1925. Source: Angus Konstam, *Yangtze River Gunboats 1900–49*, 38. Reprint with permission by Osprey Publishing.

a memorandum to the other powers, inviting them to open negotiations with the Chinese as soon as China had a government with any degree of authority over the country as a whole.[151]

The leftist elements that were now increasingly in control of 'Red Hankow' had no patience for such diplomatic scheming. The revolutionary spirit was strong and there were daily parades and demonstrations. On 4 January 1927 a crowd attempted to rush into the British Concession, demanding the immediate departure of its foreign occupants.[152] The Royal Marines, already in position with fixed bayonets, took charge of the situation and a stand-off ensued. The Chinese had an ally in the Yangtze; it was low-water season and the larger foreign gunboats had had to withdraw downstream. Foreign banks and businesses closed and all foreign women and children were advised to leave by whatever means they could. The Europeans and Americans who remained were herded into the Asiatic Petroleum Co. building on the bund.[153] This was considered capable of being defended, and had an escape route to the river just across the road. The following day the mob returned. The British had repeatedly asked for Chinese troops to help control the crowd, but to no avail. The Nationalists had already pre-empted the outcome and established a Committee of Administration for the concessions. Towards the evening of 5 January an offer was made to the besieged British: if the Royal Marines were returned to their ships, and if the Hankow Volunteers were disbanded, then Chinese troops would enter the concession and take responsibility for its protection. Rather than risk the consequences of a shot being fired, the offer was accepted.[154]

The immediate crisis being thus resolved, attention turned to the longer-term question of the existence of the British Concession. The British government had to accept the inevitable, and withdraw with as much dignity as possible. Even though the British mercantile community was becoming tired of the regularly staged anti-British demonstrations,[155] there was a high degree of resentment about the management of recent events. They had witnessed the ignominy of seeing members of their volunteer corps disarmed by the Royal Marines.[156] They also asked why there were fewer Royal Navy ships in this time of crisis than there had been a year ago.[157] British Consul-General Herbert Goffe was instructed to open negotiations with the experienced Eugene Chen Yujen, the Foreign Minister of the Nationalist government and leader of the left-wing element.[158] However, in view of the potentially far-reaching consequences— the British Concessions at Kiukiang (Jiujiang) and Wuhu had also been overrun—on 11 January[159] Sir Miles Lampson, the British Minister in Peking, sent Owen O'Malley to be his personal representative in Hankow and lead the British side.[160]

Given the tension that prevailed, there was a great deal of pressure on the negotiators to reach an understanding—more so on the British side as their case was weak. On 27 January[161] O'Malley was instructed to issue a memorandum to the rival Chinese governments in Peking and Hankow, stating that Britain would be prepared to accept the application of Chinese law to British subjects in China, provided a satisfactory resolution was reached for the Hankow and Kiukiang concessions.[162] This conciliatory measure then paved the way for continued discussions. What has since been referred to as the Chen–O'Malley Agreement was signed on 19 February 1927. News of the accord was greeted with loud cheers from the safe distance of the House of Commons in London.[163] It provided for the immediate handover of the British Concession to the Chinese, which would become known as Special Administrative District No. 3.

Now only the French and Japanese concessions remained. Chen assured France and Japan that while there was no plan to resume their areas, it had to be recognized that there had been no plan to take back the British Concession—it was a spontaneous act by the Chinese people.[164] The Treaty Powers accordingly started to boost their naval presence at Hankow, just in case. By late April there were 35 warships moored alongside the bund in a line that stretched for over two kilometres: eleven of them were British, ten Japanese, nine American, three French and two Italian.[165] The Japanese in addition armed their remaining 800 male residents, determined to defend their concession if needed.[166]

The delicate task of extricating the British from their comfortable concession had been achieved relatively peacefully. Militants in Chiang's team complained that things were being made too easy for the foreigners and demanded more robust action, but Chiang wanted business to resume and knew for that he needed the foreigners. Without being officially in charge of the country, he still managed to direct some of the vital customs revenue towards Kuomintang coffers.

Under new management

Apart from hurt pride, the rendition of their concession was not a great loss to the British, who recognized the impracticality of maintaining concessions in the Yangtze ports.[167] Business had been brought to a standstill by the events of 1927 but trade figures for 1928 were surprisingly good.[168] Foreigners were not subjected to any Chinese taxation other than normal ground rent; rates charged by the new municipal council were strictly to meet the expenditure incurred within the concession area. The four largest British firms were based outside the concession and most British people lived in either the former German or Russian concessions.[169] Nor did the change mean the end of Hankow as a treaty port; none of the foreign powers wanted to abandon the treaty port system until China had a legal system that was free from arbitrary interference.[170] Hankow, with its bund and strong foreign presence, was still the commercial centre of Wuhan.

The new municipality that was now running the former British Concession was required to have three British and three Chinese councillors, under a Chinese director. The British had seen representation as a right, not a special concession, and some found it hard to adjust.[171] Even so, the director rarely took any major decisions without consulting British advisers.[172] More adjustment was necessary when tension grew between China and Japan in the early 1930s. The murder of a Japanese consular policeman inside the Japanese Concession on 21 September 1936 prompted swift retaliatory action. Two Japanese destroyers were dispatched from Shanghai, bearing a large contingent of marines as a 'permanent landing party'.[173] These were to join the five Japanese warships and 300 marines already in the port.[174] Naturally, the entire foreign community of Hankow was alarmed by these events. Later in the month it was announced that all non-military Japanese were to quit Hankow for Shanghai.[175] A rumour that the British were to follow suit was quickly denied.[176]

Japan embarked on a full-scale invasion of China in July 1937. Although the invaders initially concentrated their attention nearer the mouth of the Yangtze, Hankow was not unaffected. On 16 July the Japanese Concession was surrounded by a force of 3000 Chinese troops, facing the Japanese marines on the opposite side of the street, but no further action was taken.[177] In August all Japanese civilians left for Shanghai, leaving only the military and able-bodied men who had been drafted to help defend the concession. The Japanese Consul departed, expressing the naive hope that Japanese property in Hankow would be adequately protected.[178] The many Japanese shops had been closed for some time because of the impossibility of doing any business.[179] Japanese advances in the east meant Hankow was again virtually cut off from the outside world. As only Japanese steamers could safely navigate the lower stretches of the river, people could only travel to and from Hankow at the whim of the Japanese.

By 11 August all the Japanese had left, including the marines. The 60 Chinese policemen given

Postcard of rooftop view of the bund in the 1930s. Source: Zhe Fu, ed., *Late Qing and Early Republic Wuhan Images*, 76.

the task of protecting the concession saw evidence everywhere of extremely hasty departure.[180] Later that month the aerial bombing started.[181] Initially doing little damage, raids by Japanese aircraft became more regular and effective during September and October. The efforts by the Chinese air force to repulse the Japanese were strengthened when six volunteer American pilots joined them, as did a dozen Russians.[182] The stakes increased significantly for all parties when on 1 December Hankow once more became the capital of China, so as to be safer from more concentrated Japanese attacks in the east.[183] Chinese refugees flooded in, and many in the foreign community tried to leave. Four days before Christmas 1937, the British cruiser HMS *Capetown* sailed from Hankow for Shanghai with 1 man, 21 women and 26 children. Other Europeans tried to escape by train to Canton; four arrived on 7 October, dodging many Japanese attacks along the way and travelling the last 100 kilometres in a chartered car.[184]

Many foreigners remained and had no intention of leaving. Indeed, some aspects of expatriate life carried on as if nothing untoward was happening. The bars and other nocturnal establishments were still busy. For the more sedate, the Race and Recreation Club was also in full swing.[185] Then, in June 1938, at a time when *The China Mail* was carrying an advertisement for 'Fast and Comfortable Daily Air Services between Hong Kong & Chungking via Hankow',[186] the Chinese government announced that it was evacuating itself to Chungking (Chongqing). All the panoply of government was moved, along with all non-combatant staff, and most of Hankow's railway and industrial assets were destroyed as part of a 'scorched earth' policy.[187]

The exodus was not a moment too soon. On 10 June it was reported that the Japanese navy had gathered 60 warships at Anking (Anqing) for an advance up the Yangtze.[188] On 13 July, with the fleet still battling against the flooding river, Japanese aircraft bombed Wuchang, leaving many dead.[189] The day before, the British Ambassador to China instructed all British Consuls not to evacuate 'unless it is absolutely essential'. He feared that it would be much harder for the British to return once they had left, and that their property would be looted as soon as they departed. He told the British in Hankow to shelter in the Hongkong Bank and Asiatic Petroleum buildings, secure in the knowledge that a gunboat of the Royal Navy was standing by.[190]

Two hundred additional British marines had been brought in from Hong Kong, and they paraded on the bund at 6:00 a.m. on 19 August[191] but already the Chinese part of Hankow was under heavy aerial attack.[192] The air raids increased in intensity over the following two months and on 25 October, an advance party of two Japanese motorboats carrying 20 marines drew alongside the Japanese Concession.[193] While their buildings elsewhere in the concession area had been saved through the intervention of the foreigners living there, the Japanese found that the majority of those in their own concession had been destroyed. On 13 August the Chinese municipal authorities had taken formal repossession of the Japanese Concession, calling it Special Administrative District No. 4,[194] but just over two months later it was back under the control of its former tenants.

There were mixed feelings about the return of the Japanese. At least, the suspense was over and there was considerable relief among the foreign population that the Japanese had retaken their concession without firing a shot, ignoring for a moment the heavy bombing. Everybody recognized that things were not going to be as they were. In SAD No. 3 the Royal Marines were in charge. After assessing the situation for six days the Marines recognized the inevitable and, despite the strong protestations of the British community, handed control to the Japanese forces.[195] Immediately there were cases of foreigners being stopped and searched by Japanese patrols.[196]

Taking stock of their position, the Japanese carried out a census of the foreign population. There were 1163 people from 30 different countries. The biggest group were the British with 279, followed by White Russians, Americans, French, Italians, Germans and others. The total included 236 missionaries, 20 female dancers and 15 White Russian musicians.[197] All had seen 'normality' crumble and faced humiliation and danger. Some, inevitably, were soon to lose their lives. In 1941, the Hong Kong–incorporated Hankow Club was put into liquidation; an era had ended.

Further reading: Archer, *Hankow Return*; Johnston and Erh, *Far from Home*; Lee, *China's Recovery*; Rowe, *Hankow: Commerce and Society*; Salkeld, 'Witness to the Revolution'; Tolley, *Yangtze Patrol*; Zhe, *Wuhan Images*.

HARBIN (HARBIN) 哈爾濱

Heilongjiang, 45.47° N, 126.39° E
Open City, 1905 Japanese Treaty

When Russia's expanding empire reached Manchuria in the 17th century, it diverted northwards to avoid encroaching on Chinese territory. Such niceties were not to last. Taking advantage of China's various troubles in the mid-19th century, Russia entered into two treaties, in 1858[1] and 1860,[2] which, by appropriating Chinese land, extended Russian territory to the Pacific seaboard and the new port of Vladivostok. Russia was keen to consolidate its hold on this remote outpost by linking it directly to St. Petersburg by railway. In 1891 work began simultaneously at both ends of the largest railway project in the world, almost 10,000 kilometres long. The line would have been even longer had not Russia exercised a diplomatic sleight of hand at China's expense.

Russia had been one of the three powers that persuaded Japan to give up the territory it had won from China in the 1894–95 war. To cement the 'friendly relations' that now existed, Viceroy Li Hongzhang was in 1896 coerced into agreeing a secret 'mutual defence' treaty with Russia. Each party agreed to come to the other's aid in the event of a Japanese attack. Of course, insisted the Russians, such help would be much easier to provide if their railway could cut straight through Manchuria. China agreed, thereby granting a double benefit to Russia: not only were the Russians able to shorten their railway by 1000 kilometres, but they also obtained a foothold in China without having to fight for it. In due course Russian engineers erected a steel bridge across the Sungari (Songhua) River in the middle of nowhere. In less than a generation the place became the modern metropolis of Harbin.[3]

The 1896 treaty gave rise to the Chinese Eastern Railway Co. (CER) to manage the railway's construction and operation. Two years later Russia leased the Liaodong Peninsula. The deal included the right to build a branch line from Harbin south to Port Arthur (Lüshun). The agreement also stated that the railway concession would never serve as a pretext for the Russians to seize Chinese territory.[4] They did not need to, as in the contract for the building of the railway China undertook to hand over to the CER all the land necessary for the line's construction and operation, and to grant the company the absolute and exclusive right to administer that land for the next 80 years.[5]

This entity was unique among the foreign settlements in China. The whole length of the railway line was effectively leased to Russia, together with as much land on either side of the track as Russia deemed 'necessary'. Included in the lease was Harbin, a new town with no indigenous population. By 1901, when the main railway construction was complete, there was a Russian population of 12,000. By 1903, when the line opened for regular traffic, this had increased to 35,000.[6] Not all the Russians were merchants, but there was much business to be done. The vast Manchurian plain was rich in agriculture, especially in beans and wheat. The stage was set for Harbin to become a Russian commercial centre for the whole of northern Manchuria.

The Boxer Rebellion enabled Russia to tighten its grip on Manchuria in general and Harbin in particular. In contravention of the terms of the Peace Protocol, Russia kept large numbers of troops in Manchuria long after the rebels had been defeated. The other powers were concerned about a possible Russian annexation. In an attempt to maintain the 'open door', America demanded the creation of at least two treaty ports in the region, Harbin being one of them.[7] The Russians said that they did not oppose the opening of selected Manchurian towns, but Harbin could not be included; situated in the railway zone, it was not China's to concede.[8] The United States settled for Mukden (Shenyang) and Antung (Dandong) instead,[9] but the matter was not resolved.

After Japan defeated Russia in the war of 1904–5, a post-war agreement with China required the opening of Harbin to international residence and trade, along with 15 Manchurian towns.[10*] Russia still controlled northern Manchuria, but Japan became master of the south. The CER branch line south of Changchun was handed over to Japan, becoming the South Manchuria Railway. The CER remained firmly in Russian hands, with Harbin as its headquarters. During the conflict the city had grown as a supply base and military mustering point. Already by 1905 there were 'old' and 'new' towns.[11] The former was the Pristan (Daoli), the wharf area, the latter was around the railway station. A small Chinese town also appeared.[12] In 1906 there were 200,000 Russian soldiers in Harbin, unconvincingly claiming a lack of transport to take them home;[13] it was their railway that had brought them there. The number shrank to 28,000 later in the year, renamed 'railway guards'.[14]

Not quite Paris

A Custom House opened on 1 July 1907,[15] followed by the consulates of Russia, America and Britain.[16] Factories of a non-railway nature began to appear, all related to agriculture—sawmills, flour mills, bean-crushing plants[17] and, naturally, vodka distilleries. Land in the railway zone was leased by the Russian government, but only to Russians or Chinese, making things difficult for other foreigners.[18] Most businesses were, inevitably, Russian, but there were also some British, German and Japanese firms, including many familiar treaty port names.[19] Commercial and residential properties appeared in large numbers, along with dozens of Russian Orthodox and other churches. Many of these buildings from the early 20th century remain, giving modern Harbin a very Russian character. The Russians wanted to create a new St. Petersburg, and in some ways they did, winning grudging admiration from visitors.[20] The city was later dubbed 'The Paris of the Far East', although Peter Fleming, visiting in 1933, wrote that anyone who had stayed there would not have bestowed this title.[21]

Harbin was dominated by the CER, which had become more of a colonial administration than a railway operator.[22] The area of the city under the company's direct control was vast, including housing, hospitals, hotels, schools, a daily newspaper[23] and the city's telephone exchange.[24] The company operated three river steamers, and 20 tugs for towing lighters.[25] In 1914 it undertook a large reclamation project, creating a new dock at Fujiadian which soon attracted customs and shipping operations. The company provided a railway police force, with a reach as far as that of the track. The whole operation was underwritten by the Russian government and was not expected to make a profit, which was perhaps as well.[26]

Controversial municipal government

It was inevitable, however, that the Russians would seek to charge Harbin residents and businesses for the many benefits provided by the CER. To do this a structure was needed. In May 1909 Russia and China agreed to the establishment of municipal bodies in Harbin and all 'commercial centres of importance' along the railway line.[27] A Harbin town council was formed with members elected by landowners. Yet many foreigners, including the Germans and British, did not recognize the council's right to tax non-Russian residents.[28] This was not finally resolved until late 1914.[29] In fairness, the Russian municipal authority was doing a good job. The attractive city was soon boasting nearly 30 hectares of public parks and gardens.[30]

Firmly under Russian control, Harbin was not affected by the 1911 revolution.[31] However, the effects of the 1914–18 war were felt. Germans were the third-largest foreign population in the city after Russians and Japanese,[32] and their numerous

---

* See entry on Japanese Stations in the North-East for the others.

businesses closed. Worse came when Russia mobilized and the railway was only available for troop movements.[33] The city's fortunes changed again when the Russian Revolution of 1917 brought an influx of 'White Russians' (Tsarist loyalists), bringing skills, money and a willingness to work hard. Harbin became larger than any Russian city within a radius of 1000 kilometres.[34] Rapid growth and inter-factional Russian conflict caused a breakdown in law and order.[35] The consular body met with the Russian director-general of the CER and announced that, if order was not restored, they would bring in troops. The Chinese responded by sending a force of their own. There was fighting between them and 1500 Soviet Russians.[36] When the Russians surrendered on 27 December 1917, peace was restored and Harbin found itself increasingly under Chinese control.[37] Meanwhile in Moscow a furious Leon Trotsky rather impotently ordered the arrest of the entire Russian administration of Harbin for allowing 'foreign' troops into the city.[38]

Other effects of the Russian Revolution left Harbin untouched. For example, in 1918 the concept of the 'workers' paradise' was redefined when railway employees struck for more pay. The CER told them that they would continue to accept the same pay, otherwise they would be shot.[39] For the upper strata of society life was much more agreeable. Tourists started to include Harbin on their itineraries. Social life rivalled Shanghai's. Business hours were from 8:00 a.m. until 3:00 p.m., leaving much of the day solely for enjoyment.[40] There were 64 hotels, 13 clubs, and 12 theatres and 'picture palaces'.[41] The British consular service found Harbin to be the most expensive posting in the Far East, thanks to the Russians' love of banqueting and drinking.[42]

By 1921 Harbin's foreign population included 70,000 Russians, 3500 Japanese and Koreans, and 400 of other nationalities. Beans and their products remained the dominant business. In 1912 there had been two major bean-oil plants; ten years later there were 40, spurred on by the European demand for soap, candles and paint. The CER built new docks and there was extensive reclamation of the riverfront.[43]

The overly grand British Consulate in 1911, supporting Harbin's reputation as 'the most expensive posting in the Far East'. Reprinted with permission by the National Archives.

The railway company remained a major force in the city, but was undergoing transformation. In the aftermath of the revolution, Russian railways had fallen into a state of dilapidation. In 1919 the Soviet government invited a number of foreign powers to assist in the railway's restoration. The result was the Inter-Allied Railway Committee, comprising Britain, China, France, Japan, Russia and the United States. This body took over the Trans-Siberian and CER lines, with the object of making them commercially viable. Ironically, the new socialist masters' pursuit of profit meant a reduction in the philanthropic and social aspects. A cleaner and more efficient CER passed back into Sino-Soviet control in 1924.[44]

This transfer was part of the brief honeymoon period in Soviet-Chinese relations. Two years later Chiang Kai-shek dismissed his Russian 'advisers'. One effect in Harbin was the abolition of the Russian Municipal Council, which was replaced by a Chinese self-governing body.[45] Chiang continued to flex his new-found Nationalist muscle. Noting that the Japanese in South Manchuria appeared too strong, he decided to challenge the Russians in the north. In a sudden move, he ejected the Russians from the CER. To his surprise, Moscow reacted swiftly, sending troops with an ultimatum for restoration of the *status quo ante*. The Chinese backed down.[46] They were equally powerless when the Japanese marched in and took the city in February 1932. The Western press was more concerned with events in Shanghai and Harbin's occupation was hardly noticed in the outside world.[47]

Further reading: Bard, *Light and Shade*; Carter, *Creating a Chinese Harbin*; Johnston and Erh, *Far from Home*; Latané, *Our Relations with Japan*; Putnam Weale, *Manchu and Muscovite*; South Manchuria Railway: *Manchuria: Land of Opportunities*.

Hokow (Hekou) 河口

Yunnan, 22.30° N, 103.57° E
Treaty Port, 1896 French Treaty

French territorial aggression in 1885 resulted in a number of treaties and conventions. One such, in 1887, opened the Red River town of Manhao as a treaty port.[1]* Another convention in 1896 exchanged Manhao for Hokow,[2] where a French Vice-Consulate was opened in August 1896 and a customs station the following July. Hokow was picturesque but as a place of foreign commerce very short-lived.[3]

Situated opposite the French Tonkin town of Laokai, Hokow facilitated supervision of the extension of the Annam railway into China, and curbed the 'river pirates' who opposed French ambitions in the region;[4] the French referred to any rebel as a 'pirate'.[5] They were quelled in 1898 by being converted into regiments of Chinese soldiers, obviating the need for a consul.[6] Railway construction brought a brief period of activity, and one or two French merchants.[7] But when it was finished in 1908 there was nothing left to do. The vice-consul remained into the 1930s, processing passports for French nationals travelling into China.[8] The last remaining foreign resident was a customs man, in post until 1934.[9]

---

* See entry on Mengtse for further details.

Hong Kong (Xianggang) 香港

Hong Kong SAR, 22.16° N, 114.09° E
Colony, 1842 British Treaty

Known to European sailors since at least the late 18th century, Hong Kong's main attraction was its sheltered deep-water harbour. Contemporary maps indicate there was no certainty that Hong Kong was an island. Lord Amherst's mission in 1816 visited only the south coast, taking on fresh water from the waterfall that is today next to the Wah Fu housing estate. By 1829 the East India Company was interested in the harbour's potential as a refuge for its operations.[1] Five years later Lord Napier suggested that Britain take possession of Hong Kong as a less restrictive base for mercantile activity in comparison with Canton (Guangzhou).[2] In 1837, anticipating this possibility, European and American opium hulks were moved away from Lintin (Neilingding) Island towards Hong Kong—initially to Capsuimoon (Ma Wan) and later the harbour proper. Then in 1839, at the outbreak of the First Opium War, the entire British community from Canton, having been refused permission to sojourn at Macao, sailed their ships to Hong Kong's harbour to await developments. Trade, including opium, continued during the conflict, largely thanks to intermediary services provided by the Americans. Some forays were made onto the Kowloon Peninsula, but the British were otherwise confined to their fleet.

British occupation

Hong Kong was ceded to Britain in the 1842 Treaty of Nanking (Nanjing). British sailors and officials, led by Captain Charles Elliot, had already landed on the island on 25 January 1841, claiming formal possession the following day; Elliot had been offered either the island or Kowloon—but not both.³ Possession Street in Sheung Wan supposedly marks the place where they came ashore, although the Union Jack was probably raised inland at what is today Hollywood Road Park, then a rocky outcrop. Occupation was initially a negotiating tactic by Britain; it was not intended that the island be retained. But Sir Henry Pottinger, having taken over from Elliot, believed its possession was both necessary and desirable as a base for British operations in China, in particular because of the ongoing military activities further north.⁴

Elliot had declared Hong Kong to be a duty-free port and Pottinger reaffirmed that status, initially a hollow gesture. Hong Kong's small population had no need of imports, and the island had little to export. Britain intended to use Hong Kong as a base from which it could promote and protect the trade that was expected to develop in the five treaty ports. That trade came far short of expectations, leaving Britain to wonder whether it really needed Hong Kong. The colony was widely believed to have no commercial value of its own, although it did have the advantage of being unquestionably under British control. The challenge was how to convert that advantage into tangible results when the colony was itself dependent upon the success of the treaty ports.

There was some fertile soil on the island, but little flat land. Fresh water was scarce. A settled population of 3000–4000, scattered among 20 or so villages, was engaged mainly in fishing, farming and quarrying.⁵ Nevertheless, Pottinger confidently declared that within six months the new colony would become a 'vast emporium of commerce and wealth'; a correct prediction but wrong timing. After an initial spurt of interest, as shown for example with the first land auction in August 1841, most foreign merchants returned to the familiar, if uncomfortable, environment of Canton.⁶ Yet even while Britain and China were still at war, there was an influx of Chinese to Hong Kong. By the end of 1841 the population had soared to 15,000.⁷ Some were small-time entrepreneurs who had profited from supplying the British forces, and therefore needed to escape China. But the majority were unemployed labourers, driven from home by economic hardship. This transient mass of people was to prove both a boon and a headache for the young colony.

As a demonstration of intent, in early 1842 Pottinger removed the Superintendency of Trade from Lintin Island to Hong Kong. Jardines, who had started building in Hong Kong, responded by moving their headquarters from Macao. Appreciating the increased security of operating from a British colony, Dents and others soon followed.⁸ Opium was the main business of these firms in the early years. Even though the drug had been one of the causes of the war, the Treaty of Nanking made no mention of it. Hong Kong became the distribution centre for all the opium being brought into China. Accustomed to palatial living in their Canton factories and Macao mansions, the wealthy *taipan*s built 'magnificent pretentious homes . . . usually the size of the average Florentine palace'.⁹

If trade in other items remained disappointing, Hong Kong and its magnificent harbour grew as intended to be the service centre for the fledgling treaty ports, particularly those in the south of China. Shipping and its support industries were the first to develop—building, repairing, fitting out and supplying vessels. In 1844 it was recorded that 538 ships visited Hong Kong.¹⁰ Within the protection of British jurisdiction and military defence, the colony

East Point, Hong Kong, with the godowns and offices of Jardine Matheson, c. 1845. Pencil, by unknown British artist. Courtesy of Martyn Gregory Gallery, London.

became the headquarters for firms operating in the other ports.

As the base of Britain's chief representative in China, Hong Kong was the conduit through which official dialogue between the two empires took place. However, its geographical location made such communication inconvenient, and the Hong Kong governor's dual and occasionally conflicting roles of promoting both the colony and the treaty ports was consequently challenging. The problem was not resolved until the Second Opium War. In 1859 the Superintendency of British Trade was moved to Shanghai,[11] and from 1860 there was a British Minister in Peking (Beijing). Thus Hong Kong's diplomatic role was removed, enabling its rulers to concentrate solely on the development of the colony.

The development of a Chinese city

Hong Kong's birth as a colony witnessed one misfortune after another—typhoons, dysentery, fires and fever. Furthermore, given the doubts over whether or not Hong Kong was to be a permanent British possession, it is not surprising that the initial development of the new town was far from satisfactory. The site for Queen's Town (later renamed Victoria by Pottinger)[12] was chosen on the north-west shore of the island, a place where the steep hillside met the sea, with only the narrowest margin of sloping beach between the two. It was not anticipated that there would be much demand for land. To this confined area came three groups of people, each with conflicting requirements: the British military, wanting space for accommodation, parade grounds and docks; foreign merchants, requiring waterfront sites with private access to the sea; and Chinese immigrants, needing work and shelter. Competition between these three groups was to define the physical development of the city for the remainder of the century.

The British military were, naturally, in a position to get what they wanted. The Royal Navy took the area now known as Tamar. The army barracks were placed just inland in what has become Hong Kong Park. In later years, with neither party willing to move, the narrow road between the two, today's Queensway, became a major bottleneck, restricting access from Victoria to the east. The government offered to buy out the military in 1921, but the price demanded was too high;[13] only in the early 21st century was the congestion properly addressed. London's instructions that there should be no permanent structures other than military arrived too late. The land sale in 1841 saw almost all the available lots taken up by British, American, Indian and Parsee firms, and buildings started to appear in a line stretching along the harbour front. Further auctions in 1844 and 1847 consolidated the merchants' hold on the area. The only break was a lot commandeered by the government for Central Market (still occupying its 1841 site).

The merchants built their 'Florentine palaces' on the hillside above, with private paths leading up to them.[14] Their business premises were bounded on the landward side by Queen's Road. However, lack of foresight and rivalry between the merchants meant there were only one or two lanes connecting this road to the sea, another problem that was to challenge the city's planners for many decades. Perhaps the thinking had been based on a Canton precedent, where all that was needed was a waterside stronghold from which business could be done. Expansion in the tightly packed commercial area could only be seawards. The resulting piecemeal reclamations made the waterfront messy, dangerous and increasingly unhealthy.

Then there was the third group of people, by far the largest. The 1843 Supplementary Treaty of the Bogue provided that all Chinese 'shall be at full and perfect liberty' to come to Hong Kong for business.[15] In fact, all were welcomed whether for business or not. No restrictions were imposed even when, in 1949, there was further mass immigration; a quota was introduced only in 1950.[16] Initially almost all the arrivals were men, coming to Hong Kong looking for work. With the building and road-laying projects that were now at hand, there was much work to be done. Wages were very low. These men were willing to live in the most basic housing and suffer appalling conditions to maximize the money they could send back to their families. Others, more fortunate, profited by charging them for the privilege. Inevitably, disease and crime were rampant. Their perceived 'needs' also presented a business opportunity. By 1844 in the Chinese area there were 8 gambling houses, 20 opium dens and 31 brothels.[17]

Faced with such an influx, the government had to move fast. In 1843 Pottinger laid out a proper network of streets south of Queen's Road, the area becoming known as Taipingshan. What is now core Central, to the east of Pottinger Street, was cleared of its shabby squatter houses and effectively reserved for European use; the Chinese were moved into the new area. By 1847 all the lots between Queen's Road and Caine Road had been sold. Three years later they had all been built upon, mainly with wooden tenement houses. No wheeled vehicles were anticipated, and so the streets were very narrow and steep, in many cases stepped.[18] Their presence today gives the city yet another planning problem, but also much charm.

A major fire in 1851 allowed for reassessment and more redevelopment, this time with a stretch of proper sea wall at Bonham Strand. Yet the continued flood of immigrants from Guangdong meant that the government was always in the position of trying to catch up, never able to plan ahead.[19] In 1848 the population had reached 22,000. A year later it was 28,000. The growth of Hong Kong and the treaty ports, albeit initially slow, was taking business away from Canton and putting people out of work, particularly those in the carrying trade.[20]

With the outbreak of the Taiping Rebellion in 1851, Hong Kong's apparent stability and prosperity attracted yet more male migrant labourers, fleeing the chaos. However, given the threat to their livelihoods that the rebellion posed to Chinese businessmen in Guangdong, a number relocated to the British colony. They were of a different class from the existing population, although some of the latter were accruing wealth through various business activities.[21] In addition to tenements, shop-houses started to appear. More land was made available in Sai Ying Pun, to the west of Taipingshan, where the streets were wider and better laid out.[22] The Chinese population of Hong Kong almost doubled in the two years to 1855, when it reached 72,000.[23]

The abolition of slavery by the British Empire in 1833 coincided with phenomenal growth in the plantation colonies of America, the West Indies and South-East Asia. Then gold was discovered in California in the late 1840s and in Australia soon afterwards. Rumours abounded of the rich pickings to be had. Workers were needed for the necessary, back-breaking labour to make the various ventures successful. Tens of thousands of labourers from Guangdong and Fujian saw golden opportunities, and Hong Kong became one of the most important ports from which these fortune-seekers departed. Chinese businesses based in Hong Kong developed in order to meet the needs of these travellers: transitory housing while they awaited shipment; transporting them back and forth to California and Australia; and servicing their needs while abroad. These were many and various, including food (particularly rice) and other necessities, opium, repatriation of the dead, remittance services and the provision of female company.[24]

Whereas the labouring masses tended to group together based on the dialect they spoke or their village, the increasing number of Chinese merchants forged associations based on the nature of their business. The Nam Yeung Hong dealt mainly with the Chinese diaspora in South-East Asia. The Kam Shan Hong supplied those in California, while the Nam Pak Hong acted as a general 'south and north' conduit for China's imports and exports.[25] The benefit to Hong Kong of all this activity was immense. It turned

Taipingshan, late 1860s/early 1870s. Courtesy of Ko Tim-keung.

attention eastwards, across the Pacific, away from the traditional focus on India and Europe. Hong Kong became an oceanic trade centre, with a growing shipping fleet to prove it.[26]

Coupled with this new mercantile activity was the emergence of a Chinese elite within the colony. Unlike the treaty ports, Hong Kong had had no commercial institutions or hierarchies when the British arrived,[27] providing an opportunity to achieve social standing through individual effort. Rigid British attitudes concerning class and race meant that there was never a 'level playing field' in Hong Kong, but some Chinese entrepreneurs managed to advance themselves and their families and gain recognition from the colonialists for their achievements.[28]

THE EMERGENCE OF A CHINESE ELITE

Sir John Bowring was appointed governor in 1854. Some argue that his jingoistic response in 1856 to events in Canton, where he had been consul for five years, led to the Second Opium War. Although in Hong Kong there was no co-ordinated uprising among the Chinese, foreigners' supplies were largely cut off, placards appeared in the streets and there were a number of acts of terrorism. The most notorious was an alleged attempt by a Chinese baker to poison the entire foreign community with bread laced with arsenic. It was followed by an 'order' from the Guangdong authorities for all Chinese to leave the colony. China discouraged its people from leaving the country and regarded any that did as traitors. Hong Kong's Chinese were placed in a difficult position, torn between different allegiances. The majority had families in China; rather than risk reprisals, 20,000 obeyed.[29]

Once peace had been restored, together with the 20,000 returnees and normal trading conditions, Hong Kong continued on its path of growth. The additional eleven treaty ports created by the postwar treaties did not threaten Hong Kong as some had feared. On the contrary, Hong Kong gained an important asset as a result of the war—the Kowloon Peninsula. There had always been concerns that, although British Hong Kong specifically included the harbour, it was impossible to control or defend it; potentially enemy territory started at the Tsim Sha Tsui shoreline. British and Americans began building in Kowloon in the 1840s, until stopped by Governor Davis.[30] Now the peninsula was British. Initially leased in perpetuity from China, the 1860 Convention of Peking ceded Kowloon to Britain absolutely. A proposal that Kowloon be cleared of Chinese and kept purely for European settlement was not pursued.[31]

With the acquisition of Kowloon the Chinese population of the colony increased to 119,000 in 1861.[32] The new area of Sai Ying Pun was completely built upon by 1865,[33] yet the demand for housing increased and rents rose. The streets had by now assumed the teeming and crowded appearance that is associated with early Hong Kong.[34] Meanwhile European residences were spreading further up the hill; Robinson Road was built in 1861 and soon became lined with attractive mansions.[35] The challenge for the colonial government was to continue to attract 'the better class' of Chinese to come and settle, while at the same time controlling the masses.[36]

The initial dialect-driven groupings began to give way to neighbourhood associations (*kai fong*) and temple committees. These bodies influenced public order and constituted a rudimentary form of self-government, providing structures with which the colonial government could communicate. Hence, a degree of cooperation arose.[37] The Hong Kong Chinese were reconciled to living under a foreign administration—as long as their livelihoods, customs and culture were left alone. In this they were much like the foreign merchants, who had a similar reluctance to become involved with politics unless their businesses were impacted.[38] Chinese labourers responded to impositions such as curfews, pass laws and excessive police interference with strikes and other forms of passive resistance.[39] In 1872 all 19,000 cargo coolies stopped work.[40]

The newly emergent Chinese commercial elite were a very different matter. Gradually, alternative power structures were developed within the Chinese community that gave opportunities for the

China. The Tung Wah became the focus of embryonic Chinese political power, managing Chinese affairs within the colony. People brought disputes to the committee for negotiation and arbitration as was usual in Chinese communities. They preferred to avoid British courts, where both the language and the 'justice' meted out were incomprehensible. Only as a last resort were unresolved cases referred to the 'official' legal process.[42] In this manner the Chinese elite served an extremely useful function for the colonial government. Nevertheless, their activities were closely watched to ensure they did not exceed proper boundaries.[43]

By the late 1870s it became apparent that, although the British maintained a strong administrative hold over their colony, the Chinese held the balance of economic power.[44] The Chinese elites were willing to support continued rule by Britain because their commercial success rested on political stability, and that the British provided.[45] Even so, they were frustrated by the unwillingness of the British to involve them in government. A paradigm shift began to take shape under the influence of Governor Sir John Pope Hennessy. He assumed office in 1877 with the belief that Chinese should have the same rights as Europeans,[46] a view not widely shared but Hennessy persevered. He appointed Ng Choy (Wu Tingfan) to the Legislative Council in 1880.[47] Ng was educated at one of Hong Kong's leading English schools, and the first Chinese to qualify as a barrister in London.[48] Ho Kai, also a barrister (and physician), brother-in-law of Ng, was another early prominent member of the Chinese community; he was appointed to the Legislative Council in 1890 and in 1912 became the first Chinese to be knighted.[49] It gradually became easier for Chinese to rise to prominence. One such was Robert (later Sir Robert) Ho Tung. Hong Kong–educated, Ho joined the Maritime Customs before becoming comprador to Jardines. By the age of 35 he was the richest man in Hong Kong.[50] Although of mixed parentage Ho considered himself to be Chinese, as such becoming in 1906 the first Chinese to be allowed to live on Victoria Peak, despite the law prohibiting this.

One of many narrow, steep streets running upwards between Central and Sheung Wan, 1900s. Courtesy of Ko Tim-keung.

acquisition of status and position as well as providing culturally appropriate facilities. One of the first was the Tung Wah Hospital, founded in 1869. Chinese people were reluctant to submit to Western medicine, particularly the abhorred, invasive practice of surgery. The formation of a hospital run by Chinese for Chinese was encouraged by the foreign community.[41] In addition to providing Chinese doctors practising Chinese medicine, the hospital built housing for the poor, gave free burials to those whose families could not afford this most important of Chinese rituals, or repatriated the dead to China where this was preferred. In 1878, the Tung Wah Committee, comprising the leaders of the Chinese community, founded the Po Leung Kuk to give shelter to destitute women and children. The Committee's work also extended beyond Hong Kong, such as in raising money for disaster relief and providing free vaccinations in

Successive British governors came to rely heavily on men such as these to act as communicators and mediators between them and the Chinese population. By 1897 that population was approaching a quarter of a million. Even after the acquisition of Kowloon in 1858, there were arguments that more land was needed, especially for defensive purposes. London resisted such calls for fear of upsetting its trading relationship with China.[51] However, Japan's surprise victory over China in 1895 encouraged other powers to be aggressively acquisitive of Chinese territory. Britain negotiated a 99-year lease of an additional 1000 square kilometres for Hong Kong—the 'New Territory'; the island and Kowloon measured only 128 square kilometres. The New Territory was largely undeveloped, with a scant population engaged in fishing and agriculture. It was the impending expiry of this lease that triggered the return to China of the whole colony in 1997.

The rule of law

By the time of the handover, the principle of 'the rule of law' had been firmly embedded in Hong Kong, but it was not always so. Shortly after taking possession of Hong Kong Captain Elliot proclaimed, on 2 February 1841, that pending Her Majesty's pleasure 'the natives of the island of Hong Kong and all natives of China thereto resorting, shall be governed according to the laws and customs of China, every description of torture excepted'.[52] This would have been in accordance with British practice elsewhere, notably India. China had a well-articulated criminal code but its guiding principles bore little relation to British notions of justice and its administration.

China offered to supply magistrates to exercise jurisdiction over Hong Kong's Chinese British subjects; a similar practice was of long standing in Macao. Imperial Commissioner Qiying visited the colony in June 1843 to exchange ratifications of the Treaty of Nanking. He was entertained royally, as befitted his station, but when he suggested a 'Macao-style' solution for Hong Kong Pottinger rejected the idea;[53] he later agreed to liaise with a Chinese official stationed in Kowloon regarding dealing with Chinese outlaws.[54]

Hong Kong was a British colony and had to function as such, which meant introducing the full panoply of English law—magistrates, courts and trial by jury. In 1843 a Legislative Council was created, charged with advising the governor on the making of laws. Simultaneously an Executive Council was formed to assist the governor to carry out those laws, make grants of land, and appoint and suspend officials. This was the standard British colonial structure. All appointees were government officials of one sort or another. In 1846 the Europeans asked for an elected body to govern them, but this was refused by London.[55] From 1850 the legislature was opened to appointed 'non-officials'—leading members of the foreign non-government community. The result was an executive-led government—a (mostly) benevolent dictatorship.

Governor Bowring immediately applied his reforming enthusiasm to the field of law and order. He investigated corruption in the police force and contemplated allowing suitably qualified Chinese lawyers to plead in the Supreme Court. Many of his efforts were frustrated by scandals among some of his most senior officials and general lack of support from the European community. The problems associated with crime grew with the colony's increasing wealth. Early laws distinguished between Chinese and others. Examples included a nightly curfew and the outlawing of undue noise.[56] When public security was involved, the colonial government had no qualms about using force. In 1855 a fleet of Taiping war junks entered the harbour, intent on mischief against the imperial troops stationed in Kowloon City. They were ordered away by the Royal Navy.[57] The navy was also used regularly for the extermination of pirate fleets on the high seas.

A safe haven

The security offered by this albeit imperfect legal system was unique in China, giving Hong Kong the status of a safe haven. Some of the colony's earliest Chinese entrepreneurs were fleeing likely reprisals for having helped the British in the First Opium War. More came to escape the Taipings. Hong Kong's border was virtually open, so the colony continued to attract Chinese who wanted to escape personal or political trouble. Compared with the rest of China, Hong Kong was stable, orderly, peaceful, prosperous and governed by a relatively small number of generally fair-minded administrators.[58] A Chinese press had developed from the earliest times, enabling Chinese people to express views that would be treasonable just a few kilometres to the north.[59]

It is ironic, therefore, that this combination of factors was to attract to the colony activists and reformers who had on their agendas the scrapping of all foreign privileges in China. The Xingzhonghui (Revive China Society) was founded in Hawaii in November 1894 by Sun Yat-sen and held meetings in Hong Kong soon afterwards. The group's objective was to restore China's prosperity through revolutionary action against the Qing rulers, who had been shown to be inept and corrupt. The strategy was to seize power in Canton and go on from there. An attempt to do that failed due to an informer, and all members were banished from Hong Kong. A later request by Sun to return to Hong Kong was answered with an assurance that he would be arrested, demonstrating that havens have their limits, although Sun made a number of secret visits.

The Boxer movement had no effect on Hong Kong, but between 1895 and 1911 at least eight mainland revolutionary attempts were organized in the colony.[60] Sun and his accomplices achieved their main goal when the Xinhai Revolution began on 10 October 1911 in Wuchang. There were mixed reactions among the Chinese in Hong Kong, although many hoped that Hong Kong would be reunited with a new China.[61] On 18 October a crowd of 400 stormed the office of the Bank of China, forcing the removal of the imperial dragon flag that was still flying there. Elsewhere, barbers' shops in Queen's Road had a three-day free offer removing men's queues, the hated symbol of Manchu rule. Curiously, another group of refugees appeared at this time—30,000 Manchus.[62] So long as they did not plot an imperial comeback, they too were welcomed. One effect of the revolution was that Chinese copper coins lost much of their underlying value. When their use was banned on Hong Kong's trams and ferries, these services were boycotted as a gesture of solidarity with the revolutionaries over the border.[63]

Labour activism had already begun to appear in the 1890s and 1900s. There was evidence of growing militancy and there were strikes. Allegations of poor treatment of Chinese in the United States led to an American boycott in 1905.[64] Japanese businesses were boycotted in 1908 as a reaction to Japan's encroachment into commerce and manufacturing in China.[65] Although this resulted in a riot, none of these activities had a particularly serious effect on Hong Kong's trade.[66]

COMMERCE AND INDUSTRIAL GROWTH

Hong Kong was founded with the intention of creating a commercial emporium. Its early days were unpromising, followed by an over-dependence on importing opium and exporting labourers. Ultimately, however, the goal was achieved. Britain governed Hong Kong as an economic centre for the promotion of the China trade. The colonial government tried not to interfere in business directly unless it thought it absolutely necessary. In later years this approach was to be expressed as 'positive non-interventionism', a doctrine that lasted until the late 20th century. With the appearance of a growing Chinese mercantile community in the 1860s, Hong Kong's economy diversified into that of an entrepôt and distribution centre. There was nothing home-grown that could be exported, but an increasing amount of China's trade passed through Hong Kong's harbour.

Initial industrial efforts related to shipping. Hong Kong's first Western-style vessel, the *Celestial*, was launched in 1843 from a dockyard at East Point owned by a Captain Lamont. By the 1850s there were 240 ships' chandlers, two rope-makers and two cannon factories. In 1857, following the destruction of the docks at Whampoa (Huangpu), Lamont and Douglas Lapraik built a dock at Aberdeen, increasing Hong Kong's attraction as a centre for repair and refitting; there were few such facilities on the China Coast.[67] In 1863 a number of dock operators amalgamated to form the Hongkong and Whampoa Dock

Connaught Road waterfront, 1912. Source: Peter Moss, *Passing Shadows, Hong Kong* (Hong Kong: FormAsia Books Limited, 2005), 116. Reprinted with permission by FormAsia Books Limited.

Co. The P&O line established a regular service to London in 1845. Locally, Jardines operated one of the largest fleets, and by the 1860s they had competition from Lapraik's steamers, particularly on the passenger-carrying coastal routes.

Then there was the coastal junk trade. Estimated to be 80,000 tonnes in 1847, this grew to 1.35 million over the next 20 years.[68] An increasing number of these vessels also used the repair and other services available in Hong Kong. By 1871 the colony was handling 15 percent of all China's exports and 33 percent of its imports. Twenty years later this had grown to 40 percent and 50 percent respectively. Hong Kong's role as the transshipment port for China was affected in the early years of the 20th century by the growth of treaty ports such as Tientsin (Tianjin) and Dairen (Dalian), but the colony remained second only to Shanghai.[69] Victoria Harbour recorded over 500,000 commercial vessel movements in 1907, not counting lighters, passenger boats and fishing craft.[70]

The Oriental Bank issued Hong Kong currency notes in 1846, the Chartered Mercantile Bank of India, London and China in 1858, and the Chartered Bank of India, Australia and China in 1863.[71] But many transactions were still measured in Spanish or Mexican silver dollars, sterling, Chinese copper cash and silver sycee, or colonial Indian currency. The British Indian banks that came to Hong Kong all had an external focus. In 1865 a group of foreign merchants in the colony founded the Hongkong and Shanghae [sic] Banking Company, with the specific purpose of financing trade between the open ports of China and Japan. The new bank issued its own notes in Hong Kong in 1867, and later in some of the treaty ports. This institution later became the globally powerful HSBC. Chinese merchants had a need for banks to service their particular requirements. By 1886 there were 20 local banks,[72] a number of them still in business today.

Hong Kong's reputation as an opium centre proved difficult to discard. In 1868 Sir Rutherford

Alcock, Britain's Minister in Peking, described the colony as being 'little more than an immense smuggling depot'.[73] The legalization of the drug in 1858, and the consequent charging, and evasion, of customs duty meant that Alcock's comments were not entirely unjustified. Although Hong Kong was a free port, the others along the coast were not. Duty had to be charged on any opium that passed over the border into China, and naturally great efforts were taken by the unscrupulous to avoid doing so. The capture in 1867 by the Chinese Customs of a Hong Kong junk carrying undeclared opium intensified the authorities' efforts to stop the smuggling. Customs cruisers, often under British captains, maintained a virtual blockade of Hong Kong harbour. This was not lifted until 1886, when full cooperation was agreed between the two sides.[74*] That did not mean that use of opium ceased. The drug continued to feature as an important commodity; in 1906 an estimated 10 percent of the Chinese population were thought to be addicts.[75] The Hong Kong government profited in that the lucrative monopoly on the distribution of opium was periodically sold to the highest bidder. The proceeds were an important part of fiscal revenue. Dealing in opium was condemned by the British Parliament in 1891, but to no effect. A ruling in 1907, when opium provided almost one-third of the colonial government's income (it peaked at 46 percent of government revenue in 1918),[76] led to a gradual cessation of exports from India, hence imports to China. Hong Kong's opium dens started to close in 1907, and had vanished by 1910. However, use of the drug was not made illegal until 1945.[77]

By the 1880s most foreign firms in Hong Kong had stopped dealing in opium. The blockade, coupled with political pressure, encouraged the former importers to look for other business. Jardines, the leader of the foreign business community, turned to a variety of new ventures—textiles, property, sugar-refining and infrastructure.[78] The company's shipping interests, still substantial, were facing stiff competition from a newcomer—Butterfield & Swire. Most ships were handled if not owned by one or the other.

Taikoo Sugar Refinery, 1911. Photograph by Warren Swire. © Image courtesy of John Swire and Sons and Historical Photographs of China, University of Bristol.

Swires were particularly successful in the coastal trade, which led them in 1884 to start a sugar factory, sourcing the product from up the coast at Swatow (Shantou). By the early 1900s their Taikoo Sugar Refinery was the world's largest.[79] In 1902 the firm commenced construction of a large dock at Quarry Bay. Although the dock has long gone, Swires continue to draw significant income from the housing and commercial buildings that have replaced it.

With the focus in Hong Kong's early days on trade rather than manufacturing, other industries were slow starters. There had been some small-scale businesses making such things as cigars, glass, matches and soap.[80] Manufacturing was boosted when war engulfed Europe in 1914. A number of small Chinese-owned factories served the needs of those countries whose industry became focused on the war effort—Hong Kong–made torches, batteries and enamelware became popular.[81] Chinese banks also benefited from this new activity. The foreign-dominated shipping and sugar industries flourished, along with a new line in cement manufacture. The population swelled to 600,000.[82]

However, many of the colony's needs became difficult to satisfy, owing to wartime shortages. Hong Kong underwent a period of severe inflation. When a shortage of rice, one of the most important commodities for Chinese people, led to significant price rises and profiteering, the government broke from

---

* See entry on Kowloon for more details.

its non-interventionist principles and entered the market, ensuring a steady and reasonably priced supply.[83] A bigger impact was caused by another necessary commodity—silver. Hong Kong's economy, like that of China, was still based on the silver standard. Worldwide demand for silver coins in the years 1914 to 1918 caused the silver price to rise by over 80 percent. The exchange rate of the Hong Kong dollar to sterling rose by a similar amount as a consequence, increasing a further 45 percent during 1919.[84] Then, with the global depression of the 1920s, the value of silver fell to almost its pre-war level.[85] Silver dollars had for long been the favoured medium of settling accounts among the Chinese. A trader's shroff, or cashier, could tell the quality of silver by touch. It was a difficult decision to abandon silver in place of the globally more popular and stable gold. Another major slide in the price of silver, and the Hong Kong dollar, prompted a government commission in 1931 to look at the whole question of Hong Kong's currency. It concluded that, as long as China remained on the silver standard, Hong Kong had no choice but to follow suit. Then in November 1935, triggered by economic moves by the United States in 1934, China abandoned the silver standard. Hong Kong immediately moved to base its currency on the value of sterling, supported by a specially created exchange fund.[86]

A stock exchange was established in 1888. This proved very popular with the Chinese in particular and they became major investors.[87] Later the city would boast four separate exchanges. The person to make the most spectacular use of the new exchange was Paul Chater. Arriving from Calcutta in 1864 at the age of 18, Chater first became a broker, then turned his talents to property and eventually became a leader in just about everything. He died in 1926 and had long been the colony's richest man, whose efforts were recognized by a knighthood. Among the still existing Hong Kong companies that Chater founded, or was instrumental in founding, are Hongkong Land, the Hong Kong & Kowloon Wharf & Godown Co. and Hongkong Electric. Hong Kong was the first city in Asia to have electric street lighting. Powered by a generator in Ship Street, Wanchai, the first 50 lamps were lit in December 1890. Another power station was built in 1903 in Hung Hom to serve Kowloon's needs.[88]

The need for cheap and efficient transport within Hong Kong was met in a number of ways. A cross-harbour ferry service was first established in 1842 by Abdoolally Ebrahim & Co., an Indian trading firm still in business today. A regular service was started in 1880 by another Indian, Dorabjee Naorojee, becoming the iconic Star Ferry in 1898.[89] In 1901 there was a proposal for a bridge over the harbour.[90] The idea was revisited in 1921,[91] but eventually emerged as the Cross-Harbour Tunnel in 1972. Rickshaws were introduced from Japan in 1874 and proved to be very popular on the urban area's narrow, cramped streets. The wealthy preferred the more sedate sedan chair, with larger households employing their own teams of liveried bearers. Until the Peak Tram appeared in 1888, the sedan chair was the only means of getting to and from the secluded mansions on the heights above the city. A street tram service was introduced on the island in 1904 and is still a popular and convenient form of public transport. From 1911 the journey time to Canton was much reduced by the opening of the Kowloon-Canton Railway. The 1920s and early 1930s saw a proliferation of private bus operators; in 1933 the government awarded franchises to just two—one each for Hong Kong Island and Kowloon. Kai Tak Airport opened in 1925 with a grass runway on reclaimed land in Kowloon. From 1928 the flying boats of Imperial Airways included Hong Kong in their global service network.

Back in 1854, one of Sir John Bowring's goals had been to tidy the central waterfront with the creation of a bund. Private mercantile interests frustrated this effort. Governor Sir Hercules Robinson managed to create a footpath along the harbour-side in 1862. Bowring's dream was only realized long after his departure, when the path became Des Voeux Road in the 1880s.[92] This was only a temporary solution. It took the vision of Paul Chater to resolve the issue. He backed what became the world's biggest reclamation project, when in 1890 he started to create a new praya stretching from the navy docks to Shek Tong Tsui in the west, constructing 25 hectares of new land. Once completed in 1904 Hong Kong started to see its first skyscrapers: stately buildings of four or five storeys now commanded the waterfront, dwarfing their two-or three-storey predecessors.[93]

The economic problems of the late 1910s and early 1920s fuelled an increase in labour militancy. In April 1920 dock workers demanded a 40 percent pay increase. Electricity, tram and other workers joined their strike.[94] Wages were increased as a result—not by the amount demanded, but enough to increase inflation. High increases in rents prompted the government again to step into the market; rents were frozen in June 1921, a measure that remained for five years.[95]

In January 1922 Hong Kong's seamen struck for higher pay, and were joined by dock workers and coolies. As happened in the 1850s, the strikers were 'ordered' to go to Canton for the duration of the strike. This was not as unusual as it may seem. According to an annual report of the Hong Kong General Chamber of Commerce: 'For many Chinese Hongkong† and Canton are alternative places of residence . . . A daily ebb and flow of 50,000 people between the two places is not uncommon.'[96] On 4 March the situation worsened when police at Sha Tin shot at a group of strikers attempting to walk back to China; four were killed. Canton had always envied the commercial success of Hong Kong; Sun Yat-sen had even announced an ambitious plan to make Canton into the Great Southern Port. Any opportunity to damage Hong Kong's economy was seized, and Canton played a key role in organizing and prolonging the strike.[97] The colonial government's response was robust, and the dispute gradually dissipated.

Worse was to come with the shooting by British-controlled police in May 1925 of demonstrators in Shanghai, prompting the seamen to walk out again on 19 June, although not for more pay. When news came of 50 Chinese killed four days later by shots fired from the British Concession at Canton, the situation worsened. By July practically all Hong Kong businesses were affected, and an estimated 250,000 workers and their families departed for Canton. In Hong Kong the military and the Volunteer Corps ran essential services, assisted by a number of Chinese who chose not to side with the strikers.[98] The colonial government attributed the action to Communist agitators, of whom a number had come to Hong Kong seeking to further their aims. Most businesses were open again by September, albeit on a reduced scale. Then the continuing strike turned into a Canton-sponsored boycott of all Hong Kong trade. Foreign ships were banned from carrying Hong Kong or British goods, and checks were made at ports along the coast. The number of ships entering the harbour fell by 60 percent, and the stock market dropped by 40 percent. There were many bankruptcies, and Hong Kong businesses were estimated to have lost hundreds of millions of dollars. Governor Sir Edward Stubbs called for strong action against Canton, but was ordered by London to sit and wait.[99]

While Chiang Kai-shek was distracted in the north of the country, a British gunboat appeared in Canton in September 1926 to clear British wharves of strike pickets. This was enough to bring the boycott to an end. A formal conclusion was achieved through British acceptance of tariff increases, the only concession made during the whole affair.[100]

China had long complained about lacking control over its import and export tariffs, a right removed in 1842. When the foreign powers agreed to return autonomy to China in 1929, import duties rose and Hong Kong's trade suffered. As about a quarter of China's imports still came through the colony, smuggling increased. When requests by the Nanking government to have a Chinese Maritime Customs presence in Hong Kong were refused, another blockade was threatened. This time Canton came to the colony's rescue; vested interests among senior members of the Canton government ensured that the threat was removed, and the smuggling remained.[101] Despite all this political tension, there was no serious attempt to overthrow the colonial government. As with the political upheavals in China in the 1950s and 1960s, Hong Kong's commercial contribution to the country was too important to jeopardize.

---

† The name was formally changed to 'Hong Kong' in 1926.

By the early 1930s Hong Kong's manufacturing industry had started to diversify. The 1931 census showed that 19 percent of workers were engaged in manufacturing, ahead of the 15 percent employed in transport and only a little behind the 21 percent in the core commerce and finance industries.[102] Knitwear, hosiery and footwear were becoming important, but the global depression hit these and all of Hong Kong's other economic activities. The volume of trade in 1935 was half of what it had been four years previously. One-third of imports and half the exports were still with China, but chaos reigned over the border. Conditions improved in 1936 and 1937, and by 1939 there were 857 factories registered in Hong Kong, one-quarter of them engaged in knitting and weaving.[103]

JAPANESE OCCUPATION

At first, Japan's actions in China benefitted Hong Kong's economy. With the occupation of Shanghai by the Japanese, much of the country's war materiel and other trade diverted to Hong Kong. Even when the colony's attraction as a safe haven brought refugees flooding in, doubling the population to over two million, there was a boom in land sales.[104] Hong Kong was firmly in the hands of the British, and it was widely assumed that it would be defended vigorously. But when the invaders advanced southwards so speedily, capturing Canton in October 1938, many of Hong Kong's Chinese preferred to take their chances in their villages. The Japanese attacked on 8 December 1941. By the time the colony surrendered on 25 December, more than half of the population had fled. The world as Hong Kong knew it had come to an end.

Britain resumed possession of its colony when the Japanese surrendered in 1945 and a whole new world of possibilities opened up.

Further reading: Carroll, *A Concise History of Hong Kong*; Eitel, *Europe in China*; Endacott, *A History of Hong Kong*; Munn, *Anglo-China*; Nield, *The China Coast*; Sayer, *Hong Kong 1841–1862* and *Hong Kong 1862–1919*; Tsai, *Hong Kong in Chinese History*; Tsang, *A Modern History of Hong Kong*.

ICHANG (YICHANG) 宜昌

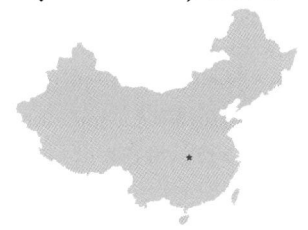

Hubei, 30.41° N, 111.16° E
Treaty Port, 1876 British Treaty

In 1869 Robert Swinhoe, British Consul in Taiwan-fu (Tainan), accompanied a group of British merchants travelling up the Yangtze. Their gunboat, HMS *Opossum*, was the first steamer to reach Ichang, the furthest such a vessel could travel.[1] They concluded that Ichang was insignificant commercially but, as the head of navigation, it should be opened as a treaty port until somewhere better could be found.[2] Swinhoe's separate report included the full Chinese text of a placard he had seen, offering rewards for attacks on foreigners and their property:[3] rewards were scaled for killing foreigners, destroying their steamers, etc. Death was the penalty for any locals who were 'selfish enough' to sell land to foreigners.[4] Such deep-rooted antagonism was to erupt repeatedly in the coming decades.

Despite these disadvantages, Ichang was a step towards Chungking (Chongqing) and the imagined opportunities of trade with Sichuan Province. Ichang was opened by the Chefoo Agreement of 1876. Walter King was appointed British Consul and he set out in February 1877 on his 500-kilometre voyage from Hankow (Hankou). After a difficult journey he was received with hostility and had to withdraw. Returning a month later he established the British consular presence on a junk in the river.[5] King recommended the purchase of a plot of land for a British Concession and identified a site near the city's south gate, away from the riverbank and stretching southwards for 500 metres.[6] However, an angry mob prevented him from erecting boundary stones. Complaints to the Chinese authorities went unheeded.[7] In 1880 Britain renounced plans for a concession.[8] Pragmatically, hostility and the absence of commercial opportunity rendered it unviable.

The Americans had a pleasanter introduction. Consular Agent Nelson Bryant arrived on 1 April 1877 just in time to see a temple opened as the Custom House. To the chagrin of his British counterpart, Bryant raised his flag at a house that had been prepared for him.[9] Despite this warm welcome, the Americans withdrew, preferring to handle their consular needs from Hankow.

In 1882 the British Consul moved from his floating abode to one on land. Openly referred to as 'Her Britannic Majesty's Cowshed',[10] this was a simple Chinese house. A government report in 1889 stated that it would be 'difficult to get any first-class European servant' to live in it, putting the incumbent at the time firmly in his place. The same report concluded that, despite high prices, land should be bought to construct a proper residence.[11] This was completed in 1892,[12] allowing the consul to live in a 'comfortable family residence' overlooking the Custom House and the Yangtze.[13] Today's view is limited to Hongxing Road but the building, at No. 42, is there, currently used as a restaurant. An early priority was a tennis court for the consul and other foreign residents. Fresh meat was scarce, so the grass court doubled as grazing for sheep, managed by a Mutton Club.[14]

In 1878 the entire foreign population comprised ten missionaries, four customs officers, the British Consul and one merchant, the representative of Butterfield & Swire; he had left by the following year. As far as business was concerned, there was none.[15] Ichang's *raison d'être* derived from its position a few kilometres short of the famed Yangtze Gorges. Currents and submerged obstacles prevented both steamers and the larger junks from the lower river going further. Ichang therefore had grown as a transshipment station, where goods were passed between the larger boats and the smaller craft that were pulled by armies of trackers through the upper reaches.

The foreign powers were already providing steamers to transport goods between Ichang and the lower ports. Extending operations to the upper river remained a challenge for many years. The story of Archibald Little's pioneering efforts and ultimate

The paddle-steamer *Pioneer*, dominating the Ichang (Yichang) skyline, c. 1900. Source: *Journal of the Hong Kong Branch of the Royal Asiatic Society*, vol. 16, 1976, Plate 20.

success is told in the entry on Chungking. Little was the first independent foreign merchant to reside at Ichang (indeed, one of the few ever to do so), moving there in 1887. When, largely as a result of his determination, Chungking became a treaty port in 1890, Ichang's transshipment trade received a major boost. Two other foreign merchants joined Little. Agents for Jardines and Swires erected large warehouses, and the foreign population, mainly missionaries but including eleven in the customs service, rose to 42. Swires later installed their own manager; his 1918 house stands at No. 13 Hongxing Road.

By the 1930s foreign vessels were running from Chungking to Hankow and beyond, bypassing Ichang, but the technical obstacles were replaced by others. Ichang's sole purpose was as a place for moving cargoes from small vessels to bigger ones, and vice versa. If these vessels sailed on by there was nothing for Ichang's labourers to do. The coolies' unions managed to require ships to make unnecessary stops and the shippers were then charged the equivalent of the unloading and reloading fees before being allowed to continue. This unusual situation went on for years, the only compromise being that in 1931 some, but only some, of the direct shipments were allowed to pass through unmolested.[16]

Returning to the foreign-settled area, in the absence of a formal concession there was little central planning. Separate bunds were built by Jardines, Swires, the Roman Catholics and the customs.[17] A General Improvement Committee was formed in 1894 to manage drainage and roads.[18] It also leased a plot of land for a recreation ground.[19] Hockey and football were played there, especially against visiting navy crews.[20] Golf was restricted to the winter when, as a result of the low level of the river, a 300-metre-wide sandbank appeared, stretching for two or three kilometres and providing 'good, though rather monotonous exercise'.[21] From the mid-1890s a few new European-style buildings appeared, including a new Custom House and residence for the commissioner.[22] The small foreign community was at last living in proximity.[23] Today the area is bounded by Yanjiang Avenue and Hongxing Road on the west and east, and Erma and Yima roads on the north and south. Three unidentified European buildings have been preserved at Nos. 99 to 101 Yanjiang Avenue. Between this area and the old city walls, a large plot was occupied by the Franciscans. A few of their buildings remain on Erma Road, along with a very large church—one of two to be found in Ichang; a Protestant church stands at No. 60 Yanjiang Avenue.

The need for togetherness was not just for social reasons. Anti-foreign feelings were ever present. The customs temple was overrun by a mob in 1884, and three or four more times in following years. In 1891 a riot destroyed a number of foreign residences, and severely damaged the almost completed British Consulate.[24] Similar disturbances were common in the remaining years of the old century.

The 1911 revolution, on the other hand, had little effect on Ichang, with the Republican army quietly occupying the Chinese city around midnight on 18 October.[25] It had been feared at the time that Ichang might be crushed between rival factions,[26] but the small city proved too insignificant. Ichang escaped the immediate effects of the Shanghai troubles of 1925, but the boycotts of 1927 brought trade to a halt.[27]

The Japanese opened a consulate at Ichang in 1919, and by 1923 there was a consular police force of three officers.[28] In November 1937 the British Consulate closed as Japanese forces swept up the Yangtze valley. By June 1940 they reached Ichang, but could penetrate no further.[29] Nor could the Japanese stop the heroic evacuation of millions of people upstream to Chungking, along with hundreds of thousands of tonnes of plant and machinery, enabling China's industry to continue in skeleton form. A large and impressive monument to this feat stands on the riverfront.

Further reading: Bromfield and Lee, 'Captain Plant'; Little, *Through the Yang-tse Gorges*; Parkinson, 'The First Steam-Powered Ascent'; Simpson, 'Hell and High Water'; Stevens, 'A Tale of Sour Grapes'.

Kashkar (Kashgar) 喀什

Xinjiang, 39.28° N, 75.58° E
Treaty Port, 1860 Russian Treaty

Situated 3000 kilometres from the nearest stretch of navigable Chinese water, Kashkar is the place that stretched the term 'treaty port' to the absolute limit. Peking (Beijing)'s hold over the far west of its empire was tenuous and fraught with difficulties, both cultural and geographical. Authority was difficult to exert over a resentful, rebellious, predominantly Muslim population. In 1835, to stop the eastward spread of neighbouring Kokand, China allowed a Kokand diplomat to be based at Kashkar.[1] In an attempt to appease Russian aims, a Sino-Russian treaty in 1860 opened Kashkar to Russian trade 'as an experiment'.[2]

Trade was not the Russians' main interest. The unstable region around Kashkar attracted them as a base from which to threaten British India and Chinese Turkestan. When the Muslim adventurer, Yaqub Beg, led another rebellion in 1865, Russia quickly recognized his new kingdom, Kashgaria, which rapidly became a rallying point for Muslim disaffection.[3] It was rumoured that, while simultaneously uttering soothing words to China, Russia was providing military support for Beg.[4] Britain, co-player with Russia of 'The Great Game' for paramount regional influence, also recognized Beg's state, sending missions to his capital, Yarkand (Yarkant) in 1870 and 1873,[5] as did Turkey.[6] At great expense and difficulty, Peking despatched General Zuo Zongtang, sponsor of the Foochow (Fuzhou) Arsenal, to reclaim the rebel state. Zuo and 2000 men took two years to reach the 'barbarously remote' outpost. After a bloody campaign he was successful, and China ruled once more.[7]

Kashkar, an oasis, was well placed to capture a share of the Silk Road trade. Situated a pleasant 1500 metres above sea level, the town commanded two Central Asian mountain passes—one into Russia and one into Afghanistan and eventually India. The main commodity was brick tea, brought up from China by camel train for the Russian market.[8] Muslin, chintz and tea were imported from India.[9]

However, for the foreign powers Kashkar's importance was political. Russia opened a consulate in 1881. Britain's Government of India established a consular agency in 1890 and a full consulate in 1908.[10] Apart from Swedish missionaries, the only foreigners resident in Kashkar were the members of the two consulates.[11] By all accounts, the characterful old areas of Kashkar have been obliterated in the name of progress. However, I believe the former Russian Consulate remains, as does the Chini-Bagh (Chinese Garden), the former residence of the British Consuls.

Further reading: Fleming, *News from Tartary*.

The very impressive entrance to the Chini-Bagh, c. 1900. Source: Lady Macartney, *An English Lady in Chinese Turkestan*.

Kiukiang (Jiujiang) 九江

Jiangxi, 29.43° N, 115.58° E
Treaty Port, 1858 British Treaty

Kiukiang never lived up to foreigners' expectations. Opened as a treaty port by the 1858 Treaty of Tientsin (Tianjin), it was not even mentioned in the treaty. As the Yangtze valley was still plagued by Taiping rebels, Britain secured the right to open Chinkiang (Zhenjiang) and two others, to be identified 'so soon as Peace shall have been restored'.[1] The chosen two were Hankow (Hankou) and Kiukiang. For the British, the main attraction of Kiukiang was its position near the mouth of the Po Yang (Boyang) Lake, the large stretch of water from which all the exports of Jiangxi Province flowed. The newcomers were chiefly interested in tea, particularly green tea that had previously journeyed overland to Foochow (Fuzhou) or Ningpo (Ningbo), and porcelain. Kingtehchen (Jingdezhen), a town on the east shore of the lake, had for centuries supplied the imperial palace with the finest porcelain available anywhere.

In 1858 Lord Elgin was awarded the rare privilege of sailing up the Yangtze to Hankow. Based on what he saw, his instructions to Harry Parkes, who led the port-opening mission in March 1861, were to favour Hukow (Hukou) over Kiukiang. Hukow was at the entrance of the channel leading to the lake, whereas Kiukiang was 25 kilometres upstream.[2] However, Parkes found Hukow was too small and had neither flat land suitable for godowns nor a good anchorage. Instead he selected Kiukiang, already in decline before the Taipings left it in ruins. Parkes knew it had been 'brought to a very high state of perfection by the Chinese in more prosperous times'.[3]

Parkes, as usual, selected a plot of ground for the British Concession. Unusually for a Chinese city, Kiukiang's walls lined the riverbank for over 400 metres, leaving only a towpath. Parkes obtained a site of 500 by 200 metres, leased in perpetuity, to the west, upstream from the city. The concession was split into four blocks of seven lots each, two blocks on the river and two behind, each separated by a road. Initially only the front blocks were settled; the rear of the concession was dominated by a large pond, the former outline of which can still be seen in the pattern of today's streets.[4] Its presence meant the exact location of the concession's southern boundary was still contested in the 1920s.[5] A bund was included and two riverside lots were designated for a British Consulate. Interpreter Patrick Hughes (aged 27) was installed as vice-consul on 8 March 1861, in temporary accommodation.

The tiny foreign community may have been resented but it suggested a degree of security to the local population, and the city started to be reoccupied. Still far short of the previous number, inhabitants increased from 10,000 when the British arrived to 40,000 a year later. By then most of the concession lots had been sold, on 99-year leases from the British government. The first meeting of land-renters occurred in April 1862, a committee elected, and agreement reached to tax each lot to finance necessary infrastructure work. In the winter season's low water the riverbank was exposed to a depth of 15 metres, making the building of a bund possible. By 1866 European-style houses had been built on most lots facing the river, including a British Consulate.

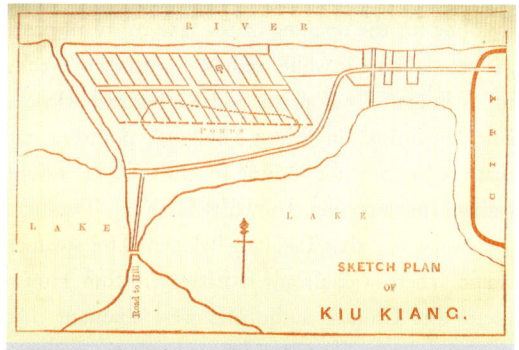

1867 sketch plan of the British Concession, complete with pond. Source: Mayers, Dennys and King, *The Treaty Ports of China and Japan*, 430.

Not counting the junior members of the customs outdoor staff, who were generally excluded from all aspects of 'society', the foreign population numbered between 20 and 25. There were eight British firms, three American, one missionary, one doctor and one British police inspector.[6]

Early frustrations

It was soon realized that the new treaty port was not destined for greatness. Despite Shanghai being over 700 kilometres away, Chinese merchants preferred to go there for whatever foreign imports they needed, principally opium and cotton goods.[7] Of exports there was only one—tea. The production of wonderful porcelain had been largely abandoned in favour of utility kitchen pieces, for which there was high demand after the wreckage caused by the Taipings. Tea was big business in the early years, the only commercial activity involving foreign merchants. On the opening of Kiukiang, there had been a rush of 'youthful foreigners, expectant of rapidly-made fortunes', but their enthusiasm led to overtrading and bankruptcy.[8] Furthermore, as steam navigation on the Po Yang Lake was forbidden, all the tea for export was brought to Kiukiang by junk. Given the Yangtze's strong flow, junks sometimes had to wait for weeks for a wind to bring them the few kilometres upstream from Hukow to load the waiting steamers. Hukow was now being seen as the better option after all, but it was too late to make a change.[9] Its destiny was to become a port-of-call.

Jardines, Russells and Gibb Livingstone started to lobby for the opening of the lake to steam navigation, claiming it would reduce a journey of weeks to 24 hours.[10] They petitioned Rutherford Alcock, British Minister in Peking (Beijing), pointing out that the junks, while waiting to exit the lake, would gather at an anchorage known as Takutang (Datang). They suggested that Takutang be opened for steamer traffic. There was already a native Custom House there. The Chinese authorities were adamant that the lake remain closed to foreign activity, ensuring the tea-producing areas stayed as remote as they had been for centuries. Jardines pulled out in frustration in 1871, preferring to conduct their Kiukiang business from Hankow, 250 kilometres upriver. Gibb Livingstone left the following year and Russells a few years later. Many of the ten new houses along the bund became vacant and dilapidated.[11]

The position of Kiukiang as a staging post between the much larger ports of Shanghai and Hankow nevertheless ensured that there was a continuous stream of foreign shipping calling at the port. Even if the cargoes were not developing as hoped, the number of passengers travelling along the river kept shipping agents busy. The British lines, Indo-China Steam Navigation (Jardines) and China Navigation (Swires), took the largest share, but the China Merchants line was a major competitor, as later were Japanese operators. In 1882, the two British companies started to moor hulks off the bund for use as landing stages, connected to the shore by wooden pontoons.[12] Jardines returned to Kiukiang in 1886 to manage their own shipping affairs.

Showing a brave face

Despite commercial disappointments, the concession showed a brave face. Unlike Chinkiang, for example, it was well run. The chair of the municipal council was occupied at various times by the Commissioner of Customs, the British Consul and missionaries as well as merchants. It kept its area clean and tidy and the well-maintained bund was lined with trees. There were small churches catering to both Protestants and Roman Catholics, and that essential of any gathering of two or more Englishmen abroad—the club.[13] Street lighting was introduced in 1883. During 1885 the bund was extended citywards, funded by a voluntary wharfage charge managed jointly by Chinese and foreign merchants.[14] A public garden was laid out in the concession in 1888.[15] The pond, although a malaria risk in the hottest months, provided a popular venue for ice-skating in the winter.[16] The 'happy monotony of this charmingly situated riverine port' was also broken whenever a foreign gunboat called. Full use was made by the small community of the social possibilities presented by the visiting crews, which could dwarf the number of residents

The bund in 1872, already very well established. Courtesy of Wattis Fine Art.

by a factor of three or four to one.[17] Eventually the municipal council also provided a small theatre in its office building.[18]

Commercial foreign residents were few. Apart from the two British shipping companies, by the late 1880s there were only two British firms in Kiukiang, gathering tea exports for shipment. In 1886 three steamers loaded direct for London, but the experiment was not repeated.[19] In 1875 a Russian company from Hankow set up a branch, followed a few years later by another. They each operated a factory in the concession making brick and tablet tea. This way of packaging tea for long-distance travel was uniquely Russian, and kept the China tea market going much longer than it would have done otherwise. The two firms employed several thousand workers[20] until closing in 1917.

THE OPENING OF THE LAKE AND OTHER DEVELOPMENTS

The foreign community still saw running steamers on Po Yang Lake as the port's salvation. But China was determined not to lose out once more to foreign expertise and capital. By 1897 there were six Chinese steam launches operating, forbidden to tow any cargo junks except those carrying tea. Passenger boats could be towed freely, and these quickly became popular.[21] The breakthrough came in 1898 when the long-awaited Inland Steam Navigation Regulations were issued, opening all China's navigable waters to foreign steam traffic.[22] Despite lobbying so long for access, the foreign operators were slow to take advantage of their new privileges. Within the next ten years China Navigation began to run small riverboats on the lake, and the Japanese NKK line brought tea out to Kiukiang. Asiatic Petroleum operated small motorboats to take its products direct to inland customers. The new regulations precipitated an increase in trade, but the effects were not as anticipated when Jardines had pressed their case over 30 years previously.[23] Perhaps it was all too late.

Missionaries exceeded all other sectors of the foreign population, using Kiukiang as a base for penetrating the provincial interior. In 1898 a large Roman Catholic cathedral was inaugurated on Lot 1 at the eastern (city) end of the concession, dwarfing the Protestant St. Paul's Church;[24] neither remain. The next largest foreign group consisted of customs employees, about 20 in the 1890s. The service occupied several concession lots by 1903;[25] their Lot 13 building remains. In 1898, customs' responsibilities were expanded to include the collection of *likin* for the Kiukiang prefecture. In 1901 the terms of the Boxer Protocol brought all native customs operations near the treaty ports under the foreign-run service, including the native Custom House at Takutang.[26] These developments were a learning opportunity for the commissioner and his staff. Not until 1913 was he able fully to control 'native' operations. He demonstrated this by reducing the number of staff in the local customs operation from 248 to 89.[27]

Standard Oil and Asiatic Petroleum were the only new foreign firms to open in Kiukiang, arriving in 1905 and 1909 respectively. Both built handling facilities a few kilometres downstream, at a place still occupied by large storage tanks. Standard Oil also built the imposing office building still present at the western end of the bund. Other modern innovations had little effect on Kiukiang. A railway line to Nanchang, the provincial capital, was approved in 1904; while only 130 kilometres long it remained unfinished until 1916.[28] Factories took even longer to arrive.

The walled city never regained its pre-Taiping bustle. Even by 1901, only the western quarter was built on; the rest was used for cultivation. It was the area adjacent to the British Concession that became the focus of development. In 1898 the 'stinking pond' on the concession's southern perimeter was at last filled in[29] and became a public park. The area to the west received greater attention. The concession's upstream edge was marked by Lungkai Creek (Longkai He), a small waterway used as a junk anchorage whenever it was not too silted. There had been various schemes to deepen the creek. In 1885, following the success of the Sino-foreign collaboration to enlarge the bund, the same group extended it along the creek,[30] although silting continued to be problematic.

In 1917 a new town, Pinhingchow (Binxing Zhou) appeared on land that had been drained, reclaimed and well laid out. The railway station was already there, and was soon joined by a number of factories, new roads and houses. By 1921 there was an electric power station, a four-storey hotel and a thriving business district, connected to the concession by a wooden drawbridge.[31]

Revolution and rendition

Kiukiang city authorities transferred their allegiance to the new Republican government within weeks of the 1911 revolution but in July 1913 local leaders rebelled against Yuan Shikai.[32] Order was not fully restored until experienced troops appeared from Wuchang, determined to exert central authority.[33]

The small foreign community was often concerned about security; there were riots in 1888, 1891 and 1909. In 1915 student-led protests against Japan's notorious 'Twenty-One Demands' led to a boycott of the newly established Japanese presence in Kiukiang. They had six nationals at their consulate, on a lot shared with a branch of the Bank of Taiwan.[34] The boycott was poorly planned and ineffective. A repeat in 1919, however, brought all trade and passenger movements to a standstill until the overriding requirements of commerce prevailed in September 1920.[35] At the height of these troubles, the British Consul requested that American marines be landed.[36]

When news arrived of the shooting of Chinese demonstrators by municipal police in Shanghai on 30 May 1925, there was an anti-British riot in Kiukiang. The Chinese constables of the Kiukiang municipal force refused to intervene and were dismissed.[37] City authorities assured the British of the concession's safety, but students broke into the British and Japanese consulates on 13 June. There is no trace today of the British Consulate, but features of the Japanese Consulate are still visible in the renovated building that is still there. The mob also burned down the Bank of Taiwan; soon rebuilt, its replacement remains. The arrival of Japanese marines halted further destruction.[38]

The rest of the country was now in turmoil. Chiang Kai-shek's Revolutionary Army captured Kiukiang in November 1926, causing the remaining foreign population to flee to ships in the river. On 5 January 1927, taking a lead from their brothers in Hankow, coolies refused to unload a China Navigation vessel. When sailors from HMS *Wyvern*, a British destroyer, started unloading it there was fighting, and a mob advanced on the concession. Warning shots were fired from the *Wyvern*. T. V. Soong, Chiang's Finance Minister, was in Kiukiang at the time. He advised restraint, but on 7 January the concession was overrun and the British Consul and staff evacuated.[39]

The formal end of the treaty port came a few weeks later with the signing of the so-called 'Chen–O'Malley' Agreement on 20 February, similar to that signed on 19 February regarding Hankow. The document formally recognized handing the British Concession to the provisional committee set up by Chen Yujen, the Nationalist government's Minister for Foreign Affairs.

The British can hardly have been too upset at losing this disappointing concession for which, 66 years earlier, there had been such high hopes. The Kiukiang concession became a Special Administrative District, like Hankow, and when even this was abolished in 1930 the British hardly noticed.[40]

Further reading: Lee, *China's Recovery*; Munro-Faure, 'The Kiukiang Incident'.

Kiungchow (Qiongzhou)
瓊州

Hainan, 20.00° N, 110.21° E
Treaty Port, 1858 British Treaty

Kiungchow was an outpost where for over a thousand years Chinese officials were banished for offending their emperor. The Haikou Museum is full of their stories. In its early years as a treaty port foreign residents would have been able to appreciate their sense of abandonment. Virtually all the British consular officials who were posted there during the 50 years of the consulate's existence became seriously ill, although only one died in post.[1] Even in the early 21st century Kiungchow was listed by one American multinational as one of only two 'hardship postings' in China.[2]

In 1665 British Captain John Weddell tried but failed to open trade at Canton (Guangzhou). Instead, he recommended that Britain seize Hainan as a trading base.[3] Had this happened, the history of the China Coast would have been very different. It was two hundred years before Hainan reappeared on Britain's agenda. In 1858 Britain and France included Kiungchow as a treaty port in their respective treaties of Tientsin (Tianjin). The 'port' was five kilometres inland, but being the prefectural headquarters the consuls would be near the seat of local government. Kiungchow's actual seaport, Hoihow (Haikou), became the de facto treaty port, although it was some time before Britain or France bothered to develop their new trading post. One reason was that local authorities were unwilling to grant facilities to foreign merchants. Another was the almost prohibitive regulation of the Imperial Maritime Customs whereby any foreign vessel bound for Hainan had to obtain clearance in Canton, requiring an unprofitable detour of over 200 kilometres. A memorial from the Hong Kong General Chamber of Commerce in October 1867 recommended appointing a consular agent at Kiungchow from among any willing British merchants in order to handle the necessary paperwork.[4] No such merchants existed.

Ten years went by and the new treaty port remained effectively closed. In 1869 Sir Rutherford Alcock, British Minister in Peking (Beijing), tried to exchange Kiungchow for Wenchow (Wenzhou).[5] Hong Kong's business community, and its London representatives, were not supportive, preferring to remove the barriers faced by Kiungchow. Memorials poured in to the British Foreign Secretary, urging him to pursue opening the port. One from Hong Kong pointed out that Kiungchow was the only treaty port on China's south-west coast and that it would benefit from the passing trade between Hong Kong and the French interests in Indo-China;[6] still no merchants came, and the port remained closed. Only in 1872 was an application made to the Tsungli Yamen to have a 'competent interpreter' appointed to Kiungchow as vice-consul.[7]

No great expectations

It was not until 1 April 1876 that the British Consulate and the Custom House were opened. The customs staff established themselves in a roomy but tumbledown building. The consular men were put up in the North Fort, described as 'rickety and manned by about 40 Chinese "soldiers" and the usual compliment [sic] of seedy-looking mandarins'.[8] The inappropriateness of his lodgings meant the consul was soon moved to rented premises, but these were no better—a disused warehouse that had become a piggery and a public convenience,[9] 'a Disgrace, all damp and dirty'.[10] An official report to London described the consul's residence as 'a miserable hovel'.[11] A purpose-built consulate would not be provided until another quarter-century had passed.

The port was open, yet no foreign merchants accepted the challenge of going there. Shallow water required even small vessels to anchor four kilometres from shore. At low tide a man could wade out to sea for over a kilometre without wetting his knees.[12] In addition, the approach to the anchorage was hazardous, with no navigational aids, and it experienced summer and autumn typhoons. Unusually, the tides were very irregular. Sometimes there were two a day, sometimes one, and occasionally none.[13] In his idle moments, of which he had many, Consul Edward Parker wrote to a scientific journal with his observations on the subject.[14] In 1876 *The China Mail* noted that the port 'does not warrant the forming of any great expectations'.[15]

This proved correct. The appearance of foreign steamers helped only Chinese merchants, who dealt in sugar, silk, cotton piece-goods and tobacco. The first foreign merchant was an employee of Edward Herton, founder of one of the larger hongs in Swatow (Shantou). Herton moved to Hoihow himself in about 1878.[16] He was a determined man and became the principal protagonist in the foreigners' fight to rectify weaknesses in the transit pass system.

Herton took on the agency for the Hongkong & Shanghai Bank and for a couple of years was commercial king of this small domain. In 1879 Augustus Schomburg, a German clerk from Shanghai,[17] moved to Hoihow and set up a rival business.[18] With few exceptions, these two firms represented the entire foreign mercantile community for the next 15 years. Sugar was the most important export,[19] and the foreign merchants had to induce steamer operators to load up with it at Hoihow.

Pigs and the 'pig trade'

The larger, faster and safer foreign steamships sparked an expansion in another export trade. Known unpleasantly as the 'pig trade', the shipment of coolies to work South-East Asia's plantations was a lifesaver for the struggling treaty port. From a total of 6000 emigrants in 1885[20] numbers expanded to over 15,000 by 1889. The majority went to Singapore,[21] many tempted by fraudulent promises.

Exporting real pigs also grew in importance during the 1880s. Hainan pigs were considered to be of particularly high quality[22] and Hong Kong's appetite was insatiable. Like all lucrative business ventures, it gave rise to its own ingenious fraudulent practices. The animals were sold by weight at the time of embarkation. The temptation to feed them to bursting point just before embarkation was irresistible. They arrived at their destination 18 hours later, hungry and lighter.[23] Another fraud was to wait for a departing ship to be out of sight, then bring a junk alongside and exchange the cargo of bigger pigs for smaller ones. The correct number of porkers would arrive, and the fat ones could be sold many times.[24]

In 1887 the enterprising Mr. Herton obtained a transit pass to export 20 pigs, only to have them impounded by the authorities, who were afraid that if foreigners were to enter this market there would be a loss of revenue.[25] In fact the Englishman was not considering a full-scale pig-export business; he was trying to pay a Hong Kong merchant, in pigs, for a shipment of yarn he had received.[26] Herton's business in Pakhoi (Beihai) had just been forced to close because he was not allowed use of the transit passes to which he was entitled by treaty. He claimed for wrongful confiscation of his pigs, giving rise to enormous amounts of correspondence and rallying of support from foreign merchants in Hong Kong. Finally, late in 1892 it was announced that pigs would be included on the list of dutiable commodities under the treaties.[27] A doubtless exhausted Herton closed his Hoihow business soon afterwards.

Other difficulties hampered foreign business expansion in Hainan. Kiungchow was named in the treaty but Hoihow was its port. Consequently, the Chinese authorities denied foreigners the right to trade at Kiungchow and attempted to establish 'the recognized bounds of the Treaty Port of Hoihow'.[28] The *likin* office claimed Kiungchow to be 'in the interior' and levied tax on goods moving from one to the other.[29] However, these important principles hardly mattered considering the almost total absence of foreign trade. At the beginning of 1887 the foreign population stood at only 17,[30] not even double the number on the port's opening. There had been no improvements in drainage, lighting or bunding,[31] and the silted approach to the port still presented almost insuperable problems. The Viceroy of Guangdong and Guangxi made a formal visit in 1888. Despite his exalted status, it took three hours to transport him the five kilometres from his moored ship to the shore. He was so incensed that immediately he arrived home he gave instructions for a European engineer to survey the necessary improvements. This was done, but there was no follow-up action.[32]

The problem of buying land

Another problem facing foreigners in Hoihow was the inability to buy land. Attempts were made in 1883 to procure a site to erect a British Consulate, but they met with local opposition and got no further.[33] Some 15 years after the opening of the port, no foreign trader or consul had been able to acquire any site on which to build. Slowly that began to change. A Foreign Office study in 1889 noted the gross inadequacies of the consular premises. To rectify this state of affairs, three sites were considered for purchase. One was the current location, but the price proved exorbitant. The second was at Fort Egeria (named after a visiting British naval vessel and today the site of Binhai Hospital) on Coconut Island (now part of the mainland),[34] to the west of the existing site. Schomburg had acquired land there, as had a Portuguese mission, and it was where the unsuccessful attempt had been made in 1883. The third was on the opposite side of the creek that formed the sea entrance to Hoihow. This plot was smaller but far from Chinese houses, and the one that the report favoured. However, it concluded 'the fact of the matter is that the Chinese do not want us to have any site at Hoihow. They have fought us for 13 years and will continue to do so'.[35] Meanwhile the British Consul 'continues to dwell in a dilapidated barn-like structure'.[36]

Eventually they acquired Coconut Island.[37] However, despite having as a neighbour one of the

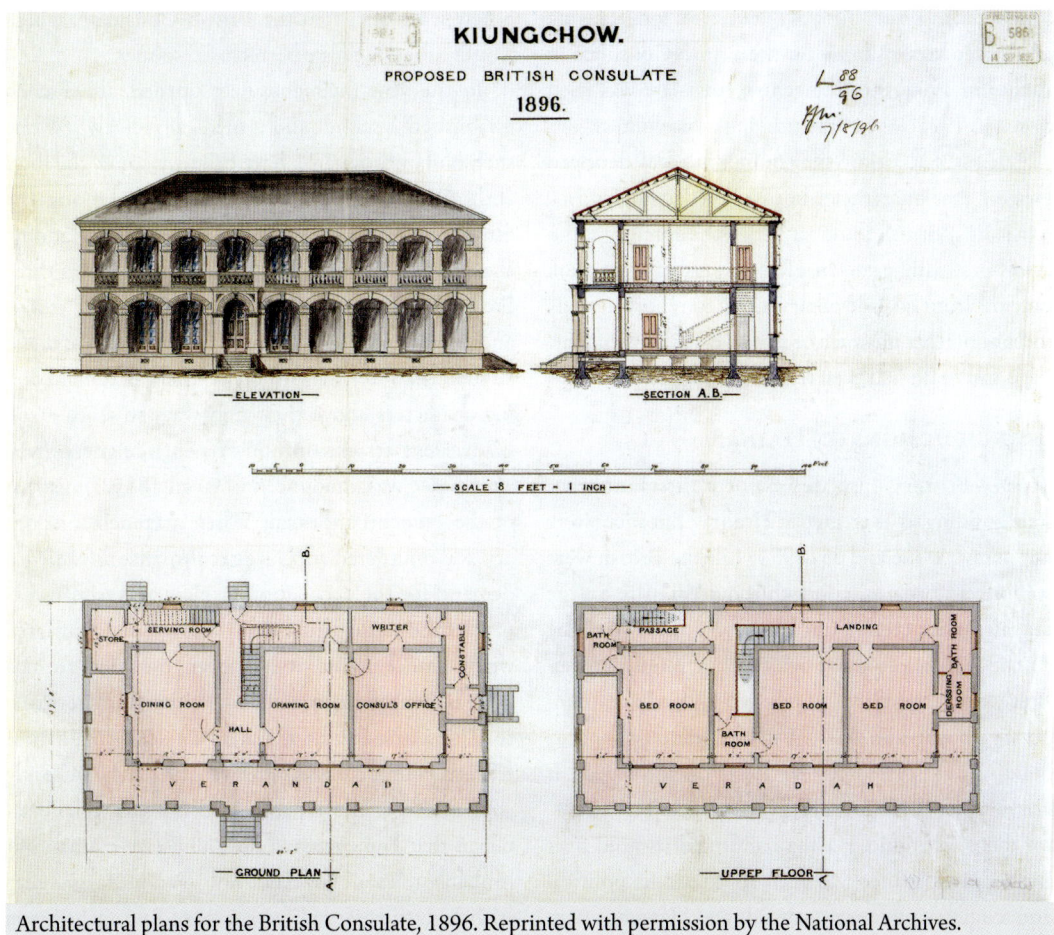

Architectural plans for the British Consulate, 1896. Reprinted with permission by the National Archives.

only two foreign firms operating in Hoihow, it was declared to be unsuitable,[38] perhaps because it was low-lying and prone to flooding. A new site was suggested in 1896, but it was not long before this too was rejected. In 1897 an area was surveyed to the west of Fort Egeria, amid low-lying saltpans behind the American Presbyterian Mission hospital. It became known as the Salt Pan Site. Plans for a colonial-style, three-bedroom consular residence had already been drawn up,[39] waiting only for a final decision on where it should be built. With the Salt Pan Site now confirmed, a foundation stone–laying ceremony was held on Monday 18 September 1898. Doing the honours was the wife of Pierre Essex O'Brien-Butler, who, despite his grand name, was only acting consul. The couple were surrounded by the entire British community of twelve, while flapping above them was a Union Jack big enough to cover them all.[40] The building was completed in 1900[41] but was not used for long. Having taken over responsibility for the British Consulate in Pakhoi in 1904, the Kiungchow consulate was itself closed in 1925, long after outliving its usefulness.

For years at a time the community was deprived even of that guaranteed booster of flagging spirits, a visit by a British gunboat.[42] But the foreign population gradually grew. In 1893, Consul Parker took time off from his tide observations to report joyfully to London that for the first time a British birth, marriage and death had been registered in the same year.[43]

French designs on Hainan

The new British Consulate was not the first European-style building to be erected at Hoihow, but there were not many. At the end of 1897, while the British were still prevaricating, the French acquired a site on the far side of the creek from Hoihow, possibly the one Britain had rejected, on which they built a consulate.[44] It was completed in July 1899,[45] and a contemporary photograph shows it to be a grand two-storey building but isolated 200 metres across the water.[46] It was not there to support French commercial interests, for there was none. Having confirmed its hold over Indo-China, France was keen to extend its political and religious influence eastwards and Hainan was an

An 1898 photograph of the French Consulate, standing in splendid isolation. © SOAS. Image courtesy of Historical Photographs of China, University of Bristol.

important step. Suspicions of French intentions gave a new lease of life to the British Consulate, which would otherwise have been closed sooner.[47]

In the year their consulate opened, the French established a school and a medical facility.[48] While such philanthropy may have been welcome, the local authorities distrusted French motives. During the Sino-French War France was believed to be planning the invasion and occupation of Hainan. When three French warships appeared in July 1884, local troops and militia were mobilized. In September, the *taotai* advised all foreigners to write their nationality in big characters above their doorways so as to avoid inadvertent attacks on non-French foreigners. Even after peace was announced in April 1885,[49] mistrust of the French continued. When a French missionary was murdered in Guangxi Province in 1897, a demand for the occupation of Hainan was feared as part of the settlement claim.[50] Less than a year later, when France found it had been excluded from a large indemnity loan made by Britain and Germany to China, the French threatened to take Hainan in reprisal.[51] Immediately afterwards French bickering with Russia at the expense of China led to a declaration that France would not only seize Hainan but probably the Luichow (Leizhou) Peninsula as well.[52] Although they settled for a lease of Kwangchowwan

(Zhanjiang) in April 1898, rumours of something bigger remained.[53] It was not until the Boxer uprising that the attention of all the powers shifted to the situation further north.

The port comes into the 20th century

With almost all trade in the hands of Chinese merchants, all the foreigners could contribute were their ships, if only they could approach close enough to be efficient and useful. A lack of navigation lighting near Hainan led to a number of shipping accidents, both in the strait and on the south coast.[54] Things improved when buoys and lighthouses appeared in 1894, under the Maritime Customs service,[55] but these did nothing to help the harbour. It was still taking passengers two hours to come ashore from a moored steamer.[56] In 1908 a British engineering firm surveyed the harbour and formulated a plan,[57] but by 1910 the project had been shelved indefinitely. Pigs and coolies remained the chief exports, with the annual total of the latter doubling to 40,000 in the first ten years of the new century.[58]

By 1900 the combined foreign population of Hoihow and Kiungchow had grown to 60,[59] including missionaries and their families. Such a small group made little impression on the treaty port. The French Consulate remained aloof over the water. Most of the foreign buildings were near the British Consulate on the Hoihow waterfront.[60] There were also the Customs Commissioner's residence and some buildings for his assistants, as well as the Customs Club; customs staff formed the largest group within the foreign population. None of these buildings remains today, although a later (perhaps 1930s) Custom House occupies the site of its predecessors, currently a police station.

The Chinese had also been active. New forts were built in 1891 to the west of Hoihow, the side the French were most likely to attack, and the latest Krupp guns installed.[61] The few roads began to be lit by kerosene lamps in 1892 and a telephone system was introduced, although this only linked the telegraph office in Hoihow to the *taotai*'s yamen in Kiungchow.[62] A telegraph link to the mainland had been introduced some years before, but it was never satisfactory; typhoon warnings from Hong Kong arrived days after the storm.[63] A severe typhoon in 1907 wrecked two of the three steamers that serviced Hoihow and the third was disabled. Trade stopped for weeks.[64]

A Kiungchow Electric Light Co. was established in 1914, but it could only run 1000 lamps. Mismanagement and frequent breakdowns soon saw it close. Hoihow's walls were largely demolished in the 1910s to make way for wider streets.[65] Kiungchow's walls also began to disappear, but their former position remains discernible. Until the 1920s the two places were separated by five kilometres of low hills, dotted with graves. The road was improved in 1918 and a handful of decrepit Ford vehicles operated a bus service between the two.[66]

A 20-metre bund was built at Hoihow in 1925. Just behind this, rows of small two-and three-storey commercial buildings remain, giving an impression of what the Chinese business centre was like then. Also in 1925, rubber-wheeled rickshaws were introduced and there were, at last, proper electricity and telephone systems. A final attempt at harbour improvement was made in 1928 with the appointment of the Netherlands Harbour Works Co. but, as previously, the plan was not adopted.[67] Hainan experienced the usual skirmishes between Nationalists and Communists in the 1920s and 1930s. The 1961 film and later ballet *The Red Detachment of Women* was based on one such Hainanese battle.[68] These troubles were to pale compared with the Japanese blockade and subsequent occupation of Hainan as the 1930s ended.

A 1902 British Foreign Office map of Hainan's natural resources bore the legend 'Pigs Everywhere',[69] so important were they to the island's economy. The passing of an era was marked when the *Directory & Chronicle* recorded that during 1940 no pigs were exported at all. That was effectively the end of the treaty port.[70]

Further reading: Halcombe, *The Mystic Flowery Land*; Michalk, 'Hainan Island'; Nield, 'China's Southernmost Treaty Port'.

Kongmoon (Jiangmen) 江門

Guangdong, 22.36° N, 113.06° E
Port-of-Call, 1897 British Treaty
Treaty Port, 1902 British Treaty

Kongmoon, 'The Gate of the River' in Chinese, used to be on the coast. The same silting process that has today left it 50 kilometres inland also created a prosperous alluvial plain, and Kongmoon became one of its chief distribution centres.[1]

The Burmah Convention of 1897 opened Samshui (Sanshui) as a treaty port and designated Kongmoon as a port-of-call. It was hoped Samshui, 75 kilometres upstream, would become the great commercial centre for foreign trade on the lower West River. When Samshui disappointed expectations, the British 1902 Commercial Treaty conferred full treaty port status, and Britain's hopes, on Kongmoon.

Kongmoon was situated about five kilometres up a creek, one of the lateral waterways linking the West River delta. The creek, although navigable for small steamers, was so crammed with Chinese vessels that passage through it was sometimes impossible. Local trade was declining, owing to the growth of nearby Canton (Guangzhou), Macao and Hong Kong, and to a lesser extent the new treaty ports of Kiungchow (Qiongzhou) and Pakhoi (Beihai).[2] Yet the creek remained an extremely busy stretch of water.

In May 1901 Lt. Webster, the commander of a passing British frigate, HMS *Robin*, noticed comparatively deep water at the West River end of the creek, and that there was a suitable site for creating a settlement on the right bank of the river, at a place known as Pakkai (North Street), where there was already a Custom House.[3] A British report suggested that the opening of Kongmoon as a substitute for Samshui 'would be of great and lasting benefit' to British interests. Once this news leaked out, most of the river frontage was bought by local speculators, leaving little room for a British Consulate.[4] But the consular presence was to be even shorter-lived than that at Samshui.[5]

On 7 March 1904 the port was declared open,[6] the last British treaty port to be opened in China proper. As trade in foreign goods was the province of Chinese merchants, there was no need for foreigners to reside in the lesser treaty ports and maintain their expensive consulates. Accordingly the British Consulate, the only official foreign presence to be established at Kongmoon, closed in 1905, never having moved off its houseboat. As for foreign businessmen, despite reports in February 1904 of 'hurried preparations being made',[7] hardly any came. A Mr. Grote appeared and disappeared in 1905, and four Portuguese from

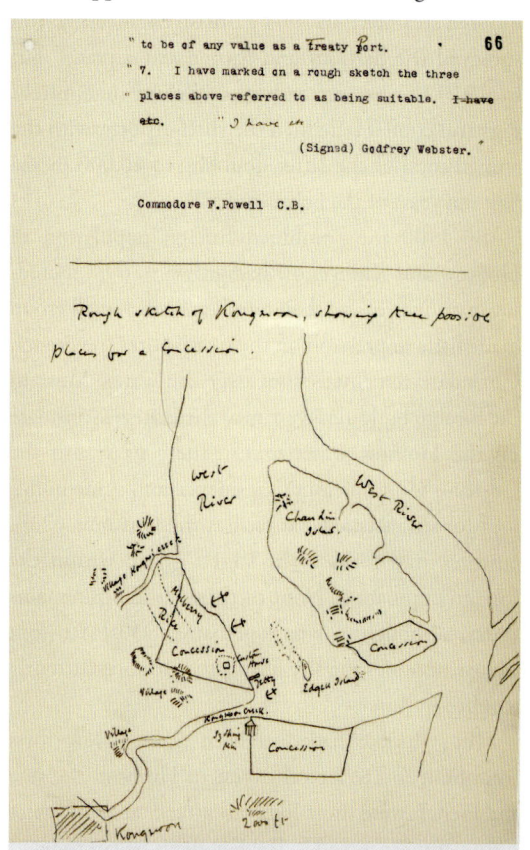

Lt. Webster's rough sketch of 1901, showing the anchorage and three possible sites for a British Concession. Reprinted with permission by the National Archives.

Macao started a manufacturing business in 1906, but were gone a year later. In 1904, Commissioner Maze reported: 'At present there are no indications that . . . the overestimated commercial possibilities of the place will be speedily, if ever, realized.'[8] Opinion had not changed 20 years later.[9]

The customs had maintained a presence in Kongmoon since its port-of-call days; in 1904 theirs was the only European-style house.[10] This formed the nucleus for building offices and residences in what became a sizeable compound. The location is still discernible, although only one building remains. This appears to have been the commissioner's residence; in about 2009 it was moved from its central position to make way for a new residential tower block.* Other foreign buildings appeared in the settlement area, including the residence of the Asiatic Petroleum agent, now resplendent in garish pink, at the south end of Haibang Street. Joining the small community that was beginning to develop were the men and women of the Canadian Presbyterian Mission. They built several dwellings and, in 1912, a 'commodious hospital'.[11] Beautifully renovated for its hundredth birthday, this is still in use as part of a large modern hospital complex. At the south end of the former settlement is an active religious centre, originally built by Americans of the Maryknoll order.

There was a daily steamer service from Hong Kong, a journey of eight hours; today's high-speed ferry takes just over two. There was also a regular service to Wuchow (Wuzhou) and Macao. The main exports carried were fresh fruit and vegetables, tobacco, palm-leaf fans and softwood poles, the latter having been floated down the river from the interior. Imports comprised the usual cotton piece-goods and sundries.[12] In 1912 Kongmoon became the terminus of the Sunning Railway, the country's only private railway, entirely financed and constructed by Chinese. The line ran 100 kilometres from Doushan, in the south of the province.[13] The owner of the line,

Chen Yixi, made his fortune in Seattle. So pleased was he with his success that he commissioned a statue of himself in his home town, Taishan, where he lived with his six wives, not trusting that this would be done posthumously.[14] The Kongmoon station was a few hundred metres north of the Custom House, and a wharf was constructed to link to the steamer service. In 1920 a new bund was completed, linking the railway station to the rest of the settlement. Almost 800 metres long and ten wide,[15] this is today recognizable as Haibang Street.

Kongmoon's trade continued a modest expansion, and manufacturing began—first silk[16] and fruit-canning,[17] and later paper-making[18]—the only foreign input being the machinery and, initially, river transportation. Kongmoon suffered with the rest of the country during the turbulent 1920s and 1930s. In 1937 the exit to the sea was closed because of hostilities, then all communications with the outside world ceased on 29 March 1939, when Kongmoon was occupied by Japanese forces.[19]

Kowloon (Jiulong) 九龍

Hong Kong SAR, 22.19° N, 114.11° E
Customs Station, 1886 British Treaty

From its inception as a British colony, Hong Kong was a duty-free port and, inevitably, a base for smuggling. Profits could be made smuggling anything into China but the most attractive commodity was opium, especially after its trade was legalized by the 1858 Treaty of Tientsin (Tianjin) and abnormally high rates of duty and *likin* were set. In 1867 the Guangdong customs authority established customs stations along the coast near Hong Kong. Unable to tax at source the Chinese were obliged to patrol both Hong Kong waters and land borders, and tax whomever they apprehended.[1]

---

* This was the third time I had seen evidence of historic buildings being physically moved in order to preserve them. The others are the Cathedral Seminary in Foochow (Fuzhou) and the British Consulate in Pakhoi.

1868 map showing the Chinese customs stations near to Macao and Hong Kong. Reprinted with permission by the National Archives.

Their efforts were so successful that by 1868[2] Hong Kong merchants were resentful of this 'fiscal blockade' and damage to their perceived legitimate activities. The methods employed, combining threatened or actual violence with 'squeeze', only added to their anger and frustration. Robert Hart demurred from intervening, seeing the actions of the native customs agents as Chinese officials taxing Chinese people in Chinese waters. The British Foreign Office agreed. In 1871, as a conciliatory gesture, Hart placed a foreign officer on each of the native customs cruisers to ensure proper procedures, but the blockade continued.[3]

Also in 1871 a customs station was established in the walled-city garrison of Kowloon.[4] A stone pier, the Lung-chin Jetty, was constructed to link the station to the sea, some 200 metres away.[5]* In 1876 Hart suggested that a Custom House under foreign management be established in Kowloon to better facilitate the collection of duty. The idea was rejected[6] and the difficulties continued. The 1876 Chefoo Agreement established the principle that both duty and *likin* on opium would be collected simultaneously by the same agency, but there was no agreement about the method. It was not until 1887 that Hart's Custom House was established in Kowloon, following the signing of the 1886 Opium Agreement.

The operation was based at Laichikok, a hamlet opposite the western tip of Stonecutter's Island. Two hulks were moored there as bonded warehouses, and buildings erected for the accommodation of foreign and Chinese staff.[7] Four sub-stations were established, under foreign management. One was at Capsuimoon (Ma Wan) at the western entrance to the harbour, where a stone plaque marks the site; Capsuimoon had been used intermittently in the 1820s as a safe anchorage for opium hulks when Macao and Whampoa (Huangpu) were closed to foreigners, and in 1839 it was where the entire British fleet took refuge when they were evicted from Macao.[8] The other three sub-stations were Kowloon City, Changchow (Cheung Chau) and Fotochow (Fat Tong Chau), a few miles outside the eastern entrance to the harbour, what is now the southern tip of the Tseung Kwan O Industrial Estate. These four had been functioning for 20 years as bases for the provincial customs authorities' hated cruisers.[9] Over the following few years, stations were added at Samshuipo,

---

* Parts of this structure were unearthed in 2008 during the Kai Tak redevelopment project.

Chinlanshu (possibly Tai Lam), Mayautang (possibly Yau Tong), Kautaushek (perhaps Ngautaukok) and Ngaushiwan (Ngauchiwan).

The foreign inspectorate were intended to be responsible for the collection of duty on opium, and for handling complaints made by junk operators about the actions of the native customs cruisers. It became obvious that two taxing authorities operating side by side were both inefficient and confusing. So for the first time foreign customs staff were put in charge of controlling junk traffic and collecting *likin* as well as customs duty. A few *likin* 'farmers' remained, causing difficulties; vested interests ensured that they were not completely removed until 1890. As most of the stations were collection points, not ports, there were no residents apart from the customs people, nor any trade.[10] For everyone's convenience, the indoor staff were based in Queen's Road Central, Hong Kong.

In addition to their water-borne responsibilities, and their responsibility for *likin* collection, the Maritime Customs had to control the movement of goods across the land border. An armed force of six foreigners and 150 Chinese maintained a round-the-clock patrol of the frontier, marked today by Boundary Street. A 2.5-metre-high bamboo fence was erected, with a gate for each of the six highways connecting south with north. Land-based smuggling was eradicated, but only after several serious encounters and deaths. The huge junk population meant that contraband activities at sea were more difficult to control. A fleet of three ocean-going steamers and ten support vessels was hardly sufficient for the task. By 1891 the Kowloon customs operation employed 67 foreigners and 700 Chinese.[11] The expense of operating such a service was enormous, matched by the volume of trade conducted—and China needed the revenue produced.

The presence of a Chinese taxing authority within a free-port British colony required acclimatization by all parties, from junk captains to foreign customs officers. The foreign Hong Kong Chamber of Commerce was anxious that their freedoms not be impinged upon, fearful that their home would 'sink to the level of just another Treaty Port'.[12] Showing sensitivity, Hart advised his staff to carry out their duties with a light but firm hand. Nevertheless it was an odd situation for all concerned. Ultimately, convenience won the day. Although lacking official recognition by the colonial government, the customs presence was tolerated and the commissioner allowed to live in suitable accommodation among his expatriate peers.[13] Of immediate practical relevance was that Hong Kong vessel owners were allowed to complete all formalities before sailing, saving valuable time.

Notwithstanding this tacit acceptance, Hart recorded that Hong Kong was 'tired of having our office there'. In 1890 it was moved from Central to Laichikok, then a journey requiring $5.00 and two hours.[14] Hart suspected that this was prompted by a desire among Hong Kong merchants to put the Chinese service in its place, despite the convenience of having it there.[15] However, further moves were to come shortly afterwards. The extension of the British colony after leasing the New Territory in 1898 meant the Chinese customs stations found themselves on the wrong side of the border. Hart wanted to keep them where they were, but the Hong Kong Chamber of Commerce was bitterly opposed.[16] With what Hart described as 'indecent haste', the colonial government insisted that they be moved back into China.[17] Accordingly, a string of 17 new stations was established fringing expanded Hong Kong. From west to east these were: Lintin Island (Neilingding); Taisan (Dachandao); Chakwan (Chiwan); Kwaimiao (Yuehai); Shatau; Lungtsunku (Longchuanxu); Samchun (Shenzhen); Lofeng (Luofang); Lentong (Liantang); Shataukok; Yimten (Yantian); Kaichung (Xichong); Sangchung (Shayuyong); Tipfuk (Diefu); Hasha (Xiasha); Namo (Nan'ao); and Samun (Sanmen Dao). Foreign staff were based at a number of these stations, their temporary matshed dwellings being gradually replaced by brick or concrete structures.[18]

In 1905 the customs office moved again to Central, to the newly constructed York Building. With the opening of the Kowloon-Canton Railway in 1911, Kowloon City enjoyed the anomaly of becoming a Maritime Customs station proper, collecting duty on the increasing quantity of goods arriving by rail.[19] In the 1920s the writ of the Kowloon operation included all junk traffic entering and leaving Hong Kong, all towed craft, the railway and steamers plying between Hong Kong and inland ports, but not trade between Hong Kong and the treaty ports, if by steam or motor vessels of 100 tonnes or more.[20] These tortuously defined responsibilities were a compromise between correct jurisdiction on the one hand and commercial practicalities on the other. In this manner, the hybrid Kowloon operation of the Chinese Maritime Customs service continued its strange existence into the 1940s.

KULING (LUSHAN) 廬山

Jiangxi, 29.34° N, 115.58° E
Hill Station, 1895

British missionary Edward Little started his career in China in Chinkiang (Zhenjiang) in 1886 and later became the founding entrepreneurial force behind the mountain resort of Kuling, a pun on 'cooling'.[1] In 1895 he started acquiring over 200 hectares of land in the Lushan Mountains, 15 kilometres south of Kiukiang (Jiujiang) and 1000 metres above sea level. His claim to be merely renting land in the 'immediate vicinity' of a treaty port exasperated both the Kiukiang British Consul and the local authorities.[2] Both the Chinese authorities and local people were aghast at the scale of his ambitions although not denying his right to rent. Placards on the Kiukiang city gates in July 1895 threatened the destruction of missionary property. In August a note was left at the Custom House, announcing that all foreigners would be exterminated.[3]

Nevertheless, the land was handed over. Little's plan was always to develop it as a commercial venture (he later gave up his missionary calling for a job in commerce), and he was happily surprised by the speed with which the sub-lots on his estate were bought by foreigners. The Chinese were less pleased, claiming that some of the lots were outside the loosely defined boundary. In a compromise, Little agreed to return part of what he thought had been his, and then erected 60 boundary markers to ensure there was no uncertainty about the rest.[4] The new resort proved popular. During its first summer season, in 1897, there were 300 foreign residents—almost equal numbers of Americans and British, comprising missionaries, business people and officials.[5] So successful was the venture that Little immediately started negotiating for an extension. In 1904 he secured an additional area, doubling the original number of lots.[6]

Management was vested in an estate council, on similar lines to the municipal councils in some of the treaty ports.[7] The body oversaw a foreign community that became larger than in most treaty ports combined. A census was taken each summer: in 1913 there were 1187,[8] rising to 1731 four years later.[9] Holidaymakers came from Shanghai and the Yangtze ports, some from as far away as Canton (Guangzhou), to occupy the 500 houses and bungalows and scores of hotel and guesthouse rooms. The facilities, for which they paid a modest charge, included tennis, swimming, hiking, a public library and an auditorium. There were hospitals, British and American schools, churches, a dairy and branches of several Hankow (Hankou) and Shanghai stores.[10] Kuling became both a summer and winter resort, and some people chose to retire there permanently.[11] For a few years, the British Consul-General in Hankow decamped to Kuling every summer, possibly imagining himself to be in Simla.[12]

The peculiar nature of the place, being a privately owned resort rather than a formal settlement or concession, was to Kuling's advantage during the turbulent mid-1920s. When the British Concessions at Hankow and Kiukiang were returned in 1927, all that happened at Kuling was that British and American residents made a tactical withdrawal, leaving only Germans and Russians; there was a parallel Russian resort known as Luling.[13] But others came. In July

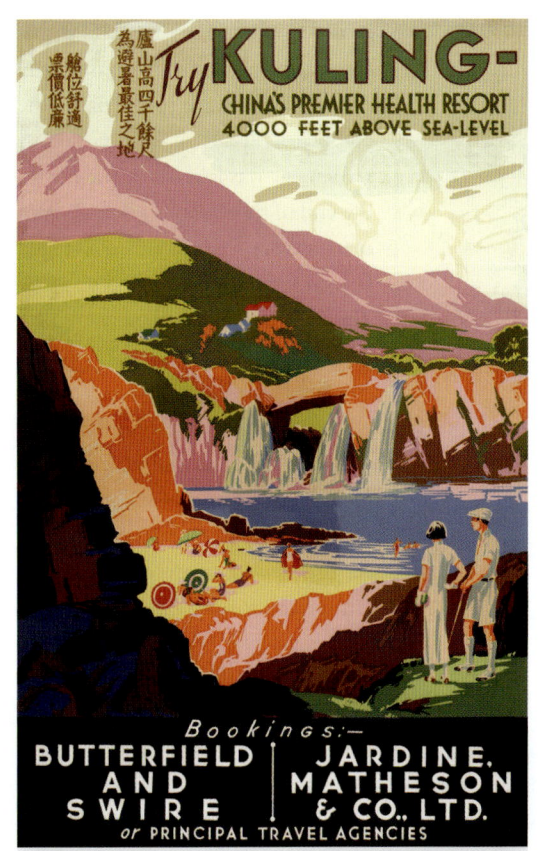

Travel poster from the 1930s, showing the delights of Kuling (Lushan). Source: http://www.flickr.com/photos/trialsanderrors/3751523499. From the Artist Posters Collection at the Library of Congress. [Public domain.]

1927 Mikhail Borodin, Chiang Kai-shek's Marxist mentor, ensconced himself in the Fairy Glen Hotel, surrounded by Russian 'civilians' carrying automatic weapons. A number of senior Chinese took up residence, including Chen Yujen, T. V. Soong and later Chiang himself.[14] The year 1927 saw the first of the annual 'Kuling Conferences', at which it was decided to move the national capital from Hankow to Nanking (Nanjing).[15]

Foreigners returned in 1928, and there was an uneasy coexistence between the foreign-owned mountain resort and what was becoming known as China's Summer Capital. In 1929 an attempt by the Chinese to take control was resisted by the Estate Council on legal grounds.[16] In 1930 the resort was closed to all foreigners 'because of military operations',[17] but 1932 saw 1400 foreign summer residents, in addition to Chiang and his team at their annual meeting.[18] This surreal situation could not last. At a formal, amicable ceremony in April 1936, the chairman of the Kuling Estate Council handed a symbolic key to the estate office building to the director of the Bureau of Administration of the Lushan Settlement, and the Summer Capital was once more part of China.[19]

Further reading: Johnston and Erh, *Near to Heaven*; *Kuling Estate Directory*; Little, *The Story of Kuling*; Molloy, *Colossus Unsung*.

KWANGCHOWWAN (ZHANJIANG)
湛江

Guangdong, 21.11° N, 110.24° E
Leased Territory, 1898 France

French hopes for this leased territory on the Guangdong coast failed to materialize. Comprising a sheltered bay, the immediate islands, a strip of coast and a patch of ocean, some 800 square kilometres in total, Kwangchowwan served only as a base from which the French flag could be flown. Having consolidated its hold on Indo-China after the war of 1884–85, France claimed a sphere of influence over China's south-west provinces. In 1896 French vessels were surveying the harbour at Kwangchowwan, hoping to establish more than just influence.[1] They were attracted by the sheltered harbour, over 30 kilometres long and up to 8 wide.

The scramble among the foreign powers in 1898 to obtain concessions in China gave France the leverage it sought and it made its demands known to Peking (Beijing) regarding Kwangchowwan,[2] a warship having landed troops there in February. In

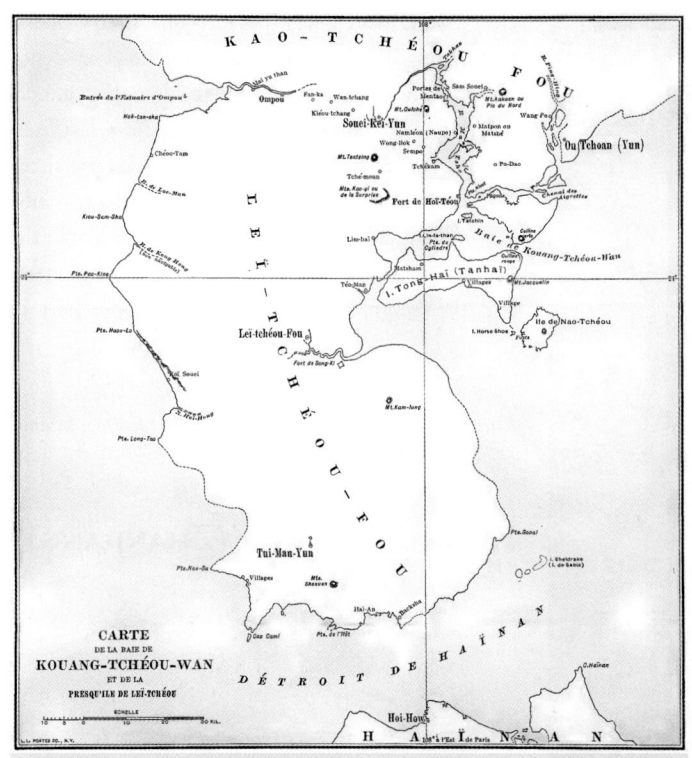

1898 map of the Luichow (Leizhou) Peninsula, showing the 'Baie de Kouang-Tchéou-Wan'. Source: MacMurray, *Treaties and Agreements*, 128.

April the *tricolore* was raised and France took possession.[3] Details of the intended terms of occupation were kept from Peking until 27 May;[4] before settling the proposed boundary, French soldiers laid down marker stones. Ill feeling was rife among the local population, and in November 1899 two junior French officers were captured and beheaded.[5] French outrage led to harsh reprisals, with 300 Chinese killed,[6] and threats that France would seize the entire coast from Yeungkong (Yangjiang), halfway between Kwangchowan and Macao, west to Indo-China. A senior official came from Peking to agree the borders, and a convention was ratified on 5 January 1900, giving France a lease for 99 years.[7]

This desolate outpost did nothing to uphold French prestige; the French press ridiculed the country's lack of influence in China. When the annexation of Guangdong was hinted at, *The China Mail* retorted that 'Hong Kong as an island off the coast of a French colony is too dreadful to contemplate'.[8] These fears subsided and the French began sorting out their new possession. Administration was placed under the colonial structure of Indo-China. A settlement was laid out at the northern end of the harbour some 20 kilometres from the sea and christened Fort Bayard after a visiting warship. The area was well planned, with wide tree-lined roads, proper drainage and public gardens. A residence was built for the French Administrator as were several other public buildings, including a police station.[9] This is still used by the Chinese police, but looks very grubby when compared with the glistening former Administrator's Office, both on Yan'an Road. Ten kilometres up river from Fort Bayard was the Chinese port of Chihkan (present-day Zhanjiang), with a sizeable trade exporting rice, sugar and pigs to Macao and Kongmoon (Jiangmen).[10] The military settlement, opposite Fort Bayard, was even more impressive, with its large barrack blocks and military hospital.[11] Any surviving buildings remain unseen behind the gates of the Chinese navy barracks now occupying the site.

Development was expensive, the French being determined to make the place both beautiful and prosperous, with plans for docks, coal wharves, an arsenal and fortifications.[12] Paul Doumer, Governor-General of Indo-China, paid a visit, proclaiming that the fledgling possession had 'a brilliant future as a port of commerce'. Overly optimistic, perhaps, as at the time of his visit the foreign commercial population comprised two storekeepers.[13] There were never more than a handful of foreign merchants in Kwangchowan and, until the oil companies arrived, all of them were French. The *Chronicle & Directory* for 1901 stated that the settlement's trade was 'expected to develop considerably', the expectation remaining unchanged for almost 30 years. In contrast, the number of officials and missionaries multiplied. Another building from the French period is the Catholic Cathedral of St. Victor, also on Yan'an Road and still an active place of worship.

The early arrival of regular steamers was a blessing, linking Kwangchowwan with Hong Kong and Haiphong, and calling at Hoihow (Haikou) and Pakhoi (Beihai).[14] The place was, by default, a free port. Negotiations to establish a Custom House were interrupted by the Boxer troubles in 1900,[15] and fell into abeyance. The idea was raised again by China in 1928. It was thought unfair for Kwangchowwan to divert trade that had previously gone through nearby Chinese ports, where it was exposed to duty. These ports were suffering, and the imposition of duty at Kwangchowwan would redress the imbalance.[16] In 1936 Kwangchowwan was included in the Chinese customs system when a collecting station was established at Luichow (Leizhou), at the south end of the French area.[17] When Japanese activities in southern China closed many of the usual trade routes, business through Luichow grew remarkably.[18]

Rendition of the territory was promised by France during the 1922 Washington Conference, regardless of what action other powers might take.[19] When France realized that Britain was keeping the New Territory of Hong Kong and Japan was retaining Manchuria, the promise was withdrawn. China argued that Britain's agreement to hand back Weihaiwei (Weihai) was sufficient precedent, but the French answer was still *non*,[20] and there the matter rested. With the advent of the Pacific War, France was in an odd position as regards exposure to Japanese aggression. While Indo-China came under the control of the Vichy government, Kwangchowwan claimed loyalty to Free France.[21] Such confusion bought a few years of isolation from the hostilities, but on 17 February 1943 Kwangchowwan was occupied by Japanese forces.[22] Formal rendition took place in 1946.

Further reading: Cunningham, *The French in Tonkin and South China*; Montague, *The Leasehold of Kouang-Tcheou-Wan*.

KWEILIN (GUILIN) 桂林

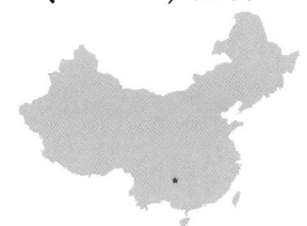

Guangxi, 25.16° N, 110.17° E
Consular Station, 1942 Britain

A canal link northwards to the Yangtze justified Kweilin as the provincial capital of Guangxi, until Nanning took the title in 1914. The Nationalist government made Kweilin their capital in 1936, before moving to Chungking (Chongqing) in December 1937. Never a significant centre of foreign trade, from 1937 Kweilin was the halfway stopover for Hong Kong-to-Chungking flights. Its geographical location made it a base for monitoring Japanese activity in China, so Britain established a consulate-general in August 1942. The station closed on 5 November 1944. Five days later the Japanese captured the city, linking their occupied territories in China and South-East Asia.[1]

LAPPA (HENGQIN DAO) 橫琴島

Guangdong, 22.11° N, 113.31° E
Customs Station, 1886 British Treaty

The genesis of Lappa as a customs station is similar to that of Kowloon (refer to the Kowloon entry for background and rationale). Lappa, once an island and now part of Zhuhai, is situated opposite Macao's Inner Harbour. It was one of several islands over which Portugal claimed a loose sovereignty as dependencies of Macao.[1] The Opium Agreement of

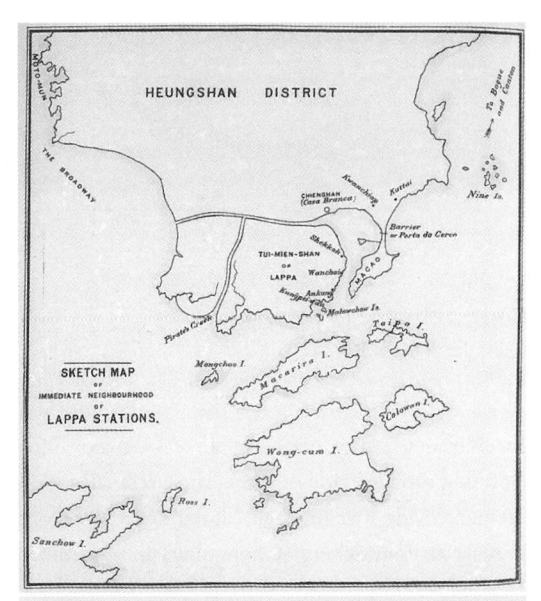

1891 map showing Macao and the adjacent island of Lappa (Hengqin Dao). Source: Customs Decennial 1882–91.

1886, although signed in Hong Kong, resulted in a Custom House being established there in 1887.

There were also two principal supporting stations: Malowchow (today a small hill east of Lianping), at the western entrance to the Inner Harbour, and Chienshan (Qianshan), called Casa Branca in Portuguese. The latter had three strategically located sub-stations to monitor passing junks: Kwanchiap (in the vicinity of Paotaishan Park); Kuttai (to the northeast of the Barrier Gate); and Shekkok (Shijiaoju). Another was added at Kungpei-wan, the bay south of Lappa in which Malowchow Island lay,[2] plus one in the West River delta—Wangmoon (Hengmen). By 1897 there was a sub-station at Mongchow (a separate island but now absorbed into Hengqin Island).[3] Three more were added in 1899, at Tungho (Dong'ao), Gaemoon (Yamen) and Naiwanmoon (Jinwan) in the delta.[4] In 1901 another opened at Nine Islands (Jiuzhou Dao) north-east of Macao.[5] Lappa and its string of twelve small stations and sub-stations became responsible for an area stretching along the south-west coast as far as Hainan.[6]

Many staff were needed to manage such a busy district. When the Custom House was opened there was a foreign commissioner, assisted by 22 European staff, mostly Portuguese, and even more Chinese.[7] By the turn of the 20th century the number of Europeans had increased to 54, assisted by 27 Sikhs. Additionally there were four patrol vessels under foreign command.[8] Lappa's area of responsibility decreased in 1902 with the opening of Kongmoon (Jiangmen) as a treaty port with Wangmoon and Gaemoon attached.[9] Further reductions followed when, in accordance with the Anglo-Chinese Agreement of May 1911, legitimate trade in opium diminished and then ceased altogether. As opium duty had been the principal source of revenue for Lappa, its absence lessened the workload considerably.[10] By 1918 the Lappa customs operation was headed by an assistant commissioner, who oversaw a European staff of 16.[11] A number of the smaller sub-stations closed, and the *1912–21 Customs Decennial Report* admitted that 'the frontier is no longer seriously patrolled by our preventive officers'.[12] Lappa remained as a customs station under foreign management until the 1940s, by which time the European staff had been reduced to two.[13]

Lappa customs' main administrative office was in Macao, at 2 Rua dos Prazeres.[14] There were also a number of senior and junior staff residences on Lappa, as well as the Custom House itself. These have all been swept away by the spate of development in the area surrounding Macao.

Lintin Island (Neilingding Dao) 內伶仃島

Guangdong, 22.24° N, 113.48° E
Opium Receiving Station, 1820s

Lintin's day came and went before the Treaty Port Era. This solitary outcrop, barely four kilometres by two, was claimed for Portugal by Jorge Alvares in 1513[1] but not pursued. The island later became popular with ships of all nations waiting for permission to proceed to Canton (Guangzhou).[2] Lintin's importance increased in 1821 when Whampoa (Huangpu) and Macao's opium business was curtailed, forcing a move to the 'outer anchorage' of Lintin,[3] where for the next 20 years commercial activity seethed. The opium hulks, moored in the island's bays, received and distributed the drug. Whenever winds became too strong, the ships took refuge in the more sheltered anchorages of Capsuimoon (Ma Wan) and Cumsingmoon (Jingxingmen).[4]

The volume of business justified the Chief Superintendent of British Trade moving to Lintin in 1840, conducting his duties from the vessel *Louisa*.[5] James Matheson suggested that Britain annex Lintin as a permanent base;[6] Hong Kong was selected instead. On the cessation of hostilities most of the opium business moved to the new colony and Lintin faded into obscurity. It remained popular for a while as a pirate base; HMS *Surprise* lived up to its name and destroyed a large pirate fleet there in 1858.[7]

Nothing remains to remind us of the activities of the early 19th century, except for a solitary 1831 European gravestone that was seen being used as a table in a village in the late 1990s.[8] In 1950, after the period covered by this volume, remnants of the Nationalist government imposed a blockade on the Pearl River Delta from a base on Lintin.[9] The island is described today as a nature reserve and is inaccessible.

Jardine Matheson's opium ship *Jamesina* at Lintin Island (Neilingding Dao), 1838. Oil on canvas, by William John Huggins. Courtesy of Martyn Gregory Gallery, London.

Lungchow (Longzhou) 龍州

Guangxi, 22.20° N, 106.51° E
Treaty Port, 1887 French Treaty

France selected Lungchow as a treaty port following the demarcation of the Tonkin–Guangxi border in 1887.[1] The town was a Chinese military post, its erratic walls constructed in the same year,[2] perhaps with the French in mind. The Custom House was opened on 1 June 1889. The foreign population of seven in 1891 consisted entirely of consular and customs staff.[3] It was not the potential of Lungchow itself that attracted the French. The plan was to extend the Haiphong railway into China, thereby capturing the Guangxi trade from the West River. The first part of this plan was fulfilled in December 1894 when the line reached Langson, 50 kilometres to the south.[4]

However, the Chinese merchants doubted this new route would make westward transportation any quicker or cheaper. Initial experience regarding trade with Canton (Guangzhou) showed that the route via Haiphong was up to 16 times more expensive than taking the West River.[5] Their products were mainly agricultural—sugar, beans, timber and aniseed—and they had already seen the trade in the last killed by the punitive rates of duty for crossing French territory. Instead they relied upon junks to take their goods up and down the Zuo River to Nanning, where it joined the West River. The French completed the track from Langson to the border in early 1902, but it got no further.[6]

French trade did nothing to boost the fortunes of Lungchow. More European goods passed from China into Tonkin than vice versa. In 1893 these even included those French gastronomic essentials red wine and mustard.[7] In 1896 the newly appointed French Consul missed a public relations coup by travelling to his post via the West River rather than the French railway.[8] Yet Lungchow remained a strategically important post for France, part of the constantly simmering French plans for expansion into Guangxi. The first French Consulate stood outside the town, on the right bank of the Li River, moving to land opposite the town where this most impressive building still stands.

The turmoil of the mid-1920s increased the port's trade when the West River was closed by fighting between Guangxi and Guangdong.[9] In 1939, when the southern ports were disrupted by Japanese activity, the volume of trade increased a hundredfold[10] but only for a short while. In June 1940 the whole area was occupied by the Japanese and the treaty port's life came to an end.[11]

Further reading: Lee, *France and the Exploitation of China*.

Lungkow (Longkou) 龍口

Shandong, 37.38° N, 120.19° E
Open City, 1914 Presidential Mandate

For centuries Lungkow was the sea port for much of Shandong. Going north across the Gulf of Chihli to Manchuria were fruit and vegetables. Coming back were beans and beancake (used for fertilizer). Lungkow's vermicelli was famous; then a cottage industry, now an international brand. Economic ties were strengthened by the summer migration of 60,000–80,000 agricultural workers from Shandong to northern Manchuria.

Lungkow came to international prominence through Japan's actions in the First World War. Japan sided with the Allies, undertaking to 'capture' Tsingtao (Qingdao), a German possession. To this end, on 3 September 1914 Japan landed 50,000 troops at Lungkow from 18 transport ships.

Although contravening all principles of sovereignty, this move was expected; Japan had asked permission for its troops to enter China, and been refused.[1] Instead, China instructed its forces not to resist the invaders. When the Japanese landed, the Chinese commander at Lungkow made a polite request that they leave, which, with equal politeness, they disregarded. There were no hostilities, and the Japanese marched towards Tsingtao.[2]

At Japan's prompting, Lungkow had been 'voluntarily' opened on 8 January 1914 by Presidential Mandate.[3] A customs presence was established on 1 November 1915. Subsequent development of the port was half-hearted. The anchorage, with a bed of clay, not sand, was protected to the north by the Qimu promontory. But a population of 6000 was insufficient to create a thriving settlement. A plot of land north of the old town was bought and laid out for development by the New Settlement Development Co.[4] One of its first actions was constructing a concrete wharf and pier. This was completed and handed over in May 1920.[5] The customs office moved to be near this new facility and, for the first time in the service's history, had a Chinese officer in charge.[6] Godowns were erected and a small, man-powered railway track linked the new town to the old. But nothing else happened and the new pier decayed through lack of use.[7]

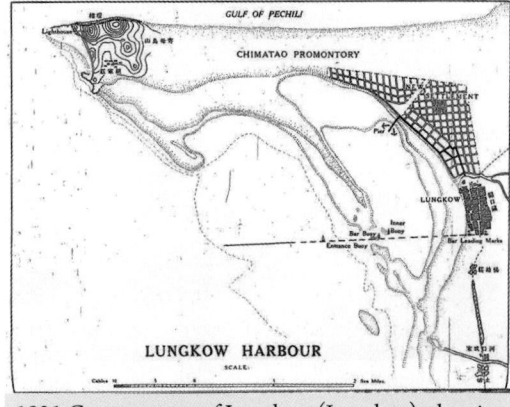

1921 Customs map of Lungkow (Longkou), showing the proposed New Settlement. Source: Customs Decennial 1912–21.

Migrant workers continued to go to Manchuria for the season; 120,000 in 1927 and 149,000 in 1929.[8] Vermicelli exports increased, from 1600 tonnes in 1916[9] to almost 16,000 tonnes in 1927.[10] These activities had expanded since the port opened, but predated it. The commercial focus gravitated inland and hopes rested on the new highway. This commenced in 1921, joining Lungkow to Chefoo (Yantai) in the east and Weihsien (Weifang) in the south, where it linked with the Tsinan (Jinan) to Tsingtao railway. The road increased Lungkow's usefulness slightly, and there were hopes that a railway would follow.[11] None did. Excluding Japanese, there were never more than three foreigners—all working with the customs.[12]

The connection to Manchuria dominated Lungkow's brief existence as an open port. The Russian rouble was in free circulation in the town's markets,[13] later replaced by the Japanese yen;[14] the Japanese Bank of Lungkow opened in 1909.[15] Japanese forces, a presence in nearby waters in the 1930s,[16] blockaded the town in 1938,[17] then occupied it on 2 March 1939, thereby closing the open port.[18]

There is no sign today of Lungkow having ever been anything other than a prosperous, albeit somewhat small Chinese port.

Macao (Aomen) 澳門

Macao SAR, 22.11° N, 113.22° E
Occupied Territory, 1557 Portugal
Colony, 1887 Portugal

Portuguese traders visited Macao in the early 16th century, establishing formal occupation in 1557. For almost three hundred years this outpost provided the only nearby refuge for foreign merchants when they were obliged to depart Canton (Guangzhou) at the end of the November-to-May trading season. Twice in the 18th century successive emperors suggested

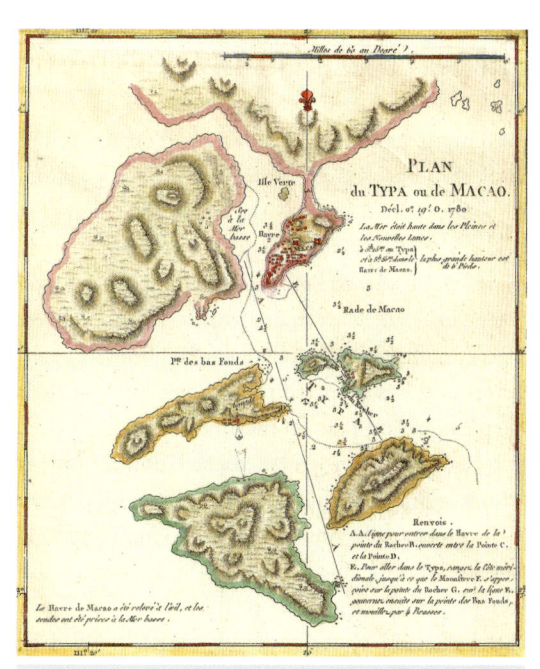

1780 sea chart of Macao and its surrounding islands, by Rigobert Bonne. From the author's collection.

making Macao the centre of all foreign trade. Twice the offer was declined.[1] When the British mercantile community was forced to leave Canton in 1839 they sought refuge in Macao, but were refused. Macao's commercial status declined once the British colony of Hong Kong was created in 1842.[2]

Portugal claimed possession of Macao by right while paying 500 *taels* in annual rent to the Chinese. This reinforced the Chinese view that China was the sovereign power, as did the taxing stations they maintained.[3] The relationship was uneasy. The outcome of the First Opium War in 1842 encouraged Portugal to flex its muscles. It refused to pay the annual rent, the taxing stations were closed and all signs of Chinese authority were expelled. Portugal persisted in seeking Peking (Beijing)'s recognition of its ownership of Macao. Following the Second Opium War, a treaty was signed in Tientsin (Tianjin) in 1862 giving Portugal the right in perpetuity to occupy and govern Macao, tantamount to recognition of sovereignty;[4] China did not ratify it.

The leverage the Portuguese needed finally presented itself in 1886 in China's Opium Agreement with Hong Kong. A device to control smuggling in the British Colony, this agreement was conditional upon China procuring Macao's adoption of similar measures to control its opium trade. Portugal found itself, for once, in a strong bargaining position. Lisbon presented virtually the entire 1862 treaty for Peking's reconsideration. Again negotiations nearly foundered, owing to Portugal's insistence that Lappa (Hengqin Dao) be included within Macao. Robert Hart considered the Portuguese to be obstinate negotiators and was prepared to abandon hope of their cooperation and take on the smugglers without it.[5] Eventually, the Portuguese backed down, content with recognition of their sovereignty over Macao. On 1 December 1887 the Treaty of Peking confirmed Macao as Portuguese territory.[6] The agreement also recognized as dependencies the islands of Taipa (Dangzai) and Coloane (Jiu'ao Shan), claimed by Portugal in 1851 and 1864 respectively.

However, Macao had been eclipsed by its bigger, more successful British neighbour. No longer having much purpose, trade dwindled to insignificant levels and Macao was largely left to reflect on past glories.

In the late 1930s Macao claimed neutrality in connection with Japanese advances into China. Japan initially respected this stance but when Hong Kong fell in 1941, Macao was isolated. While it ostensibly remained free, the Japanese bullied the Macao government into accepting 'advisers'. When the United States discovered that these advisers were party to the provision of fuel to Japanese forces through Macao, American aircraft bombed the fuel storage hangars. There were other, mistaken attacks by American pilots who thought they were over Japanese territory;[7] by then it had become quite hard to tell the difference. Compensation of US$20 million was paid by Washington after the war. Little damage had been done to Macao's historic core, which continues to be a very special place.

Further reading: Braga, *The Western Pioneers*; Boxer, *Seventeenth Century Macau*; Coates, *Prelude to Hong Kong*; Ljungstedt, *An Historical Sketch*; Nield, *The China Coast*; Puga, *The British Presence*.

MENGTSE (MENGZI) 蒙自

Yunnan, 23.22° N, 103.24° E
Treaty Port, 1887 French Treaty

France's war of 1884–85 with China opened the Tonkin borders with Guangxi and Yunnan provinces for Sino-French trade. As those borders remained undefined, the 1885 Treaty of Tientsin (Tianjin) merely said that trade would be conducted at 'certain spots which shall be settled later'.[1] It was two years before an Additional Convention defined the 'spots' as the treaty ports Lungchow (Longzhou), Mengtse and Manhao.[2] Manhao was the head of junk navigation on the Red River, 40 kilometres south of Mengtse, and was later exchanged for Hokow (Hekou).

The short journey from Mengtse to its river port of Manhao took two days.[3] Yunnan's many major river systems each carved out deep valleys and gorges, separated by high mountain ranges. Communication was a constant challenge to those who would open this undeveloped province to modern commerce. Consequently, railways were a thing more frequently discussed than seen. When a line eventually reached Mengtse it was first the making, then the breaking, of it as a business centre.

There seemed to be little enthusiasm for opening Mengtse. No French Consul arrived until 30 April 1889, having travelled up the Red River. The customs staff—three Europeans and three Chinese—arrived on 15 July, after a 103-day journey from Canton (Guangzhou). The Custom House was opened on 24 August, together with a branch at Manhao.[4] To encourage two-way trade, the French relaxed some of their import duties and waited for commerce to flow.[5] To French chagrin early trade in foreign goods largely involved Hong Kong and India, not Tonkin and France.[6] A consulate was built in 1893, outside the East Gate, along with quarters for customs staff;[7]

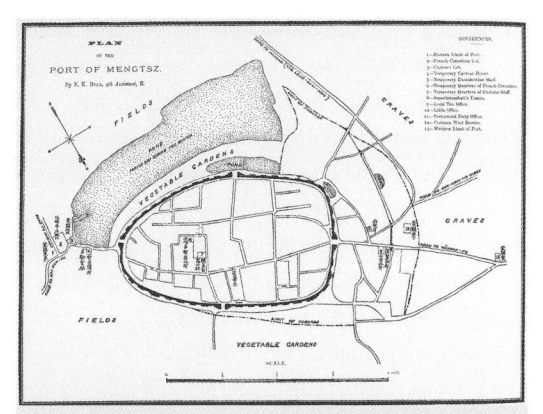

1891 Customs map of Mengtse (Mengzi), showing the French Consular Lot (2) and the Customs Lot (3) on the extreme left. Source: Customs Decennial 1882–91.

a new Custom House followed two years later.[8] The consulate can still be seen, looking like the *mairie* of a large provincial French village. A small, ornate Chinese building, purporting to be the Custom House, stands in the erstwhile customs compound. After looting during an anti-French riot in June 1899, the French demanded a concession, confident they would get one. They did not.[9]

Mengtse's staple export was tin, representing 80 percent of China's output.[10] Mines had been worked for centuries at Kochiu (Geju) 30 kilometres west, using age-old methods. The traditionally minded owners refused to experiment with machinery until the 1920s[11] yet were happy to consider using more modern means of distribution; the French railway line from Haiphong was extended, in 1909, to Pishihchai (Bisezhai), ten kilometres north of Mengtse and close enough to the tin mines to be an attractive alternative to using pack animals.

Construction of the railway was a massive undertaking, involving surveying the challenging terrain, building tunnels and bridges, and laying track. By 1902, 50 French engineers and other staff were living in Mengtse.[12] Four years later there were 800–900 working in the province, and the amount they spent on beer, wine and household effects was having an impact on the trade figures.[13] French merchants followed, and by 1910 all the major Indo-China firms had offices at Mengtse. There were seven French staff at the consulate, and 14 foreign customs men.[14] Seven foreign hotels appeared at various points along the railway[15] and the town boasted a French Club.

The prosperity that follows railways made the northward journey, affecting locals and foreigners alike. The line reached Yunnan-fu (Kunming), the provincial capital, in 1910. The 60,000–70,000 pack animals that had been employed in 1908 had reduced to twelve in 1911. The number of junks on the river fell from 10,000 to 2000.[16] There followed a gradual drift of foreign business and merchants to Yunnan-fu. By the 1920s the flame of Mengtse's commercial success had all but flickered out. The final blow came in 1932, when the role of the customs stations was reversed—the former branch at Yunnan-fu became the regional head office, Mengtse an increasingly insignificant appendage.[17]

Further reading: Lee, *France and the Exploitation of China*.

Mokanshan (Moganshan)
莫干山

Zhejiang, 30.36° N, 119.53° E
Hill Station, 1890

Foreign missionaries in China were skilled in finding resort areas at which they could hide from the rigours of the summer months. Mokanshan was such a resort, about 40 kilometres north-west of Hangchow (Hangzhou) and perched on a 600-metre-high hilltop. The first Western-style house was built there around 1900.[1] Many more followed and by 1917 there were over 100, accommodating a summer population of 700, almost half of them children.[2] The facilities were run by the Mokanshan Summer Resort Association,[3] which looked after sanitation, road maintenance and medical services, also providing recreation facilities

The tennis courts during what seems to be a children's sports day, early 1930s. Courtesy of Mark Kitto.

such as tennis courts and a swimming pool. A kindergarten ensured parents could relax.[4]

There were Protestant and Catholic churches, various stores and a post office. The oddly named (for a hilltop settlement) Railway Hotel took its name from the Shanghai-Hangchow-Ningpo Railway Co., which organized transportation to the resort by a mixture of rail, road, canal and sedan chair.[5] Mokanshan's more illustrious visitors included Chiang Kai-shek in 1927—honeymooning with his bride, Song Meiling[6]—and Du Yuesheng, an infamous Shanghai gangster.[7]

Less welcome were the Japanese soldiers who occupied the resort in December 1937.[8] By then most owners had sold their properties, if they could, or abandoned them. Many are still inhabited today—and some are available for rental as holiday homes.

Further reading: Johnston and Erh, *Near to Heaven*; Kitto, *China Cuckoo*.

MUKDEN (SHENYANG) 瀋陽

Liaoning, 41.47° N, 123.25° E
Open City, 1903 American and Japanese Treaties

Taking advantage of China's defeat by Japan in 1895, Russia extended its Trans-Siberian Railway across Manchuria to Vladivostok. Two years later it forced another concession for a branch line south, through Harbin and Mukden to Dalny (Dalian) and Port Arthur (Lüshun). In 1900, with China preoccupied by the Boxer Rebellion, Russia used its new railways to occupy large tracts of China's north-east. Japan was deeply concerned about the Russian advances and enlisted American support to object.[1] The two countries signed separate treaties on 8 October 1903, requiring the Chinese government to open Mukden as a place of international residence and trade.[2] Japan was planning action that was more direct. When war broke out between Russia and Japan in 1904, the Japanese army discovered that the Russians had made Mukden into a stronghold, from which they were driven out only after a major battle.[3] Mukden was opened to foreign trade after the Japanese army left in 1906. Consuls from America, Britain, Germany and Japan took up residence immediately, to be told by China that the treaties only required Mukden to be opened on terms 'to be discussed later'. There was no mention of tax and duty concessions and there was to be no foreign-managed Custom House. However, whether Mukden was an open city or a treaty port hardly mattered to the foreign powers. The initial four consulates were joined in 1909 by France and Russia, all there solely because the others were. In 1907 Mukden became the seat of the Viceroy of the Three Eastern Provinces, as the Chinese called Manchuria,[4] making the consular posts political, not commercial.[5]

Yet Mukden did have some commercial importance. The Japanese had inherited the Russian railway infrastructure south of Changchun, naming it the South Manchuria Railway (SMR), and Mukden became its operational centre. Today's main station in Shenyang is easily recognizable as the old SMR station. Mukden was at the junction of two other major lines—to Antung (Dandong) and Peking (Beijing), each with its separate station.

The city contained a royal palace and ancient imperial tombs, requiring the railway to be kept two kilometres west of the city. This allowed the Russians the advantage of commandeering the entire area between the city wall and the station as their concession.

The West Wing of the South Manchuria Railway Headquarters Building in 1922. It looks just the same today. Source: *Manchuria: Land of Opportunities*, 76.

The Japanese inherited this area, and built using the Russians' plans. It came to be known as the Railway Concession and was vast—over six square kilometres. Its outline and distinctive street layout are still clearly visible. Some of the finest foreign buildings in the city are to be found on the grand Zhongshan Square: the SMR's Yamato Hotel (now the Liaoning Hotel, still impressive); the former Yokohama Specie Bank (now a Chinese bank); and the Japanese (now Chinese) Police Station.

By the end of their first year there was a Japanese population of 2500.[6] While the Chinese wanted to keep all foreigners in the Railway Concession, or at least outside the city wall, the Treaty Powers disagreed.[7] Foreign merchants established themselves wherever they could, some giving their addresses as 'inside the Small South Gate'.[8] An unofficial foreign settlement grew on a patch of land between the western wall and the Railway Concession. It was not strictly a settlement, being administered by the Chinese city authorities,[9] but the foreign consulates congregated there.[10] Today there is an otherwise inexplicable sight on a triangle of land to the west of Qingnan Main Street: six houses of European design, huddled together. Some are unoccupied and others residences of officials.

Missionaries had been the first foreigners to arrive in Mukden. French Catholics built a church outside the South Gate in 1878. In 1892, the city became the seat of the Bishop of Manchuria. His church was destroyed in 1900. Taking its place in 1912 was the twin-spired grey brick and stone cathedral that stands there today. Preceding the Catholics by a year was John Ross, a Scottish Protestant who built a church just outside the Great East Gate. His enlarged structure of 1889 is still a popular place of worship.

The foreign merchants also left a mark on the city. After the First World War the number of foreign firms grew. British-American Tobacco alone employed 24 expatriates for its manufacturing and distribution activities.[11] In 1919 the foreign population of the city was over 2600, mainly Japanese, with a further 22,000 Japanese in the Railway Concession.[12] Substantial new houses were built for the managers of the bigger companies.[13] The city was now a major industrial centre.

During 1931 Manchuria came increasingly under the control of the Japanese army, acting on its own authority.[14] The Tokyo government attempted to restrain the rapacity of its troops. The Japanese commander received a warning that orders were coming that would end his glory days. On 18 September 1931 a small Japanese bomb blew up part of the railway line.[15] Now known as the Mukden Incident, this provided a perfect excuse for 'retaliation'. Japanese troops poured out of the concession, and the annexation of the north-east began. By 1932 Manchuria had become the 'independent' state of Manchukuo, with the unfortunate Henry Pu Yi as its emperor.

Further reading: Brooks, *Japan's Imperial Diplomacy*; *Manchuria: Land of Opportunities*; Putnam Weale, *Manchu and Muscovite*; Ranger, *Up and Down the China Coast*.

Nanking (Nanjing) 南京

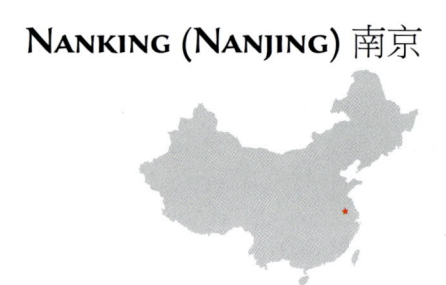

Jiangsu, 32.05° N, 118.43° E
Treaty Port, 1858 French Treaty

In 1858 the French Treaty of Tientsin (Tianjin) gave treaty port status to Nanking, but it was not formally opened; the surrounding country was occupied by the Taiping armies, and since 1853 Nanking had been their capital. Establishing a foreign trading post was considered neither possible nor desirable. The rebels were defeated in 1864 with much loss of life. In an orgy of looting and terror, the incoming Hunan troops completed the destruction of the city and its people. Women and small children were run through for sport, not for the last time in Nanking's history. The imperialists inherited a pile of rubble where there had been a proud and wealthy city.[1]

In 1865 British and French officials arrived to mark out their respective concessions. Their chosen sites were disputed by the city authorities. The matter was referred to Peking (Beijing), and ten years later a 'resolution' was announced: the requested areas 'had been washed away by the river', closing the case.[2] This was untrue but not implausible.

Nanking's major export was silk, an industry on which one-third of the population was dependent.[3] Chinese merchants obtained whatever foreign goods they needed from Chinkiang (Zhenjiang), 70 kilometres downstream and a treaty port since 1858.[4] The foreigners knew that Nanking would be of more political significance than commercial. This had been demonstrated by the British in 1842 when they threatened the ancient city to gain the Imperial Court's attention.

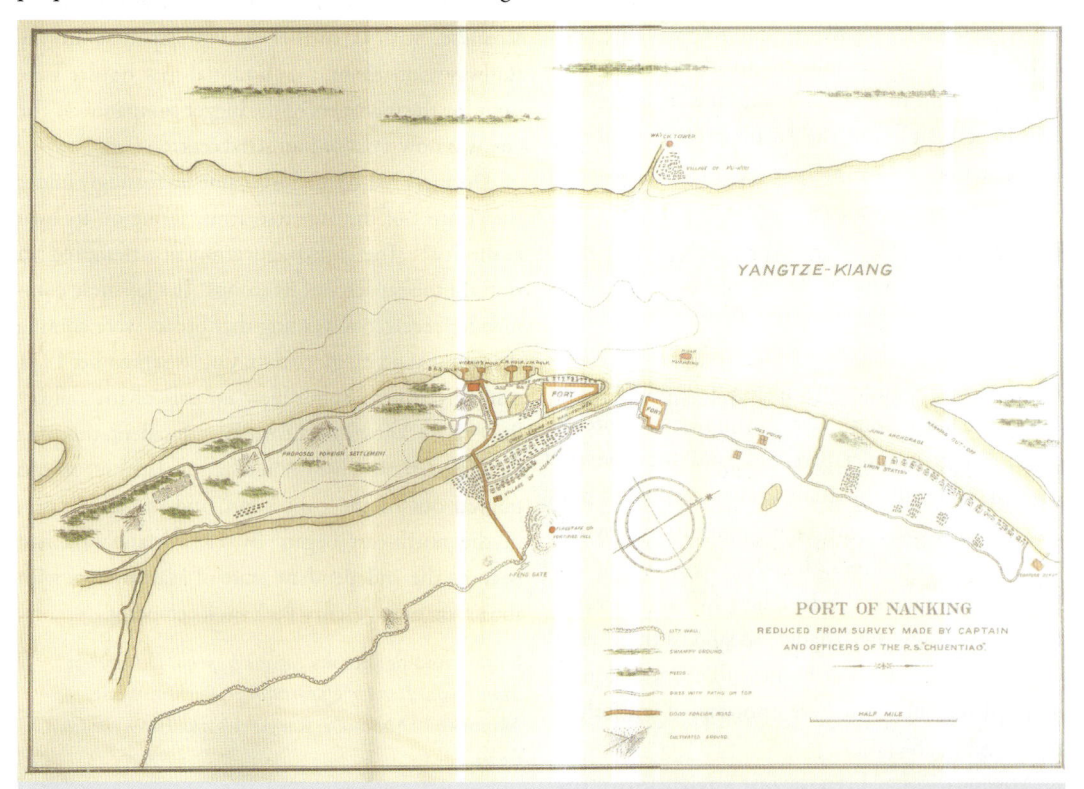

1901 Customs map of Nanking (Nanjing), showing the foreign steamer jetties and the site for the proposed foreign settlement. Source: Customs Decennial 1892–1901.

In 1899, as France tried to revive its dormant claim to a concession at Nanking,[5] Peking established a Custom House. After 40 years, Nanking formally assumed treaty port status. At this time the various foreign powers were hovering like vultures picking off the choicest pieces of a collapsing Chinese state. The Chinese preferred the treaty port outcome, and the accompanying international quasi-protection, to possibly more damaging demands from foreign powers. The area designated for foreign settlement, Hsiakuan (Xiaguan), was on the upstream side of the creek where foreign steamers had called since the 1870s, effectively becoming the port for Nanking.[6]

A significant number of foreigners resided in Nanking, almost exclusively British and American missionaries living within the city walls. Hsiakuan primarily provided a site for the Custom House, and a base for the shipping companies. Then, without warning, in January 1903 a large part of Butterfield & Swire's riverfront lot fell into the river. It happened at a busy time and, with an entire iron godown and all its contents, 150 Chinese coolies were washed away. The warehouse site was now a torrent of rushing water over twelve metres deep. In February, 60 metres of the customs frontage similarly disappeared, prompting discussion about whether the entire area should be abandoned.[7] Instead, the Custom House was moved from its temporary quarters to a new building further inland and the bund was patched up, although there were further collapses in later years.[8]

Hopes for commercial development rested on the railways. Nanking was accessible by the largest ocean-going steamers all year round, and therefore a feasible transshipment port for the mineral-producing provinces in the north. Foreign firms appeared in Nanking in anticipation of coming prosperity. After Swires came Standard Oil in 1905. The first railway project, a line from Shanghai, had been awarded in 1903 to the British & Chinese Corporation, a joint venture between Jardines and the Hongkong Bank. The track was to traverse some of the country's richest tea, silk and cotton regions.[9] However, although popular with passengers, the opening of this line in 1908 did little for Nanking's trade figures as it could not compete with the established steamer services.[10]

A greater impact was made by the Tientsin-Pukow Railway. Work on its southern section commenced in 1909 at Pukow (Pukou), the village immediately over the river from Nanking, and was completed three years later. Pukow became a major port in its own right with a better anchorage than Nanking-side. A Pukow Custom House was established in July 1915, and Nanking's port limits were extended to include it. Nanking started to export produce from the north directly to both the southern ports and foreign countries.[11] Many new government buildings appeared in the city. Two impressive examples remain: the former post office in Da Ma Road and the former Yangtze Hotel, at the corner of Baoshan Street and Zhongshan North Road, now a police station.

Just as the new railways raised hopes, they were dashed by the political events of 1911. The revolution was violent and bitter and few cities in China suffered more than Nanking. Half the population fled in panic in the first few days and all business stopped. The revolutionary army laid siege to the city. For a short time Imperial forces withstood the onslaught, even when faced by a revolutionary uprising from within, but were forced to surrender on 2 December. Damage and looting during the siege and the failed internal uprising was nothing compared with the havoc wreaked by the incoming soldiery. The Manchu quarter was destroyed and, again, many lives lost. The revolution was a double blow to Nanking's commercial prospects. The complete change in both the style and appearance of China's leadership meant the market for exotic silk garments disappeared overnight.[12]

Nanking became the nation's capital, but was far from being out of harm's way. An army mutiny in July 1913 quickly became an armed rebellion against the central government when the mutineers took control of the city. Loyal government troops laid siege to Nanking from 15 August to 1 September. Much of Hsiakuan was burnt and looted.[13] A British government report in 1914 described what happened, and what was to recur twice: 'Wanton murder, looting, rape, and incendiarism have been the unchecked amusements of the victorious soldiery . . . Up to last night [3 September] hell unrestrained has reigned in the city.' Tardy attempts to restore order led to mass executions. Three days proved sufficient to loot the whole city. Women and children were shot as they fled. The rebel leaders escaped, so penalties were borne by the inhabitants, who had opposed the rebellion. The commanding general of the vengeful government forces apologized for any inconvenience that may have been caused to British residents.[14]

In 1912 Sun Yat-sen moved the capital to Peking, but Nanking remained at the forefront of developments in China, including the general commercial modernization and industrial development of the following decades. However, it had a less desirable role in the political chaos that shook the country in the later 1920s. Chiang Kai-shek's Kuomintang seized Nanking in March 1927. One of his declared national objectives was to cancel the 'unequal treaties' and the consequent rights and privileges given to foreigners in China. In February he recovered the British Concessions at Hankow (Hankou) and Kiukiang (Jiujiang). There was no concession in Nanking that could be taken back, but Chiang had other plans.

In the early morning of 24 March 1927 Chiang's troops surrounded the residence of the British Consul-General, the grand structure that still stands on Huju South Road. It was attacked and robbed of everything of value. The American and Japanese consulates suffered the same fate. The Japanese Consul was shot at and his British counterpart injured.[15] In other attacks seven foreigners were killed—from America, Britain, France, Italy and Japan. Women were assaulted and all foreign property was ransacked.

A mustering station for foreign residents was arranged on Socony Ridge. This was a small hill inside the city's north-east corner where a few foreign houses clustered, the main one belonging to the Standard Oil Co. Once all the refugees had gathered, they escaped over the intervening half-kilometre of ground under covering fire from gunboats in the river.[16] This was probably the last example of gunboat diplomacy in action in China.[17]

The foreign powers lodged the strongest possible protests with Chiang's government, demanding reparations and indemnities. The artful leader announced that it had not been his men who were responsible. It had been Communist insurgents within his ranks, and he promised that they would be duly punished, pleased to legitimate his planned purge of his former allies. He kept his word and another bloodbath ensued. Chiang held public mass executions of Communists, suspected Communists and others who were just unlucky. The process took many days and tens of thousands are reported to have died.[18] Mao Zedong and Zhou Enlai were key targets, but escaped. The foreign powers were aghast at the brutality, but decided they could not press further for redress. If anything, Chiang's actions increased his international standing as a man it was dangerous to cross.[19]

For Japan the story was not yet finished. It had been making steady inroads into north-east China. Once full-scale war broke out between the two countries, it was not long before Nanking fell. December 1937 saw the fifth mass slaughter of its civilians in less than a century. The brutality equalled that of the previous four occasions but, because this time it was carried out by a foreign power, it left an indelible mark on this most unfortunate of cities.

Further reading: Chapman, *The Chinese Revolution 1926–27*.

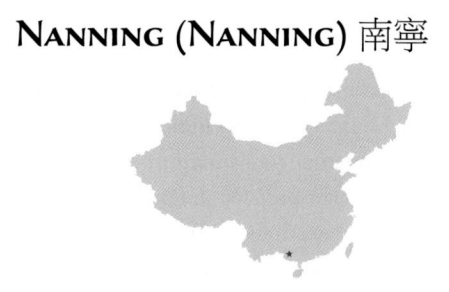

NANNING (NANNING) 南寧

Guangxi, 22.48° N, 108.19° E
Open City, 1899 Imperial Decree

Nanning's opening for foreign trade had numerous false starts but never achieved prominence. French excursions from Indo-China after the war of 1884–85 were thought to threaten Britain's commercial and political interests; France intended diverting Guangxi's trade towards Tonkin. In 1885 Britain proposed a railway from Nanning to Canton (Guangzhou), keeping foreign trade within its sphere of influence. This did not happen.[1] Instead the Burmah Convention of 1897 acquiesced to Britain's request to open the West River. By a separate note, the Tsungli Yamen confirmed the opening of Nanning as soon as commercial interests justified it.[2] Britain interpreted this as agreement to open Nanning if France extended its Tonkin railway into China.[3] France countered with a threat to annex Hainan Island and more.[4]

A more rational French demand was met, namely the right to build a railway from Nanning to Pakhoi (Beihai), a treaty port with significant British interests.[5] Naturally, France had no intention of building a line for Britain's benefit. Britain therefore pressed for Nanning to be opened. On 3 January 1899 an Imperial Decree was issued.[6] However, nothing happened, owing to the dilatoriness of local officials.[7] In June 1900 the British gunboat HMS *Sandpiper* left Wuchow (Wuzhou), carrying Consul Henry Little to facilitate the opening of the port,[8] but he returned empty-handed. In August 1901 the Wuchow Customs Commissioner, A. H. Harris, tried again and was equally unsuccessful.[9]

Only on 1 January 1907 did a clear statement emerge from Peking (Beijing) confirming the port was open. It took several months before the Maritime Customs, that essential feature of open status, was in place. The pontoons and Custom House needed for the customs to function were being made in Wuchow, to be taken upriver and reassembled.[10] As a foretaste of things to come, these were to be towed up the river by steamer, but the water proved too shallow. Instead they were hauled by coolies, taking almost three weeks.[11] The formal opening ceremony took place on 17 March 1907. The customs flag was the only one raised as no foreign power had yet established a consulate.[12]

The floating Custom House, 1913. © SOAS. Image courtesy of Historical Photographs of China, University of Bristol.

The Chinese authorities identified a plot of 50 hectares as a commercial settlement for occupation by both foreign and Chinese merchants. Wide concrete roads were laid and a bund created.[13] Maintenance and law and order were vested in a Board of Works, headed by the Chinese Superintendent of Customs.[14] Following usual practice, a set of land regulations was drawn up. These were initially not accepted by the Treaty Powers,[15] but became representative of the way things were to be done.

One of the first buildings was a large foreign-style house for the Chinese customs superintendent, dominating the middle of the plot.[16] Another grand building was erected for the customs indoor staff; the outdoor staff made do with the floating facility until it was replaced in 1920 by a permanent structure. A tiny yet imposing Chinese post office was also built.[17] Initially there was little else. The only foreign businesses ever in Nanning were the oil companies— Standard Oil and Asiatic Petroleum—and British-American Tobacco. These three built enormous residences-cum-hongs on the bund for their expatriate managers, possibly as compensation for their unsatisfactory existence.[18] They left after a few years; the employment of local agents was cheaper.

The old city of Nanning, the site the settlement now occupied, had been a kilometre south of the newer walled city that greeted the arrivals in 1907. The city was moved because of frequent landslips into the Tso (Zuo) River.[19] The settlement was soon to share its fate. The bund, built by inexperienced Chinese contractors, collapsed into the river within the first year.[20] It was to do so repeatedly, threatening the stability of buildings that had once stood far back from the water.[21]

By 1907 the pattern of business was fixed. Chinese merchants imported cotton yarn and piece-goods from Wuchow or Hong Kong, and exported star anise, Yunnan opium, sugar and groundnut oil.[22] The only value foreigners contributed was efficient river transportation. This was the same river that repeatedly demolished the settlement's stonework and was unnavigable for steamers. Initially the Hong Kong firms of Banker & Co. and Edwards & Co., as well as Jardines, chartered Chinese junks to transport their goods to Nanning.[23] The 600-kilometre journey from Wuchow still took 20 days. In 1908 Banker pioneered motorboats, and soon had a fleet of five that could do a round-trip in five or six days. Other firms followed, and by 1914 there were 22 such vessels,[24] increasing to over 40 by 1920.[25]

Even with this activity, Nanning was still a backwater. France established a vice-consulate in 1910,[26] and in 1911 demanded to station troops in Nanning 'for the protection of French merchants'. There were none there, although others had been subjected to robbery elsewhere in the province.[27] By 1912 the French Vice-Consul had moved to Lungchow (Longzhou) and his residence was occupied by the European postmaster.[28] The British never installed a consul at Nanning, choosing instead to place the port under the supervision of Wuchow.[29]

The decision to move the provincial capital from Kweilin (Guilin) to Nanning in 1914[30] increased the standing of the city, but had no impact on prospects for foreign trade. The negative effects of almost continuous rebel activity in Guangxi, and civil war in the 1920s with neighbouring Guangdong, meant that Nanning was increasingly unattractive as a base for foreign business.

NEWCHWANG (YINGKOU) 營口

Liaoning, 40.40° N, 122.13° E
Treaty Port, 1858 British Treaty

The first British Consuls at Newchwang would write their dispatches from 'The Port of Newchwang' rather than simply 'Newchwang'. Manchuria consisted of three north-eastern provinces, largely unknown to the foreign powers in the mid-19th century. They did know that the region had one major river, the Liao, and near its mouth was a commercial city called Newchwang (Niuzhuang). Its name in Chinese, 'Cow Village', should have raised doubts, but the British planners decided this was the place to establish a treaty port so Newchwang was inserted in their 1858 Tientsin (Tianjin) Treaty.

They were unaware that Newchwang, over 100 kilometres up the tortuously winding river, had been abandoned owing to heavy silting. The Chinese moved to Yingtze (Yingxi), just inside the river mouth. This tiny settlement, then also known by today's name of Yingkou, had been created in the 1820s as a military camp and possessed a few muddy forts. The land had been half-heartedly reclaimed from the river, and was frequently submerged during spring tides.[1] Nevertheless, it was the last relatively dry ground before the sea.[2]

When the first British Consul, Thomas Taylor Meadows, arrived on 24 June 1861, he found his assistant, Arthur Davenport, at Yingkou on board the gunboat HMS *Woodcock*. Davenport had tried but failed to reach the town of Newchwang,[3] and was awaiting further instructions.[4] A subsequent expedition to Newchwang found it devoid of commercial importance, and almost unpopulated.[5] To make it appear that the terms of the treaty were being honoured, the British selected Yingkou as the treaty port, renamed it Newchwang, and carried on.[6] I propose to do likewise.

Meadows's consular district was enormous, covering all of Manchuria, many times the size of the United Kingdom and whose riches were only just beginning to be discovered by outsiders.[7] The only accommodation available was a mud temple, then a standard introduction to local consular living. Meadows was to stay there for many years.

An 1867 guide to the treaty ports described Newchwang as 'dreary in the extreme [with] no advantages to correct this feeling subsequently'.[8] I had the same impression when I visited 145 years later. In the 1860s the only commercial activity related to soya beans and their products. Vast quantities were transported downriver from the fertile plains of Manchuria. At Newchwang the beans were pressed for their oil, which was highly prized for cooking purposes. The remaining mush was fashioned into round flat beancakes, a fertilizer in demand in southern sugar plantations. Thousands of seagoing junks massed in the river, waiting to load oil and cakes. So important was this trade to the Chinese that the Tariff Agreement, detailing the 1858 treaty, specifically prohibited British ships from carrying beans and beancake from Newchwang. As this was about the only trade available at the new port, the 31 foreign vessels that called in 1861[9] found it difficult to make it worth their while. The British Minister in Peking (Beijing) pointed out to the Chinese rulers that it was Chinese merchants who would benefit from the faster and more efficient steamers. Accordingly, the prohibition was lifted on 24 March 1862[10] in time for the new season. In that year 86 foreign ships arrived, 201 in 1863 and 302 in 1864.[11]

Bean oil junks unloading at the bund, c. 1922. Source: *Manchuria: Land of Opportunities*, 28.

This did nothing to make living at Newchwang attractive. Meadows staked out an area for a British Concession along a 1000-metre stretch of the riverbank upstream from the town,[12] arranging for the eleven-hectare site to be leased in perpetuity to the British government on 2 September 1861.[13] A concession was preferred over a settlement, avoiding the problems arising from dealing with individual local landlords in such a remote place.[14] It was the only one of the Tientsin Treaty concessions that was not chosen by Harry Parkes.[15] Whether the more experienced man would have selected a better location cannot now be determined. The site possessed deep water but it was fast-moving, being on the outside of the bend, and seemed determined to take the riverbank with it on its way past. However, the concession did benefit from having the river on one side and the only road into the interior on the other—all trade passed by either its front or back doors.[16]

A DISAPPEARING CONCESSION

Nominally the concession had ten lots which, as they kept falling into the river, were never formally laid out. Three were taken by British merchants, of whom only one lasted, Henry Bush. His firm, later Bush Brothers, became the leading foreign concern in Newchwang, latterly with more agencies than all other firms combined.

A 23,500-square-metre plot was reserved for a British Consulate[17] although it was not used. Major Crossman, conducting a review of all British consular properties in China, referred to Newchwang as a 'wretched port'. He also described Meadows's temple

The home of Henry Edward Bush. Source: http://s810.photobucket.com/user/thebushfamily2010/media/HEBHomeChina.jpg.html

as 'not at all adapted for the residence of a family—requiring as it does, a walk in the open air to go from one [room] to another'. He nevertheless determined the arrangement would do for the moment.[18] Of course, Meadows explored the possibility of building a consulate but found no one in Newchwang capable of doing so.[19] The unfortunate man was able to win one small victory. His request in late 1867 to replace the stoves that had been heating his temple since 1861 was accepted.[20] The grand sum of £78[21] was spent on shipping them to Chefoo (Yantai), thence overland to Newchwang.[22] They arrived in time for Meadows's death on 14 November 1868,[23] just as the river was starting to freeze again. Only in 1875 did work commence on a consular residence and supporting buildings on a new lot, safely away from the river.[24] In 1889 the Foreign Office was able to report that the consular compound of single-storey buildings, surrounded by trees and looking rather like holiday homes,[25] was suitable in every respect.[26] So it remained, until Britain's consular presence was terminated in 1934. Unfortunately, the residence and other buildings were occupied in 1946 by Chinese Nationalist troops and were left derelict.[27] Nothing remains today to indicate where the buildings once stood.

ATTEMPTS AT MODERNIZATION

Chinese merchants had been quick to grasp the benefits of foreign shipping to transport their products. Of the 274 foreign vessels that called in 1865, only 37 were consigned to foreign merchants.[28] When it came to manufacturing methods, they were much slower to change. The crushing of beans and the making of beancakes was exclusively done by hand[29] in a large number of small factories. Jardines were the first to build a modern bean mill,[30] but it was poorly designed and had to be closed.[31] The area to the west of today's city centre was until recently largely given over to manufacturing. Still there are one or two small factories, many tiny houses that used to accommodate workers and the occasional larger house of European design, presumably for factory managers.

The ravages of the Taiping rebels were not felt in the north-east, but there were still bandits in the area creating havoc in an increasingly prosperous Manchuria. Thanks to the efforts of the American Consul, in 1868 a garrison of foreign-drilled Chinese troops was stationed in Yingtze.[32] But this was not enough. The small foreign community was constantly concerned that during the four months the river was frozen they could not enjoy the protection of a gunboat; any moored vessel could be crushed by ice.[33] British gunboat HMS *Grasshopper* managed to survive the winter of 1870, but it was considered unwise to repeat the experiment.[34] The threat of violent invasion persisted. Before departing in the winter of 1873 another gunboat offloaded a field gun and three soldiers to handle it, together with a supply of rifles and ammunition. These three trained a force of a dozen Europeans in the use of the weaponry, and displaying the field gun on the parade ground had a deterrent effect on would-be troublemakers.[35] This winter arming of the concession became an annual event.[36] In addition, Robert Hart sanctioned the forming of a military police force from the boatmen and other Chinese employed by the customs;[37] a foreign-managed Custom House had been established on 9 May 1864.[38] Under the command of the Customs Commissioner, the force numbered 60.[39] Finally, there was a credible deterrent and the community felt safer.

But the winter presence of a gunboat would have been better still. A general meeting of the entire foreign community in 1884 agreed to request the ministers and admirals in Peking for a gunboat, useful also at this time as a defence against the French. As a sign of sincerity a subscription was raised for the preparation of a dry dock.[40] The result can still be seen at the eastern end of Liaohe Park. The protrusion into the riverfront wall, not quite 100 metres by 15, might still be big enough for the job, should the Chinese navy be so inclined.

Pilots, the bar and other developments

The 1867 guide also described Newchwang as 'little more cheerful than an Arctic swamp'. There were 25 foreigners,[41] plus 8 or 10 members of the customs service and about 30 pilots.[42] The land around the river estuary was flat, making the river mouth invisible to incoming ships. In 1867 a lightship and marker buoys were introduced by the Maritime Customs, making the approach much safer, but the hazardous sandbar across the entrance remained. Licensed pilots were necessary, and they waited for business at the river entrance.[43] Every incoming vessel was required to engage one.[44] Owing to the sandbar, it became the practice for captains partially to offload in the open sea. Only when they were light enough did they risk crossing the bar into the port.[45]

By the mid-1870s there were over 500 shipping arrivals during the season.[46] Among them, Butterfield & Swire's China Navigation Co. soon dominated the beancake cargo market, introducing specially designed vessels known as 'Taikoo Beancakers'. Indeed Swires' early success in shipping is attributable to this one activity.[47] In 1884 the company opened its own sugar refinery in Hong Kong so its ships were able to carry sugar to the north, and bring beancake south to Amoy (Xiamen) and Swatow (Shantou). Being assured of full cargoes in both directions, Swires kept their rates so low that nobody else could compete.[48] Initially using Bush Brothers as agents, by the end of the 1880s Swires opened their own operation. The firm built godowns and offices along the riverfront. Fortunately, one still remains—a pleasing two-storey red-brick office building near the western extremity of the old foreign area. Today it is occupied by an art gallery.

In 1870 *The New York Times* commented: 'Who, except a crack-brained Sinologue, would have ever chosen Newchwang as a commercial emporium? To anyone proposing to settle there, the best advice is an emphatic "don't".'[49] Yet by 1883 there were over a hundred foreigners at Newchwang,[50] including missionaries living inland. In 1884 there were six or eight European houses and three or four stores supplying the visiting ships.[51] Cut off from the outside world during the frozen winter, residents needed to entertain themselves. The first pony races were held in September 1863,[52] and meetings happened sporadically thereafter. Ice-skating was popular on the consular pond, and duck-shooting in the surrounding wetlands. Indoors there were social evenings and amateur theatricals at the British Consulate.[53] In the early 1880s, the consular courtroom was fitted out as a theatre; this lasted for six years until it was restored to its former dignity.[54] Following an initiative by Consul Meadows in 1866, the winter post was brought overland from Chefoo by customs courier.[55] The service remained a good one, and the Sunday morning arrival of the runner was eagerly anticipated.[56]

The river frontage still caused concern. All but four of the concession lots had disappeared into the river by the end of the 1880s. Half-hearted efforts to shore up the bank were unsuccessful.[57] Only the customs property was properly protected.[58] A Foreign Office report in 1889 stated that something ought to be done, but not by Her Majesty's Government.[59] A handwritten note 31 years later by the British Minister in Peking summed it up: 'The real fact is that the so-called British Concession in Newchwang has never been taken seriously.'[60]

The foreign business community took matters into its own hands. A bund was created to the west of the concession, and was gradually improved out of funds subscribed by the foreign residents, consulates and the customs. In 1890 a committee was appointed with responsibility for its maintenance, plus the introduction of public footpaths and lighting.[61] There were still only four sizeable foreign firms but given the volume of product they loaded on and off steamers their need for storage and handling space was considerable. In 1882 the foreign merchants were joined by the China Merchants Steam Navigation Co., the brainchild of Li Hongzhang, keen to attract some of the lucrative shipping business. The company built wharves, godowns and offices between those of Bush Brothers and the Custom House.[62]

THE JAPANESE

Japan became a major buyer of Newchwang's beancake. In 1870, three-quarters of the ships leaving the river were bound for Japanese ports.[63] Mitsubishi bought a piece of river frontage in June 1894, big enough to berth two vessels,[64] possibly with imminent developments in mind. War broke out later that year between Japan and China. When the area around Newchwang fell to the Japanese on 6 March 1895[65] the period of uninterrupted growth in trade naturally came to a halt.[66] Although Newchwang's Swire man, W. de St. Croix, thought that the invaders should be 'spanked and sent home',[67] the chief of the Japanese administration was considered to be understanding and helpful to the foreign community.[68] The end of the occupation was agreed in the Treaty of Shimonoseki in April 1895, but the Japanese troops did not leave until November, having been in possession for nine months.[69]

When trade resumed there was a considerable backlog. The year 1896 recorded the highest trade volume ever.[70] The Chinese town was 'thick with beancake mills', the Japanese purchasing ever-increasing amounts.[71] A new mill was built with steam machinery imported by Swires from Hong Kong.[72] Unlike the earlier attempt, this enterprise was an instant success; another one was constructed soon afterwards.[73] Swires, with a fleet of 35 steamers, made 250 trips to Newchwang in 1897. Jardines made a similar number. When Lord Charles Beresford visited in 1898, representing British chambers of commerce, he counted 20 steamers in the river and 2000 junks.[74] In 1899 the value of trade was up by 49 percent over the previous year.[75] Unfortunately, more trouble was heading towards Newchwang.

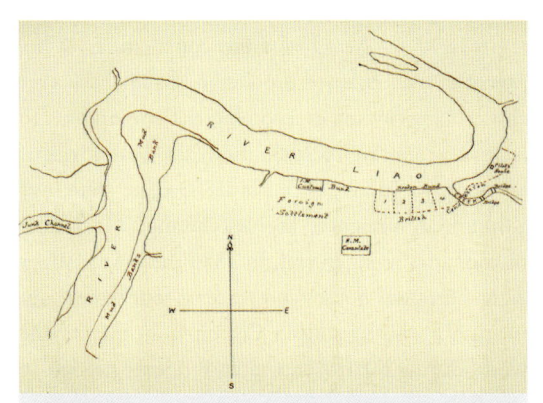

1888 sketch of the treaty port, showing Lots 1 to 4, the Custom House and the British Consulate. Reprinted with permission by the National Archives.

Russians and railways

Newchwang was affected by the Boxer troubles that spread across the north-east in 1900, but the Russians were a graver threat. As a result of their lease of the Guandong peninsula in 1898, there had been an increasing Russian presence in Newchwang. Russia gained the right to both build a railway line to the end of the peninsula and defend it. This the Russians interpreted very broadly. Taking advantage of the strained relations between Britain and France, a Russian regiment occupied the forts at the mouth of the river. A nearby British gunboat did nothing.[76] Incoming railway material fuelled a boom in imports. The line would be closest at Tashichao (Dashiqiao), 20 kilometres to the east. The extension of a branch line to Newchwang would benefit the port, and enable the Russians to transport their material to the main line more speedily. By 1898 an estimated 36,000 tonnes of railway equipment had been landed to the east of the concession area, at a site rapidly becoming a de facto Russian Settlement.[77] This plot of land, with almost two kilometres of river frontage,[78] became a hive of activity, with locomotives, wagons and carriages being assembled.[79] Disregarding treaty obligations, Russia made it clear that it would not pay the required import duty. The Customs Commissioner was ordered not to interfere.[80] The British merchants told Lord Beresford that they felt as though they were living in a Russian province.[81]

Meanwhile British interests were building another line for the Imperial Chinese Railway, from Shanhaikwan (Shanhaiguan) on the western shore of the gulf. The geography was such that the terminus for this line, which was expected to be open by early 1900,[82] had to be on the opposite side of the river. A railway concession stretched for four kilometres, allowing the material for this line to be offloaded and processed in the same way as the Russians were doing to the east.[83] To make up for the shrinkage of its original concession, Britain applied for a new one on the north bank, to be near the end of its railway line. Fearing that whatever they did not manage to get the Russians would grab,[84] the British boldly applied for a tract of land with frontage of almost a kilometre that stretched back to a point where it rejoined the river, 20 kilometres upstream;[85] this was the last meandering sweep of the Liao before it met the sea. The peninsula that was encompassed by the British plan was a malarial swamp, but would provide a useful buffer.[86] So confident was the British Consul that his report for 1898 stated the concession had been granted, although saying that the exact position and extent had not been settled.[87] A Japanese application for a concession with a similar length of river frontage, between the British claim and the railway, was also reported as agreed in principle. The Russians contemplated building a bridge over the river to link their Chinese Eastern Railway with the Imperial Chinese line, and ultimately Peking. They applied for a concession on the opposite bank to the one they had already commandeered.[88] The natural reluctance of the Chinese to grant all these claims enabled negotiations to be extended until the next 'excitement' struck Newchwang.

The Yingkou *taotai* had done well to keep the more enthusiastic elements of the Boxer movement at bay. But when, spoiling for a fight, Russian troops attacked the Chinese garrison on 26 July 1900 he was understandably shaken. On 3 August the Russian Consul informed him that the resident Russian gunboat would fire a 31-gun salute to mark a state occasion. Naturally, the *taotai* was alarmed, fearing that the anti-foreign element, already roused by the attack eight days previously, would interpret this as aggression. This was exactly what happened. On 4 August a mob, comprising Boxers as well as Chinese regulars,[89] approached the barricades surrounding the concession; the British Consul had already ordered that defensive steps be taken.[90] The crowd was repulsed by a combined force of Russian troops and the crews of two Japanese gunboats that were in the river at the time.[91] Also joining the defence were the civilian Newchwang Volunteers, under the command of the Customs Commissioner.[92] The Russians seized possession of the treaty port, including the foreign areas, and established a civil administration, assuring the community that treaty privileges would be honoured.[93] Ominously, they raised their navy's flag over the Custom House.[94]

The world was focused on the main theatres of Tientsin and Peking, where the Russians were hailed as heroes, and paid little attention to the 'protective security' measures taken in Newchwang. Trade came to a standstill while the new regime settled into place.[95] It did not take long for changes to become apparent. On 9 August the civil administration was subordinated to the Russian military authority and, more importantly, so was the Maritime Customs. The exchange on 4 October of the naval flag for the Russian Customs flag was a clear statement of intent.[96] The *taotai*, who had tried so hard to maintain peace, decided to absent himself when the Russians took over. With him went all the staff of the native customs office. The Russians therefore assumed this function as well, detaching foreign staff from the Maritime Customs to manage the *likin* collection office.[97] No matter from which office revenue was collected, it was all diverted by the Russians to defray the costs of their occupation and the building of their railway. A Newchwang branch of the Russo-Chinese Bank was opened for the purpose, and grew rapidly.[98]

Despite its unpropitious beginning, the Russian administration effected considerable improvements to Newchwang, particularly at the eastern end.[99] The railway station is still there and recognizable, as is the wide boulevard that leads from it perpendicular to the river. There was talk of extending the port limits to include the two new railway termini. Once trade picked up, having been only slightly dented by the diversion of business to Port Arthur (Lüshun) via the railway,[100] a Newchwang Tug & Lighter Co. was formed. This soon expanded its capacity; continuing insufficient wharfage made its services indispensable.[101] The most significant improvement the Russians made was in the running of the treaty port. Regulations for the Provisional Civil Administration of Newchwang were formulated. A representative of the foreign consuls had a seat on the council, and other non-Russians were invited to participate. For example Dr. Daly, the resident British physician, was made Sanitary Inspector with a Mr. Dunn, a British engineer working with the Russian railway, as his assistant. These two played a prominent part in all discussions relating to municipal affairs.[102] The Russians were making it clear that they intended to keep Newchwang for as long as possible.

But Sir Ernest Satow, the British Minister in Peking, remarked in September 1901 that it was time to hand over the customs and *likin* revenue so that it could be used for its agreed purpose, financing the repayment of China's growing indemnity debt. Russia had undertaken to collect revenue on behalf of China until their relations could be normalized by treaty,[103] but unsurprisingly the Russians felt no sense of urgency. By a Sino-Russian convention of 1902, the Russians agreed to evacuate Newchwang by 8 April 1903.[104] A few months later the civil administrator started to plan a building designed to hold all the Russian offices. The site was in the centre of the foreign settlement near the other consulates and, to their annoyance, encroached on land used as a public square.[105] The rather ornate building, small considering its former status, is now in protective custody inside the grounds of a police training facility.

The Russians did not evacuate the treaty port on the agreed date, giving a variety of reasons. Underneath them all was the fear of Japan's intentions in a region big enough for only one aggressive, expansionist power.[106]

THE JAPANESE AGAIN

The outbreak of the Russo-Japanese War in February 1904 convinced Newchwang's foreign population that Japan would attack as soon as the ice melted.[107] Foreign families were not the only ones to leave. The Russian troops and their entire administration also fled. When the Japanese army arrived in July, they met no opposition.[108] Following a familiar pattern, the Japanese began administering the Custom House, siphoning off the revenue, although subsequently they accepted a commissioner appointed by Sir Robert Hart.

The Japanese were said to have 'a talent for organization which amounts almost to genius'. In a few days they were totally in control and working hard. Within a week there was, according to one observer, no remaining sign of the Russian occupation.[109] By the end of 1905 the Japanese population numbered over 7000, and other foreigners almost 300.[110] Trade revived quickly, and 1905 broke all records both for volume and value.[111] The usual multinationals of the early 20th century started to appear—Asiatic Petroleum, Standard Oil and British-American Tobacco. But Newchwang, once Manchuria's sole port, now faced stiff competition. The Japanese revived Dalny (Dalian), and under its new name of Dairen it was impacting the trade of Newchwang. Antung (Dandong), at the mouth of the Yalu River, opened by the Americans in 1903, also made its presence felt.

An agreement was signed in December 1906 for the Japanese rendition of the port.[112] In spring 1907 local civil control was returned to the *taotai*, and the Custom House flew the IMC flag for the first time since 1900.[113] Japanese investment still boomed, and for the moment the small non-Japanese foreign community felt secure. There had been a cricket ground since 1894,[114] and a typically colonial club before that. Meyrick Hewlett, Acting British Consul in 1913–14, managed to secure a site for a golf club and for a new Newchwang Club building.[115] He left before the new building was completed in 1915, but we can still enjoy it. Standing on Shifu Road it now houses a restaurant, and has been tastefully restored. A trust was created in 1918 for a new recreation ground, the trustees being the British Consul, W. R. C. Ford of Jardines and J. Edgar, a long-standing British merchant.[116] They did not know they were witnessing the twilight of their world.

Nothing could be done about Newchwang's river icing over in winter but the silting was another matter. The sudden appearance of a market in Europe for Newchwang's chief export, soya beans, led to efforts to deal with the sandbar at the river mouth. But the larger ocean-going ships that serviced this demand now preferred to use Dairen's better facilities and deeper water.[117] The new railway lines had taken business away from the junk operators; an estimated 20,000 junks before 1904 had shrunk to 3000–4000 ten years later.[118] Steamer owners did not want to suffer a similar fate due to silting. Discussions started in 1907 on possible improvement schemes. In 1909 the foreign Chamber of Commerce approved a levy on goods and tonnage to pay for the work, and to establish a River Conservancy Board.[119] Deliberations continued into 1910, and the port limits were extended to include the two railway termini.[120] Only in 1924 did the board announce that the bar had been dredged to a depth of eight metres along its entire length.[121] Too late—in the late 1920s the southern sugar farmers started using different forms of fertilizer, and the seemingly unstoppable export of beancake petered out.[122]

In the early 1920s Newchwang ranked eighth among the 46 treaty ports in terms of value of trade,[123] but Manchuria was about to undergo significant changes. The British Consulate, the first to open in 1861, was the last to close 73 years later,[124] by which time the European population was almost non-existent.[125] Newchwang's fate was inextricably tied to the Japanese and their perception of Manchuria as a tasty appetizer, ripe for consumption.

Further reading: Coates, *China Races*; Drage, *Taikoo*; Putnam Weale, *Manchu and Muscovite*.

Ningpo (Ningbo) 寧波

Zhejiang, 29.53° N, 121.33° E
Treaty Port, 1842 British Treaty

Ningpo's early prosperity as a fishing port attracted the attention of pirates, both domestic and Japanese. The islands of the Chusan (Zhoushan) Archipelago both protected the river entrance to Ningpo and provided hiding places for seaborne robbers. Consequently Ningpo, like many Chinese coastal cities, is situated 30 kilometres up a river, the Yung (Yong). The Portuguese arrived in the early 16th century and perhaps were a welcome deterrent to the Japanese.

The British fleet attacking Chinhai (Zhenhai), 9 October 1841. ©National Maritime Museum, Greenwich, London. Reprinted with permission.

They chose to encamp at Chinhai (Zhenhai), at the mouth of the river, the first European colony in China. By 1533 there was a permanent Portuguese settlement,[1] named Liampo, that grew rapidly.[2] Success led to arrogance, the colonists' downfall. In 1545 a deteriorating relationship with the local population prompted the Jiaqing Emperor to order the colony's destruction.

At the end of the 17th century the English East India Company began sending ships to Ningpo, attempting to restart the old Portuguese trade, especially the export of Nanking (Nanjing) silk.[3] It became apparent they were as disadvantaged as they had been in Canton (Guangzhou).[4] Besides, Chinese merchants were moving away from Ningpo towards Shanghai, with its easier access to Yangtze trade. This trend gained momentum as the 18th century progressed.[5] Yet when Hugh Hamilton Lindsay visited in 1832 he observed the sale of European woollen goods, indicating a ready market.[6] A personal recommendation from William Jardine to Foreign Secretary Lord Palmerston in October 1839 ensured Ningpo was included in the Treaty of Nanking's list of ports to be opened.

No flood of business

The first non-military British resident in Ningpo was Rev. W. C. Milne, a missionary who moved from Chusan in 1842.[7] In 1843 a British merchant arrived, Charles Mackenzie,[8] followed by the first British Consul, Robert Thom.[9] Formerly with Jardines, Thom had resided in China for ten years and spoke the language; he had been interpreter to Sir Henry Pottinger during the recent campaign.[10] Focusing on trading potential, Thom chose not to exercise his right to establish the consulate inside the city. Instead, he rented a Chinese merchant's house over the river from the city's north-east wall.[11] The new treaty port was officially declared open on 1 January 1844.[12]

The hoped-for business did not materialize. In 1845 the British community comprised Thom, his assistant and a student interpreter at the consulate, and two lady missionaries. Mackenzie was about to give up the struggle and leave.[13] The superior location of Shanghai, 150 kilometres to the north, meant little happened in Ningpo. By 1846 the foreign population had almost doubled,[14] inflated by missionaries.[15] The year's trade amounted to imports of just under £12,000 and exports of even less, carried by six small ships, the only foreign vessels to visit.[16]

For the purposes of consular jurisdiction the official limit of the treaty port was fixed at Chinhai.[17] When the import trade did improve after the British evacuated Chusan in 1846, much of it was illegal. As ever, Jardines and Dents traded opium illicitly from hulks moored just outside the port limit. Thom and his early successors would have been uncomfortable that these two firms provided the only means of sending and receiving official mail.[18]

In 1851 Sir Samuel Bonham, Hong Kong Governor and Superintendent of British Trade in China, suggested to the Foreign Office that

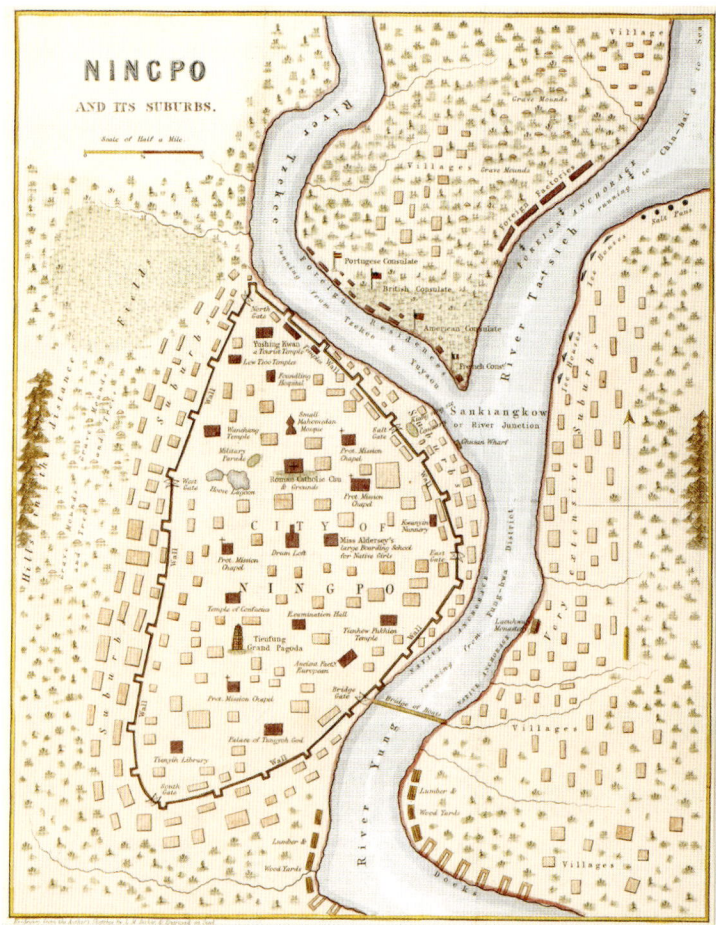

1853 map showing four foreign consulates opposite the north-east wall of the Chinese city. Reprinted with permission by Antique Print and Map Room, Sydney.

buildings, interspersed with paddy fields and Chinese graves, spread to the west and north of where a tributary joined the Yung. A map from 1853 shows, from left to right on the western arm, the consulates of Portugal, Great Britain, America and France. Portugal was represented by Dents, so the marked building was probably the Dents agent's residence. The first United States Consul, Charles Bradley, arrived in 1857;[24] the Americans maintained a Ningpo consulate until the early 20th century. French interests were managed either by their consulate in Shanghai or, after 1884, by the British in Ningpo. The place where the French Consulate is marked is close to the French cathedral, known today as Christ Church, which was the focus of the French presence in Ningpo.*

Piracy was one reason why so few vessels risked coming to Ningpo. Portuguese from Macao with their fast, armed lorchas had been providing a service protecting convoys of Chinese fishing junks. As is often the case, the party providing the protection came to be feared more than those from whom protection was sought. It was big business and high fees were paid by the unfortunate junk operators. It was also competitive, with a rival Cantonese gang offering a similar service. Disputes between the two became more of a menace than the pirates.

The Chinese authorities decided that the Cantonese and their leader, A-Pak (Pu Hsing-yu), were the lesser of the two evils. In 1854 the *taotai* enlisted A-Pak and his men into the Imperial Navy, and told him to sweep the Portuguese from the seas.[25]

underperforming Ningpo be swapped for somewhere with more potential. Peking (Beijing) rejected the idea.[19] Meanwhile, foreign trade stagnated while missionaries multiplied. By 1855 there were 14—4 English and 10 American—but only 5 merchants.[20] The official British presence was downgraded to a vice-consulate.[21] An account of Ningpo from this time describes it as 'the quietest place under the sun. A handful of merchants lived there, buried without the trouble of dying.'[22]

No formal settlement was marked out.[23] The missionaries preferred to live and work within the walled city. Other foreigners gravitated to the opposite side of the river where a loose arrangement of European

---

* Unfortunately, the cathedral was destroyed by fire in July 2014.

In the middle of 1857 A-Pak forced his adversaries into the river as far as Ningpo. A battle took place on 26 June. Overwhelmed, the Portuguese abandoned their lorchas and fled. Appeals for sanctuary at the British Consulate went unheeded for fear of provoking an anti-foreign riot, so they tried hiding among the surrounding Chinese graves, where many were butchered. An assault by A-Pak on the Portuguese Consulate was halted only by the chance appearance of a French frigate, the *Capricieuse*. The ship's captain saw the consulate of an ally apparently under attack, and opened fire on the assailants. The fighting stopped. The French captain received the surviving Portuguese on board, not in friendship but because of treaty obligations. He sent them to Macao to face Portuguese law.[26]

Matters did not stop there. Some time later a Portuguese brig of war came up the river in the company of twelve armed lorchas. Reparation was demanded from the *taotai*, who said that it had nothing to do with him (A-Pak was by now a civilian again). The two rival gangs would have to negotiate between themselves. Another battle seemed imminent, but was stayed by another chance arrival—the British naval steamer HMS *Nimrod*. Its captain, Commander Roderick Dew, explained to the Portuguese that he and his vessel were neutral, but if any shot were to come near his ship or the British residences on shore he would retaliate. Public opinion was strongly against the Portuguese and they departed, leaving no Portuguese presence in Ningpo.

Captured by the Taipings

In 1861 the city was captured by the Taiping rebels. They had tried, and failed, to take Hangchow (Hangzhou) and were in desperate need of access to the sea.[27] Harry Parkes, one of the joint commissioners governing Canton, was accustomed to travelling around China as a diplomatic 'fireman'. When Ningpo seemed under threat of capture, Parkes was ordered to negotiate with the Taipings. The city fell before he arrived, but routines were surprisingly normal. Rebel leaders assured foreigners of the safety of their persons, consulates, businesses and residences. They even established a Custom House and an appropriate set of regulations to govern the continuing trade.[28] The missionaries living and working inside the walled city were reassured that as co-religionists they would remain untouched.[29]

The Chinese residents of the city took a different view. Of the population of 400,000 it was estimated that all bar 20,000 fled,[30] either to Shanghai or across the river to the foreign area, where some 70,000 took refuge.[31] The rebels kept their promises and foreigners remained unmolested, but it was clear that the country's future stability required that the usurpers be defeated. Anticipating trouble, the British tried to train the Ningpo garrison of imperial troops to defend the city, but this had proven unsuccessful.[32] Now it was the rebels who were strengthening the city's defences. However, when a salute was fired from the city wall to honour the return of a Taiping commander, it was claimed some Chinese in the foreign area were killed.[33] The British responded with some firing of their own; when news arrived of the death of Queen Victoria's consort Prince Albert, the resident British warship showed its respect by firing a salute.[34] The combined message, of the prince's death and British power, was unmistakable.

On 6 March 1862, loyal seaborne forces (in fact, A-Pak and his reformed gangsters) recaptured Chinhai from the Taipings,[35] giving an opportunity to reassert imperial control over the city. On 10 May A-Pak's fleet were deliberately provoking the rebel defenders as they sailed between the city and the foreign settlement.[36] Naturally, stray bullets fell among the foreigners—and across the decks of HMS *Encounter*, under the same Commander Dew. Also moored was a French warship. This time Dew gave the order to fire. He and his French colleague bombarded the city walls and the rebels fled.[37] A-Pak and his men did more damage and took more plunder in the following few hours than the Taipings in the previous six months.[38]

The combined British and French force returned the city to grateful Imperial representatives. With proof of how weak Ningpo's defences were, the British started to train a local militia. This was achieved by Major-General James Cooke, who had served with Charles Gordon in Shanghai. Cooke's Anglo-Chinese Force, with a number of junior British officers, comprised some 200 well-drilled Chinese soldiers and was entirely funded by the city authorities.[39] Their barracks and much-used parade ground (the soldiers were 'perfect in their drill') was just inside the city's Salt Gate.[40] They acted for many years as a semi-official defensive army.

The *taotai* of Ningpo caused a monument to be built to honour the British and French who had died in defence of his city. This tall pyramid-like structure had pride of place on the right bank of the river, opposite the east wall. It was restored in 1906 and again in 1932, when it was removed to the Foreign Cemetery; a rededication ceremony was held there in 1933.[41] This and all the other memorials in the cemetery, currently the peaceful Baisha Park, were destroyed in the Cultural Revolution.

Ningpo took time to settle down after the Taiping occupation. One factor that aided this process was the establishment by Commander Dew of a foreign police force[42] under the overall auspices of the Maritime Customs.[43] Initially comprising a British sergeant and 16 Chinese constables, by 1867 a British superintendent commanded a much larger force that included British constables.[44] Its purview extended beyond the immediate foreign-settled area, and its size grew to 40. From 1880 the force was employed directly by the *taotai*,[45] although still under a British officer, who combined the role with that of magistrate.[46] In 1890 a new police station was built near the French cathedral.[47] The smart and purposeful building is still there. The police force remained under foreign supervision until 1907 when its last commander, Major Watson, died; it was then amalgamated with the civil police force of Ningpo.[48] Foreign buildings had been appearing in various places along the southern banks of the riverine peninsula to the north-east of the city. Half a dozen gems still remain, although the present city authorities lack diligence in the placing of plaques.

THE GOVERNMENT OF THE SETTLEMENT

On 13 January 1862 the Ningpo consuls of Britain, America and France met to consider how the foreign settled area should be governed. No agreement was reached, but they declared the triangular area between the two stretches of river should be recognized as the foreign settlement.[49] Unsatisfied, later in the year the French tried to secure an exclusive French Concession by making a formal request to the *taotai*. The other powers objected at ministerial level in Peking, and nothing came of it.[50] The result was a haphazard spread of residential buildings and hongs, interspersed with Chinese houses and businesses.[51] European-style roads were planned for the area known as the Campo, Portuguese for 'field'. The first was a generous twelve metres wide and over a kilometre long, running parallel to the Yung River about a hundred metres inland. These days it is called Zhong Ma (Middle Horse) Road. In 1864 it represented a unique opportunity; on 24 May, Queen Victoria's 45th birthday, the new road hosted Ningpo's first race meeting. The *taotai* donated a silver cup for one of the races.[52] Part of the northern end of the settlement was for some years known as 'the racecourse'.[53] There were rumours that a club was about to be started,[54] in the true British tradition. Like many things in Ningpo, this never got beyond the thinking stage.

Foreign trade was dwindling, not that it had ever been impressive. The proximity of Ningpo to its 'big brother', Shanghai, cast a long, deep shadow over business. Dents and Jardines kept their hulks just out of sight and maintained hongs in the Campo. As Jardines moved out of opium, others moved in; both Sassoon companies† had a sizeable presence in Ningpo. The American Civil War of 1861–65 gave a brief boost to the cotton traders, but this only lasted until the better-quality American supplies to Britain once more became available.[55]

In early 1868, the British Minister in Peking sought input from merchants in all the treaty ports to the renegotiation of the Treaty of Tientsin (Tianjin). Ningpo's response came from the eight leading

---

† The rival family firms of David Sassoon & Sons and E. D. Sassoon & Co.

Protestant missionaries; there was no means of collecting the businessmen's views. When asked in 1869 to comment on the nationwide trend of trade falling from British hands into Chinese, Consul William Fittock politely pointed out that in Ningpo it had always been in Chinese hands. In support of this statement, Fittock reported that all British goods entering the port came via Shanghai through Chinese merchants. The cost to British merchants of bringing items to Ningpo from Shanghai, a 150-kilometre journey, was half that of shipping them to Shanghai from Britain.[56]

Even such minimal business required a team of between 15 and 20 customs staff for the necessary inspections and measurements. Most were based in Ningpo, with a few at Chinhai. The customs service also manned the lighthouses appearing on the nearby coast from the mid-1860s. With the expansion of the responsibilities of the service well beyond revenue collection, a new three-storey Custom House was built, now a museum to the Ningpo Customs. A photograph from about 1870 shows the commissioner's residence, a very handsome two-storey house on the riverbank, with a verandah and walled garden.[57] Enviously, the British Consul reported in 1868 that the commissioner enjoyed this 'commodious house for his exclusive use', whereas the consul had to justify hiring sedan chairs and boats, needed because his unsuitable and rented accommodation was so remote.[58] Something had to be done.

And it was—in part. In 1864 the British government purchased a plot of land measuring 80 metres by 50 at the north end of the settled area. Elaborate plans were made to build residences in the compound for the consul, his assistant and the interpreter, as well as offices and a gaol.[59] All these buildings were to be tastefully set out in a large gardened enclosure. Construction started in 1866, beginning with a solid river wall and embankment. The consul's residence cost £4000,[60] a very large sum for a very unbusy port. Whether or not it was worth it can be judged by peering through the gates of the People's Liberation Army barracks that now occupies the site, where the former consular residence can clearly be seen. Its twin,

Dents' hong on the bund, 1870s. © RSAA. Image courtesy of Historical Photographs of China, University of Bristol.

planned to house the office and the consular assistants, was never built. There was no point. During the following two decades there were only one or two dispatches a year to Ningpo from the British Minister in Peking. In the early 1890s, Consul Herbert Giles had so much spare time that he was able to compile the first proper Chinese-English dictionary, building on earlier work by Thomas Francis Wade.‡

Nevertheless, appearances had to be maintained. There were one or two hotels catering for visiting sailors and the lower end of the trade.[61] Then in 1865 an advertisement appeared for the Queen's Hotel. With 18 en suite bedrooms, this establishment boasted that it was 'the finest in the East',[62] although it did not seem to remain open for long. Neither did Hatchard's, the Astor House or Swanberg's, all making a brief appearance in the 1860s. There were ten foreign firms in 1872,[63] and the same number ten years later.[64] Russells started a regular steamer service from Shanghai in 1867. When it withdrew the China Merchants line continued the service. In 1878, Swires' China Navigation started a service in competition, offering fares that were 50 percent cheaper. When the passengers on the incoming China Merchants ship heard of this, they demanded a 50 percent refund. Unperturbed, the captain moored his vessel in midstream until calm returned, only then allowing his passengers to disembark.[65] Thereafter, the two lines ran their ships on alternate days, except Sundays, when there was no service.[66]

‡ The Wade-Giles system of romanization of Chinese words and names was a standard for much of the 20th century.

Very little prospect

By the beginning of the 1880s the foreign merchants of Ningpo grudgingly accepted the paucity of their prospects. At that time there were three areas where the foreigner could add value in the absence of Chinese expertise: shipping, insurance and banking. Ningpo was a David to nearby Shanghai's Goliath (but without the fire-power) in relation to shipping and insurance. As for banking, Ningpo merchants had their own expertise, having long since pioneered the widespread use of paper money.[67] They had also developed a system of settling accounts between themselves by way of adjustments to each other's accounts with Chinese banks, equivalent to a cheque payment system. They even spread this novel type of business to Shanghai and beyond;[68] Ningpo merchants were the leaders of Shanghai's Chinese mercantile community. So, mostly, the foreigners sat back and watched.

One European managed to secure a job that had for centuries been performed by Chinese. Marco Polo described a 'Bridge of Boats', even then an ancient institution. This floating toll-bridge, about 200 metres long, consisted of a line of junk hulls lashed together. As the only link to the eastern suburbs, it was very popular. When a second, similar bridge was installed some time in the 1860s or early 1870s, joining the foreign settlement to the city, its management was placed in the hands of a foreigner, Antonio Rossich. A toll would be collected from all who crossed except Chinese government officials and soldiers in uniform, exempted in accordance with long-established custom. One day in 1877 Rossich inadvertently took the four-cash toll from a soldier, then made a bad situation worse by questioning the authenticity of one of the coins. The resulting disagreement became a riot, and he ran for it. Major Watson and his Chinese constables managed to restore order, but the affair revealed the dissatisfaction felt for years with the bridge's foreign management. When he demanded too high a price to be bought out, the city authorities started a free ferry service immediately alongside.[69] A few months later,

The old Bridge of Boats, 1906. Source: *The East of Asia Magazine*, Vol. 5 (Shanghai, 1906).

Rossich admitted defeat and the bridge passed into Chinese hands.[70]

Missionaries continued to come to Ningpo. Most were French, servicing not only Ningpo but also the surrounding country as far as Hangchow. It was French of a different persuasion that next caused a stir in the sleepy treaty port. In the summer of 1884 it seemed the Sino-French War would spread to Ningpo. The river mouth was barricaded with wooden piles and sunken stone-laden ships. Two French warships came close to Chinhai and exchanged shots with the forts, but little damage was done on either side. The only effect on Ningpo was that Chinhai became the terminal for cargo and passenger operations, linked by small river craft. No anti-foreign feeling was apparent throughout the crisis. Indeed, many Chinese fled once more to the foreign area. The *taotai* even lent 50 of his policemen to Major Watson's force, in case of trouble.[71]

In many of the coastal treaty ports a flourishing business developed exporting labour to the rising economies of South-East Asia and Latin America, but not in Ningpo. In 1886 the British North Borneo Company opened a Ningpo office; it closed within a few years. When rumours spread of mistreatment of 500 Ningpo men in the Straits Settlements, a wealthy Chinese businessman hired a ship to go to Singapore and bring them back. Independent of their veracity the rumours were firmly believed. There was no more emigration.[72]

Throughout the 1880s on average one steamer a day called at Ningpo. The value of trade at the end of the decade was the same as at the beginning. Imports were still mainly opium and cotton, and tea the biggest export. However, this one-time staple was in terminal decline. By 1891 there were only two foreign firms still operating in Ningpo: Gustav Kutzlau, a recently arrived German who managed to survive for ten years, and E. Wadman, a British merchant who had been in business in Ningpo since 1868 but who lasted only another year.[73] There now being no other choice, the attention of both was focused solely on the export of rush and straw hats and mats.[74]

It is not surprising that matters of infrastructure were not given much attention. Occasionally individual merchant houses took the initiative to improve the settlement. In 1873 Russells started a new bund. When completed it would have given an uninterrupted promenade all the way from the Foreign Cemetery to the American Consulate on the upper reach of the river—but it never was. In 1874 an ambitious project was undertaken to drain and level the main street in the Campo from the Bridge of Boats to the British Consulate.[75] Such sanitary arrangements in the Campo made the foreign area different from its surroundings[76] and were the responsibility of a voluntarily financed Public Works Committee of five foreign and four Chinese members. In 1884 the Customs Commissioner backed another scheme to create a bund for the whole length of the Campo. This plan was shelved. Instead the waterfront remained, apart from Russells' unfinished bund, a hotchpotch of wharves belonging to various owners, with wilderness in between. In 1887 a less ambitious plan found favour, and what appeared the following year was a half-mile 'bund of simple construction and somewhat heterogeneous appearance'.[77] A more comprehensive bunding project was completed in 1902,[78] attaining its present form in the 1930s.

Chinese growth

It was the Chinese businessmen that kept Ningpo growing. In 1887 a steam-powered cotton-ginning machine was introduced to the city with Chinese capital, one of the first pieces of Western industrial machinery to be used in China.[79] This was followed by similar investments in cotton and flour mills, Chinese-owned but using British or Japanese expertise and equipment.[80] In 1905 there was an attempt at using Western technology when a Chinese entrepreneur, wishing to modernize the fishing industry, bought a steam trawler. The jealous and traditional fishing guilds noticed that this newcomer did not know where the best fishing grounds were—and they did not tell him. The experiment failed.[81]

Hangchow, halfway between Ningpo and Shanghai, opened as a treaty port in 1895. This had a negative effect on Ningpo's business, and prompted Britain to consider closing its Ningpo consulate in favour of Hangchow.[82] However, it was quickly realized that Shanghai was having an equally deadening effect on Hangchow as Ningpo; more so given its greater proximity. The newer consulate was closed in 1922 and the Ningpo consul became responsible for both places.[83]

Ningpo was taken over without bloodshed by the revolutionaries in 1911.[84] Nor did it become a battleground in the turmoil of the 1920s.[85] However, the small foreign community could not escape the anger of the anti-foreign movement later in that troubled decade. Anti-British demonstrations on the bund in 1926[86] turned into a full boycott of British goods the following year.[87] All foreigners were evacuated in March 1927.[88] While the numbers were not many, the principle involved was weighty. Ningpo had faded so completely from foreign public perception that newspapers felt obliged to remind readers in reports that mentioned the city that it was 'a port in Chekiang, south of Shanghai'.[89] The last foreign businessman departed in April 1932.[90] The British closed their consulate at the end of 1933 and sold the splendid consular building to a Chinese merchant in 1934.[91] As it was before Europeans arrived, Ningpo remained a major fishing port.[92] The banks of the river, from Chinhai to the city, were still lined with thatched huts used for centuries to store winter ice for the fishing industry.[93] And it was difficult to say to what extent, if any, Ningpo benefited from its 90 years as a treaty port.

Further reading: Bredon, *Sir Robert Hart*; Bruner, Fairbank and Smith, *Entering China's Service*; Coates, *China Races*; Cooke, *China*; Johnston and Erh, *The Last Colonies*; Nield, *The China Coast*; Tiffen, *Friends of Sir Robert Hart*; Uhalley, 'The Taipings at Ningpo'.

Pakhoi (Beihai) 北海

Guangxi, 21.29° N, 109.06° E
Treaty Port, 1876 British Treaty

When Pakhoi opened as a treaty port on 1 April 1877 the Union Jack flew over a fisherman's shack, raised on stilts, squeezed between similar ramshackle structures and surrounded by open sewers.[1] Consular assistant Alexander Harvey could not even enjoy the comparative comforts of the mud temple available to his counterpart in Newchwang (Yingkou).

Pakhoi was one of the four treaty ports created by the 1876 Chefoo Agreement. Its opening was sought for many years by Daniel Robertson, a former East India Company man and now a veteran of 33 years with the British consular service in China. Robertson should have been an expert, but whatever his hopes for this dot on the Guangdong coast, they were never fulfilled. *The China Mail* described Pakhoi as 'a wretched hole; the people are surly and dirty; the streets are stinking lanes, and the shops are dirty'.[2] Even Chinese from other provinces were appalled at conditions prevailing at Pakhoi.[3] The port was, however, famous for two things. First, due to its remoteness and poor communication with the interior, Pakhoi was a favourite resort of pirates. When the Canton (Guangzhou) Hoppo dispatched a mandarin to Pakhoi in 1869 to introduce the idea of paying taxes and duties like everybody else, the residents beheaded him.[4] Second, Pakhoi was plague-ridden, as the handful of foreign inhabitants discovered in the summer of 1877.[5] Plague came every two or three years and was a fact of Pakhoi life.[6]

US Navy Commander George Perkins visited the port in July 1877 aboard the USS *Ashuelot*. His impression that business 'must be inconsiderable'[7] was not entirely correct. Pakhoi residents were well disposed towards foreigners: the local Deputy Superintendent of Trade even insisted on helping to hoist the British flag.[8] Why would they not be? The local merchants were already enjoying a thriving trade, including the import of foreign goods, and they were confident that these newcomers were no threat. They were quite right.

Foreign goods were purchased in Macao and Hong Kong, and brought to Pakhoi by junk. Rice and sugar were the major exports.[9] Four foreign trading ships visited in 1877; what they carried could have been fitted into one of them, with room to spare.[10] The following year there were none.[11] Even though there was inherent risk in using junks for sea transport—their slow speed made them vulnerable to pirate attack and bad weather—Pakhoi merchants preferred them to the foreign steamships. That was until they met one they liked. In September 1879 Russells introduced a small, fast and economical steamer, the *Hainan*. It offered three or four round-trips in the time it took

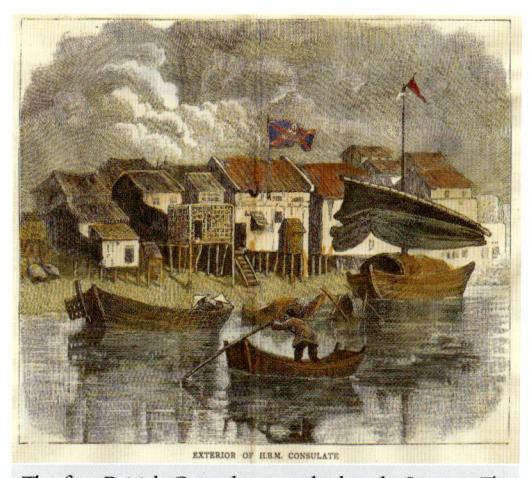

The first British Consulate, on the beach. Source: *The Graphic*, 5 March 1887.

a junk to do one.[12] Jardines and China Merchants followed, their vessels calling at Pakhoi on their runs between Hong Kong and French Indo-China. By the end of the year there was lively competition.

Of the first foreign merchants to arrive, the most successful was Herton, Ebell & Co. This firm developed the trade in *cassia lignea* as one of Pakhoi's major exports. Growing wild in the hills of Guangdong and Guangxi, this cinnamon-like tree bark produced an aromatic essential oil. Herton, who was part-owner of the *Hainan*,[13] taught the growers how to collect the product and pack it. He was forced out of the business as a result of preferential tax arrangements in favour of local traders. Herton was also the builder of the 1885 British Consulate[14] and possibly a number of other buildings of similar style that remain, but his business in Pakhoi closed in 1887.[15]

The purpose-built Custom House, a commanding three-storey structure dating from 1883, can still be found inside today's customs compound, at the east end of Zhuhai Road. Nearby is the former Imperial Chinese Post Office building. This service was started in 1897 with the Pakhoi branch initially located in the Chinese town.[16] The present building dates from a few years later.

A BLUFF BUT NO CONCESSION

Pakhoi, located on China's extreme south coast, actually faced north, hence its name in Chinese, 'North Sea'. The Chinese settlement was at the foot of a ten-metre-high bluff that stretched inland. This bluff deprived the town of the south-westerly sea breezes in the summer, while exposing it to the north-easterly winter monsoon. By choosing to build their houses on top of the bluff, the foreigners benefited from the cooling effect of the one and the welcome bracing effect, at least to the English, of the other. At the end of their gardens was the beginning of a large and empty common, a useful place for exercise, relaxation and game-shooting. No British Concession was established in Pakhoi for fear there would be insufficient interest to make it pay.[17] The bluff had plenty of space, and so these marooned expatriates consoled themselves with well-built villas and spacious gardens.[18] Of course, today all this land has been built upon and even the bluff itself has disappeared.

Among the new residents on the bluff was the British Consul. The fisherman's shack was determined to be the cause of the continuing poor health of its occupants. In 1884, Consul Clement Allen was authorized to acquire a generous plot measuring eight hectares for £80, a bargain even then. Mrs. Allen laid the new consulate's foundation stone on 24 May 1885, but was never to live there. Her husband was transferred to Amoy (Xiamen) just before the new granite and brick building was completed. His successor, consular assistant Lionel Hopkins, professed himself to be delighted with, in his view, the strongest foreign building in China.[19] It was a splendid edifice, of typical colonial design, housing both the consul's residence and offices. A testament to the building's strength was provided over a hundred years later, when the entire structure was moved 50 metres to the south-west to make way for a road-widening project. It now stands just as solidly within the grounds of the Beihai No. 1 Middle School on Beijing Road. Some of the British land was sold to a French missionary body; their church and administration building still stand nearby. Another tranche was passed to the British Church Missionary Society, and two of their buildings remain in the school compound. Yet a further parcel of land was offered to the French for their consulate, but the offer was not accepted. The

The new British Consulate in 1898. It was later moved to its present location. Reprinted with permission by the National Archives.

remainder became a recreation ground for the foreign community.[20]

Hopkins, the sole resident of the new consulate, became acting consul and made an international name for himself with his annual report for 1887. He gave an overview of the treaty port's performance during its first decade, and his comments were not flattering. Thanks to the new steamers local producers were better off because their eggs and pigs could now be marketed in Hong Kong, and at 50 percent higher prices. For foreign businessmen Pakhoi had been a failure. There had never been three, and there were seldom two foreign businesses there simultaneously. Hopkins asked whether it would have been better for foreign trade had Pakhoi not been opened.[21] His controversial and, for some, disloyal remarks garnered much publicity. An editorial in *The Hong Kong Daily Press* commented on Hopkins's 'extraordinary expression of opinion' and highlighted the benefits that steamers had brought to British trade as a whole.[22] The poor experience of Pakhoi would 'not be without its use if it prevents the formation of similar extravagant ideas' in connection with the opening of further treaty ports. This produced a strongly worded article in the Hong Kong press supporting Hopkins's unenthusiastic views.[23] There was even editorial comment in *The Times* in London.[24]

Despite this verbal spat, in terms of on-the-spot activity 'British trade remained obstinately non-existent'.[25] Ten years after the port's opening the foreign population stood at eleven, seven of whom were in the customs service and two in the British Consulate. Edward Herton had passed his mantle as sole foreign merchant in Pakhoi to Augustus Schomburg, from Bremen, whose firm remained until forced into liquidation in 1914 by events in Europe. The German's former hong, dating from 1891, is now an arts museum within the Municipal Cultural Department's compound. Schomburg's business meant that the majority of ships that called were German. The main commodity they brought in was cotton yarn, and they took out indigo, tin, sugar and aniseed.[26] Schomburg later pioneered importing kerosene, which he stored in a specially built facility at the extreme west end of the beach.[27] Although it was short-lived, the sudden growth in German commercial activity prompted the building of a German Consulate in 1905. This impressive structure is now used as part of a school.

Blockaded by the French

During their war with China in 1884–85, the French blockaded Pakhoi, and all trade ceased. Their action panicked the local population, particularly when a French warship opened fire on what it thought was an armed force planning retaliation; it was in fact a large gathering paying their respects to the dead in the Qingming festival. Fortunately, no additional ancestors were created that day.[28] After the war, the French returned to Pakhoi with different intentions. In 1887 they built a consulate on the bluff, just to the north-east of the British Consulate and equally conspicuous.[29] It is now used as a government guesthouse, recognizable although somewhat altered. The French were not simply there for trade. Since 1870 there had been a French cathedral on the small island of Waichow (Weizhou), about 50 kilometres due south. Now French missionaries concentrated their activity on the mainland, building hospitals, schools and churches. The British also built hospitals in Pakhoi. A number of buildings from 1886 and 1905 can be found within the grounds of the Beihai People's Hospital on Heping Road, most of them doing the jobs for which they were designed.

A larger French aim was to divert the trade of Yunnan and south-west China to the upper reaches of the Red River, whence it would flow to French ports in the Gulf of Tonkin. The effect of this began to be felt on Pakhoi's trade in 1890.[30] By 1900 a large proportion of the foreign shipping at Pakhoi had become French.[31] Another, undeclared, aim was to ensure no other nation achieved success in the region that the French increasingly considered their exusive sphere of influence. Successive British Consuls had recommended that a railway from the West River south to Pakhoi would add significantly to the port's business. Any effort to achieve this was met with vigorous French protests, claiming they alone had the right to such projects. Meanwhile they did nothing.[32] The only inland transportation was either bullocks pulling wagons or, on the narrower paths, coolies pushing wheelbarrows.[33]

However, a railway became pointless when, in June 1897, the West River was opened to steam navigation.[34] This development had been anticipated for many years; in 1890 Consul Benjamin Scott predicted that when it happened, 'nothing can save Pakhoi from actual insignificance'.[35] Now no longer a rumour, it provided one more nail in Pakhoi's commercial coffin and deflated foreign merchants' aspirations. The French opening of Kwangchowwan (Zhanjiang), 130 kilometres to the east, as a free port in 1900 was another blow, as was the opening to foreign trade in 1907 of Nanning, 160 kilometres to the north-west and one of the largest cities on the West River. Pakhoi had been sidelined.

There were other reasons for Pakhoi's lack of appeal. Piracy was ever-present, as was inter-provincial rivalry and fighting between Guangdong and Guangxi. Guangxi people saw Pakhoi as a symbol of their lack of access to the coast. (Before the provincial border was moved in 1952, Guangdong stretched all the way to Indo-China.) Foreigners, particularly missionaries in the interior, experienced violence: in November 1905 five American missionaries were killed and their hospital burned down.[36] A police force was established the following year, but made little difference. Townspeople could not understand why men in uniform were 'parading the streets without any special object'.[37] Local people were not used to accommodating any authority higher than themselves. As Consul Edward Allen commented scornfully in 1896: 'the highest native civilian within 20 miles [is] an officer of the rank of sub-district deputy magistrate, armed with an amount of authority that barely enables him to call in question the theft of a match-box'.[38]

The French kept their consular presence in Pakhoi until the late 1930s, but the British withdrew in May 1904, giving responsibility for Pakhoi to the Kiungchow (Qiongzhou) consulate.[39] It is difficult to say exactly when the treaty port of Pakhoi ceased to exist, but it finished pretty much as it had started. A British naval intelligence guide from 1945 describes the port as having very inadequate facilities, with all boats anchoring a kilometre or more offshore. There was, as before, little in the way of fuel supplies or available provisions. The town was described as dirty and devoid of modern sanitation.[40] Visitors from those days would not recognize the pleasant modern city that still goes by the same name.

Further reading: Rydings, 'Problems of the China Trade'.

Peitaiho (Beidaihe) 北戴河

Hebei, 39.48° N, 119.30° E
Seaside Resort, 1890s

Two sources are credited with the discovery of Peitaiho as a seaside resort in the early 1890s. Some say a group of foreign missionaries found its beautiful beaches while escaping the interior's heat. Others credit Claude Kinder, a British railway engineer engaged by the Chinese government to supervise the building of the line from Tientsin (Tianjin) to Shanhaikwan (Shanhaiguan). By 1893 Kinder had built a holiday cottage in an area that came to be known as West End. Ownership of property by foreign non-missionaries was prohibited, so one of his local contractors became nominal owner.[1] Others followed as news spread about how much pleasanter was the climate at Peking-sur-Mer or Tientsin-by-the-Sea.

The resort had only just started to develop when it was destroyed during its occupation by Chinese troops in the Sino-Japanese War. Once rebuilt its growth was rapid.[2] The 20 residences in 1896 grew to 100 in 1899, spaced along ten kilometres of beach, with a summer population of 400. Peitaiho Station was on the line that Kinder had built, and all visitors came by this route, despite it being eight kilometres

Kinder's rebuilt bungalow. Source: Crush, *Imperial Railways of North China*, 110. Courtesy of P. A. Crush Chinese Railway Collection.

from the resort. Holiday accommodation was reached by sedan chair, donkey cart or on foot.[3] This made for tedious beginnings and endings to vacations, but the promise of healthy relaxation and excellent bathing from May to October ensured popularity.

The accommodation formed three main clusters: West End, Rocky Point and East Cliff. The luxurious holiday bungalows of the senior customs officials, including Sir Robert Hart and Gustav Detring, were in West End. To the east were those of the British Minister and Jardines. Rocky Point was largely missionary territory. Being allowed to own their properties, they formed the Rocky Point Association, which, with voluntary subscriptions, looked after sanitation and leasing arrangements.[4]

All this effort was for nothing. On 20 June 1900 30 to 40 foreigners were whisked to safety by a British gunboat just as a horde of Boxers, Chinese soldiers and local people appeared and destroyed everything. Nothing was left, except for a surprising number of foreign articles that appeared in local markets for many years.[5]

A positive outcome from the devastation was that when rebuilding took place, almost immediately, the boundary of the open city of Chinwangtao (Qinhuangdao), 15 kilometres away, was extended to include Peitaiho. Thus all foreigners could own the land on which their houses stood.[6] East Cliff Land Co. was formed to purchase 46 hectares to build houses and a hotel.[7] Other hotels followed: the Strand, the Oriental and the Peitaiho.[8]

Another beneficial effect of the Boxer troubles was that a contingent of German troops took up residence in 1901 in a ten-hectare camp.[9] They soon became dissatisfied with marching from the railway station, and there were insufficient sedan chairs and donkeys for them. So they built a small railway, connecting the settlement to the main station, and offered holiday-makers free travel. When the Germans departed it was found they had no legal title to the land on which their railway stood; their offer to sell the line to the Peitaiho residents could not be accepted. For a while a push-trolley service was maintained.[10]

The influential community petitioned widely in Peking (Beijing) for a replacement railway, having experienced a convenience they were loath to relinquish. In 1917, their pleas heard, a branch line was built to a new Peitaiho Beach Station. This brought yet more people to the resort; that year there were 300 homes and a summer population of 2000.[11]

By 1923, despite efforts to create an overall municipal body, there were five separate residents' associations, including one catering to a growing Chinese community.[12] There were more than 400 residences and, during August and September 1921, a weekly air service to Peking.[13] An assembly hall was built on the area vacated by the Germans, run by missionaries for the staging of wholesome concerts.[14] Fashionable shops and restaurants from Tientsin established branches in Peitaiho for the season. This

The temporary push-trolley service on the old German tracks. Source: Crush, *Imperial Railways of North China*, 112. Courtesy of P. A. Crush Chinese Railway Collection.

sophisticated community could not survive the ravages of the Pacific War, nor those of the Chinese civil war that followed. By 1949 very few of the smart holiday homes were still habitable.

In an ironic twist, Beidaihe is today a very popular summer resort, not least for the highest echelons of the Communist Party. Vast tracts of the town were totally redeveloped during the early years of the 21st century. All that can be seen for kilometre after kilometre along the west beach is a continuous wall, occasionally broken by heavily guarded entrances, behind which are just visible roofs of detached, comfortable villas. Elsewhere in the town are a number of sanatoria for miners, railway workers and the like. Few buildings survive from the European era, although a new foreign age is dawning. Almost all signs, including street names, are in two languages—Chinese and Russian.

Further reading: *China Sanatorium*; *Peitaiho Directory*; Johnston and Erh, *Near to Heaven*.

PEKING (BEIJING) 北京

Beijing Municipality, 39.54° N, 116.23° E
Diplomatic Station, 1858

In the eyes of the Chinese, Peking was the imperial capital, the seat of the Son of Heaven and the centre of the known world. All envoys were by definition from vassal states, expected to kowtow and bring tribute. Foreigners were barbarians and, with few exceptions, best kept at bay. In the 16th century, Jesuit missionaries so impressed the palace with their knowledge of astronomy and ability to predict solar eclipses they were permitted to stay, some rising to high positions. In 1727 the Treaty of Kiakhta permitted four Russian Orthodox priests to live in the capital, as well as six students to learn Chinese.[1] At the time Roman Catholics were being persecuted in China, but Russians, who did not proselytize, were tolerated.[2] All other attempts by foreign powers to gain access to Peking failed, as witnessed by the spurning over the centuries of official delegations from Portugal, Holland, Britain and elsewhere.

This only increased Peking's desirability to foreigners, who concluded that if access was not given it must be taken through armed conflict, and so it was. The various 1858 treaties of Tientsin (Tianjin) provided for foreign envoys to live in Peking 'for the better preservation of harmony'.[3] Lord Elgin, chief negotiator of Britain's treaty, was pressured into agreeing to delay the fulfilment of that provision, the Chinese naturally believing that harmony would be better preserved if no foreigners were allowed anywhere near Peking.[4] Elgin's position changed in 1859 when he and his colleagues were stopped at Taku (Dagu) on their way to ratify the treaty in Peking. This resulted in the forcible entry into Peking by the Allies in 1860—resident diplomatic missions were established immediately. Against its will China became a member of the Western-style comity of nations.

A legation area was designated in the south of the inner city, near the new Tsungli Yamen, equivalent to a Ministry of Foreign Affairs, and means of formal intercourse were established. Immediately, each nation's minister in Peking became the senior point of reference in China for communication and resolution of disputes. For Britain, the roles formerly played by the Governor of Hong Kong and, since 1859, the Superintendent of British Trade in Shanghai were transferred to the British Minister. This was a diplomatic mission, not to be confused with the roles of the consuls, who were primarily concerned with matters of commerce.

Foreign nations were permitted to build or rent houses and offices in the agreed area for their diplomatic missions, and this became known as the Legation Quarter. It was not a settlement, as had become common in the treaty ports; Peking was certainly not a treaty port. Britain's 1858 treaty allowed British subjects to travel anywhere in China on business, provided they had a proper passport.[5] However,

Legation Street, the principal road in the Legation Quarter, c. 1900. Courtesy of Chester Cheng.

the tariff rules agreed supplementary to the treaty specified that access to the capital for trading purposes was forbidden.[6]

In 1864 the headquarters of the Imperial Maritime Customs relocated to Peking from Shanghai, under the management of Robert Hart.[7] Hence, with diplomats, customs people and missionaries there was soon a sizeable foreign population in the capital. Inevitably, some commercial activities evolved to satisfy foreigners' needs. By 1877 there were four hotels and a number of stores, all technically illegal.[8] The foreign merchants began to behave as if they *were* in a treaty port, assuming rights that did not exist. The Chinese government objected, but to no avail.[9] For practical reasons such activities were unavoidable. Over time 'tolerance may be said to have created a prescriptive right',[10] but the resentment remained.

Anti-foreign feelings erupted violently in the spring of 1900 with the Boxer uprising. Keen to ensure that the rebels did not turn against them, the Imperial Court offered the use of the palaces as Boxer headquarters.[11] Relations between the court and the legations deteriorated. Frequent and violent anti-foreign demonstrations by an armed mob of thousands prompted the foreign powers on 29 May to ask permission for more guards to be brought up from Tientsin, where they were held in readiness. Assent was grudgingly given and on 31 May a force of 400 foreign troops took up positions in their respective legations.[12] The demonstrations continued, with the full connivance of the palace.

On 4 June a much larger force was called up from Taku, for which permission was certainly not given. The 2000 men from eight countries, led by British Rear Admiral Seymour, set out by rail from Tientsin on 10 June. After two days, and only half way to Peking, Seymour found the track had been destroyed and was forced to turn back.[13] Meanwhile the British Legation was burned down, and a Japanese diplomat and the German Minister killed. Boxer reinforcements poured into Peking, causing destruction to friend and foe alike. On 21 June the popularity of the Empress Dowager soared when she declared war on all foreign powers, calling it a war 'against foreign violence masquerading as civilized diplomacy'.[14] The legations were under siege.

It was not until 4 August that an enlarged Allied force of over 18,000, having taken Tientsin, was able to set out for Peking.[15] The siege was broken on 14 August, by which time the empress and her court had fled. Li Hongzhang was left to negotiate a peace settlement, the Boxer Protocol. One of its terms was the recognition that the foreign powers had exclusive control of the Legation Quarter, including the right to provide their own police.[16] This effectively extended the concept of extraterritoriality to the foreign area of the capital, while not going as far as making Peking a treaty port. Indeed, in October 1901 Prince Chung wrote to the American Minister, Edwin Conger, complaining again about foreign merchants establishing themselves in the capital. They should, said the prince, go and do their business in the treaty ports. Conger replied by suggesting that Peking be opened like so many other cities in China. The idea was rejected.[17]

The Japanese took things further with their Supplementary Treaty of Commerce and Navigation in 1903. They procured China's agreement to a specified area outside Peking's inner city to be opened to foreign trade and residence as soon as all legation guards were withdrawn.[18] However, with memories of the vulnerability of the legations still fresh, the guards stayed. Peking's status remained as it was, with no further attempts at changing it.

Further reading: Fleming, *The Siege at Peking*.

Port Arthur (Lüshun) 旅順

Liaoning, 38.48° N, 121.13° E
Leased Territory, 1898 Russia

For centuries, coastal trading junks used Port Arthur's bay to escape bad weather. There were mud huts, some simple shops and a few inns to cater for visiting sailors.[1] When the British fleet called in 1860, en route to attack the Taku (Dagu) forts, Admiral Seymour named the bay after Lt. William Arthur, commander of HMS *Algerine*, the first British ship to shelter there.[2] Inability to adequately defend itself against Seymour's fleet confirmed China's conviction that it needed its own modern navy. In 1881 Li Hongzhang was charged with creating a credible naval force, with Port Arthur as its main base.

Li was distracted by other responsibilities and let the local *taotai*s manage the project. They failed, owing to their complete lack of experience. In the words of *The China Mail*: 'Never was a high official surrounded by a set of more useless creatures than Li Hungchang, and he is really greatly to be pitied.'[3] Matters improved when Li took control, visiting the developing showpiece regularly,[4] determined to create a world-class facility. In 1884, the actions of the French, particularly at Foochow (Fuzhou), once more exposed the empire's vulnerability.[5] Li engaged foreign engineers and military men whom he thought best qualified for the various aspects of the enormous job. Fortifications came under the Prussian Major Constantin von Hanneken. The chief instructor of navigation was American, a British officer taught seamanship and a German was in charge of gunnery training.[6] In October 1886 a visiting German admiral proclaimed the base to be impregnable from the sea, and praised Li and von Hanneken.[7]

In a surprising move, in November 1886 Li removed the Germans and appointed a French syndicate at Port Arthur.[8] The Germans had completed one major task—building and arming the forts that encircled the base. The French were given the job of improving the harbour and a dozen French engineers took up residence.[9] By 1890 their job was complete. The naval base had a dry dock, extensive wharves, a deep harbour, foundries and all the necessary plant for building and repairing warships. The entire facility was lit by electricity.[10] Port Arthur hosted an impressive fleet of eleven cruisers and other large ships, and eight gunboats and smaller vessels.[11] More were based at Weihaiwei (Weihai). At last, it looked as though China had a battle fleet that could match that of any potential enemy.

The new Chinese hardware was impressive; the command structure and experience of those commissioned to operate it was not. Japan's modernization was much more effective than China's; this was proven when war broke out between the two over Korea. On 21 November 1894, the Japanese captured Port Arthur, China's supposedly impregnable base and a key point from which to threaten Peking (Beijing). The invaders found large supplies of coal and ammunition, as well as fortifications and dockyard plant left entirely intact.[12] Presaging similar atrocities in the following century, the Japanese troops went on a killing orgy. The correspondent of the London *Standard* described it as three days of 'cold-blooded butchery'.[13] An estimated 20,000 were slaughtered.[14]

In the 1895 Treaty of Shimonoseki Japan gained the cession of the Liaodong Peninsula, an area contiguous with another of its spoils, Korea. Japan thus controlled a significant part of southern Manchuria, territory for which Russia also had plans. Chief among the attractions for Russia was the prospect of the ice-free harbour of Port Arthur.

Japan temporarily outwitted

With the enthusiastic support of France and Germany (Britain watched but remained uninvolved),[15] Russia expressed a concern that the Japanese presence in

Manchuria would destroy the political balance in the Far East. Force was hinted at.[16] By a convention of 8 November 1895 Japan agreed to hand the peninsula back, in return for an increased indemnity.[17]

Later in November rumours[18] about the 'Port Arthur Coup' proved to be true. A pact had already been devised giving Russia advantages in return for its support of China during the war with Japan, ineffective though that support had been. This agreement allowed Russia to extend its Chinese Eastern Railway network all the way to Port Arthur, and occupy the port for a period of 20 years as 'guardian' in certain circumstances,[19] such as if Russia 'should find herself suddenly involved in a war'.[20] This was going to happen anyway but Russia was impatient. A squadron of 13 Russian warships arrived at Port Arthur on 29 October before the Japanese had vacated, or even signed the convention.[21]

Russia received permission to build winter quarters for its navy,[22] and military surveyors set to work.[23] By December 1897 Russia was in full military occupation, in response to the occupation of Kiaochow (Jiaozhou) by the Germans in November.[24] The arrival of two British cruisers in January 1898 prompted the Russian ambassador in London to demand their withdrawal, to 'avoid friction'.[25] Events moved quickly and, for China, disastrously. First the Germans formalized their possession of Kiaochow Bay with a lease, granted on 6 March. Three days later the Russians issued an ultimatum, demanding a similar arrangement for Port

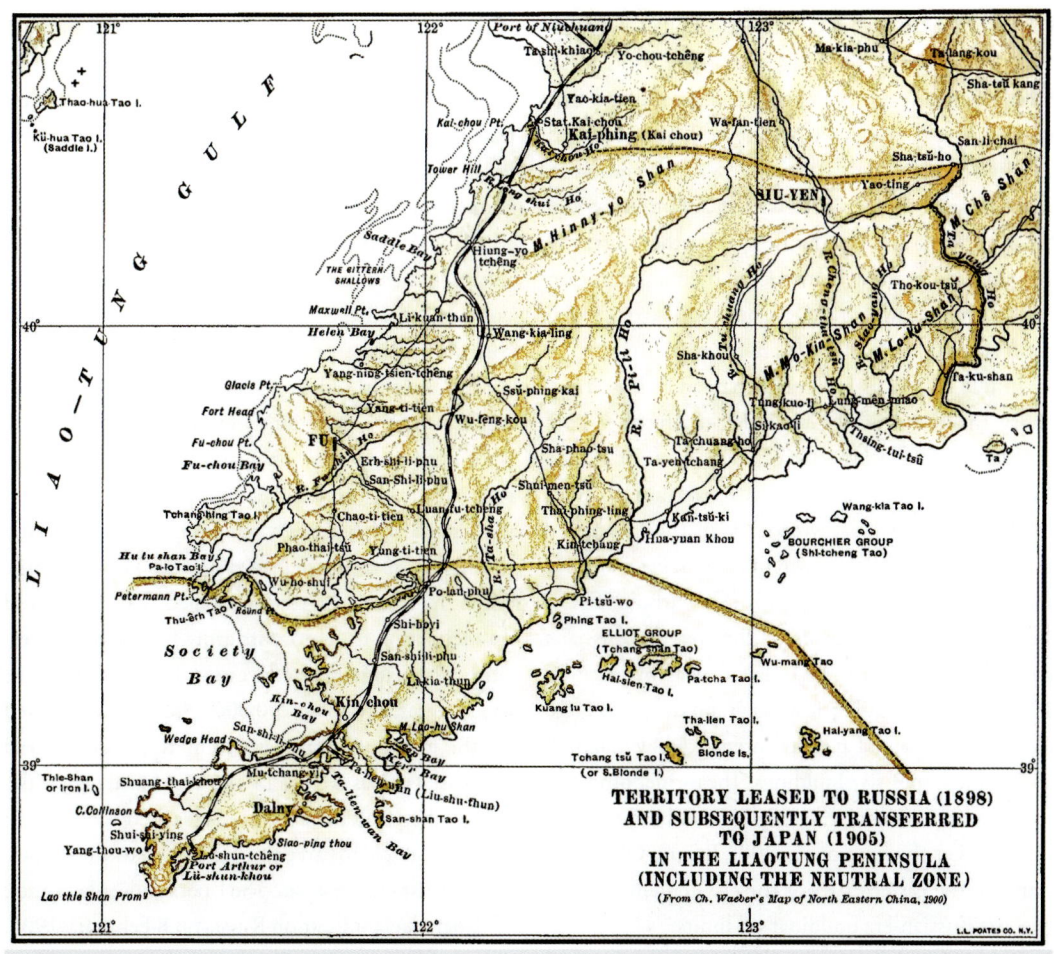

1898 map of the Liaotung (Liaodong) Peninsula, with Port Arthur (Lüshun) at the southern tip. Source: MacMurray, *Treaties and Agreements*, 128.

Arthur and Talienwan (Dalianwan); their lease was signed on 27 March. The French followed with a lease for Kwangchowwan (Zhanjiang) in April, and the British with Weihaiwei and Hong Kong's New Territory in May and June respectively. Japanese protests were ignored.[26]

The Russian lease was for 25 years, renewable indefinitely. Assurances that the port would be open to foreign trade proved false.[27] It was announced in July that Port Arthur was for the exclusive use of Russian and Chinese warships.[28] Clearly Russia did not want to share their new colony with anybody except the Chinese, and there they had no choice. Previous harsh treatment of the local population had caused 90 percent to leave. Now the Russians realized that to produce the model settlement they wished would require help. The new Russian governor announced that Chinese willing to settle with their families would be given work and free housing.[29] Furthermore, the Japanese had not only removed all their ammunition and armaments when they left, but had also destroyed the fortifications.[30] There was much work to do.

In July 1899 Russia formally named its leased territory the Kwantung (Guandong) Prefecture. Port Arthur was made the seat of the Governor of the Far East, an area that included Kwantung, Russian Manchuria, and Vladivostok and the Maritime Provinces. The Chinese town of Lüshun grew around the naval base at the eastern end of the harbour. To the west, separated by a stream, is the area the Russians chose to develop. The basic layout was in place by 1902, and is used still.[31] It was a grand design of large circular roads, broad avenues intersected by diagonal streets and impressive buildings. The former offices of the governor remain. Although partially opened to foreigners at the time of the 2008 Beijing Olympics, much of the eastern part of the city remains a naval base, its Russian-era buildings off limits.

There was an embryonic, underfunded municipal government: no water supply, drainage or police. Yet by 1900 there were more than 100 foreign merchants representing a dozen firms, including Americans, British and Germans.[32] Four years later the number had more than doubled. Mainly contractors to the Russian navy, they operated from a small bund, less than 100 metres long, that stretched from the naval dockyard to the stream.[33] The all-important railway connection to Harbin (thence to Europe) was completed in 1903 and regular trains started running in July,[34] further swelling the civilian population.[35] The port was guarded by 15,000 Cossacks[36] and was the base of the Russian Pacific Fleet.

The Boxer troubles of 1900 gave Russia an opportunity to display its military might. Japan and Russia were both members of the international force that relieved the legations in Peking. Russia's contribution was significant, but not when compared to the many thousands of troops it had stationed in Manchuria. After the Boxers had been quelled, Russia showed no inclination to remove its army from Chinese territory. Russia's railway concession included the right to protect it, and some 200,000 soldiers were detailed for the job. Japan was alarmed by this unnecessarily large presence as well as by the very existence of the Trans-Siberian Railway. Once it reached Vladivostok it would be able to carry Russian troops to within easy striking distance of Japan. The Japanese decided to act.

Japan declared war on Russia on 8 February 1904. A few hours before the declaration was received in St. Petersburg the Japanese fleet attacked Port

The development of the Russian harbour facilities, c. 1900. Courtesy of Régine Thiriez.

Arthur. Attempts to block the narrow entrance by sinking ships having failed, the Japanese commenced a blockade of the port in April. Unable to defeat the Russian defences in a head-on attack, the Japanese cut communications to the north.[37] There then followed a war of attrition. With heavy losses, the Japanese forces slowly made their way south. When the Russians surrendered on 1 January 1905, Japan gained not only the port and its harbour, but also 59 defending fortresses.[38] Today every hill overlooking the city has either a ruined fort on top, or a military memorial, or both.

Port Arthur becomes Riojun

In possession again, the Japanese renamed the place Riojun. The governor's offices were converted to the Japanese military headquarters. An impressive museum-cum-government office building was constructed on the foundations of an uncompleted Russian officers' club and a town hall was built on the adjacent lot. All this fitted in well with the Russian master plan, and the result is still most attractive to the modern visitor.

Port Arthur was partly opened to commerce on 1 July 1910. The Japanese population grew rapidly, outnumbering the Chinese inhabitants 9000 to 8000 by 1913,[39] but there were few other foreigners.[40] The sublime weather generated some interest in Port Arthur as a holiday resort. In 1923 there were 20 beachside houses for rent, built by the government.[41] As the 1920s gave way to the 1930s, Port Arthur was subsumed in the chaos that raged over the north-east.

At the Yalta Conference in February 1945, Roosevelt, Churchill and Stalin agreed that Russia could once more 'lease' Port Arthur at the conclusion of the Pacific War.[42] When the Japanese surrendered, the Russians lost no time. They parachuted troops into Port Arthur, and followed up with tanks and a heavy naval presence.[43] They finally withdrew in 1955.[44]

Further reading: Bland, *Li Hung-chang*; Nield, 'Bits of Broken China'; Otte, *The China Question*; Villiers, 'The Truth about Port Arthur'.

Port Hamilton (Geomun-do)
巨文島

South Korea, 34.02° N, 127.18° E
Occupied Territory, 1885 Britain

Almost surrounded by two islands, and with a diameter of two kilometres, Port Hamilton lies 50 kilometres off South Korea's southern coast. A survey was carried out by Sir Edward Belcher in 1845, who named the harbour for Captain William Hamilton, Secretary of the British Admiralty. In 1857 Russia obtained permission to establish a coaling station there, but nothing happened. The desirable harbour was to be a key feature of Anglo-Russian relations in the coming decades. In 1875 Sir Harry Parkes, British Minister in Japan, sent another survey team, which concluded the desirability of Port Hamilton's occupation by Britain was 'too obvious to need remark'. But again, nothing happened.[1]

In 1884 rumours emerged of an imminent Russian occupation of Port Hamilton; Russian officers were already training the Korean army.[2] In 1885 the uneasy peace following the Afghan War of 1878–79 collapsed, raising tension between Britain and Russia.[3] Russia's aid for an insurrection at Kashkar (Kashgar)[4] made war between Britain and Russia look certain. French attacks in the south distracted China, making Russian aggression in the north a likely element of any conflict. If this were to happen, China thought its best hope was Britain rather than its acquisitive neighbour;[5] Russian troops had already moved to the Korean border. Li Hongzhang proposed an Anglo-Chinese agreement whereby Britain would lease Port Hamilton;[6] Korea had been a vassal state of China since 667.[7] The Russian Minister in Peking (Beijing) declared that if this were to happen, Russia would seize Port Lazareff (Wonsan) on Korea's east coast as compensation, whereupon the Chinese offer was withdrawn.[8]

Faced with this threat to its interests in the Far East, Britain sent a fleet to Port Hamilton. The Union Jack was raised in May 1885 in response to the appearance of a Russian gunboat.[9] There were protests from Russia, Japan and China—and Korea, which had not been consulted. Before agreeing to withdraw, Britain required guarantees of Korea's territorial integrity, something China was unwilling to support as it called into question China's suzerain position. The Korean government suggested both Port Hamilton and Port Lazareff be opened as treaty ports. Instead, China undertook that no part of Korea would be occupied by a foreign power, following the receipt in Peking of a similar Russian undertaking. Agreements were signed in November 1886 and Britain withdrew the following February,[10] leaving behind 18 wooden huts, comprising the Royal Marines officers' quarters, a hospital and other barrack buildings.[11] Also remaining was a British cemetery, rededicated in 1998.[12] The agreements lapsed in 1895 when Korea came under Japanese rule.

Port Hamilton again came to British attention in March 1898 when its seizure was considered to counter the territorial acquisitions by other powers at China's expense.[13]

Further reading: Coy, *The British Occupation of Komundo, 1885–1887*.

Saddle Islands (Shengsi) 嵊泗島

Zhejiang, 30.42° N, 122.37° E
Seaside Resort, 1900s

The Saddle Islands, an archipelago with sheltered anchorages at the mouth of Hangzhou Bay, provided a base for foreign pilots watching for sailing vessels approaching Shanghai. When the North Saddle Lighthouse was built in 1871 it boasted the most powerful light in China.[1] In 1884 the islands were connected by cable to Port Hamilton, enabling the British to monitor Russian activities. In the spring the islands were home to a Chinese fishing fleet. When they left in mid-June, foreign holidaymakers came to enjoy weather significantly cooler than in Shanghai, eight hours away by steamer.[2]

Further reading: E. S. Little, 'The Saddle Islands'.

Samshui (Sanshui) 三水

Guangdong, 23.09° N, 112.50° E
Treaty Port, 1897 British Treaty

Samshui is an example of a treaty port whose opening, in retrospect, was probably a mistake. The trade potential of the West River was a focus of Britain's dealings with China in the late 19th century, not least to block French regional aspirations. The 1897 Burmah Convention listed three new treaty ports. Two of them, Samshui and Kongkun Market (Jianggen), were close neighbours and were treated as the same place.[1]

The first British Consul at Samshui, Herbert Brady, arriving at night after a twelve-hour journey from Canton (Guangzhou), found there was no accommodation. The Customs Commissioner let him use the Fulu Hu Temple, which had been allocated as a customs residence.[2] It was formally opened as the British Consulate on 26 November 1897.[3] From here Brady had a fine view of the nine-storey Kuigang Pagoda. The consul's former residence has been demolished (unusual for a Chinese temple), along with everything nearby except the pagoda, now standing in the middle of Wenta Park.

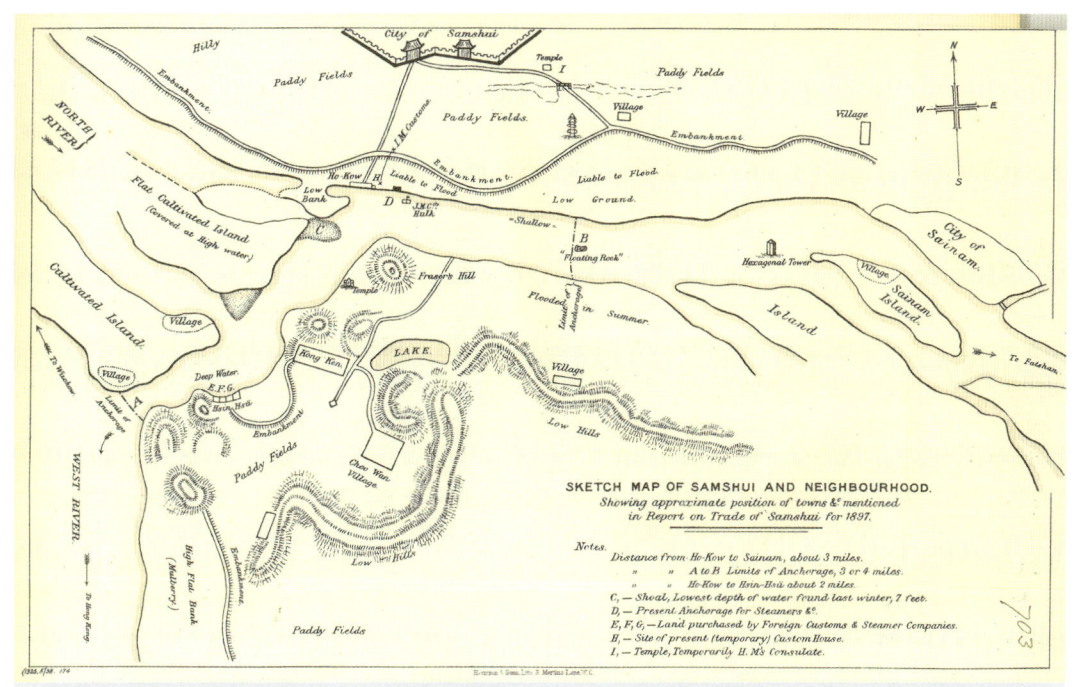

Sketch of Samshui (Sanshui) and surrounding area. 'Kong Ken' is on the river to the left. Source: *Foreign Office Report for Samshui*, 1897.

Samshui's walls had a circumference of only two kilometres, and much of the enclosed ground was given over to cultivation. The population of 4000 lived in small, dilapidated buildings and there was little business of any kind. The nearest commercial centre was Sainam (the city that now bears the name Sanshui; the old Samshui is now known as Sanshuicheng), about five kilometres downstream. This was considered as a potential treaty port, but the water was too shallow.[4] Samshui was on rising ground, about a kilometre from the riverbank, so an even smaller place at the water's edge acted as its port. This was Hokow (Hekou), which Brady called an indescribably dirty, poor place with 'one straggling street'. The 50 or 60 tumbledown shops and shanties 'bear witness to the annual immersion to which they are subjected'. There was some boat-building and rope-making, but no other commercial activity.[5] Nevertheless it was at Hokow that the tiny foreign community was to be based.

In 1898 Brady built a two-storey wooden house in Hokow, which he financed himself, opening it as the consulate on 1 July.[6] By the end of the year he had been transferred elsewhere[7] and the customs bought his house as a Custom House.[8] Before departing, Brady was negotiating to purchase land on which a proper consulate could be built. His successor, Harry Fox, took over the project. He completed the purchase in 1899, just before being sent to Hong Kong to recover from malaria. The following year Acting Consul Henry Little continued Fox's work. He constructed a four-roomed wooden bungalow as his residence on the consular lot.[9] But after all this effort, the consulate was closed in 1902.

A Maritime Customs presence was established in June 1897,[10] but acquired a commissioner only in 1901.[11] The Custom House recorded a small but satisfactory level of foreign trade. Fox expressed a hope for a steady increase 'provided that no disturbing elements in the shape of novel forms of taxation intervene'.[12] The port limits were identified as extending halfway to Sainam, where most local trade was centred. *Likin* would therefore be payable on goods going between Sainam and Samshui. However,

Jardines won the right to import and export at Sainam as if it were part of the treaty port area.[13]

Jardines were the first and for almost 20 years the only foreign firm to have a presence at Samshui. Through a local agent they represented the Hong Kong, Canton & Macao Steamboat Co. and Butterfield & Swire, the first two ship operators to service the new treaty port.[14] Neither owned vessels suitable for the shallow river, so chartered what they could from Hong Kong. They used a system of flat barges towed behind steam launches, until purpose-built steamers could be introduced. In this manner a tri-weekly service was established from Canton and Hong Kong, calling at Samshui en route to Wuchow (Wuzhou), 200 kilometres further up the West River.[15] Jardines had the only pontoon moored off Hokow. Other shipping companies loaded and unloaded from anchorages in the river.

The humble beginnings of Samshui as a small transhipment port were sufficient to transform Hokow. In 1898 thatched huts started to be replaced by more substantial shops and houses made of brick,[16] some still there. In 1899 foreign imports and exports were double the previous year, and there were 14 steamers visiting on a regular basis.[17] Samshui remained, however, a backwater, inconvenient and dangerous; in 1898 Consul Fox reported there was no telegraph and the river was infested with pirates.[18] In 1903 the Customs Harbour Master was shot in the face when he and his team attempted to capture some bandits.[19] Notwithstanding these problems, and the continuing lack of any foreign business presence, some of the essentials of a treaty port gradually came into existence. A 'poor man's bund' ran for a few hundred metres along the riverfront at Hokow, consisting of a double row of granite slabs. In 1905 a residence was built there for the Customs Commissioner, along with an examination shed, both long gone. But the imposing and apparently overly large Custom House, built in 1910,[20] is a protected building, glowering over the 200 metres of mud flats that separate it from the river.

Although technically a treaty port, Kongkun Market never featured more than its mention in the 1897 convention. Situated a couple of kilometres down the West River from Hokow, Kongkun consisted of two tiny villages, surrounded by attractive pine-clad hills and paddy fields. It was unsuitable in all respects, having no anchorage and no available building land. The even smaller village of Hsin Hsu (Xinxu), a kilometre further on, had both.[21] However, being on the opposite side of the river and even further away from Sainam, the anchorage was used only in times of exceptionally low water. Plots of land at Hsin Hsu were bought by the Maritime Customs, China Merchants and the Hong Kong, Canton & Macao Steamboat Co.[22] but, apart from some oil storage by Jardines,[23] were never used. Now known as Jianggen, this tiniest of all the treaty ports is in danger of isolation from the outside world. In 2012 the road leading to it from opposite Hokow had disappeared within a vast construction site.

In 1904 Samshui was boosted by a railway connection to Canton.[24] From the line's opening on 26 September,[25] five trains a day enabled the much faster and more efficient movement of goods and people. The river route to Canton was almost 150 kilometres and took twelve hours; by rail it was only 50 kilometres away.[26] A collection of crumbling buildings remain in Samshui station, still used for goods transport. They may not date from the line's opening but enjoy protected status.

In 1917 Hokow's first foreign businessman became resident—P. Drummond, manager of Asiatic Petroleum's expanding activities.[27] The company had had a floating kerosene store since 1907.[28] Drummond oversaw the upgrading of this facility into four 40-tonne, shore-based storage tanks, completed in 1920.[29] Standard Oil followed and in 1918 doubled the foreign mercantile community by stationing their man in Hokow.[30]

A new post office building was erected in 1921.[31] This is still there, at the western end of Qiaodong Street, with the Custom House 200 metres away at the other end. Still recognizable as Consul Brady's 'one straggling street', one or two newer buildings cannot remove the impression of being at the back end of beyond. Foreign trade fell throughout the 1910s,[32] falling further in the 1920s as a consequence of boycotts and general strife in China. Long-overdue work on the present 200-metre concrete jetty started in March 1937.[33] Designed to link the railway station to the river, this was completed just in time for the Japanese occupation in October 1938.[34]

SANMUN BAY (SANMEN WAN) 三門灣

Zhejiang, 29.03° N, 121.44° E
Naval Station (attempted), 1899 Italy

In March 1899 Italy, desiring recognition as a 'Great Power', demanded a lease on Sanmun Bay for use as a naval and coaling station. Its harbour was 'capable of sheltering the navies of the world'.[1] Also demanded were three nearby islands, mining and railway rights, and the establishment of Italian influence over much of Zhejiang Province.[2] Italy had negligible interests in China but its demands were thought to be supported by Britain and Germany.[3] China decided enough was enough (even Denmark was reported to be preparing a similar claim)[4] and refused. America adopted a position of 'disinterested neutrality' regarding Italy's demand, although a friendly power opening Sanmun Bay would aid American interests in the Philippines.[5] It was believed Japan supported China's bold response because it did not want other powers near its interests in Formosa (Taiwan) and claims on Fujian.[6] Five Italian cruisers sailed for China to demand an apology for the refusal.[7] Before they could press their case the Italian Minister in Peking (Beijing) was recalled, ostensibly because he had exceeded his instructions.[8] Italian claims for Chinese territory were quickly forgotten.

SANTUAO (SANDU) 三都

Fujian, 26.38° N, 119.39° E
Open City, 1898 Imperial Decree

The island of Santuao was declared an open city by Imperial Decree on 5 April 1898.[1] It was situated in Samsah Bay (Sansha Wan) one of the many large, sheltered, deep-water harbours found along China's south-east coast. Those factors made Samsah Bay very attractive to acquisitive foreign powers. In 1897 there had been rumours that China had offered Germany Samsah Bay for helping to remove the Japanese from the Liaodong Peninsula.[2] The Germans conducted a thorough examination of the bay[3] but chose to lease Tsingtao (Qingdao) instead. The Chinese decided it preferable to declare Santuao an open port rather than allowing one predatory power sole access to the bay. Better that foreigners' energies should be directed at fighting each other than opposing China.

However, there was some confusion about the identity of the place. Chinese practice was to refer to a city when meaning the city's port; the two could be kilometres apart, as with Canton (Guangzhou) and Whampoa (Huangpu). The official Chinese

View of the bay at Santuao (Sandu), c. 1903. Source: National Institute of Informatics – Digital Silk Road Project. Digital Archive of Toyo Bunko Rare Books. http://dsr.nii.ac.jp/toyobunko/III-2-B-233/V-1/page/0281.html.en

announcement referred to Funing, the Fujian prefectural city now known as Ningde, some 15 kilometres to the west of Santuao. Reuters immediately announced that the city of Funing in the Gulf of Chihli was open to foreign trade.[4] *The China Mail* agreed, welcoming British success in checking rising Russian influence up north.[5] Once the identity had been clarified, the names Santuao, Funing and Samsah became more or less interchangeable.

A customs presence was opened on 8 May 1899 on the west side of Santuao's south coast.[6] The foreign commissioner and two colleagues, initially confined to a hulk, were later given proper accommodation ashore. The island was not large, with one straggling village and no trade at all. Basic supplies were difficult to obtain, forcing visitors to bring their own. The area in the vicinity of the customs accommodation was designated for a foreign settlement.[7]

The inlet chosen for the Custom House, a muddy flat at low tide, had an anchorage sufficient for large vessels. It was there that steamers came to collect tea for onward shipment to Pagoda Island (Mawei), a hundred kilometres to the south. Much of the tea exported from there was grown around Samsah Bay and carried overland by coolies. These men at first feared a threat to their livelihoods,[8] but found they were still needed. They carried the tea to a number of places along Samsah Bay's extensive coastline, whence it was loaded onto small local craft and taken to Santuao for reloading onto coastal steamers.[9] It was a laborious process, but it worked.

Volumes increased and the major shippers established agencies at Santuao. The Japanese line OSK was the first to run a regular service in 1900; others operated during the tea season. A public board was established in 1900 under the joint control of the Chinese authorities and the customs service.[10] This body improved the roads and stood poised to provide infrastructure for the foreign settlement that never came. Imposing a two percent wharfage charge it reclaimed 150 metres of the foreshore and built a jetty.[11] In 1905 a telegraph cable was laid to the mainland. As it was severed by a typhoon in 1917, for four years telegrams were carried across by boat. The Custom House was damaged by another typhoon in 1919,[12] and destroyed by a third in 1931.[13] Apart from customs men, the only other foreigner to reside briefly at Santuao was the agent of Asiatic Petroleum.[14]

Despite the typhoons Samsah Bay appealed as a potential naval base. In 1900 Secretary of State John Hay, under pressure from the US Navy to acquire a coaling station, negotiated for the right to establish a base in the bay.[15] The Japanese, keen to protect their new possession of Formosa (Taiwan) just across the straits, objected and by 1904 the idea had been shelved.[16] The Chinese themselves were the next to show interest, sending a team of senior naval officers to survey the area in 1907.[17] Nothing came of it. In 1915 the Japanese included in their notorious 'Twenty-One Demands' claims for special mining, railway and other infrastructure rights in Fujian. They also insisted that no other power could build a naval base in Samsah. There matters rested until 23 July 1939 when a Japanese destroyer arrived in the bay and ordered all foreign ships to leave as the Japanese were going to mine the harbour.[18]

Apart from a customs residence, the only remnants of European influence in Santuao concern the missionaries, who were active there long before it was formally opened. A large monastery and two or three churches are in good repair. Two large churches and some foreign-style buildings can be found on the mainland in the vicinity of Guiqicun.

SHANGHAI (SHANGHAI) 上海

Shanghai Municipality, 31.14° N, 121.29° E
Treaty Port, 1842 British Treaty

Mongol encroachments into northern China, particularly in the 13th century, forced the Han Chinese to flee southwards. This led to Shanghai's prominence both as a coastal port and a terminus for an inland shipping network. On the edge of a large alluvial plain and near the mouth of the Yangtze, the town became a distribution centre for the products of the surrounding area. In the Ming period, much of this land grew cotton, and many were engaged in cottage-based spinning and weaving operations. Shanghai's city walls were built in the 16th century to protect what had become a thriving town with its own municipal government.[1]

Ningpo (Ningbo), a larger and prefectural-level city 150 kilometres to the south, was the area's major city. By the late 18th century the greater potential of Shanghai had been recognized by the merchants of Ningpo themselves. By 1832 Shanghai's star was rising and Jardines and the East India Company made exploratory visits. Shanghai was a major trade centre for three products in which they were particularly interested—cotton, silk and tea. The Huangpu River was crowded with thousands of junks.[2] The decision to include Shanghai as a port to be opened by the 1842 Treaty of Nanking (Nanjing) was easy.

Three foreign settlements

The treaty port of Shanghai was opened on 17 November 1843 by British Consul Captain George Balfour. With no practical alternative, Balfour intended to establish his consulate inside the walled city, a decision vehemently opposed by the city authorities—until a Mr. Yao appeared. Yao was a merchant and partner in a Hong Kong business. He offered Balfour his large and elegantly furnished house in the city. Balfour accepted, making this the most comfortable of all the first British Consulates in China. With Yao the unofficial 'keeper of the foreign devils' in Shanghai, others took up residence in the city. Yao's motives were not wholly altruistic as he wanted the British merchants to use his godowns and handling facilities exclusively.[3]

Within a week of arriving, Balfour had established the treaty port limits and the cargo handling area. However, faced with a quasi 'co-hong' arrangement whereby all foreign goods transited through the hands of Yao and his associates, it became increasingly urgent to obtain land designated for foreign use.[4] Besides, the pleasant autumn weather of November soon became an oppressive Shanghai summer. The foreigners came to see the walled city as 'a wretched little place', served by streets no better than open sewers.[5] Some considered living in the countryside, away from the smells and crowds.[6]

In 1842 a 900-metre strip of riverbank, north of the city, had been identified for British occupation, and attention was now directed towards developing it. Stretching from present-day Beijing Road in the north to the Yangkingpang Creek in the south (today's Yan'an Road), the eastern boundary was the Huangpu; the western limit was vague, pending a needs assessment.[7] The sparsely populated 55-hectare plot was filled with cotton trees, mulberry bushes and graves. Both Shanghai's authorities and citizens anticipated a bonanza from the diversion of part of the Canton (Guangzhou) trade. Settlement area landowners demanded prices far above real value, forcing Balfour to negotiate a fixed rate per *mou* of land with the *taotai*.[8] Purchases were made, but foreign merchants were reluctant to commit until tenure had been defined.

Their concerns were met in November 1845 when a set of land regulations were issued. These were drafted by Balfour, in discussion with London, but issued as a Chinese pronouncement with an English translation. Thus they did not amount to an agreement between the two countries, but a declaration by the Chinese.[9] Foreigners' obligations included keeping the streets clean, building bridges where needed, fire precautions and drainage. The Chinese authorities were content to leave the newcomers alone. In this spirit the regulations prohibited Chinese landowners in the settlement from selling or renting land to other Chinese.[10] Applications for land purchases (leases in perpetuity) were made through the British Consul. Although non-British applications were permitted, the area was a British Settlement.[11] In 1846 Balfour negotiated the lease of a plot for his consulate outside the northern limit of the settlement, between the boundary and Soochow (Suzhou) Creek.[12] That year the western limit was fixed roughly at today's Henan

Road, giving an area of 72 hectares. Despite the goodwill that existed on both sides, the foreign community felt concerned for safety. A settlement bounded on three sides by defendable stretches of water was comforting. A further agreement in 1848 extended the settlement westwards to the present-day Xizang Road—then a ditch called Defence Creek.[13]

Some non-British settlers came to resent British dominance—particularly when France and America emerged as Treaty Powers in 1844, expecting to rank equally with Britain in everything. Although French missionaries had long been active in and around Shanghai, France did not send a consul until 1848. Not wishing to recognize British superiority by accepting the land regulations, he applied both for a house outside the British Settlement and a separate French Concession. This he obtained through some sleight of hand.

French pressure had led to an Imperial Edict in 1846 reversing the previous prohibition of the promotion in China of Christianity. It incorporated an understanding that French Catholics could recover property seized when their activities had been declared illegal in 1724. One such property became Shanghai's Temple of the War God—and France wanted it back, or so they said. Instead they were offered a tract of land[14] which in 1849 became the French Concession. Smaller than the British Settlement, it was wedged between the walled city and the Yangkingpang Creek.

In 1846 Shanghai's only American merchant, Henry Wolcott, became United States Vice-Consul; some say he appointed himself, without reference to Washington.[15] The American flag above his house was the only foreign emblem flying in the settlement. Both British and Chinese officials thought Wolcott's action inappropriate, and Balfour requested he remove it. Wolcott refused to accept an instruction from a foreign consul. The flag remained. Later in the year, Balfour was succeeded by Rutherford Alcock, who obtained an amendment to the land regulations, forbidding the flying of any flag other than the Union Jack. Non-British were welcome but only as a courtesy extended by Britain.[16] The Americans resolved

The house of Franklin Delano Williams, co-founder of Wetmore, Williams & Co., in Mission Road (now the junction of Fuzhou and Sichuan Roads). Oil on canvas, by Chow Kwa. Courtesy of Martyn Gregory Gallery, London.

the issue by occupying land in Hongkew (Hongkou), north of Soochow Creek, to build a hospital and a mission. An informal American Settlement developed through private agreements with Chinese landowners.[17] Even so, when a fully accredited American Consul was posted to Shanghai, he preferred to establish his consulate near the centre of business in the British Settlement.[18]

Proximity to the Yangtze was a major draw for foreign business interests. By 1850 Shanghai's foreign trade had exceeded Canton's, including tea and silk exports.[19] Credit should not go solely to the foreign merchants; Cantonese traders moved up to Shanghai and soon rivalled those from Ningpo for dominance of the local market.[20] But it was the foreign presence that had the greatest visible effect on Shanghai. By 1850 there were a number of foreign houses in the settlement, many of them prefabricated in Hong Kong and brought up by sea; local artisans had not as yet acquired the skills to build in the foreign manner.[21] There was also a church, a club, racecourse, hotel, public garden and cemetery. In 1853 the foreign population stood at 170 men and 14 women.[22] And there was the British Consulate, completed in 1852, taking pride of place at the northern end.

1850s and 1860s: One drama after another

The treaty port was but ten years old when it was drawn into a series of events that had an impact far beyond Shanghai. The Taiping Rebellion broke out in 1851 in the south, bent on overthrowing the Manchu dynasty. In 1853, encouraged by Taiping activities, an unrelated group called the Small Swords took over the walled city of Shanghai. The Taipings themselves had by this time captured Nanking, 250 kilometres to the west, and were now looking eastwards.[23] With so much confusion, the foreign powers adopted a policy of armed neutrality.

With rebels in control of the city immediately to their south and an ill-led band of some 20,000 Imperial soldiers on the British Settlement's northwest boundary, the foreign consuls agreed in April 1853 to the formation of the Shanghai Volunteer Corps. In December the *taotai*, suspecting that the Small Swords were supplied from the settlement, attempted to invade the foreign area. He was driven off. He then requested foreign help to take back the city, but was reminded of the policy of neutrality; foreign merchants had indeed been supplying both sides. Meanwhile the soldiers were making repeated forays into the settlement. Alcock demanded that they withdraw, otherwise they would be attacked. His bluff was called. On 4 April 1854 the British and Americans, with sailors from their warships augmented by the Volunteers, managed to raise a total of 380 men. Vastly outnumbered, they went on the offensive. When contingents of the Small Swords joined the fray (at the probable invitation of the foreigners), the government troops fled.[24] The Battle of Muddy Flat, as it was known, was a pivotal moment in the independence of the British Settlement.

Meanwhile the walled city was still occupied by the Small Swords. The French feigned disgust at the demonstration of neutrality by the British and Americans. So when the *taotai* asked them to join government troops in a combined assault on the rebel-held city they obliged. In February 1854 the Small Swords evacuated, leaving government troops to wreak terrible revenge. One problem had been resolved, but the Taipings remained. Their effective closure of most of the Yangtze ports had a severe effect on foreign imports (apart from opium), although exports of tea and silk continued expanding.

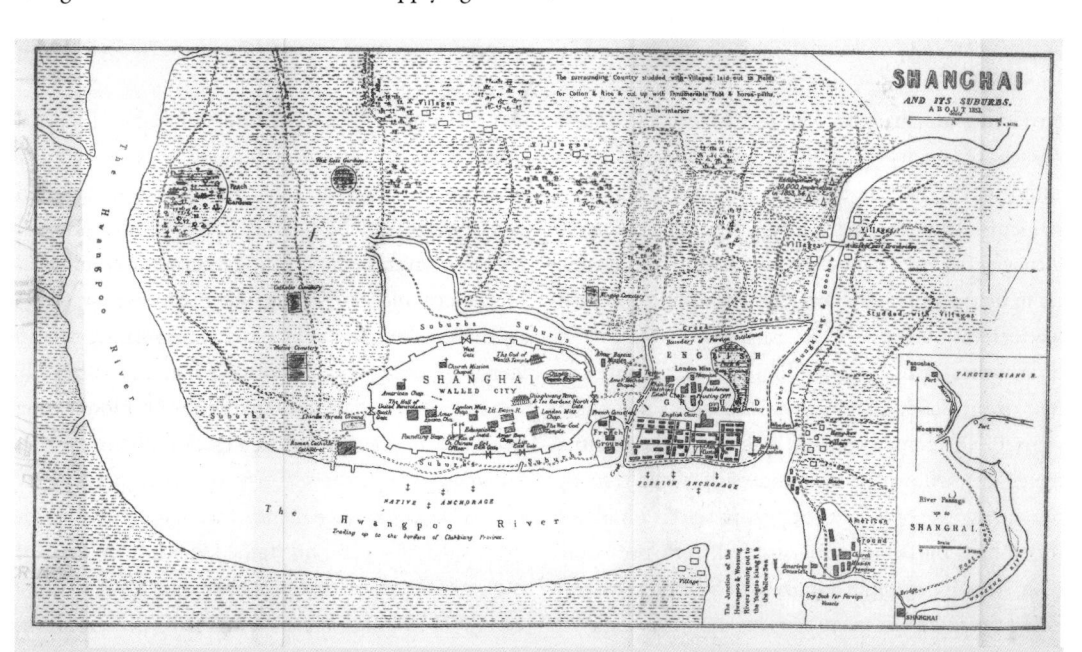

Shanghai as it was at the time of the Battle of Muddy Flat, 1853. Source: Lanning and Couling, *The History of Shanghai*, 304.

During their occupation of the city the Small Swords had destroyed the Custom House. Various foreign consuls saw this as an opportunity to avoid customs dues. The British and Americans thought otherwise, stating that rebel activity should not absolve the Treaty Powers from their obligations—and their view prevailed. In July 1854 a new Custom House was established in the settlement, but under foreign management and control.[25] This supposedly temporary arrangement proved successful beyond expectations. Peking (Beijing) received far more revenue from Shanghai than ever before, now that intermediaries were prevented from taking their share. It was not long before the new foreign-managed system was replicated in all the other treaty ports.

Recent experience had convinced Shanghai's foreign residents that the Chinese government could not offer protection. They needed to strengthen their own municipal arrangements. The 1845 land regulations required the British Consul to appoint three leading members of the community to a Committee on Roads and Jetties, an embryonic municipal government empowered to raise revenue.[26] In 1854 the British, American and French consuls drafted another set of land regulations. These were approved by the *taotai* and put to a meeting of land-renters. The Committee on Roads and Jetties was dissolved, and on 11 July the Shanghai Municipal Council (SMC) was elected in its place. This new body was given authority over all three foreign areas and all foreign residents. Applications for land were now to be made through the applicant's own consul. The original claim by the British for complete jurisdiction in such matters was waived.[27]

Another change was that Chinese were allowed to rent or buy land. This was realistic, given that there were 20,000 of them resident, including some wealthy merchants, following the capture of the walled city by the rebels. The 300 foreigners were uncertain about this influx, but those who profited from providing their housing strongly approved.[28] Shanghai experienced the first of its many property booms.

A period of peace and prosperity ensued. The foreign population were, as ever, happy to ignore what was happening in the rest of the country.[29] Besides, the 1858 Treaty of Tientsin (Tianjin) had legalized the trade in opium, and so the hulks were moved from Woosung (Wusong) to moorings opposite the Shanghai settlements. Business thrived. In June 1860, when the Taipings took Soochow, 70 kilometres to the west of Shanghai, concerns were expressed about how the settlements could be defended if directly threatened. The *taotai* made an opportunistic suggestion. He proposed that British and French forces then in Shanghai combine to repulse the rebels. Britain and France were at war with China, and the forces in question were on their way to the Peiho (Hai) River to fight. Despite the apparently preposterous nature of the proposal the Allies agreed, provided their military assets were used for defence not attack.[30]

The Taipings were surprised, approaching the walled city in August 1860, to see foreign flags flying and Allied soldiers shooting at them.[31] (Even more surprising was that simultaneously another Allied force was attacking the Imperial forts at Taku [Dagu].)[32] Repulsed, the rebels turned towards the settlements, only to face bombardment from the Allied warships moored in the river. The Taipings withdrew, but not before about 300,000 refugees had flooded the settlements. In true Shanghai style, property prices soared.[33]

In February 1861 Admiral Sir James Hope, a leader of Allied forces in China, went to Nanking to visit the Taiping leaders. He guaranteed them Allied neutrality provided the rebels stayed at least 50 kilometres from Shanghai. Peace and prosperity returned once more, and the Taipings allowed foreign steamers up the Yangtze as far as Hankow (Hankou). However, Zeng Guofan and Li Hongzhang, respectively Viceroy of Nanking and Governor of Jiangsu, made overtures to the foreign powers for help in finally eliminating the rebels.[34] This was prompted partly by the successes of American adventurer Frederick Townsend Ward and his trained, disciplined force of multinational mercenaries.[35] In January 1862 an army of 30,000 Taipings, approaching the settlements from the north in breach of the understanding with Hope, halted when they saw the ranks of the Volunteers and an Indian battalion. Another group approaching from the west was stopped by Ward.[36]

Britain had shied away from giving direct military support to China in its struggle with the Taipings. Neither London nor Peking relished the idea of British and Chinese troops fighting side by side; the memories of the recent war were too fresh. However, the rebels' refusal to disperse led to doubt about continued neutrality. An Imperial Edict in 1862 resolved the issue. It said that as Shanghai was so important to the foreigners, it was only right that they defend it.[37] Almost immediately Hope set about clearing the Taipings from his 50-kilometre zone, and British and French troops joined Ward's men on their forays. Ward, who by this time had assumed Chinese citizenship, was promoted by the emperor, and his band of fighters given the soubriquet the 'Ever-Victorious Army'. After a series of campaigns that saw the rebels come within three kilometres of the settlements' boundary,[38] and the death of Ward and his succession by British colonel Charles Gordon, by the end of 1862 the Taipings were no longer a threat to Shanghai.[39]

WHEN THE DUST SETTLED

These various dramas changed the Shanghai foreign settlements. The turmoil had given birth to a new municipal council and a foreign-managed customs service and, now with 500,000 refugees, a population problem of gigantic proportions. The settlements also had become more autonomous. Britain and France had been fighting Russia in the Crimean War and had little energy to spare for monitoring events in Shanghai.

The French Consul had signed the 1854 land regulations, but in 1862 claimed that he was not bound by them as they had not been ratified by Paris. (Nor were they ratified by London until 1868.) On 13 May a separate municipal council was established to run the French Concession. While Britain and America accepted that extraterritoriality did not impinge on overriding Chinese sovereignty, France believed leasing land to a foreign power gave that power all the rights of government.[40] Whereas the other settlements were governed by the combined will of their residents, France ran its concession as an absolute French possession. The French Consul reigned supreme, answerable only to the colonial governor in Indo-China.[41] Whereas the British claimed to treat all nationalities equally, French nationals were given priority in all matters in the French Concession, including land allocation.[42] But by this time almost all business was being done in the British Settlement, leaving the French area without revenue—except for licence fees from the opium dens, brothels and gambling houses that soon made the concession their home.[43]

Originally a place for missionary activities, the status of the American Settlement at Hongkew was uncertain, recognized neither by Washington[44] nor, until 1863, by the Chinese authorities.[45] It had grown to include a dockyard and places of entertainment for foreign sailors. A Hongkew Municipal Committee existed, but its activities were limited by lack of revenue. Its police force of six struggled to maintain law and order, especially over criminals evicted from the adjacent British Settlement. In order to gain the latter's cooperation the Americans agreed that the two police forces be amalgamated. Soon a full merger of the two settlements was proposed. This happened on 21 September 1863. In many respects a British takeover, the new entity became known as the International Settlement.[46] In 1866 a new set of land regulations was devised.

In 1862 the leaders of Shanghai's foreign commercial community had suggested making the settlements an independent republic. But this proposal, removing the equally unwelcome attentions of the *taotai* and of the foreign consuls, was unrealistic and contravened the treaties.[47] However, the International Settlement was not far short of independence. Not under the jurisdiction of any one country, it governed itself. A later British Minister in Peking described it as an 'anachronism [but] a most useful one'.[48] Others described it as a 'poorly camouflaged British colony'.[49]

In keeping with contemporary reformist thinking in Britain, the right to vote in the settlement was attached to property and property tax. The qualifying level of tax paid was set not so high as to make the electorate too exclusive, but not so low as to enfranchise 'undesirables'.[50] By-laws issued under the land regulations had to be approved by the SMC, by ratepayers at a public meeting and by a majority of the foreign ministers in Peking. The system was unwieldy, but allowed a fine balance between independence and the appearance of recognizing consular authority. Most of the meetings of ratepayers were chaired by the British Consul; the British still accounted for the largest part of the treaty port's commerce. Members of the council were elected, their number limited to nine. The heads of major British firms were almost guaranteed a seat. In addition there was usually one American and one missionary—but no Chinese.[51]

The main duties of the SMC related to law and order, sanitation, public works and the like. However, the presence of a huge refugee population demanded that special attention be given to Chinese interests; Chinese were by now paying half the taxes collected by the SMC.[52] The 1866 land regulations contained some controversial terms and were not finally approved until 1869.[53] One was the proposal that Chinese residents be given the franchise, on certain conditions, and be eligible for election to the council. Alcock, by now British Minister in Peking, objected and the proposals dropped.[54]

The independent tendencies of the settlement meant that the SMC resisted attempts at interference by Chinese authorities. In 1862 the Chinese city government tried to levy a poll tax on the settlement's Chinese population, common practice elsewhere. The British Minister in Peking stated that the treaties could not prevent the Chinese government from taxing its own people. However, Consul Medhurst in Shanghai refused to allow Chinese tax collectors to roam the settlement. After a year's stalemate a compromise was agreed whereby the SMC collected the tax through the rates system, and paid it over to the *taotai*.[55]

The question of exercising jurisdiction over the Chinese in the settlement presented similar problems. The principle of extraterritoriality established that Chinese in the treaty ports were subject to their own legal system, but nowhere else were so many living in a foreign-managed area. The *taotai*'s suggestion of setting up fully fledged Chinese courts within the settlement caused horror. The emergence in 1863 of the Mixed Court was another compromise. Cases involving only Chinese parties would be presided over by a Chinese magistrate. In cases involving both a foreigner and a Chinese, the Chinese magistrate would be joined by an assessor, a member of the consulate of the foreign party; the concept of 'innocent until proven guilty' did not exist in the Qing legal code.[56]

Civil and criminal cases where both parties were non-Chinese continued to be tried by the respective consuls. In recognition of its increasingly important role, in 1865 Britain established in Shanghai a Supreme Court for China; the Superintendency of Trade had already been transferred to Shanghai in 1859, leaving Hong Kong responsible solely for its own legal and commercial affairs.[57]

In 1863 it was estimated that Shanghai was the sixth-largest port in the world. The American Civil War created international demand for Chinese cotton, fuelling further growth. As happened in other boom towns like Chicago, San Francisco and Melbourne, building land that could have been bought very cheaply in 1850 now changed hands at many hundreds of times that price.[58] However, once the Taiping threat was over large numbers of Chinese left the refuge of the settlement and returned to their homes. Shanghai experienced its first slump with whole streets of new housing standing empty.[59] Economic problems were not to beset only Shanghai. A global depression in 1866 was to add to the port's woes. The powerful house of Dents collapsed and six of the eleven banks in the International Settlement failed. Even the SMC was facing bankruptcy.[60]

The strengthening of Shanghai and of China

Having tasted the fruits of success the foreign business community did not intend to give up. Much else was happening that gave the settlement momentum and comfort. In 1862 the racecourse was relocated to its third (and final) site; parts of its outline can still be recognized in today's Renmin Park. The same year saw the rebuilding of the Shanghai Club on a very extravagant scale. The Holy Trinity Cathedral was consecrated in 1866.[61] There had been a danger that the river frontage of the International Settlement, a former coolie towpath, would become an eyesore like the one in the French Concession—a line of sheds, wharves, ugly functional buildings and sewers that did not reach the low-water mark. Instead it started to become what we know as the iconic Bund, today one of the most beautiful and impressive stretches of city waterfront in the world.

After the failures and wild speculations of the previous decade, business in the post-Taiping years developed on a much sounder basis. Imports of foreign goods between 1864 and 1874 almost doubled. There were no deep-water ports to the north, securing Shanghai's role as a distribution and transshipment centre. In 1863 work started on a long-overdue project to make navigation in the river safer, especially near the notorious Woosung Bar.[62] The Hongkong & Shanghai Bank was formed in Hong Kong in 1865, and a Shanghai branch opened the same year. Jardines eased itself out of the opium trade around this time, focusing instead on real estate, insurance and shipping and, later, manufacturing. John Samuel Swire arrived in Shanghai in 1866; Butterfield & Swire would grow into one of the largest firms on the China Coast. Russells founded the Shanghai Steam Navigation Co. in 1867, a third of the capital coming from Chinese investors.[63] Initially it enjoyed an almost complete monopoly of foreign traffic on the Yangtze.

It was not just foreigners who were determined to grasp opportunities. Having to seek British and French help to defeat an internal rebellion, so soon after their loss in a war against the same British and French, had shaken the Chinese world-view. There was a strong current of opinion in China that the country must modernize. One of the main proponents of the Self-Strengthening Movement was provincial governor Li Hongzhang. Armaments were seen as the first priority, and Li was behind the founding in 1865 in Shanghai of the Kiangnan (Jiangnan) Arsenal, a munitions factory and later shipyard;[64] the first ship was launched in 1868.[65] Li attached to this facility a school for teaching Western languages and science.[66] Another Li initiative was the China Merchants Steam Navigation Co., one of the first Chinese ventures under the 'government-supervised merchant enterprise' (*kuan-tu shang-pan*) formula.[67] Starting in 1872 with an old P&O vessel,[68] financed entirely by Chinese capitalists, the fleet numbered twelve in 1876. The following year it more than doubled when China Merchants bought the entire Shanghai Navigation fleet. Under the command of British captains, this line became the largest in the coastal and river markets, with branches in the key treaty ports.[69]

Established in 1878, the Shanghai Cotton Cloth Mill was another Li-sponsored venture using the same formula.[70] Although extremely capable, Li was also very busy and was not able to give the cotton mill the attention it deserved. Despite being guaranteed a ten-year monopoly[71] the project languished, owing to 'gross waste and mismanagement'. For fear of upstaging Li, no other cotton mill appeared for some time.[72] Li's factory was operating successfully in 1889[73] (it even paid a 25 percent dividend in 1893),[74] allowing others to follow.[75] By 1894 there were six.[76] The settlement provided a business environment free from government interference, something unfamiliar to but greatly welcomed by Chinese entrepreneurs. These men knew how to make capital work within treaty port conditions. Increasingly there were Chinese-owned ventures using Western models, including warehousing, insurance, paper mills and telegraphy.[77]

The foreigners' presence attracted businesses to Shanghai, yet foreigners were prohibited from

The French Bund, 1911. Courtesy of Régine Thiriez.

manufacturing. European and American merchants claimed the right, under the treaties, to engage in manufacturing at the treaty ports. The Chinese government steadfastly refused, instructing customs officers to forbid the landing of any manufacturing machinery intended for foreign use.[78] The Sino-Japanese War resolved the matter. The 1895 Treaty of Shimonoseki allowed Japanese manufacturing rights at any treaty port. By application of the Most Favoured Nation principle, this right extended to all Treaty Powers. Foreign merchants could now compete with their Chinese counterparts, and Shanghai benefited from the ensuing rivalry.[79] British and German companies led the way; the Japanese were slow to capitalize on their gain, but soon overtook the others. Chinese capital continued to pour into Shanghai. Flour mills, chemical works and many other factories spread along the banks of the Huangpu towards Woosung.[80]

The industrial boom triggered a rapid rise in land prices[81] and an increase in population. The Chinese silk industry, for years a staple of the national economy, was collapsing in the face of better-quality competition from Japan.[82] Shanghai's thriving cotton industry attracted skilled workers made redundant by the silk factories of Soochow and Hangchow (Hangzhou).[83] The settlement was filling up, prompting the SMC in 1896 to ask Peking for another extension to its boundaries. At the same time the French applied for an extension to their concession. Both applications included land in Pudong, some having already been acquired by British and American shipping firms. The resulting disputes delayed the process. Besides, the Chinese government was in no mood to give further land away to foreign powers, having just lost a war with Japan. Finally, approval was announced in July 1899. The International Settlement grew from 7 square kilometres to almost 22, and the French Concession more than doubled to 144 hectares.[84]

Revolutionaries and riots

Commercial success brings employment and opportunities to many. It also generates large disparities in wealth and working conditions that are frequently unpleasant and often dangerous, for which the wages paid are no compensation. The end result is dissatisfaction among the working classes, manifesting itself in a variety of ways from riots to unionization. In Shanghai outward displays had been few: a riot in the French Concession in 1874 over a plan to build a road through a cemetery;[85] and another in the International Settlement in 1897 prompted by an increase in wheelbarrow licence fees.[86]

Disaffection among the working poor was exacerbated by anti-foreign feeling, although to a lesser extent than elsewhere. Apart from posters in the streets exhorting people to attack the city's major missions, Shanghai largely escaped the anti-foreign disturbances that spread along the Yangtze in 1891.[87] Yet the settlement symbolized all that was becoming increasingly resented when Chinese people saw the power and influence foreigners wielded. One of the many ironies that permeate treaty port history is that, with its free Chinese press and general laissez-faire attitude, the International Settlement provided a safe base for people to meet and share grievances. Furthermore it was largely through the missionaries' schools and other activities that foreign ideas were being introduced to an increasingly politically aware student population.[88]

In 1900 provincial leaders and the foreign consuls met in Shanghai to discuss the threat of the Boxer rebels. The foreigners were anxious about the possible closure of the Yangtze to foreign shipping and its effect on trade. In return for the foreign powers undertaking to restrict their military activities to the north, Li Hongzhang, Sheng Xuanhuai and the other viceroys undertook to regard the Empress Dowager's declaration of war against all foreign countries as a forgery; brave men, they ignored it.[89] The river stayed open and the rebels were repelled.[90] However, a number of radical anti-Manchu and anti-imperialist societies sprang up in the wake of the rebellion, and these were supported by Shanghai's Chinese press. The *Shun Pao* was particularly vocal, urging its readers to both overthrow and murder the Qing. This was too much even for the SMC, but they refused the Chinese authorities' demand in 1903 to enter the settlement and close the offending publication. After an awkward stand-off, settlement police arrested the editors and they were subjected to the due process of Chinese law.[91]

Two years later Japan defeated Russia in the war of 1904–5. That an Asian country could humiliate a European power in this manner provided impetus to the Chinese anti-imperialist movement. A dispute in the Mixed Court in 1905 over jurisdiction resulted in a fight inside the courtroom between Chinese and settlement police. With encouragement from propagandists, this flowed over into the streets, causing a riot. The SMC offices were attacked and the Louza police station burned. Order was restored only when sailors were landed from foreign warships.[92] Later in the year there was a boycott of American trade, following a decision by Washington to restrict immigration from China, concerned, for example, that nine percent of the population of California was Chinese.[93] This petered out when Chinese merchants faced bankruptcy.[94] Yet it was another example of the Chinese flexing their newly found muscles.

Much of this muscle was provided by students returning from studying in Europe, America and Japan. One of their immediate concerns was that Chinese residents were denied representation on the SMC, despite owning about 90 percent of the settlement's real estate, thereby contributing a similar portion of the SMC's revenue.[95] In 1906 the SMC repeated its mistake of 1866 and refused to allow Chinese members.[96] (This happened again in 1915, when the ratepayers voted in favour but were overruled by the foreign ministers in Peking.)[97]

Meanwhile business continued to thrive. More factories and houses were built by foreigners outside the settlement boundary, and in 1909 the SMC applied again for an extension. The growing nationalism in the country meant the request was refused. An appeal met a very different sort of barrier—the 1911 revolution. The Chinese city of Shanghai declared for the republic on 4 November, evidenced by the sudden appearance of white flags all over the settlement. While no violence was connected to the revolution, there was a breakdown in law and order among jubilant Chinese as Imperial officials fled. Among them were the magistrates of the Mixed Court, prompting the foreign consular body to take over its operation.[98] Pre-revolutionary banknotes became worthless and there was a run on Chinese banks. Of the 36 in operation in Shanghai, 14 failed in the course of three days, and many of the remainder reduced their capital.[99]

The Great War brought prosperity to Shanghai as its factories supplied the needs of the warring nations. Industrial growth was retarded only by the difficulty in obtaining foreign plant and equipment.[100] A number of Chinese became millionaires but postwar settlements breathed new life into ever-present anti-foreign sentiments. The decision of the 1919 Paris Peace Conference to recognize Japan's claims over the formerly German areas of Shandong gave rise to strikes and a boycott of Japanese trade; anti-Japanese feelings had already been stoked by Japan's issue in 1915 of its 'Twenty-One Demands' on China. The failure, also in 1919, of yet another attempt at Chinese representation on the SMC strained Sino-foreign relations further. The ratepayers' meeting at which this radical change was proposed agreed instead to create a Chinese Advisory Committee of five, to be nominated by the Chinese community. Disagreements over nominating procedures meant the committee did not meet until May 1921.[101]

The Chinese Communist Party was founded in Shanghai in 1921. The real power behind the Chinese delegation to the 1921 Washington Conference—at which Shandong was returned to China, but no commitment was made to ending extraterritoriality—was not the disunited Chinese government but the increasingly engaged body of

The Shanghai Municipal Council Building in 1922—larger than the town halls of most Western cities. Source: *Shanghai Municipal Council Annual Report 1922*.

left-leaning students and intellectuals. Shanghai was becoming the national centre for their activities. The number of strikes in Shanghai had increased steadily between 1918 and 1924, apparently with Bolshevik support.[102] On 15 May 1925, seven agitators were shot by the Japanese foreman of a cotton mill, one later dying from his injuries.[103] The SMC did not prosecute the Japanese, but arrested six Chinese students when they staged a protest a week later. This prompted further outrage, and on 30 May three thousand chanting students marched through the settlement. They approached the Louza police station on Nanking Road, where their colleagues were held, and found it defended by armed Chinese and Sikh constables under a British officer. Believing his position was about to be overrun, the officer ordered his men to shoot into the crowd.[104] Twenty-four were killed or died subsequently, and 36 were injured.[105]

A general strike was called for 1 June. It was widely supported by workers, students and merchants and financially underwritten by the (Chinese) General Chamber of Commerce.[106] By 10 June 130,000 workers had walked out, forcing the temporary closure of 107 foreign-owned factories, as well as the cargo-handling wharves.[107] Later in the month the strike ran out of steam as its backers ran out of money. When the SMC cut off the power supply to the still functioning Chinese factories, things gradually returned to normal.[108] The settlement's foreign community of 'Shanghailanders' had been proud of their unique, efficient municipal administration. They did not want to provide an excuse for diplomats in Peking or their home countries to question the wisdom of the settlement's continued existence. After the events of 1925, this seemed increasingly likely.[109]

In 1914 the French Concession admitted two prominent Chinese into the municipal government, albeit under the absolute authority of the French Consul. In the International Settlement, a ratepayers meeting in early 1926 voted in favour of three Chinese being elected to the twelve-man SMC. The 1925 census showed that there were 29,947 foreigners living in the settlement, and 810,299 Chinese. The Chinese thought three were insufficient, but the new members eventually took their seats in May 1928. At that meeting it was agreed that the Mixed Court be returned to Chinese jurisdiction.[110]

To add to its troubles, Shanghai was seen as a prize by the factions continuously fighting in much of the rest of the country. As combat approached the city an estimated 200,000 sought refuge in the settlement.[111] By November 1926 the National Revolutionary Army had captured Hankow and Kiukiang (Jiujiang) on the Yangtze. A total of 40,000 foreign troops arrived to defend Shanghai, 20,000 of them British. A long line of foreign warships stood ready in the river.[112] The loss of the British Concessions at Hankow and Kiukiang in February 1927 caused alarm in the International Settlement, as did the frequent demonstrations and rallies.[113]

In March 1927 Chiang Kai-shek's forces entered the Chinese city. The French Concession and International Settlement raised barricades, prepared for the worst.[114] But Chiang did not preside over a united army. Communist elements managed to form a city government, until a combination of Chinese bankers, businessmen and gangsters financed a bloody campaign allowing Chiang's Kuomintang to seize power.[115] With the creation of a Greater Shanghai Municipality later in the year, Chiang gained the support of all elements of the business community.[116] Despite continuing turmoil elsewhere, Shanghai settled down to what it did best—making money. Remarkably, trade for 1926 showed a record high, with Shanghai contributing 41 percent of the national customs revenue, the port still the world's sixth largest.[117]

THE GOLDEN AGE: A LAND OF SILK AND MONEY

From a foreign perspective, Shanghai was always a comfortable place to be posted. Life was good and the rewards were plentiful. In the turmoil of the 1920s, many preferred to avert their eyes and pretend nothing was changing. Shanghai was the centre for all the central and northern treaty ports. Junior staff, known as 'griffins', worked there for a few years before being sent 'up country' for experience. Those who survived returned after many years to senior positions at headquarters; more foreign companies had their China base in Shanghai than in Hong Kong. Despite the manifest problems, the 20 years prior to 1932 are considered Shanghai's golden age.

Numerically the Japanese had been the largest non-Chinese community since about 1918 but the British still dominated the government, the police and 'society' in general. The epicentre of power and privilege was the Shanghai Club, where a man's standing in the community determined where he could stand at the bar. Shanghai was not a colony, but nobody seemed to have informed the British residents of that vital fact; they treated the Chinese as colonial subjects. The increasingly wealthy Chinese elite built houses and drove cars that matched those of the foreign *taipan*s. But within the private clubs and public spaces discrimination was rife. There was very little social mixing between Chinese and non-Chinese—even between one group of foreign nationals and another.[118]

At the lower end of the foreign social scale, even the rawest recruit was paid more than he ever earned at home; at least his money went further. Junior police constables employed Chinese servants to look after them.[119] An SMC report in 1923 cautioned that Shanghai had a style of living that was 'extravagant beyond all necessity' and new arrivals were 'tempted to maintain a standard beyond both their needs and their means'.[120] It was said that a man's position was 'not ruled so much by what he can earn as by what he can owe and still remain at large'.[121] Many in the police abused their positions for financial gain. Another 1923 report suspected that half the force was involved in some degree with opium smuggling. Organized crime, especially armed robbery and kidnapping, was exacerbated by the ease with which suspects could cross jurisdictional boundaries and escape capture. The French Concession was obviously run in a more lax manner than the International Settlement. One can see why when Du Yuesheng (Big-Eared Du), a leading gangster, was admitted to the French Municipal Council.[122]

Racing was one activity that was open to all. During the twice-yearly season all banks and businesses closed at 11:00 a.m. to enable everybody to participate.[123] Other forms of entertainment abounded, with Foochow (Fuzhou) Road being the centre for tea-houses, 'sing-song' houses, opium dens, restaurants, brothels and theatres.[124] Nearby Nanking Road was (and is) the premier shopping district. Spurred on by the vibrant Chinese film industry, local people adopted Western dress and habits. The opening of new Chinese department stores, such as Sincere (1917) and Wing On (1918), transformed shopping into entertainment. When the foreign elite indicated that they did not wish to be served by Chinese, the major stores recruited European sales assistants—and advertised the fact.[125]

The population had doubled to a million between 1895 and 1910, and then tripled again by 1930.[126] By then there were over 70,000 foreigners. Jewish and White Russian immigrants were new and significant communities, fleeing persecution in Europe.[127] Sir Victor Sassoon, a member of the Baghdadi Jewish opium-trading family, had no need to flee London but was simply irresistibly attracted to Shanghai and the opportunities it presented in the late 1920s. Using his vast resources to buy real estate, he created another fortune in Shanghai, leaving his signature on its skyline. Monuments to his success still exist in the form of Broadway Mansions, the Peace Hotel and others. Land prices tripled in five years in the early 1930s, making Shanghai's land the most expensive in the world.[128] By then the Bund had assumed the appearance that it still has today, thanks to the efforts and commitment in recent years of the city government to restore it to its 1930s grandeur. The confidence generated by this line of powerful buildings suggests that nobody thought the party would ever end.

An island in a Japanese sea

Increasing international pressure for the abolition of extraterritoriality and foreign concessions in China led, in 1931, to the drafting of a treaty that would do just that. The treaty was not signed because in September Japan started its invasion of Manchuria, prompting another anti-Japanese boycott in Shanghai, where there were about 20,000 Japanese residents.[129] Most lived in Hongkew, a virtual Japanese colony.[130] The boycott continued into 1932, when, in January, the Japanese provoked an incident in neighbouring Chapei (Zhabei) in which a Japanese monk was killed by a Chinese soldier.[131] The Japanese Consul-General threatened to take over Chapei unless a series of demands were met, including the arrest of the soldier and an immediate end to the boycott. The mayor accepted all the terms, but the Japanese invaded anyway. Three thousand troops had already been landed for the purpose.[132] After five weeks of bombing from carriers in the river, 85 percent of the area was destroyed.[133] Despite the death and destruction at its perimeter, the International Settlement was hardly affected by Japan's actions. Indeed, they were supported by most foreigners who felt 'China should be taught a lesson'.[134] The mood changed when a Japanese 'Naval Landing Party', comprising tanks, armoured cars and 2000 men, established itself in barracks in Hongkew and assumed policing powers. Non-Japanese crossing into the area were stopped and searched.[135]

This unpleasant state of affairs remained while Japan completed its designs on China. In 1937 they were ready. The full invasion of China by Japan produced rapid results. By August there were 400,000 more refugees in the settlement and 26 Japanese warships in the Huangpu.[136] Some 30,000 Chinese troops took up positions on 12 August to defend the city. The first shots were fired the next day, followed by a heavy artillery bombardment of the Chinese city,

The eight-inch guns of HMS *Suffolk* guarding the Bund, 1932. Courtesy of Wattis Fine Art.

with much loss of life.[137] On the 14th, Chinese aircraft, intending to bomb the Japanese flagship *Izumo*, panicked under fire and released their bombs on Nanking Road. Deaths amounted to 729, with 861 injured. Another Chinese plane dropped its load on the French Concession, killing 1011 and wounding 571.[138] Thousands of British and Americans left as an estimated 1.5 million Chinese arrived. Although the settlement was not targeted, Japanese military action was much less restrained than it had been in 1932. Unconcerned about international opinion, Japanese aircraft machine-gunned the car of the visiting British Ambassador; the USS *Panay* was bombed and its survivors strafed as they swam away. The two sides fought to a bitter stalemate, broken only when simultaneous landings of Japanese reinforcements to the north and south of the city forced the Chinese army to flee.[139]

Despite all this, Japan was still a Treaty Power. Their request to hold a victory parade in the International Settlement on 3 December 1937 could not be denied.[140] Later in the month Japan established a civil government in Pudong, and then the following October a Special Municipal Government for Shanghai.[141] The foreign settlements became an island in a Japanese sea. Showing unusual respect for democratic principles, in the light of its recent behaviour in China, Japan requested more representation on the SMC. As votes were attached to property ownership, the Japanese in the settlement subdivided their registered properties; by March 1940 they had created 4000 out of the 1300 properties that had existed the previous September. However, the British followed suit and kept their dominant position.[142] Trouble was clearly not far away.

At the ratepayers' meeting of January 1941 the Japanese contingent objected to proposed budget measures. When the vote went against them, the senior Japanese representative shot and wounded SMC Chairman Sir William Keswick. The council and business leaders met and suspended the land regulations. A Shanghai Provisional Council was created, its members nominated by the foreign consuls. For the first time, municipal affairs in the settlement were not dominated by Britain.[143] The inevitable Japanese takeover did not take long. Having formally entered the Second World War on 8 December 1941, Japan's troops marched into the International Settlement. The Japanese Consul-General called on the chairman of the Provisional Council and asked him to 'cooperate with Imperial forces and carry on as usual'—but to do so under the Japanese flag.[144] Thus Japan realized a long-cherished dream of the Chinese—to have all of Shanghai united under one government. It was just the wrong government.

Further reading: Bickers, *Empire Made Me*; Dong, *Shanghai 1842–1949: The Rise and Fall of a Decadent City*; Hibbard, *The Bund: Shanghai Faces West*; Johnston and Erh, *A Last Look* and *The Last Colonies*; Lanning and Couling, *The History of Shanghai*; Nield, *The China Coast*; Pott, *Shanghai: A Short History*; Wei, *Shanghai: Crucible of Modern China*.

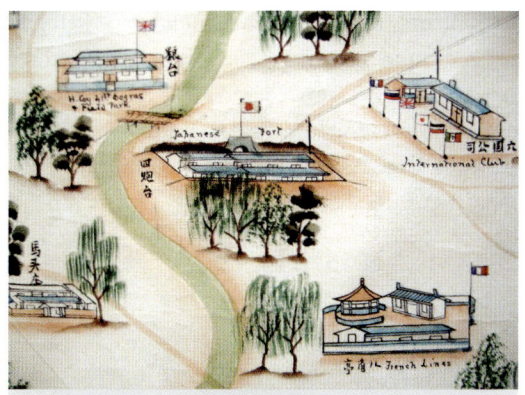

Detail from bird's-eye view of Shanhaikwan (Shanhaiguan), c. 1905, showing some of the foreign barracks and the International Club. Pen, ink and gouache on linen, by unknown Chinese artist. Courtesy of Martyn Gregory Gallery, London.

SHANHAIKWAN (SHANHAIGUAN)
山海關

Hebei, 39.57° N, 119.47° E
Military Station, 1894 Japan

Its name means 'Barrier between the Mountain and the Sea'. Shanhaikwan is where the Great Wall meets the ocean, and where China used to meet Manchuria; it was the required entry port for bringers of tribute.[1] When the British captured Shanghai in 1842, the Chinese assumed they would approach Peking (Beijing) by way of Shanhaikwan, the way barbarians always did. The garrison was strengthened accordingly.[2] Instead the British arrived via the Taku (Dagu) forts. In 1894 the Japanese used Shanhaikwan as a base from which to threaten the capital, and a reported 100,000 Chinese troops were mobilized.[3]

Another crisis soon arose. Allied soldiers landed in 1900, on their way to relieve Tientsin (Tianjin) and Peking from the Boxer rebels, and Shanhaikwan was caught up in the posturing between Britain and Russia.[4] In July the British cruiser HMS *Terrible* was dispatched preparatory to bombarding Shanhaikwan's coastal forts.[5] Then the Russians seized the Tongshan coal mines[6] and the Tientsin-to-Shanhaikwan railway.[7] In response, the British increased their land forces[8] at the same time as the Russians were approaching the coast from the west. In the face of this escalating game of dare, the Chinese evacuated the forts, and the British took them without a shot being fired.[9]

The influx of large numbers of foreign troops meant a business community evolved. A station hotel was built in 1900 and a narrow-gauge railway connected it to the beach, five kilometres away.[10] A small seaside resort developed, the northernmost of the 'Chinese Riviera', more secluded and restful than its southern neighbours.[11] Two churches were built,[12] and a branch of the Chinwangtao (Qinhuangdao) customs station established. But it was the foreign military presence that made the biggest impression, with thousands of British, French and Italian troops stationed there for many years after the Boxer troubles. Even in 1937 there was still a small French garrison, with a British presence in the summer season.[13]

The large, sprawling fort at the end of the Great Wall, now known as Lao Long Tou (Old Dragon's Head), has been restored, with waves lapping against

Shasi (Shashi) 沙市

Hubei, 30.17° N, 112.15° E
Port-of-Call, 1876 British Treaty
Treaty Port, 1895 Japanese Treaty

A newspaper in 1876 proclaimed that Shasi was 'beyond all doubt the largest mart on the Yangtze beyond Hankow [Hankou]'.[1] This seemed possible as its riverbank was hidden by a densely packed line of junks stretching several kilometres. Shasi was made a port-of-call by the 1876 Chefoo Agreement, enabling foreign steamers to take on and set down goods and passengers, and then given full treaty port status by the 1895 Treaty of Shimonoseki. Japanese Consul Eitaki performed the opening ceremony on 1 October 1896 and established a consulate with three staff. In 1897 Britain sent Walter Clennell as acting consul; he took up residence on a junk on 29 May.[2]

Shasi's early promise for foreign merchants was found to be illusory. The myriad junks seen on the river were found to be involved in the transshipment of goods from Chungking (Chongqing) to a network of canals and inland waterways, over which Shasi commanded a key position. Significantly, the canal route to Hankow was much shorter than via the Yangtze. Shasi had been an efficient transshipment centre for centuries, and the Chinese saw no advantage in changing to foreign steamships.

The foreign presence was resented throughout the Yangtze valley. In Shasi an argument between two Chinese workers became an anti-foreign riot on 9 May 1898. The Custom House, the commissioner's residence and almost everything else 'foreign' were destroyed.[3] Ironically, the mob was assisted by a new-fangled foreign import—kerosene.[4] The Japanese had been negotiating for a settlement almost two kilometres long and near the Custom House.[5] The conclusion of these discussions became part of their post-riot compensation demands. In July an area was set aside as a Japanese Concession and money was guaranteed to create an embankment in front of it.[6] The underlying antipathy to foreigners was always there. Some years later a foreign resident described Shasi as a 'non-active volcano'; it could go off at any time.[7]

The Custom House reopened on 1 July 1898, but the British were ready to leave. Their consular presence was closed six months later. In optimistic anticipation some British businesses had bought lots in the Japanese Concession, but none were developed.[8] The Japanese, with more invested in Shasi, were determined to succeed.[9] Shasi was a manufacturing centre for a particularly durable cotton fabric.[10] But Japanese attempts to develop cotton mills along modern lines failed. Neither were any of the other activities normally associated with treaty ports successful. The steamers that called dropped anchor in the river, there being no hulks or pontoons. In addition, the current was so strong that engines had to be kept running in order not to slip backwards. Cargo- and passenger-handling was difficult and dangerous. The bund, financed from the riot compensation, was completed in 1905, but most of it collapsed in 1908.[11]

Not until 1910 was there a proper mooring facility. The bund was repaired and a public pontoon erected.[12] Later a second was provided by the Japanese NKK line, and a third by Butterfield & Swire.[13] But

The Bund, 1910. Photograph by Warren Swire.
© Image courtesy of John Swire and Sons and Historical Photographs of China, University of Bristol.

most cargo was still handled by junks using the canal system.[14] In the words of British Consul Harry Fox, supervising things from Ichang (Yichang): 'While foreign steamers ring vainly at the front door, trade comes in and goes out at the back!'[15]

The revolution of 1911 was felt less in Shasi than in the adjacent city of Kingchow (Jingzhou), home to the largest Manchu population outside Peking (Beijing).[16] This diverted the attention of the revolutionaries away from Shasi.[17] Chaos engulfed both the Yangtze and the country in the 1920s. Shasi, if it ever was, had ceased to be an effective treaty port. Today the former foreign commercial area is represented by a line of nondescript muddy buildings along Linjiang Road, the former bund. One warehouse alone bears testimony to that age, marked with a '2'. Presumably there used to be at least one other.

Soochow (Suzhou) 蘇州

Jiangsu, 31.17° N, 120.38° E
Treaty Port, 1895 Japanese Treaty

Soochow flourished for almost 2000 years as a centre of civilization, beauty and learning, then was almost totally destroyed by the Taiping rebels in the mid-19th century. When it opened as a treaty port in 1895 one of the first foreign firms was a brickworks; repairs and rebuilding had been slow and there was a ready market for the products of E. Brass and his Wuli Brick Factory.[1]

Treaty port status was conferred by the Treaty of Shimonoseki. Soochow was a major centre for producing the finest silks and satins in China. Its clientele included the Imperial household.[2] In the days when most of China's trade was internal, Soochow's business dwarfed that of Shanghai, then referred to as the port for Soochow.[3] As the country's trade became increasingly external, Soochow was relegated to the position of supplier to Shanghai, almost as a suburb.

The Custom House opened in September 1896 near where the Grand Canal skirted the city's south wall. This building is now almost hidden behind the Suzhou Youth & Children's Center at 45 Nan Men Road, along with the impressive former commissioner's residence and a few ancillary structures. From the Custom House the foreign settlement ran west for two kilometres, and inland from the canal about 500 metres. The city government built a road[4] connecting the settlement to the railway station at the northwest corner of the city wall. The Japanese demanded an exclusive concession.[5] Eventually,[6] it was agreed in March 1897 that the western part of the settlement be reserved for them,[7] largely irrelevant as most of the foreign population was Japanese. Other Treaty Powers reserved but did not exercise their right to exclusivity.[8] The Japanese laid out lots for a hundred houses[9] and built an imposing consulate, now inside the First Suzhou Silk Factory at 94 Nan Men Road. Britain was the only other country to open a consulate, a two-man affair based in a rented house[10] from 1896 to 1902, when it was subsumed by Shanghai.[11]

In terms of foreign trade, Soochow's story as a treaty port is fairly typical. Almost all of it was handled more cheaply and efficiently by Chinese merchants, as was the shipping;[12] transport was by canal so there was no scope for foreign vessels. The Japanese Taito Sinri & Co. was the only foreign steamboat company to open in Soochow, operating two launches in 1896 with the aid of a subsidy from the Japanese government.[13] By 1921 there were six local steam launch companies running upwards of 50 craft between Soochow and Shanghai, Hangchow (Hangzhou) and Wusih (Wuxi).[14] A railway line connected Soochow to the national network in 1906,[15] initially having an adverse effect on water transport. The two learned to coexist;[16] the railway increased the volume of business to the port, in which all could share.[17] However, the combined effects of improvements in the railways and neglect of the canals meant that by the early 1930s the six boat companies had been reduced to two, with only one boat each. At the same time a landing stage

Soochow (Suzhou) city walls, late 19th century, as seen from the foreign settlement. Pastel and watercolour, K. Miyake. Courtesy of Martyn Gregory Gallery, London.

was built near the Custom House for the seaplanes of Shanghai-Hankow Airways.[18]

Soochow had long been a popular destination for visitors because of the beauty of its gardens and canals. By the early 1930s, to cater for the continuing stream of tourists, now including foreign visitors, there were several hotels in the city. All under Chinese management, they had, as Charles Crow pointed out, 'their ups and downs'.[19] If arriving by train, tourists found a station that was state-of-the-art for its time, complete with a dispensary and medical officer's consulting room, a ladies' waiting room, a refreshment facility and a kitchen.[20] On leaving modernity they would then have been besieged by drivers of carriages, rickshaws and donkeys, vying keenly for their business.[21]

Silk prompted Soochow's opening as a treaty port, and its manufacture was the only foreign commercial activity of note. The British-owned China-European Silk Filature was built inside the foreign settlement, and two other joint-venture operations opened nearby.[22] Moreover, foreign manufacturing methods were adopted by Chinese operators, with large-scale steam-powered factories edging out the traditional cottage-based artisans. Local merchants built a 15,000-spindle cotton mill in late 1895, using the latest British machinery.[23] All this produce found a ready market in Shanghai, now only a short distance away by rail. The silk industry, once a world leader, fell victim to the vagaries of fashion and the availability of cheap, artificial, easy-care alternatives. By 1931 all the steam filatures had closed, even the newest and best-equipped Japanese venture.[24]

Foreign commerce in Soochow was unsuccessful. In 1911 the settlement was described as a wilderness, with many of the new roads overgrown with grass.[25] Other activities prospered. Shortly after the port was opened, the mainly American missionaries outnumbered all other foreign residents by three to one. Three years later there were over 50 of them. One of their main interests was the founding of a university. Three former educational institutions came together in 1900 as Soochow University, organized under an American charter but largely financed by local interests.[26] Magnificent Western-style buildings still grace the busy campus. In 1925 the faculty included more than 20 Americans, compared with the 8 foreign members of the customs service and 6 European and American businessmen.[27] Other missionaries were running a hospital and a number of schools.

As with many Chinese cities, security was often a concern for the foreign population. In 1910 Chinese soldiers attacked foreigners, an action that provoked a riot.[28] The city walls, last restored in 1662, proved useful when further unrest threatened in 1925.[29] Fighting in the area surrounding Soochow led to a partial evacuation.[30] Soochow was captured by the Nationalists two years later.[31] The Japanese wreaked the final havoc on their treaty port. Their occupation of the Yangtze delta in 1937 led to a complete cessation of trade.[32] Later that year their planes rained bombs on Soochow.[33] No doubt this brought welcome business to Mr. J. A. Snell and his Soochow Brick & Tile Co., the last foreign business to be listed in the 1941 directory,[34] following in the footsteps of Mr. Brass almost 50 years earlier.

Swatow (Shantou) 汕頭

Guangdong, 23.21° N, 116.40° E
Treaty Port, 1858 British Treaty

The early history of Swatow as a treaty port is defined by the less desirable activities in which foreign merchants were heavily involved. The east coast of China is heavily indented with bays, estuaries and islands, hiding places for the conduct of nefarious activities with little fear of official interference. One such place was Namoa (Nanao).

Namoa

When the European and American opium traders started running their fast clipper ships up the coast from Canton (Guangzhou) in the 1820s, the island of Namoa was one of the bases they chose for unloading their goods. About 20 kilometres north-east of Swatow and three or four kilometres offshore, this substantial, irregularly shaped, hilly island offered sanctuary. Today it can be reached by ferry from Laiwu.

The opium merchants were not the first foreigners to appreciate the attractions of this location as a base for illicit trade. The Portuguese came here in the early 16th century. Japanese pirates were frequent and unwelcome visitors in the late Ming dynasty. In 1562 they occupied the island, using it as a base for attacking the adjacent coastline.[1] In response the Chinese established a Namoa garrison in 1575 and a fort the following year at Shenao, near the island's north-east tip. In 1646, Namoa was conquered by Zheng Chenggong, sometimes known as Koxinga, the leader of the local resistance against the newly established Qing dynasty. Many of Zheng's soldiers were recruited and trained at Shenao. His barracks remain intact, most of its attendant buildings renovated to a high standard in 1998. A huge statue of Koxinga stands there looking suitably threatening, alongside a 4000-kilogram iron cannon.

Notwithstanding the military presence, and in full breach of Imperial law, the opium ships anchored at the western tip of the island, a place known as Clipper Point, where they could be spotted easily by waiting customers. A small fort still overlooks this anchorage, one of many that used to cover the island. Known as Chang Shan Fort, it was built in 1717 and rebuilt in 1814, but it did not last long as an effective military installation. Foreigners took up residence inside the tiny citadel for the trading season, from October to May, and remains of the walls of their small and uncomfortable houses can still be seen inside. While the clipper captains built more commodious residences on the coast, the watchers at the abandoned fort had a clear view over Clipper Point anchorage. A description of the transactions that took place there can be found in the writing of William Hunter.[2]

The war of 1839–42 had no effect on Namoa's business, which continued expanding. From the 1820s to the 1850s, Jardines and Dents both had sumptuous (if illegal) establishments on Namoa,[3] and the small walled town nearby grew prosperous. In 1843 Sir Henry Pottinger, Hong Kong's first governor, expressed concerns that the new colony was a refuge for opium smugglers. This increased the attraction of Namoa, and similar places, as a base far away from the official gaze. When local Chinese officials reported to Peking (Beijing) that the barbarians were building on Namoa, without mentioning why, a formal investigation was launched. This reported that all such buildings had been removed. Of course they had not, but the investigating mandarin's pockets were heavier when he left.[4]

When Imperial Commissioner Qiying visited Hong Kong in June 1843, Pottinger made the pragmatic suggestion that Namoa and the others become semi-official opium trading stations, keeping the drug out of the new treaty ports. Qiying agreed, proposing an annual rent of 2.1 million *tael*s of silver, to be paid five years in advance. Pottinger refused the offer, nothing changed and the trade continued unabated.[5] In 1844 the Chinese complained again about the European houses on Namoa, giving details of their number and dimensions. Pottinger replied that they were there with the connivance of the local authorities, so they should force them out. He highlighted the irony whereby Europeans in Canton faced personal violence by being there legally, whereas those illegally on Namoa were openly encouraged to remain. Nevertheless, the Chinese gave the settlers six months to quit. To demonstrate compliance, a house was demolished so that a report could be sent to Peking claiming the barbarians had been repulsed. It was intimated there would be no objection to an immediate replacement,[6] so once again nothing changed. Receiving ships continued to be stationed at Namoa, with the shore facilities to service them.

The 'pig trade'

Another business activity came to Namoa, more odious even than the drug trade. Fujian was one of the poorer provinces of China, and so when the men of the region were told of paid work overseas on the plantations of South-East Asia, the Caribbean and America, they were interested. Thus was born the coolie trade with its attendant horrors. The newly opened treaty port of Amoy (Xiamen), 200 kilometres to the north-east, established itself as a centre for the export of coolies. Britain banned owning or transporting slaves anywhere in the British Empire from 1833. This made it increasingly difficult for British firms like Muir & Syme and Tait & Co. to operate their coolie business. These concerns maximized their profits by providing the minimum conditions to sustain life, and not always that. They needed to operate outside the jurisdiction of British treaty ports and they looked towards Namoa and Double (Mayu) Island, just outside Swatow.[7]

If there was ever humanity in what was most unpleasantly termed the 'pig trade', it soon vanished. The European firms, far from any official control, either British or Chinese, began kidnapping unwary men. The only 'service' the holding ships performed was to prepare the kidnapped labourers for the conditions that they would suffer during the voyage and their subsequent 'employment'. A large white house stood on the south side of the river at Swatow; this was used as a storage facility for waiting emigrants and latterly as a navigational aid.[8]

Official British objections to the coolie trade had been circumvented by the spurious use of vice-consular appointments. In 1846 James Tait in Amoy procured his appointment as Spanish Vice-Consul. In 1856 he appointed the master of Dents' receiving ship as Spanish consular agent in Swatow, stationed on Double Island.[9] Not only the British were involved in the trade. Between 1852 and 1858 American ships transported 40,000 from Double Island, not including the 8000 that died there from either plague or starvation.[10] The Germans were also engaged in this sordid but lucrative business.

In 1855 a British law attempted to regulate the conditions in which Chinese were transported on British ships, but ensuring compliance was extremely difficult. Furthermore, British shippers complained that they were disadvantaged; vessels of other nations carried 1500 souls, compared to the 240 that would have been allowed on a British ship of similar size.[11] A similar American law was not enforced. The application in Swatow of German regulations in the 1860s was the responsibility of the German Vice-Consul, a partner in the firm handling most of the emigration business. Conditions gradually improved as the export of coolies expanded. In the early 1900s about 100,000 sailed every year; in 1936 alone, 132,579 left Swatow, mostly for Hong Kong (for transshipment) and Siam.[12] Even in the present century investigations continue. A report to the Californian State Legislature in May 2002, in connection with insurance claims made during the slavery era, detailed the 1854 case of a New York clipper, *Sea Witch*, engaged to transport 700 coolies from Swatow to Panama. During the 65-day voyage 14 died but the insurance company paid only one-quarter of the insured sum, pocketing the rest; another example of how would-be respectable businessmen found ways of profiting from the traffic in human life.[13]

Double Island

Europeans were attracted to Double Island after the opening of the first treaty ports in 1842. This small, picturesque island acquired its English name from its two low peaks, neither more than 50 metres high. With its neighbour half a kilometre to the south-east, Sugarloaf (Dezhou) Island, Double Island guarded the boundary between the Han River estuary and the sea. On its larger peak a lighthouse still stands, a modern replacement for the one there when the Europeans first arrived.

In the 1840s Swatow was no more than a small collection of huts along the muddy northern bank of the estuary. More important was the city of Chaochow (Chaozhou), some 50 kilometres upstream. As usual with Chinese cities at that time, all focus was inland. The entrance to the river was therefore a convenient place to establish operations meant to avoid official notice. Apart from providing a suitable mooring for the opium hulks, it was a convenient place to which unwilling emigrants could be taken, pending shipment. For the Europeans it was more than convenience. Kidnapping had made them so unpopular it was unsafe for them to be anywhere else. They stayed there a number of years, even after Swatow was opened as a treaty port under the 1858 Tientsin (Tianjin) Treaty.

By 1851 Double Island had a sizeable foreign as well as local community; Chinese businessmen always found a way of servicing a market, even if their customers were universally unwelcome. A village grew next to the foreign houses.[14] Missionaries arrived, even though they had to rub shoulders with drug merchants and kidnappers. In 1857 no fewer than 120 foreign vessels entered and cleared the little port.[15] A settlement grew on the western side of the island, sheltered from the prevailing winds.

In view of the pervading hostility on the mainland to Europeans, Double Island was chosen as the site for the Custom House when Swatow was opened by Horatio Nelson Lay on 1 January 1860. As a precaution, he ensured that the customs had two armed lorchas, under British officers;[16] the possibility of renewed hostility between Britain and China was always present. When the first British Consul, George Caine, arrived six months later, he established himself on Double Island, as did the American Consul.[17] The area around Swatow was well known for its lawlessness and independence of spirit, exacerbated by the foreigners' own lawlessness. It was not until about 1872, when the foreign population had risen to 120,[18] that it was considered safe to move the customs installation to the city, leaving Double Island as a subsidiary customs station and warehousing facility.[19] It also remained the base for pilots, whose job was to guide ships through the treacherous approaches to the harbour. A few kilometres inland from the cape that marked the entrance to the river was Signal Hill, just over 100 metres high,[20] from where approaching vessels were announced by semaphore. The pilots would have lived at the southern end of Double Island, in sight of Signal Hill. The ruins of a line of small houses, possibly in Western style, can be seen there. Any view of Signal Hill, however, is obliterated by an ugly flyover.

A quiet village now occupies much of Mayu Island. A very small harbour has a stone protecting wall of some apparent antiquity. Nearly all the houses are new and tile-covered, in the popular lavatorial style. One, however, stands out as being different—square-looking, of two storeys and not of a typical Chinese design, occupying the place shown on old maps as the Custom House. The big city is visible across the water, giving the impression that this small island still stands sentinel at the harbour entrance.

Kialat

The sparkle of Swatow as a treaty port proved illusory. In 1860 Swatow was a small, dirty town on the northern banks of the Han River, which was fast-flowing and very muddy. The highest settled area was only two metres above the level of the river. From the town, the river bank stretched to the east for a kilometre or so, then curved north and back to a point directly opposite Double Island, making a large bay. It was at the head of this bay, in an area called Kialat (Jielu), that a small European community developed. An 1867 account refers to 'several handsome houses'.

The customs establishment was at the south-western tip of the bay, adjacent to the Chinese town. As the bay and the river were edged by oozing mud, long jetties, up to 200 metres, were needed in order for ships to handle passengers and goods.[21] Between 1877 and 1914 about eight hectares were reclaimed from the bay and put to use for shops and warehouses. The foreign community financed the building of a proper road along the foreshore, which by 1910 had electric lighting.[22] This reclamation and development was the beginning of a process that continues, moving the centre of the city steadily eastwards. Pressure to redevelop the original centre thus reduced, many old buildings remain.

Kakchio

The British Consul was not among the early residents of Kialat. Between the provocation provided by the kidnappings and the not infrequent inter-village warfare in the surrounding area, it was nine months before the consul dared to visit Swatow, and three years before he moved his consulate away from Double Island. When he did so, it was not to Kialat but to Kakchio (Jiaoshi), a hilly promontory on the south bank of the river. By the early 1870s a substantial, attractive building was built for his use along with a house and offices for his staff.[23] This is still there, tastefully renovated and occupied by various government agencies. Adjacent is the former shipping office. The consular pier is still visible, although it is now a road, the water on each side having been reclaimed. Over a hundred metres long, eight metres wide and stone flagged, it leads to the new riverside road that was created in the early years of the present century. The pier had the capacity to moor up to 30 tugs and lighters.

Kakchio became the fashionable place to live. The wealthier businessmen and the more affluent missionaries chose to build grand houses there, with extensive gardens and tennis courts. The leading firm Bradley & Co. constructed another jetty to the west of the British Consulate, slightly shorter and with capacity for 15 boats. This was visible as a landlocked road until it was redeveloped in the 1990s. At that time

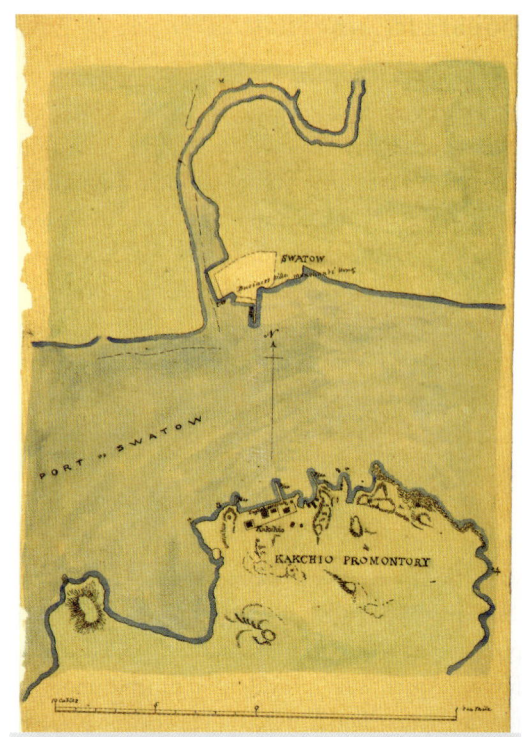

1876 map of Kakchio (Jiaoshi), showing piers and buildings. Reprinted with permission by the National Archives.

other European buildings could be seen;[24] most have gone, but there is one fine exception. In about 1918 Butterfield & Swire constructed 'Swatow Claymore' as a residence for their *taipan*. The striking building is still there; now inside a military establishment it is definitely off limits to strangers.

In the early years, the Americans were the only other nation to establish a full consulate in Swatow. Having initially used C. W. Bradley Jr. as vice-consul (fluent in the local language; his father had been American Consul in Amoy), in 1866 they appointed a full consul, keeping Bradley as vice-consul. The consulate was probably housed in Bradley's Kakchio premises as the Americans were notorious for not providing adequate housing, or even remuneration, for their consular officials. The arrangement was short-lived as the consulate closed in 1877, and Swatow's American interests were managed from Amoy. The United States set up another full consulate in 1911, which closed in the Pacific War.

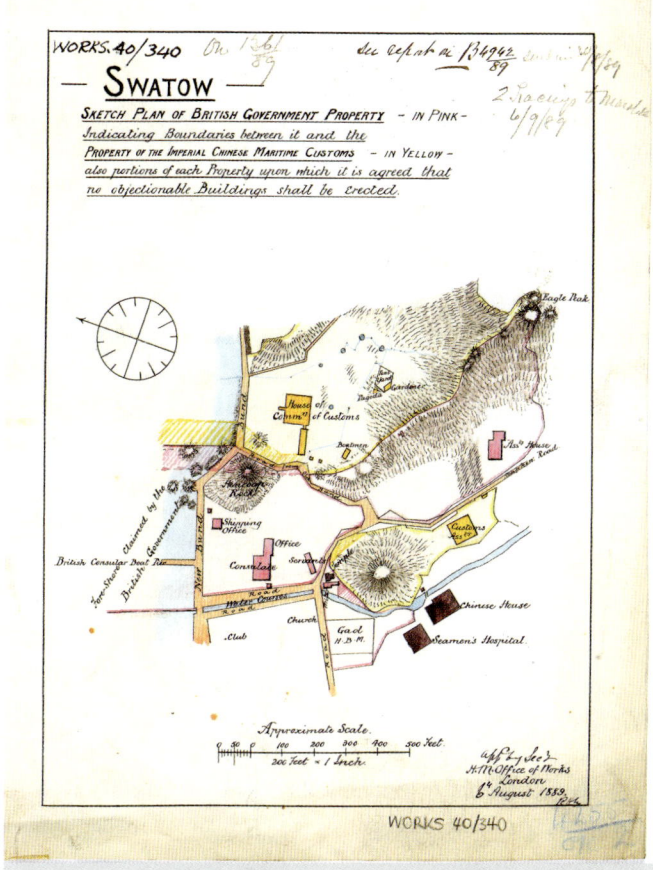

1889 map of the British and Customs properties at Kakchio (Jiaoshi). Reprinted with permission by the National Archives.

THE EARLY GROWTH OF THE TREATY PORT

One factor that restricted the early growth of the treaty port was lingering local hostility. Britain tried to secure the lease of a plot of land near the Chinese town for the creation of a formal concession, but was initially thwarted. A lease was eventually obtained, but neighbouring villagers took to threats and demonstrations when steps were taken to occupy the site. The British were loath to use force and the Chinese government claimed it was unable to control its people, so the scheme was abandoned.[25]

Two additional factors militated against plans to form a settlement. First, it was apparent that all trade in the new port was, apart from opium, firmly in the hands of Chinese merchants from Singapore and Canton, acting on behalf of Hong Kong principals; there seemed little scope for foreigners to participate other than in shipping and insurance. Second, the Treaty of Tientsin referred not to Swatow as the treaty port but Chaochow, the seat of local government. It was unclear whether the treaty extended any rights of occupation and residence to Swatow. Without a formal settlement, foreign residence tended to be widely scattered, as we have seen.

Precarious residence was at least possible at Swatow; even entering Chaochow was not—especially for the British Consul, who technically lived there. This unfortunate official made several attempts between 1861 and 1863 to pass through its gates, but was always repulsed by armed townspeople. Again, the Chinese government maintained they could do nothing. In September 1865 Robert Hart indicated clearly that if the situation did not improve, the British might feel they had just cause to resort yet again to arms.[26] Two months later, Caine was escorted into the city by an armed Chinese guard and made the point of acquiring consular premises there.[27] Nevertheless he experienced unpleasantness and violence during his brief stay.[28] It came to British attention in January 1869 that the villages along the way to Chaochow were trying to prevent contact with the provincial capital, even to the extent of attacking any British boat making the passage. Chaloner Alabaster, Acting British Consul, took a contingent of marines and sailors and destroyed some of the villages involved; the rest submitted.[29] In 1871 HMS *Dwarf*, presumably a vessel with no pretensions of size, made its way peaceably as far as Chaochow.[30] Although the British consular premises were retained for the use of visiting consuls until 1911, Chaochow was never realistically a place of foreign residence.

In 1859, the year before it formally opened to foreign trade, Swatow (meaning at that time Double

Island) had a foreign population of twelve.[31] The year after opening, this figure had risen to 33.[32] Regular steamer services, by 1867 linking Swatow to Hong Kong, Amoy and Foochow (Fuzhou),[33] encouraged more to come. By 1873 there were 75 foreign residents, of whom 8 were missionaries. By 1884, 30 of the 90 foreign residents were missionaries.[34]

As in many ports the Maritime Customs was the largest employer of foreigners. Even after moving the Custom House to the mainland, some outside staff—tide-waiters, boat officers, etc.—continued to be based on Double Island. The rest, including the examiners and administrative staff, moved to the new Custom House and its surrounding inspection yards and other facilities. A fine new road, Customs Road (now Waima Road), was built to connect the Custom House in the south to the edge of the Kialat community to the north. In later years this thoroughfare was sufficiently important to house major banks, several hotels and the post office, which is still there. Starting with a total of eight European staff in 1861, the number of foreign customs employees increased to about 20 by 1873. In 1865 Hart decreed that the commissioner should move from Double Island to occupy a large house in Kakchio. Of all the grand houses, his was by far the grandest. The mansion, outhouses, enormous garden and tennis courts occupied a site east of the British Consulate but, sadly, nothing remains.

THE GERMAN CONNECTION

The Germans were among the first to show interest in Swatow's potential. In 1861 Hinrich Dircks set up as a general commission agent. Dircks left Swatow in 1878 but his firm lived on, becoming one of the major mercantile players. Since 1871, the Dircks senior partner had been ex officio vice-consul for the new German Empire. Naturally it was expected that this included the keen promotion of the new country's interests. However, Dircks's successor went too far. A plot of land, allocated for use by the customs, was claimed by Dircks & Co., based on an old title deed transferred to them by their comprador. Legal wrangling ensued. Far exceeding his consular powers,

1897 view of the Customs Commissioner's palatial residence. Source: Macgowan, *Pictures of Southern China*, 211.

senior partner Bernhard Schaar called in the German navy and, on 25 November 1882, an armed party of 50 officers and men took possession of the property, hoisted the German flag and laid out boundary markers. The sailors departed, leaving two guards to patrol the perimeter. There were diplomatic exchanges at the highest level between London and Berlin. In Peking Robert Hart was further alarmed to hear that 400 armed German sailors had landed in Amoy to retake possession of goods seized by the *likin* office there.[35] Use of German armed forces to settle commercial disputes seemed habit-forming.

By late January 1883 the Swatow matter was still unresolved. Hart noted that Schaar was pushing the matter in a 'high-handed and very aggravating style'.[36] In April it became apparent the German Chancellor, Bismarck, had disapproved of the use of his navy for such purposes, and Schaar was removed from his consular position. Then it was revealed that the firm's comprador, Kwok, had 'sold' the land in question for $500 to Dircks & Co. when it was not his to sell. Dircks had then tried to sell it on to Jardines for $25,000. The truth emerged and the Germans helped Kwok to escape justice. Dircks & Co. was declared bankrupt and Schaar attempted suicide, but survived.[37] Businessmen have short memories and forgiving natures; the following year saw him establishing the firm of Schaar & Co., effectively taking over the business, insurance and shipping agencies of Dircks.[38]

Schaar & Co. did not last long. In 1886 two other former Dircks men—J. T. Lauts and L. Haesloop—formed a new partnership and took over Schaar's key German connections.[39] Trading as Lauts & Haesloop, this new firm led the German business community for the next 25 years. It also became the leading practitioner of the coolie trade. In 1890 the firm acquired the Swatow agency for the Association of Deli Planters, a consortium of the five largest tobacco growers in Dutch Sumatra. (So important was this body that the Dutch Minister to Peking relocated to Swatow in 1888–89.)[40] A regular labour supply service was established the following year, with fellow German Jebsen & Co. providing a fleet of three or four coasters to transport workers south to the plantations.[41] Lauts & Haesloop flourished, and a branch was opened in Formosa (Taiwan).

Events in Europe in 1914 put a temporary end to all German business in the treaty ports. There was a resurgence between the two world wars, but when German firms were forced to close again in 1939, foreign business in Swatow was already in a state of terminal decline.

The Germans opened a full consulate in 1883, which remained in operation for the next 30 years. Its former premises, on Dahua Road, are in excellent condition. Once the home of Hinrich Dircks before becoming the consulate,[42] it now houses the offices of several government agencies.

INDUSTRIES AND INFRASTRUCTURE

In 1878 Jardines established the Oriental Sugar Refinery in Kakchio.[43] Changing its name in 1880 to the China Sugar Refinery,[44] this grew quickly to be the employer of eleven European staff and an untold number of Chinese. Swatow was a major sugar-producing region, with fields of cane stretching for hundreds of kilometres. When in 1862 the arriving foreign ships found that demand exceeded supply more plantations were laid out, doubling capacity.[45] The refinery was equipped with the latest machinery and prospects were good. However, the venture was short-lived. Within ten years the business collapsed, owing to the combination of crippling Chinese taxation and cheaper competition. Sugar could be brought from the Dutch East Indies and refined in Hong Kong for a lower price. By 1902 Hong Kong sugar was even imported into Swatow.[46] For years the factory was a white elephant, 'temporarily closed'.[47] The name finally disappeared from the directories in 1904. A flour-milling initiative in 1908 was similarly frustrated by competition from nearby Hong Kong.

An industry coexisting with the sugar refinery was beancake manufacture. Soya beans were grown in huge quantities in China's north-east. This was a very versatile crop; even when the beans had been crushed for their oil, the remainder could be used as fertilizer for the sugar and orange plantations of Swatow. The pulp was therefore compressed into blocks, known as beancakes, and sent down to Swatow in exchange for sugar. Butterfield & Swire entered this trade in 1874, becoming extremely successful. They built their China Navigation Co. fleet with the profits.[48] In 1882 a factory was started in Swatow to make the beancake there. Reversing northern practice, the oil was the useful by-product.

Other initiatives were to be hampered by the sensitivities of the local people. In about 1890 a Chinese company was formed to operate mines in the nearby hills. The belief that local women would become barren if the ground were opened up gained credence and the project was abandoned. In another venture, Bradleys backed a scheme to provide fresh water to Swatow; only river water was available, and of dubious quality. Again, money was subscribed and the required land was purchased. But when the locals objected that this interference with nature would deleteriously affect the area's *fengshui* the *taotai* refused to intervene.[49] The project was abandoned.

The independent and rebellious Swatow people were unwilling to upset the gods. Confronting the government was a different matter entirely. A spectacular case of disobedience occurred in the closing years of the 19th century. The Chinese government noticed Swatow paid less tax than other regions, and attempted to increase the *likin*. However, when a new office was erected to oversee tax collection the people simply demolished it.[50]

Only shipping and its adjuncts of insurance and banking were genuinely open to foreigners, all of them activities that the Chinese were slow in developing. In 1863 an average of two ships arrived daily in Swatow, 70 percent British and 20 percent German. Before long, 15 shipping companies had agencies there. Douglas Lapraik & Co. opened a branch in 1881; their efficient ships had kept Swatow in touch with the outside world for many years.[51] In 1882, building on their successful coastal trade, Butterfield & Swire opened an office.[52] There had been ships' chandlers from the very beginning, one of the first rejoiced in the name Drown & Co.[53] Yet despite the volume of foreign shipping, there were no dockyards. Furthermore, the tides were not sufficient even to allow vessels to be beached on the muddy banks and have their bottoms inspected at low tide. The nearest place for major repairs was Amoy.

In terms of railways, Swatow fared little better. As early as 1888 it had been agreed that a line between Swatow and Chaochow would be economically viable. Jardines surveyed the proposed route,[54] but did not proceed. Bradleys then applied for permission to build, but received no reply. Eventually a concession was granted to a long-term Chinese resident of the Dutch East Indies[55] for a half-metre-gauge railway line to run 15 kilometres north-west from the city. It was to be for passengers only—and man-powered. Negotiations extended the line as far as Chaochow, and allowed steam engines to be used instead of coolies. A construction contract was awarded to the Japanese, with rails and engines to come from America and rolling stock from Japan. Work started in September 1904. Progress was slow, owing to disputes over land prices, but the railway finally opened in November 1906. Planning myopia meant that this little railway never joined any main trunk line, and at Swatow the station was located unnecessarily far away from the town centre. It disappeared in the 1920s in the devastation of the civil war.

For a few years in the 1930s, until prevented by hostilities, seaplanes of the China National Aviation Corporation added a touch of romance to travel, landing in the north-west corner of the harbour en route between Canton and Shanghai.[56] Apart from this and the railway, shipping was the only means of entering and exiting Swatow.

In the late 19th century a large cottage industry emerged for the manufacture of embroidery and lace, and this expanded into the 20th century. Major stores in England and America had 'Swatow Departments' which sold fine napkins, table linen, delicate embroidery and lace from these small workshops.[57] The name 'Swatow' became synonymous with expert craftsmanship in this field and for a number of years the business flourished, largely with American backing.

Social life in the treaty port

The foreign community in Swatow was never large, and was split between Swatow-side and Kakchio-side; much of the entertainment and social life was home-grown. Some of the larger houses were able to stage 'private theatricals'.[58] Outdoors, the wide flat estuary of the Han provided scope for game shooting in the winter, particularly ducks and geese, a popular pastime. Weekend parties would go upriver on small boats and return with impressive hauls. Sailing was not very popular owing to strong currents and tides,[59] but there were good walks in the rough hill country above Kakchio.

Swatow developed a reputation as one of the healthiest ports in China, and Double Island became a popular weekend beach resort in the summer; the beach remains popular with bathers. The Masu Retreat Club was a large bungalow on the hill above the beach, facing the morning sun and the cooling sea breezes.[60] In the early 1920s plans were drawn up for a substantial bungalow on Double Island for the Customs Commissioner, and a slightly smaller one for his deputy. These were probably never built as things were becoming increasingly difficult for the British in China, even when they were employees of the Chinese government. On the bright side, there were the visits of friendly warships to anticipate, providing excuses for parties and entertainments. The crews of American naval vessels would insist the British community play them at softball. This was agreed, provided the British could then thrash the Americans at cricket.[61]

Although there were in Swatow as many as five or six social clubs at various times, none of them enjoyed a reputation of being 'the place to go'. The Swatow Club stood over the road from the British Consulate in Kakchio, but it was described as 'a poor affair'. The club house was a bungalow with a verandah. There was a piano, but no bar to stand up at. The gentlemen members could therefore not mingle, but had to sit and order drinks to be delivered.[62] It did have a tennis court and a large garden, and there was another feature that appealed to some: its library. The club had been founded by early British and American consuls and they loved to read. Herbert Giles spent some years there as British consular assistant; he went on to become Professor Giles, co-inventor of the Wade-Giles system of Romanization of Chinese and the second professor of Chinese at Cambridge University. Over the river, the Kialat Club boasted a bowling alley as well as a billiard room and library. The wives of members of both institutions were permitted to use them on certain afternoons for their 'at homes'. Another club was established by the Maritime Customs for its European staff. These three were to survive until 1940. In the years between the world wars there was a Taikoo Club, serving the needs of the officers and European crew of the China Navigation Co.

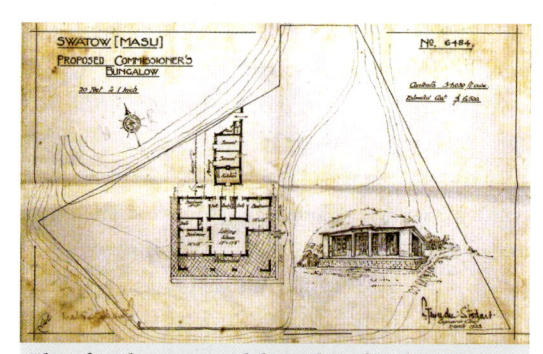

Plan for the proposed bungalow for the Customs Commissioner. Source: Shantou Customs Museum.

The relatively small size of the foreign community and its lack of a geographical centre led to certain challenges when obtaining life's necessities. As early as 1867 there were two or three stores that provided for basic needs, but clothes, for example, had to be ordered from Hong Kong. Spiritual needs were also poorly served; the large missionary community directed its attention to the as yet unconverted Chinese population. Divine services for the foreign community were held at the British Consulate on Sundays.[63]

Swatow's first hotel opened in 1866. Founded by a group of European chandlers, this was probably a billiard room and a bowling alley with residential facilities attached.[64] It appears not to have lasted very long. In later years the need for a hotel was met by Mr. F. H. Hyde, an auctioneer and commission agent. From 1903 he was the proprietor of the Swatow Hotel[65] and from 1911 the Astor House Hotel. Some time in the mid-1920s the Palace Hotel opened, and these two continued to vie for business along fashionable Customs Road. In the 1920s and 1930s there was also a profusion of bars and night spots. The Kialat Cinema opened in 1924, and the Capitol Theatre ten years later.

20TH-CENTURY SWATOW

As the new century dawned the Boxer uprising was in full swing. Although the troubles were confined to the north, the foreign population in Swatow felt exposed with no concession or other area

1920s view of the modest Swatow (Shantou) Club – 'a poor affair'. Photograph by Warren Swire. © Image courtesy of John Swire and Sons and Historical Photographs of China, University of Bristol.

that was easily defendable. The official sailing directions for Swatow continued to describe 'the natives' as 'generally rebellious and wicked in the highest degree'.[66] Despite its rather disappointing performance as a treaty port, in the opening years of the 20th century Swatow had a foreign population, including missionaries, of some 200.[67] And it was ranked fifth in terms of the value of trade among the 35 open ports of China,[68] a relative triumph reflecting the depressing performance of the others. In his decennial report for 1892 to 1901, Customs Commissioner Smollet Campbell wrote: 'The history of Swatow during the period covered by the present Report has been singularly uneventful—perhaps happily so.'[69] The port had for a while been declining in its importance for the Europeans. The Chinese businessmen were comfortable, but there was still little scope for foreigners. Foreign business was in the hands of just four firms—Bradleys, Butterfield & Swire, Jardines and Lauts & Haesloop.[70]

The foreigners and the Chinese led separate lives, and relations between them could become strained. An example arose in 1902. Butterfield & Swire (B&S) had brought in a cargo of rice and wanted it unloaded at night to enable the vessel to get away on the early morning tide. Swires were concerned that the coolies would steal some of the cargo under the cover of darkness, so they insisted on it being weighed into the hands of the purchaser. The dock workers refused to comply, resenting such public lack of respect and trust. They sent telegrams to all ports from Newchwang (Yingkou) to Singapore, ordering a boycott of all B&S ships. (Sometimes, newfangled Western inventions proved useful.) The action was called off only when Swires agreed to dismiss their Swatow agent and the local comprador.[71] It was reported the following year that the comprador had not left, nor had the agent been dismissed.[72] But both sides had made their point. The formation in 1904 of a Swatow police force of 300 was willingly financed by voluntary subscription.[73]

The most visible signs of early 20th-century Swatow that remain are to be found in the old town centre. Whole streets of shabby and crumbling shop-houses and other buildings date from the 1920s and 1930s. Fortunately, the street names have not been changed since the treaty port days; addresses can be located using old maps. The decorative plaster-work on the upper storeys of the shop-houses appear to be bold statements of affluence, made by newly wealthy returning emigrants. Another gem is the old Nam Sang department store with its eccentric roof adornments.

The area immediately surrounding the Custom House was the hub of the commercial activity of the treaty port in the late 19th and early 20th centuries and the site of extensive inspection and storage facilities. Still standing at the time of my visit in 2010 were large warehouses, formerly owned by Butterfield & Swire and rebuilt using reinforced concrete supports following a particularly severe typhoon in 1922;[74] any earlier examples would have been destroyed in an earthquake in 1918. The Custom House has been 'renovated', retaining its architectural integrity beneath its rather startling white exterior. The year '1919' has been carved on a stone tablet next to the main entrance, which implies it survived the 1922 deluge, but its predecessor did not withstand the earthquake. Inside is a museum dedicated to customs activities past and present. Just up the road the post office's exterior is the same as ever, although inside is more a philatelic products shop than a functioning post office. Nearby is a former customs residence within a building site, but it was not possible to determine if it was being pulled down or renovated.

The combination of the 1918 earthquake and the 1922 typhoon left a devastating mark on Swatow. Altogether there were an estimated 2000 deaths in the first disaster and 50,000 in the second, the storm being the worst then on record. Ships were left on the surrounding hillsides, and the Sugarloaf Island and Good Hope Cape lighthouses were swept away.[75] Houses that avoided being blown down were destroyed by the storm surge that followed.[76] The riverfront was flooded to a depth of two metres.

The Hong Kong Telegraph, in its report a few days later, described the event as a 'calamity which almost beggars description'.[77]

Large-scale street widening had begun in 1922, but work stopped as funds were redirected to typhoon repairs. It was resumed the following year at a slow pace, not restarting in earnest for another ten years.[78] In 1923 a Bund Construction Bureau was established to build a 25-metre-wide bund, financed by the sale of reclaimed foreshore lots. The bureau also reserved the right to build an electric tramway and wharves along the new river frontage.[79] However, the following year saw a complete stoppage, not only on this project but also on all work relating to the handling of ships. British shipping formed the lion's share of the tonnage that visited the port, and the anti-British activities of 1925 extended here also. Swatow had to be provisioned from Hong Kong, also experiencing severe difficulties for similar reasons.[80]

Swatow could not escape the factional fighting and civil war that were to engulf the whole country as the century progressed. Rival bands of Communists and 'Nationalists', the latter usually thugs in the employ of one local warlord or another, pursued their bloody battles in the area around the port. Many local people were shot. One serious effect on the commercial life of Swatow was that banknotes were honoured one day but not recognized the next, depending upon which warlord was behind the issuing bank. Silver dollars therefore once more became the currency of choice for business. Despite the hardships, local business continued and was quite successful in some cases. Swatow became the linen port for South China and the embroidery business continued to flourish, thanks to the American market. On the negative side, even in the early 1930s the electricity supply was rationed. Electric lighting was only available between 5:00 p.m. and 12:00 p.m. every day, with an extra three hours' supply on weekends and holidays. Furthermore shops could no longer supply the needs of the foreign population. Ice and most food had to come up by overnight steamer from Hong Kong.[81]

The ultimate disaster was Swatow's capture by the Japanese. The initial Japanese presence had been innocent enough. In 1903 there had been just one Japanese resident. In 1905, of a total foreign population of 523, almost half (232) were Japanese.[82] Many were working on the railway project, but there was now a new type of Japanese. Since occupying Formosa in 1895, Japan had given citizenship to the island's residents, many of whom had strong ties to Swatow. The Japanese Consul spent much time trying to decide who was and was not considered Japanese.[83] A strong Japanese presence had been established—and was to continue. The year 1907 saw the simultaneous arrival of the Japanese-owned Bank of Taiwan and *zaibatsu* Mitsui Bussan Kaisha, as well as a branch of the Imperial Japanese Post Office.[84]

As the 1930s progressed it became clear that Japan's interest in China was no longer commercial. When neighbouring treaty ports Canton and Amoy were captured by the Japanese in 1937, Swatow remained free and prospered but not without difficulty. From September 1937 Japanese aircraft dropped bombs on the city, and then strafed the bund and the shipping in the harbour.[85] These efforts were assisted the following February by the Japanese navy, shelling the railway and the power station. Japanese attention was engaged elsewhere and Swatow was temporarily reprieved. Trade was almost back to normal at the close of 1938, but many had fled inland or south, to the perceived safety of Hong Kong.

Attacks recommenced in earnest in 1939. A visiting American noted that the Japanese 'come in any time they wish as the Chinese seem to have given up any idea of defending the place'. He saw an American destroyer lying off the large Standard Oil storage and residential compound near the Custom House. A British destroyer was also busying itself around the harbour. Nevertheless, the Japanese fleet entered the port unchallenged in June and shelled indiscriminately. On 21 June the city was captured.[86]

Further reading: Bruce, *The Story of Old Swatow*; Johnston and Erh, *The Last Colonies*; King, *In the Chinese Customs Service*; Moseley, *From Swatow to Hong Kong*; Yiu, 'Idealizing Space'.

Szemao (Simao) 思茅

Yunnan, 22.46° N, 100.58° E
Treaty Port, 1895 French Treaty

The conviction that Yunnan Province had trade potential was strong but misplaced. France had 'collected' Mengtse (Mengzi) and Manhao as treaty ports in 1887. Szemao, 250 kilometres to the west, was added eight years later.[1] This brought the French within 100 kilometres of British Burma. Britain responded by also nominating Szemao as a treaty port in its 1897 Burmah Convention.[2] The Most Favoured Nation principle would have sufficed, but its specific inclusion raised Szemao's status. It was a hollow gesture.

A village[3] on a malarial plain, Szemao's only function was strategic; the two powers could watch each other's movements. Even that limited aim proved difficult owing to inaccessibility. Szemao's only import was cotton and its sole export Pu'erh tea. All business was securely in Chinese hands and conducted by mule caravans to Indo-China and Burma.[4] Britain suggested Szemao as the terminus of a new railway line from Bangkok, but the geographical challenges proved too great and the economic prospects too small.[5]

A French Consul arrived in 1896, with three foreign Maritime Customs staff.[6] The first British Consul arrived in February 1898, after a two-month journey from Hong Kong. He was set upon by a crowd shouting 'Kill! Kill!'[7] During the winter of 1898–99 the Burma–China border was largely fixed, the main object of the 1897 convention. Difficulties arose where the line crossed the territory of the Wa, a fearless tribe of headhunters. Trouble was not long coming.[8] Sometime in 1901 British Consul George Litton and two British members of the Frontier Commission were attacked by the Wa when visiting a nearby market. Litton escaped after witnessing the decapitation of his two companions. Joint Sino-British reprisals included the destruction of 60 Wa villages.[9]

The only business in Szemao was transacted in a small section of one street.[10] It is not surprising that the British left in 1901 and the French in 1902.[11] The Custom House was the only foreign presence that remained. Its effectiveness was always hampered by the uncontrollable trade routes through the mountains, allowing the mule train drivers to escape paying duty.[12] The service remained determined, opening increasing numbers of sub-stations in the mountain passes even into the 1930s,[13] a triumph of will over reason.

Buffalo carts in the main street of Szemao (Simao), c. 1900. Photograph by Frederick William Carey. © 2011 Ann Kinross. Image courtesy of Historical Photographs of China, University of Bristol.

TACHIENLU (KANGDING) 康定

Sichuan, 30.03° N, 101.57° E
Consular Station, 1913 Britain

The town of Kangding, in Sichuan Province, lies 200 kilometres west-south-west of Chengdu, huddled in a steep river valley at an altitude of 3000 metres. The town was known as Tachienlu and in 1913 became one of the most remote of Britain's Chinese consular stations. On the geographic and ethnographic boundary between China and Tibet, all trade between the two passed through Tachienlu. Lord Curzon, British Viceroy of India, pursued a 'forward policy' with respect to the northern frontier of the Raj, culminating in the invasion of Tibet and the occupation of Lhasa in 1904. Until then, the Chinese had been satisfied with the arrangement of 1727, whereby the eastern part of Tibet became part of Sichuan, hence China, while the rest remained a vassal state.[1]

After withdrawing from Lhasa, the British remained interested in Tibet, ready to fill the power vacuum following the Chinese revolution in 1911, when Tibet proclaimed its independence.[2] A British-sponsored conference in 1913 in Simla, attended by British, Tibetan and Chinese officials, attempted to clarify the border between British India, on one hand, and China and Tibet, on the other. China did not ratify the resulting Simla Accord of 1914, but Britain took the opportunity to station a consular agent at Tachienlu to watch Chinese military activities in the region, a political lookout post.

The journey from Chengtu (Chengdu) to Tachienlu involved a trek of twelve days,[3] with most goods being carried by coolies. The principal export westwards was brick tea. The year 1910 saw almost 8000 tonnes being carried into Tibet.[4] Owing to the high altitude, coolies could not go beyond Tachienlu and so the burden had to be taken up by yaks, mules, ponies and sometimes camels for the lengthy and arduous journey to Lhasa.[5] One oddity of the tea export trade was that it could only be done with a licence, each allowing the export of five 'packages' of tea. With no definition of a 'package', there was a bewildering array of different sizes and weights. The commodity travelling in the opposite direction was musk. One French firm had an agency at Tachienlu and a principal of the firm would come once or twice a year from Chungking (Chongqing) to take delivery of this valuable substance.[6]

A British consular report in 1913 said that Tachienlu was too remote to be the focus for Chinese-Tibetan trade and that, once they were free of political restrictions, Tibetan merchants would turn to India. That freedom never came. The year of 8000 tonnes of tea, 1913, turned out to be the peak year for trade at Tachienlu.[7]

Always a single-person posting, the consular agency remained until 1922. In 1928 the name of the town was changed to Kangding when it was made the capital of the newly created province of Sikiang (Xikang). This was abolished in 1950 and the 1727 border was restored, along with Chinese suzerainty.[8]

TAIWAN-FU (TAINAN) 台南

Taiwan, 23.00° N, 120.09° E
Treaty Port, 1858 British Treaty

Taiwan-fu became a treaty port in the 1858 Treaty of Tientsin (Tianjin). As the capital of Formosa (Taiwan), it naturally attracted foreign interest. The Dutch built Fort Zeelandia on the coast in 1624 during their brief occupation of the island.[1] Remnants of this rambling fortification still stand, as do those of a smaller fort, Provintia, built in 1653[2] inside the walled city. From these bases, the Dutch eliminated

Spanish and Japanese opposition and ruled for almost 40 years. They were forcibly removed in 1662 by the Ming loyalist Koxinga (Zheng Chenggong), who, fleeing the mainland, chose to make Formosa his stronghold. In 1670 the English East India Company established a factory at Anping, the port for Taiwan-fu. Their interest was in hides and sugar, but they found the conditions too tough. In 1681 the factory closed.[3]

Commercial interest in Takow

It was 150 years before foreign interest resurfaced. In the 1830s the British, frustrated by the restrictions of Canton (Guangzhou), considered making Formosa a base for their China operations. Americans also cast acquisitive eyes at the island in 1853, but were distracted by their civil war.[4] However, it was an American merchant who first started to explore the commercial opportunities offered by Takow (Kaohsiung). In 1855 C. D. Williams obtained the right to export camphor in exchange for suppressing local piracy. He shared this right with fellow American W. M. Robinet. The latter also set up a sugar exporting business the following year.

In 1856 another American, Matthew Rooney, became the first foreign merchant to settle in Takow. As agent for Robinet, Rooney peddled opium, supplied to him by Jardines, from his hulk moored in the lagoon. In 1859, arch-rival Dent & Co. bought out Rooney and his business. By now this included Robinet's godown at Shao Chuan Tou (Shaochuan), on the north shore of the harbour entrance. To deter competition, particularly Jardines, Dents then leased most of the remaining land in the area.[5] This forced other foreign interests to Takow on the south side of the entrance (an area now known as Qijin).

In 1861 Robert Swinhoe arrived off Taiwan-fu as the first British Consul, but his ship could not touch land owing to a heavy swell.[6] He was forced to pull in at Takow, the only sheltered anchorage on that part of the coast. He then made an arduous overland journey to Taiwan-fu, where he opened a vice-consulate on 29 July. Swinhoe returned to Takow in 1864 after a decision to relocate the consulate there. Lack of any suitable accommodation obliged him to take a six-month lease on Dents' receiving ship and hoist his flag there.[7] In May 1865 he leased a building in the Chinese town,[8] and later took over Takow's only foreign-style house, built by a recently bankrupt British merchant. Throughout, the consulate continued to be listed officially in Taiwan-fu.

As for trade, in 1863 a total of 52 foreign vessels visited Takow. The place was not a treaty port, so visiting ships had first to call at Tamsui (Danshui) or Amoy (Xiamen) to complete the necessary formalities. Imports consisted of 90 percent opium, the remainder being cotton and woollen goods. Exports were almost entirely sugar. The majority of the ships were German; it was not until 1872 that the British started to dominate.[9] In 1864, Britain obtained China's agreement that Takow would be formally recognized as a dependent port of Taiwan-fu.[10] This enabled a Custom House to be opened on 5 May, although the commissioner was in the invidious position of having to live on a Jardines opium-receiving

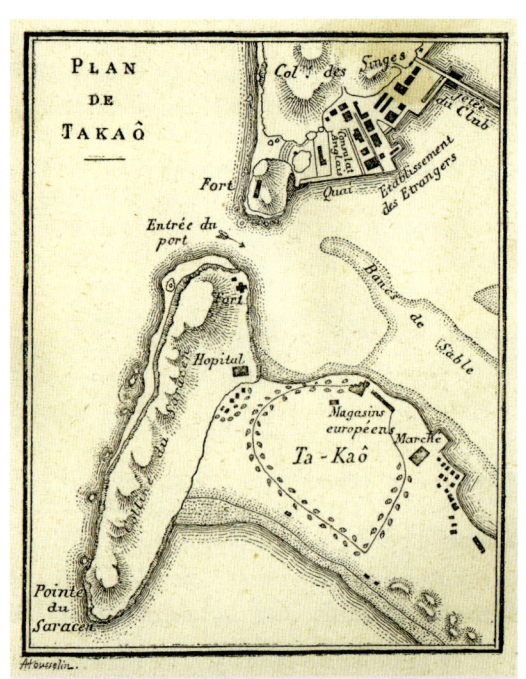

1893 French map of the entrance to the lagoon, with the Chinese village of 'Ta-Kao' to the south and the foreign settlement to the north. Courtesy of Reed Digital Collections.

Hildebrand engraving based on an 1865 photograph by William Pickering, showing ships at the small Shao Chuan Tou (Shaochuan) bund. Courtesy of David Oakley.

ship.[11] The new facility made a significant difference to vessel operators: in 1865, 152 ships visited.

Despite Takow being in most respects a distant, end-of-the-line outpost of commerce, sugar kept it going. There was already a long tradition of exporting sugar to China and Japan. The area of land under sugar cultivation was large, but there were no water or road links with the sugar-growing interior. As foreign vessels were prohibited from loading anywhere but at a designated treaty port, the frustrated merchants had to wait for the product to come to them via pack animals or coastal junks. They suggested that ten small ports along the south and west coasts of Formosa be opened to their ships.[12] It was not to be. The British Trade Report of 1879 referred to the 'clumsy contrivances of the sugar farmers', who showed no enthusiasm for better transportation. It was suggested that the ill-fated railway plant recently uprooted from Woosung (Wusong) near Shanghai be put to use instead of rusting in a Taiwan-fu godown.[13] Exports nevertheless rocketed, with 1880 being the highest on record. A steady increase in Japanese production stemmed the rise, but Formosa remained a significant exporter of sugar to Japan.

Indicative of the sugar-driven confidence is the decision by Britain to build a new consulate and a proper residence for its consul. These were completed between 1877 and 1879[14] and both buildings still stand, with a flight of brick steps connecting the two. The former consular office building is in a very bad state of repair and access is only by special permission.* The residence on Ape's Hill (Shou Shan) is in excellent shape, commanding one of the best views for miles; it is now open as a museum. In the late 1870s, between the foot of Ape's Hill to the west and the customs jetty to the east a little bund was formed,[15] behind which were the foreign hongs and godowns.

* I am grateful to David Oakley for arranging this.

Some evocative remains are still evident—a brick gateway here, a heavy stone entrance there, a much altered but still recognizable sugar godown or two. The delightful Takow Club has disappeared; this, with its billiard room, bar and reading room, used to sit at the seaward end of a long pier.[16] Walking home after a good night at the club must have been a risk.

The Germans still used Takow as, without the easy access to coal that their rivals enjoyed, they relied on sailing vessels. Having a relatively shallow draught, these ships were not troubled by the increasingly hazardous sandbar at the harbour mouth. Starting in 1872 other merchants, with their larger steamers, started to move north to Anping. An editorial in *The Hong Kong Daily Press* in 1886 extolled the good weather enjoyed by Takow, encouraging people to go there for a holiday and stay 'in one of the many empty hongs'.[17] A more practical Foreign Office report three years later reported that the harbour had been surveyed for the third time in ten years—and still no dredging had started.[18]

The attraction of Anping

The silt washed down by the many rivers from Formosa's mountainous centre was why Anping was initially overlooked in favour of Takow. By the time the British came in 1861, the harbour at Anping had lost the attraction it once held for the Dutch. However, problems with Takow—silting, encroachment by oyster farmers and salt-panners, the ever-expanding sandbar—made Anping's proximity to the centre of power the more attractive proposition. The small area of flat land at Anping where the ruins of Fort Zeelandia still lay had once been the port, and would become so again. Ships had to lie offshore for loading and unloading, but the merchants built houses along the bund.[19]

Some aspects of this activity can still be seen. There is no trace of the 1881 bund,[20] but there is a stretch of protective sea wall that is even older, dating from 1778. There are two former merchants' houses from the Treaty Port Era: the modest former house of German merchant Julius Mannich, trader in camphor and sugar and a shipping agent; and the much grander building of Tait & Co. Also identified by plaques placed by the authority behind the Anping Harbor National Historic Park are the sites of three other firms.

A branch of the Takow Custom House was opened in Anping as early as January 1865,[21] and the general move of business from Takow enhanced its importance; by the end of the 1870s there were five European customs men based at Anping.[22] In 1885 the *taotai* set aside a plot of land for a British Consulate,[23] facing the Tait building, although the only sign of this today is an attractive stone pictorial plaque in the grounds of the Simen Elementary School, which was built on the consulate site.

The foreign residents of Anping did not feel as isolated as they had at Takow, now that they were located on the outskirts of a city. Besides, by 1877 there was a thrice-weekly steamer service and a telegraph line linking the two places.[24] Later there was a regular service linking Anping to Hong Kong, Swatow (Shantou) and Amoy.[25] Yet the proximity of a major centre of population had its drawbacks. When Swinhoe had arrived in 1861 and installed himself in a temple outside the city walls, the attentions of an unruly mob forced him to accept the invitation of a kindly Chinese merchant to move to safer quarters within the city.[26] Missionaries still preferred to live inside the city, although they had to flee to Takow for four months in 1868 when threatened by angry rioters.[27] On a good day, the walled city of Taiwan-fu was a pleasant place to be. There were many open spaces, giving it a refreshing rural aspect.[28]

In 1887 Formosa became the Province of Taiwan, its capital the newly created northern city of Taipei. This precipitated a change of name from Taiwan-fu to Tainan-fu, later simply Tainan. But more far-reaching changes were in the offing. Southern Formosa managed to escape the effects of the 1884–85 war between France and China. The coast was blockaded, which naturally disrupted trade, but there was no bombardment. There was, however, much shelling by the Japanese ten years later; both Anping and Takow were attacked. Resistance quickly collapsed following Japanese victories in the north. When the new colonizers arrived on 21 October 1895 their occupation effectively brought an end to the Treaty Port Era in southern Formosa.[29]

Further reading: Davidson, *The Island of Formosa*; Oakley, 'The Foreign Cemetery at Kaohsiung' and *The Story of the British Consulate at Takow*.

TAKU (DAGU) 大沽

Tianjin Municipality, 38.58° N, 117.42° E
Consular Station, 1862 Britain

Taku holds a special place in China's history, now represented by the solitary remains of one tiny fort, overlooking a vast expanse of reclaimed land, massive docks, container-handling facilities, multi-lane highways and soaring bridges. The forts, originally a large complex, guarded the mouth of the Peiho (Hai) River, the sea entrance to Peking (Beijing). In some respects the entrance did not need much guarding, being very difficult to spot from the sea. To the north and south of the river's mouth was a bleak, flat and muddy wasteland. The British fleet managed to find it in 1840, before being persuaded to return to Canton (Guangzhou) to continue its warlike negotiations.[1] A more determined effort was made in 1858 when a combined British and French force captured the forts en route to Tientsin (Tianjin). In 1859, when the Allies brought their ambassadors to sign the treaties of Tientsin, they were forced to withdraw by the Chinese, suffering heavy losses. The situation was reversed in 1860 when, after a third battle, the forts were taken and rendered harmless.

A British Vice-Consulate opened in 1862 at Taku in a rented house,[2] two kilometres up from the river's mouth, set back from the water.[3] It processed the papers of sailing ships trading at newly opened Tientsin. The few steamers that called could negotiate the river, but sailing vessels struggled with the many bends in the 90-kilometre passage. In 1867 a residence, gaol, constable's quarters and offices were built[4] on a riverfront plot a few kilometres inland from the rented premises.[5] But its existence was short-lived. By 1877 the preponderance of steamers meant that it was no longer worthwhile keeping a consular presence simply for the few sailing ships, and it was closed. During its short life, the vice-consulate became known as the 'ugly duckling' of the treaty port postings; incumbents asked for a special allowance to enable them to buy a large supply of books to fill their days.[6]

The forts were again taken in 1900, and the British, Germans, Japanese and Russians occupied one each until the Boxer Protocol of 1901 required them to be razed. The small remnant that stands sentinel today is a token rebuild. Adjacent to this symbolic monument is a large museum describing the history of the forts, once the proud front line of the empire's defences. The narrative is fair, and the English captions of high standard. One statement caught my eye: 'The lesson learned by later generations from the experiences at Dagu Fort is that a weak nation will inevitably be bullied; and only a strong country can thrive in peace.'

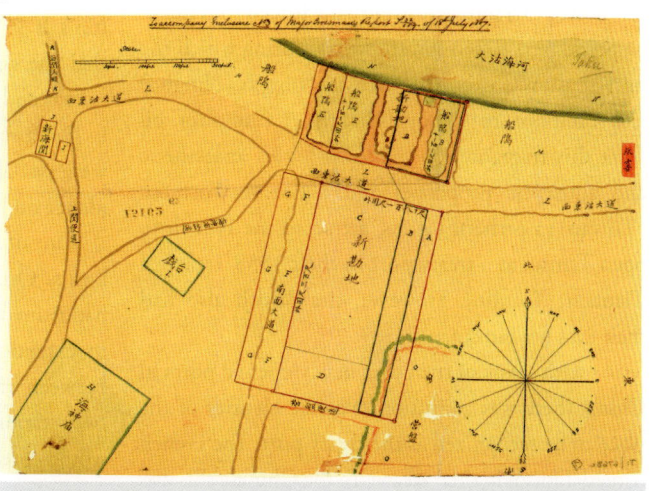

1867 plan of the new British consular site. Reprinted with permission by the National Archives.

Tamsui (Danshui) 淡水

Taiwan, 25.10° N, 121.25° E
Treaty Port, 1858 French Treaty

The Japanese tried three times to establish a colony at Tamsui in the 16th and 17th centuries.[1] Where Japan failed, Spain succeeded. In 1627 the Spanish built Fort San Domingo to deter Japanese designs on the Spanish Philippines. The Spanish were unwelcome and their wooden fort was burned down in 1636. A stone structure replaced it, but no sooner was it finished than the Spanish themselves dismantled it, recognizing their exposed position in relation to Holland's rising regional dominance. These fears were justified when the Dutch defeated the Spanish in a sea battle off Keelung (Jilong) in 1642. The victors built Fort Anthony on the site of the Spanish fortification, presumably finding much useful building material to hand. Their presence was also short-lived. Following Dutch defeat in the south of the island by Koxinga (Zheng Chenggong) in 1662, the Tamsui population rebelled again. The Dutch were able to hold out for a few more years but were eventually forced to retreat.[2]

So matters rested for 200 years, during which the only trade was exporting rice to Ningpo (Ningbo) and camphor to Amoy (Xiamen).[3] Camphor oil from this fragrant wood, known for its anaesthetic and antiseptic properties and native to Formosa (Taiwan)'s northern forests, attracted the French to open Tamsui as a treaty port in their 1858 Treaty of Tientsin (Tianjin). However, the British also had their eyes on Tamsui.

As with many of the other newly opened ports in China, there was confusion over the identity of the place to be recognized as the treaty port. The French named Tamsui in their treaty. To the Chinese this was the name of the river or estuary; there was no such town. At the entrance to Tamsui River there was only a small fishing village, Huwei, opposite the foreign anchorage. The nearest market town was Banka (Wanhua), 20 kilometres upriver and an important city. So which was to be the treaty port?

Banka and Twatutia

Obviously, it was the city of Banka (sometimes known as Manka) that the foreign merchants chose to assume was the open port. But when John Dodd, one of the first foreign merchants to establish himself there, leased a hong the local people objected strongly.[4] Even when an imperial official confirmed the lease, he proved powerless to control an angry mob that prevented Dodd from taking occupation. A compromise was reached permitting foreign merchants to lease land and buildings a few kilometres downstream at Twatutia (Dadaocheng).[5] The two places have now been completely absorbed by Taipei. Nothing remains from these early European days, apart from the patch of open grass that separated the commercial houses of Twatutia from the river. In Dihua Street there are dozens of highly decorated Chinese shop-houses from the beginning of the 20th century, a reminder of earlier commercial activities.

In 1858 the British Treaty of Tientsin named the southern city of Taiwan-fu (Tainan), the capital of the island, as a treaty port. It was there that the first British Consul, Robert Swinhoe, established himself in July 1861. Within months, he decided that the commercial future of the island lay in the north, and he removed his establishment to Tamsui in December.[6] As was usual, no shore-based quarters were available, so he had no choice but to take up residence on Jardine Matheson's opium-receiving ship.[7]

One of Swinhoe's first tasks was to define the port limits. On 7 July 1862 he announced that Britain had gained permission for the boundary of 'Tamsui' to extend to Banka.[8] Geographically, Twatutia lay between the two but was excluded as there were *likin* stations there; to have these within a treaty port would present jurisdictional problems and create confusion for Chinese and foreign merchants. Some years later, in 1890, British Vice-Consul William

Holland highlighted the anomaly by renting a house in Twatutia. He hoisted the British flag and, as a courtesy, notified the city officials what he had done. The embarrassed mandarins accepted Holland's right to reside there.[9] Another request three years later to include Twatutia within the treaty port of Tamsui was quashed by the Chinese merchants.[10] By then there were 20 foreign merchants established there, but 30,000 Chinese residents.[11] The anomaly was ignored.

A SLOW START

Once the treaty port opened, the foreign merchants interpreted very broadly rules which were supposed to bind them. The imprecision concerning the location of the port was helpful in this respect. After 1858 they took their ships into numerous anchorages and roadsteads along the west coast. Although not large, the foreign trade was awarded a Custom House in October 1863 and Robert Hart ordered that all trade be restricted to Huwei.[12]

For the first ten years Jardines, Dents and Dodd & Co. were the only major firms at Tamsui[13] but the number of foreign vessels coming and going increased fourfold. Most were British, with the Germans in second place, trading mainly with other treaty ports on the mainland. Opium constituted some 75 percent of the value of imports, with cotton goods adding a further 10–15 percent. Thanks to the pioneering work of John Dodd, tea became an increasingly important export—80 percent of the total by 1872—with camphor and coal accounting for much of the rest.[14]

Dodd, who came to Formosa in 1860, was the first foreign merchant to realize the potential of Formosan tea. In 1865 he started encouraging local growers by offering them loans to expand their production. Bringing skilled workers over from Amoy and Foochow (Fuzhou), he started his own tea-firing operation in Banka, later expanding to Twatutia.[15] Within five years, shipments of Formosa tea had risen tenfold[16] and Dodd was joined by four Amoy firms in the expanding business.[17] Exports of camphor were increasing but the growers were not replanting,[18] suggesting its future was doomed.

CONSULS AND CUSTOMS MEN

In 1866 the British Vice-Consul's accommodation was upgraded to a temple, still hardly ideal.[19] The old Dutch fort was in reasonable condition, adapted by the Chinese military for their own use.[20] Believing it preferable to the temple, the British leased it as a consulate and residence.[21] Plans were put in hand to fit out the fort with office and living space, as well as a gaol. Work stopped in 1870, pending a proposal to abolish the British consular presence in Formosa;[22] the cost of maintaining consulates in such faraway places was questioned.

Uncertainty vanished when Prime Minister Benjamin Disraeli ruled that Britain could not endanger its international prestige. In 1876 the converted fort, inadequate for its combined uses, was supplemented with a single-storey wooden residence, built close by.[23] The depredations of humidity and termites led to its replacement in 1891 with a two-storey red-brick building, enlarged in 1905. It remains today in all its glory, an enormous and imposing structure standing on a hilly rise. It served as a consulate until 1972.

Although the Custom House has long gone, the 1869 former residence of the commissioner remains. Now know as 'The Little White House', this too has been lovingly renovated and still commands a southerly view over the river.

1869 view of Tamsui (Danshui) by William Pickering, with the British Consulate in the foreground. Courtesy of David Oakley.

Keelung

Keelung, some 30 kilometres to the west of Tamsui, and twice that by sea, boasted one of Formosa's few sheltered harbours. It may have had a Portuguese presence in 1590[24] but Spain put the place on the European map. Naming the port Santissima Trinidad in 1626, the Spanish developed it into their main base on Formosa. Fort San Salvador had a garrison of 500, the biggest in East Asia.[25] However, Keelung suffered the same fate as Tamsui, falling to the Dutch and then to Koxinga.

France obtained consent in 1861 to add Keelung as a dependent port of Tamsui,[26] their interest being the nearby coal mines. Three years later the foreign population was only three—one merchant and two customs officers;[27] a Custom House was opened there on 1 October 1863.[28] Britain was also interested in the coal, mostly as a source of supply for Hong Kong's new gasworks.[29] The British opened a consular sub-station in Keelung in 1869, but there was so little to do that it closed two years later.[30]

Although there was a long history of exporting coal to Amoy and Foochow,[31] the mines were not operated efficiently. It was left to Robert Hart to improve matters. In 1874 he arranged for a mining engineer from England to investigate the mines' potential profitability. The findings were favourable and permission given for modern mining methods to be introduced in June 1876, the first such operation in China.[32] Hopes that the Keelung Colliery would form the nucleus of a thriving mercantile community were disappointed. Keelung was joined to Tamsui by rail in 1887,[33] but a request two years later for the mine to be taken over by a foreign company was refused by Peking (Beijing). Within a few years production ceased.[34] No trace remains in Keelung of any European commercial presence.

Non-commercial activities

Non-commercial European activities in Tamsui have left a stronger impression. Many missionaries came, the most active being Dr. George Mackay, who arrived in 1872. From then until his death in 1901, Mackay built a large number of churches in the interior. He is best remembered, and still revered, for his work in education in Tamsui. In 1882 he founded Oxford College, now a part of Aletheia University, and the Tamsui Girls School, today part of Tam-Kang High School. Mackay's college building remains; his school building was replaced in 1916.

Just to the west of the school and university compound are three fine buildings. The first is Mackay's former residence, painted brilliant white and possibly looking better than when he moved there in 1875. Sharing the same grounds are two red-brick former missionary dormitories built in 1906 and 1909 respectively, now offices of various university departments.

Mackay and members of his family, together with some merchants and sailors, are buried in a separate enclosure within the Foreign Cemetery, at the junction of Xinmin Street and Lane 3, Zhenli Street. The cemetery is in the grounds of Tam-Kang High School and its condition bears witness to the careful attention of the students.

Bombardment by the French

The tiny foreign community must have been concerned when Formosa became a pawn in the tussle between France and China in 1884. In an attempt to seize the island, the French fleet approached Tamsui and started a bombardment on 2 October.[35] Fortuitously, the sandbar that was such a menace to visiting merchant vessels meant that the French warships could not come close enough to do serious damage.[36] An attempted landing on 8 October was repulsed.[37] Frustrated in their main plan, the French blockaded the entire west coast.

The attackers had had more success in Keelung two months previously. The forts were overcome and the port captured, giving the French steamers a vital supply of coal.[38] France occupied the port for some months with a force of 3000 men.[39] But Keelung's surrounding hills are high and rugged. Unable to penetrate the rest of the island, the French negotiated a settlement instead. They withdrew on 21 June,[40] after the 1885 Treaty of Tientsin, having lost some 700 officers and men, largely through disease. Their small enclosed cemetery remains.

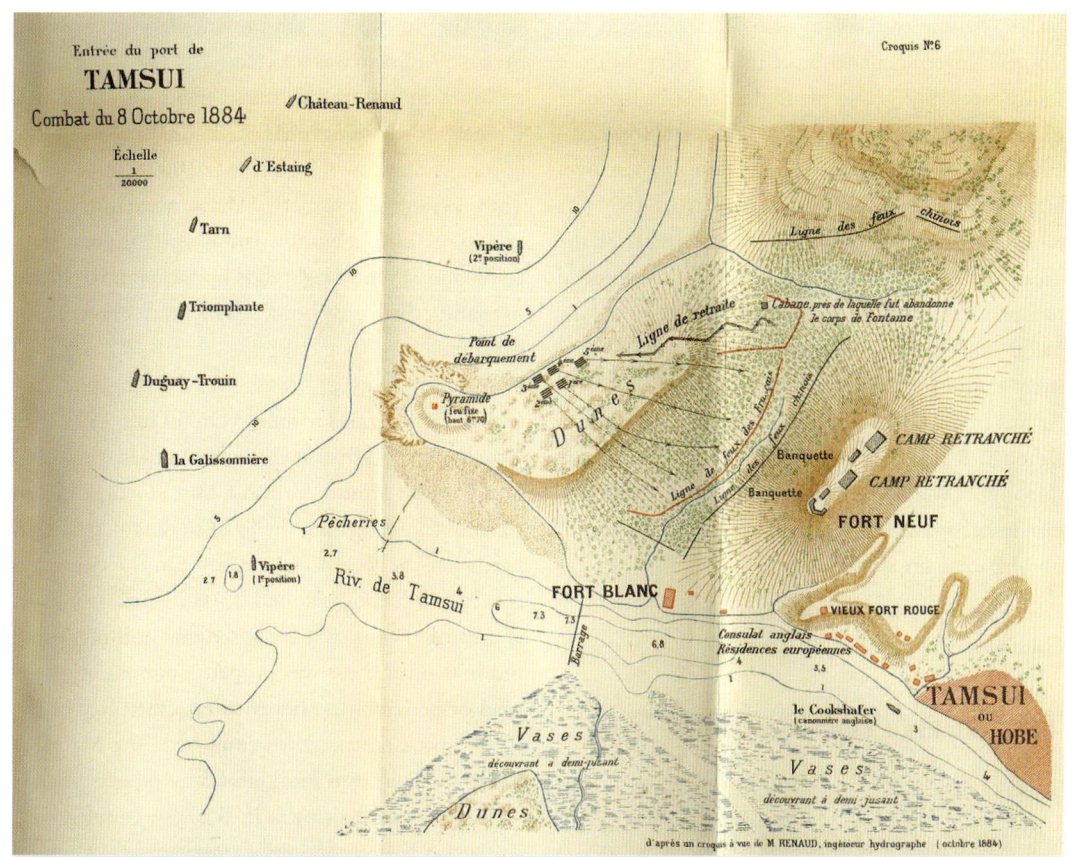

1884 plan of the French bombardment of Tamsui (Danshui) River, by Eugene Germain Garnot, 1894. Courtesy of Reed Digital Collections.

A SHORT PERIOD OF OPTIMISM

As a treaty port, Tamsui had seen its best days by the time normality returned. The foreign merchants of Twatutia, having fled to the comparative safety of Tamsui, returned to their businesses. All of these were on or near the new bund,[41] as was their club, said to be the smallest in the world.[42] Douglas Lapraik's regular steamer service to Hong Kong resumed[43] and prospects still looked reasonably good for the principal commodity, tea. Charles Halcombe observed that Twatutia was 'full of bold and ugly red-brick buildings and tea boxes everywhere—even the air seems impregnated with tea, and hardly anything else can be got there'.[44]

Furthermore, the French assault had been a shot in the arm to the Chinese rulers of Formosa. The general who had vigorously opposed the attackers, Liu Mingchuan, remained as governor and pursued his attempts to modernize the island. Having completed the railway between Tamsui and Keelung, he extended it to the cities in the south and commissioned two coastal steamers to boost trade with the mainland.[45] Unfortunately this progressive official, a protégé of Li Hongzhang, retired because of ill health in 1891,[46] leaving his ambitious plans to languish under his successor's unenthusiastic stewardship.[47] Before he left, and perhaps in recognition of the support they rendered during the recent conflict, Liu ensured that there was a 'commodious' clubhouse for the foreign merchants at Twatutia to enjoy.[48]

ANOTHER FOREIGN INVASION

The Japanese landed a number of armed men in Formosa in 1874 to punish the local people for the murder of Japanese sailors, shipwrecked on the island's remote east coast.[49] This action caused the Chinese government to push its frontiers into the 'savage' area, but it also planted an idea in Japanese minds that they might like the whole island for themselves, it being a geological extension of their own home islands. The Sino-Japanese War of 1894–95 took place elsewhere, but one of the terms of the Treaty of Shimonoseki was that Formosa was ceded to Japan. An army of occupation landed on 3 June 1895[50] and the Tamsui Custom House closed six days later, handing its responsibilities to the Japanese.[51] At this point Tamsui lost its status as a treaty port, although it and Keelung remained open to foreign shipping.[52] While the Japanese did not ban foreign business activities, it became increasingly difficult for non-Japanese firms to continue.[53]

Further reading: Davidson, *The Island of Formosa*; Halcombe, *The Mystic Flowery Land*.

Tengyueh (Tengchong) 騰衝

Yunnan, 25.02° N, 98.29° E
Treaty Port, 1897 British Treaty

Britain's empire in South Asia reached its zenith in 1885 with the annexation of Upper Burma, bringing British interests to the Chinese frontier. Not until nine years later did Britain and China reach agreement about the definition of the border. The Burmah Convention of 1894 provided that Manwyne (Manghuan) be opened as a treaty port.[1] An agreement in 1897 settled further details about the frontier, and allowed Britain to substitute Manwyne for either Shunning-fu (Fengqing) or Momein, whichever it preferred.[2] Manwyne was about ten kilometres from the Burmese border and infamous as the place British official Raymond Margary was murdered while surveying possible trade routes in 1875.

Shunning-fu was the sub-provincial capital, way to the east; Momein was selected.

Momein was the Burmese name for the small Chinese town Tengyueh, 50 kilometres from the border as the crow flies, but over 100 by mule track. The town was on a small river that crossed into Burma and joined the Irrawaddy. It was up that great river to Bhamo, seven or eight days by pack animal thence overland, that cross-border trade was expected to develop.

Within Tengyueh's walls was nothing but government offices and temples.[3] On 30 July 1899 they were joined by a British Consulate[4] and in May 1902 by a Custom House.[5] British Consul George Litton set about investigating the local trading patterns, in particular the *likin* arrangements. On the two main routes to Bhamo he found 13 tax barriers on one, and 21 on the other.[6] He advised that nothing would improve until there was proper communication—a road or preferably a railway to take the place of the 75,000 pack animals then employed. The Maritime Customs countered local efforts by establishing six sub-stations of their own; in this way, coupled with the successful promotion of transit passes, it gradually took control. Imports from Burma, principally cotton, would be rushed up as far as Manwyne before the summer rains commenced and stored there in customs godowns. Once the river rose, the onward journey would be as far as possible by dugout river craft, and then finally by mule to Tengyueh.[7] The main product of Yunnan at that time, opium, could not be imported, leaving the major exports as skins, live animals, fruit and vegetables.[8]

Tengyueh's remoteness gave its residents a detached attitude to political events in the outside world.[9] As long as Britain continued to rule Burma, Tengyueh's consular presence was considered a necessity, subsidized by the Indian government.[10] The same remoteness made for extreme difficulties in constructing a consulate. Litton recorded in 1905: 'The local masons & stonecutters are really the most hopelessly idle, stupid & happy-go-lucky crowd I ever had to deal with.' Meanwhile he lived in a 'glorified mud hut'.[11] The foundation stone for the new consulate

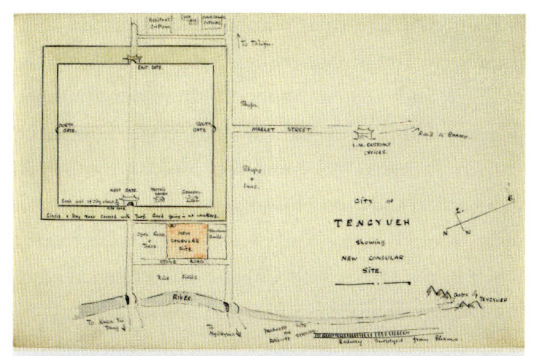

1910 plan of the city, showing the old (east) and new (west) sites of the British Consulate. Reprinted with permission by the National Archives.

was not laid until 1921, on a site outside the West Gate.[12] The rather earthy-looking stone building can still be seen to the north of Jihong Street, undergoing a much-needed facelift. The Japanese closed it in 1942.[13]

TIENTSIN (TIANJIN) 天津

Tianjin Municipality, 39.08° N, 117.11° E
Treaty Port, 1860 British Treaty

Historically, Tientsin was a gatekeeper for Peking (Beijing). The city's Chinese name translates as 'Heavenly Ford', meaning the river crossing on the way to the seat of the Son of Heaven. Access to the capital was rarely granted to foreigners, and Tientsin was often as close as was allowed. This happened in 1858 when a combined British and French force, under Lord Elgin, disabled the forts at Taku (Dagu) and came up the river to Tientsin, arriving on 30 May.[1] The Chinese, to avoid the humiliation of foreign armies in their capital, agreed to negotiations. Treaties were concluded in June with Britain and France, as well as America and Russia.

The treaties opened ten treaty ports—but not Tientsin. Elgin argued that if Tientsin were opened it might be used deliberately to overawe Peking. Elgin prevailed, but his delicacy and poor judgement were criticized by many.[2] If Tientsin had been included, it could have been garrisoned pending treaty ratification and two further years of conflict avoided. Instead, the foreign embassies withdrew in mid-July.[3]

When the Chinese changed their minds regarding the treaties, hostilities resumed. The Allies returned to occupy Tientsin on 25 August 1860 and found the Chinese had taken advantage of their absence to install defences. Their general, Sengelinqin, a Manchu prince,[4] had built a high encircling mud wall several kilometres long, creating as an additional line of defence a tidal ditch seven metres wide—wasted effort because the defenders vacated the premises. The wall was dubbed 'Sam Collinson's Folly' by the British troops.[5] After the Allies had avenged themselves on Peking and availed themselves of its treasures, the long-drawn-out conflict was brought to an end with the British and French Conventions of Peking, signed on 24 and 25 October respectively. These provided for the opening of Tientsin as a treaty port.

A DIRTY LITTLE HOLE

In 1863, Eric Bowra of the Imperial Maritime Customs described Tientsin as 'a dirty little hole of a town with about six Europeans and a hostile population of half a million'.[6] Riverside concessions had been marked out for occupation respectively by the French, British and Americans, starting a kilometre south of the walled city, but no one was living there. The British Concession was a marshy swamp, home to mosquitoes in summer and ice in winter; it required considerable work before it became habitable. The ground needed draining and raising to a level free from flooding. Until the concessions were ready, the foreigners had to live and work in the city.[7]

The 25-hectare British site was selected by Harry Parkes[8] and was mapped and marked out by Captain Charles Gordon of the Royal Engineers (later to become General 'Chinese' Gordon of the 'Ever-Victorious Army'). The French Concession, 24 hectares, was surveyed by a French army officer but no further action taken for some years. In August 1861

99-year leases on lots in the British Concession were auctioned and the lessees made responsible for their share of the costs of draining and policing the land.[9] By 1865 a large number of buildings had appeared, including those of Jardines and Sassoons and, on the riverfront, Dents,[10] the first substantial house to be built in the foreign style.[11] In 1866 a set of land regulations was introduced to govern the British Concession.[12]

A major commercial activity in Tientsin at the time was salt, an important source of Chinese government revenue. The city had the largest salt store in the empire.[13] Brine was brought upriver from the coastal flatlands in specially designed boats. The foreign merchants found the river less obliging. The sandbar at its mouth rose and fell at whim. The first British consular report, in 1862, noted: 'The navigation of the Tien-tsin River... from its entrance all the way up to the city, might be very much improved at a trifling expense.'[14] Time was to prove this confident statement laughably optimistic.

The early British merchants in Tientsin quickly realized that the Chinese traders were purchasing foreign goods direct from suppliers in Shanghai.[15] In 1867, the British responded by importing goods to Tientsin direct from England. One such vessel arrived that year, three the following year and six in 1869.[16] The foreign merchants were not discouraged by the commercial and physical obstacles they encountered, and their numbers increased. By 1867 there were 100 foreigners living there, excluding the military, and Tientsin ranked fifth among the open ports of China. A regular steamer service connected it with Shanghai.[17] A bund was built in the British Concession and a jetty for steamers. The rudiments of what would become the Tientsin Club were created when in the early 1860s Captain Laen opened a billiard hall and clubhouse. Horse racing started in 1863 on a course a kilometre back from the concessions.[18] Meetings were held every May and October, but staging them was no easy matter. The venue had to be changed at short notice when a dust storm obliterated the course, or when a burst dyke flooded it. By 1868 the organizers were on their third racecourse.[19]

The British Consulate also faced a succession of different venues. From unsuitable rented premises in the city, Consul James Mongan had supervised the auctioning of the new concession's lots. He reserved a large riverside one for the consulate[20] at the southern end, while looking covetously at Dents' magnificent house at the other. Parts of this were already rented for consular purposes and in 1867 Mongan negotiated the purchase of the whole compound. However, immediately the purchase was completed there were regrets. A Treasury report rued that 'it might have been cheaper if we had waited as Dent is now bankrupt'.[21]

FRENCH TROUBLES

France was less concerned with the commercial potential of the port than with promoting Catholicism. As early as 1866 *The New York Times* issued a prescient prediction: 'Beyond all question there will sooner or later be trouble... on account of the French. While foreigners are generally hated because they are foreigners, the French are in general disrepute everywhere in China... because of their insolent character and overbearing conduct.'[22] In Tientsin this manifested itself in a way that guaranteed local resentment. On the opposite side of the river to the walled city, at the junction with the Grand Canal, there stood a complex of Imperial structures that were part temple and part palace. The Allied commanders occupied

The former Dent hong that became the British Consulate in 1867. Reprinted with permission by the National Archives.

them in 1858 for the treaty negotiations, the British in one part and the French in another. On returning as part of the occupying force in 1860, the French seized the whole complex and established their consulate in an Imperial apartment. Moreover, they started work on a massive cathedral, Our Lady of Victories, on the site of the Imperial temple, completing it in 1869. Consequences followed this display of cultural insensitivity in 1870.

An order of French nuns ran an orphanage for the abandoned, sick and dying children of Tientsin's poor, just outside the city's East Gate. The nuns offered a small payment to anybody bringing a child to them. The Chinese questioned their motives and came to believe that the nuns were removing the children's eyes and hearts to make potions for diabolical purposes.[23]

Rumours of trouble brewing had been circulating[24] when, on 21 June, a large mob surrounded the French Consulate and attacked the cathedral. The outraged French Consul, Henri Fontanier, armed himself and his assistant and rushed to the *taotai*'s *yamen*. In a heated exchange, the Frenchman accused the Chinese official of instigating unrest and fired one of his pistols to demonstrate his anger. Fontanier was, not unreasonably, detained. The mob switched its attention to the *yamen*. The consul was advised not to leave. Ignoring this counsel he tried to shoot his way out and was immediately set upon and killed. The frenzied mob returned to the French area and set fire to it. They killed 21 of the nuns and mutilated their bodies. With cries of 'Kill the French first, then the other foreigners', the mob went on to murder three Russians. A fortuitously heavy thunderstorm calmed tempers.[25]

Locally, order was rapidly restored, but wider consequences were ongoing. An Imperial Decree was issued on 25 June, ordering a full investigation and proper punishment of the guilty. High officials arrived in Tientsin to assist the viceroy. Foreign gunboats were dispatched, the first arriving on 29 June. Soon there was a naval force of five French, one American and three British warships, with more gathering at Chefoo (Yantai). The other foreign powers wanted to

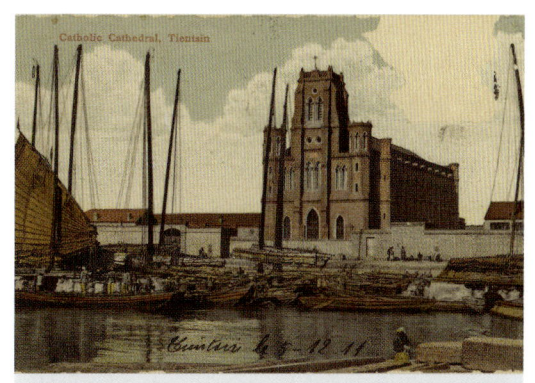

1911 view of the twice rebuilt French Cathedral. Courtesy of Régine Thiriez.

show solidarity with France, but were shocked when the French demands were made known: two senior Chinese officials to be decapitated, or the French navy would be instructed to take whatever steps it considered necessary.[26]

Meanwhile, an inspection of the ruined orphanage produced the conclusion that no irregularities had occurred.[27] Regarding the French demands, a message was brought from Peking (by no lesser personage than Li Hongzhang) that to comply would be 'almost impossible' and no heads could be delivered without a proper trial.[28] At about this point French interest waned, distracted by the outbreak of the Franco-Prussian War on 19 July. A number of people, considered more or less guilty, were beheaded and some senior officials stripped of their rank and banished to the icy northern frontier, and there the matter ended.[29] France's overwhelming defeat by the little-known (in China) Prussians left them with no standing to pursue the matter further.[30] The ruins of the cathedral stood as a reminder of mutual distrust and misunderstanding for more than a quarter-century.

LI HONGZHANG AND GUSTAV DETRING

The only positive outcome from the 1870 massacre was that Li Hongzhang was appointed Viceroy of Chihli and Imperial Commissioner for the Northern Ports, based in Tientsin. Li had delivered the diplomatically sensitive 'almost impossible' verdict from Peking, a case of the messenger being of equal significance to the message. He was to produce many far-reaching and important reforms in China, any one of which would have been considered 'almost impossible'.

Humbly born in 1832, Li's status grew as a scholar and a military leader. Forces under Li fought with Gordon's 'Ever-Victorious Army', giving him an early encounter with foreign methods. He was the ideal candidate to come to Tientsin immediately after the massacre. As a tangible demonstration of the growing importance of Tientsin as a proxy for Peking in matters relating to foreigners, Li left Paoting-fu (Baoding), the provincial capital, and moved to Tientsin when he took up his appointment.[31]

By 1872 Li had engaged European drill instructors to give Western-style training to the Tientsin-based Chinese infantry, artillery and cavalry.[32] As for the navy, the Beiyang (North Sea) Squadron of ten vessels was based at Tientsin under Admiral Ding, but Li engaged a British admiral and twelve junior officers to assist.[33] Li took time out from his heavy responsibilities to conclude the negotiation of the Chefoo Agreement in 1876, thereby putting Sino-British relations back on the track from which the Margary affair* had derailed them.

Following China's defeat by France in 1885, Li was even keener to improve his country. Foreign capitalists flocked to Tientsin and presented Li with scheme after scheme for his consideration. For a period of 20 years, from 1874 to 1894, Li acted as the emperor's prime minister, making Tientsin the focus of new learning, national reform and foreign contact. In the 1880s Jardines started to coordinate their many dealings with the Chinese government via their Tientsin office.[34] Li was at the centre of everything.

Coincidence brought Li into contact with a very different official, also dedicated to reform in general and Tientsin in particular. These two were to forge a close personal relationship that lasted for 25 years. In 1865 Gustav Detring, German and ten years Li's junior, joined the Imperial Maritime Customs. After a spell as student interpreter in Peking, Robert Hart wrote in 1869 that he found Detring 'pugnacious and hot-headed',[35] an opinion that long experience gave him no cause to change. Detring's rise in the service was fast. From 1875 to 1876 he was the commissioner at Chefoo,[36] where he first came into contact with Li during the agreement negotiations. Predictably, Detring's next posting was as commissioner at Tientsin, Li's power base. He was to stay for 27 years, almost completely overlapping Li's period of prominence. Initially Detring balanced the dominance of the British,[37] but fast became Li's most trusted adviser in matters relating to foreign affairs and China's development.

Both Hart and Detring were keen to be seen as trustworthy friends of China, but whereas Hart's style was subtle, Detring was inclined to be blunt and assertive. The first major collision between the two came in 1884, and was related to China's conflict with France. Against Hart's advice, Detring visited Paris while on home leave and involved himself in diplomacy. Returning to China he found himself posted to Canton (Guangzhou). Within weeks, Li ordered Hart to return Detring to Tientsin to assist with negotiations that would conclude the war.[38]

In 1894 Li sent Detring to Japan to attempt to delay another seemingly inevitable war. He came back empty-handed. The Japanese refused to recognize the credentials of this German employee of the Chinese customs to negotiate so serious a matter, and ignored him.[39] In Tientsin, concerns were expressed about Detring's apparent partiality regarding German interests.[40] In 1895 he had arranged for the Taku forts to fly the German flag should they be threatened by Japan.[41] Then, following China's defeat by Japan, Detring tried to form a German syndicate to lend money to help Peking pay the indemnities. In return Germany would gain a measure of control over the northern railways forming the security for the loan.[42] The deal did not proceed.

In 1896 Detring went over Hart's head when submitting a proposal to the Tsungli Yamen for the creation of a unified Imperial Bureau of Railways. Hart did not consider this part of the Maritime Customs' brief.[43] As we shall see, there was a further error of judgement by Detring that destroyed Hart's

---

* See entry on Chefoo for details.

confidence in him. Nonetheless, Detring was owed an enormous debt of gratitude by the people of Tientsin, both Chinese and foreign, for whom he worked tirelessly. He was responsible for many good works and improvements. At Detring's instigation China's first postage stamps were issued in Tientsin in 1878, from the former Imperial Post Office that still stands on Jiefang North Road.[44] In 1879, after only two years' residence, he was elected Chairman of the British Municipal Council, a measure of how cosmopolitan that body was,[45] and held that position for 13 years.[46]

Detring invested his own money as freely as that of the council in a number of major projects. One close to his heart, and his palatial home, was the new racecourse, opened in 1887[47] to the south-west of the concessions. This became immensely popular, featuring many more sports than horse racing. The clubhouse, renovated to a very high standard, still stands, as do many of the former stables, although the tracks have become an ornamental water feature.

In 1889, following a suggestion by Li Hongzhang, Detring promoted the building of Gordon Hall as the virtual town hall of the British Concession,[48] the first of its kind in China.[49] The imposing building was opened in May 1890. Considered by many as a white elephant, the project was criticized as a 'woeful waste of public money and a striking example of the Council's ineptitude'. However, it grew to be the centre of life in many respects: it housed the seat of municipal government, a public library, meeting rooms, a theatre and a dance hall. A 1922 plan to erect a bigger building for the municipal council was dropped in favour of keeping Gordon Hall.[50] A remnant has been incorporated into a new hotel built in the Edwardian style. Immediately in front of Gordon Hall was an area of scruffy park. Detring transformed this into Victoria Park, opened in 1887 to mark the Queen's Golden Jubilee. It became a favourite place for relaxation and 'being seen'. Band concerts were held most afternoons in the season.[51] As the Municipal Committee Park it remains a popular, peaceful facility in the middle of the busy city.

In 1886 Detring founded Tientsin's first English newspaper, the *Chinese Times*. During its five-year

Postcard showing an aerial view of Victoria Park in the 1920s. Gordon Hall is at the top, the Astor House Hotel on the right. Source: unknown.

life, the paper was edited by an English merchant turned writer, Alexander Michie, and was noted for its probing editorials. Also in 1886 Detring started the Tientsin Printing Co., which published the city's first Chinese newspaper, the *Shih Pao*, and later *The Peking & Tientsin Times*.[52]

Detring received honours from nine nations (notably Great Britain was not one of them), including a number from China. On his death in 1913 no statue was raised to him, although some thought such a memorial appropriate.[53] Had he lived a little longer, he would have faced the ignominy of being detained as an enemy alien.

THE KAIPING COAL MINES

There had been coal mines in the Tangshan area of north-east Hebei since the Ming dynasty. The coal produced was of good quality but the methods employed were primitive, the shafts shallow. Li Hongzhang realized the importance of coal in the modernization of his country. In 1873 he summoned Jardines' long-serving comprador, Tang Jingxing, from Shanghai, to see if he could operate the Kaiping mine using Western machinery. Li needed the coal to supply another of his new self-strengthening ventures, China Merchants Steam Navigation Co.[54] Tang's conclusion was positive, adding that transportation costs could be reduced by building a short railway to the canal and river system, thence to Tangku (Tanggu) on the river between Tientsin and Taku.

A new company was formed for the purpose—the Chinese Engineering & Mining Co.—with foreign shareholders and managers but under Chinese control.[55] The company needed to acclimatize to alien operational methods but by 1882 most difficulties were resolved.[56] The railway line, however, was a success from its commencement in 1881. Six years later, Li presented a memorial to the throne requesting that the short Kaiping line be extended to Tientsin and the coast. He wisely stressed military over economic advantages and received approval. The Kaiping Railway Co. thus became the China Railway Co. The 130-kilometre line to Tangku was completed in 1887[57] and extended to Tientsin in 1888.[58] Coal production soared, satisfying all local demand and allowing surpluses to be exported to Japan. Later the government opened the new port of Chinwangtao (Qinhuangdao) specifically for handling Kaiping coal.

The new facility's development was disrupted by the Boxer troubles, and the mines themselves were very nearly lost. In 1900, with foreign armies in evidence province-wide, the Kaiping operations were dangerously close to areas Russia and Japan were claiming as their respective spheres of influence. Li ordered Detring to oversee placing the coal interests under the safe umbrella of a British holding company, to be held equally by British and Chinese interests. No sooner had this been done, in 1901, than the British half of the company issued new shares to raise capital, thereby making the Chinese minority shareholders.[59] Li was incensed, as was Yuan Shikai, who was now in the ascendant.

Yuan ordered the new arrangement cancelled and the *status quo ante* restored. Unfortunately it was not that easy. English company law now had to govern the company's conduct, and annulling agreements went beyond 'almost impossible'. There then followed a long court case with Detring, the mastermind of the reorganization, as a key witness. It was disclosed that he had received a salary, bonuses and shares from the Kaiping company, facts of which Hart was unaware. The Inspector-General was shocked at this breach of faith and customs regulations by his most senior lieutenant.[60] International relations were such that Hart, a Briton, could not take public disciplinary action against Detring, a German, despite both being employed by the Chinese government. However, Yuan refused further contact with Detring. After much deliberation, Hart allowed Detring to remain in Tientsin, but no longer as a member of the customs service.[61]

The coal business flourished. In 1907, Yuan Shikai, still angry at the loss of 'his' mine, established the Lanchow Official Mine Co. Its mine was just to the north of that of the Kaiping company, and its mission was to become a serious competitor of the now foreign concern. But even Yuan could see that the Kaiping operation was bigger, stronger and, with better infrastructure, more efficient.[62] Rather than face the prospect of Lanchow being forced out of business, Yuan allowed a merger of the two rivals (effectively a Kaiping takeover) under the name of the Kailan Mining Administration (KMA).[63] A mighty body needed a mighty headquarters to prove it, and in 1921[64] the new KMA Building was completed on Meadows Road in the British Concession. By 1931, the company had grown to operate five mines and employed 35,000. Coal production that year reached 5.3 million tonnes.[65] In addition, huge investments had been made in staff welfare, housing, hospitals and schools, bathhouses and a savings bank. The KMA owned the railway rolling stock that was used to carry its product to Chinwangtao and owned or chartered a fleet of 21 steamers to transport it from there to customers at other ports. This vast empire was managed from the building that still stands in Tai'an Road. The columned edifice appears to have no function these days and is locked and guarded. There is no plaque, but below the pediment over the huge pillars can still be made out 'KAILAN MINING ADMINISTRATION'.

Keeping the river navigable

Tientsin's Hai River provided convenient transport and an abundant water supply, but it tended to flood and deposit silt. This latter problem was exacerbated by the numerous bends between the city and the sea; Tientsin and Taku were 50 kilometres apart, but the journey along the river was almost double that.[66] Silt carried down the river was dumped once it reached the sea, creating the infamous Taku Bar. Summer floods caused the mud level of the riverbed at Tientsin to rise faster than the water level of the surface,[67] so that people could wade from one bank to the other.[68] Some years were better than others, but the general trend was one of deterioration. Any attempts at dredging were always defeated by nature. In 1887 Detring described the river as 'the bugbear of the port' and requiring strong action.[69] He persuaded Li Hongzhang to commission a river survey, while preparing him for the inevitably expensive remedial work.[70] Danish engineer Albert de Linde was engaged to produce recommendations.

The first of these saw the establishment, in 1898, of the Sino-foreign Haiho Conservancy Board. This body immediately started building locks to close the many canals and creeks leading out of the river that slowed down the flood tide and allowed the river to drop its silt. One such waterway was the Wei Tze Canal, the ditch that had been formed in 1860 by 'Sam Collinson'. The river end of this canal can be seen just downstream of the Qufu Dao Bridge, the lock, although much newer than de Linde's, still doing the same job.

An article in the 1901 Boxer Peace Protocol gave significant funding to the Conservancy Board to enable it to continue its work. A loan was raised in 1902 to finance the cutting of the five most difficult bends.[71] Vested interests in the lighterage business complained about a potential loss of revenue. But the river-straightening operations proceeded, reducing the distance from the Tientsin Bund to the sea by around 16 kilometres.[72] Later efforts reduced the original 90 kilometres to 56.[73] The smoother flow of the river diminished the silt deposits, but the Taku Bar remained.

It will be remembered that in 1862 Consul Gibson predicted the expense would be 'trifling'. Forty years later it became clear how ill judged was his statement. Everyone agreed the bar should be dredged but there was no unanimity about who would pay. The shipping companies, by now heavily invested in land and facilities at Tangku, claimed it was the merchants in the concessions who would benefit most. In June 1905, to break the impasse, the land-renters of the British Concession agreed to raise a loan.[74] Consistent and focused effort paid dividends. By 1921 clearance at the Taku Bar had been increased from 3.5 metres to 5 metres.[75] It sounds insignificant but for ships at that time it represented the difference between accessing the river or staying outside.

Tangku, the alternative port

Tangku was a small town sheltered inside the first bend of the Hai, about five kilometres from the sea. In 1865 it was described as the inner anchorage for Taku,[76] the outer one being the open sea. A customs tide-surveyor was based there and lived, very appropriately, in a temple of the Sea God.[77] From small beginnings a commercial community grew that served Tientsin well.

The first to be established were a number of pilots, living in a 'ship-shape little colony of mud huts' known as Pilot Town.[78] A dock was built in 1880 for repairing Chinese warships.[79] Tangku received a major boost when the Kaiping railway was extended there in 1887. The delightful Tangku South station was built in 1888;[80] it still services the occasional freight train. By then there was a foreign population of over 50,[81] many of them working for the Taku Tug & Lighter Co.

Because all sailing ships, as well as many ocean-going steamers, had to offload their cargo at the Taku

Postcard of the railway station at Tangku (Tanggu). Source: Crush, *Imperial Railways of North China*, 40. Courtesy of P. A. Crush Chinese Railway Collection.

Bar, a lighterage service was needed to transport goods between the river mouth and Tientsin. Initially in 1872 this was an ad hoc arrangement.[82] By the 1890s the company had a fleet of over a dozen vessels. For years it enjoyed a monopoly and all that went with it: complaints about inefficiency, high cost and poor security.[83] Meanwhile it paid dividends of up to 174 percent to its investors.[84] Swires started a long-overdue rival operation in 1904—the Tientsin Lighter Co. The new concern mainly serviced Swire vessels, but prompted all-round service improvement.[85]

These commercial activities, combined with the river's continued silting, ensured Tangku's prosperity. Captain James Watts, the manager of the Tug & Lighter Co., opened a hotel in 1886.[86] It was hoped that the new Taku Hotel would entice holidaymakers away from Chefoo,[87] but it is unlikely that this happened often. Tangku was a place of business. By the early 1900s a number of Tientsin's major hongs had Tangku branches, with investment increasing in proportion to the river's silting. Asiatic Petroleum built a large storage and handling facility at the southern end of Tangku; there is still an oil storage plant on the same site. Standard Oil had its tanks at nearby Hsinho (Xinhu). The bund and wharves that once stretched along the river's left bank have been completely replaced. Near the old railway station are a number of brick buildings dating from this period but in late 2011 they looked to be joining the surrounding building site.

The 1880s and 1890s: Coming of age

The pioneering work of Li Hongzhang and Gustav Detring, the Kaiping coal mines and the efforts to keep the river open to traffic all form the background against which foreign business started to take off in the 1880s and 1890s. The British interest had always been trade. Tientsin was the gateway to a vast hinterland, stretching to Tibet. The major export was cotton[88] but there were none of the usual staples of tea, silk and porcelain. Hence exports always lagged behind imports.

At the beginning of the 1880s about 900 foreign vessels arrived annually, mostly British.[89] The foreign population, including missionaries, was 262, half of whom were women and children.[90] Of the men, about 20 were Russians, importing brick tea from their factories in Hankow (Hankou) for dispatch by camel to Siberia.[91] Another 20 Chinese Engineering & Mining Co. employees headquartered in Tientsin, and 24 were employed by the Maritime Customs. There were 26 foreign businesses, including 4 German, 8 Russian and 9 British.

Most of the streets in the British Concession were properly surfaced, and gas and electric lighting started to appear in the 1880s.[92] A bund ran the full length of the concession[93] but was not destined to become a grand statement for disembarking steamer passengers. Instead, it was used as an open-air godown. Local matting was found to be impervious to rain, and so goods were piled onto the bund under its protection to await sale. Commodities could be bought and sold many times without ever being handled.[94]

Foreign investors saw potential in China's railways, especially once the Kaiping line was extended to Tientsin in 1888. Railway construction and management, together with the import of the hardware, provided Tientsin with major commercial impetus; the Imperial Chinese Railway Administration was to become a significant employer of foreign staff,[95] and a plethora of new shipping agencies appeared.[96]

The French started to develop their concession following the unpleasant experience of 1870. Space was under pressure in the British Concession and the French boundary, previously of no interest to anybody, suddenly became a hot issue. An angry and hostile dispute was settled only when Li Hongzhang intervened.[97] The movement of foreigners out of the city into the concessions created housing shortages that were to continue for some time.[98] A new Custom House was built in the French Concession.[99] A later incarnation still stands on the same site.

Hotels had mixed luck. In 1867 the Hotel d'Europe was described as providing good accommodation and 'a fair table'.[100] Other hotels, such as the Globe on the bund, came and went but one was to remain and become a much-loved landmark. A small hostelry erected by missionary John Innocent in 1863 became, in 1874, the Astor House. In 1886 the one-storey structure was converted into the lovely three-storey building[101] that forms the centrepiece of the hotel today. It still provides the best accommodation in Tientsin.

In 1885 the Chinese city started improvements to its streets and drains.[102] These efforts were possibly encouraged by what had been visibly achieved in the foreign areas—until recently unhealthy, undrained swamps, but now transformed beyond all recognition. Life there was following the usual pattern, with a Tientsin Club for the *taipan*s and other associations catering to a wide variety of sporting, spiritual or intellectual interests. In 1896 the Race Club absorbed the adjacent Country Club and, guided by Detring, developed the latter's large park into the best of its kind in China.

Communication with the outside world remained a problem, especially in the winter when the river froze. In 1881 Li Hongzhang introduced a telegraph link to Shanghai.[103] Detring's new postal service provided a thrice-weekly courier to Chinkiang (Zhenjiang), 900 kilometres to the south on the Yangtze River. There was also a weekly connection to Newchwang (Yingkou) and a daily service to Peking, between four and eight days away by horse-drawn cart and riverboat.[104] When a railway link to the capital was opened in 1897 the journey time was reduced to three hours.[105] The effect on business was, naturally, positive, but then disaster struck.

Besieged by the Boxers

The foreign concessions were besieged by the Boxer rebels for 27 days in the summer of 1900. Tientsin's foreign-inspired modernization initiatives encouraged the rebels to concentrate their activities there. They arrived at the beginning of June and quickly pressed the city authorities into supplying them with food and funds. The Imperial troops joined the rebels and the combined, much better armed force destroyed all missionary buildings, including the French cathedral; this had been in ruins from 1870 to 1897, when it had been rebuilt and freshly consecrated.[106]

Defending the concessions were 560 marines of various nations, rapidly brought onshore from their vessels. There were also 1700 Russian troops, including artillery units, who had arrived too late to accompany an abortive mission to relieve the foreign legations in Peking. A volunteer force of concession residents brought total defenders to about 2400. Against 10,000 determined zealots this number was woefully insufficient. On 17 June the Chinese shelled the French and British concessions from heavy batteries mounted on the city walls. Being closer, the French area suffered more. A quarter of the houses there, mostly Chinese, were destroyed and two-thirds of the population fled. An estimated 4000–5000 were killed.[107] Foreign women, children and non-combatants were herded into the capacious cellars of Gordon Hall.[108] If necessary, this bastion was to be the site of a last stand.[109] Fortunately, its Scottish architect had built it rather like a baronial hall and its battlements would have been useful.[110]

A contingent of Russians was detailed to defend the railway station, which proved to be auspicious.[111] Not designed to be defended, the concessions were severely exposed. Godowns were plundered and makeshift barricades of bales of cotton, sugar, rice and peanuts were erected. The future 31st President of the United States, Herbert Hoover, at that time a mining engineer, was among the defenders.[112] So was young Englishman James Watts, son of Tangku's Captain Watts, a private in the Tientsin Volunteer Corps[113] and successful amateur jockey.[114] On 20 June Watts volunteered to ride his best horse at the gallop to Taku, 50 kilometres away, to summon help from the naval forces that were waiting there for news. He and three Cossacks rode through the night, thundering past enemy soldiers. Thanks to them, a multinational relief force of 8000 was immediately dispatched to Tientsin. Five days later the siege was lifted. Watts was decorated by the British government and appears in later directories as J. Watts Jr., CMG.

Foreign reinforcements continued to flood in, eventually becoming an expeditionary force of some 18,000 men, almost half of them Japanese. On 13–14 July the walled city was taken by a frontal attack in the face of heavy defending fire.[115] Loyal members of the relief force included the Chinese Regiment, local soldiers recruited by the British in Weihaiwei (Weihai).[116] It was fitting, therefore, that when the city walls were later torn down some of the stones were taken to Weihaiwei for building material.[117]

Under military rule

Once Tientsin and the immediate area had been cleared of rebel forces, the Allies found that the city's *taotai* had also disappeared. They therefore formed a military administration. Known as the Tientsin Provisional Government (TPG), it took over the government and policing of the city and its suburbs up to the Mud Wall, but excluding the foreign concessions. The TPG was headed by a council, initially comprising the Russian, British and Japanese military commanders, later increased by the addition of French, German, American and Italian representatives.[118]

The body's immediate priorities were sanitation and security, but they had another job to do first. The city of Tientsin had been permitted the privilege of defensive walls during the reign of the Ming Yongle Emperor.[119] Five hundred years later the TPG decided that they had to go. This was not only a punishment for the city, although the loss of face would have been significant to its residents. The walls were by now offering no protection to the Chinese commercial quarter that had grown outside the city. Moreover, the enormous barrier prevented much-needed fresh air from circulating in the tiny streets. Some 20 or 30 years ahead of most Chinese cities, Tientsin's walls were replaced by wide boulevards. This was not the only demolition work carried out by the provisional government. Article VIII of the Peace Protocol decreed that not only were the Taku forts to be destroyed, but also any others 'which might impede free communication between Peking and the sea'. This was interpreted broadly and the TPG was entrusted with the work. It was handled in a business-like manner, and contracts were drawn up for the destruction of 25 forts, including those at Shanhaikwan (Shanhaiguan).[120]

Postcard showing the International Bridge letting traffic through, 1920. Source: unknown.

The TPG set to, unfettered by any concern for local objections—an effective benevolent dictatorship. They erected an iron swing bridge, the International Bridge, leading from the French Concession to the railway station. The bund was improved, widened and extended to run from the concessions all the way round the city's north-west corner, laying the foundation for the attractive arrangement that exists today. Those in the way of such improvements were evicted, but compensated with either money or land.[121]

The military government also introduced a freshwater supply to the city, but a principal focus was to improve the river. The TPG were granted an extension of authority down the river to the sea. The locks that had been built by de Linde were repaired.[122] The straightening projects that had been promoted by Detring now became much easier. Opposition was ignored[123] and the Haiho Conservancy Board was taken under the TPG's wing.[124]

Another role assumed by the TPG was that of managing the local customs duty arrangements. The collection system was comprehensively reorganized. A combined foreign-Chinese staff was installed and Peking began to receive approximately 14 times the previous amount of revenue.[125] It was the easiest local customs station to transfer to the foreign-run Maritime Customs when this became a requirement in 1901.[126]

The reign of the TPG came to an amicable end on 15 August 1902. At its last meeting, the council handed over all the minutes and accounts to Yuan

Shikai, the newly created Viceroy of Chihli. A presumably surprised Yuan also received a list of judicial sentences not yet completed, a schedule of works on hand and cheques for the amounts required to complete the projects to which the TPG had committed itself. Furthermore, there was a healthy balance in the city's bank account.[127] At the time, a local journal expressed the opinion that Tientsin 'had witnessed more civic improvements in one year than in its previous five centuries'.[128] The success of the arrangement was in large measure attributable to the TPG being, at heart, a military body, and one in which nobody in Peking took much interest.[129] It is fortunate it achieved its goals so quickly. The Allies' unity of purpose, engendered by the Boxer threat, faded once the danger passed, to be replaced by jealousies over the granting of concessions.[130]

Concessions for all

China's various troubles 'afforded splendid opportunities' for foreign powers to obtain further quasi-territorial rights.[131] Nowhere was this more so than in Tientsin, where the original 3 grew to between 9 and 15 foreign areas, depending on how you define the term—more than in any other treaty port. Their combined area was eight times that of the Chinese city.[132] They are best considered separately because once established each developed along different lines.

The British Concession

The original British Concession stretched 1000 metres along the riverbank and 250 metres inland.[133] Administered by an elected municipal council, it was the only foreign concession in Tientsin not under consular control. Although very British in its institutions and social habits, the concession was also international; the council included Russian as well as British members, and its chairman for many years was Gustav Detring, a German. The first concession to be actively developed, it became the focus for foreign business.

Commercial and population growth led to purchases of land to the west of the concession. By 1892 Detring had spent large amounts of his own money, plus that of the municipal council, and was being ridiculed for creating another 'folly'.[134] The additional area (the British Extension) was properly drained and began to look like part of the original concession even though it was not. There was a need for policing as well as sanitary and lighting arrangements, and so a *taotai*'s proclamation in 1897 gave the British permission to exercise such powers. The area stretched to the Mud Wall (today marked by Nanjing Road), and comprised almost 100 hectares. The land remained individually owned, making the British Extension a settlement, not a concession.[135] Owners of property in the extension were required to comply with British municipal regulations. These were vested in a separate municipal extension council, a body junior to the main municipal council but composed of substantially the same people and with a common staff.[136]

Continuing pressure for land led to a further area being granted for British administration in 1900. Known as the British Extra-Mural (i.e., beyond the Mud Wall) Extension, this was enormous—230 hectares, making the total British area 3.5 square kilometres. Acquiring such a large plot was opportunistic as it was not immediately needed. Much of it was unreclaimed swamp and remained so for some time. In terms of government, the new area was left to itself, but the ponds and other wet areas were filled in, using the mud and sand dredged out of the river.[137] In the early 1920s what became known as the Five Avenues area was laid out, and some 2000 foreign-style homes were built there.[138] Many still exist, in an area looking more like a suburb of London than a Chinese city.

There was a general willingness to combine the British areas. The stalwarts of the original concession considered their enclave superior to the upstarts; indeed, 98 percent of Tientsin's foreign business was conducted or headquartered there.[139] But now they were outnumbered by the population of the additional areas. H. G. W. Woodhead, influential editor of *The Peking & Tientsin Times*, brought matters to a head by starting an intensive newspaper campaign, in 1915, to bring about the amalgamation of the three areas.[140] His efforts prompted many heated discussions in the inner sanctum of Gordon Hall. One of

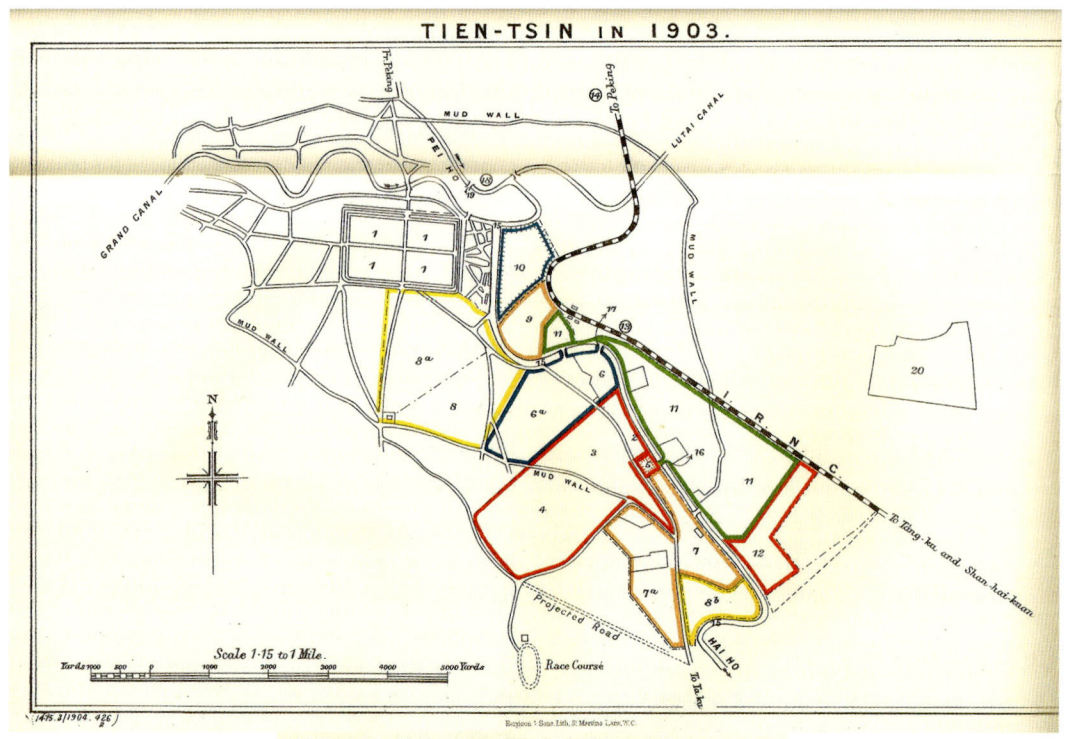

Explanation of Sketch of Tientsin in 1903.

1. Chinese city (walls pulled down to form roads). 2. British original concession. 3. British extension (settlement). 4. British extension (extra mural). 5. American concession. 6. French concession. 6A. French extension. 7. German settlement. 7A. German extension. 8. Japanese settlement. 8A. Japanese extension. 8B. Japanese additional extension (8A and 8B administered by the Chinese Government). 9. Italian settlement. 10. Austro-Hungarian settlement. 11. Russian settlement. 12. Belgian settlement (not occupied). 13. Railway station (Tientsin settlement). 14. Railway station (Tientsin city). 15. Hai ho. 16. Proposed Russian bridge. 17. International bridge. 18. Yamen of the Governor-General. 19. Iron bridg . 20. East Arsenal (French barracks).

1903 map of the foreign concessions, also showing the Mud Wall. Source: *Foreign Office Report for Tientsin*, 1903.

the trickiest issues was the tenure rights of the original concession's land-renters. When their leases expired in far-off 1960, this small but influential body of people would be faced with having to pay a potentially high premium to renew them, simply to continue enjoying the same residence benefits as people living on the other side of Taku Road, whose tenure was permanent. A solution was negotiated and new land regulations came into effect on 1 January 1919.[141]

In 1927, aligned with the realities of the times, Britain started rendition negotiations and an agreement was initialled. The Chinese government became distracted by pressing internal affairs so it remained unsigned. The British Municipal Council stayed in charge for a few more years.[142]

The French Concession

When development of the French Concession started in the 1880s it was mainly residential. In 1896 the French sought an extension to their concession, but the process was complicated by substantial British interests that had accumulated in the earmarked area. The Boxer crisis delayed matters, but on 20 November 1900 France was granted an additional 86 hectares, extending their site to the Mud Wall.[143] A number of Chinese banks made their offices in the French area, as did many retail stores; today's pedestrianized

Binjiang Road, the former rue Marechal Foch, is Tianjin's main shopping street. There remain a number of visible reminders of the period of French occupation, not least the imposing former municipal council building and the former French Consulate, both in Chengde Road. Very close to the latter is a large sprawling complex of former French military barracks. France handed back its concession in 1946.

The American Concession

The Americans played no official part in the war leading to the Tientsin concessions, yet were granted one of 13 hectares in 1860. No active American control or jurisdiction was exercised, and this plot, adjacent to the British Concession, became 'a sort of no-man's land and a focus for disorder'.[144] On 12 October 1880 the Americans advised that they no longer wanted the concession, while reserving their future right to revive their claim.[145] In the following years almost the whole area was acquired by the Chinese Engineering & Mining Co. and the China Merchants Steam Navigation Co. During the post-Boxer period, the concession was home to the United States military.[146] Subsequently, in the absence of clear responsibility for this rough area on its border, Britain offered to assume it. On 23 October 1902 it was formally absorbed within the British Municipal Extension.[147]

The German Concession

Following the Sino-Japanese War of 1894–95, Germany was quick to emphasize its assistance in containing the victorious Japanese regarding acquisition of Chinese territory. Thus, in October 1895, it obtained some for itself in Tientsin. The thin strip of land measuring some 70 hectares had about 1500 metres of river frontage.[148] Nearer the sea than the British Concession, and with a potentially much longer bund, it threatened the established interests in the treaty port. The Germans were determined to exercise tight control over their acquisition. A commercial arrangement allowed the Deutsch-Asiatische Bank to acquire the land from its Chinese owners, lay out roads and a bund, then sell individual lots.[149] In 1899 everything was transferred to a specially created management company. In 1901 Germany claimed an extension to its concession, more than doubling its size with a large plot on the western side of Taku Road.

A municipal council was formed in 1905, chaired by the German Consul.[150] Initially, development was slow; Germans living in the British and French areas were reluctant to give up their comforts.[151] Eventually, the German Concession became the most popular and best maintained of the foreign residential districts,[152] with shaded, tree-lined roads.[153] In 1907 a new German Club was erected on Wilhelm Strasse, the continuation of Victoria Road. It is still there and recognizable, despite much of its Teutonic glory being hidden by later alterations. In 1911 the German Consul moved from the British Concession into a grand new building opposite the club.[154]

When diplomatic relations between Germany and China were broken in March 1917, the concession reverted to the city as the First Special District.[155]

The Japanese Concession

Having defeated China in the war of 1894–95, the Japanese exercised their newly won right to be granted an exclusive concession. In August 1898 they marked out an area of 113 hectares adjoining the western boundary of the French Extension.[156]

In 1879 Mitsubishi became the first of the *zaibatsu* with representation in Tientsin.[157] Coal trader Mitsui was next in 1881, followed by a gradual increase of Japanese business interests in the port, especially with the creation of the Japanese Concession. Japan played a key role during the Boxer troubles and rewarded itself by announcing in December 1900 its assumption of the remaining land between its concession and the city walls, plus a small plot between the southern end of the German Concession and the Hai River.[158] The latter area hugged a bend in the river and gave the Japanese the advantage of the first landing place for incoming vessels. The total Japanese area exceeded 400 hectares.[159]

They soon found it impracticable to administer three separate areas as one. Claiming jurisdiction over a hostile population living immediately outside the city wall also had its problems. Accordingly, in 1903 the southern plot and most of the northern extension were given up.[160] What remained grew as a commercial centre as more Japanese businesses were established. About half the advertisers in a 1908 tourist guide to Tientsin are Japanese, promoting products and services including photography, musical instruments and silk goods.[161]

The Russian Concession

Russia opened a consulate in Tientsin as soon as it became a treaty port.[162] In 1867 it was located on the riverside, opposite the British Concession.[163] An impressive former Russian Consulate still stands there, just over the Daguangming Bridge. Russia's role in the deliverance of Tientsin from the Boxers prompted a concession claim. The large Russian military contingent had camped on the river's left bank and, on 6 November 1900, they claimed this area as theirs by right of conquest.[164]

The site was huge, over 400 hectares and with a massive river frontage. Eastwards it stretched to the railway line, and included the Tientsin East Station of the Peking-Mukden Railway.[165] This key Chinese-owned and -managed facility had been financed by the British, who consequently felt a proprietorial right over it. British objections led to some dangerous stand-offs with Russian soldiers detailed to guard the station. After fraught negotiations, the Russians agreed in February 1901 to relinquish the station.[166] Their presence was still very apparent, however, with the adjacent Russian municipal council building.[167]

Russia justified 'right of conquest' by arguing that imperial troops joined the Boxers, entitling it to claim the conflict came under rules of international warfare. Nobody shared this spurious view. Even the Russians were unconvinced. In May 1901 Russian authorities were quietly buying out the private owners of the land in their concession, land they claimed they already owned.[168]

The land Russia took was mainly either agricultural or undeveloped. However, its proximity to the railway station gave it great commercial appeal. By 1903 timber and coal yards had arrived. In later years large factories appeared, including those of Standard Oil and British-American Tobacco. A few industrial facilities remain along the riverfront of the former concession. By 1907 the Russian area was 'the prettiest spot in Tientsin', with many trees and shaded places.[169] China resumed control of the concession in 1920 after withdrawing diplomatic recognition from the Soviet Union, renaming it the Third Special District.[170]

The Belgian Concession

Belgian engineers were active in the early days of China's railway development but their country was not one of the Eight Powers that tackled the Boxers. On 7 November 1900, the day after the Russian announcement, the Belgian Consul in Tientsin made one of his own. Belgium claimed a concession of almost 100 hectares at the southern end of the Russian claim.[171] Perhaps it was the attraction of being next to the railway line that drew them, but the Belgians did little with their new possession. There was a Belgian Municipal Council[172] but the Belgian Consulate stayed in the British Concession.[173] The land was voluntarily rendited in August 1929.[174]

The Italian Concession

Italy had been one of the Eight Powers, and on 1 December 1900 it announced that it too expected some land, possibly because everyone else was getting some. Demonstrating a real need for an Italian Concession would be challenging. Nevertheless, China confirmed the 50-hectare concession's existence in June 1901. It was exceptionally well laid out by the Italians. There were broad, well-paved streets and it became a very popular refuge for Chinese politicians and warlords. Palatial residences were built,[175] many still surviving in what today is called 'Italian-Style Town'. The Italian Concession lasted the longest, formally relinquished on 10 February 1947.[176]

The Austro-Hungarian Concession

The last member of the Eight-Nation Alliance to be rewarded with a slice of Tientsin, on 7 September

1901, was the Austro-Hungarian Empire. They received a 70-hectare lot, to the north of the Italians and opposite the old city. Apart from a short distance along the city wall, this acquisition made over 20 kilometres of riverbank that was now in the hands of foreigners. Very few Austrians or Hungarians lived in their new concession. Indeed, it was almost exclusively occupied by Chinese. Municipal matters came under an administrative secretary from the consulate, supported by a council of six leading Chinese residents whose lives carried on much as before. One of the most noted residents was Yuan Shikai, who lived there from 1912 to 1916. His house still stands, looking splendid. On the day that China declared war on the Central Powers, 14 August 1917, Chinese police marched into the concession and took it over, renaming it the Second Special District.[177]

The 20th century and industrialization

At the beginning of the 20th century two innovations changed the nature of Tientsin's trade. First, the single-track railway to Peking, opened in 1897, was so successful that the line was doubled in 1898; by 1905 almost half the trade with the interior was carried by rail.[178] Second, the vexed issue of foreigners engaging in manufacturing was resolved by the Japanese Treaty of Shimonoseki.

Cotton was still the principal export but, as was the case with so many of China's commodities, when popularity rose quality fell. By 1910 it was accepted that action was necessary; raw cotton was arriving in Tientsin containing up to 39 percent moisture by weight. The following year saw the formation of the Tientsin Cotton Anti-Adulteration Society. Imperial Edicts were issued requiring all cotton coming into Tientsin to be tested, not only cotton destined for export. A central testing facility was created in the Russian Concession, under the supervision of the Maritime Customs. Moisture was reduced to a much more acceptable ten percent.[179]

Cotton was not only being exported in its raw form. From 1916, modern cotton spinning and weaving mills were established, by both Chinese and foreign investors. With European and American production being diverted towards war goods, the Tientsin factories were busy and profitable. Flour milling started about the same time, and was equally successful. Match factories already existed, but were also re-energized.[180] Camel wool, brought to Tientsin from Tibet, was exported to the United States, where it was used for making carpets.[181] In the 1920s carpet factories began operating in Tientsin, and by the end of the decade they numbered 161. Surprisingly, apart from the four foreign-run concerns only one used machinery.[182] In 1914 the Tientsin Mint produced the first Yuan Shikai coins, under new National Currency Regulations that decreed that the Chinese currency henceforth be known as the 'yuan'.[183]

During these years of commercial growth the foreign population swelled; Tientsin was second only to Shanghai in terms of business volume. Fear of losing ground to Tsingtao (Qingdao), due to its ice-free status, proved groundless. There were powerful vested interests in Tientsin, and the Chinese much preferred to operate under their own system of government.[184] By 1914 there were 20 firms employing 10 or more European staff.[185] The foreign population in 1921 stood at over 11,000, including 1200 Japanese.[186]

Generally, Tientsin was a pleasant place to live for foreigners at that time. Churches were well established. The mainly Protestant British had All Saints Church, a classic building that still graces Tai'an Avenue. The predominantly Catholic French had St. Joseph's Cathedral, at the southern end of rue Marechal Foch, as well as the twice rebuilt Notre Dame, which found itself in the Austrian Concession. Both of these are still there, the former having been reconsecrated in 1980. For the non-conformists there was the Wesleyan Chapel just off Victoria Road, these days unused.

Roads were improved significantly as motorcars and buses became popular. An electric tram was built by a Belgian concern at the beginning of the century. The first in China, it had a network of twelve kilometres, all double-track,[187] linking the old city to the main railway station via the Japanese and French concessions.[188] The Tientsin Club, bastion of the foreign community, moved into impressive new premises in 1905, conveniently adjacent to the Astor House hotel and a short walk from Gordon Hall.[189] The club building is still there, although access is not possible. From 1901 Kiessling's had been a popular restaurant and confectioner in the German Concession. This institution, having survived all the vicissitudes of 20th-century China, now occupies a newer building on the site of the old Victoria Café and still serves good food and home-brewed beer.

A number of eye-catching buildings from the 1920s can still be seen, many in excellent condition. Next to the headquarters of the Kailan Mining Administration on Tai'an Avenue is the residence of the British Consul-General. The former Victoria Road hosts a long line of extremely grand foreign bank buildings, monuments to the glory days of treaty port commerce. The most impressive is that of the Hongkong & Shanghai Bank, from 1924.[190] This and many others are now serving the Bank of China and its affiliates. On the same road are the former residence of the British Vice-Consul and the attractive former offices of Jardines and Butterfield & Swire.

The entire city becomes a Japanese Concession

The wave of anti-British demonstrations that convulsed Shanghai and other treaty ports in the 1920s spread south, avoiding Tientsin.[191] The main threat came later from Japan. In 1937 the Japanese population had mushroomed to 45,000.[192] That year Japanese troops occupied the remaining non-foreign areas; apart from their own, only the British, French and Italian concessions remained. Next, they blockaded the British Concession, ostensibly to obtain the release of 'Chinese terrorists' held in British gaols.[193] In 1939 the British Municipal Council, in emergency session, agreed to closer cooperation with the Japanese on law and order. Specifically, it was agreed that Japanese police should be present whenever British municipal police took action 'against persons in whose criminal activities the Japanese authorities are interested'.[194] By 1941 this meant everybody.

Further reading: Bickers and Tiedemann, *The Boxers, China and the World*; Burton St. John, *Guide to Tientsin*; Coates, *China Races*; Johnston and Erh, *Far from Home*; McLeish, *Life in a China Outport*; Rasmussen, *Tientsin*; Rawlinson, *China's Struggle for Naval Development*.

Tsinan (Jinan) 濟南

Freighters at Tientsin (Tianjin) Bund, 1930s. Source: *China Proper*, Vol. 3, 414.

Shandong, 36.40° N, 116.59° E
Open City, 1904 Imperial Decree

The lease of Kiaochow (Jiaozhou) to Germany in 1898 included the right to construct a 320-kilometre railway from Tsingtao (Qingdao) to Tsinan, the provincial capital of Shandong. It was completed in 1904. In an attempt to limit Germany's influence, and prompted by Japan, an Imperial Decree of 18 May opened Tsinan to foreign trade.

Tsinan and Shandong were of great interest to Japan as well as Germany. Along with Britain and, somewhat later, America, these countries established a significant consular presence. Land for a German Consulate had already been acquired in 1903. The chief engineer of the Shantung Railway, Heinrich Hildebrand, designed the impressive building, today used as city government offices.[1] A British Consulate was opened in June 1905, the better to observe German activity. The first incumbent was given the best reception of any new consul anywhere. He was invited to a grand banquet by the governor. Just as dinner was about to be served, the band struck up 'God Save the King' then 'Rule Britannia', expressing Chinese pleasure at having such a powerful counter to the Germans.[2] An extremely grand British consular residence was built in 1918, unfortunately demolished 'illegally' very recently.[3]

The Catholic Cathedral is the most impressive of Jinan's Christian churches. When it was completed in 1908 it was the largest church in northern China.[4] The site had been a missionary centre since at least 1866. After its opening in the 1910s the Shantung Christian University was soon referred to as the premier educational institution in China.[5] Some of the early buildings still grace the modern Shandong University campus.

The Foreign Settlement, inaugurated in January 1906, was reasonably well run by the municipal authorities. A designated police force was created, initially under a European superintendent supported by 10 Indian and 40 Chinese constables.[6] Streets were well paved and a public park was created at its centre.[7] A cluster of German-era buildings can be found at the junction of Wei'er and Jingyi roads, including the German Consulate and the Chinese Post Office. The former Deutsch-Asiatische Bank building still reflects the political and economic might it was designed to portray. In 1910 a second railway added to Tsinan's importance when the city became the halfway point on the Tientsin-Pukow line, linking the city to Peking (Beijing) in the north and Nanking (Nanjing) in the south. The station serving the Tsingtao line had only been completed in 1904, but when the much more grand Tientsin-Pukow station appeared in 1912, 60 metres to the north, the old one had to go; it was an insufficiently powerful statement of German prestige. Its replacement can be seen today on Jingyi Road, built in 1914.[8] (The other station was demolished in 1992, but there is now talk of recreating it.)[9]

In November 1914 German prestige received a bigger blow, when Japan snatched Tsingtao, together

Deutsch-Asiatische Bank Building, 1908. Source: Warner, *German Architecture in China*, 189. © Wilhelm Ernst & Sohn Verlag für Architektur und technische Wissenschaften GmbH & Co. KG. Reproduced with permission.

with all German possessions, infrastructure and influence in Shandong. There was an influx of Japanese into Tsinan and much new building. Their 1916 consulate is no more, but the former Japanese Military Police Station still exudes an air of ruthless authority. Whereas Germany's aims had been mainly political and commercial, those of Japan were military and territorial. Japanese soldiers were happy to give assistance to local rebels when a riot turned into something worse in 1916. When the rebels fled to the foreign, now Japanese, settlement the Japanese did nothing to stop them, and prevented government forces from giving chase. Protests to the Japanese Minister in Peking were to no avail as Japan continued to exercise far more than 'influence' over Shandong.[10]

The 1920s saw Germans returning to Tsinan, and their consulate was reopened in 1922. By then it was the Japanese who were in charge. In 1928 the Japanese caused Tsinan to give its name to one of the many 'incidents' that punctuate early 20th-century Chinese history. In April, rumours of the imminent fall of the provincial capital to Chiang Kai-shek's Nationalists prompted an influx of Japanese troops on the pretext of protecting Japanese interests. The incident occurred in May; Chiang's forces were repulsed and the Japanese took possession of Tsinan, and much else. They were to remain in occupation for twelve months.[11] When full-scale war broke out between China and Japan in 1937, Japanese troops once more took possession of the city and remained until 1945.

Further reading: Warner, *German Architecture in China*.

TSINGTAO (QINGDAO) 青島

Shandong, 36.05° N, 120.19° E
Leased Territory, 1898 Germany

Tsingtao sits at the mouth of a bay that is one of the best harbours in China. When it was opened by Germany as a free port on 2 September 1898, flags flew from every hut.[1] Tsingtao was tiny but potentially important, not least because the quality of the locally brewed beer was about to improve. The Germans were not the first to be interested in the area. William Jardine badgered Lord Palmerston in 1840 to include Kiaochow (Jiaozhou) Bay in his list of desired treaty ports.[2] German interest was first aroused in 1866 when Baron Ferdinand von Richthofen, uncle of the future fighter ace 'The Red Baron', conducted a survey of the China Coast. The unified German state was about to be established and wanted its share of the Chinese 'cake'. Richthofen was a noted geologist, and claimed to be looking for coal.[3] His ulterior motive was to identify a suitable depot for his country's emerging navy.[4] His report was ignored for the next 30 years.[5]

Green Island (in Chinese, Qingdao) off the eastern entrance to the bay was a base against pirates.[6] A Qing garrison and some crude fortifications were on the mainland, but Tsingtao was of little importance except to fishermen.[7] After the Sino-Japanese War of 1894–95 Germany, Russia and France combined to force Japan to relinquish its newly captured territory in the Liaodong Peninsula.[8] Wanting a reward for its official entry onto the Chinese stage, Germany asked to establish a coaling station at Kiaochow Bay. The request was denied. A secret agreement between China and Russia had already conditionally promised the place to Russia, and Russian ships were wintering there.[9] The agreement was that Russia could lease Kiaochow for 15 years if 'there should suddenly arise military operations' requiring Russian involvement. Until this happened Russia was not to occupy Kiaochow 'in order to obviate the chance of exciting the jealousy and suspicion of other Powers'.[10]

But the German Emperor had already become both excited and impatient, particularly by the huge territorial gains being made by his cousin, the Russian Tsar. In November 1894 he suggested seizing Formosa (Taiwan).[11] He also wanted Amoy (Xiamen). The German fleet under Admiral von Tirpitz was ordered to Amoy in 1896, prepared to take it by force. The British presence deterred them,[12] combined with the decision that Kiaochow would be Germany's best option as no other power was much interested in Shandong. Gustav Detring, of the Chinese Imperial Maritime Customs, and Li Hongzhang visited Berlin in 1896. The Kaiser quizzed them about Germany gaining a foothold in China. Both advised him against taking such a step because of potential repercussions.[13] Undeterred, in 1896 Wilhelm sent Admiral Otto von Diederichs to survey Kiaochow. Several engineers followed in 1897 to investigate the possibility of harbour installations.[14] In London, the British government considered the opening of Kiaochow as a treaty port. British Minister in Peking (Beijing) Sir Claude MacDonald doubted Kiaochow's commercial value, but thought its opening would usefully scupper German plans.[15]

Two German Catholic missionaries were murdered on 1 November 1897 in rural Shandong, victims of armed robbers. This was no orchestrated attack on Germans or foreigners in general.[16] Chinese authorities immediately investigated the matter; local villagers had also been killed. But Kaiser Wilhelm saw only an advantage to exploit. Cloaking opportunism in righteous indignation he implemented his plans.[17]

On 14 November Diederichs returned to Kiaochow with his fleet and, landing 600 marines, occupied a position overlooking the Qing barracks and its 2000 occupants.[18] The surprised Chinese commander offered the visitors the use of his drill ground, thinking this was the purpose of landing so many men.[19] Instead, Diederichs gave his host two hours to vacate his post—or face the consequences.[20]

News of this heavy-handed action travelled quickly, and reactions were mixed. Obviously Russia and Germany had colluded.[21] *The Times* admired the Kaiser's direct approach, avoiding 'wasting time making remonstrances at Peking, which would assuredly have been met as usual by the innumerable dilatory devices of Chinese diplomacy'.[22] The paper even questioned why Britain bothered using diplomacy at all. In Hong Kong, the *Weekly Press* was equally enthusiastic: 'We congratulate our German friends upon the blow which they have struck for the freedom of foreign residents in China.'[23]

Others were less jubilant. In Peking, Li Hongzhang led the protests, astonished by the unannounced seizure of Chinese territory by a supposedly friendly nation.[24] Sir Robert Hart wrote: 'The German action simply drives me wild—it is so high-handed and opposed to all that's right, and it is so likely to attract imitation. Poor China!'[25] He added, 'having tasted "blood", I fear the Germans will want, not merely a steak, but a sirloin, round, and big!'[26] The order for the sirloin followed rapidly, showing the action was long planned. The German Minister presented his country's terms on 22 November, including the demand that the Chinese government defray Germany's occupation costs. This formula was commonly used by foreign powers whose pride had been hurt, and was agreed. China also accepted the German demand of leased territory in the bay area.[27]

The more significant demands were that Germany receive preference in the building of railways in Shandong, and the right to work any mines developed along the track. There was resistance to these proposals as they were counter to the Most Favoured Nation principle. Britain had been negotiating, unsuccessfully, for railway rights in the province.[28] By force, Germany succeeded where Britain failed.

The Germans were pleased with their achievements. On 6 March 1898, while maintaining the fiction of Chinese sovereignty, they gained a 99-year lease of both sides of the entrance to the bay, the bay itself up to the shoreline, and a number of islands—more than 500 square kilometres in all. A neutral zone was recognized in the 50-kilometre belt surrounding the leased area, extending the immediate German sphere of influence to over 7000 square kilometres.[29] (Hong Kong at that time covered a little over 100 square kilometres.)

Using nerve and brute force, Germany had upset the precarious balance between the European Powers. Lord Salisbury was reluctant to retaliate by demanding another British possession. Other nations showed fewer scruples, proving Hart's fears to be correct. Three weeks after the signing of the German lease, Russia signed a similar document covering Port Arthur (Lüshun) and Talienwan (Dalianwan). France followed on 22 April with a lease of Kwangchowwan

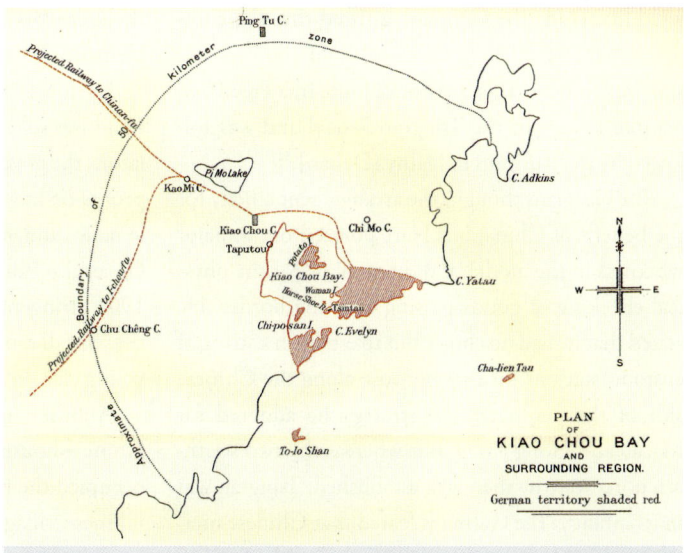

1898 map of the area leased by Germany, and the 50-kilometre buffer zone. Source: *Foreign Office Report for Chefoo*, 1898.

(Zhanjiang). Britain, feeling outmanoeuvred, took a lease on Weihaiwei (Weihai) on 24 May, and on the New Territory of Hong Kong in June. Japan, having been coerced by three of these four into giving back Liaodong three years earlier, watched and waited, knowing its time would come.

A Custom House for the free port

Although military installations were among the first to be built, the Germans valued Tsingtao's potential as a commercial port. German trade in China was second only to British, although still far behind.[30] The Germans had been granted concessions in Hankow (Hankou) and Tientsin (Tianjin) and, seeing the success of Hong Kong, they were determined to run their own colony.

However, it was British experience that prompted Germany to allow an anomalous Custom House in its new free port. Hong Kong had suffered many years a virtual blockade of its harbour by the Maritime Customs; while the port was free, the passage of goods over the border with China was not, and this gave rise to smuggling and preventive strategies, both on a large scale. On 17 April 1899 an agreement was signed to establish a Tsingtao Custom House. All goods brought into the port would be free of duty; if they subsequently passed into China, then duty would be paid. The Germans insisted that the commissioner and as many as possible of the customs staff be German. This 'Custom House in a Free Port' became known as the Tsingtao Model and was followed by the Russians in Dalny (Dalian).[31]

The Germans thought the arrangement chiefly for the benefit of China, but Hart pointed out a major weakness in the model: it did not allow for the physical checking of goods passing over the border. He stated that he had no choice but to establish a string of customs stations for that purpose along the Chinese side of the perimeter, the strategy he adopted for Macao and Hong Kong. But whereas the two southern ports were by then well established, Tsingtao was in its infancy. The Germans feared that Chinese merchants would set up their businesses on the 'wrong' side of the border, depriving the new port of much of its development potential.[32]

In 1905 a new arrangement determined the free port to be, in effect, the dock area.[33] The Custom House was moved to the dock gate and all inspection and taxing of goods was done there. As a concession to the Germans for the additional administrative burden, it was agreed that 20 percent of all revenue collected would be paid to the colonial government.[34] Business was set to boom.

A German showpiece

Germany spent vast amounts making Tsingtao a showpiece of German culture, efficiency and military prowess. During German administration, far more was spent than was earned; the colony never came even close to paying its way.[35] The German Admiralty administered Tsingtao, so the money came from the deep pockets of the navy.[36] Land auctions were held on 3 October 1898,[37] triggering a building bonanza. Enormous military barracks and hospitals appeared, as well as missionary establishments, schools and private houses. Rapid expansion in the 21st century has pushed the city centre eastwards, removing pressure to redevelop the older areas. Consequently, many German buildings remain, giving the modern city its unique flavour. As there was virtually nothing there, the Germans were able to plan a street layout complementing their vision of a physically striking city. A development plan was published in April 1899.[38] Land was sold rather than leased, but, to deter speculators, the government reserved for itself a share in the profits on any subsequent sales.[39] Hygiene was problematic, and many soldiers died of typhoid. When Governor Paul Jaeschke also succumbed in January 1901 stringent changes were made. These included the installation of two-metre drains,[40] giving the young city the highest standards in Asia.[41]

Another innovation was the way in which Chinese housing was dealt with. While the Germans occupied the picturesque coastal area of the city, the Chinese villagers were resettled in well-constructed brick-built dwellings laid out on broad streets just to the north. Regulations were issued concerning public cleanliness. The streets were not laid on the traditional Chinese east-west axis, but were rotated through 45 degrees. In this way they were aligned with the prevailing wind, and there were no cold, damp north-facing walls.[42]

The railway and other early developments

In October 1899 Prince Heinrich of Prussia, the Kaiser's younger brother, visited and opened a luxurious hotel named after him. He also cut the first sod of the new railway.[43] Surveying had been completed and progress was rapid. By June 1902, when 86 Germans worked for the railway company,[44] the line extended 130 kilometres north-west to the coal-producing area of Fangtze (Fangzi).[45] Two years later the network reached 320 kilometres to the provincial capital, Tsinan (Jinan).[46] By 1912, with the completion of other lines in China, it took only 14 days to travel from Tsingtao to Berlin.[47]

The Shantung Mining Co. was formed in Berlin in 1899 and was quick to capitalize on the possibilities opened by the railway. The company's 1902 former head office building still stands next to that of the Deutsch-Asiatische Bank on Taiping Road. The extension of the railway to Tsinan enabled access to the better quality output of the Hungshan (Hongshan) mines.[48] Coal became an important export, and the company a major employer of foreign staff—144 of them by 1905. Beancake and straw braid also grew in importance as the railway attracted these items away from their traditional port of Chefoo (Yantai).[49]

Construction of Tsingtao's harbour began in March 1901. By 1903 the colony had the most modern facility in Asia.[50] It was lit by electricity, and the railway tracks extended right up to the wharves. In due course, the timing of the trains was synchronized with the shipping schedules so as to minimize waiting time.[51] By the end of 1905 there was also a dry dock capable of taking the largest ships then sailing in eastern waters.[52]

The government and the governed

Despite the investment Berlin was making in its colony, a German Foreign Office report in 1900 stressed the importance of the independence of the Tsingtao administration from the home government. A municipal council was created, under the direct supervision of the governor. A modest residence was built for him near the eastern entrance to the bay.[53] Work began in October 1905[54] on the large mansion still standing today. In 1907 the fourth governor, Oskar von Truppel, had an uninterrupted view of the burgeoning commercial city to his right and the military barracks to his left.

Of the two main barracks, it was commenced in October 1899. This was for the navy; the governor and all his senior officers were naval men. It serves today as a People's Liberation Army Navy base. Bismarck Barracks, built from 1903 to 1909 on the site of the earlier Qing equivalent,[55] was for the army. It now houses the Ocean University.

Closer to the governor's residence was the town hall, the administrative centre of the colony. While built on a grand scale in 1904–6,[56] it still had to be enlarged years later. The additions to the original building are such that it is virtually impossible to 'see the join' today. The enlarged building still carries on the functions it was designed for.

From its earliest days, Tsingtao attracted all the major German firms operating in China. One of the

The 'modest residence' built for the first governor. Source: Warner, *German Architecture in China*, 293. © Wilhelm Ernst & Sohn Verlag für Architektur und technische Wissenschaften GmbH & Co. KG. Reproduced with permission.

most important was Carlowitz & Co., whose office building still stands on Taiping Road. Imports comprised everything to get the city and port up and running. Exports included groundnuts, vegetable oil, silk, cotton and beer. In 1905 the Anglo-German Brewery Co. of Hong Kong opened the Germania Brauerei.[57]

Seven years old as a German colony, Tsingtao was preparing in 1905 for its first season as a tourist destination. The Auguste-Victoria Bay beach, east of the city, was very popular with bathers. The Prinz Heinrich Hotel opened an annex there in 1904, the Strand Hotel, now commercial offices. There were holiday villas for rent, the racetrack was being widened and returfed, there was a sports ground and good walking in the newly wooded hills.[58] A tourist guide from 1906 called the place 'Tsingtao' instead of Kiaochow. The new name was becoming official.[59] The foreign population in 1907 had risen to 1654, excluding the military, of whom 1412 were German.[60] The revolution of 1911 hardly affected Tsingtao, apart from creating a building boom accommodating wealthy Chinese who were escaping the troubles.[61] By 1911 the small fishing village had become the sixth-largest port in China.[62]

A CHANGE OF OWNERSHIP

In 1911 the Socialist opposition in the German Reichstag demanded the retrocession of Tsingtao. Tirpitz, by then Minister for the Navy, the rulers of the colony, countered by saying if Tsingtao were given back 'Germany would surrender her whole position in China.'[63] This was about to happen, but in a way neither Tirpitz nor his opponents could have imagined.

As Europe collapsed towards war in July 1914, Japan saw a potential reward for its long years of patience. Defeat of the Russians in 1905 had given the Japanese confidence to mount the world stage. An increasingly suspicious Britain nevertheless renewed and strengthened its alliance with Japan in 1911, giving the Japanese the platform they needed. As war plans were discussed, Britain reluctantly accepted the Japanese marching into Shandong, provided the

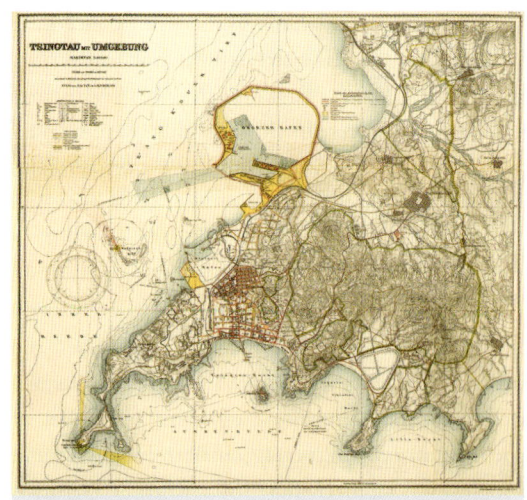

1913 map showing the impressive results of 15 years of German development. Reprinted with permission by the National Archives.

German colony was handed back to China eventually. Japan agreed; 'eventually' could be a very long time.[64]

Tsingtao's defences had been strengthened in early 1914 and martial law was imposed on 1 August. On 15 August Japan, acting as an ally of Britain, issued an ultimatum to Germany: hand over Kiaochow unconditionally, or action will be taken to secure its transfer. Seizure of the territory, Japan maintained, would be a step towards its eventual return to China. A deadline of 23 August was given.[65] At this late stage Germany offered to retrocede its colony but, faced with Japanese threats, China refused the offer.[66] Japan was not about to be cheated out of its long-awaited vengeance.

On 26 August the Japanese fleet appeared off Tsingtao accompanied by a token British destroyer; Britain wanted to be involved, in the hope of influencing the final outcome. A blockade of the port was enforced. On 3 September a force of 50,000 Japanese troops landed at the small port of Lungkow (Longkou), 170 kilometres to the north.[67] This army captured all the towns and cities it came across on its relentless march south. By 18 September the Japanese were ready to commence the assault on Tsingtao. On the 26th they were joined by 1300 British and Sikh soldiers, sent from Tientsin.[68] The defenders numbered 1600 troops, augmented by 3000 conscripts, almost every able-bodied German who could be found in China.[69]

A difficult and bloody battle followed. German defences proved to be thorough, but the invaders' strength of numbers told. The Japanese marked their emperor's birthday on 31 October by firing the traditional salutes, using untraditional live rounds. During the night of 1–2 November the Germans blew up their prized dock installations.[70] A white flag appeared over the governor's residence on 7 November.[71]

The British troops stayed for another fortnight before being sent to France via Hong Kong.[72] Britain and its allies immediately asked when the Japanese would honour their pledge to return Tsingtao to China. Carl Crow, an American journalist who had been in Shanghai since 1911, claimed that it was common knowledge that Japan, although an ally of Britain, was hoping for a German victory in the war as this would give Tokyo the freedom of action in Asia that it sought.[73] In early 1915 the British Cabinet recognized that, useful as the Japanese contribution had been to the Allies' war effort, there were unlikely to be any others.[74] Indeed, it was feared that to press the Japanese to send their troops to the European theatre would come at a high price concerning Japan's ambitions as a world power.[75]

No one was prepared for what Japan did next. On 18 January 1915 Tokyo issued its infamous 'Twenty-One Demands' to China. These included the consolidation of Japanese gains in Shandong and Manchuria. With particular respect to Kiaochow, Japan demanded that China give full assent to arrangements that Japan and Germany might reach regarding territorial and development rights. Most of the demands were encapsulated in two Sino-Japanese treaties, signed on 25 May 1915.

The Japanese attacks had targeted the forts and other defences, carefully avoiding damage elsewhere, thus saving that beloved institution—the Tsingtao brewery.[76] Dai Nippon Beer Co. bought the remaining British shares and promised to leave the flavour unaltered, a tradition that still survives.[77] More factories were built in the later war years, including silk, soap, canned goods and cotton.[78] Work began reclaiming a 47-hectare site near the harbour for further industrial expansion.[79] A new commercial focus grew in what is now Guantao Road, where many buildings from the period survive, including those of Hongkong Bank and Butterfield & Swire.

Customs arrangements were agreed on the same lines as the former German scheme;[80] the 1914 Custom House still stands on Xinjiang Road. Japan administered its new possession efficiently and sensibly. Twenty years of vitriol against Germany in the Japanese press came to an abrupt end on the taking of Tsingtao. The Germans were portrayed as the real criminals behind the forcing of Japan from Port Arthur in 1895 as, unlike Russia and France, they had had no prior interest in China.[81] That crime was purged, but the question of ultimate sovereignty remained unanswered.

China declared war on Germany in 1917, not in anticipation of fighting the enemy but in the hope of gaining a seat at the victors' table. At the Paris Peace Conference in 1919 China was given a seat, but no voice. To China's dismay the conference upheld the Japanese occupation of Chinese territory. This insult gave rise to the May Fourth Movement, named after a student protest that year in Peking. British Cabinet papers reveal that 18 months before the war ended Britain had assured Japan it would support the latter's claims in Kiaochow and elsewhere north of the equator, in return for Japanese non-interference with British claims in the southern hemisphere.[82] There was nothing China could do except refuse to sign the peace treaty. It was not until the Washington Conference of 1921–22 that reason prevailed and the former German territory was restored to Chinese sovereignty.

In 1898 the Chinese government had lost a fishing village. In 1922 it regained a major port and a well-planned, attractive and efficiently run city. The Japanese remained a strong presence; during the war years their number had increased from 1000 to 24,000,[83] buying land all over the city[84] and continuing what the Germans had started. The business profile was more international than under German administration and trade already exceeded pre-war levels.[85]

Between the Germans and the Japanese, major industrial zones developed along the railway lines north of the city: iron and coal mining, as well as textile, brick, cement, silk and vegetable oil manufacturing.[86] There were locomotive and carriage works. Shandong produced 30 percent of China's tobacco, which supplied the large Tsingtao factories of British-American Tobacco.[87] By the 1930s the port's volume of trade was behind only Shanghai, Tientsin and Dairen.[88] Henan and Zhongshan roads still host impressive bank buildings from this time.

Tourists and holidaymakers flooded back. The Prinz Heinrich Hotel had become the Grand, with the Grand Strand as its annex. The Edgewater Mansions Hotel was completed in 1937, in time to host a coronation ball in honour of King George VI.[89] This ultimate statement in luxury boasted a sea-facing balcony and private bathroom for each of its bedrooms.[90]

Another change of ownership

Tsingtao was remarkably little affected by the boycotts and disturbances of the 1920s. Even in 1931, during another anti-Japanese boycott, Tsingtao's commercial relations with Japan remained 'almost normal'.[91] But rumours of the fall to rebel forces of the provincial capital in April 1928 saw Japanese troops sent to Tsinan, ostensibly to protect Japanese nationals. A clash between these troops and the Nationalist army prompted the deployment of heavy Japanese reinforcements, who occupied not only Tsinan, but also the railway line and Tsingtao. They withdrew twelve months later.[92] Trouble at the city's Japanese cotton mills in December 1936 precipitated the landing of 1000 Japanese marines. They not only patrolled the manufacturing district, but also occupied the wharf, the airfield and the railway station.[93] More was to follow. As part of their invasion of China, Japanese forces occupied Tsingtao on 10 January 1938. This time they stayed over seven years.

Further reading: Hoyt, Johnston and Erh, *Far from Home*; *The Fall of Tsingtao*; Nield, 'Bits of Broken China'; Otte, *The China Question*; Schrecker, *Imperialism and Chinese Nationalism*; Warner, *German Architecture in China*.

Wanhsien (Wanzhou) 萬州

Chongqing Municipality, 30.48° N, 108.22° E
Open City, 1917 Presidential Mandate

Situated on the Yangtze halfway between Ichang (Yichang) and Chungking (Chongqing), Wanhsien was listed as a treaty port in the 1902 British Commercial Treaty. The relevant clause depended upon China abandoning *likin*. When this proved impossible, the clause lapsed. In 1917, the Chinese government opened the port on its own initiative and on 16 March a foreign-managed Custom House was established.[1] The small walled town was a distribution centre for eastern Sichuan. Except for the import of kerosene, business was exclusive to Chinese merchants. The dominant export was wood-oil.[2]

Apart from a few customs men and missionaries, the only foreigners were the crews of gunboats and commercial steamers. This otherwise insignificant place gave rise to two 'incidents', so common in early 20th-century Chinese history. In 1924 an American was killed during a riot among lightermen. HMS *Cockchafer*'s British commander ordered local officials to execute those responsible. Two men were beheaded, but questions were asked in the House of Commons about the officer's conduct. The Royal Navy supported his actions and the matter lapsed.[3]

The second, more serious incident happened in 1926. A local warlord tried to requisition two Butterfield & Swire steamers to transport his troops. The company refused.[4] Soon afterwards, when a junk full of soldiers was upturned by the wash of a passing steamer, the general seized the vessels, together with their six European officers, and held them captive.[5] Negotiations for their release were heated and inconclusive.[6] HMS *Cockchafer* was again on station, but its crew were seriously outnumbered by the Chinese

Dramatic depiction of the 1926 Wanhsien (Wanzhou) Incident. Source: WikiSwire.

soldiers holding the two ships. When British reinforcements arrived on 5 September they attempted to board the vessels and free the captives. In a strong Chinese response, seven British sailors were killed. The British gunboats opened fire, shelling the shore batteries and some civilian areas. Five Swires employees were rescued and one lost overboard.[7]

This quintessential piece of gunboat diplomacy came at an inopportune moment. Chiang Kai-shek was busy galvanizing his forces along the lower stretches of the Yangtze. News of the incident enabled him to instil even more enthusiasm into his men.[8] The anti-British boycott that followed the shelling, and the evacuation of its few foreign residents the following year, effectively closed this open city.[9]

Weihaiwei (Weihai) 威海

Shandong, 37.30° N, 122.07° E
Leased Territory, 1898 Britain

The British were not strangers to the Territory of Weihaiwei when, in 1898, they signed the lease. In 1816 Lord Amherst, while on his ill-fated mission to Peking (Beijing), had dropped anchor in 'Oei-aei-oei' bay but moved on, unable to obtain supplies.[1]

Lindsay's mission of 1832 concluded that Shandong had little to offer in exchange for foreign imports, describing the walled town of Weihaiwei as 'merely a small village'. An inscription indicated that the town and its wall had been built in 1400 to protect the area from Japanese pirates.[2] As Chinese walled cities go, Weihaiwei was tiny, despite the grand meaning of its name—Garrison City of the Majestic Ocean.[3]

Weihaiwei next came to British attention during the Anglo-French expedition to Tientsin (Tianjin) and Peking in 1860. HMS *Actaeon* anchored off Liukungtao (Liugongdao), the main island in the bay, in April, allowing General Wolseley a brief reconnoitre of the harbour. He found it too exposed to easterly winds and lacking fresh water.[4] No fuel or supplies of any sort could be obtained, apart from a few sheep and poultry.[5] Notwithstanding, a British government paper of 1869 expressed the opinion that Weihaiwei might be a useful port of refuge.[6]

Weihaiwei becomes a naval base

A plaque in Liukungtao commemorates a Chinese naval machinery facility in 1879, and a coaling station in 1881. The action of the French, in particular their destruction in 1884 of the new shipyard and arsenal they had helped to build at Foochow (Fuzhou), added a sense of urgency to China's modernization efforts. Prompted and sponsored by Li Hongzhang, Peking ordered that Weihaiwei be used as a base for its Beiyang (North Sea) Fleet. As Germany was seen as the rising power in Europe, German military engineers were engaged to advise on fortifying Liukungtao.

Twelve stone and concrete fortresses, many of which survive today, were built on the island under the supervision of military engineer Constantin von Hanneken.[7] The admiral commanding the Beiyang Fleet, Ding Ruchang, also headed the new Naval College, opened in 1890. Five senior British and American naval officers were attached to the college in various supervisory positions, plus a further 27 on the ships anchored in the harbour.[8]

These preparations were timely, as on 1 August 1894 the Sino-Japanese War commenced. Admiral

Ding's fleet engaged the Japanese on 17 September at the mouth of the Yalu River near the border between China and Korea. Both sides suffered heavy casualties and the Chinese were forced back to Weihaiwei, where Ding was ordered to remain. Rather than risk the wrath of the huge guns pointing at their warships, the Japanese landed troops inland and captured the fortresses on the mainland. From there they could fire at the Chinese, knowing that the guns on the island were fixed and posed no threat.

Japanese torpedo boats broke through the curtain of mines, and enemy vessels poured through the breach, intent on destruction. The flagships of the British and German eastern fleets stood close by and could only watch as the newly repaired Beiyang ships were annihilated, along with most of the naval facilities on Liukungtao.[9] When Ding's ammunition ran out, he ordered the white flag to be raised[10] and swallowed a lethal dose of opium, as did a number of his senior officers—a sad end to such high hopes.[11] The Articles of Surrender of 14 February 1895 allowed the admiral's coffin to be removed without interference from the Japanese 'solely out of respect for the soul of Admiral Ting [sic], who did his duty towards his country'.[12] The brave man's remains were taken to Chefoo (Yantai), where they were received with all due reverence.[13]

Britain takes a lease

Japan took formal possession of Liukungtao on 17 February 1895 and, under the terms of the Treaty of Shimonoseki, was to remain there until China paid its war indemnity. The final payment was made on 7 May 1898[14] but long before then the international community was wondering what would happen next. The Qing government was on the verge of collapse and likely to take the country with it. A scramble for Chinese territory seemed inevitable. The British wanted neither to lag behind nor take the lead. On 25 February 1898 the Chinese government indicated to Sir Claude MacDonald, British Minister in Peking, that it would be willing to lease Weihaiwei to Britain as a counter-balance to Russian, German and Japanese ambitions in northern China. London turned down the proposal, fearing Russia would seize Port Arthur (Lüshun); Weihaiwei and Port Arthur faced each other across the Gulf of Chihli, guarding the entrance to Peking. Despite supporting the concept of Chinese territorial integrity,[15] Britain's hand was forced when Russia announced it had indeed extracted from China a lease of Port Arthur for 25 years, seriously altering the regional balance of power.

On 2 April, having obtained Japan's consent, MacDonald accepted the offered lease of Weihaiwei on the same terms as had been agreed with Russia for Port Arthur.[16] As the Japanese troops started to withdraw on 9 May 1898, the British navy moved in. By 23 May the Japanese had gone.[17] The following day, which happened to be Queen Victoria's 79th birthday, the Union Jack was raised on the south-western tip of Liukungtao, although the lease was not effective until 1 July.

Britain and Russia had long mistrusted each other, particularly over Russia's intentions towards India. Fearing that Russia might extend its lease of Port Arthur, the wording of the British lease stated that Weihaiwei should be held by Britain 'for so long a period as Port Arthur shall remain in the occupation of Russia'.[18] This ploy came back to haunt them.

Responsibility for government of the territory was shared between the army and the navy. One of the first acts by the newly appointed commissioner, Lt. Ernest Gaunt RN, was to close most of the businesses that had sprung up on the island. *The China Mail* reported that a few foreigners (not, the paper hastened to add, Englishmen) had opened drinking establishments without permission. As the last Japanese left, Gaunt marched round the small town with a body of guards and 'peremptorily closed' them all.[19]

There was much evidence of the Japanese bombardment of 1894. The few foreign residences were dilapidated and had to be demolished, as did many of the former shops.[20] The three Japanese military camps on the mainland were in good order, as were four of the forts on the island. However, Lord Charles Beresford, visiting Weihaiwei in late 1898 as part of a fact-finding trip to China, remarked that there was

The raising of the Union Jack next to the Imperial Dragon flag on 24 May 1898. Reprinted with permission by Weihai Municipal Archive.

not a gun to be seen whereas the Russians, in their short time at Port Arthur, had installed 70.[21] Another visitor in 1898 was Prince Heinrich, younger brother of the German Emperor. Reportedly he remarked to Beresford: 'You English are the most extraordinary people... The Russians are working with great energy fortifying their port... and the British are employed with great industry making a cricket ground.'[22]

He was correct, and it must have been a good one: in June 1899 the Weihaiwei XI beat a visiting team from Shanghai by a convincing eight wickets.[23] There was also a nine-hole golf course at the island's eastern end.[24] A regatta was held in September 1898,[25] and by the end of the year there were hockey and tennis clubs.[26] There was a parade ground for the garrison of 800,[27] which, having sorted out the sports facilities, began putting the fortifications back into proper shape. The plan was that Weihaiwei would be developed into a major naval base—perhaps the finest in the East, or at least a northern Hong Kong. Then in the middle of 1901 orders came from London to stop all work.[28]

Britain, reeling from the unexpectedly high cost of the Boer War in South Africa, was unwilling to pay the estimated £2–3 million for the required breakwater[29] (£100–150 million at today's values). The territory was to be retained only as a summer base and sanatorium for the navy's China Squadron and the island was handed over to the Admiralty.[30] In 1899 the Admiralty had purchased all private land on the island, allowing the few Chinese who lived there to remain as tenants, and requisitioned some former Chinese government buildings.[31] One was the former *yamen* of the Qing naval commander, the largest building on the island. Repaired and renamed Queen's House it became the centre for almost everything: a council chamber, the commissioner's residence, a canteen for the Royal Navy, the British post office and the initial site of the Union Chapel. This building still stands and is the main focus of any visit to Liukungtao. Impressive new buildings were erected, many of which remain. Among them are the former Royal Marines barracks in the south-west of the island and, built partly on the site of the ruined Qing naval academy, the British naval commander's residence and offices. Another very distinctive building from this period, visible from the ferry to the island, is the water distillery, an essential early investment.[32]

EARLY MERCANTILE ACTIVITY

Notwithstanding that the Royal Navy lost no time in claiming Liukungtao as its own, the initial commercial activities in Weihaiwei were on the island. The first business was started in 1898 by Duncan Clark, a customs tide-waiter from Chefoo. He set up as a general merchant, providing the navy and its supporting establishment with food, water and coal. Every year, from April to October, the Royal Navy's China Fleet moved north from Hong Kong, frequently hosting the navies of America, Austria-Hungary and France. Business was brisk for Clark in the season. By 1902 he was advertising his firm as manufacturer of aerated water, land agent, foreign fruit and vegetable grower, proprietor of the Weihaiwei Water-Boat Co., supplier of bunker coal and fresh water to visiting steamers, and provider of the ferry launches *Spray* and *Foam*—with a branch on the mainland. He also

Duncan Clark at his pier with his launch *Spray*, c. 1907. Courtesy of Duncan Clark.

operated the British post office. Clark built the stone pier that stands just to the west of today's ferry terminal on Liukungtao. In 1903 a silk factory joined his portfolio. By 1908 Clark's water plant was producing 1500 dozen bottles a day and his steam bakery could make 500 kilograms of bread every hour.[33] However, the most visible aspect of the firm's activities was the management of hotels.

Weihaiwei was quickly recognized as a place for rest and relaxation. The climate was the best on the China Coast and people started to go there for holidays from the southern cities. Clark's first hotel opened on the island in 1900 in small bungalows, previously Chinese navy officers' quarters. These were soon demolished and replaced by the very grand Island Hotel, facing the sea. This building is still the first that visitors to Liukungtao see on alighting from the ferry. A second storey was added to the original in the 1930s, increasing the capacity to 40 rooms, and the hotel remained in the proprietorship of D. Clark & Co. until 1949. The present structure is magnificent and beautifully cared for but, like much of the island, is now owned by the Chinese navy and is inaccessible.

When the Chinese Regiment (see below) disbanded in 1906 Duncan Clark converted the officers' quarters and regimental mess block into Clark's Mainland Hotel. This, the second of his hotels, continued until the mid-1920s. Clark was not the only person to see potential in the hotel industry. In 1900 the Weihaiwei Land & Building Co. built Queen's Hotel on the mainland, overlooking the southern tip of the island. Initially used by the military as a hospital,[34] it reverted to its original purpose under the management of Shanghai's famous Astor House.[35] It, too, became too small. In 1902 the capacity was doubled to 80 large bedrooms with en suite bathrooms.[36] In 1908 Queen's Hotel, now renamed King's Hotel, became Clark's third hotel, giving him a virtual monopoly of the Weihaiwei hotel market.

One other firm that features prominently in British Weihaiwei's early history is Lavers & Clark. The two principals, formerly businessmen in Chefoo (this Clark was unrelated to Duncan Clark), set up in Weihaiwei in March 1899, establishing the Weihaiwei Land & Building Co. to build holiday properties for letting on the mainland.[37] The firm was the agent for the Hongkong & Shanghai Bank and manager of the Weihaiwei Lighter Co.; in the absence of proper wharves and piers, lighters were the only means of servicing ships. The only export of note from Weihaiwei in the earlier years was groundnuts, known today as peanuts. Lavers & Clark understood the crop's importance to the port's prosperity and organized a local producers' guild to better manage production and distribution;[38] the guild had 92 members by 1922.[39] The firm's harbourfront building also housed the Port Edward Club. It still stands, but inside a People's Liberation Army (PLA) Navy base. However, the verandah is visible from a distance overlooking the harbour; it must have been a good spot to enjoy evening cocktails. Ernest Clark's handsome bungalow, built in 1916, also survives. Formerly known simply as 'The Bungalow, Weihaiwei',[40] it stands above the harbour at Port Edward. This is also Chinese navy property and not easy to access.

Masters of all they surveyed

The businesses so far described started out on Liukungtao, but a very small part of the leased territory. The British now controlled all the other islands in the Bay of Weihaiwei, plus a swathe of land 16 kilometres wide along the bay's entire coast. Britain also had the right to erect fortifications, station troops or take any measures necessary for defensive purposes east of the line 121° 40' east of Greenwich. In a similar way to the Kowloon walled city in Hong Kong, the walled town of Weihaiwei was left outside British jurisdiction.

Britain did not exercise its authority inland until the exact boundary was agreed, and for this purpose an Anglo-Chinese team was appointed.[41] The total leased area was almost 750 square kilometres and contained some 300 villages. Adding the area where Britain had fortification rights, the total came to almost 4000 square kilometres. It was estimated that 80,000 people lived within the leased territory.[42] Major Penrose of the Royal Engineers headed the British side of the boundary team. As usual they named all the ridges and peaks after the leading naval and military men of the day. Within a year Penrose and his team had produced a large-scale map of the territory. During the initial stages of this challenging exercise, which commenced in 1898, the surveyors met with not one incident.[43] However, with the Boxer troubles brewing in 1900, it was inevitable that some disturbance would affect Weihaiwei. The trigger was rumours about how tax was to be levied on the villagers; reports of armed resistance[44] soon became fact. Major Penrose was attacked and injured[45] and some Chinese were killed.[46] Order was restored, after a period of martial law, in July.[47]

Any hopes that Weihaiwei might turn into a northern Hong Kong were crushed as a result of the survey. Penrose saw little but very dry and rocky hillsides. Some land was terraced, with crops of wheat, barley, millet and sweet potato.[48] Silkworm cocoons were raised for the Chefoo market. Even taking into account the main crop, groundnuts, it was difficult to envisage a prosperous hinterland supporting a busy commercial port. There were very few trees for either fuel or building material; these had been felled over the centuries by the villagers and not replanted. Furthermore, there was no industry at all and roads into the interior were non-existent.

As the Admiralty dominated Liukungtao, it became clear that the centre of civil administration would have to be elsewhere. Matou (Chinese for 'ferry pier') was chosen for the purpose as it was the part of the mainland closest to the naval base. With effect from 1 January 1901 responsibility for Weihaiwei was transferred from the War Office to the Colonial Office, thereby enabling non-military personnel to be appointed as commissioners (equivalent to governors).[49]

James Stewart Lockhart

In December 1901 James Stewart Lockhart was appointed. A member of the Hong Kong government since 1879, Lockhart was a respected scholar of Chinese language and culture and was Hong Kong's Colonial Secretary. He had overseen the mostly successful assimilation of the leased New Territory with the rest of the colony, and was seen as uniquely qualified to administer Weihaiwei. His appointment was greeted with universal enthusiasm. *The China Mail* remarked that Lockhart's 'well known energy and efficiency . . . will soon put life into the place' and create in Weihaiwei a flourishing commercial possession;[50] that he failed to live up to these expectations was not his fault.

A colleague of Lockhart referred to Weihaiwei as being 'a local Margate instead of a Portsmouth', the former being a pleasant seaside town on England's south coast, the latter being the bastion of Britain's global naval supremacy. When Lockhart took up his new post on 3 May he would not have expected the standard of accommodation enjoyed by Hong Kong's governor, but he was not prepared for the house of the former military commissioner's assistant.[51] This comprised seven small rooms, without internal sanitation, running water or electricity. It was to be many years before any budget was available for improvements.[52] By the end of his tenure in 1921, Government House was impressive enough although never as grand as he wished. Nothing remains of the building; its unmarked site is now a street parking lot opposite No. 1 Nanchang Street.

Despite irritation about his living conditions, Lockhart immediately set about organizing the young territory. A legal system and a postal service were required. Births, marriages and deaths had to be registered and a taxation system introduced. Roads

Government House, Weihaiwei (Weihai). Courtesy of David Mahoney.

needed to be built and business to be encouraged and grown. One of the first jobs to be tackled was the renaming of Matou. King Edward VII ascended the throne on 22 January 1901. A new town and a new king, combined with a touch of patriotism, made 'Port Edward' an obvious choice. Naturally, the renaming ceremony should coincide with Edward's coronation on 26 June 1902. On 24 June the king was whisked into hospital for emergency surgery and so the renaming (and the coronation) did not take place until 9 August.[53]

Although answerable to London, Lockhart largely acted as he thought appropriate. The Order in Council under which Britain governed Weihaiwei required the British courts, in civil cases between Chinese, to be guided by Chinese law or custom.[54] Thus Lockhart used the local population and their existing procedures to govern themselves. By and large the idea worked, although Lockhart was puzzled by some of what he saw. In his report for 1902 he noted that a villager had walked 30 kilometres to tell the magistrate that he could not keep his wife in order; while another walked 15 to complain that a neighbour had stolen six handfuls of grass, imploring 'the great man to help him, in which case his gratitude will be as the ocean in depth, and the vault of heaven in height'.[55]

Lockhart extended the principle of self-government to revenue collection. A system existed whereby village headmen apportioned the taxation burden between their villagers, and Lockhart was quite happy to perpetuate this arrangement, especially as it cost him nothing.[56] The commissioner embarked on programmes of tree-planting and road-building, with many thousands of the former and over 60 kilometres of the latter being introduced in the first year.[57] He realized that if Weihaiwei was to attract investors and prosper, both would be needed.

Although Lockhart's official title was not as senior as that of governor of a colony, in some respects he had more power. For example, he was not obliged to establish the colonial structure of legislative and executive councils to advise him. He did form an advisory council of leading businessmen, noting in his report for 1903 that he had not found it necessary to hold regular meetings with them.[58] As for legislation, the Weihaiwei government passed 116 ordinances between 1901 and 1930, including the Margate-sounding 1904 Rowing Boat Ordinance, a measure to license such craft and control their charges.[59]

At the end of his first year Lockhart reported the construction of an improved pier on the mainland as the original had a tendency to disappear at high tide, although he recognized the need for a deep-water pier if trade was to develop. A market and an abattoir were built—the right to operate the latter was sold as a monopoly, as were the opium and Chinese wine distribution businesses. These three brought the new government much needed revenue. An example of Lockhart's 'can do' approach concerns Weihaiwei's printing arrangements. Before he arrived, the government purchased a printing press from the navy but, as there was nobody to operate it, the machine was idle and even the *Government Gazette* was handwritten. Lockhart lent the printing machinery to a Protestant mission, at no charge, for them to print religious tracts, and in return asked for the occasional printing of government papers.[60]

The territory was well managed, but very small and not financially self-supporting. The remedy lay in a steamer service and a railway. The former was soon achieved; the latter remained a dream. Press reports in 1899 that Nippon Yusen Kaisha and China Merchants were to open regular steamer services proved false.[61] Weihaiwei remained a sporadic port-of-call for vessels going elsewhere. Butterfield & Swire announced in 1901 that two of their steamers would call in the summer on their way to and from Shanghai.[62] In 1902 the government subsidized an all-year service to carry mail and passengers between Weihaiwei and Chefoo[63] but Lockhart still pushed for a regular year-round service to Shanghai.[64] In 1903 Butterfield & Swire agreed to run a weekly service, in return for an annual subsidy of £1000.[65]

The absence of a rail link was a result of political not commercial considerations. When Germany secured the lease of Kiaochow (Jiaozhou) in March 1898, the terms included the right to develop railways throughout much of Shandong. Britain's lease of Weihaiwei, in the same province and only 200 kilometres away, was interpreted as a threat. To gain German acquiescence Britain declared it had no interest in competing in Shandong.[66] Britain was at this time courting Germany as a possible partner in an alliance against France and, in the context of China, Russia. Accordingly Lord Salisbury, Britain's Prime Minister in 1898, announced 'it is not possible to make Weihaiwei a commercial port, and it would never be worthwhile to connect it with the interior by railway'.[67] Arthur Balfour, later himself Prime Minister, added that a railway to Chefoo was a physical impossibility. Joseph Walton, a British Member of Parliament making a fact-finding tour of China in 1899, was scathing of Balfour's opinion, especially as Balfour had never been there. On his return, Walton suggested in the House of Commons that Weihaiwei be handed over to Germany so that a railway could be built. Ultimately, Weihaiwei had to make do with its cart track connection to Chefoo.

Sir James Stewart Lockhart retired in 1921. His governance of Weihaiwei was seen as fair and enlightened. Among the retirement gifts and presentations he received was one from the Chinese mercantile community, which presented him with a bowl of pure water, symbolizing the purity of his administration.[68]

The Chinese Regiment

An early consideration of the British towards their new possession was its defence. Following a recommendation from London, local men were recruited in 1899 into a Chinese Regiment. Shandong men had a reputation for loyalty and trustworthiness, and the new recruits initially met these expectations. The regiment was commanded by British officers and NCOs and grew to 1300 men by early 1902.

The Chinese soldiers responded well to the disciplined training, becoming a professional force. The regiment's first taste of active service put these local men in a potentially difficult position. When Major Penrose and his party were attacked on 5 and 6 May 1900 while marking out the boundary, they looked to the Chinese Regiment for support. The soldiers performed so well there was no hesitation about including 200 of them in the Expeditionary Force sent to relieve Tientsin and Peking at the height of the Boxer Rebellion the following month.[69]

Impressive though the regiment was there were some problems, including desertion. Chinese militias in Shandong Province were suddenly achieving previously unknown levels of excellence. A number of the Weihaiwei soldiers shared their training with the armed bands in the surrounding countryside to use for more patriotic purposes than supporting the British government.[70] Another problem for the regiment, in post–Boer War Britain, was its cost. In 1902 when London announced its decision to disband it there was criticism from the press and elsewhere.[71] Initially Lockhart could still call upon the regiment when his small police force needed assistance, and even on the officers to assist him with administrative work,[72] but recruitment stopped and numbers shrunk. The regiment was disbanded in 1906, by which time only 600 soldiers remained. Some of the men joined the police forces of Weihaiwei and Hong Kong; others became anti-piracy guards on British ships.[73] Their buildings were handed over to the government, and the main barracks block became Clark's Mainland Hotel. This can just be seen through the gates of the PLA base on the west side of Beishan Road.

Gold and other business ventures

Chinese had been prospecting for gold around Weihaiwei before the British period.[74] The leasing of the territory enabled many hopefuls from overseas to participate. In 1899, it was reported that a surveyor prospecting for gold had discovered a coal mine, a poor consolation.[75] Lockhart issued 34 gold prospecting licences in 1903,[76] and the Weihaiwei Gold Mining Co. was formed; its $600,000 of shares were 100 percent oversubscribed[77] and profits were hungrily anticipated. Gold was found in the bed of the stream now known as the Wuzhu River, and in the south-west hills, present-day Fanjiabu, where the mining company established its operations. Crushing plant was installed in 1904.[78] The following year there was a European management of 9, and 400 Chinese workers. Gold-bearing rock was sent to San Francisco for processing, but the small quantities and high cost of shipment meant the business could not pay its way. In 1906 the company went into liquidation.[79]

Another business venture intended to change the face of Weihaiwei was fruit growing. The climate was seen as appropriate for cultivating apples, pears, peaches, cherries, plums and nectarines. Soil quality had already been established, despite the unpromising appearance of the hillsides, by Lockhart's tree-planting programme. A fruit-growing specialist, Mr. Gibbons from London's Kew Gardens, arrived in 1905 to advise on how best to manage the project. One of the first things he did was to plant an orchard next to Government House as a divider between Lockhart's residence and the rest of the city.[80] However, despite Gibbons's considerable efforts, and he stayed in Weihaiwei until 1909, overseeing several successful harvests, there was no commercial interest. The idea was dropped.[81]

In 1904 British-American Tobacco (BAT) were experiencing difficulties with the customs authorities over the import of tobacco into Shanghai. They considered Weihaiwei as a possible source of supply and base for manufacturing;[82] the territory was a free port, so no customs issues would arise. However, it was only in the summer of 1913 that some BAT representatives came up from Shanghai and established an experimental farm.[83] Lockhart reported that the farm 'had a better year' in 1915,[84] but after that nothing more was heard. Once more, Weihaiwei's size and lack of infrastructure scuppered a potential source of employment, business and revenue.

There had been virtually no trade before the British lease period and, being a free port, there was no customs service to provide details of what was subsequently imported and exported. As we have seen, groundnuts were the biggest export crop. Salt and rice grew to prominence, and cotton yarn and piece-goods, sugar and kerosene were initially the chief imports.[85] Standard Oil erected an oil storage godown in 1908, which it supplied by barge from its facility in Chefoo.[86] Almost despite itself, Weihaiwei's commercial activities increased and more shipping, insurance and banking agents appeared in Port Edward. There were still no wharves and piers and all goods had to be loaded and unloaded by lighter, but the business community grew and soon there were several Chinese and Japanese shops.[87]

The Chinese Labour Corps

It is inevitable that people in a poor area, such as eastern Shandong was then, will look elsewhere for gainful employment if none is to be had close by. This economic fact of life was behind one of Weihaiwei's most famous exports. In 1902 the Witwatersrand Native Labour Co. bought a site on the sea front and constructed a compound capable of holding 2000 labourers pending shipment to the mines in South Africa. However, this facility was unused as the British public were deeply uncomfortable about whether the coolie trade was slavery in a new guise.[88] Some Chinese did work in the South African mines, but by about 1910 they had mostly returned home.

The processing centre found a new use in 1916. As a result of the carnage in France, Britain needed all able-bodied men to fight in the trenches. None could be spared for non-combat roles. They decided to recruit 150,000 Chinese for support duties like maintenance, transport and manual work. Many of these were to be hired in Weihaiwei, and so the Witwatersrand company offered its site. Recruiting started in October 1916 and the following January the first batch of what was later to be known as the Chinese Labour Corps (CLC) left Weihaiwei for Europe via Canada. Following China's declaration of war against Germany in 1917, and the consequent occupation of Germany's Chinese possessions by the Allies, the headquarters of the recruiting operation moved to Tsingtao (Qingdao). The main reason was the absence of a railway linking Weihaiwei to the recruiting grounds.[89]

Nevertheless, a total of 44,000 left from Weihaiwei. Although guaranteed not to face enemy fire, some CLC members died in France and Belgium. Part of each volunteer's wage was paid direct to his family. Of benefit to the community as a whole was the construction of a much-needed pier to accommodate the volunteers' departure. This was built in 1916 and formally opened in 1918 as Victory Pier.[90]

Post-war growth

This new pier was one outward sign of a growth in Port Edward's commercial activity around this time. It was funded by additional shipping dues[91] gladly paid by the commercial community as finally they could land their goods directly. By the end of 1918[92] there was a line of new buildings from the eastern end all the way to the walled town over a kilometre away.[93] In terms of industry, a Chefoo firm established a hairnet business in 1913, employing 500 people.[94] Hair was collected from local women and sent to Germany for treatment, before returning to Weihaiwei to be made into hairnets. On the subject of hair Reginald Johnston, in his report as Acting Commissioner for 1917, remarked that even six years after the 1911 revolution the queue (the hated symbol of Chinese subservience to their former Manchu rulers) 'is still cherished by multitudes of the people of this Territory' although rarely seen elsewhere in China.[95]

An embroidery factory started in 1912; there were twelve by 1927.[96] A soap works opened in 1917 and a silk filature the following year.[97] By 1919 there were eight filatures, although the bulk of the territory's cocoons still went to Chefoo for processing. One reason for this growth in activity was the influence of Lockhart. He had from the outset encouraged Cantonese businessmen to come to Weihaiwei. It is hard to explain otherwise why, in 1918, a Cantonese Club appeared in this northern port. Another important industry was fishing, receiving a boost in the 1920s when motorized trawlers and an ice factory were introduced, enabling it to serve Shanghai's huge market.[98] Despite these advances, the 1921 census found only 20 percent of males aged nine or over were engaged in industry and commerce; groundnut farming remained the dominant activity and provided 90 percent of the exports,[99] chiefly to Hong Kong and Canton (Guangzhou).[100] In 1922 Weihaiwei no longer had to ask London for handouts. Its revenue was greater than its expenditure, and would remain so.[101]

Sixteen vessels of the Royal Navy's China Squadron at anchor. Courtesy of David Mahoney.

The Cinderella of the Empire

Writing in 1938 after a career in China with the Foreign Office, Sir Eric Teichman referred to Weihaiwei as the 'Cinderella of the Empire',[102] never invited to the ball. The summer months were and are extremely pleasant. The foreign resident population, including government and military people, was never more than two hundred but in summer the arrival of tourists and the fleets of many nations increased this number significantly. Religious needs were met by St. John's Church at Port Edward and St. James' Church and the Union Chapel on the island, now used as a kindergarten. There was also a Roman Catholic Church on the mainland run by French missionaries, still standing and in excellent condition. Membership of the Port Edward Club, founded in 1902 with Lockhart as president, was open to civilian residents and officers of the army or navy of any European power, plus those of the United States and Japan.[103] On Liukungtao there was the nine-hole Weihaiwei Golf Club. Again, the commissioner was president and membership was open to military men and resident foreigners. A rule was added in 1908 whereby 'the putting greens and tees are closed when the Negative Signal for Tennis is hoisted'; if the weather was unsuitable for playing tennis then neither could they play golf.[104] It is hard to imagine the sort of community that would raise a signal warning against playing tennis.

The Weihai Municipal Archive Bureau maintains that today there are 170 buildings remaining from the British period, although many of them are concealed (therefore largely protected) within one military establishment or another. One of the more accessible British buildings on the mainland is the Wilkinson Villa. This former holiday house is one of a small cluster built by Shanghai lawyer E. S. Wilkinson in about 1921.[105] Standing next to the Dongshan Hotel on the sea front is the 'Four Holes Building', so called because of four round windows that adorn its dormer roof. This was owned by J. R. Elias and appears to have been a hotel or boarding house. The former office of the British Junior District Officer can be found in a backstreet between Beishan and Suzhou roads, waiting for the same loving renovation that so many others have enjoyed.

Standing on a small cliff just above the seafront is another fine building with a special history. In January 1901 Herbert Beer founded a school for European boys in a Chinese house on the island. There were initially four pupils, but the school became so popular that Beer needed larger premises. He purchased the present site in 1903 and built accommodation for 40 boarders. The new Weihaiwei School was ready for occupation in 1904 and quickly filled to capacity. By 1917 he was teaching the sons of businessmen from Mukden (Shenyang) to Canton and Kobe to Chungking (Chongqing), preparing them for the English public school system.[106] The school was considered by some to be the best British preparatory school in the Far East. In addition to its high standards, young boys could stay relatively close to their parents, enjoy good weather and still be within British jurisdiction. During the 1920s the school went into decline and closed in the autumn of 1925.[107] In 1929 the building became the East Cliff Hotel.

Although the British community was small, the inevitable social rankings were reflected in where people lived. On the island's waterfront are some gorgeous houses, still inhabited but now in serious disrepair. These were the residences of the Royal Navy senior officers. Further east, towards where the golf club was, are smaller houses possibly for lower-ranking officers or holidaymakers. In this part of the island is East Village, the only Chinese settlement allowed to remain when the British took charge. Comprising two rows of single-storey terraced houses, it is still occupied. A villager offered me large figs fresh from the tree when I visited.

In the evenings there were dinners and musical get-togethers. The men met at the Masonic Lodge, still standing on the former High Street. When they were not engaged with running the home, supervising their children and charity work, the British wives occupied themselves with tennis, prodigious quantities of letter-writing, visiting each other and shopping. Shops and other commercial concerns were located along Seymour Street, to the west of Queen's House.

Seymour Street on Liukungtao (Liugongdao), showing one of Ah Fong's 'branches' on the left and the roofs of Queen's House in the centre, 1909. Courtesy of Chester Cheng.

The Japanese firm I. Kataoka & Co. had two shops there, at Nos. 36 and 70, selling Japanese curios, silks, screens and 'picture frames of every description'.[108] Ah Fong, who ran a photographic studio, sold a selection of postcards. Ah Fong was adept at what must have been an early version of Photoshop; he superimposed his name on so many old photographs of Weihaiwei's buildings that it looked as if his were the only business there. There was the cheekily named 'Sin Jelly Belly & Co.—Naval Tailor and General Outfitter', so named because the proprietor resembled a reincarnation of the Laughing Buddha.[109] Two ghostly remains exist of business names on these buildings. One is totally illegible, and of the other all that can be read is that the business was '[ESTA]BLISHED 1898'.

Beyond the shops of Seymour Street were the naval support facilities. Large shells, torpedoes and other heavy items were moved from the storage buildings by way of a tiny railway track out to the iron pier, from which they were loaded onto ships. The rails, the buildings and the pier are still there, and the majority of the buildings can be identified on detailed maps from that period.

There was a naval cemetery on Liukungtao and a small civil burial place on the western tip of the island. A tree today marks the position of the latter,[110] but of the former there is not the ghost of a trace. I understand that whatever was left of these cemeteries was destroyed in the Cultural Revolution. An interested visitor in recent years told me she had seen a number of gravestones stacked up beside a government building, and noted the details; they mostly related to young soldiers and sailors who died in the early 1900s, but the most recent was dated 1934.

GIVING IT ALL BACK

Almost since the lease of Weihaiwei was signed there were rumours, as well as the occasional high-level serious discussions, about returning it. The lease was not for a defined term so the question of when the territory would be relinquished was always present. As early as 1902 G. T. Hare, Acting Commissioner before Lockhart, suggested to the Colonial Office that it should all be handed back except for Liukungtao and Matou.[111] Rumours that the territory was to be handed over to Germany, following the 1901 decision not to create a naval fortress, were covered widely in the press at the time.[112] In 1905, when Japan forced the Russians from Port Arthur, the rumours intensified; Russia's presence across the Gulf of Chihli had been the fact on which Britain's lease was based. However, Britain managed effectively to have 'Russia' replaced by 'any other power' in the lease and carried on as normal. Indeed, Japan wanted Britain to stay, as a counter-balance to the German presence to the south. There was even a rumour in 1906 that Weihaiwei would be handed to China in return for control of a proposed Tientsin-Chinkiang Railway.[113]

For people trying to develop business such political manoeuvring and the prevailing uncertainty made life difficult. The fledgling merchant community wrote to Lockhart in mid-1906 asking for clarification of Weihaiwei's status. A frustrated Lockhart replied that he could not provide it.[114] The following year Ernest Clark wrote to Sir John Jordan, British Minister in Peking, asking if China would compensate British businesses in Weihaiwei on rendition, having heard that the British government would not.[115] His question was not easily answered. The new Republican government of China was reported to be raising funds for the repossession of Weihaiwei and its development as a naval base, but this did not happen either.[116]

The trigger for serious discussion was provided by the aftermath of the Great War of 1914–18. China had declared war against Germany in 1917 but took no part in any warlike activity. China saw all the powers who had been occupying Chinese territory squabbling among themselves, and realized that whatever the outcome there would be changes on the international political scene. China wanted to take advantage of the opportunities this would offer. At the Washington Conference of 1921, Japan was forced to give the former German possession of Tsingtao back to China, and Britain volunteered to relinquish Weihaiwei, provided it remained as a holiday destination and a convalescence station for the Royal Navy. Die-hards among the sizeable British community in China argued that this would lead to the end of British prestige in the East and collapse of British commercial interests in China.[117] Nevertheless, a Sino-British committee was formed in September 1922 to recommend suitable rendition terms. Its first meeting was held the following month in Weihaiwei.[118]

The prospect of rendition had been announced in the Weihaiwei *Government Gazette* on 20 March 1922. For the rest of that year, the commissioner noted that there was in the community 'a general feeling of impending change'.[119] This uncertainty was to continue for some time. A provisional agreement for rendition was agreed by the Sino-British committee on 31 May 1923, and a retrocession treaty was drawn up the following year.[120] But by that time China was in a state of acute confusion. Civil war and warlordism made it unclear which was the appropriate Chinese body to whom Weihaiwei should be returned. So Britain waited for the Chinese dust to settle. The by now reluctant possession enjoyed a period of tranquillity while disorder reigned in the rest of the country. Commissioner Johnston was even able to open a public park in 1928 to mark the birthday of King George V.[121]

It took Sir Claude MacDonald a week to negotiate the lease; giving it back took almost eight years. The Convention for the Rendition of Weihaiwei was signed on 18 April 1930 and ratifications were exchanged in Nanking (Nanjing) on 1 October. China was concerned about lingering imperialist ambitions on the part of Britain, perhaps with good reason. Fears were stilled and the Chinese allowed Britain to continue using the naval base for ten years, with a renewal option, together with a large number of buildings and other facilities, including the golf course. Other land and buildings in Port Edward were to be leased to Britain for 30 years, again renewable, at no charge. Otherwise the entire territory was to be handed back to China, without compensation to the British government.[122]

London could afford to be generous, but the British mercantile community could not. For them, compensation was an extremely important issue. In the event, the terms of rendition included an undertaking that, if the Chinese government ever bought out the interests of foreign businessmen, this would be done at amounts to be agreed by another joint commission. Of course, in the end this did not happen but the immediate anxieties of the business community were assuaged. In addition, foreigners were granted perpetual leases for all properties formerly held on Crown leases from the British administration.

Port Edward's small bund, 1930. The Lavers & Clark building is on the left. Reprinted with permission by Weihai Municipal Archive.

Weihaiwei was handed over with due ceremony on 1 October 1930. At the beginning of the day, the Chinese flag was run up the flagpole at Government House next to the Union Jack. This marked the first occasion the two had ever flown alongside each other. At the end of the day the Chinese flag flew alone.

The process was smooth and amicable, but there were a number of consequences, foreseen and otherwise. First, British Weihaiwei had been a free port with no customs duties payable on any goods. On 9 October 1930 a Custom House was opened. What had not been foreseen was the impact the imposition of customs payments would have on local businesses; about 30 firms closed as they could no longer make a profit. A second effect was that, in anticipation of the handover of the territory, the Chinese merchants wanted the outgoing British government to spend its carefully husbanded surplus—some $300,000. Accordingly, this was largely used for a new stone pier and roads in Port Edward as well as improved street lighting.[123]

Included in the lots identified for 30-year lease under the rendition agreement were the senior district officer's house, grounds and stable, and the non-commissioned officers' mess and grounds. The first of these was to be used for the residence of the now required British Consul; this building is no more. The second was to provide consular offices, and is still there, marked by a plaque at 62 Beishan Road.

Weihaiwei enjoyed good administration and security in the years immediately following rendition. Chinese banks opened branches and new industries were established. There was no rush to replace the colonial-era street names; addresses were still given as 'The Bund' or 'Dorward Road'.[124] However, a visitor in January 1937 found Weihaiwei 'disappointing'. He stayed 'at a huge barnlike summer hotel that was almost empty. It was cheerless, uncomfortable and morgue-like'.[125] Just over twelve months later Japanese marines landed, and once more Weihaiwei was under foreign occupation.

Further reading: Airlie, *Thistle and Bamboo*; Atwell, *British Mandarins and Chinese Reformers*; Bruce-Mitford, *The Territory of Wei-Hai-Wei*; Inouye, *Japan-China War*; Johnston, *Lion and Dragon in Northern China*; Lethbridge, 'Sir James Haldane Stewart Lockhart'; Nield, 'Bits of Broken China'; Tan, *British Rule in China*; Zhang, *Weihaiwei under British Rule*.

WENCHOW (WENZHOU) 溫州

Zhejiang, 28.01° N, 120.38° E
Treaty Port, 1876 British Treaty

The modern, affluent city of Wenzhou lies on the south bank of the River Ou, 30 kilometres from the sea. Its location is attractive, but in former days it was isolated. Meandering through a plain, interspersed with canals, but surrounded by hills, only the river allowed entry to the provincial interior. Small vessels could travel west from Wenchow for 50 kilometres, the tidal limit, until meeting impassable rapids. The city developed as the collection and distribution point for the produce of south-east Zhejiang Province. Many of its streets were and are lined by canals.

Sir Rutherford Alcock signed a convention in 1869, adding Wenchow to the list of treaty ports, substituting for unexciting Kiungchow (Qiongzhou). However, the British government refused to ratify Alcock's document. Wenchow re-emerged in 1876 when the Chefoo Agreement made it a treaty port but foreign commercial development never came. Before the ports of Foochow (Fuzhou) and Ningpo (Ningbo) were opened in 1842, Wenchow had been a major tea exporter, being close to the main growing areas. When the tea trade gravitated to those other ports, Wenchow's capacious anchorage was left with nothing. Today the expectation that trade thriving in new ports would return to Wenzhou appears extremely unrealistic, but that was the idea at the time.

Nowhere to live and little to do

The Custom House was opened on 1 April 1877,[1] and the British Consulate ten days later,[2] but disillusion was almost immediate. Furthermore there was disagreement about the settlement's location, even whether there was to be one. In February Shanghai British Vice-Consul Arthur Davenport had inspected a site outside the East Gate. At 900 by 300 metres this was sufficiently large, and had the river to the north and a canal to the south. The ground, consisting of paddy fields, needed to be raised—an expensive prospect. Nevertheless an agreement was drawn up, and owners told that they might have to sell to the British. The *taotai* and a number of Wenchow merchants had already been buying land there in anticipation of quick profits.[3] However, Davenport did not initiate any purchases in the agreed area. Having seen foreign goods available in Wenchow, he concluded that benefits arising from its treaty port status were likely to be slim,[4] a correct judgement.

The only other power to show interest in Wenchow at the time was America. The US Consul at Ningpo, Dr. E. C. Lord, came in April 1877 to see where the best site would be for an American Settlement. He rejected an island in the river where the only ground safely above the water level was occupied by two pagodas.[5] Reluctantly he marked off an area downstream of the British site.[6]

British Consul Chaloner Alabaster was sent from Amoy (Xiamen) in April to take temporary charge of Britain's presence in Wenchow. Despite the *taotai*'s earlier assurances, he was unable to find any accommodation. The only suitable temple had been taken by the Customs Commissioner; Alabaster was obliged to accept an invitation to occupy its spare room.[7] Neither was he impressed by Davenport's site for a settlement. Its generous size meant the cost of raising it by the required two metres would be prohibitive.[8] Wanting a second opinion Alabaster inspected the site with William Paterson of Jardines, then the only

1877 Chinese map of Wenchow (Wenzhou), showing the original site of the British Consulate (the red marker at the bottom), the later site on 'Conquest Island' in the river, and Davenport's proposed site of the British Settlement (the left-most of the right-hand cluster of red markers). Reprinted with permission by the National Archives.

foreign hong potentially interested in Wenchow. The two concluded that the site would be good for shooting snipe, but little else.[9] Instead the consul recommended following the lead of the Maritime Customs. The Custom House had been established on the thin strip of land between the north wall and the river; a modern—perhaps 1930s—replacement still occupies the site, now used as a police station. On 2 May 1877 a new agreement was drawn up with the *taotai*, covering this narrow area between where two bulges of the wall almost touched the river.[10]

Alabaster's temporary home was in the extreme south-west of the walled city, distant from the river.[11] Jiangxin Island, in the river and opposite the north wall of the city, had been rejected by Lord as a settlement site, but appealed as a place of residence. Alabaster therefore rented part of a temple complex on the island to serve as both his home and his office.[12] All supplies, including fresh water, had to be brought across the river. The island is now accessible by a ferry every 20 minutes and is home to a number of temples, memorials to revolutionary martyrs, a large Ferris wheel and other attractions. For Alabaster it was blissfully peaceful but far from ideal, and compared poorly with the smart structures other foreigners were building in Wenchow. The temple was in danger of imminent collapse through the combined agencies of weather and termites.[13] Even Eeyore's 'heap of sticks' would have been better.[14] Successive incumbents complained bitterly about their living conditions. The quiet island was a consolation, although insufficiently large for serious exercise. A few minutes' walk to the west, standing on a small rise, was one of the island's two ancient pagodas. The West Pagoda dates from 969 although renovated many times, most recently in 1982. A plaque on the East Pagoda dates it to 869. Just over a thousand years later, after the signing of the Chefoo Agreement, the plaque records that the British invaders forced the building of a customs office in its bottom floors, necessitating the removal of all its decorative features. If true, the resulting office would have been no more than two metres wide.

The island became known as 'Conquest Island'. The first foreign vessel to call at Wenchow after its opening was the *Conquest* on 18 April 1877. This steamer, owned by F. Bulkeley Johnson, a director of Jardine Matheson, made the run between Shanghai, Ningpo and Wenchow three or four times a month, bringing in full cargoes of goods but taking out virtually nothing. It was taken off the unprofitable route at the end of July.[15] Jardines' withdrawal was a fatal blow to the new port.[16] A German merchant, H. B. Meyer, made a brief appearance in 1878, but almost immediately withdrew to Ningpo.[17] Malcampo & Co., a long-standing Spanish firm from Amoy, set up a branch in Wenchow in 1893,[18] but four years later they too had gone.

Required to gather revenue, the five or six European customs officials were by far the largest community of foreigners, but the volume of business in the treaty port was never great. James Mackey, the assistant in charge of the customs, states in his report for 1879: 'Life is naturally dull and monotonous in the extreme . . . Rumours of the events passing in the great world outside reach this quiet place with a muffled sound.'[19] In 1880 the first British consular report described Wenchow as having once been a major trading centre but now 'sunk in hopeless apathy'.[20] This was not a reference to the foreign businessmen, because there were none. The local population was described as lethargic and unenterprising.[21]

Related to the lack of activity was the Ningpo Chinese merchants' fear that their business would suffer; Ningpo was only 200 kilometres north of Wenchow. And Foochow's tea merchants imposed restrictive barriers immediately it seemed the tea trade might return to Wenchow. What local enterprise there was in Wenchow comprised mainly the export of wood, charcoal and bamboo poles. The surrounding area also cultivated bitter oranges and opium.

One-third of the Chinese population was considered to be opium users, and another one-third addicted. This possibly explains Wenchow's reputation as an unfocused, lazy town.[22] By the end of 1878 the entire European population comprised the assistant in charge of the customs, James Mackey, and his staff of four despondent tide-waiters; Her Britannic Majesty's Consul Robert Forrest, and his assistant Pelham Warren; Dr. Wykeham Myers, a medical practitioner; three pilots—William McKay, E. Sandstedt and Charles Schmidt; Herr Meyer, when he was visiting from Ningpo; and the Revs. Stott and Jackson, missionaries from the China Inland Mission—14 people in total.[23] (It is not known whether the entire community met together, but with a Mackey, a McKay, a Myers and a Meyer, it would have been a confusing party.) By the following year the pilots had been redeployed and Dr. Myers had departed. This pattern remained for almost the entire life of the treaty port. Only the missionaries were a growth area.

There had been a Roman Catholic presence in Wenchow since at least 1874. By 1883 the missionaries outnumbered all other foreigners. They were mostly British, but their number included Americans, Germans, Italians and one or two French. It was the French who were to trigger one of the very rare anti-foreign outbursts in Wenchow. During the Sino-French War of 1884–85, placards were put up around the city urging the population to massacre all Catholics, the British Consul, all foreigners and even all mandarins. There was no British military presence, and Wenchow was too remote for the Royal Navy to be deployed. On the night of 4 October 1884, all the foreign buildings in the city were destroyed. The foreign community managed to escape to the island and were safe. Nevertheless they considered it expedient to move to a place well downstream to await the outcome. All except the consul, Edward Parker. He donned his full dress uniform, seated himself outside the consulate, and waited to face the mob. Thanks to the forethought of the Chinese officials, the rioters found that all boats had been removed. Unable to cross the river, the riot evaporated. The ringleaders were punished, damage was compensated and things soon returned to sleepy normality.[24]

Successive British Consuls, whose job included the promotion of British trading interests, complained that there was no regular foreign-owned shipping service to Wenchow.[25] In December 1878 the first foreign sailing vessel to visit the new treaty port, the German 320-tonne vessel *Hans*, arrived in search of export cargo. For a week the ship's master tried unsuccessfully to secure business.[26] Nobody had anything they wanted to dispatch that could not be sent by trusted junks. The following year in January a regular steamer service started between Wenchow, Ningpo and Shanghai, under the ownership of the recently formed China Merchants Steam Navigation Co. However, the wooden-hulled vessel was decrepit and constantly broke down. It made the journey three times a month, carrying the mail and whatever other business it could get. In the 1890s it was replaced by a converted Chinese warship, equally unreliable.[27]

The absence of foreign-owned ships continued to be an issue. Some years not a single one entered Wenchow. With no competition, the sole regular carrier could charge whatever the owners wished. The few attempts to open up the market always failed. A small British steamer, the *Fookching*, tried trading between Wenchow and Foochow in 1888. At only 77 tonnes it was too small to compete with the junk trade, on which duty was lower.[28] In August 1893 the *Pekin*, another small foreign-owned steamer, started a regular service to Foochow, Amoy and Hong Kong.[29] Malcampo was the agent in Wenchow, but this service stopped when he returned to Amoy in 1897. By 1898 *The China Mail* was saying that 'it is somewhat difficult to assign any reason for keeping the port open except for the protection of the missionaries'.[30] Yet still Wenchow lumbered on. In 1904 a Norwegian steamer was chartered by a Chinese person to try and break the China Merchants monopoly. On the vessel's second visit to Wenchow it was unable to secure a single package of merchandise. There was no third visit.[31] If only, Acting Consul John Pratt reported to London in 1905, a firm like Butterfield & Swire would enter the market, then there would be a change.[32] They didn't, and there wasn't. Instead the few foreign residents continued to live 'under the same social conditions as Robinson Crusoe'.[33]

A NEW HOME, BUT STILL NOTHING TO DO

Against this backdrop of disappointment and inactivity the British Foreign Office, surprisingly, financed the construction of a new consular residence. National prestige must have been a consideration, as by 1894 an impressive three-storey, grey brick building was erected on Conquest Island,[34] with a smaller building about 30 metres to the west for the constable and his gaol. Both of these still stand on the bund to the right of the ferry jetty, beautifully cared for and now used as the Jiangxin Island International Mansion—'Since 1894' as the establishment's logo claims. These buildings served their original purposes for only a few years. A third building, of a slightly earlier date, formed a welcome enhancement to the lives of the half-dozen or so customs tide-waiters and other staff who had been living in makeshift accommodation. (Their superior, the Customs Commissioner, still lived happily in a picturesque old temple within the city.)[35] A coffee shop now services a few tables on the riverside, where a contemplative hour can be enjoyed.

Externally impressive, the new residence's interior was damp. Water leaked through the roof and walls and ran down the stone staircase. A good breeze usually blows along the river, but this passed straight by the house, allowing no circulation of air within. The brick structure was in no danger from white ants, but the place was unhealthy; many of its occupants suffered from fever. One of the first consuls to live in the new residence was William Ayrton, whose career was marked by 'idleness and negligence'.[36] Wenchow must have been the perfect posting for him. His duties were so few and his house so large that he was able to entertain visitors, such as his sister-in-law Millicent McClatchie.[37] Born in Hankow (Hankou) to a missionary father, and therefore no stranger to China, Miss McClatchie stayed in Wenchow for almost four years and, happily for us, wrote a detailed journal of her experiences. She also contributed articles to newspapers, including Hong Kong's *China Mail*, under the pen-name of 'Gwenda'.

From her we learn that the presence of numerous temples gave the island, in Chinese minds, a sacred quality. Furthermore, the last Song emperor took refuge there when fleeing from Kublai Khan and his Mongols in the 13th century.[38] Wenchow's population never forgave the British occupation, nor for erecting a consulate that could be seen from every part

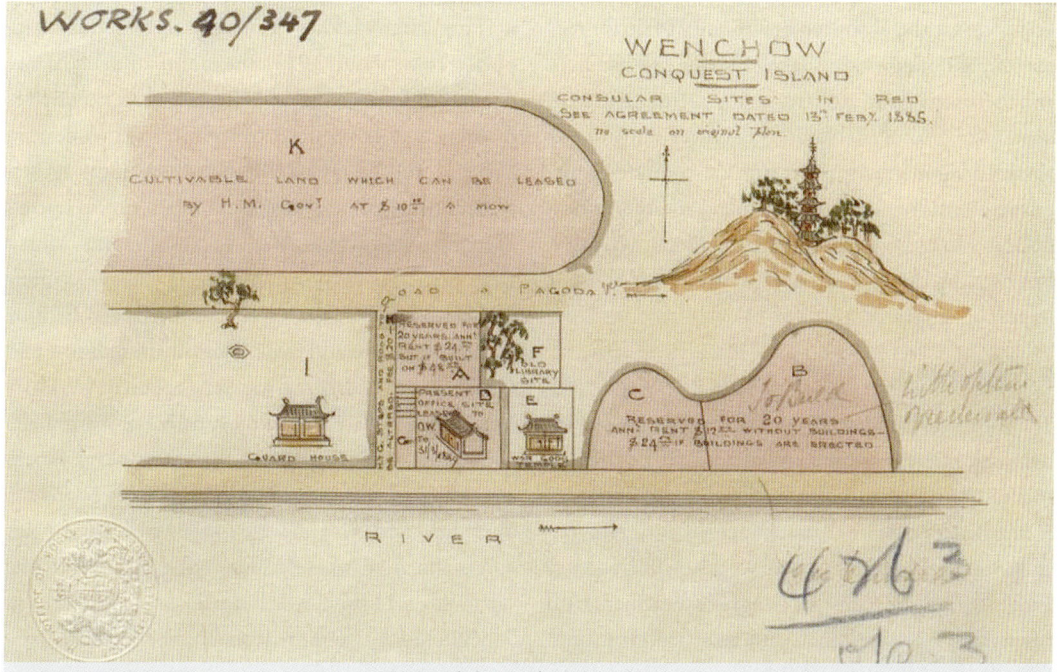

1885 plan of the plots reserved on Conquest (Jiangxin) Island for the British Consulate (marked C and B). Reprinted with permission by the National Archives.

of the ancient city walls across the river. McClatchie describes the island as very pretty and rich in trees, which it still is.

Life on the island was lonely, as would have been life for a foreigner in any part of Wenchow. The small community called the place 'the Cinderella Port', with perhaps more justification than the folks in Weihaiwei (Weihai), and considered it the most isolated of all China's open ports. Four boatmen could be engaged to row to the mainland, taking ten minutes on a good day. But longer-distance communication was difficult. A courier took six days to reach the nearest treaty port, Ningpo,[39] and there was no telegraph connection with the outside world. In 1897, therefore, on the occasion of Queen Victoria's Diamond Jubilee, it was impossible for her loyal subjects marooned in Wenchow to send a traditional congratulatory telegram. Instead, they wrote a letter and hoped that it would arrive. The following year saw the island once more playing host to the entire foreign community when the absence of rice in the shops caused a riot. This could hardly be blamed on the foreigners but they constituted an easy target for discontent.

Apart from walking round the island, there was very little for the European community to do for recreation. Shooting was available, for those so inclined, and there were goose, snipe and duck. These and wild boar were also available at the Lower Anchorage, about 15 kilometres downstream. Customs tide-waiters were occasionally stationed there, and there was a holiday cottage, owned by the China Inland Mission but used by the consul and his family for the hot month of August.

Early closing

The consulate had been occupied for only a few years before closure was recommended by the Tower Report in 1900; the post had long outlived its usefulness, if it ever had any. In 1902 it was merged with Ningpo, from where the consul visited Wenchow for one day a month. Only the consular constable remained, with his staff of one watchman and two boatmen, until formal closure in June 1907.[40] The consular properties were sold to the customs in 1924.[41]

The missionaries, while potentially benefiting from the protection of the consulate, had always conducted their activities outside the official life of Wenchow and were unaffected by the consulate's closure. Their church was destroyed in the disturbances of 1884, but the Catholics were not deterred. They immediately started to build a new cathedral, completed in 1889 in time to celebrate Easter.[42] This very attractive stone and brick building still stands, surrounded by a vibrant Chinese Christian community, but in a sorry state.

In 1900 the number of missionaries resident in Wenchow increased significantly; 30 were attached to the China Inland Mission alone.[43] In about 1901 the English Methodists built a church in the eastern quarter of the city, capable of seating 1000. This incorporated a hospital and dispensary. In 1903 a college was added, with a capacity for more than 200 students, half of them as boarders.[44] The church is still there, in a small street off Gongyue Road, and is used by the local Christian community, who are much in evidence. Along a small alley to the east the attractive college buildings also survive, now used as public housing.

Having no foreign official presence beyond 1902, it is arguable whether Wenchow remained a treaty port. From about 1911, the multinationals penetrating other parts of China established themselves in Wenchow—Asiatic Petroleum, British-American Tobacco and Standard Oil—but used local agents. Reflecting the times, Japanese companies also started Wenchow branches. Iwai, Kabayashi and Mitsui were forerunners of a more sinister Japanese interest. From the mid-1930s Japan's intentions became increasingly clear and their determination to conquer China's whole coastline was very apparent by 1939. In mid-1939 there were almost daily bombardments by Japanese aircraft, and a stringent naval blockade which severed communications with Shanghai. Wenchow and Ningpo were the last two major ports to remain in Chinese hands.[45] The city fell to the Japanese on 11 July 1942, but retaken five weeks later. It held out for two more years but became a Japanese possession again in September 1944 and remained so until the end of the Pacific War.[46]

Whampoa (Huangpu) 黃埔

Guangdong, 23.05° N, 113.24° E
Consular Station, 1843 Britain

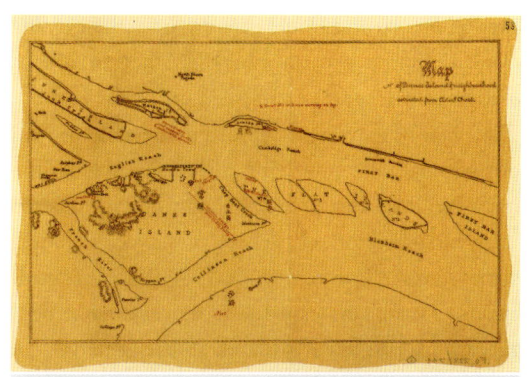

1884 map showing Danes Island (Changzhou) and all the main features in the area of Whampoa (Huangpu). Reprinted with permission by the National Archives.

The places collectively known as Whampoa served, in the early days of European commercial intercourse with China, as the port for Canton (Guangzhou), 20 kilometres upstream. An observer in 1844 noted that there were seldom fewer than 30 or 40 sailing vessels lying there, and often more than a hundred,[1] because they were unable to sail further.

Over many years, all aspects of the complex river system were minutely charted by foreign navigators, with every headland, water passage and island identified and named. French Island, now Shenjing Island and almost entirely occupied by the South China Normal University, was the place designated in 1756 by the local authorities for French sailors to walk and take exercise. It kept them away from the British, with whom, the Chinese observed, the French seemed to be always at war.[2] Danes Island, present-day Changzhou, derived from the Danish East India Company in the early 18th century and became the main focus of foreign activities.

The British installed a consular agency at Danes Island in 1843, upgrading to a vice-consulate in 1854.[3] There were never more than two staff, but they had a major responsibility. The British community numbered 96 in 1851, slightly more than at Canton. But when the sailors on the visiting ships were included, the vice-consul found himself responsible for thousands. Visiting mariners swarmed off their ships seeking entertainment. They found this aplenty in the grog shops and brothels of Bamboo Town, an English corruption of the Portuguese name for Whampoa—Bampo. This rough collection of Chinese stilted dwellings occupied the eastern tip of the island. The wooden stilts have been replaced by concrete, the vices of old long gone, but this small village holds no appeal today as a place to linger.

It was many years before a site for the British Vice-Consulate was designated, owing to Chinese objections to providing land for it. The first consular agent was obliged to live on a naval vessel,[4] although as a retired sea captain he may have thought this normal.[5] His successor did not.

The ship was both ancient and leaky and official pleas were made in 1849 that land be set aside for a permanent residence.[6] Xu Guangjin, the newly appointed Commissioner for Barbarian Affairs, replied that if the consul needed land he should lease it himself, adding that the Chinese government never interfered with such matters.[7] For many years a stalemate continued. Xu insisted he was unable to force Chinese landowners to lease property to the British.[8] Yet, when a certain Tseng Ping-kao did just that in 1852, he was arrested.[9] Only in 1858 was a lease agreed.[10]

The foreign cemeteries

In one respect, the foreign community was more dead than alive. In 1837 French Island was described as 'little more than a handsome cemetery'.[11] The numbers of people visiting the port, coupled with the primitive sanitary arrangements, necessitated a suitable burial site. A survey of 1938 lists 256 mainly European and American graves scattered over three sites on French and Danes islands, the earliest dating from 1748.[12] It was only in 1847 that an official foreign cemetery was established on Danes Island.[13] There may be gravestones hidden in the undergrowth of two small hills now lying within the island's military facilities, but access is impossible. However, many old gravestones have been preserved, including some from the 18th century. In 1980 the government created a small landscaped terrace near the northern tip of what was French Island, and relocated 30 or more stone memorials there.

The rise and fall of Whampoa's docks

The creation of the Colony of Hong Kong threatened the usefulness of Whampoa. Furthermore, the new foreign steamers could bypass Whampoa and go straight to Canton. Yet its extensive dock and ship-handling operations continued to give the place purpose. In the 1840s and 1850s, almost the entire foreign community was involved in supplying and servicing ships. The first docks, known as 'mud docks', were cut into the banks of the river at places deemed firm enough for vessels to be hauled up without sinking in ooze.[14]

The mud docks were owned by Chinese, with the work overseen by the ships' foreign masters. With the more exacting standards required for steel-hulled steamers, changes were necessary. Impetus came from the insistence of the Peninsular & Oriental Steam Navigation Co. (P&O) that its steamers be serviced under qualified European supervision. In 1846 P&O sent John Couper from Scotland to take on the management of their docking needs. Couper was soon followed by his son, who became the manager of a mud dock. The younger man inherited the ownership of his dock and built one of stone. More foreign dock managers followed, mainly Americans, and by 1856 the entire Whampoa dock complex was under Western control and management.[15]

In 1857 the foreign commercial establishment at Whampoa was largely destroyed, a consequence of the Second Opium War. This only led to the creation of bigger and better docking facilities.[16] Couper sold his new granite dock in 1863 to the newly formed Hongkong & Whampoa Dock Co. (HWD),[17] a joint venture between Jardines, P&O and Douglas Lapraik.[18] There were by this time four foreign owners of dock operations, employing more than 20 European engineers and foremen.[19] After HWD, the largest was the Union Dock Co. This company started business in Hong Kong in 1865, and the following year began acquiring docks in Whampoa.[20] In 1870, after many offers and counter-offers, HWD acquired the business of Union Dock and became the largest docking and repair establishment in East Asia.[21]

The bonanza was not to last. The year 1873 saw the beginnings of a long-lasting economic depression in America and Europe, felt keenly in the China trade. In 1875 HWD decided to focus on Hong Kong and sold its Whampoa property to the Chinese government.[22] By 1884 the mud docks were described as dilapidated, and even the granite ones were neglected.[23] The locations of the HWD and Union docks can easily be determined on Changzhou's north shore, but are tiny compared with the enormous military yards on the west of the island.

The British Consulate and the Chinese Customs

The lease in 1858 allowed Britain to build a two-bedroom residence-cum-office for the vice-consul. In 1867 it was determined not to be big enough; nor were the arrangements for detaining offenders adequate. It was cheaper to demolish the existing gaol and build a new one, and the vice-consul was given office space in the new building.[24] He had to be satisfied with his residence being given a lick of paint.[25] The house stood on a small hill presently occupied by a memorial to Chinese revolutionary martyrs.[26]

From this vantage point, Vice-Consul Henry Hance could observe the activities at the Custom House below. Arriving in 1859, Hance continued as vice-consul until his death in 1886; the vice-consulate itself was closed three years later. On Hance's demise, his house was adopted for use by the Maritime Customs as a holiday resort and sanatorium.[27] A Whampoa branch of the foreign-managed customs service was opened by Robert Hart in October 1859,[28] also having to manage with a floating office in its early years. In 1877 it moved into a smart building on the waterfront,[29] just in time. When it opened the foreign customs had a staff of ten, headed by a tide-surveyor. As a result of the 1870s depression, the tide-surveyor became the sole occupant of the new building. In 1926 the customs staff, by then totally Chinese, moved out of the building and the adjacent military academy moved in. In 1984 the former Custom House became a museum dedicated to the history of both the Whampoa customs service and the academy.

THE WHAMPOA MILITARY ACADEMY

After taking over HWD's large dock in 1875, the Chinese military began using Whampoa as a centre for training and experimentation. An Imperial Torpedo Department was established in 1883 under a foreign superintendent. By 1889 there was a naval and military academy, employing British and German instructors. In 1911 a new industrial college opened, and this too employed a foreign professor.[30] All were forerunners of the influential and prestigious Whampoa Military Academy, established on 16 June 1924.[31] Sun Yat-sen had decided that China needed a professionally trained army and navy and sent Chiang Kai-shek to Moscow for three months of indoctrination in the then admired ways of Soviet Russia. On Chiang's return, Sun put him in charge of the new academy.[32] Within its first couple of years, the school and its staff of 40 to 50 Russian instructors turned out several thousand zealous graduates.[33]

The academy suffered significant damage in 1927 during an anti-Communist crackdown,[34] but its progress was not affected. Branches were established in Canton (in a building on the riverfront at Yanjiang Middle Road), Chaochow (Chaozhou), Nanning, Changsha and Hankow (Hankou). The academy was relocated to Nanking (Nanjing) in September 1930. To escape the Japanese it moved again, in August 1937, to Chengtu (Chengdu). In 1949 the academy officially moved to Taiwan.[35] The physical structure in Whampoa remains. Although still a military area, many parts of the large complex are open to the public.

NEW TOWN AND OVER THE RIVER

What was known as Whampoa Island is now simply the Hai Zhu District of the city of Guangzhou. The southern tip of this long tongue of land is immediately opposite the western end of Danes Island, and it is there that Whampoa's first overflow settlement, New Town, sprang up. It housed Chinese shops and sailors' boarding houses, including, in the early 1870s, the Union and Whampoa hotels, and a bowling alley.

However, it was many years before the place that is now known as Huangpu began to feature in the foreign history of Whampoa. There was nothing on the north bank of the Pearl River proper until the early years of the 20th century, when there was talk of Whampoa being made a deep-water port to rival Hong Kong. Not until 1938 was a 400-metre-long wharf constructed and reclamation work put in hand.[36] The project was brought to a halt by the Japanese invasion of Canton later that year. The Nationalists fled the mainland for Taiwan from Whampoa in 1949, by which time they would have had other things on their minds.[37]

Further reading: A. Coates, *Whampoa: Ships on the Shore*; O'Regan, *Foreign Death in China*; Tiffen, *Friends of Sir Robert Hart*.

WOOSUNG (WUSONG) 吳淞

Shanghai Municipality, 31.24° N, 121.29° E
Port-of-Call, 1880 German Treaty
Open City, 1899 Imperial Decree

Woosung might have been chosen as one of the first treaty ports if being near an existing city had not been a priority. Whereas Shanghai was 25 kilometres up a small and hazardous tributary, Woosung village was at the mouth of that waterway and on the banks of the Yangtze itself.

'Pioneer', the first engine on the Woosung (Wusong) Railway, being carried for its first test run, 1876. Courtesy of P. A. Crush Chinese Railway Collection.

In 1865 the Woosung Road Co. was formed, with Jardines as managing agent. Permission was obtained to widen and straighten the military road from Shanghai. The construction of a railway line, the real intention of the promoters, was not mentioned but the project became too expensive and the company wound up in 1867.[1]

The plan was revived in 1872 when Jardines formed a more substantial company in London. The project coincided with a new horse-drawn tram system that had been constructed along Shanghai's bund. Jardines announced that they would be laying rails for a tram along their 'roadway', and took the lack of official response as consent. A full-blown railway was constructed, China's first. It was on a tiny scale, with its less-than-one-metre gauge track and locomotives that had been shipped out from England in individual packing cases.[2] However, Jardines had misread the situation.

The Shanghai *taotai* made his position clear. In a reasonably worded, 17-point dispatch to British Consul Walter Medhurst he stated the permissions granted to the company were based on the construction of a road; a railway had never been mentioned and would never have been allowed.[3] Nevertheless, as a sign of both a marked lack of respect and a high level of optimism, the first segment of the line was opened on 30 June 1876. The *taotai*, who had been invited, did not attend the ceremony.[4] The following day was a 'free travel' day, and people thronged to have their first experience of rail travel.[5] The extension to Woosung was opened on 26 December 1876, by which time China's objections had been taken to a higher level.

British Minister to Peking (Beijing) Sir Thomas Wade was negotiating with Li Hongzhang the terms of the Chefoo Agreement, signed on 13 September 1876. Although the Woosung Railway did not feature in the formal agreement, it had been on the agenda at Chefoo—particularly when it was reported on 3 August that a Chinese man had been run over and killed while walking on the track. The purpose of the Chefoo negotiations was to decide compensation for the murder of a British official on the Burmese border. The British now found themselves with the embarrassing prospect of a counter-claim along similar lines. As a generous compromise, Li proposed that China should buy the little railway at cost, and Jardines were advised to accept the offer.[6] Jardines received payment on 20 October 1877 and stopped running the trains. The Chinese tore up the track and demolished the stations. The equipment was shipped to Taiwan-fu (Tainan).[7]

The Woosung Railway episode was emblematic of the difficulties faced by foreigners trying to introduce innovation to the supremely conservative Chinese Empire. The question of the Woosung Bar was another. The bar was a constantly moving sandbank below the surface at the entrance to the Huangpu River. From the opening of Shanghai as a treaty port it was a hazard to passing vessels, the danger increasing as ever larger ships were introduced. As ships had to give it wide berth, the Woosung Bar effectively narrowed the navigable waterway quite considerably. When asked to dredge the river mouth, Chinese authorities stated 'the bar was placed there by Heaven and cannot be removed'.[8] Half-hearted schemes were proposed and foreign surveyors engaged but it was not until the Boxer Peace Protocol of 1901 that things changed. Taking advantage of the opportunity to force terms on a weakened China, this multinational agreement included a requirement that China establish a properly funded and professionally managed Whangpu River Conservancy Board. By then Woosung had been upgraded to a quasi–treaty port.

A Supplementary Convention between China and Germany in 1880 had given Woosung the status of a port-of-call. German ships, and through the Most Favoured Nation principle those of any Treaty Power, became able to take on or discharge merchandise originating from or bound for Shanghai. Foreigners were not permitted to erect landing stages, residences or business premises.[9] Ports-of-call had been introduced four years earlier along the Yangtze River by the Chefoo Agreement as a means of facilitating internal trade. The concept did not apply easily to Woosung, a place of direct shipment to and from foreign countries.[10] To address the customs ramifications, a halfway-house arrangement enabled customs officers to board ships at Woosung and complete formalities there.[11] The Germans had other plans. In 1898 they held secret discussions in Peking to establish an exclusive concession at Woosung.[12] When this information was leaked to the British Legation, Minister Sir Claude MacDonald acted immediately. Possession by any one power of the gateway to the largest port and paramount commercial centre in China would be disastrous. He persuaded the Tsungli Yamen to open Woosung to all nations as an open city.[13]

No formal declaration was made until 8 May 1899.[14] Some saw the delay as evidence of a lack of sincerity on China's part, possibly true. The plan for the new 'foreign settlement' showed virtually the entire foreshore reserved for the Imperial Chinese Railway Administration. Foreigners were expected to build their houses and offices on the far side of the railway yards. An old fort would be removed, but not the village that occupied the centre of the 'foreign' area.[15] When a municipality was established, it became clear that foreigners had no say in its management.[16] Ultimately, none of this mattered. Woosung was so dwarfed by its gigantic neighbour that the concept of a separate existence was meaningless.

Further reading: Crush, *Woosung Road*.

WUCHOW (WUZHOU) 梧州

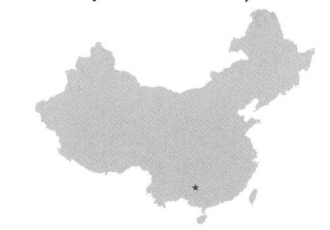

Guangxi, 23.28° N, 111.19° E
Treaty Port, 1897 British Treaty

The Burmah Convention of 1897 between Britain and China opened Wuchow as a treaty port. Almost 300 kilometres up the West River from Canton (Guangzhou), Wuchow was the head of navigation for ocean-going vessels, just inside Guangxi. Wuchow was not expected to be a significant centre of foreign trade, but the principle of opening the West River was important. In Britain's view, the main thrust of the 1897 Convention was to stem French influence in south-west China, diverting trade down the West River rather than overland to French Indo-China. In this respect, Wuchow was a success.

The port was opened in June 1897. By year's end there were eleven foreign firms established at Wuchow, all bar two represented by a Chinese agent.[1] This benefited the British and German firms concerned; local agents were the best commercial travellers when it came to marketing foreign goods. In turn, the agents gained a degree of consular protection for their questionable 'foreign' status.[2] In 1904, the British Consul reluctantly recognized those agencies claiming to be British, if only to prevent them looking elsewhere; any apparent lessening of British influence on the West River did not serve Britain's purpose.[3]

The Chinese business quarter was located on two streets outside the city walls, on the left bank of the West River where it was joined by the Fu, flowing from the north.[4] Upstream from Wuchow the West River was beset by rapids. A transshipment business had evolved, loading merchandise onto smaller craft for the onward journey to Nanning. The junction of the two rivers was the scene of much activity, with the Fu providing shelter from the stronger currents of its larger neighbour. The advent of foreign vessels required a different approach. The West River, like many in China, is prone to seasonal flooding—the water level can rise ten metres in hours. The steamers had to moor against a floating pontoon, linked to the bank by a gangplank. This was usual in a number of riverine ports, but Wuchow's pontoons, known as *pai*, were different. Local design decreed they be decorative wooden two-storey structures surrounded by a walkway—a Chinese answer to Swiss chalets.[5] Before long there was a long line of them, including one for the Maritime Customs and for each of Wuchow's shipping companies.[6]

The first foreign firm to abandon their *pai* was Jardines, which bought a substantial tract of riverfront land east of the city. A large building was constructed housing both offices and the residence of their senior man. Despite this ostentatious start the firm withdrew their representative after a few years, leaving a local agent to run their affairs.[7] To travellers coming up the river this new hong, the first foreign building they would have seen for days, signalled arrival at Wuchow. The customs bought a site next to Jardines for a residence for their commissioner; other staff remained living on the water. By 1903 there were nine foreign houses clustered round a central tennis court and cricket pitch.[8] There was in addition the Wuchow Club, housed in a neat little wooden building.[9] In 1922 the customs erected seven fine buildings to accommodate their offices and residences for 16 foreign staff.[10] Most are still there.

The British Consul also lived and worked on a *pai* until land was acquired for building.[11] The shoreline below the city walls was taken by a mass of Chinese businesses and boats, and Jardines and the customs had taken the best land to the east. So in 1899 the British controversially decided to build their premises on a hill on the far side of the Fu, over which there was no bridge. Such a small community might more wisely have chosen proximity, but the top of the 100-metre-high hill was flattened and the consul's residence built on its summit; the offices and constable's residence were at the foot of the hill.[12] The consulate's opening ceremony in July 1903 was a suitably grand occasion.[13] The first raising of the flag had taken place discreetly a few days earlier to avoid suggesting the British were 'taking possession'.[14] The residence is still there, although the commanding view is now obscured by vegetation.

1915 view from the British Consulate looking east, c. 1915. © Peter Lockhart Smith. Image courtesy of Historical Photographs of China, University of Bristol.

Steamers soon took much of the carrying trade from the junks, and the import-export volume passing through the Maritime Customs grew impressively. By 1903 Wuchow ranked 11th of the 34 treaty ports in China.[15] The main imports were cotton—piece-goods from England and yarn from India—with Wuchow serving as a distribution centre for the rest of the province. Rice was the staple export, along with timber, essential oils, indigo and livestock.[16] The only industry of note was boat-building. During the low-water winter months the foreshore became covered in matsheds, and wooden craft of all shapes and sizes were made by an army of craftsmen.[17] Steamers connected daily with Canton and Hong Kong, and after 1907 with Nanning. The journey from Canton had been reduced from 35 days to 3. The return took only a day.[18] The 1910s saw the arrival, as elsewhere in the country, of the foreign oil and tobacco companies. Asiatic Petroleum and Standard Oil built storage facilities on the far side of the river.

But Guangxi was a troubled place. As early as 1900 anti-foreign placards were posted around the city stating that kerosene, a foreign import, was made from human bones and should be avoided. Many people threw away what they had and reverted to nut oil for their cooking.[19] There had been a small rebellion in the area in 1898 and more were expected at any time.[20] A combination of political unrest and unusually severe flooding in 1917 caused much unhappiness, with a number of local firms bankrupted.[21] In 1921, matters took a more alarming turn when the two provinces of Guangxi and Guangdong declared war on each other.[22] Wuchow was on the border. Frustrations were inevitably vented against foreigners, and the anti-British boycott of 1925 caused the consulate to close. Continued fighting and heavy taxation took their toll as the 1920s gave way to the 1930s. When Japanese activities closed the lower West River in 1938, the little trade remaining had to use the land route to French Indo-China.[23] Things appeared to have come full circle.

Further reading: *A Handbook to the West River*.

Wuhu (Wuhu) 蕪湖

Anhui, 31.20° N, 118.21° E
Treaty Port, 1876 British Treaty

Wuhu was occupied by the Taiping rebels in 1853. The distribution centre for the vast rice crop of Anhui Province, it was considered to be the most prosperous of their possessions.[1] When Lord Elgin's mission called in for supplies in October 1858, they found that it had been almost totally destroyed.[2]

Frederick Bruce requested in 1862 that Wuhu be opened to British steamers for the collection of tea exports, the overland route to Shanghai having been closed by the Taipings.[3] His request was refused, but in 1876 the Chefoo Agreement added Wuhu to the list of treaty ports. By then Britain had been trading on the Yangtze for 15 years, so why did they see potential in Wuhu? Perhaps its possession emphasized British dominance. The foreign merchants in Shanghai were reported to be excited by Wuhu's prospects[4]—a misplaced emotion.

The port was opened on 1 April 1877. Two weeks later *The China Mail* reported that the main export 'seems to be rice' but that tea and silk 'were expected'. They had not appreciated that the trade, admittedly significant, belonged to Chinese merchants, leaving little scope for foreign enterprise. Arthur Davenport, British Vice-Consul in Shanghai, was sent to secure a tract of land on the river for a British Concession. This he did, although he advised against immediate occupation. He thought it wiser to see how the river behaved in the summer before building. Many summers would pass before further progress was made.[5]

It was missionaries who were the first to develop land at the new treaty port. In 1877 the Jesuits bought a site on the first of a line of small hills that stretched back from the river, downstream of the creek that led to the walled city a kilometre or two inland.⁶ Their intentions were not entirely spiritual. Immediately below their mission were the office and residential premises rented by the Maritime Customs. This became the nucleus of the small foreign business community. The Jesuits later reclaimed four hectares of riverfront and erected a stone bund and a number of foreign-style residences and warehouses. At the time of the port's opening, however, the 14 foreign residents were obliged either to live on ships in the river or occupy whatever land-based premises they could secure.⁷ The 14 included the representative of just one foreign firm. Alexander Man, Commissioner of Customs, had the following to say in his Trade Report for 1879: 'Although some progress has been made . . . it cannot be said that the outlook in this direction at all inclines as yet to the optimist view. Rather, I fear, is the contrary the fact.'⁸ How delicately bad news was phrased in those days.

The trade of the port was substantially in Chinese hands and imports were obtained directly from Shanghai. The only export to speak of was rice, and sending this most important of commodities out of the country was prohibited. The only scope for foreign involvement was providing fast and efficient transport in the form of steamships. Owing to peculiarities of the river current at Wuhu, the hulks that the shipping companies used could not be linked to the shore by pontoons. Instead goods and passengers had to be ferried back and forth in small junks and sampans.⁹ The first hulk to be moored, in 1877, belonged to the China Merchants Co. It was placed at the mouth of the creek to be near the Custom House. George McBain followed in 1882, and then Butterfield & Swire and Jardines in 1884 and 1886 respectively.¹⁰ As each hulk floated in isolation, customs examiners were assigned to each one. Foreign customs staff more than doubled in the first ten years, from 8 to 18, supported by a much greater number of local staff.

The concession site remained untouched after being identified in 1877. It was plain there was insufficient commercial interest to recoup the cost of laying it out formally. The site started at the outflow of another small creek 1500 metres to the north of

1933 view of the Custom House and surrounding commercial area. Photograph by Warren Swire. © Image courtesy of John Swire and Sons and Historical Photographs of China, University of Bristol.

Wuhu Creek (the Taokia, long since disappeared) and ran north for 1200 metres to a small hill, I Chi (Yiji) Shan. The site was in many ways ideal and had good, deep anchorage facilities. However, between it and the Custom House much of the foreshore was occupied by Chinese timber merchants who refused to allow an access road. Timber was an important industry, with large log rafts floating down the river from above Hankow (Hankou), to be broken into smaller ones at Wuhu for onward journeys up the many canals and creeks.¹¹

China Merchants acquired part of the site, as did other Chinese firms. They bunded their properties, although with no central plan.¹² Apart from the American Methodists, who occupied I Chi Shan, it was many years before there was any further foreign occupation of the settlement area. No businesses wanted to go there without convenient access to the Custom House. But by 1901 the shipping companies were becoming increasingly dissatisfied with their hulk arrangements, and despite its shortcomings they began looking at the settlement area.¹³ Interest grew such that in 1904 the city authorities issued regulations for the General International Settlement of Wuhu, formally established on 16 May 1905.¹⁴

This major development prompted the filling-in of swamps and the building of roads. A unified bund was discussed and buildings were expected to spring up. Jardines and Swires acquired lots, but initially it was only Swires that built—four substantial rice-storage warehouses. Photographs even as late as 1911 show them standing in splendid isolation. A faithfully reproduced replica of Swires' China Navigation office stands there now. In 1919 a new Custom House and supporting buildings were erected on the plot south of the Taokia Creek allocated for the purpose 42 years previously;[15] it is still there, looking grand. Notwithstanding, the settlement remained a wasteland for the most part before other warehouses were added. The last remaining example could still be seen in mid-2007, but now the whole site is given over to residential blocks.

The settlement's slow progress did not mean lack of development elsewhere. In 1882 the Customs Commissioner had a fine house built on the hill behind that occupied by the Jesuits. The magnificent result still stands, freshly restored but with no apparent purpose. Only slightly less magnificent is the Assistant Commissioner's dazzling white residence, on the same hill and slightly to the south-east.

The foundation stone for the British Consulate was laid on 30 April 1887 on the Jesuits' hill and a two-storey residence-cum-office finished before year's end.[16] Only three years later a British government report questioned the need for a consulate at all in such a quiet port. Yet the presence remained until 1922, when its responsibilities were taken over by Nanking (Nanjing).[17] By happy chance the building is still there, although looking rather sad.

The next hilltop mansions to appear were an impressive residential block for the Jesuit missionaries in 1888 and another for their Methodist brethren two kilometres away on I Chi Shan in 1889. The Methodist hospital burnt down in 1923, but its 1927 replacement is still used.[18] In the absence of a formal foreign municipal body, a voluntary group known as the Wuhu Roads Improvement Society, chaired by the British Consul, assumed responsibility for laying and improving roads and pathways. All the foreign community were subscribers, as were a few Chinese merchants.[19] The society was still functioning until at least 1921.[20]

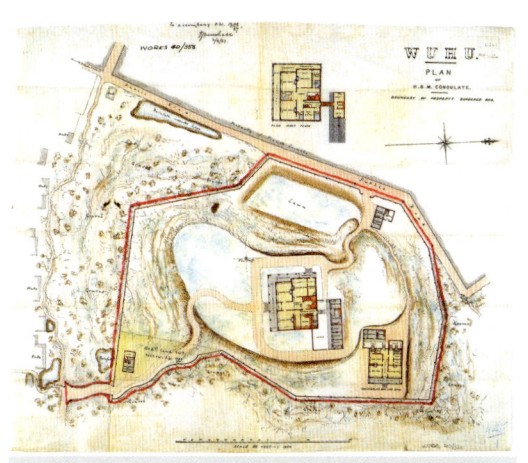

1887 plan of the site reserved for the British Consulate. Reprinted with permission by the National Archives.

The only foreign business activity was shipping, and in terms of cargo this was confined to transporting rice to other treaty ports. The trade could be booming one year and in the doldrums the next, according to the vagaries of the rice crop either locally or at the port of consumption. Additional extraneous factors also affected the level of trade. During the Sino-French War of 1884–85, France declared rice to be 'contraband of war' and threatened any foreign steamers that were found carrying it. Shipments from Wuhu therefore diverted to the inland waterways, carried by junk.[21] Political game-playing also had an effect on the shippers' ability to trade. In 1890 the viceroy prohibited foreign vessels (but not Chinese junks) from carrying rice, claiming it was needed to feed the local population. It became clear that the authorities were using that year's bumper crop to boost provincial revenue; goods carried by foreign vessels paid duty to the central government, whereas the duty on goods carried by Chinese vessels went to the province.[22] Another example arose in 1898 when a similar ban was imposed as a device to reduce the price of rice. The foreign shippers suffered, but not as much as the farmers.[23] With all this excitement it is hard to understand how the Butterfield & Swire representative could report that Wuhu was 'unspeakable in its dullness and lack of resources'.[24]

An outbreak of anti-foreign disturbances along the whole of the Yangtze occurred in 1891. Wuhu was one of the first and most terrifying flashpoints, with anger directed against Roman Catholic missionaries for allegedly boiling babies alive and cutting out children's eyes and hearts to make potions. The entire Jesuit compound was destroyed. The British Consulate was stoned, and Consul Colin Ford and his family escaped by dressing in Chinese clothes. The Custom House was threatened, and only the arrival of three Chinese gunboats prevented further violence.[25] Once it was over, a token two unfortunates were beheaded, and an indemnity was paid to the Jesuits.[26]

The riots of 1891 were neither the first nor the last directed against foreigners at Wuhu, but they were the most serious. Paradoxically, the foreign imprint that remains in Wuhu, apart from the secluded European-style mansions, is thanks to the missionaries: the former Methodist hospital at the northern end of the settlement and the magnificent Cathedral of St. Joseph at the southern end. Midway between them is the red-brick St. James School, nowadays functioning as the No. 11 Middle School. The indemnity money was well spent.

YOCHOW (YUEYANG) 岳陽

Hunan, 29.26° N, 113.08° E
Open City, 1898 Imperial Decree

The wealth and river network of Hunan, a centre of anti-foreign sentiment, was irresistible to foreign commercial interests. Britain was negotiating opening Siangtan (Xiangtan) as a treaty port, over 200 kilometres up the Xiang River from where it joins the Yangtze. Instead the Chinese government opened Yochow by Imperial Decree on 5 April 1898.[1]

As often happens with compromises, neither party was satisfied. The British saw it as at least a step in the right direction, even though Yochow was only just inside the Hunan border—but British merchants protested that penetrating deeper was preferable. The Chinese were unhappy about foreigners forcing their way into Hunan at all—but at least they were far removed from the provincial heartland. In 1899 Sir Robert Hart sent H. B. Morse to open the Custom House, advising him to 'go slowly, see everything and be reasonable'.[2] Under Morse's direction the Custom House was opened in November with a staff of four Europeans.[3]

Yochow was generally seen as a place of no political or commercial importance, but it was expected to attract all the trade of Hunan that passed by to or from the Yangtze. This did not happen. The trade continued to pass by. The site of Yochow was unsuitable for steamer traffic; the anchorage was poor and there was no shelter for moored vessels. An alternative was Chengling, eight kilometres to the north and only a kilometre from the Yangtze. A small creek provided the required shelter and the Chinese government designated land for a foreign settlement. Municipal work was to be under the joint control of the *taotai* and the Commissioner of Customs.[4] Roads were marked out and lots put up for auction. To appease local sensitivities, land was let on yearly leases rather than give the impression of permanent possession.[5] A foreign customs tide-surveyor became superintendent of police.[6] A survey was conducted for the construction of a bund, but work was suspended due to the Boxer troubles further north.[7]

The customs were the first to build. The Custom House and outdoor staff quarters were built on land six or seven metres above the general ground level. The housing for the more senior staff was built to the north, on slightly higher ground still.[8] These buildings, in particular the commissioner's 'palatial mansion', dominated the immediate countryside and could be seen for miles around.[9] The British Consul was less fortunate. He arrived too late for the auction and could secure only a 'third rate' site. This was the opinion of Reginald Tower, who was reviewing Britain's consular needs in China. Tower recommended that the lease not be signed. The British Consulate therefore closed before it opened.[10] The Japanese, who had attended the auction, obtained a

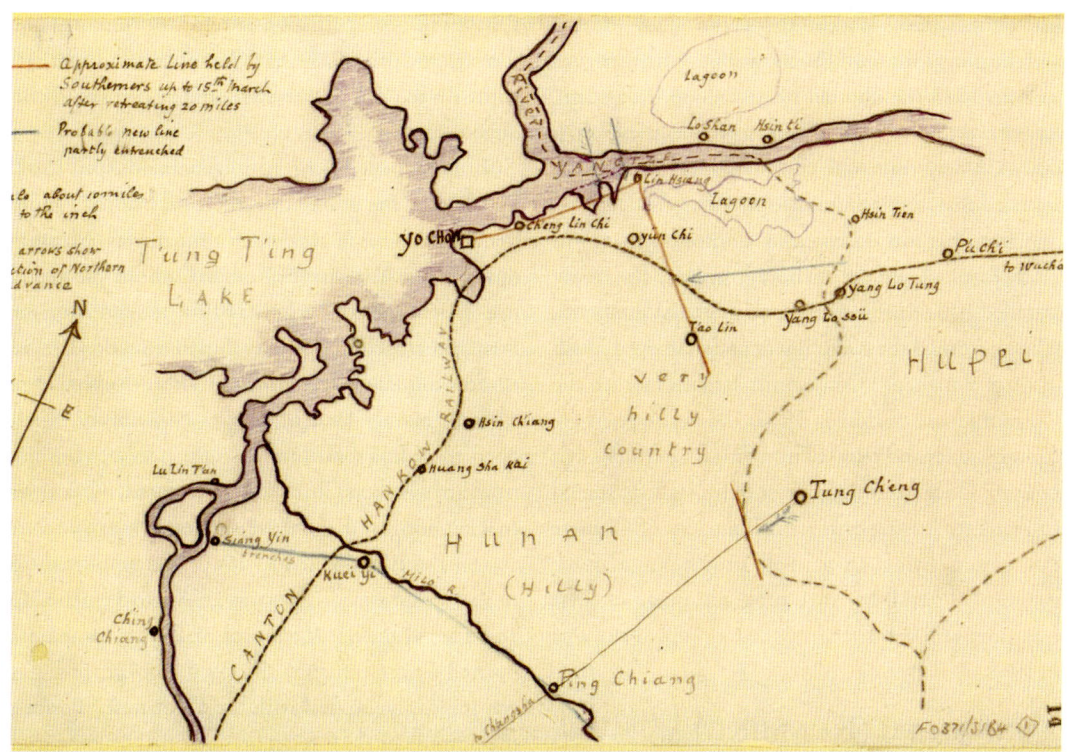

1918 map showing the position of Yochow (Yueyang) and Ch'eng Lin Chi (Chengling) at the entrance to the Tung Ting (Dong Ting) Lake. Reprinted with permission by the National Archives.

much better plot. Furthermore, following destruction of Japanese property at Shasi (Shashi) during a riot in July 1898, Japan demanded that it be granted an exclusive settlement at Yochow.[11] Neither this nor their consulate came about.

The section of Tower's report dealing with Yochow was very long, considering his recommendation to close it. Yochow as a quasi–treaty port, he said, was more of a hindrance than a help to foreign trade. Before its opening, steamers could sail direct from Hankow (Hankou) to Changsha, a much bigger city and well within Hunan's borders, under the Inland Steam Navigation Rules. But those rules governed navigation beyond the limit of the nearest treaty port. As Yochow had achieved open status, steamers were forbidden to bypass it en route to or from a non-opened port. Any foreign-shipped cargo from the interior, principally raw cotton, tea and rice, was now required to be transshipped at Yochow onto a steamer operating under the Yangtze River Regulations. This involved an unjustifiable level of expense, delay and inconvenience. The British merchants had foreseen this, but their government had not. Furthermore Yochow, or rather Chengling, was tiny and totally without handling facilities.[12]

This bizarre situation was resolved in 1903 when Changsha became a treaty port, rendering Yochow defunct. The major shipping companies—Jardines, Swires, China Merchants and NKK—maintained a presence at Chengling using local agents. And of course the Custom House remained, but there was no other activity. When the new Hankow-Canton Railway passed close to Yochow in 1918 it had no more effect than to provide some welcome company for the tiny foreign community; two foreign railway engineers were briefly based at Yochow. Of much greater import was the turmoil that grew during the 1910s and 1920s. The district became a battleground.[13] When each of the competing armies realized it was about to be ousted, and this happened many times, they marked the occasion by looting and burning not only Yochow but Chengling as well. In 1923 the unusual phenomenon of 'foreign' trade reverting to junks was observed as these obviously Chinese craft were considered less likely to be attacked than foreign steamships.[14]

Chengling was occupied by Cantonese troops in 1926, fortified and the anchorage mined. The newly installed batteries fired on passing foreign gunboats, which returned the compliment and destroyed much of what remained.[15] Communist activities forced the Custom House to close in 1930. They kidnapped the commissioner and released him only on payment of a ransom. Once free he and most of his staff evacuated to Hankow, leaving only a small nucleus of Chinese tide-waiters living on a small launch for a quick getaway.[16] Presumably they took advantage of their transport well before the Japanese occupied the area in 1938.[17]

Yunnan-fu (Kunming) 昆明

Yunnan, 25.02° N, 102.43° E
Consular Station, 1902 Britain

British interest in Yunnan-fu was prompted by French designs on south-west China, thought to threaten British concerns in Burma. In a convention of 7 August 1896, France secured the opening of Szemao (Simao) as a treaty port, close to the Red River, to encourage trade between China and French Indo-China. Even if this had happened, Szemao would only have been a step on the way to the provincial capital, Yunnan-fu. In 1897 France was granted permission to build a railway to Yunnan-fu from Haiphong. The British felt obliged to match this with one from Burma along the route investigated by Raymond Margary a generation earlier. The French completed theirs, the first train arriving in Yunnan-fu on 1 April 1910[1] after a three-day journey.[2] The British did not,[3] perhaps as a result of comments by the Viceroy of India; Lord Curzon scoffed that the entire Burma-to-China trade could be carried on two dugout canoes.[4]

Britain opened a consulate-general in April 1902, but despite the grand title there was seldom more than one official in residence. Yunnan was a dangerous province. Yunnan-fu's Roman Catholic Cathedral had been burned down in May 1900 in retaliation for French encroachments, and religious functionaries of all denominations were forced to flee.[5] Nevertheless a small, mainly French, foreign community developed, including some businessmen. Access to the city from anywhere in China was convoluted, by steamer to Haiphong and then the single-track railway.[6] A customs station opened in 1910, and employed up to six foreign staff.[7] There was an Anglo-French club and a small hotel.[8] A handful of British companies opened offices, but they all closed in 1922, saying it was impossible to deal with the Yunnanese.[9] Besides, the purpose of the foreign presence had become strategic rather than commercial. Britain closed its consulate in December 1947.[10]

Russian Frontier Stations

(See Map 2 'The Russian border area' on page xxii.)

The first recorded treaty between China and a foreign power is the 1689 Treaty of Nipchu (Nerchinsk in Russian). This dealt with border delineation (a matter agreed only over 300 years later), and reciprocal rights of trade and travel. A second attempt to settle the boundary was the 1727 Treaty of Kiakhta, an agreement opening two trading stations on the frontier—Kiakhta (now just inside Russia on the border with Mongolia) and Nipchu (700 kilometres to the east and now well inside Russian territory).

Cross-border trade with Russia had been conducted since 1847 at Ili (also known as Kuldja or Yining, in Xinjiang) and Tarbagatai (near the Xinjiang border with Kazakhstan and now known as Qoqek). Ili was in the 'cold country', a place of banishment for Canton (Guangzhou) Hong merchants who failed to pay their debts.[1] Even Commissioner

Lin Zexu found himself there, having failed in his duties in Canton.[2] The 1851 Treaty of Kuldja regularized trading arrangements and allowed for Russian settlement at the two towns.[3]

Further steps were taken to agree the border in treaties of 1858 and 1860. The latter, signed in Peking, opened Urga (Ulaanbaatar) and Kalgan (Zhangjiakou) for Russian trade, with a consul to be stationed at the former. The two treaties transferred to Russia the territory to the south and east of the Amur (Heilong) River, an area they named the Maritime Province. In 2013 Russia's prime minister claimed, apparently without irony, that his task was to protect the province 'from excessive expansion by bordering states.'[4]

A Muslim rebellion in Xinjiang in 1871 prompted Russia to intervene when Chinese imperial authority collapsed. The 1881 Treaty of St. Petersburg restored Qing sovereignty, but at a high price. In addition to a large payment to Russia, six more towns were opened for Russian trade and consulates: Hami (Kumul in Xinjiang); Kobdo (Khovd in Mongolia); Kucheng (Qitai, Xinjiang); Suchow (Jiuquan, Gansu); Uliassutai (Uliastai, Mongolia); and Urumchi (Urumqi, Xinjiang). The treaty also gave Russia the right to open a consulate at Turfan (Turpan, in Xinjiang). Russia extended its influence further in Manchuria by developing railways, principally the Chinese Eastern Railway, each line and major station being 'protected' by Russian troops. Despite signing a convention confirming Chinese authority in Manchuria in 1902,[5] Russia continued gaining territorial and commercial advantages, losing most of them following a war with Japan in 1904–5.

Further reading: Foust, *Muscovite and Mandarin*.

JAPANESE STATIONS IN THE NORTH-EAST

(See Map 3 'Manchuria' on page xxiii.)

Japan had been pressured into signing its own one-sided treaties with the major Western powers in 1858 and felt the need to restore national pride by exerting itself over its larger, yet enticingly weak, neighbour. In 1871 Li Hongzhang refused to grant Japan the same concessions won by the Europeans and Americans. However, he did sign a treaty in Tientsin (Tianjin) giving Japan trade and commercial privileges, plus extraterritoriality for its citizens. For the first time, grudgingly, China treated Japan as its equal.[1]

Japan's wholehearted embrace of Western technology, particularly military, led to victory over China in 1895. The resulting settlement gave rise to the opening of four treaty ports—Hangchow (Hangzhou), Shasi (Shashi), Soochow (Suzhou) and Suifenho (Suifenhe). Japan's 1903 Commercial Treaty opened Changsha as a treaty port, and Mukden (Shenyang) and Tatungkow (Dadonggou) as open cities. Suifenho was of no importance commercially, apart from being the border post between Manchuria and Russia's Maritime Province, and Tatungkow remained insignificant.

Faced by a probable Japanese victory over Russia in the war of 1904–5, China bowed to Japanese pressure and opened in May 1904 by Imperial Decree three cities in Shandong, where Japan sought dominance—Choutsun (Zhoucun), Tsinan (Jinan) and Weihsien (Weifang).[2] Choutsun was a sub-station to Tsinan, a city growing in importance. Weihsien, another sub-station, became famous as the site of one of the largest Japanese internment camps of the Pacific War.

In December 1905 Japan and China entered into a treaty recognizing all the transfers and assignments, mainly of railways, made in the Treaty of Portsmouth, from Russia to Japan. Additionally, Japan required China to open a further 16 towns and cities in the north-east for international trade. Most were, or would become, stops along the ever-increasing railway network in north-east China. Only Aigun (Aihun) and Harbin became significant. Of the remainder, six were in Liaoning Province: Fakumen (Faku), Fengwangcheng (Fengcheng), Hsinmintun (Xinmin), Liaoyang, Tiehling (Tieling) and Tungkiangtzu (Tongjiangkou). Three were in Heilongjiang, near the Russian border: Hailar (Hulunber), Manchouli (Manzhouli) and Tsitsihar

(Qiqihar). Five were in Jilin: Changchun, Hunchun, Kirin (Jilin), Ninguta (Ning'an) and Sanhsing (Yilan). Changchun was on the boundary between the Russian and Japanese parts of Manchuria. The city had separate 'railway towns' for each nation, and different time zones; Russian time was 23 minutes earlier than Japanese.[3] Changchun grew as a distribution centre for the produce from the surrounding plains. The Japanese installed major support facilities there for the South Manchuria Railway, including factories and engineering works, plus housing, hospitals, schools and the luxurious Yamato Hotel. Kirin, on the navigable Sungari River and 1000 kilometres from its mouth,[4] became a distribution centre for timber from the Manchurian forests.[5]

Japan annexed Korea in 1905 and almost immediately entered into a dispute with China about the location of the Sino-Korean border. In 1907 Japanese troops crossed into the Gando (Jiandao) region, home to many Korean refugees. The dispute was resolved with the Gando Convention of September 1909. In return for recognizing the region was part of China, Japan was granted further railway rights in Manchuria and the opening of four more towns as places of international trade: Chuitzuchien (Yanji), Lungchingtsun (Longjing, the only one to become a customs station), Paitsaokou (Baicaogou) and Toutaokou (Toudaogou).[6]

A Presidential Mandate in January 1914 recognized that open ports in China had resulted in 'benefits to all' and conferred that status on seven more towns and cities. Five, all railway towns, were in a line parallel to those opened to Japan in 1905. They were, from west to east, Kueihuacheng (Hohot), Kalgan (Zhangjiakou, already opened by the Russian treaty of 1860), Dolonor (Duolun), Chihfeng (Chifeng) and Taonan. The sixth was Hulutao (Huludao), at the northern end of the Bohai Sea. Work began there in 1910 to create an ice-free harbour, but was interrupted by the 1911 revolution. The mandate of 1914 attempted to revive the project but it only began in earnest in 1930.[7] The seventh was Lungkow (Longkou) in Shandong.[8]

The First World War diverted the attention of the European powers with a presence in China. Japan saw an opportunity to strengthen its position and, in January 1915, issued the 'Twenty-One Demands' to the government of Yuan Shikai. In a thinly disguised step towards colonizing the entire province, seven additional towns and cities in Shandong were opened, along with eight in Inner Mongolia. Those in Shandong were Ichow (Linyi), Lintsingchow (Linqing), Poshan (Boshan), Tehchow (Dezhou), Tsining (Jining), Yangkiokow (Yangkou) and Yenchow (Yanzhou). Newly opened in Mongolia were Chinpeng (Jinpeng), Hsiao Kulun (Kulun), Kailuhsien (Kailu), Lichuan (Fuli), Linsi (Linxi), Pingchuan (Pingquan), Talai (Dalai Nuori) and Wuchanghsien (Wuchang). Later agreements established customs stations at Pitzuwo (Pikou) and Pulantien (Pulandian, also known as Port Adams), both within the Japanese leased territory of Dairen, and at Chinchow (Jinzhou) at the head of the Bohai Sea.[9]

Japan's efforts to develop Manchuria centred on the successful South Manchuria Railway. This was a huge organization developing major centres of its own, including: Anshan, a centre of steel production; Fushun, then and now a significant coal-mining city; Penhsihu (Benxi), near large iron mines; and Kaiyuan, Kungchulin (Gongzhuling), Ssupingkai (Siping), Tashihchiao (Dashiqiao) and Wafangtien (Wafangdian), all important railway junctions. Each had large Japanese populations.[10]

Japan's earlier encroachments were made under the pretence of the established system of opening ports by treaty. Consequently, Japan created more treaty ports and open cities than any other nation. However, in March 1932 the Japanese created the 'independent republic' of Manchukuo, which absorbed and annexed Manchuria. Changchun was made the capital, given the new name Hsin King, and the last Emperor of China was installed as 'Chief Executive Henry Pu Yi'.[11] Subsequent Japanese actions brought about the end of the whole treaty port system.

Further reading: Auslin, *Negotiating with Imperialism*; Brooks, *Japan's Imperial Diplomacy*.

Yangtze River Ports-of-Call

(See Map 6 'The Yangtze River' on page xxvi.)

In the twilight of both the 19th century and the Qing dynasty, Britain found itself in danger of being outflanked by its rivals among the Treaty Powers. Dominant since its first treaty in 1842, Britain wished to demonstrate it remained so. Accordingly, it declared a sphere of influence over the entire Yangtze valley, including Shanghai's hinterland and effectively half of China. The 1858 treaties of Tientsin (Tianjin) had opened Chinkiang (Zhenjiang), Nanking (Nanjing), Kiukiang (Jiujiang) and Hankow (Hankou), stretching 1000 kilometres upriver from Shanghai. However, Lord Elgin's goal was that the privilege should not be restricted to the named ports. He wanted all the river's trade opened to British merchants.[1] This was to remain a wish.

The British Treaty of Tientsin allowed for its commercial terms to be revised after ten years. As this deadline drew near, views were sought from concerned parties in China and Britain, generating a huge amount of correspondence. A Supplementary Convention was signed in 1869, allowing British merchants to go virtually anywhere on China's rivers with vessels 'resembling Chinese craft, and propelled by oars or sails'. Furthermore, the merchants would be permitted to rent property for residence and storage, but not be allowed to display any signs describing their business, nor could their vessels fly their house flag.[2] Despite Sir Rutherford Alcock's view that these concessions went far beyond reasonable expectations,[3] they were met with derisory comments from the British mercantile community. The convention was not ratified by the British government.[4]

The main Chinese fear was that their merchants would be disadvantaged if foreign steamers, with greater speed, carrying capacity and efficiency, were to enter home waters. Britain pressed its case again during the negotiations surrounding the 1876 Chefoo Agreement. This convention identified three more treaty ports on the Yangtze—Wuhu, Ichang (Yichang) and Chungking (Chongqing), the last being conditional on the navigational challenges presented by the upper river being overcome. Thus the number of open ports on a now 2000-kilometre stretch of the river rose to eight. The agreement identified another class of port, referred to as a 'port-of-call'. Six were listed—Anking (Anqing), Hukow (Hukou), Lukikow (Luxi), Shasi (Shashi), Tatung (Datong) and Wusueh (Wuxue). The Commercial Treaty of 1902 upgraded Anking to a treaty port, but its opening was dependent upon *likin* reforms which were unacceptable to China. Shasi became a treaty port under the 1895 Treaty of Shimonoseki. Tatung had been identified by Frederick Bruce in 1862 as a potential collection depot for tea exports.[5] It was stipulated that the six were not open ports and that foreign merchants were not authorized to trade there. However, foreign steamers could 'touch' for the purpose of picking up or setting down passengers or cargo, provided the ship-to-shore transfers were done solely by native boats.

In 1898 the Inland Steam Navigation Regulations were issued, opening all inland waterways to foreign steamers registered for the purpose. They were allowed to 'proceed to and fro at will', but could only land cargo 'at places ordinarily recognized as places of trade for native vessels'.[6] The application of these regulations to the Great River was clarified by the issue, also in 1898, of the Yangtze Regulations. These reaffirmed the status of the six ports-of-call already identified, and added eight 'landing stages', where the handling of cargo was prohibited, but passengers and their baggage could be taken on or discharged. The eight were Chinghokow (Yidu), Hsinti (Xindi), Hwangchow (Huangzhou), Hwangtzekang (Huangshigang), Iching (Yizheng), Kiangyin (Jiangyin), Luchingchiang (Lujinggang) and Tienhsingchiao (Tianxingqiao).

Arranging for 22 places along the river (including Chungking) to be at least partly open to foreign shipping was a considerable feat of negotiation. Still, dissatisfied merchants grumbled. The various rules for registering, reporting and settling the *likin* and other duties payable were seen as 'a mountain of unworkable regulations' likely to smother the gift of freer access. Thus, in the first months of the new system, 'not one package of cargo has ever been landed'.[7] Passengers were quick to benefit from the faster means of transport, but Chinese merchants were 'more or less indifferent to a day or so' delay in carrying goods, preferring the cheaper and traditional modes of transport.[8] Looking at the river today, with the thousands of vessels of all description racing up and down, it is hard to reconcile the views of just over a century ago.

WEST RIVER PORTS-OF-CALL

(See Map 8 'The Pearl and West Rivers' on page xxviii.)

Since the creation of Yangtze River ports-of-call in 1876, much had happened in China's south-west. In particular, France had defeated China in a brief war over control of Tonkin, which in French eyes was a step towards opening trade in China.[1] The French had threatened to annex Hainan Island and the entire Guangdong coastline, which at that time bordered the French colony. Paul Doumer, the Governor-General of Indo-China, even drew up plans for the invasion of Yunnan.[2]

Seeing the West River as potentially drawing trade from the Upper Yangtze and directing it away from French territory, Britain established a foothold there by replicating the formula it had applied successfully on the Yangtze. In a Special Article in the 1897 Burmah Agreement, Britain obtained the opening of Kongkun Market (Jiangken), Samshui (Sanshui) and Wuchow (Wuzhou) as treaty ports, and created four ports-of-call—Kumchuk (Ganzhu), Kongmoon (Jiangmen, later to become a treaty port), Shiuhing (Zhaoqing) and Takhing (Deqing). British steamers were free to ply between Wuchow and Hong Kong or Canton (Guangzhou) along certain routes that were to be advised.[3] The ports-of-call could be used for the picking up and setting down of passengers and cargo, under regulations identical to those operating on the Yangtze.

Some degree of regulation was necessary but there were complaints and irritations. The main frustration was that a steamer plying from one treaty port to another could not conduct any business at intermediate ports. Hence the British Commercial Treaty of 1902 laid down a set of new regulations and established three more ports-of-call, for use by passengers and cargo, and ten 'landing stages', for passengers only. The ports-of-call were Paktauhau (presently part of Jiangshui), Lotinghau (Nandukou) and Dosing (Yunan). The landing stages were Fongchuen (Fengkai), Howlik (Dinghu), Kaukong (Jiujiang), Kulow, (Gulao), Lukpu (Lubu), Lukto (close to Dahe), Mahning (Maningwei), Wingon (Yong'an), Yuetsing (Yuecheng) and Yungki (Suixiang).

The regulations were cumbersome, and revised again in 1904. But there were now 20 places along the river system, plus Canton, where foreign steamers could conduct business.

Further reading: *Handbook to the West River*; Lee, *France and the Exploitation of China*.

TIBETAN PORTS

(See Map 4 'Tibet' on page xxiv.)

The British in India wanted to establish trade ties with Tibet on their northern frontier. Such a move would help to keep Russian interest at bay, a constant fear. Tibet, nominally a vassal of China, was ruled by a powerful lama elite, who for centuries had isolated their population from corrupting foreign influences.

An article in the 1876 Chefoo Agreement allowed for a British exploratory mission to Tibet. The first attempt was countermanded by an Anglo-Chinese convention in 1886 which, while mainly concerned with matters relating to Burma, agreed trade with Tibet would not be pressed 'unduly'.[1] Interpreting this as British weakness, the Tibetans immediately launched an attack on Sikkim. The British response was to ask China, as the suzerain power, to remove the unwanted visitors. When the deadline expired in March 1888, with no action taken, the British forced the invaders back into Tibet. Another convention was signed in 1890, confirming Britain's hold on Sikkim and its border with Tibet.[2]

Regulations agreed in 1893 for cross-border trade included the establishment of Yatung (Yadong) as a trade mart for British merchants.[3] Yatung was selected by the Tibetans and proved to be an insignificant village, but it was formally opened for trade on 1 May 1894. Tibetan traders were allowed to travel all over India, and the British expected Yatung would facilitate some degree of reciprocation. It did not. Nor did the Tibetans seem to have any intention of honouring the new agreement, claiming that as they had not been party to the negotiations they had no obligation to abide by the outcome. Britain concluded that Chinese suzerainty was nothing but 'a political fog into which the Tibetans could dodge and hide when so inclined'.[4] However, tea was to the Tibetans what opium had been to the Chinese, and the British felt confident that they could break the Tibetan tea monopoly and introduce their own product.

In 1904, while Russia was at war with Japan, Britain decided that the time for shying away from undue pressure was over. Colonel Francis Younghusband headed an armed mission to Lhasa in 1904 which led to the opening of two more cities—Gartok (Gar Yasha) and Gyantse (Gyangze).[5] Gartok was extremely remote, once the summer capital of western Tibet and 450 kilometres north-east of Delhi. Gyantse, on the other hand, was conveniently located between Yatung and Lhasa. By then it was obvious that lucrative trade over the Indian-Tibetan border was a lost cause. Today it is as if none of this had ever happened, apart from the wonderfully named museum in one of Gyantse's old forts—'Memorial Hall of Anti-British'.

Further reading: Allen, *Duel in the Snows*; Fleming, *Bayonets to Lhasa*.

Appendix

Places visited by the author during the preparation of this book:

Amoy: February 2009
Anping: June 2011
Banka: June 2011
Canton: October 2008, April 2009, March 2012
Capsuimoon: April 2011
Changsha: September 2011
Chefoo: October 1999, September 2008, September 2010
Chengtu: September 2012
Chinkiang: January 2013
Chinwangtao: December 2011
Chungking: February 2012
Chusan: October 1999
Dalny/Dairen: October 1999, June 2012
Double Island: February 2010
Foochow: April 2009
Gyantse: April 2006
Hangchow: October 2012
Hankow: June 2010, November 2012
Hoihow: February 2009
Hokow (West River): March 2012
Hong Kong: my home since 1980
Ichang: November 2012
Keelung: June 2011
Kiukiang: November 2012
Kiungchow: February 2009
Kongkun Market: March 2012
Kongmoon: March 2012
Kowloon: frequent visits
Kulangsu: February 2009
Kuliang: April 2009
Kuling: November 2012
Kwangchowwan: February 2012
Liampo: October 2009
Lungkow: September 2008
Macao: frequent visits
Mokanshan: 1996
Mukden: June 2012
Namoa: February 2010
Nanking: January 2013
Nantai: April 2009
Newchwang: June 2012
Ningpo: October 1999, October 2009
Pagoda Island: April 2009
Pakhoi: February 2012
Peitaiho: December 2011
Peking: 1997
Port Arthur: October 1999, June 2012
Samshui: March 2012
Shanghai: 1982, 1999, 2006, November 2008
Shanhaikwan: December 2011
Shasi: November 2012
Soochow: March 2011
Swatow: February 2010
Taiwan-fu: June 2011
Takow: June 2011
Taku: December 2011
Tamsui: June 2011
Tangku: December 2011
Tientsin: November 2007, December 2011
Tinghai: October 1999
Tsingtao: October 1999, September 2008, June 2013
Twatutia: June 2011
Weihaiwei: October 1999, September 2008, September 2010
Wenchow: February 2010
Whampoa: March 2012
Wuchow: February 2014
Wuhu: January 2013
Yunnan-fu: April 2006
Zakow: October 2012

Notes

Introduction

1. Bickers 2011, 5–6.
2. Beardson, 10.
3. *South China Morning Post*, 11 May 2014, 'Push to Reappraise Defeat by Japan'.
4. Osterhammel, passim.
5. Beardson, 14.
6. Wood, 55.
7. Wood, 17.
8. Woodhead 1925, 243.
9. 1843 The Bogue, Article VIII.
10. Nolde, 300.
11. *The Friend of China*, 22 December 1842.
12. Murphey 1970, 14.
13. *The Friend of China*, 4 May 1843.
14. *The Colonial Gazette*, quoted in *The Friend of China*, 6 April 1843.
15. M. Wright, 179.
16. Bickers 2011, 44.
17. Osterhammel, 482.
18. M. Wright, 265.
19. C. See, 183.
20. Cohen, 209.
21. M. Wright, 290.
22. C. See, 185.
23. M. Wright, 286.
24. C. See, 187.
25. A. Little 1899, 330.
26. *The Colonial Gazette*, quoted in *The Friend of China*, 6 April 1843.
27. FO Foochow 1908, 8.
28. Boulger, 174.
29. Beresford, 448.
30. Rawlinson, 30.
31. Rawlinson, 131.
32. M. Wright, 210.
33. Osterhammel, 712–24.
34. Feuerwerker, 5.
35. Osterhammel, 661.
36. M. Wright, 196.
37. Murphey 1970, 21.
38. Feuerwerker, 98.
39. Chu and Liu, 4.
40. Chu and Liu, 218.
41. Chu and Liu, 85.
42. Dikötter, 42.
43. Dikötter, 84.
44. Osterhammel, 661.
45. O. Rasmussen, 101.
46. Bland, 9.
47. O. Rasmussen, 226.
48. Wei 1981, 150.
49. Abend 1944, 16.
50. Abend 1944, 9.
51. Bodde and Morris, 186.
52. Dikötter and Brown, 269.
53. Morse 1910, 1: 110.
54. Tai, 7.
55. Karabell, 53.
56. Tai, 7.
57. *The Friend of China*, 15 December 1842.
58. *The Friend of China*, 15 December 1842.
59. 1689 Nerchinsk, Article IV.
60. Munn 2001, 358.
61. M. Wright, 138–39.
62. M. Wright, 257.
63. Alabaster, 5.
64. Clark, 126.
65. M. Wright, 33.
66. Cohen, 251.
67. M. Wright, 274.
68. 1871 Correspondence, 187.
69. TNA, FO 663/18 #19, Bowring to Backhouse, 11 March 1856.
70. 1902 Commercial, Article XII.
71. M. Wright, 289.
72. Feuerwerker, 13.
73. Dikötter, 82.
74. *The China Weekly Review*, 19 June 1926.
75. 1943 Chungking.
76. Osterhammel, 286.
77. FO Chungking 1891, 8.
78. M. Wright, 179.
79. Tai, 9.
80. M. Wright, 254–55.
81. M. Wright, 167.
82. FO Foochow 1897, 11.
83. FO Amoy 1901, 8.
84. 1902 Commercial, Article VIII.
85. Hall, 15.

86. Imperial Maritime Customs Service List 1907, v.
87. Kwong, 22–23.
88. Murphey 1970, 1.
89. Cook, 105.
90. Maugham, 31–32.
91. Trade Report 1897, 5.
92. Otte, 24.
93. TNA, FO 17/1903, report by Howard, 31 December 1889.
94. Schrecker, 251.

Aigun

1. Customs Decennial 1922–31, 198.
2. *The Hong Kong Daily Press*, 12 September 1900.
3. Couling, 9.
4. Customs Decennial 1922–31, 198.
5. *The Hong Kong Telegraph*, 27 January 1910.
6. *The Hong Kong Telegraph*, 18 February 1910.
7. Teichman, 22.
8. *The China Yearbook 1924–5*, 354.
9. Customs Decennial 1922–31, 197–98.
10. Customs Decennial 1922–31, 197–203.

Amoy

1. Legarda, 36.
2. Haffner, 16–19.
3. J. Davis 1846, 46.
4. Legarda, 35.
5. Fairbank 1953, 66.
6. Greenberg, 47.
7. Greenberg, 140.
8. S. Ball, 201.
9. Bingham, 2: 236.
10. G. Hughes, 47.
11. Fortune 1847, 40.
12. TNA, FO 663/49/9, Thom to Pottinger, 8 December 1843.
13. Fortune 1847, 35–42.
14. A. Coates 1983, 14.
15. Fairbank 1953, 163.
16. TNA, FO 663/1/283, Pottinger to Gribble, 25 March 1843.
17. TNA, FO 663/49/7, Gribble to Pottinger, 4 December 1843.
18. TNA, FO 663/48/4, Gribble to Neville, 2 November 1843.
19. TNA, FO 663/49/2, Gribble to Pottinger, 10 November 1843.
20. TNA, FO 663/49/6, Gribble to Pottinger, 4 December 1843.
21. TNA, FO 663/1/69, Pottinger to Gribble, 11 December 1843.
22. TNA, FO 663/48/17, report by Gribble, 3 July 1844.
23. Lane-Poole, 59.
24. TNA, FO 663/49/10, Alcock to Davis, 12 February 1845.
25. Lane-Poole, 62.
26. TNA, FO 682/1978/25, Qiying to Davis, 6 May 1845.
27. TNA, FO 663/49/61, Lay to Davis, 11 August 1845.
28. Lane-Poole, 97.
29. TNA, FO 663/1/33, Davis to Lay, 3 April 1845.
30. TNA, FO 663/49/62, Lay to Davis.
31. TNA, FO 663/49/78, Sullivan to Davis, 6 November 1845.
32. TNA, FO 228/60/22, Layton to Davis, 21 April 1846.
33. P. Coates, 19.
34. Costin, 116.
35. Blue, 94.
36. Fairbank 1953, 159.
37. Campbell, 98.
38. Morse 1910, 1:363.
39. Costin, 169.
40. A. Wright, 820–27.
41. TNA, FO 228/60/61, Layton to Davis, 18 December 1846.
42. TNA, FO 228/70/11, Layton to Tait, 18 February 1847.
43. TNA, FO 663/54/12, Layton to Davis, 25 February 1848.
44. Costin, 169.
45. *Old Photos of Xiamen*, 83.
46. Campbell, 95.
47. *The New York Times*, 5 August 1852.
48. Bickers 2011, 104.
49. Campbell, 103.
50. Sinn 2013, 225.
51. Costin, 171.
52. Campbell, 97–104.
53. Morse 1910, 1:363.
54. Lane-Poole, 63.
55. Chen 2008, 33.
56. TNA, FO 663/15/48, Bowring to Backhouse, 9 March 1855.
57. Cooke, 87.
58. TNA, FO 678/14, 20 February 1852.
59. Chen 2008, 33.
60. Morse 1910, 1:449.
61. G. Hughes, 27–28.
62. Fairbank 1953, 411.
63. Morse 1910, 1:449.
64. G. Hughes, 26.
65. Fairbank 1953, 412.
66. Fairbank 1953, 413.
67. G. Hughes, 36.
68. TNA, FO 682/1984/9, Xu to Bonham, 18 April 1851.
69. TNA, FO 682/1984/12, Bonham to Xu, 26 April 1851.
70. TNA, FO 682/1984/15, Xu to Bonham, 2 May 1851.
71. Trade Reports 1865, 63.
72. Commercial Report Amoy 1862, 67.
73. Commercial Report Amoy 1867, 67.
74. 1868 Memorials, 17.
75. Trade Reports 1867, 69.
76. Trade Reports 1868, 71.
77. Davidson, 373.
78. Mayers, Dennys and King, 243.
79. G. Hughes, 120.
80. A. Wright, 819.
81. Gerson, 117.

82. Chen 2008, 34.
83. TNA, FO 228/84/33, Layton to Johnston, 30 June 1848.
84. P. Coates, 93.
85. TNA, FO 228/251/14, Pedder to Bowring, 10 February 1858.
86. TNA, FO 663/63/38, Pedder to Bruce, 6 August 1861.
87. TNA, FO 663/63/39, Pedder to Bruce, 6 August 1861.
88. TNA, FO 663/63/41, Pedder to Bruce, 10 August 1861.
89. TNA, FO 228/304/42, Pedder to Bruce, 12 August 1861.
90. TNA, FO 228/304/45, Pedder to Bruce, 20 September 1861.
91. TNA, FO 663/63/50, Pedder to Bruce, 20 December 1861.
92. Legation Buildings, 3.
93. TNA, WORK 40/127, building plans, 27 June 1874.
94. Mayers, Dennys and King, 262.
95. Trade Reports 1867, 71.
96. *China Directory 1867*, F 1–3.
97. Cribb, 154.
98. Cribb, 128.
99. *The Hong Kong Daily Press*, 3 April 1873.
100. Fairbank 1975, 187.
101. *The Hong Kong Daily Press*, 25 September 1875.
102. Chen 2008, 36.
103. Customs Decennial 1882–91, 507.
104. Chen, 21. 'Land, Title Deed, and Urban Transformation: Foreigners' Acquisition of Real Property in Xiamen (1841–1945)', 21.
105. P. Coates, 205.
106. *The Hong Kong Daily Press*, 2 March 1886.
107. C&D 1879, 274–80.
108. *The Hong Kong Daily Press*, 1 October 1875.
109. *The Hong Kong Daily Press*, 2 November 1876.
110. *The Hong Kong Daily Press*, 26 January 1882.
111. *The China Mail*, 19 September 1889.
112. *The Hong Kong Telegraph*, 4 January 1883.
113. Fairbank 1975, 446.
114. Customs Decennial 1882–91, 495.
115. FO Amoy 1886, 11.
116. P. Coates, 205.
117. *The China Mail*, 30 January 1889.
118. FO Amoy 1888, 3.
119. C&D 1897, 206–13.
120. FO Amoy 1899, 8.
121. Brooks, 105.
122. Beresford, 184.
123. FO Amoy 1900, 4.
124. Beresford, 185–88.
125. FO Amoy 1899, 7.
126. FO Amoy 1886, 3.
127. FO Amoy 1896, 16–21.
128. FO Amoy 1906, 7.
129. FO Amoy 1898, 11.
130. Morse 1920, 276.
131. Morse 1910, 3:163.
132. Pitcher, 123.
133. Drage, 59.
134. Pitcher, 123.
135. Drage, 59.
136. FO Amoy 1900, 7.
137. Brown, 228.
138. Drage, 151.
139. P. Coates, 206.
140. TNA, FO 228/565, Proposed Municipal Regulations for Kulangsoo, 30 December 1876.
141. Pitcher, 122.
142. Customs Decennial 1902–11, 111.
143. C&D 1904, 334–41.
144. Hewlett, 151.
145. Pitcher, 10.
146. Brown, 226.
147. Brown, 212.
148. A. Wright, 828.
149. C&D 1911, 1025–32.
150. C&D 1924, 918–25.
151. *China Proper*, 3: 275.
152. *The Hong Kong Daily Press*, 25 November 1886.
153. FO Amoy 1901, 8.
154. FO Amoy 1886, 9.
155. FO Amoy 1902, 6–7.
156. C&D 1911, 1025–32.
157. C&D 1914, 1044–51.
158. Customs Decennial 1902–11, 109.
159. C&D 1924, 918–25.
160. FO Amoy 1906, 6.
161. S. Wright, 810.
162. Chen 2008, 34.
163. FO Amoy 1898, 11.
164. Marriner and Hyde, 79.
165. TNA, FO 678/21.
166. Customs Decennial 1912–21, 155.
167. *Old Photos of Xiamen*, 97.
168. Hewlett, 152.
169. Haffner, 90.
170. Hewlett, 154–80.
171. P. Coates, 471.
172. TNA, FO 93/23/37, Rendition of British Concession at Amoy, 17 September 1930.
173. TNA, FO 676/313.
174. *Advocate of Peace*, vol. 83, no. 12, December 1921, 422.
175. Hewlett, 152.
176. Endacott 1978, 57.
177. C&D 1940, A400–408.
178. *China Proper*, 2: 276.

Antung

1. *The China Mail*, 3 July 1906.
2. *The New York Times*, 10 April 1904.
3. FO Antung 1907, 3.

4. *The New York Times*, 9 June 1907.
5. FO Antung 1907, 4.
6. C&D 1920, 671–72.
7. *The Hong Kong Telegraph*, 20 August 1909.
8. *The China Yearbook 1924–5*, 504.
9. 1905 Manchuria, Article VI.
10. C&D 1912, 802–3.
11. C&D 1912, 802–3.
12. *The China Yearbook 1924–5*, 100.
13. Customs Decennial 1922–31, 263–64.
14. C&D 1912, 802–3.
15. Drage, 239.
16. Customs Decennial 1912–21, 59–62.
17. C&D 1921, 673–74.
18. *The Korean Times*, 28 March 2010.
19. C. Lee, 138.
20. *The Straits Times*, 26 August 1920.
21. C. Lee, 138.
22. *The Hong Kong Telegraph*, 15 November 1929.
23. C&D 1941, A107–8.
24. Williams, 332.
25. *The New York Times*, 9 June 1907.
26. C&D 1923, 666–67.
27. *The Hong Kong Telegraph*, 3 November 1914.
28. *The China Yearbook 1924–5*, 319.
29. C&D 1923, 666–67.
30. C&D 1935, A114–15.
31. *The Hong Kong Daily Press*, 4 July 1932.
32. *The Hong Kong Daily Press*, 5 September 1932.

Baku

1. Morse 1920, 299.
2. Davidson, 240.
3. Note of French, German and Russian Ministers to Japanese Minister for Foreign Affairs regarding Retrocession of Liaotung Peninsula, 18 October 1895.
4. A. Wright, 654.
5. Blue 1982, 251.

Canton

1. Greenberg, 212.
2. Collis 1965, 13.
3. *The Chinese Repository*, No. 18 (1849), 277.
4. Wong 1983, 4.
5. TNA, FO 682/1976/103, Pottinger to Qiying, 25 July 1843, etc.
6. 1846 Bocca Tigris, Article I.
7. Manchester Correspondence.
8. A. Coates 1978, 89.
9. 1847 Canton, Article 1.
10. 1847 Canton, Article 4.
11. Nolde, 305–11.
12. Morse 1910, 1:397.
13. P. Coates, 104.
14. P. Coates, 104.

15. Wong 1998, 113–14.
16. Leibo, 17.
17. Leibo, 17.
18. Morse 1910, 1: 504–6.
19. V. Garrett, 106.
20. S. Wright, 137–38.
21. Leibo, 18.
22. Leibo, 21–24.
23. S. Wright, 138.
24. Leibo, 25.
25. TNA, MFQ 974, Royal Navy survey, March 1858.
26. Lane-Poole, 192.
27. Lane-Poole, 279.
28. Staples-Smith, 9.
29. Mayers, Dennys and King, 132.
30. V. Garrett, 126.
31. *The China Mail*, 20 September 1866.
32. TNA, WORK 10/56/3, report by Crossman, 21 February 1867.
33. TNA, FO 17/1093, report by Howard, 31 December 1889, 18.
34. V. Garrett, 126.
35. Staples-Smith, 16.
36. TNA, FO 228/2325, Land Regulations of British Concession, Shameen, approved 25 September 1871.
37. Bruner, 179.
38. Bredon, 36.
39. Ljungstedt, 228.
40. V. Garrett, 119.
41. V. Garrett, 127.
42. Consular Establishments, 25.
43. TNA, WORK 10/56/3, report by Crossman, 21 February 1867.
44. Gordon Cumming, 27.
45. Bird 1883, 45.
46. V. Garrett, 134.
47. Kerr, 3.
48. Staples-Smith, 19.
49. Michie, 2:326.
50. Customs Decennial 1882–91, 544.
51. TNA, FO 17/1093, report by Howard, 31 December 1889, 18.
52. P. Coates, 191.
53. C&D 1893, 184–91.
54. Conner, 257.
55. Turner, 24.
56. V. Garrett, 133.
57. FO Canton 1886, 3.
58. A. Wright, 784.
59. Customs Decennial 1902–11, 146.
60. Hutcheon, 23.
61. FO Canton 1906, 1.
62. V. Garrett, 168.
63. Staples-Smith, 20–24.

64. Staples-Smith, 4.
65. V. Garrett, 168–69.
66. Angus, 75.
67. FO Canton 1900, 10.
68. FO Canton 1887, 7.
69. 1902 Commercial, Article V.
70. C&D 1908, 903–17.
71. C&D 1904, 345–55.
72. A. Wright, 784.
73. FO Canton 1899, 12.
74. FO Canton 1908, 4.
75. Staples-Smith, 26.
76. Customs Decennial 1912–21, 190–92.
77. Customs Decennial 1912–21, 191–94.
78. Chapman, 11.
79. Customs Decennial 1912–21, 193–98.
80. Brunero, 60.
81. Staples-Smith, 30.
82. C&D 1925, 952–73.
83. Brunero, 69.
84. C&D 1927, 862–78.
85. C&D 1927, 862–78.
86. Customs Decennial 1912–21, 171.
87. *China Proper* 3: 256.

Changsha

1. Hewlett, 51.
2. C&D 1906, 791.
3. FO Changsha 1905, 3.
4. Fairbank 1973, 374.
5. Couling, 88.
6. *The China Mail*, 14 September 1904.
7. Lo and Bryant, 56–57.
8. Hewlett, 49.
9. Lo and Bryant, 56.
10. TNA, WORK 40/145, building plans, 1910.
11. C&D 1906, 791.
12. *The Hong Kong Daily Press*, 19 August 1905.
13. *The China Mail*, 8 March 1907.
14. Tai, 146.
15. FO Changsha 1905, 4–8.
16. A. Wright, 719.
17. Hewlett, 65.
18. FO Changsha 1910, 3.
19. *The New York Times*, 18 April 1910.
20. P. Coates, 391.
21. Couling, 88.
22. FO Changsha 1910, 11.
23. Crow 1933, 224.
24. FO Changsha 1908, 5.
25. FO Changsha 1909, 3.
26. Tolley, 127.
27. C&D 1919, 780–82.
28. Customs Decennial 1922–31, 523.

29. Cook, 141.
30. C&D 1941, A365–70.

Chefoo

1. Michie, 1: 221–22.
2. Lane-Poole, 208.
3. Michie, 1: 221–22.
4. Morse 1910, 589.
5. Mayers, Dennys and King, 457.
6. Fisher, 202–6.
7. Fisher, 208.
8. *The New York Times*, 29 January 1861.
9. Oliphant, 178.
10. Lo and Bryant, 70.
11. Lo and Bryant, 67.
12. Commercial Report Chefoo 1862, 52.
13. Dean, 82.
14. Dean, 80–81.
15. Mayers, Dennys and King, 461.
16. Commercial Report Chefoo 1862, 51.
17. Mayers, Dennys and King, 462.
18. Consular Establishments, 101.
19. C&D 1866, 223–24, and *The China Directory* 1867, N1–2.
20. Consular Establishments, 101.
21. Mayers, Dennys and King, 461.
22. Commercial Report Chefoo 1862, 54.
23. P. Coates, 172.
24. TNA, FO 228/335/11, Morrison to Bruce, 15 April 1862.
25. TNA, FO 228/335/13, Morrison to Bruce, 8 August 1862.
26. TNA, FO 228/414/14, Lay to Wade, 21 June 1865.
27. TNA, FO 228/335/16, Morrison to Bruce, 6 October 1862.
28. TNA, FO 228/350/3, Bruce to Morrison, 27 February 1863.
29. TNA, FO 228/350/12, Morrison to Bruce, 5 May 1863.
30. TNA, FO 228/391/10, Lay to Wade, 17 June 1865.
31. TNA, FO 228/376, Morrison to Wade, 2 August 1864.
32. TNA, FO 228/414/4, Alcock to Middleton, 8 May 1866.
33. TNA, FO 228/391/10, Lay to Wade, 17 June 1865.
34. Morse 1920, 241.
35. TNA, FO 228/414/16, Middleton to Alcock, 28 December 1866.
36. Legation Buildings, 2.
37. TNA, WORK 40/161, plan of consulate, 1911.
38. *Old Pictures of Chefoo*, 27–30.
39. Tiffen, 148.
40. Customs Decennial 1882–91, 56.
41. C&D 1872, 288–89.
42. FO Chefoo 1893, 18.
43. Customs Decennial 1882–91, 56.
44. FO Chefoo 1893, 15.
45. A. Wright, 767.
46. *The China Mail*, 12 September 1899.
47. TNA, FO 228/961, *taotai* to British Consul, 20 July 1899.
48. *Chefoo Daily News*, 7 October 1906.

49. TNA, FO 228/2137.
50. Customs Decennial 1902–11, 231.
51. Customs Decennial 1912–21, 200.
52. Customs Decennial 1902–11, 228.
53. Customs Decennial 1882–91, 75.
54. FO Chefoo 1894, 13.
55. Customs Decennial 1902–11, 228.
56. Mayers, Dennys and King, 459.
57. 1871 Correspondence, 105.
58. Osborne, 176.
59. J. Ball, 581.
60. Customs Decennial 1882–91, 75.
61. FO Chefoo 1903–5, 5.
62. Customs Decennial 1902–11, 230.
63. FO Chefoo 1890, 6.
64. FO Chefoo 1891, 7.
65. *The China Yearbook 1924–5*, 529.
66. Customs Decennial 1922–31, 429.
67. Trade Reports 1879.
68. Customs Decennial 1882–91, 45.
69. Customs Decennial 1882–91, 66.
70. FO Chefoo 1888, 3.
71. FO Chefoo 1907, 6.
72. FO Chefoo 1897, 9.
73. A. Wright, 770.
74. Cribb, 162.
75. Presbyterian Heritage Center: www.phcmontreat.org.
76. Couling, 90.
77. C&D 1902, 169–73.
78. International Genealogical Index.
79. C&D 1898, 116–21.
80. C&D 1897, 113–17, and 1901, 158–62.
81. C&D 1916, 764–69.
82. Couling, 90.
83. Trade Reports 1879.
84. FO Chefoo 1893, 17.
85. FO Chefoo 1893, 14.
86. FO Chefoo 1909.
87. FO Chefoo 1907, 3.
88. Couling, 90.
89. Couling, 90.
90. FO Chefoo 1906, 16.
91. Customs Decennial 1902–11, 226–28.
92. Customs Decennial 1922–31, 433.
93. Customs Decennial 1912–21, 196.
94. *The China Yearbook 1924–5*, 324.
95. *China Proper*, 3: 401.
96. Mayers, Dennys and King, 458.
97. A. Coates 1983, 79.
98. *The China Mail*, 31 May 1866.
99. Donnelly, 19.
100. P. Coates, 401.
101. Letter to the author from Duncan Clark, 7 June 2009.
102. C&D 1914, 823–28.
103. A. Wright, 769.
104. Bray, 10–14.
105. Couling, 90.
106. G. Martin, 52.
107. *The China Mail*, 5 December 1894.
108. *The China Mail*, 28 January 1895.
109. *The New York Times*, 24 January 1895.
110. *The China Mail*, 7 February 1895.
111. *The China Mail*, 12 February 1895.
112. *The New York Times*, 21 January 1895.
113. *The New York Times*, 29 January 1895.
114. FO Chefoo 1896, 1.
115. C&D 1907, 699–704.
116. FO Chefoo 1900, 3.
117. Atwell, 233.
118. FO Chefoo 1900, 3.
119. FO Chefoo 1903–5, 3.
120. P. Coates, 402.
121. Atwell, 84.
122. FO Chefoo 1911, 6.
123. Atwell, 85.
124. *The New York Times*, 24 June 1912.
125. Customs Decennial 1902–11, 231.
126. Atwell, 124–26.
127. Customs Decennial 1922–31, 428.
128. G. Martin, 64.
129. Drage, 239.
130. Directory & Chronicle 1924.
131. *North-China Daily News,* 10 April 1937.
132. Customs Decennial Report 1922–31, 432.
133. Cook, 67–68.
134. G. Thomas, 88.
135. Osborne, 181–85.
136. G. Martin, 92.
137. Bray, 11.
138. G. Martin, 41.
139. Angus, 127.
140. Brunero, 149.
141. Osborne, 218.

Chengtu

1. *China Proper*, 2: 310.
2. *The New York Times*, 1 October 1895.
3. *The Hong Kong Daily Press*, 10 June 1926.
4. Stursberg, 159.
5. P. Coates, 395.
6. *The China Mail*, 12 September 1911.
7. Johnston and Erh 1998, 66.
8. TNA, FO 228/1615.
9. Service, 175.
10. Lo and Bryant, 86.
11. Stursberg, 164.
12. *The Hong Kong Daily Press*, 12 June 1926.
13. Lo and Bryant, 82.

Chimmo Bay
1. Fairbank 1953, 228.
2. Lubbock 1933, 292.

Chinchew Bay
1. Fairbank 1953, 46.
2. Morse 1910, 1: 42.
3. Fairbank 1953, 69.
4. Bickers 2011, 31.
5. Fairbank 1953, 144.

Chinkiang
1. Bingham, 2: 344.
2. Ouchterlony, 345.
3. Fairbank 1953, 96.
4. Oliphant, 497.
5. Lane-Poole, 261.
6. Lane-Poole, 261.
7. Mayers, Dennys and King, 423.
8. TNA, MFQ 1/1036.
9. 1861 Correspondence, 12.
10. *China Proper*, 3: 330.
11. 1871 Correspondence, 4.
12. Mayers, Dennys and King, 423.
13. TNA, WORK 10/56/3, report by Crossman, 29 November 1866.
14. P. Coates, 254.
15. TNA, FO 17/1306/196, Boyce to Wade, 20 March 1876.
16. Trade Report 1867, 36.
17. Consular Establishments, 82.
18. TNA, WORK 10/39/2, Boyce letter, 6 November 1872.
19. Lo and Bryant, 92.
20. Oliphant, 491.
21. *The Hong Kong Daily Press*, 31 July 1875.
22. Trade Reports 1879.
23. *The China Mail*, 6 August 1878.
24. C&D 1910, 945–48.
25. C&D 1906, 764–67.
26. FO Chinkiang 1909, 13.
27. C&D 1925, 869–71.
28. Blue, 190.
29. TNA, FO 228/674, minutes of meeting, 23 September 1890.
30. P. Coates, 257.
31. Customs Decennial 1882–91, 303.
32. P. Coates, 256.
33. *The China Mail*, 3 September 1888.
34. Bird 1899, 55.
35. C&D 1886, 457–59.
36. P. Coates, 259.
37. A. Rasmussen, 11.
38. *The Hong Kong Daily Press*, 27 September 1873.
39. *The Hong Kong Daily Press*, 7 June 1872.
40. *The China Mail*, 11 February 1889.
41. *The Hong Kong Daily Press*, 14 October 1889.
42. A. Rasmussen, 37.
43. Customs Decennial 1902–11, 421.
44. C&D 1910, 945–48.
45. Customs Decennial 1902–11, 421.
46. FO Chinkiang 1909, 14.
47. Customs Decennial 1902–11, 411.
48. Hewlett, 199.
49. TNA, WORK 10/39/2.

Chinwangtao
1. J. Ball, 688.
2. Couling, 109.
3. Crow 1933, 313.
4. *The Hong Kong Daily Press*, 24 April 1899.
5. Fairbank 1975, 1187.
6. Customs Decennial 1912–21, 117.
7. Hyde Lay, 85.
8. C&D 1935, A90–92.
9. Customs Decennial 1922–31, 330.
10. C&D 1925, 666–68.
11. *The Hong Kong Telegraph*, 31 March 1906.
12. C&D 1911, 814–15.
13. Customs Decennial 1912–21, 136.
14. Donnelly, 17.
15. McLeish, 49.
16. Customs Decennial 1912–21, 136.
17. Customs Decennial 1922–31, 335.
18. C&D 1930, 654–56.
19. Customs Decennial 1912–21, 136.
20. Customs Decennial 1922–31, 335.
21. *China Proper*, 3: 426.
22. C&D 1938, A87–89.

Chungking
1. C&D 1882, 384.
2. 1876 Chefoo, Section III(i).
3. *The Hong Kong Daily Press*, 27 December 1877.
4. *The New York Times*, 2 May 1880.
5. P. Coates, 305–13.
6. A. Little 1910, v–vi.
7. A. Little 1910, vi.
8. C&D 1888, 467.
9. A. Little 1887, 283.
10. Fairbank 1975, 773.
11. 1890 Chungking, Article V.
12. A. Little 1887, 285.
13. A. Little 1887, 288–99.
14. TNA, FO 228/1253, report by Tratman, 1 July 1897.
15. Blue, 203.
16. Bromfield, 409.
17. Blue, 204.
18. Blue, 207.
19. C&D 1921, 888–91.
20. Customs Decennial 1912–21, 238.
21. Simpson, 26.

22. Bromfield, 411.
23. Fairbank 1975, 802.
24. FO Chungking 1891, 1.
25. *The Hong Kong Daily Press*, 17 December 1890.
26. TNA, FO 228/886, Fulford to Walsham, 16 November 1890.
27. FO Chungking 1892, 2.
28. Fairbank 1975, 764.
29. *The Hong Kong Daily Press*, 9 September 1890.
30. *The China Mail*, 26 February 1892.
31. *The China Mail*, 15 May 1891.
32. *The Hong Kong Daily Press*, 4 March 1896.
33. FO Chungking 1893, 5.
34. FO Chungking 1891, 4.
35. FO Chungking 1897, 18.
36. C&D 1882, 384.
37. C&D 1891, 156–57.
38. C&D 1898, 201–4.
39. FO Chungking 1894, 9.
40. *The China Mail*, 24 December 1886.
41. *The China Mail*, 15 April 1889.
42. TNA, FO 17/1047, Walsham to Salisbury, 23 February 1887.
43. Trade Reports 1896.
44. Oxford, 37.
45. FO Chungking 1898, 12.
46. TNA, FO 228/886, Fulford to Walsham, 16 November 1890.
47. TNA, FO 228/1064, Fulford to Walsham, 19 February 1891.
48. TNA, FO 228/1115, report by Fraser, 7 February 1893.
49. TNA, FO 228/1115, report by Fraser, 3 November 1893.
50. TNA, FO 228/1253, report by Tratman, 1 July 1897.
51. FO Chungking 1896, 10.
52. FO Chungking 1903, 8.
53. FO Chungking 1905–6, 10.
54. *China Proper*, 3: 375.
55. Customs Decennial 1912–21, 233.
56. Customs Decennial 1922–31, 475.
57. Danielson, 175.
58. 1943 Chungking, Article 2.

Chusan

1. Bernard, 2: 207.
2. Blake, 47.
3. J. Davis 1841, 1:17.
4. As told to me by Keith Stevens on a visit to Zhoushan in 1999.
5. Fortune 1847, 70–72.
6. Fortune 1847, 315.
7. Hong Kong Papers, 9–14.
8. Hong Kong Papers, 3.
9. Munn 1997, 83.
10. D'Arcy-Brown, 263.
11. Bruner, 55.
12. Munn 1997, 104.
13. Wood, 86, quoting from an unstated source.
14. Stevens and Welch, 384.
15. Otte, 101.
16. Bridge, 227.

Cumsingmoon

1. Fairbank 1953, 66.
2. Morse 1910, 1: 541.
3. S. Wright, 397.

Dalny/Dairen

1. Lane-Poole, 208.
2. Bickers 2011, 261.
3. 1898 Correspondence, 11.
4. 1898 Correspondence, 33.
5. 1898 Correspondence, 46.
6. Customs Decennial 1882–91, 33.
7. Greener, 301.
8. Pelissier, 200.
9. *Old Fashions of Dalian*, 61.
10. *Old Fashions of Dalian*, 11.
11. C&D 1904, 183–84.
12. *The Hong Kong Daily Press*, 22 April 1903.
13. C&D 1906, 651–52.
14. Couling, 138.
15. C&D 1907, 697–98.
16. Fairbank 1975, 1334.
17. 1907 Dairen.
18. FO Dairen 1906, 4–6.
19. FO Dairen 1909, 5.
20. FO Dairen 1906, 7.
21. FO Dairen 1909, 6.
22. Customs Decennial 1922–31, 287.
23. Johnston and Erh 1996a, 60.
24. 1915 Manchuria, Article 1.
25. FO Dairen 1910, 5.
26. Customs Decennial 1922–31, 288.
27. *Manchuria* 1922, 51–53.
28. Customs Decennial 1912–21, 85.
29. Lo and Bryant, 446.
30. Crow 1921, 259.
31. Customs Decennial 1922–31, 283.
32. Crow 1933, 325.
33. Brunero, 140.
34. Fairbank 1958, 287.

Foochow

1. Morse 1910, 1: 42.
2. G. Hughes, 5.
3. Morse 1910, 1: 47.
4. Pitcher, 233.
5. A. Coates 1966, 37.
6. Fairbank 1953, 67.

7. S. Ball, 194.
8. Costin, 101.
9. *The Friend of China*, 10 November 1842.
10. Bickers 2011, 94.
11. P. Coates, 16.
12. *The Times*, 13 February 1845.
13. Michie, 1: 118.
14. Hyde Lay, 5.
15. J. Davis 1852, 2: 72.
16. Fairbank 1953, 204.
17. Morse 1910, 1: 362.
18. J. Davis 1852, 2: 75.
19. J. Davis 1852, 2: 72.
20. J. Davis 1852, 2: 114.
21. Pong, 32.
22. TNA, FO 228/52/3, Lay to Davis, 15 February 1845.
23. TNA, FO 682/1978/44, Davis to Liu, 4 August 1845.
24. Morse 1910, 1: 375.
25. Blue, xxi.
26. Fairbank 1953, 169.
27. Costin, 149.
28. TNA, FO 682/1984/11, Xu to Bonham, 19 April 1851.
29. J. Davis 1852, 2: 117.
30. Pong, 32.
31. A. Wright, 66.
32. Crow 1921, 303.
33. Fairbank 1953, 292.
34. Fortune 1857, 220.
35. P. Coates, 121.
36. Morse 1910, 1: 360.
37. P. Coates, 122.
38. Hibbert, 232.
39. Roche and Cowen, 6.
40. Stursberg, 41.
41. *The China Sea Directory*, 321.
42. S. Wright, 308.
43. Lubbock 1914, 177.
44. Customs Decennial 1882–91, 407.
45. Pickering, 8.
46. TNA, FO 228/1369, draft report by Tower, 26 August 1901, 91.
47. Consular Establishments, 66.
48. Lo and Bryant, 322–23.
49. Lo and Bryant, 316.
50. Lubbock 1914, 106.
51. Lubbock 1933, 322.
52. Lubbock 1914, 132.
53. Lubbock 1914, 234.
54. Trade Reports 1868, 65.
55. Commercial Report Foochow 1872, 46.
56. Commercial Report Foochow 1885, 3.
57. FO Foochow 1886, 6.
58. FO Foochow 1890, 6.
59. FO Foochow 1896, 9

60. Commercial Report Foochow 1872, 44.
61. FO Foochow 1908, 6.
62. Smith, Fairbank and Bruner, 255.
63. P. Coates, 122.
64. TNA, WORK 10/56/3, report by Crossman, 30 December 1866.
65. P. Coates, 98.
66. C&D 1872, 244–48.
67. Trade Report 1867, 62.
68. Mayers, Dennys and King, 281.
69. Mayers, Dennys and King, 279–82.
70. *The Hong Kong Daily Press*, 28 January 1869.
71. Fairbank 1975, 212.
72. Cannon, 37.
73. Fairbank 1954, 80.
74. Rawlinson, 45.
75. Fairbank 1954, 80.
76. S. Wright, 462.
77. *The China Mail*, 27 July 1868.
78. Giquel, 14.
79. Rawlinson, 49.
80. Cannon, 38.
81. S. Wright, 462.
82. Giquel, 15.
83. Rawlinson, 48.
84. Fairbank 1975, 253.
85. Roche and Cowen, 12, etc.
86. Fairbank 1975, 1092.
87. A. Wright, 837.
88. *The China Mail*, 27 October 1869.
89. Macgowan, 94.
90. C&D 1910, 987–94.
91. Crow 1933, 384.
92. C&D 1941, A388–99.
93. C&D 1938, A406–16.
94. C&D 1910, 987–94.
95. C&D 1910, 987–94.
96. Zhou, 24.
97. *Foochow Herald*, 18 February 1875 (quoted in *The Straits Times*, 6 March 1875).
98. Allen and Donnithorne, 269.
99. Donnelly, 56.
100. Customs Decennial 1882–91, 410–16.
101. FO Foochow 1886, 3.
102. FO Foochow 1887, 4.
103. FO Foochow 1898, 6.
104. Customs Decennial 1882–91, 416.
105. C&D 1882, 319–25.
106. A. Coates, 1983, 145.
107. FO Foochow 1888, 6.
108. P. King, 256.
109. FO Foochow 1891, 3.
110. FO Foochow 1898, 3.
111. FO Foochow 1896, 13.

112. FO Foochow 1900, 6.
113. Customs Decennial 1912–21, 139.
114. FO Foochow 1906, 5.
115. www.gcatholic.com

Haichow

1. Williams, 314.
2. FO Chinkiang 1906, 10.
3. China Proper, 3: 383.

Hangchow

1. Polo, 213.
2. TNA, FO 682/1984/10, Bonham to Xu, 19 April 1851.
3. TNA, FO 682/1984/11, Xu to Bonham, 22 April 1851.
4. FO Hangchow 1896, 4.
5. Customs Decennial 1912–21, 71.
6. *The Hong Kong Telegraph*, 20 April 1897.
7. Morse 1920, 271.
8. *The Hong Kong Telegraph*, 1 December 1896.
9. *The China Mail*, 24 February 1897.
10. *The Hong Kong Weekly Press*, 28 April 1897.
11. FO Shanghai 1897, 30.
12. C&D 1897, 174.
13. A. Wright, 632.
14. C&D 1898, 181–82.
15. P. King, 112–13.
16. FO Hangchow 1905, 3.
17. A. Wright, 634.
18. Customs Decennial 1912–21, 95.
19. TNA, FO 228/1369, draft report by Tower, 26 August 1901, 85.
20. Lo and Bryant, 142.
21. *The China Mail*, 27 June 1904.
22. *The New York Times*, 5 October 1905.
23. FO Hangchow 1899, 16.
24. FO Hangchow 1911, 6.
25. P. Coates, 402.
26. Customs Decennial 1912–21, 95.
27. Fitch, 53.
28. Blue, 277.
29. Gammie, 122.
30. *The Straits Times*, 11 May 1935.

Hankow

1. Rowe, 23.
2. Zhe, 7.
3. Rowe, 20–21.
4. Rowe, 22.
5. Osterhammel, 294.
6. Rowe, 26–28.
7. Costin, 277.
8. Oliphant, 565.
9. Rowe, 62–76.
10. Mayers, Dennys and King, 440.
11. Dean, 36.
12. Oliphant, 560.
13. Lane-Poole, 266–68.
14. P. Coates, 162.
15. Rowe, 48.
16. Rowe, 46–47.
17. Dean, 58.
18. S. Wright, 214.
19. Bruner, 248.
20. S. Wright, 216.
21. Mayers, Dennys and King, 444.
22. Blue, 163.
23. Commercial Report Hankow 1862, 41.
24. Smith, Fairbank and Bruner, 224.
25. TNA, FO 228/476, Caine to Alcock, 23 June 1869.
26. Mayers, Dennys and King, 443–49.
27. Legation Buildings, 2.
28. TNA, WORK 10/56/3, report by Crossman, 29 November 1866.
29. Blue, 199.
30. Osterhammel, 294.
31. A. Coates, 1983, 58.
32. Mayers, Dennys and King, 444.
33. A. Little 1887, 17.
34. T. Lindsay, 44.
35. Rowe, 46.
36. Rowe, 131–32.
37. Rowe, 132.
38. Dean, 58.
39. Commercial Report Hankow 1872, 58–59.
40. Rowe, 145–47.
41. Rowe, 148–51.
42. FO Hankow 1887, 7.
43. Rowe, 153.
44. J. Ball, 648.
45. Rowe, 45.
46. Customs Decennial 1882–91, 172.
47. Rowe, 49.
48. Customs Decennial 1882–91, 172.
49. Customs Decennial 1902–11, 359.
50. Customs Decennial 1892–1901, 303.
51. Rowe, 124.
52. Beresford, 154.
53. Zhe, 147.
54. Rowe, 124.
55. FO Hankow 1906, 14.
56. Archer 1941, 21.
57. Blue, 167.
58. Smith, Fairbank and Bruner, 208.
59. FO Hankow 1887, 14.
60. Rowe, 45.
61. TNA, FO 228/494, Caine to Wade, 4 May 1870.
62. FO Hankow 1887, 14.
63. Customs Decennial 1882–91, 167.
64. Customs Decennial 1892–1901, 315.

65. A. Wright, 710.
66. A. Wright, 709.
67. A. Wright, 586.
68. Warner, 145.
69. *New-York Tribune*, 14 October 1905.
70. Customs Decennial 1922–31, 573.
71. Tolley, 95.
72. Customs Decennial 1922–31, 573.
73. A. Wright, 702–4.
74. Abend 1944, 174.
75. Customs Decennial 1892–1901, 294.
76. Customs Decennial 1912–21, 322.
77. FO Hankow 1902, 6.
78. FO Hankow 1905, 6.
79. FO Hankow 1907, 6.
80. Customs Decennial 1892–1901, 294.
81. Customs Decennial 1922–31, 573.
82. A. Wright, 693.
83. C&D 1902, 264–75.
84. C&D 1898, 191–99.
85. Warner, 142.
86. Blue, 200.
87. Customs Decennial 1912–21, 319.
88. Walton, 117.
89. Hankow British Chamber of Commerce Papers.
90. Customs Decennial 1892–1901, 306.
91. J. Ball, 539.
92. C&D 1904, 302–12.
93. C&D 1915, 981–99.
94. C&D 1920, 837–60.
95. A. Wright, 95.
96. *The Hong Kong Telegraph*, 5 February 1936.
97. *The Hong Kong Sunday Herald*, 7 October 1937.
98. Field, 57.
99. FO Hankow 1907, 19.
100. FO Hankow 1891, 15.
101. Walton, 122.
102. Beresford, 164.
103. C&D 1907, 835–48.
104. Crow 1921, 171–75.
105. Osterhammel, 661.
106. FO Hankow 1892, 10.
107. Beresford, 300.
108. Customs Decennial 1882–91, 175.
109. C&D 1902, 264–73.
110. C&D 1906, 775–87.
111. Customs Decennial 1922–31, 564.
112. FO Hankow 1904, 11.
113. Blue, 189.
114. Customs Decennial 1902–11, 358.
115. C&D 1922, 876–99.
116. Customs Decennial 1922–31, 563.
117. C&D 1922, 876–99.
118. Customs Decennial 1892–1901, 305.
119. Customs Decennial 1902–11, 359.
120. C&D 1912, 972–87.
121. Field, 60.
122. Tolley, 66.
123. F. King, 2: 320.
124. F. King, 2: 462.
125. Tolley, 66.
126. Salkeld, 133–34.
127. *The China Mail*, 11 June 1931.
128. Crow 1921, 171–75.
129. C&D 1916, 923–43.
130. FO Hankow 1905, 17.
131. Blue, 200.
132. *China Proper*, 3: 349.
133. Customs Decennial 1892–1901, 295.
134. Customs Decennial 1912–21, 299.
135. *The China Mail*, 11 June 1931.
136. C&D 1914, 1000–1018.
137. Zhe, 162.
138. A. Coates 1983, 60.
139. A. Wright, 696.
140. A. Wright, 700.
141. C&D 1919, 759–76.
142. C&D 1914, 1000–1018.
143. *The China Mail*, 16 June 1925.
144. *The Hankow Riot of June 11th, 1925*.
145. *The Hankow Riot of June 11th, 1925*.
146. Ross, 783, passim.
147. *The Independent Herald*, 27 June 1925.
148. Tolley, 133.
149. Collis 1965, 181–84.
150. *China Proper*, 2: 113.
151. *China Proper*, 2: 158.
152. Dong, 173–74.
153. Cook, 106–7.
154. Chapman, 34.
155. Teichman, 142–45.
156. Bickers 1999, 16.
157. *Peking & Tientsin Times*, 6 January 1927.
158. Pelissier, 305.
159. E. Lee, 15.
160. Chapman, 121.
161. E. Lee, 17.
162. Chapman, 122.
163. *Peking & Tientsin Times*, 7 April 1927.
164. E. Lee, 14.
165. Chapman, 124.
166. Chapman, 161.
167. Wood, 185.
168. Customs Decennial 1922–31, 353.
169. P. Coates, 471.
170. *China Proper*, 2: 159.
171. Bickers 1999, 139–40.
172. Hewlett, 244–49.

173. *The China Mail*, 21 September 1936.
174. *The Hong Kong Daily Press*, 22 September 1936.
175. *The Hong Kong Telegraph*, 28 September 1936.
176. *The Hong Kong Daily Press*, 7 October 1936.
177. *The China Mail*, 16 July 1937.
178. *The China Mail*, 5 August 1937.
179. *The China Mail*, 6 August 1937.
180. *The China Mail*, 9 August 1937.
181. *The China Mail*, 23 August 1937.
182. *The China Mail*, 22 October 1937.
183. *The China Mail*, 1 December 1937.
184. *The China Mail*, 7 October 1937.
185. Tolley, 253.
186. *The China Mail*, 9 June 1938.
187. *The China Mail*, 7 June 1938.
188. *The China Mail*, 10 June 1938.
189. *The China Mail*, 13 July 1938.
190. *The China Mail*, 12 July 1938.
191. *The China Mail*, 19 August 1938.
192. *The China Mail*, 13 August 1938.
193. *The China Mail*, 26 October 1938.
194. Zhe, 110.
195. Bickers 1999, 139–40.
196. *The China Mail*, 31 October 1938.
197. *The China Mail*, 13 December 1938.

Harbin

1. 1858 Aigun.
2. 1860 Peking (Russia).
3. Carter, 3.
4. 1898 Liaotung, Article VIII.
5. 1896 Railway, Articles 6 and 12.
6. Couling, 226.
7. Latané, 588.
8. Latané, 589.
9. 1903 American, Article XII.
10. 1905 Manchuria, Article I.
11. Putnam Weale, 138.
12. Williams, 333.
13. *The China Mail*, 23 June 1906.
14. *The Hong Kong Telegraph*, 3 November 1906.
15. Fairbank 1975, 1531.
16. C&D 1910, 794.
17. Jernigan, 345.
18. *The China Mail*, 13 June 1904.
19. C&D 1916, 751–54.
20. Jernigan, 376.
21. Fleming 1934, 68.
22. Carter, 14.
23. C&D 1918, 673–77.
24. C&D 1925, 678–84.
25. Jernigan, 345.
26. Customs Decennial 1912–21, 6–16.
27. 1909 Municipal, Article 6.
28. *The China Mail*, 8 April 1909.
29. 1914 Municipal.
30. Customs Decennial 1912–21, 18.
31. Carter, 128.
32. *The Hong Kong Daily Press*, 28 August 1914.
33. Customs Decennial 1912–21, 1–2.
34. C&D 1921, 665–69.
35. *The China Mail*, 19 December 1917.
36. Carter, 70.
37. *The Hong Kong Daily Press*, 3 January 1918.
38. *The China Mail*, 28 December 1917.
39. *The China Mail*, 24 September 1918.
40. Crow 1933, 324.
41. Customs Decennial 1912–21, 18.
42. Williams, 171.
43. Customs Decennial 1912–21, 6.
44. Customs Decennial 1922–31, 216.
45. Customs Decennial 1922–31, 221.
46. Teichman, 66.
47. Brooks, 148.

Hokow

1. 1887 Additional, Article II.
2. 1887 Complementary, Article II.
3. C&D 1898, 242.
4. R. Lee, 141.
5. Victoir and Zatsepine, 209.
6. *Report on a Journey from Hong-Kong to Ssumao*, 7.
7. C&D 1906, 852.
8. C&D 1930, 994.
9. C&D 1935, A503–4.

Hong Kong

1. Morse 1926, 3: 261.
2. Sayer 1937, 31.
3. TNA, FO 682/1974/20, Qishan to Elliot, 15 January 1841.
4. Endacott 1958, 21–22.
5. Hayes 1988, 117.
6. Endacott 1964, 69.
7. Sayer 1937, 119.
8. Tsang, 56.
9. Abend 1944, 158.
10. Endacott 1964, 70.
11. Munn 2001, 335.
12. Courtauld and Holdsworth, 13.
13. Miners, 11.
14. Hase 2008a, 155.
15. 1843 The Bogue, Article XIII.
16. Endacott 1964, 95.
17. Bard 1993, 39.
18. Hase 2008a, 156.
19. Hase 2008a, 157.
20. Tsai, 22.
21. Tsai, 44.
22. Hase 2008a, 160.

Notes to pages 124–135

23. Sayer 1937, 220.
24. Sinn 2013, various.
25. Courtauld and Holdsworth, 26.
26. Sinn 2013, various.
27. Sinn 1989, 7.
28. Sinn 2013, 302.
29. Tsai, 52–55.
30. Endacott 1964, 39.
31. Munn 2001, 339.
32. Sayer 1937, 220.
33. Hase 2008a, 160.
34. Tsai, 22.
35. Hase 2008a, 161.
36. Munn 2001, 330.
37. Tsai, 38.
38. Munn 2001, 58.
39. Tsai, 57.
40. Tsai, 78.
41. Sinn 1989, 31.
42. Tsai, 68–69.
43. Tsai, 77.
44. Munn 2001, 368.
45. Tsai, 89.
46. Courtauld and Holdsworth, 31.
47. Pomerantz-Zhang, 58.
48. Pomerantz-Zhang, 47.
49. Tsai, 86.
50. Courtauld and Holdsworth, 32.
51. Tsang, 36.
52. Sayer 1937, 201.
53. Munn 2001, 39.
54. TNA, FO 682/1977/52, Pottinger to Cheng Yu-tsai, 20 April 1844.
55. Munn 2001, 61.
56. Munn 2001, 125.
57. Tsai, 51.
58. Tsang, 73.
59. Sinn 2013, 303.
60. Tsai, 238.
61. Miners, 4.
62. Tsai, 243–44.
63. Miners, 5.
64. Tsai, 182.
65. Tsai, 209.
66. Tsai, 95.
67. Blue 1982, 125.
68. Tsang, 61.
69. Tsai, 33.
70. A. Wright, 194.
71. Cribb, 17.
72. Tsang, 60.
73. Blue, 126.
74. Courtauld and Holdsworth, 27–28.
75. Courtauld and Holdsworth, 42.
76. Miners, 232.
77. Miners, 276.
78. Courtauld and Holdsworth, 33.
79. Courtauld and Holdsworth, 41.
80. Tsang, 61.
81. Endacott 1964, 82.
82. Tsang, 87.
83. Miners, 8.
84. F. King, 2: 560–61.
85. Tsang, 109.
86. Hong Kong General Chamber of Commerce Report for the Year 1931, 39.
87. Tsai, 87.
88. Waters, 250–51.
89. Endacott 1964, 93.
90. Endacott 1964, 122.
91. Miners, 10.
92. Hase 2008a, 158.
93. Waters, 224.
94. Miners, 9.
95. Miners, 11.
96. Hong Kong General Chamber of Commerce Report for the Year 1925, 14–15.
97. Miners, 12–14.
98. Way and Nield, 69.
99. Miners, 16–17.
100. Miners, 18–19.
101. Miners, 21–22.
102. Report on the Census of the Colony of Hong Kong, 1931, 151 Table 39.
103. Report on Labour and Labour Conditions in Hong Kong, 1939, 129–32.
104. Miners, 121.

Ichang

1. Parkinson, 150.
2. 1869 Correspondence, 4.
3. TNA, FO 1080/142.
4. *The Hong Kong Daily Press*, 23 June 1869.
5. P. Coates, 273.
6. TNA, MPKK 51.
7. TNA, FO 17/1306/299, Fraser to Derby, 16 April 1877.
8. Customs Decennial 1882–91, 148.
9. *The China Mail*, 26 May 1877.
10. *The Hong Kong Daily Press*, 7 June 1882.
11. TNA, FO 17/1093, report by Howard, 31 December 1889.
12. TNA, WORK 10/156.
13. Hewlett, 78.
14. *The Hong Kong Daily Press*, 7 June 1882.
15. C&D 1879, 346–47.
16. Customs Decennial 1922–31, 502.
17. Customs Decennial 1882–91, 142–43.
18. FO Ichang 1894, 12.
19. FO Ichang 1895, 9.

20. P. King, 185.
21. Customs Decennial 1882–91, 149.
22. *The Hong Kong Telegraph*, 20 June 1894.
23. *The Hong Kong Telegraph*, 14 August 1894.
24. *The China Mail*, 11 September 1891.
25. Customs Decennial 1902–11, 284.
26. Hewlett, 75.
27. Customs Decennial 1922–31, 501.
28. C&D 1924, 894–96.
29. *China Proper*, 3: 369.

Kashkar
1. Auslin, 19.
2. 1860 Peking (Russia), Article VI.
3. *The China Mail*, 2 February 1877.
4. *The Hong Kong Daily Press*, 8 August 1874.
5. Bland, 189.
6. Fairbank 1975, 180.
7. Fleming 1936, 157.
8. C. Bruce, 144.
9. *The Hong Kong Daily Press*, 23 October 1875.
10. Lo and Bryant, 195.
11. Fleming 1936, 331.

Kiukiang
1. 1858 Tientsin (Britain), Article X.
2. 1861 Correspondence, 3.
3. 1861 Correspondence, 12.
4. TNA, WORK 10/47/3, map from 1866.
5. TNA, WORK 10/23, Kiukiang Concession Survey and Valuation, 1922.
6. Mayers, Dennys and King, 430–32.
7. P. Coates, 262.
8. Consular Establishments, 82.
9. Trade Reports 1865, 46.
10. 1871 Correspondence, 2.
11. TNA, WORK 10/47/3, report by Boyce, 25 July 1870.
12. Customs Decennial 1882–91, 218.
13. C&D 1886, 461–62.
14. Trade Reports 1885, 72.
15. Customs Decennial 1882–91, 218.
16. *The Hong Kong Daily Press*, 7 February 1887.
17. *The Hong Kong Daily Press*, 5 December 1870.
18. TNA, WORK 10/23.
19. FO Kiukiang 1886, 2.
20. 1903 Despatch, 27.
21. FO Kiukiang 1897, 5.
22. 1898 Inland Navigation, Article 1.
23. Customs Decennial 1902–11, 367.
24. TNA, WORK 10/21, Kiukiang Concession Survey and Valuation, 1922.
25. 1903 Despatch, 27.
26. Customs Decennial 1892–1901, 327–30.
27. Fairbank 1953, 300.
28. Customs Decennial 1912–21, 338.
29. Customs Decennial 1892–1901, 348–49.
30. FO Kiukiang 1886, 2.
31. Customs Decennial 1912–21, 339.
32. *The China Mail*, 26 October 1911.
33. Customs Decennial 1912–21, 331.
34. C&D 1916, 921–23.
35. Customs Decennial 1912–21, 331.
36. *The Hong Kong Daily Press*, 25 April 1920.
37. P. Coates, 459.
38. Ross, 785.
39. E. Lee, 12–13.
40. Bickers 1999, 140.

Kiungchow
1. Lo and Bryant, 225.
2. As told to me by an American expatriate in Haikou, 16 February 2009.
3. Morse 1926, 1: 27.
4. 1868 Memorials, 23.
5. Alcock Despatch, 7.
6. Further Memorials, 12.
7. Hansard, 25 March 1872.
8. *The Hong Kong Daily Press*, 13 April 1876.
9. P. Coates, 236.
10. Milne, 155.
11. TNA, FO 228/1369, draft report by Tower, 26 August 1901, 183.
12. FO Kiungchow 1890, 9.
13. C&D 1922, 971–73.
14. *Science Magazine*, 10 June 1892.
15. *The China Mail*, 1 June 1876.
16. C&D 1879, 264.
17. C&D 1872, 237–38.
18. C&D 1880, 274.
19. Customs Decennial 1882–91, 622.
20. FO Kiungchow 1886, 2.
21. FO Kiungchow 1890, 7.
22. FO Kiungchow 1886, 2.
23. FO Kiungchow 1887, 2.
24. *The China Mail*, 7 June 1888.
25. FO Kiungchow 1888, 3.
26. FO Kiungchow 1890, 4.
27. FO Kiungchow 1892, 5.
28. FO Kiungchow 1890, 5.
29. FO Kiungchow 1887, 3.
30. *The Hong Kong Daily Press*, 4 January 1887.
31. Customs Decennial 1882–91, 630.
32. FO Kiungchow 1888, 4.
33. Trade Reports 1883.
34. FO Kiungchow 1893, 10.
35. TNA, FO 17/1093, report by Howard, 31 December 1889.
36. FO Kiungchow 1890, 10.
37. FO Kiungchow 1893, 10.
38. FO Kiungchow 1895, 4.

39. TNA, MFQ 39/1, building plans, 1896.
40. Historical Photographs of China.
41. C&D 1900, 291–93.
42. P. Coates, 238.
43. FO Kiungchow 1893, 10.
44. C&D 1899, 265–66.
45. C&D 1900, 291–93.
46. Historical Photographs of China. SOAS Collection, image 16527.
47. TNA, FO 228/1369, draft report by Tower, 26 August 1901, 111.
48. C&D 1901, 300–302.
49. Customs Decennial 1882–91, 617–18.
50. Fairbank 1975, 1115.
51. F. King, 2: 288.
52. Fairbank 1975, 1149.
53. *The Hong Kong Daily Press*, 11 January 1900.
54. FO Kiungchow 1886, 3.
55. FO Kiungchow 1894, 4.
56. FO Kiungchow 1907, 4.
57. FO Kiungchow 1908, 4.
58. Customs Decennial 1902–11, 248.
59. C&D 1900, 291–93.
60. Cunningham, 37.
61. FO Kiungchow 1891, 12.
62. FO Kiungchow 1892, 12.
63. FO Kiungchow 1909, 5.
64. C&D 1908, 928–30.
65. Customs Decennial 1912–21, 317–18.
66. C&D 1922, 971–73.
67. Customs Decennial 1922–31, 318.
68. Michalk, 126.
69. FO Kiungchow 1902, 6.
70. C&D 1941, A455–56.

Kongmoon
1. Customs Decennial 1902–11, 177.
2. C&D 1906, 841–42.
3. TNA, FO 228/1369, draft report by Tower, 26 August 1901, 65.
4. TNA, FO 228/1461, report by Little, 2 January 1902.
5. Lo and Bryant, 237.
6. *The Hong Kong Weekly Press*, 12 March 1904.
7. *The Hong Kong Telegraph*, 7 February 1904.
8. C&D 1906, 841–42.
9. Customs Decennial 1912–21, 261.
10. *The Hong Kong Telegraph*, 7 February 1904.
11. Customs Decennial 1902–11, 178.
12. C&D 1906, 841–42.
13. *China Proper*, 3: 251.
14. Hyde Lay, 38.
15. Customs Decennial 1912–21, 263.
16. C&D 1906, 841–42.
17. C&D 1911, 1056–57.
18. Customs Decennial 1912–21, 265.
19. C&D 1940, A445–47.

Kowloon
1. Fairbank 1975, 213.
2. Morse 1920, 282.
3. Fairbank 1975, 213.
4. J. Ball, 349.
5. Sinn 1990, 33.
6. Fairbank 1975, 213.
7. C&D 1891, 188–89.
8. Morse 1910, 1: 262.
9. Customs Decennial 1882–91, 681.
10. Customs Decennial 1882–91, 682.
11. Customs Decennial 1882–91, 683–93.
12. S. Wright, 706.
13. S. Wright, 585.
14. Customs Decennial 1882–91, 683.
15. Fairbank 1975, 807.
16. Welsh, 326.
17. Fairbank 1975, 1193.
18. Customs Decennial 1902–11, 155–66.
19. Customs Decennial 1912–21, 233.
20. Customs Decennial 1922–31, 217.

Kuling
1. TNA, FO 228/1030, General Correspondence, Series 1.
2. 1903 Despatch, 33.
3. TNA, FO 228/1030, General Correspondence, Series 1.
4. *The China Mail*, 21 December 1896.
5. FO Kiukiang 1897, 5.
6. FO Kiukiang 1904, 16.
7. Stone and Reed, i.
8. Blue, 192.
9. Couling, 282.
10. *Kuling Estate Directory*, 1.
11. *The Hong Kong Daily Press*, 4 December 1920.
12. P. Coates, 377.
13. Haines, 76.
14. *The Hong Kong Telegraph*, 11 August 1927.
15. *The Hong Kong Daily Press*, 26 August 1927.
16. *The Hong Kong Telegraph*, 14 September 1929.
17. *The Hong Kong Daily Press*, 21 June 1930.
18. *The Hong Kong Daily Press*, 9 August 1932.
19. *The Hong Kong Telegraph*, 24 April 1936.

Kwangchowwan
1. Fairbank 1975, 1092.
2. Bickers 2011, 327.
3. S. Wright, 688.
4. Morse 1910, 3: 112.
5. Fairbank 1975, 1208.
6. C&D 1900, 290.
7. Morse 1910, 3: 112.
8. *The China Mail*, 13 July 1899.

9. Cunningham, 10.
10. C&D 1899, 263.
11. Cunningham, 19.
12. Cunningham, 3–4.
13. Cunningham, 7.
14. C&D 1901, 298–99.
15. FO Pakhoi 1900, 4.
16. *The Hong Kong Daily Press*, 27 August 1928.
17. *China Proper,* 3: 240.
18. *China Proper,* 3: 241.
19. *The New York Times*, 2 February 1922.
20. *Advocate of Peace*, vol. 84, no. 2, February 1922, 49.
21. http://www.zum.de/whkmla/region/china/tlkwang-chowan.html
22. *China Proper,* 2: 140.

Kweilin
1. Lo and Bryant, 245–47.

Lappa
1. Fairbank 1975, 672.
2. Customs Decennial 1882–91, 582.
3. C&D 1898, 235–36.
4. C&D 1900, 286.
5. C&D 1902, 312–13.
6. Ho, 12.
7. C&D 1891, 190.
8. C&D 1900, 286.
9. Customs Decennial 1902–11, 169.
10. Customs Decennial 1912–21, 251.
11. C&D 1919, 828.
12. Customs Decennial 1912–21, 244.
13. C&D 1941, A439–40.
14. C&D 1912, 1041.

Lintin Island
1. Braga 1955, 29.
2. Morse 1926, 2: 333.
3. van Dyke, 49.
4. van Dyke, 65.
5. Morse 1910, 1: 154.
6. Keay, 456.
7. Morse 1910, 1: 406.
8. Hacker: *A Dearth of Aardvarks*. No date.
9. *The China Mail*, 19 April 1950.

Lungchow
1. 1887 Additional, Article II.
2. C&D 1891, 193.
3. Customs Decennial 1882–91, 653.
4. C&D 1896, 211.
5. R. Lee, 144.
6. Customs Decennial 1902–11, 265–69.
7. R. Lee, 145.
8. R. Lee, 156.
9. Customs Decennial 1922–31, 337.

10. *China Proper,* 3: 234.
11. *The China Mail*, 27 June 1940.

Lungkow
1. *The New York Times*, 3 September 1914.
2. *The New York Times*, 4 September 1914.
3. 1914 Presidential.
4. Customs Decennial 1912–21, 177.
5. *The Hong Kong Daily Press*, 10 May 1920.
6. *The Hong Kong Daily Press*, 12 May 1920.
7. Customs Decennial 1922–31, 421.
8. Customs Decennial 1922–31, 423.
9. Customs Decennial 1912–21, 187.
10. Customs Decennial 1922–31, 415.
11. C&D 1925, 705–6.
12. Customs Decennial 1922–31, 423.
13. Customs Decennial 1912–21, 179.
14. C&D 1933, 533–34.
15. Customs Decennial 1912–21, 181.
16. C&D 1935, A128–30.
17. C&D 1940, A126–27.
18. C&D 1941, A124–26.

Macao
1. Ljungstedt, 69.
2. Munn 2001, 40.
3. Morse 1920, 286.
4. 1862 Tientsin, Article II.
5. Fairbank 1975, 647.
6. 1887 Peking, Article II.
7. R. Garrett, 116.

Mengtse
1. 1885 Tientsin, Article II.
2. 1887 Additional, Article II.
3. C&D 1891, 192–93.
4. Customs Decennial 1882–91, 665.
5. Morse 1920, 285.
6. R. Lee, 143.
7. C&D 1895, 204–5.
8. C&D 1896, 212.
9. R. Lee, 195.
10. *China Proper,* 3: 99.
11. Customs Decennial 1922–31, 349.
12. C&D 1903, 342–44.
13. FO Mengtse 1906, 4.
14. C&D 1910, 1035–36.
15. C&D 1913, 1062–64.
16. Customs Decennial 1902–11, 275.
17. C&D 1934, A519–21.

Mokanshan
1. Johnston and Erh 1994, 12.
2. Couling, 379.
3. C&D Hangzhou 1910, 981–82.
4. Crow 1933, 176.

5. Crow 1933, 159.
6. http://www.earnshaw.com/shanghai-ed-india/tales/t-wedding.htm
7. Johnston and Erh 1994, 13.
8. *The Hong Kong Daily Press*, 24 December 1937.

Mukden

1. S. Wright, 762.
2. 1903 Japanese and 1903 American.
3. Couling, 384.
4. Lo and Bryant, 263.
5. P. Coates, 392.
6. Brooks, 126.
7. C&D 1907, 694–95.
8. C&D 1927, 617–22.
9. Crow 1933, 314.
10. Crow 1921, 248.
11. C&D 1916, 748–50.
12. Customs Decennial 1912–21, 47.
13. C&D 1923, 651–54.
14. Brooks, 143.
15. Spence, 391.

Nanking

1. Platt, 350.
2. FO Nanking 1899–1901, 3.
3. FO Nanking 1903–5, 6.
4. FO Chinkiang 1899, 4.
5. *The New York Times*, 23 August 1899.
6. Customs Decennial 1892–1901, 420–25.
7. C&D 1906, 767–70.
8. Customs Decennial 1902–11, 399.
9. Blake, 210–12.
10. C&D 1911, 976–79.
11. Customs Decennial 1912–21, 362.
12. FO Nanking 1911, 3–4.
13. C&D 1914, 992–95.
14. Further Correspondence, 51.
15. *The Hong Kong Telegraph*, 7 April 1927.
16. Chapman, 71.
17. Brunero, 84.
18. Collis 1965, 185.
19. Chapman, 132.

Nanning

1. *The New York Times*, 14 September 1885.
2. Tai, 113.
3. TNA, FO 233/237, Yamen's engagement to open Nanning-fu if French railway is extended to Po-se.
4. Fairbank 1975, 1149.
5. Hansard, 9 June 1898, vol. 58, c 1186.
6. Hansard, 9 February 1899, vol. 66, c 316.
7. Hansard, 8 March 1900, vol. 80, c 385.
8. *The Hong Kong Daily Press*, 14 June 1900.
9. *The China Mail*, 2 August 1901.
10. *The Hong Kong Telegraph*, 9 January 1907.
11. *The Hong Kong Telegraph*, 21 January 1907.
12. *The China Mail*, 18 April 1907.
13. *The Hong Kong Telegraph*, 2 August 1907.
14. C&D 1924, 960–61.
15. Couling, 392.
16. *The China Mail*, 18 April 1907.
17. Historical Photographs of China. Chinese Maritime Customs Service Collection, image 16905.
18. Historical Photographs of China. Chinese Maritime Customs Service Collection, image 16928.
19. Customs Decennial 1902–11, 215.
20. Bickers 2011, 358.
21. C&D 1923, 947–48.
22. *The Hong Kong Telegraph*, 24 February 1906.
23. *The Hong Kong Telegraph*, 17 August 1907.
24. C&D 1915, 1060–61.
25. C&D 1921, 944–45.
26. C&D 1911, 1059.
27. *The Hong Kong Telegraph*, 21 April 1911.
28. *The China Mail*, 21 February 1912.
29. Blue, 257.
30. *The Hong Kong Daily Press*, 15 July 1914.

Newchwang

1. Lo and Bryant, 284.
2. Commercial Report Newchwang 1862, 5.
3. Commercial Report Newchwang 1862, 5.
4. Lo and Bryant, 287.
5. *China Sea Directory*, 678.
6. Commercial Report Newchwang 1862, 4.
7. Commercial Report Newchwang 1862, 2.
8. Mayers, Dennys and King, 540.
9. Trade Reports 1865, 13.
10. Mayers, Dennys and King, 29.
11. Trade Reports 1865, 13.
12. Commercial Report Newchwang 1862, 5.
13. TNA, FO 669/1, Meadows to Wade, 7 January 1865.
14. P. Coates, 162.
15. P. Coates, 292.
16. Commercial Report Newchwang 1862, 5.
17. TNA, FO 669/1, Meadows to Wade, 7 January 1865.
18. TNA, T 1/6768C, report by Crossman, 18 July 1867.
19. TNA, FO 228/314, Meadows to Bruce, 11 September 1861.
20. TNA, WORK 10/437/21, Meadows to Crossman, 14 September 1867.
21. Legation Buildings, 1.
22. TNA, WORK 10/437/27, Meadows to Crossman, 15 June 1868.
23. TNA, FO 228/478, Register of Death, 14 November 1868.
24. TNA, WORK 10/80, Treasury to Office of Works, 13 March 1875.
25. TNA, WORK 55/17.
26. TNA, FO 17/1093, report by Howard, 31 December 1889.

27. TNA, FO 678/1453, Burdett to Wallinger, 26 November 1946.
28. Mayers, Dennys and King, 544.
29. Mayers, Dennys and King, 461.
30. *The China Mail*, 19 July 1868.
31. Beresford, 63.
32. *The China Mail*, 19 July 1868.
33. *The Hong Kong Daily Press*, 20 December 1865.
34. Trade Reports 1870, 10.
35. TNA, FO 228/538, Harvey to Wade, 10 April 1874.
36. TNA, FO 228/538, Harvey to Barrett, 4 November 1874.
37. *The Hong Kong Daily Press*, 19 February 1874.
38. Trade Reports 1865, 14.
39. *The Hong Kong Daily Press*, 11 March 1874.
40. *The China Mail*, 6 November 1884.
41. Mayers, Dennys and King, 540–41.
42. *The China Directory 1867*, P1–2.
43. Mayers, Dennys and King, 545.
44. *The China Mail*, 19 July 1868.
45. Commercial Report Newchwang 1862, 4.
46. Blue, xxv.
47. Marriner and Hyde, 79.
48. Marriner and Hyde, 111.
49. *The New York Times*, 18 November 1870.
50. Blue, xxvii.
51. *The China Sea Directory*, 676.
52. A. Coates 1983, 86.
53. *The Hong Kong Daily Press*, 13 February 1882.
54. P. Coates, 169.
55. *The Hong Kong Daily Press*, 29 November 1866.
56. *The Hong Kong Daily Press*, 13 February 1882.
57. Customs Decennial 1882–91, 16.
58. *The China Mail*, 25 September 1889.
59. TNA, FO 17/1093, report by Howard, 31 December 1889.
60. TNA, FO 228/3197, Bristow to Peking, 29 December 1920.
61. Customs Decennial 1882–91, 15.
62. *The Hong Kong Daily Press*, 6 July 1882.
63. *The Hong Kong Daily Press*, 9 May 1870.
64. *The Hong Kong Telegraph*, 21 June 1894.
65. Morse 1910, 2: 42.
66. FO Newchwang 1894, 6.
67. Drage, 32.
68. FO Newchwang 1895, 7.
69. Drage, 35.
70. FO Newchwang 1896, 2.
71. Putnam Weale, 504.
72. Beresford, 63.
73. FO Newchwang 1898, 10.
74. Beresford, 33–34.
75. C&D 1901, 151–54.
76. *The New York Times*, 3 November 1898.
77. Beresford, 51.
78. Morse 1920, 229.
79. Walton, 7.
80. Beresford, 44.
81. Beresford, 32.
82. Walton, 15.
83. TNA, FO 228/1328, Hosie to Ironside, 26 May 1899.
84. Beresford, 35.
85. Walton, 14.
86. Walton, 5.
87. FO Newchwang 1898, 10.
88. Walton, 14.
89. A. Coates 1983, 107.
90. Putnam Weale, 504.
91. Morse 1910, 3: 269.
92. A. Wright, 821.
93. FO Newchwang 1900, 6.
94. Morse 1910, 3: 269.
95. FO Amoy 1900, 3.
96. Morse 1910, 3: 322.
97. S. Wright, 750.
98. Fairbank 1975, 1322.
99. C&D 1904, 178–82.
100. FO Newchwang 1902, 3.
101. FO Newchwang 1901, 12.
102. Murison, 94–95.
103. Murison, 90–95.
104. Morse 1910, 3: 418.
105. *The New York Times*, 9 July 1903.
106. Morse 1910, 3: 419.
107. Fairbank 1975, 1402.
108. Fairbank 1975, 1424.
109. Greener, 231.
110. Morse 1920, 229.
111. FO Newchwang 1905, 3.
112. 1906 Newchwang.
113. FO Newchwang 1906, 15.
114. *The Hong Kong Telegraph*, 21 June 1894.
115. Hewlett, 79.
116. C&D 1919, 588–92.
117. FO Newchwang 1909, 14.
118. Customs Decennial 1912–21, 97.
119. Customs Decennial 1912–21, 101.
120. FO Newchwang 1910, 17.
121. C&D 1925, 668–73.
122. Cook, 75.
123. J. Ball, 684.
124. Lo and Bryant, 296.
125. C&D 1934, A98–100.

Ningpo
1. Morse 1910, 1: 42.
2. Mayers, Dennys and King, 329.
3. Morse 1910, 1: 53.
4. Mayers, Dennys and King, 330.
5. Hayes 2008, 180.

6. Fairbank 1953, 66.
7. Mayers, Dennys and King, 331.
8. Fortune 1847, 320.
9. Bickers 2011, 93.
10. Conner, 179.
11. J. Davis, 1852, 2: 66.
12. Fairbank 1953, 155.
13. Fairbank 1953, 332.
14. Fairbank 1953, 159.
15. Fairbank 1953, 333.
16. A. Wright, 64.
17. J. Davis 1852, 2: 69.
18. Fairbank 1953, 170–71.
19. FO 682/1984/11, Xu to Bonham, 24 April 1851.
20. Morse 1910, 1: 359.
21. Lo and Bryant, 301.
22. Bredon, 26.
23. Mayers, Dennys and King, 339.
24. Abend 1944, 80.
25. Bruner, 58.
26. Cooke, 132.
27. Morse 1910, 2: 65.
28. Uhalley, 20.
29. Lane-Poole, 286.
30. Abend 1944, 83.
31. Morse 1910, 2: 78.
32. Uhalley, 17.
33. Uhalley, 23.
34. Abend 1947, 206.
35. Morse 1910, 2: 78.
36. Uhalley, 26.
37. Mayers, Dennys and King, 334.
38. Uhalley, 28.
39. Commercial Report Ningpo 1872, 89.
40. *The Hong Kong Daily Press*, 20 September 1865.
41. C&D 1940, A380–84.
42. *The Hong Kong Daily Press*, 23 February 1864.
43. Customs Decennial 1902–11, 62.
44. *The China Directory 1867*, I1–3.
45. Customs Decennial 1882–91, 369.
46. C&D 1884, 366–69.
47. *The China Mail*, 6 November 1890.
48. Customs Decennial 1902–11, 62.
49. Tai, 73.
50. Morse 1910, 2: 119.
51. Cooke, 129.
52. A. Coates 1983, 55.
53. *The Hong Kong Daily Press*, 4 June 1864.
54. *The Hong Kong Daily Press*, 30 March 1864.
55. Mayers, Dennys and King, 343.
56. Consular Establishments, 118.
57. Historical Photographs of China. Tita and Gerry Hayward Collection, image 25104.
58. Consular Establishments, 117.
59. TNA, MPKK/50, map, 1850.
60. Legation Buildings, 3.
61. Mayers, Dennys and King, 340.
62. *The Straits Times*, 7 January 1865.
63. *Trade Statistics 1863–1872*.
64. Blue, xxvii.
65. *The China Mail*, 25 March 1878.
66. *The China Sea Directory*, 401.
67. Bruner, 36.
68. R. Smith, 28.
69. *The China Mail*, 9 April 1877.
70. *The Hong Kong Daily Press*, 23 August 1877.
71. Customs Decennial 1882–91, 346.
72. Customs Decennial 1902–11, 67.
73. Customs Decennial 1882–91, 351–69.
74. FO Ningpo 1887, 6.
75. *The Hong Kong Daily Press*, 4 June 1864.
76. Customs Decennial 1902–11, 66.
77. Customs Decennial 1882–91, 372.
78. Customs Decennial 1902–11, 65.
79. FO Ningpo 1887, 3.
80. C&D 1907, 859–62.
81. C&D 1906, 799–802.
82. FO Ningpo 1902, 3.
83. Lo and Bryant, 311.
84. P. Coates, 402.
85. Customs Decennial 1922–31, 83.
86. *The China Mail*, 18 October 1926.
87. *The China Mail*, 13 June 1927.
88. *The New York Times*, 11 March 1927.
89. *The China Mail*, 20 February 1928.
90. C&D 1940, A380–84.
91. *Old Pictures of Ningbo*, 45.
92. Crow 1921, 139.
93. Crow 1933, 188.

Pakhoi

1. P. Coates, 242.
2. *The China Mail*, 11 May 1878.
3. P. Coates, 239.
4. Commercial Report Pakhoi 1884, 34.
5. Fairbank 1975, 246.
6. Fairbank 1975, 975.
7. *The New York Times*, 16 July 1877.
8. *North-China Herald*, 9 June 1877.
9. C&D 1879, 263.
10. *The China Mail*, 13 December 1878.
11. Commercial Report Pakhoi 1881.
12. Customs Decennial 1882–91, 637.
13. Rydings, 292.
14. Plaque on the former British Consulate.
15. FO Pakhoi 1888, 2.
16. *The Hong Kong Weekly Press*, 16 June 1902.
17. P. Coates, 162.

18. Cunningham, 39.
19. P. Coates, 242.
20. FO 17/1093, report by Howard, 31 December 1889.
21. FO Pakhoi 1887, 4.
22. *The Hong Kong Daily Press*, 16 June 1888.
23. *The China Mail*, 25 June 1888.
24. *The Times*, 27 June 1888.
25. P. Coates, 239.
26. FO Pakhoi 1886, 4.
27. *The Hong Kong Weekly Press*, 7 September 1903.
28. Customs Decennial 1882–91, 638.
29. Cunningham, 39.
30. FO Pakhoi 1890, 2.
31. Cunningham, 39.
32. Customs Decennial 1912–21, 337.
33. FO Pakhoi 1907, 5.
34. FO Pakhoi 1897, 4.
35. FO Pakhoi 1890, 3.
36. Fairbank 1975, 1485.
37. Customs Decennial 1902–11, 256.
38. FO Pakhoi 1896, 6.
39. Lo and Bryant, 332.
40. *China Proper*, 3: 235.

Peitaiho

1. *Peitaiho Directory*, 2.
2. *Peitaiho Directory*, 2.
3. C&D 1900, 137–39.
4. *Peitaiho Directory*, 3.
5. *Peitaiho Directory*, 3.
6. C&D 1900, 137–39.
7. Couling, 427.
8. Crow 1933, 311.
9. Customs Decennial 1912–21, 138.
10. Crush 2013, 112.
11. Couling, 427.
12. C&D 1924, 647–48.
13. Customs Decennial 1912–21, 138.
14. Elder, 151.

Peking

1. 1727 Kiakhta, Article V.
2. Morse 1920, 212.
3. 1858 Tientsin (British), Article II.
4. Morse 1920, 22.
5. 1858 Tientsin (British), Article IX.
6. 1858 Agreement, Rule 8.
7. Morse 1920, 393.
8. Bickers 2011, 216.
9. Morse 1920, 234.
10. Williams, 328.
11. Wei 1987, 172.
12. Morse 1910, 3: 198.
13. Morse 1910, 3: 213.
14. Bickers 2011, 344.

15. Morse 1910, 3: 268.
16. 1901 Boxer Protocol, Article VII.
17. Tai, 139.
18. 1903 Japanese, Article X and Annexes 6 and 7.

Port Arthur

1. Customs Decennial 1882–91, 31.
2. Couling, 450.
3. *The China Mail*, 25 October 1886.
4. *Old Fashions of Dalian*, 145.
5. *The China Mail*, 18 November 1884.
6. C&D 1886, 485.
7. *The China Mail*, 25 October 1886.
8. *The Hong Kong Daily Press*, 3 November 1886.
9. C&D 1887, 482.
10. Customs Decennial 1882–91, 32.
11. C&D 1888, 485.
12. Bland, 240.
13. Villiers, 328.
14. *Old Fashions of Dalian*, 6.
15. Otte, 59.
16. *China Yearbook 1924–5*, 584.
17. 1895 Liaotung.
18. *The China Mail*, 7 May 1895.
19. *The Hong Kong Telegraph*, 23 November 1895.
20. 1896 Cassini, Article 10.
21. *The China Mail*, 30 October 1895.
22. Otte, 87.
23. *The Hong Kong Daily Press*, 5 October 1896.
24. Krausse, 183.
25. *The China Yearbook 1924–5*, 585.
26. *The China Mail*, 9 March 1898.
27. 1898 Correspondence, 46.
28. *The Hong Kong Daily Press*, 11 July 1898.
29. *The Hong Kong Telegraph*, 23 December 1898.
30. *The China Mail*, 25 January 1898.
31. *Old Fashions of Dalian*, 146.
32. C&D 1901, 155–57.
33. *The Hong Kong Daily Press*, 10 September 1901.
34. *Old Fashions of Dalian*, 146.
35. C&D 1903, 177–81.
36. *The China Mail*, 27 October 1903.
37. Morse 1910, 3: 427.
38. Crow 1921, 262.
39. FO Dairen 1913, 4.
40. C&D 1925, 688–89.
41. C&D 1924, 668–69.
42. Spence, 482.
43. *Old Fashions of Dalian*, 7.
44. Fairbank 1958, 287.

Port Hamilton

1. Coy.
2. Fairbank (1975), 606.
3. S. Wright, 504.

4. Coy.
5. *S. Wright*, 504.
6. Fairbank 1975, 609.
7. Morse 1920, 26.
8. Michie, 2: 303.
9. *S. Wright*, 504.
10. Michie, 2: 304.
11. *Hong Kong Daily Press*, 1 February 1887.
12. Coy.
13. Otte, 111.

Saddle Islands
1. *New York Times*, 20 February 1871.
2. E. Little 1905, various.

Samshui
1. C&D 1901, 294–95.
2. TNA, FO 228/1290, report by Brady, 3 February 1898.
3. FO Samshui 1897, 3.
4. FO Samshui 1897, 3–4.
5. FO Samshui 1897, 4.
6. TNA, FO 228/1290, report by Brady, 10 August 1898.
7. Lo and Bryant, 339.
8. TNA, FO 228/1329, report by Fox, 9 October 1899.
9. TNA, FO 228/1411, report by Little, 8 January 1901.
10. FO Samshui 1897, 3.
11. C&D 1902, 313–14.
12. FO Samshui 1898, 4.
13. FO Samshui 1897, 7.
14. FO Samshui 1897, 6.
15. FO Samshui 1897, 11.
16. FO Samshui 1898, 10.
17. FO Samshui 1899, 3.
18. FO Samshui 1898, 10.
19. *The China Mail*, 23 January 1903.
20. Customs Decennial 1902–11, 200.
21. FO Samshui 1897, 5.
22. TNA, FO 228/1290, report by Brady, 3 February 1898.
23. TNA, FO 228/1253.
24. C&D 1904, 357–58.
25. C&D 1906, 839–40.
26. A. Wright, 680.
27. C&D 1918, 915–16.
28. Customs Decennial 1902–11, 193.
29. Customs Decennial 1912–21, 274.
30. C&D 1919, 829–30.
31. C&D 1922, 961–62.
32. Customs Decennial 1912–21, 275–81.
33. *China Proper*, 3: 248.
34. C&D 1941, A443–44.

Sanmun Bay
1. Krausse, 12.
2. *New York Times*, 4 March 1899.
3. A. Smith, 114.

4. Fairbank 1975, 1193.
5. *New York Times*, 15 March 1899.
6. A. Smith, 114.
7. *New York Times*, 8 March 1899.
8. Fairbank 1975, 1191.

Santuao
1. J. Ball, 688.
2. 1898 Correspondence, 8, 12.
3. The *Hong Kong Weekly Press,* 27 May 1899.
4. *The Sydney Mail*, 2 April 1898.
5. *The China Mail*, 9 April 1898.
6. FO Foochow 1899, 9.
7. *The Hong Kong Weekly Press*, 27 May 1899.
8. C&D 1900, 256.
9. Customs Decennial 1902–11, 81–82.
10. C&D 1901, 266.
11. C&D 1902, 284.
12. Customs Decennial 1912–21, 131–36.
13. C&D 1933, 875–76.
14. C&D 1918, 879–80.
15. Tolley, 43.
16. FO Foochow 1904, 13.
17. *The China Mail*, 20 November 1907.
18. *The Hong Kong Daily Press*, 24 July 1939.

Shanghai
1. Wei 1987, 1.
2. Hayes 2008, 180.
3. Wei 1987, 34.
4. P. Coates, 26.
5. Gilbert, 165.
6. Fortune 1847, 327.
7. Pott, 12.
8. Gilbert, 166.
9. Wei 1987, 38.
10. Gilbert, 169.
11. Wei 1987, 37.
12. Pott, 20.
13. Gilbert, 167.
14. Wei 1987, 43–44.
15. Crow 1940, 157.
16. Wei 1987, 40.
17. Gilbert, 168.
18. Wei 1987, 45.
19. Tsai, 21.
20. Tsai, 34.
21. A. Coates, 1983, 22.
22. Abend 1944, 66.
23. Dong, 14.
24. Pott, 25–30.
25. Pott, 31–34.
26. Wei 1987, 39.
27. Pott, 35.
28. Pott, 37–39.

29. Pott, 42.
30. Pott, 47–48.
31. Pott, 48.
32. Dong, 16.
33. Pott, 49–51.
34. Pott, 51.
35. Dong, 17.
36. Pott, 53.
37. Wei 1987, 61.
38. Pott, 53–56.
39. Wei 1987, 62.
40. Wei 1987, 73–77.
41. Dong, 21.
42. Wei 1987, 45.
43. Pott, 63.
44. Crow 1940, 86.
45. Haan, 59.
46. Pott, 63–64.
47. Wei 1987, 74.
48. Bickers 2003, 53.
49. Bickers 2003, 103.
50. Crow 1940, 161.
51. Wei 1987, 74.
52. Crow 1940, 168.
53. Haan, 35.
54. Wei 1987, 74.
55. Wei 1987, 76.
56. Bodde and Morris, 186.
57. Munn 2001, 335.
58. Dong, 16–18.
59. Pott, 79.
60. Dong, 63–64.
61. Pott, 81–84.
62. Pott, 99–100.
63. Dong, 65.
64. Pott, 62.
65. Wei 1987, 151.
66. Wei 1987, 145.
67. Feuerwerker, 12.
68. Pott, 100.
69. Dong, 67.
70. Feuerwerker, 12.
71. Feuerwerker, 28.
72. FO Shanghai 1887, 3.
73. FO Shanghai 1889, 8.
74. Feuerwerker, 17.
75. FO Shanghai 1892, 17.
76. FO Shanghai 1894, 20.
77. Dong, 65–67.
78. FO Shanghai 1893, 21.
79. Feuerwerker, 9.
80. Pott, 133–36.
81. FO Shanghai 1895, 21.
82. Wei 1987, 112.
83. Wei 1987, 123.
84. Pott, 137–41.
85. Pott, 95.
86. Pott, 128.
87. Pott, 124–28.
88. Wei 1987, 166.
89. Feuerwerker, 72.
90. Pott, 149.
91. Wei 1987, 182–83.
92. Pott, 166–67.
93. Wei 1987, 189.
94. Dong, 82.
95. Dong, 78.
96. Dong, 83–84.
97. Haan, 49.
98. Pott, 187–91.
99. FO Shanghai 1911, 4.
100. Bickers 2003, 49.
101. Pott, 244–45.
102. Pott, 247–49.
103. Pott, 287.
104. Dong, 165.
105. Pott, 287.
106. Dong, 166.
107. Wei 1987, 224.
108. Dong, 168.
109. Bickers 2003, 174.
110. Pott, 292–96.
111. Pott, 274.
112. Bickers 2003, 177.
113. Dong, 174.
114. Pott, 300.
115. Dong, 180.
116. Dong, 185.
117. Pott, 305.
118. Wei 1987, 104.
119. Bickers 2003, 72.
120. Bickers 2003, 92.
121. Denby, 91.
122. Bickers 2003, 114–16.
123. Dong, 30–31.
124. Dong, 38.
125. Bickers 2003, 59.
126. Dong, 75.
127. Dong, 224.
128. Dong, 209.
129. Bickers 2003, 217.
130. Dong, 212.
131. Dong, 213.
132. Wei 1987, 241.
133. Dong, 213–15.
134. Bickers 2003, 221.
135. Bickers 2003, 256.
136. Dong, 252.

137. Bickers 2003, 263.
138. Dong, 253–54.
139. Bickers 2003, 269–70.
140. Dong, 256.
141. Bickers 2003, 270.
142. Bickers 2003, 306.
143. Bickers 2003, 311–12.
144. Wei 1987, 248.

Shanhaikwan
1. Fairbank 1953, 36.
2. Fairbank 1953, 86.
3. *The China Mail*, 18 December 1894.
4. Otte, 221.
5. *The China Mail*, 20 October 1900.
6. *The China Mail*, 4 October 1900.
7. *The China Mail*, 2 October 1900.
8. *The China Mail*, 11 October 1900.
9. *The China Mail*, 12 October 1900.
10. *Cook's Tourist Handbook of Peking*, 69.
11. McLeish, 49.
12. C&D 1903, 688–89.
13. Hyde Lay, 85.

Shasi
1. *The Hong Kong Daily Press*, 29 September 1876.
2. FO Shashih 1897, 5.
3. FO Shashih 1898, 4.
4. C&D 1900, 244–45.
5. FO Shashih 1897, 16.
6. *The China Mail*, 18 July 1898.
7. *The Hong Kong Daily Press*, 23 March 1906.
8. FO Shashih 1897, 16.
9. FO Shashih 1899, 3.
10. Bird 1899, 88.
11. Customs Decennial 1902–11, 287–90.
12. Customs Decennial 1902–11, 287.
13. Customs Decennial 1922–31, 512.
14. Customs Decennial 1912–21, 267.
15. FO Shashih 1905, 4.
16. FO Shashih 1897, 8.
17. Customs Decennial 1912–21, 268.

Soochow
1. C&D 1897, 174.
2. Crow 1933, 198.
3. *The Friend of China*, 28 July 1842.
4. C&D 1899, 200–201.
5. *The China Mail*, 30 December 1895.
6. Fairbank 1975, 1038.
7. *The Hong Kong Telegraph*, 12 April 1897.
8. *The China Mail*, 30 December 1895.
9. *Hong Kong Telegraph*, 9 November 1897.
10. TNA, FO 228/1369, draft report by Tower, 26 August 1901, 73.
11. Lo and Bryant, 393.
12. Blue, 278.
13. FO Soochow 1900, 7.
14. Customs Decennial 1912–21, 63.
15. *The China Mail*, 16 July 1906.
16. Customs Decennial 1912–21, 63.
17. Customs Decennial 1902–11, 29.
18. Customs Decennial 1922–31, 57–60.
19. Crow 1933, 193.
20. A. Wright, 673.
21. Crow 1933, 193.
22. FO Shanghai 1897, 31.
23. *Singapore Free Press and Mercantile Advertiser*, 24 December 1895.
24. Customs Decennial 1922–31, 59.
25. Customs Decennial 1902–11, 34.
26. Couling, 521.
27. C&D 1925, 866–68.
28. *The China Mail*, 12 and 21 February 1910.
29. Crow 1933, 194.
30. *The China Mail*, 28 January 1925.
31. Customs Decennial 1922–31, 61.
32. *China Proper*, 3:294.
33. *The China Mail*, 22 November 1937.
34. C&D 1941, A331–32.

Swatow
1. G. Hughes, 6.
2. Hunter, 40–42.
3. R. Smith, 212.
4. Fairbank 1953, 142.
5. Fairbank 1953, 144–45.
6. Fortune 1847, 33.
7. P. Coates, 65.
8. *The China Sea Directory*, 171.
9. Fairbank 1953, 214.
10. Abend 1944, 104.
11. Commercial Report Swatow 1862, 55.
12. *China Proper*, 3: 270.
13. California Department of Insurance website, www.insurance.ca.gov
14. Donnelly, 67.
15. Bickers 2011, 281.
16. S. Wright, 144.
17. Yiu, quoting Breck dispatch, 6 March 1861.
18. Yiu, quoting Helen N. Stevens, *Memorial Biography of Adele M. Fielde* (New York: The Fielde Memorial Committee, n.d.), 108.
19. P. Coates, 232.
20. *The China Sea Directory*, 169.
21. Mayers, Dennys and King, 234.
22. Customs Decennial 1902–11, 127.
23. Legation Buildings, 3.
24. P. Bruce, 14–15.

25. Mayers, Dennys and King, 233.
26. R. Smith, 321.
27. P. Coates, 227.
28. Mayers, Dennys and King, 234.
29. Michie, 2: 206.
30. *The China Sea Directory*, 173.
31. *The Hongkong Directory 1859*, 32.
32. *The China Directory 1861*, 26.
33. Mayers, Dennys and King, 231.
34. C&D 1884, 343–47.
35. Fairbank 1975, 440.
36. Fairbank 1975, 446.
37. Fairbank 1975, 461–63.
38. Customs Decennial 1882–91, 525.
39. C&D 1887, 374–77.
40. FO Swatow 1889, 7.
41. Becker, 246.
42. P. King, 245.
43. C&D 1879, 271–73.
44. C&D 1881, 281–83.
45. Commercial Report Swatow 1862, 55.
46. C&D 1908, 899–903.
47. C&D 1891, 178–81.
48. Marriner, 79.
49. Beresford, 181.
50. Beresford, 178–79.
51. A. Coates 1983, 145.
52. C&D 1883, 343–47.
53. C&D 1866, 179–80.
54. Beresford, 180.
55. FO Swatow 1903, 5.
56. *China Proper*, 3: 271.
57. P. Bruce, 19.
58. *The Hong Kong Daily Press*, 25 January 1882.
59. Cook, 122.
60. P. King, 33.
61. Cook, 121.
62. Cook, 121.
63. Mayers, Dennys and King, 235.
64. C&D 1866, 179–80.
65. C&D 1904, 342–45.
66. Drage, 58.
67. Beresford, 177.
68. FO Swatow 1902, 4.
69. P. Bruce, 27.
70. C&D 1893, 182–84.
71. FO Swatow 1902, 7.
72. FO Swatow 1903, 6.
73. FO Swatow 1904, 6.
74. Information provided to the author by John Swire & Sons Ltd. Archives.
75. Lunt, 71.
76. Moseley, 16.
77. *The Hong Kong Daily Telegraph*, 7 August 1922.
78. C&D 1928, 807–13.
79. C&D 1924, 926–32.
80. P. Coates, 465.
81. Angus, 101–2.
82. FO Swatow 1905, 7.
83. Brooks, 106.
84. C&D 1908, 899–903.
85. Moseley, 22.
86. *China Proper*, 2: 135.

Szemao
1. 1895 Complementary, Article III.
2. 1897 Special, Article XIII.
3. P. Coates, 318.
4. Customs Decennial 1902–11, 290.
5. C&D 1897, 230.
6. C&D 1897, 230.
7. *Report on a Journey from Hong-Kong to Ssumao*, 6.
8. C&D 1901, 305.
9. *The Hong Kong Telegraph*, 21 February 1906.
10. FO Report on the Trade of Yunnan, 1898, 3.
11. C&D 1903, 345–46.
12. C&D 1908, 935–36.
13. C&D 1934, A525–26.

Tachienlu
1. Lo and Bryant, 418.
2. P. Coates, 417.
3. P. Coates, 417.
4. FO Tachienlu 1913, 6.
5. *China Proper*, 3: 455.
6. FO Tachienlu 1913, 3–7.
7. FO Tachienlu 1913, 9.
8. Lo and Bryant, 418–21.

Taiwan-fu
1. Couling, 192.
2. According to information at the site.
3. A. Wright, 817.
4. Davidson, 171–72.
5. Oakley 2013, 58.
6. Oakley 2013, 1.
7. TNA, FO 228/374/25, Swinhoe to Wade, 1 August 1864.
8. Oakley 2005, 270.
9. Trade Statistics 1863–72.
10. Davidson, 174.
11. TNA, FO 228/374/25, Swinhoe to Wade, 1 August 1864.
12. 1871 Correspondence, 173.
13. Trade Reports 1879.
14. Oakley 2005, 282.
15. C&D 1882, 315–16.
16. www.takaoclub.com
17. *The Hong Kong Daily Press*, 31 August 1886.
18. FO Taiwan 1889, 4.
19. TNA, FO 678/3181, title deed for Bain & Co, 1885.

20. TNA, FO 678/3039, minutes of meeting re Anping bund, 1881.
21. Davidson, 176.
22. C&D 1879, 280–81.
23. TNA, WORK 10/210, despatch from Chen, 2 December 1885.
24. P. Coates, 321.
25. Customs Decennial 1882–91, 464.
26. Davidson, 174.
27. Le Gendre, 90.
28. Mayers, Dennys and King, 303.
29. C&D 1897, 79–81.

Taku
1. Fairbank 1953, 81.
2. TNA, T 1/6768C, report by Crossman, 18 July 1867.
3. Mayers, Dennys and King, 465.
4. Legation Buildings, 1.
5. TNA, MPD 1/210, map, 1867.
6. Lo and Bryant, 439–41.

Tamsui
1. C&D 1885, 360–61.
2. Couling, 192.
3. Fortune 1857, 237.
4. Davidson, 199.
5. Morse 1910, 2: 230–31.
6. Consular Establishments, 90.
7. Davidson, 175.
8. Davidson, 176.
9. *The Hong Kong Daily Press*, 29 November 1890.
10. Fairbank 1995, 122.
11. Fairbank 1995, 106.
12. 1871 Correspondence, 174.
13. C&D, various years.
14. *Trade Statistics 1863–1872*.
15. Davidson, 373.
16. Davidson, 206.
17. Davidson, 374.
18. Customs Decennial 1882–91, 439.
19. P. Coates, 333.
20. Mayers, Dennys and King, 315.
21. According to information at the site.
22. Legation Buildings, 4.
23. TNA, FO 17/1093, report by Howard, 31 December 1889.
24. Davidson, 10.
25. Mateo, 108–11.
26. Davidson, 174.
27. Mayers, Dennys and King, 323.
28. TNA, FO 228/374/25, Swinhoe to Wade, 1 August 1864.
29. Blue, 116.
30. Lo and Bryant, 204.
31. C&D 1879, 282.
32. *The China Mail*, 3 May 1877.
33. C&D 1888, 390–91.
34. Fairbank 1975, 182.
35. C&D 1885, 360–61.
36. Morse 1910, 2: 361.
37. Halcombe, 147.
38. C&D 1885, 360–61.
39. Davidson, 233.
40. C&D 1887, 388–89.
41. Davidson, 305.
42. *The Hong Kong Daily Press*, 1 September 1885.
43. Blue, 117.
44. Halcombe, 142.
45. Halcombe, 147–48.
46. Fairbank 1995, 107.
47. C&D 1892, 174–76.
48. Fairbank 1995, 107.
49. C&D 1885, 360–61.
50. C&D 1897, 76–79.
51. Fairbank 1975, 1022.
52. Blue, 251.
53. C&D 1928, 473–78.

Tengyueh
1. 1894 Burmah, Article XIII.
2. 1897 Special, Article XIII.
3. *China Proper*, 3: 230.
4. Lo and Bryant, 469.
5. FO Tengyueh 1904, 3.
6. P. Coates, 384.
7. FO Tengyueh 1906, 3–6.
8. *The Hong Kong Weekly Press*, 17 November 1902.
9. Customs Decennial 1922–31, 375.
10. P. Coates, 314.
11. TNA, WORK 10/633, file 'Purchase of a site for the consulate'.
12. C&D 1923, 960–61.
13. Lo and Bryant, 474.

Tientsin
1. Tai, 46.
2. W. Martin, 166.
3. O. Rasmussen, 17.
4. M. Wright, 7, 12.
5. Mayers, Dennys and King, 474.
6. A. Coates, 1983, 47.
7. O. Rasmussen, 40.
8. P. Coates, 282.
9. O. Rasmussen, 38.
10. TNA, MPKK 50/1, map, 1865.
11. O. Rasmussen, 40.
12. Bickers 1999, 137.
13. Mayers, Dennys and King, 473.
14. Commercial Report Tientsin 1862, 24.
15. Liu, 109.
16. Trade Reports 1868.
17. Blue, 104.

18. Mayers, Dennys and King, 474.
19. A. Coates 1983, 48.
20. TNA, MPKK 50/1, map, 1865.
21. TNA, T 1/6768C, report by Crossman, 18 July 1867.
22. *The New York Times*, 25 December 1866.
23. Morse 1910, 2: 241.
24. O. Rasmussen, 45.
25. Morse 1910, 2: 246.
26. Morse 1910, 2: 247–54.
27. O. Rasmussen, 48.
28. Morse 1910, 2: 256.
29. O. Rasmussen, 51.
30. Cohen, 247.
31. Lo and Bryant, 476.
32. *The China Directory 1873*, P1–3.
33. C&D 1883, 408–13.
34. LeFevour, 64.
35. Fairbank 1975, 42–43.
36. C&D 1877, 325–27.
37. Schrecker, 8.
38. S. Wright, 511.
39. S. Wright, 647.
40. *The China Mail*, 26 February 1895.
41. *The China Mail*, 11 June 1895.
42. S. Wright, 655.
43. S. Wright, 693.
44. Morse 1920, 417.
45. C&D 1880, 362–64.
46. O. Rasmussen, 76.
47. A. Coates, 1983, 92.
48. Tian, 55.
49. McLeish, 18.
50. O. Rasmussen, 63–65.
51. O. Rasmussen, 86.
52. O. Rasmussen, 85.
53. King, 73.
54. Morse 1920, 434.
55. S. Wright, 811.
56. Keswick, 129.
57. FO Tientsin 1888, 8.
58. Morse 1920, 435.
59. S. Wright, 812.
60. S. Wright, 813–15.
61. Fairbank 1975, 1481.
62. Customs Decennial 1912–21, 155.
63. Xiao, 151.
64. Xiao, 141.
65. Customs Decennial 1922–31, 371–73.
66. Oliphant, 217.
67. Morse 1920, 234.
68. McLeish, 10.
69. O. Rasmussen, 99–100.
70. O. Rasmussen, 77.
71. FO Tientsin 1900–1903, 9.
72. O. Rasmussen, 239.
73. C&D 1921, 620–53.
74. FO Tientsin 1904–5, 12.
75. Customs Decennial 1912–21, 143.
76. Trade Reports 1865, 31.
77. Mayers, Dennys and King, 465.
78. *The Hong Kong Daily Press*, 1 November 1887.
79. *The Hong Kong Daily Press*, 17 December 1880.
80. Xiao, 96.
81. Blue, xxvii.
82. *The China Directory 1873*, P1–3.
83. Blue, 288.
84. FO Tientsin 1900–1903, 8.
85. TNA, SOAS File JSSII 1/15, 1899.
86. *The Hong Kong Daily Press*, 23 April 1886.
87. *The Hong Kong Daily Press*, 7 July 1886.
88. Mayers, Dennys and King, 480.
89. Blue, xxvi.
90. Trade Reports 1879.
91. Williams, 330.
92. O. Rasmussen, 88.
93. Trade Reports 1879.
94. McLeish, 13.
95. C&D 1899, 111–24.
96. C&D 1887, 470–75.
97. O. Rasmussen, 73.
98. O. Rasmussen, 61.
99. O. Rasmussen, 74.
100. Mayers, Dennys and King, 476.
101. Tian, 42.
102. FO Tientsin 1885, 3.
103. Xiao, 86.
104. O. Rasmussen, 66.
105. O. Rasmussen, 96.
106. Morse 1910, 3: 106.
107. FO Tientsin 1900–1903, 4.
108. C&D 1901, 132–47.
109. A. Rasmussen, 170.
110. Wood, 191.
111. C&D 1901, 132–47.
112. A. Coates 1983, 107.
113. www.kaiserscross.com/304501/306501.html
114. A. Coates 1983, 107.
115. A. Coates 1983, 107.
116. C&D 1901, 132–47.
117. Burton St. John, 11.
118. Morse 1910, 3: 291–92.
119. Morse 1920, 235.
120. Morse 1910, 3: 357.
121. Morse 1910, 3: 296.
122. Morse 1910, 3: 298.
123. O. Rasmussen, 228.
124. Morse 1910, 3: 298.
125. Bickers 2007b, 136.

126. S. Wright, 750.
127. Morse 1910, 3: 365.
128. O. Rasmussen, 226.
129. Bickers 2007b, 141.
130. Bickers 2007b, 134.
131. FO Tientsin 1900–1903, 5.
132. Victoir and Zatsepine, 86.
133. FO Tientsin 1900–1903, 6.
134. O. Rasmussen, 95.
135. FO Tientsin 1900–1903, 7.
136. Morse 1920, 236.
137. *Oriental Affairs*, October 1938, 195.
138. Xiao, 48.
139. FO Tientsin 1900–1903, 6.
140. O. Rasmussen, 244.
141. Ratepayers and the Crown Leases, 10.
142. *Oriental Affairs*, October 1938, 195.
143. Morse 1910, 3: 326.
144. TNA, FO 228/1464, letter, 18 March 1902.
145. O. Rasmussen, 233.
146. Tai, 128.
147. *Oriental Affairs*, October 1938, 194.
148. Morse 1910, 3: 325.
149. *Oriental Affairs*, October 1938, 195.
150. Morse 1920, 236.
151. Warner, 61.
152. *Oriental Affairs*, October 1938, 197.
153. O. Rasmussen, 95.
154. Warner, 59–64.
155. *Oriental Affairs*, October 1938, 195.
156. *Oriental Affairs*, October 1938, 197.
157. C&D 1880, 362–64.
158. Morse 1910, 3: 325.
159. FO Tientsin 1900–1903, 6.
160. *Oriental Affairs*, October 1938, 197.
161. Burton St. John, 6.
162. *The China Directory 1863*, S2–3.
163. Mayers, Dennys and King, 475.
164. Morse 1910, 3: 324.
165. O. Rasmussen, 231.
166. Morse 1910, 3: 323–25.
167. *Guide to Tientsin 1907*, 5.
168. *Marlborough Express*, 15 May 1901.
169. *Guide to Tientsin 1907*, 5.
170. *Oriental Affairs*, October 1938, 197.
171. Morse 1910, 3:326.
172. C&D 1910, 753–82.
173. Burton St. John, 6.
174. *Oriental Affairs*, October 1938, 197.
175. *Oriental Affairs*, October 1938, 197.
176. http://en.wikipedia.org/wiki/Concessions_in_Tianjin
177. *Oriental Affairs*, October 1938, 197.
178. C&D 1907, 660–86.
179. Customs Decennial 1912–21, 142–43.
180. Customs Decennial 1912–21, 156–58.
181. McLeish, 30.
182. Customs Decennial 1922–31, 363.
183. Customs Decennial 1912–21, 145.
184. FO Tientsin 1910, 10.
185. C&D 1915, 768–802.
186. Customs Decennial 1912–21, 146.
187. FO Tientsin 1907–1908, 13.
188. Burton St. John, 12.
189. A. Wright, 730.
190. A. Wright, 732.
191. Horesh, 122.
192. Abend 1939, 37.
193. Bickers 1999, 154–57.
194. Arrangement relating to Local Issues, 2.

Tsinan

1. Warner, 186.
2. P. Coates, 391–92.
3. Information supplied by a private source in China.
4. Johnston and Erh 1996b, 42.
5. C&D 1919, 626–27.
6. C&D 1907, 720–21.
7. Customs Decennial 1902–11, 256.
8. Warner, 180–84.
9. *Sunday Morning Post*, 18 August 2013.
10. *The New York Times*, 17 May 1916.
11. Customs Decennial 1922–31, 451.

Tsingtao

1. *The China Mail*, 14 September 1898.
2. Fairbank 1953, 82.
3. *The China Mail*, 4 November 1866.
4. Customs Decennial 1912–21, 203.
5. 1898 Correspondence, 21.
6. Donnelly, 28.
7. Couling, 575.
8. Ho, 210.
9. Asakawa, 86.
10. 1896 Cassini, 9.
11. S. Wright, 683.
12. Admiral von Tirpitz's memoirs, reported in *The Hong Kong Daily Press*, 21 October 1919.
13. S. Wright, 683.
14. Customs Decennial 1912–21, 203.
15. Otte, 89.
16. Williams, 313.
17. S.Wright, 683.
18. Customs Decennial 1912–21, 203.
19. Couling, 576.
20. Customs Decennial 1912–21, 203.
21. Fairbank 1973, 369.
22. *The Times*, 16 November 1897, quoted in Fleming 1959, 29.
23. *The Hong Kong Weekly Press*, 24 November 1897.
24. 1898 Correspondence, 1.

25. Fairbank 1975, 1147.
26. Fairbank 1975, 1151.
27. 1898 Correspondence, 2–14.
28. 1898 Correspondence, 2–4.
29. Crow 1921, 266.
30. Schrecker, 11.
31. Fairbank 1975, 1362.
32. Customs Decennial 1902–11, 237.
33. Schrecker, 208.
34. S. Wright, 705.
35. Schrecker, 217.
36. Warner, 61.
37. *The China Mail*, 14 September 1898.
38. Warner, 199.
39. *The China Mail*, 4 April 1899.
40. FO Chefoo 1898, 10.
41. Warner, 197.
42. Warner, 201.
43. C&D 1900, 153–56.
44. C&D 1903, 188–96.
45. C&D 1904, 201–9.
46. A. Wright, 812.
47. Warner, 197.
48. Customs Decennial 1902–11, 249.
49. *The Hong Kong Telegraph*, 29 December 1906.
50. Hoyt, 4.
51. Customs Decennial 1902–11, 237.
52. A. Wright, 810.
53. Krausse, 217.
54. Warner, 206.
55. *Historical View of Qingdao*, 12.1
56. Warner, 210.
57. C&D 1906, 662–73.
58. *The Hong Kong Daily Press*, 9 June 1905.
59. *The China Mail*, 26 July 1907.
60. Blue, 268.
61. Further Correspondence, 17.
62. Customs Decennial 1902–11, 238.
63. *The China Mail*, 20 February 1911.
64. Hoyt, 54–55.
65. Hoyt, 60.
66. Lo and Bryant, 512.
67. Hoyt, 75–77.
68. Hoyt, 81–86.
69. Hoyt, 64.
70. Customs Decennial 1912–21, 207.
71. Hoyt, 138.
72. Hoyt, 145.
73. French 2006, 77.
74. TNA, CAB 24/1, 4, Committee of Imperial Defence Report, 29 January 1915.
75. TNA, CAB 24/28, Edwin Montagu to Lord Curzon, 28 September 1917.
76. Customs Decennial 1912–21, 203.
77. *The Hong Kong Telegraph*, 28 December 1916.
78. *The Hong Kong Telegraph*, 24 July 1918.
79. Customs Decennial 1912–21, 213.
80. *The Hong Kong Daily Press*, 9 August 1915.
81. *The Hong Kong Daily Press*, 9 September 1915.
82. TNA, CAB 24/5, 4, War Cabinet Memorandum, 14 March 1918.
83. Hoyt, 147.
84. Drage, 238.
85. C&D 1921, 694–98.
86. Customs Decennial 1912–21, 221.
87. C&D 1934, A147–58.
88. Lo and Bryant, 512.
89. G. Thomas, 115.
90. G. Martin, 127.
91. C&D 1933, 59–50.
92. Customs Decennial 1922–31, 451.
93. G. Thomas, 81.

Wanhsien

1. Williams, 315.
2. Customs Decennial 1912–21, 249.
3. *The China Mail*, 3 July 1924.
4. Teichman, 176.
5. Hyde Lay, 48.
6. P. Coates, 467.
7. *The China Mail*, 9 September 1926.
8. Stursberg, 169.
9. Customs Decennial 1922–31, 493.

Weihaiwei

1. Ellis, 2: 269.
2. Lindsay, 214.
3. R. Johnston 1910, 12.
4. A. Wright, 773.
5. *The China Sea Directory*, 565.
6. 1869 Correspondence, 2.
7. FO Weihaiwei 1902, 6.
8. C&D 1890, 223.
9. *The New York Times*, 29 January 1895.
10. Fairbank 1975, 1009.
11. Fairbank 1975, 1011.
12. Inouye, 24.
13. *The China Mail*, 26 February 1895.
14. Zhang, 18.
15. 1898 Correspondence, 41.
16. 1898 Correspondence, 61.
17. Zhang, 18.
18. 1898 Weihaiwei.
19. *The China Mail*, 6 June 1898.
20. Atwell, 19.
21. Beresford, 71–72.
22. *The China Mail*, 5 June 1899.
23. *The China Mail*, 16 June 1899.
24. Atwell, 19.

25. *The China Mail*, 27 September 1898.
26. C&D 1899, 135.
27. Atwell, 16.
28. *The China Mail*, 12 August 1901.
29. Walton, 67.
30. A. Wright, 773.
31. Tan, 20.
32. TNA, ADM 125/89, 1898 Admiralty report.
33. A. Wright, 773–77.
34. C&D 1901, 162–64.
35. Bruce-Mitford, 27.
36. Bruce-Mitford, 55.
37. Bruce-Mitford, 28.
38. Zhang, 153.
39. Zhang, 163.
40. Ernest Clark's 1939 passport application.
41. Atwell, 16.
42. J. Ball, 692.
43. FO Chefoo 1898, 13.
44. *The China Mail*, 7 April 1900.
45. Bruce-Mitford, 23.
46. *The China Mail*, 15 May 1900.
47. *The China Mail*, 4 July 1900.
48. A. Wright, 773–77.
49. Tan, 28.
50. *The China Mail*, 7 April 1902.
51. FO Weihaiwei 1902, 10.
52. Airlie, 113.
53. Bruce-Mitford, i.
54. Lethbridge, 68.
55. FO Weihaiwei 1902, 40.
56. Lethbridge, 69.
57. FO Weihaiwei 1902, 9.
58. FO Weihaiwei 1903, 5.
59. Weihaiwei Acts.
60. Airlie, 14.
61. *The China Mail*, 23 August 1899.
62. *The China Mail*, 3 August 1901.
63. FO Weihaiwei 1902, 5.
64. FO Weihaiwei 1902, 19.
65. *The China Mail*, 30 April 1903.
66. Atwell, 8.
67. Handbook 1919, 7.
68. Airlie, 197.
69. Bruce-Mitford, 23–24.
70. Lethbridge, 67.
71. *The China Mail*, 24 February 1902.
72. Airlie, 125.
73. Blue, 271.
74. FO Weihaiwei 1902, 4.
75. *The China Mail*, 23 August 1899.
76. FO Weihaiwei 1903, 20.
77. *The China Mail*, 16 February 1903.
78. FO Weihaiwei 1904, 16.
79. FO Weihaiwei 1906, 7.
80. Lethbridge, 66.
81. Airlie, 133.
82. Atwell, 68.
83. FO Weihaiwei 1913, 7.
84. FO Weihaiwei 1915, 6.
85. FO Weihaiwei 1906, 13.
86. FO Weihaiwei 1908, 6.
87. Lethbridge, 66.
88. FO Weihaiwei 1904, 40.
89. FO Weihaiwei 1918, 4.
90. Airlie, 183.
91. FO Weihaiwei 1919, 4.
92. FO Weihaiwei 1918, 4.
93. Atwell, 107.
94. FO Weihaiwei 1913, 8.
95. FO Weihaiwei 1917, 10.
96. Zhang, 159.
97. Atwell, 106.
98. Atwell, 166.
99. *China Proper*, 3: 397.
100. A. Wright, 773–77.
101. Atwell, 167.
102. Teichman, 195–96.
103. Port Edward Club Rules, 1902, courtesy of Weihai Municipal Archive Bureau.
104. Weihaiwei Golf Club Rules, 1902 and 1908, courtesy of Weihai Municipal Archive Bureau.
105. Weihai Municipal Archive Bureau.
106. FO Weihaiwei 1917, 5.
107. Zhang, 200.
108. Bruce-Mitford, 58.
109. Angulo, 137.
110. Letter to the author from Duncan Clark, 10 April 2009.
111. Tan, 30.
112. *The China Mail*, 18 February 1902.
113. *The China Mail*, 16 June 1906.
114. *The China Mail*, 18 July 1906.
115. Tan, 34.
116. *The Hong Kong Telegraph*, 8 July 1912.
117. Teichman, 196.
118. *The China Yearbook 1924–5*, 830.
119. FO Weihaiwei 1922, 2.
120. Johnston 1931, 177.
121. Johnston 1931, 182.
122. 1930 Weihaiwei.
123. Atwell, 168.
124. C&D 1933, 535–39.
125. G. Thomas, 88.

Wenchow

1. Customs Decennial 1882–91, 387.
2. *The China Mail*, 3 May 1877.

3. TNA, FO 17/1306/230, Warren to Cooper, 20 January 1877.
4. TNA, FO 17/1306/241, Fraser to Derby, 12 March 1877.
5. TNA, FO 228/598/4, Alabaster to Fraser, 16 April 1877.
6. TNA, FO 228/598/8, Alabaster to Fraser, 20 April 1877.
7. TNA, FO 228/598/3, Alabaster to Fraser, 14 April 1877.
8. TNA, FO 228/598/4, Alabaster to Fraser, 16 April 1877.
9. TNA, FO 228/598/8, Alabaster to Fraser, 20 April 1877.
10. TNA, FO 228/598/10, Alabaster to Fraser, 1 May 1877.
11. TNA, MPKK 51, 1877 map.
12. TNA, FO 228/598/8, Alabaster to Fraser, 20 April 1877.
13. P. Coates, 244.
14. Milne, 8.
15. Blue, 123.
16. *The Hong Kong Daily Press*, 15 August 1878.
17. C&D 1879, 291–92.
18. C&D 1894, 168–69.
19. Trade Reports 1879.
20. P. Coates, 243.
21. Couling, 597.
22. *The China Mail*, 14 April 1877.
23. C&D 1879, 291–92.
24. Lane-Poole, 350–52.
25. FO Wenchow, various years.
26. *The China Mail*, 18 December 1878.
27. P. Coates, 243.
28. FO Foochow 1888, 2.
29. FO Foochow 1893, 2.
30. *The China Mail*, 4 February 1898.
31. FO Wenchow 1904, 3–4.
32. FO Wenchow 1905, 3.
33. FO Wenchow 1894, 7.
34. TNA, FO 17/1047, Walsham to Salisbury, 10 November 1887.
35. *The China Mail*, 29 October 1897.
36. P. Coates, 247.
37. Hong Kong Public Records Office, HKMS No 127, D-S 1-1.
38. C&D 1879, 291–92.
39. P. Coates, 243.
40. Lo and Bryant, 542.
41. TNA, WORK 10/55/1.
42. *The China Mail*, 27 February 1889.
43. C&D 1900, 255–56.
44. C&D 1906, 802–3.
45. C&D 1940, A384–87.
46. *China Proper*, 2: 139–42.

Whampoa

1. Cunynghame, 1: 101.
2. Morse 1926, 2: 37.
3. Lo and Bryant, 547.
4. P. Coates, 112.
5. http://familytrees.genopro.com/52526/default.htm
6. TNA FO 682/1982/63, Bonham to Xu, 17 November 1849.
7. TNA FO 682/1982/66, Xu to Bonham, 23 November 1849.
8. TNA FO 682/1983/1, Xu to Bonham, 7 January 1850.
9. TNA FO 931/932, Parkes to Po-kuei, 2 November 1852.
10. TNA FO 682/1991/31b, Winchester to Po-kuei, April 1858.
11. Downing, 3: 245.
12. Staples-Smith, 50.
13. TNA, FO 682/1980/48, Qiying to Davis, 1 September 1847.
14. A. Coates 1980, 7.
15. A. Coates 1980, 13–17.
16. A. Wright, 70.
17. A. Coates 1980, 54.
18. A. Wright, 196.
19. *The China Directory 1863*, 28.
20. *The China Mail*, 17 December 1868.
21. A. Coates 1980, 4.
22. A. Wright, 198.
23. *The China Sea Directory*, 115.
24. TNA, WORK 10/56/3, report by Crossman, 21 February 1867.
25. Legation Buildings, 3.
26. Mayers, Dennys and King, 127.
27. R. Thomas, 9.
28. Bruner, 235.
29. Information provided by the Huangpu Military Academy Museum.
30. C&D 1912, 1039–40.
31. Levy, 134.
32. Fairbank 1958, 173.
33. Chapman, 48.
34. Levy, 153.
35. Information provided by the Huangpu Military Academy Museum.
36. *China Proper*, 3: 257.
37. Lo and Bryant, 546.

Woosung

1. Blake, 175–76.
2. Morse 1910, 2: 75–76.
3. Crush, 28.
4. *The Hong Kong Daily Press*, 8 July 1876.
5. *Events*, 22.
6. Blake, 175–76.
7. *Events*, 115.
8. *The Hong Kong Daily Press*, 6 June 1874.
9. 1880 Supplementary, Article I and Special Stipulation 1.
10. S. Wright, 433.
11. Blue, 196.
12. *The China Mail*, 16 April 1898.
13. *The China Mail*, 23 April 1898.

14. FO Foochow 1899, 9.
15. *North-China Herald*, 29 August 1898.
16. *The Hong Kong Daily Press*, 21 November 1899.

Wuchow

1. FO Wuchow 1897, 11.
2. FO Wuchow 1902, 10.
3. P. Coates, 370–71.
4. C&D 1898, 236–38.
5. *The China Mail*, 11 September 1903.
6. Archer 1946, 76.
7. C&D 1908, 923–25.
8. *The China Mail*, 11 September 1903.
9. *The China Mail*, 6 March 1901.
10. C&D 1923, 945–46.
11. *The Hong Kong Daily Press*, 14 November 1899.
12. *The China Mail*, 26 April 1899.
13. *The China Mail*, 5 August 1903.
14. *The China Mail*, 8 July 1903.
15. FO Wuchow 1903, 6.
16. Customs Decennial 1902–11, 203.
17. C&D 1904, 359–60.
18. Angus, 76.
19. J. Ball, 682.
20. Beresford, 265.
21. Morse 1920, 82.
22. Customs Decennial 1912–21, 283.
23. C&D 1941, A445–47.

Wuhu

1. Wolseley, 363.
2. Oliphant, 505.
3. Dean, 123–25.
4. *The China Mail*, 14 April 1877.
5. *The China Mail*, 14 April 1877.
6. *The Hong Kong Daily Press*, 27 September 1877.
7. Customs Decennial 1882–91, 254.
8. Trade Reports 1879, 75.
9. FO Wuhu 1898, 5.
10. Customs Decennial 1882–91, 254.
11. FO Wuhu 1892, 4.
12. Customs Decennial 1882–91, 254.
13. FO Wuhu 1901, 8.
14. FO Wuhu 1904, 6.
15. C&D 1921, 851–53.
16. *The Hong Kong Daily Press*, 28 January 1888.
17. Lo and Bryant, 564.
18. Customs Decennial 1922–31, 611.
19. Customs Decennial 1882–91, 254.
20. Customs Decennial 1912–21, 355.
21. Commercial Report Wuhu 1885, 59.
22. FO Wuhu 1890, 2.
23. FO Wuhu 1898, 9.
24. Drage, 67.
25. *The China Mail*, 19 May 1891.
26. Customs Decennial 1882–91, 270.

Yochow

1. J. Ball, 688.
2. Fairbank 1995, 147–49.
3. C&D 1900, 243–44.
4. Morse 1920, 251.
5. Fairbank 1995, 154.
6. C&D 1900, 243–44.
7. C&D 1902, 273–74.
8. Fairbank 1995, 153.
9. Stursberg, 79.
10. TNA, FO 228/1369, draft report by Tower, 26 August 1901, 204–7.
11. *The China Mail*, 18 July 1898.
12. TNA, FO 228/1369, draft report by Tower, 26 August 1901, 98–100.
13. Customs Decennial 1912–21, 289.
14. C&D 1924, 886–88.
15. C&D 1928, 776–77.
16. Customs Decennial 1922–31, 543.
17. C&D 1941, A361–63.

Yunnan-fu

1. *China Proper*, 3: 491.
2. Benson, Project Gutenberg website, no page number.
3. Spence, 458.
4. Lo and Bryant, 592.
5. *The China Mail*, 18 August 1900.
6. Crow 1933, 390.
7. C&D 1930, 991–93.
8. Benson, Project Gutenberg website, no page number.
9. C&D 1924, 969–72.
10. Lo and Bryant, 598.

Russian Frontier Stations

1. Auber, 126.
2. Rawlinson, 20.
3. 1851 Kuldja.
4. 'Medvedev fears Chinese influx to Russian Far East', *South China Morning Post*, 11 August 2012.
5. 1902 Manchuria.

Japanese Stations in the North-East

1. Perkins, 98.
2. Anderson, 7: 16.
3. Crow 1921, 258.
4. Williams, 330.
5. C&D 1918, 679.
6. 1909 Manchuria.
7. Customs Decennial 1922–31, 323.
8. 1914 Presidential.
9. Manchuria 1922, 9.
10. Manchuria 1922, 11.
11. C&D 1934, A116–18.

Yangtze River Ports-of-Call
1. 1861 Correspondence, 3.
2. 1869 Supplementary.
3. Alcock Despatch, 1.
4. 1869 Supplementary.
5. Dean, 123–25.
6. 1898 Inland Navigation, Supplementary Rule 6.
7. *China Overland Trade Report*, 9 July 1898.
8. *London & China Telegraph*, 3 September 1900.

West River Ports-of-Call
1. R. Lee, 1.
2. R. Lee, 231.
3. *China Overland Trade Report*, 20 August 1898.

Tibetan Ports
1. 1886 Burmah, Article IV.
2. 1890 Sikkim.
3. 1893 Darjeeling.
4. S. Wright, 616–22.
5. 1904 Tibet.

Glossary of Terms

bund: from Hindi word for artificial embankment; 'praya' used in Hong Kong and Macao

cangue: wooden frame attached to the neck as punishment for criminals

catty: traditional Chinese unit of weight, approximately 600 grams

comprador: from Portuguese, Chinese agent employed by foreign merchants to handle local transactions

concession: tract of land leased by foreign government and sub-let to its merchants

consulate: official representation of one country in another, principally charged with assisting nationals and promoting commercial and other relations

coolie: manual labourer, thought to be from the Chinese *kuli* (bitter strength)

farming: traditional means of raising tax in China, a 'farmer' was required to provide a fixed sum to the government, keeping any excess for himself

fengshui: traditional Chinese belief in importance and influence of natural elements being in harmony with their surroundings

godown: from Malay word for warehouse

hong: term applied to a trading company, and to the premises it occupies

hoppo: official in charge of imperial customs office

hulk: a retired vessel used as a permanent storage or boarding facility

IMC: Imperial Maritime Customs, the foreign-managed customs service established in 1854 in Shanghai, later expanded to all treaty ports

Inland Steam Navigation Regulations: rules issued in 1898 allowing steam vessels of all nationalities to ply China's inland waters

junk: a Chinese sailing vessel, noted for its high stern and bamboo-battened sails

landing stage: created in 1902 on the West River for the handling of passengers only; no permanent foreign presence was allowed there

li: traditional Chinese measure of length for roads, varied in different parts of the country but now accepted as being equivalent to 500 metres

likin: inland tax on the carriage of goods, introduced 1853, its unpredictability was a cause of great concern for foreign and Chinese merchants

lorcha: from Portuguese, a vessel with a Western hull but Chinese sails

mou: traditional Chinese measure of area, varied in different parts of the country but now accepted as being equivalent to 770 square metres

picul: 100 *catties*, traditionally the amount one man could carry on a shoulder pole, equivalent to approximately 60 kilograms

port-of-call: created in 1876 on the Yangtze and 1897 and 1902 on the West River as places where passengers and goods could be handled, but no permanent foreign presence was allowed

praya: Portuguese for 'beach', used in Hong Kong and Macao to mean a quay, embankment or bund

queue: the traditional plait or pigtail, forced to be worn by Chinese men to show subservience to ruling Manchu

sampan: probably from Chinese words for 'three planks', taken to mean any small boat that is not a junk

Self-Strengthening Movement: a series of semi-official reforms during 1860s to 1890s as response to China's repeated humiliation by Western arms and technological advances

settlement: a tract of land designated for foreign occupation where each occupant must enter into a separate lease with the Chinese owner

shroff: Indian origin, meaning cashier or money-changer

supercargo: from Portuguese, initially the commercial manager based on a merchant vessel, later becoming shore-based

tael: one-sixteenth of a *catty*, about 38 grams

taipan: from Chinese for 'great boss', adopted by foreign firms as a term for their senior executive

taotai: an Intendant of Circuit in the Chinese imperial government, had responsibility for a number of prefectures

Tartar: term generally applied to the Manchu; the Tartar General was the local military commander

Glossary of Terms

transit pass: introduced 1858 as means of shielding foreign imports and exports from excessive internal transit taxes

treaty port: town, city or port opened by treaty in which Treaty Powers can establish consulates and their merchants can reside and trade, and where customs duties are levied in accordance with treaty rates

Tsungli Yamen: established on outcome of the Second Opium War as government department through which foreign affairs could be managed

yamen: the official residence of a magistrate

zaibatsu: Japanese term for financial and industrial conglomerates that developed after Meiji Restoration

Bibliography

Treaties and other international agreements as referred to in the text

1689 Nerchinsk (Russia): Treaty of Peace, Boundary etc. Nerchinsk, 1689.

1727 Kiakhta (Russia): Treaty of Peace, Boundaries etc. Kiakhta, 21 October.

1842 Nanking (Britain): Treaty of Peace, Friendship, Commerce etc. Nanking, 29 August.

1843 The Bogue (Britain): Supplementary Treaty of Commerce. The Bogue, 8 October.

1846 Bocca Tigris (Britain): Convention relative to the Admission of Foreigners into the City of Canton and to the Evacuation of the Island of Chusan by the British Forces. Bocca Tigris, 4 April.

1847 Canton (China): Agreement of the Chinese Commissioner, Ki Ying, relative to the Entrance of British Subjects into Canton, the Trade at Honan, and the Erection of Churches at the Ports of Trade. 6 April.

1851 Kuldja (Russia): Commercial Treaty. Kuldja, 25 July.

1858 Aigun (Russia): Treaty of Friendship and Boundaries. Aigun, 16 May.

1858 Tientsin (Russia): Treaty of Commerce etc. Tientsin, 13 June.

1858 Tientsin (United States): Treaty of Peace, Friendship and Commerce. Tientsin, 18 June.

1858 Tientsin (Britain): Treaty of Peace, Friendship and Commerce. Tientsin, 26 June.

1858 Tientsin (France): Treaty of Friendship, Commerce and Navigation. Tientsin, 27 June.

1858 Agreement (Britain): Agreement containing the Rules of Trade made in pursuance of Article XXVI of the Treaty of 26 June 1858. Shanghai, 8 November.

1860 Peking (Britain): Convention of Peking. Peking, 24 October.

1860 Peking (Russia): Additional Treaty of Commerce etc. Peking, 14 November.

1862 Tientsin (Portugal): Treaty of Commerce etc. Tientsin, 13 August (not ratified by China).

1869 Supplementary (Britain): Supplementary Convention to the Treaty of Commerce and Navigation. Peking, 23 October.

1871 Tientsin (Japan): Friendship and Trade Treaty. Tientsin, 13 September.

1876 Chefoo (Britain): Agreement for the Settlement of the Yunnan Case, Official Intercourse, and Trade between the two Countries. Chefoo, 13 September.

1880 Supplementary (Germany): Supplementary Convention. Peking, 31 March.

1885 Tientsin (France): Treaty of Peace, Friendship and Commerce. Tientsin, 9 June.

1886 Tientsin (France): Commercial Convention between France and China. Tientsin, 25 April.

1886 Burmah (Britain): Convention relative to Burmah and Tibet. Peking, 24 July.

1887 Additional (France): Additional Convention of Commerce. Peking, 23 June.

1887 Complementary (France): Convention respecting the Delimitation of the Frontier between China and Tonkin. Peking, 26 June.

1887 Peking (Portugal): Treaty of Friendship and Commerce. Peking, 1 December.

1890 Sikkim (Britain): Convention relating to Sikkim and Tibet. Calcutta, 17 March.

1890 Chungking (Britain): Additional Article to the Agreement of September 13, 1876, declaring Chungking to be opened to Trade. Peking, 31 March.

1893 Darjeeling (Britain): Regulations regarding Trade etc. Darjeeling, 5 December.

1894 Burmah (Britain): Convention for the Execution of the Convention of 1886 respecting Boundaries etc, Burmah and China. London, 1 March.

1895 Complementary (France): Complementary Convention to the Additional Convention of 26 June 1887. Peking, 20 June.

1895 Liaotung (Japan): Convention for the Retrocession by Japan to China of the Southern Portion of the

Bibliography

Province of Feng-Tien (i.e. the Liaotung Peninsula). Peking, 8 November.

1896 Railway (Russia): Contract for the Construction and Operation of the Chinese Eastern Railway. Berlin, 8 September.

1896 Cassini (Russia): A Special Convention. Peking, 30 September.

1896 Settlements (Japan): Protocol respecting Japanese Settlements and other matters. Peking, 19 October.

1897 Special (Britain): Agreement modifying the Convention of 1894 relative to Boundaries etc, Burmah and China. Peking, 4 February.

1898 Kiaochow (Germany): Treaty respecting the Lease of Kiao-chau to Germany. Peking, 6 March.

1898 Liaotung (Russia): Convention for the Lease of the Liaotung Peninsula. Peking, 27 March.

1898 Weihaiwei (Britain): Convention for the Lease of Wei-hai Wei. Peking, 24 May.

1898 Hong Kong (Britain): Convention for the Extension of Hongkong. Peking, 9 June.

1898 Inland Navigation (China): Regulations relative to Inland Steam Navigation. Peking, 28 July.

1899 Dalny (Russia): Russian Imperial Order regarding Establishment of Dalny as a Free Port. St. Petersburg, 11 August.

1901 Boxer Protocol (Multilateral): International Protocol. Peking, 7 September.

1902 Manchuria (Russia): Convention with regard to Manchuria. Peking, 8 April.

1902 Commercial (Britain): Treaty respecting Commercial Relations etc. Shanghai, 5 September.

1903 Japanese (Japan): Treaty respecting Commercial Relations etc. Shanghai, 8 October.

1903 American (United States): Treaty respecting Commercial Relations etc. Shanghai, 8 October.

1904 Imperial (China): Imperial Edict for the opening of Weihsien, Chowcheen, Chinanfu and Choutsun. 18 May.

1904 Tibet (Britain): Convention respecting Tibet. Lhasa, 7 September.

1905 Portsmouth (Japan and Russia): Treaty of Peace. Portsmouth (New Hampshire), 5 September.

1905 Manchuria (Japan): Treaty and Additional Agreement relating to Manchuria. Peking, 22 December.

1906 Tibet (Britain): Convention respecting Tibet. Peking, 27 April.

1906 Newchwang (Japan): Agreement for the Rendition of the Port of Ying-kou (Port of Newchwang). Peking, 5 December.

1907 Dairen (Japan): Agreement for the establishment of a Maritime Customs Office at Dairen, and for Inland Waters Steam Navigation. Peking, 30 May.

1907 Political (Japan and Russia): Political Convention. St Petersburg, 30 July.

1909 Municipal (Russia): Preliminary Agreement in regard to Municipal Administration in the Chinese Eastern Railway Zone. Peking, 10 May.

1909 Manchuria (Japan): Agreement concerning Mines and Railways in Manchuria. 4 September.

1909 Gando (Japan): Agreement relating to the Chientao Region. 4 September.

1914 Presidential (China): Presidential Mandate in regard to the Voluntary Opening of Certain Ports. Peking, 8 January.

1914 Municipal (Great Britain and Russia): Agreement respecting the Inclusion of British Subjects within the Scheme of Municipal Administration and Taxation established in the Area of the Chinese Eastern Railway. Peking, 3 December.

1915 Manchuria (Japan): Treaty and Exchanges of Notes respecting South Manchuria and Eastern Inner Mongolia. Peking, 25 May.

1915 Hailar (Russia): Arrangement concerning the Situation of Houlounbouir (Hailar). Peking, 6 November.

1930 Weihaiwei (Britain): Convention for the Rendition of Weihaiwei and Agreement regarding certain Facilities for His Majesty's Navy after Rendition. Nanking, 18 April.

1943 Chungking (Britain): Treaty for the Relinquishment of Extra-Territorial Rights in China. Chungking, 11 January.

British government official papers

Arrangement between His Majesty's Government in the United Kingdom and the Japanese Government relating to Local Issues at Tientsin, June 19, 1940. London, 1940.

China etc. (Legation Buildings) – Return to an Order of the Honourable the House of Commons, dated 22 July 1870. London, 1870. 'Legation Buildings'.

Commercial Reports by Her Majesty's Consuls in China for various Treaty Ports. London: Her Majesty's Stationery Office. 'Commercial Report Ningpo 1885', etc.

Correspondence between the Foreign Office and the Commercial Association of Manchester, 1846–1848. London, 1857. 'Manchester Correspondence'.
Correspondence relating to the Affairs of China. London, 1898. '1898 Correspondence'.
Correspondence respecting the Opening of the Yang-tze-kiang River to Foreign Trade. London, 1861. '1861 Correspondence'.
Correspondence respecting the Revision of the Treaty of Tien-tsin. London, 1871. '1871 Correspondence'.
Correspondence with the Chamber of Commerce at Shanghae respecting the Revision of the Treaty of Tien-tsin. London, 1869. '1869 Correspondence'.
Despatch from HM Minister at Peking forwarding a Report by Mr WJ Clennell, HM Consul at Kiukiang respecting the Province of Kiangsi. London, 1903. '1903 Despatch'.
Despatch from Sir Rutherford Alcock respecting a Supplementary Convention to the Treaty of Tien-tsin signed by him on October 23, 1869. London, 1870. 'Alcock Despatch'.
Foreign Office Annual Series. Diplomatic and Consular Reports on Trade and Finance for various Treaty Ports. London. 'FO Hankow 1886', etc.
Further Correspondence respecting the Affairs of China. London, 1914. 'Further Correspondence'.
Further Memorials respecting the China Treaty Revision Convention. London, 1870. 'Further Memorials'.
Handbook prepared under the Direction of the Historical Section of the Foreign Office, No. 70 – Weihaiwei. May 1919.
Letter to Chambers of Commerce &c respecting the China Treaty Revision Convention. London, 1870. '1870 Letter'.
Memorials addressed by Chambers of Commerce in China to the British Minister in Peking on the subject of the Revision of the Treaty of Tien-tsin, 24 February 1868. London, 1868. '1868 Memorials'.
Memorials respecting the China Treaty Revision Convention. London, 1870. '1870 Memorials'.
Papers relating to the Colony of Hong Kong etc. 21 March 1857. London, 1857. 'Hong Kong Papers'.
Papers respecting the Agreements relative to the British Concessions at Hankow and Kiukiang. London, 1927. 'British Concessions'.
Report on a Journey from Hong-Kong to Ssumao. London, August 1898.
Report on Consular Establishments in China, 1869. London, 1870. 'Consular Establishments'.
Report on the State of Trade at the Treaty Ports of China. London, 1897. 'Trade Report 1897'.
Reports on the Trade at the Ports in China open by Treaty to Foreign Trade for various years. Shanghai: Inspector General of Customs. 'Trade Reports 1865' etc.
Return relative to Claims for Indemnity under the Convention of Peking, 1860 and the Mode of Settlement, May 5, 1870. London, 1870. 'Claims for Indemnity'.

OTHER OFFICIAL PAPERS AND DIRECTORIES

China: A Source Book of Information. Shanghai: Pan-Pacific Association, 1920.
The China Directory for various years. Hong Kong: Shortrede.
China Proper. (London): Naval Intelligence Division, 1944.
China Sanatorium, A. (no publication information available—likely to be Shanghai: *North-China Daily News*, 1899).
The China Sea Directory. London: Hydrographic Office, Admiralty, 1884.
The China Year Book 1913. London: George Routledge and Sons, 1913.
The China Yearbook 1924–5. Tientsin: Tientsin Press, 1924.
The Chronicle and Directory for China etc. for various years. After 1902 published as *The Directory and Chronicle for China etc.* Hong Kong: The Hong Kong Daily Press. Referred to as, for example, 'C&D 1886'.
Complete Atlas of China. London: China Inland Mission, 1917.
Events in Hongkong and the far East 1875 to 1884. Hong Kong: *Hong Kong Daily Press*, 1885.
A Handbook to the West River. Hong Kong: Hong Kong, Canton & Macao Steamboat Co Ltd, undated.
Hankow British Chamber of Commerce Papers – in Hong Kong University Library Special Collections.
Hansard.
Hertslet's China Treaties. London: His Majesty's Stationery Office, 1908.
Hong Kong General Chamber of Commerce Annual Reports.
Imperial Maritime Customs Decennial Reports 1882–91. Shanghai: Inspector General of Customs, 1893. 'Customs Decennial 1882–91'.
Imperial Maritime Customs Decennial Reports 1892–1901. Shanghai: Inspector General of Customs, 1903. 'Customs Decennial 1892–1901'.

Imperial Maritime Customs: Names of Places on the China Coast and the Yangtze River. Shanghai: Inspector General of Customs, 1904.

Imperial Maritime Customs Postal Index. Shanghai: Inspector General of Customs, 1904.

Imperial Maritime Customs Service List 1907. Shanghai: Inspector General of Customs, 1908.

Kuling Estate Directory and General Information for Visitors, 1925–1926. Kuling Council.

Local Regulations for the Port of Hankow. 1861.

The Maritime Customs Decennial Reports 1902–11. Shanghai: Inspector General of Customs, 1913. 'Customs Decennial 1902–11'.

The Maritime Customs Decennial Reports 1912–21. Shanghai: Inspector General of Customs, 1924. 'Customs Decennial 1912–21'.

The Maritime Customs Decennial Reports 1922–31. Shanghai: Inspector General of Customs, 1933. 'Customs Decennial 1922–31'.

Peitaiho Directory 1924. Tientsin: La Librarie Francaise, 1924.

Proceedings of Meeting following the Sungpu Massacre, 7 July 1893. Hankow Municipal Council, 1893.

Regulations for the Port of Chefoo. 10 July 1865.

Report of the Hankow British Chamber of Commerce, various years.

Report on Labour and Labour Conditions in Hong Kong, 1939.

Reports on the Census of the Colony of Hong Kong.

Trade Statistics of the Treaty Ports for the Period 1863–1872. Shanghai: Inspector General of Maritime Customs, 1873.

Who's Who in China. Shanghai: The China Weekly Review, 1925.

Journals, newspapers and periodicals

Advocate of Peace
American Journal of International Law
American Political Science Review
The Canton Register
Central Asian Society Journal
The China Mail
China Overland Trade Report
The China Weekly Review
The Chinese Repository
The English Review
The Friend of China
Geographical Review
The Hong Kong Daily Press
Hong Kong Sunday Herald
The Hong Kong Telegraph
The Hong Kong Weekly Press
The Independent Herald
Journal of Asian Studies
Journal of Oriental Studies
Journal of the Royal Asiatic Society of Great Britain and Ireland
Journal of the Royal Asiatic Society, Hong Kong Branch
The Korea Times
London & China Telegraph
London Gazette
Macau Review of Culture
Marlborough Express
The New York Times
New-York Tribune
The North American Review
North China Daily News
North-China Herald
Oriental Affairs
Peking & Tientsin Times
Science Magazine
Singapore Free Press and Mercantile Advertiser
South China Morning Post
The Straits Times
The Sydney Mail
Taiwan Historica
The Times

Archives

Beihai Municipal Archive
Historical Photographs of China, School of Humanities, University of Bristol
Hongkong and Shanghai Bank
Hong Kong Public Records Office
Hong Kong University Library Special Collections
International Genealogical Index, referred to as 'IGI'
John Swire & Sons
The National Archives, Kew, London, referred to as 'TNA'
Weihai Municipal Archive

Books and Articles

Abend, Hallett. *Tortured China*. New York: Ives Washburn, 1930.
———. *Chaos in China*. New York: Ives Washburn, 1939.
———. *My Life in China*. New York: Harcourt, Brace and Co, 1943.
———. *Treaty Ports*. New York: Doubleday, Doran, 1944.

———. *The God from the West*. New York: Doubleday, 1947.
Airey, F. W. I. *Pidgin Inglis Tails & Others*. Shanghai: Kelly & Walsh, 1906.
Airlie, Shiona. *Thistle and Bamboo: The Life and Times of Sir James Stewart Lockhart*. Hong Kong: Oxford University Press, 1989.
Alabaster, Ernest. *Notes and Commentaries on Chinese Criminal Law and Cognate Topics*. London: Luzac & Co, 1899.
Allen, Charles. *Duel in the Snows: The True Story of the Younghusband Mission to Lhasa*. London: John Murray, 2004.
Allen, G. C., and Audrey G. Donnithorne, *Western Enterprise in Far Eastern Economic Development*. London: Routledge, 2003 [1954].
Anderson, Robert. *The World Today: A Monthly Record of Human Progress*. World Review Co, 1904.
Andrade, Tonio. *Lost Colony: The Untold Story of China's First Great Victory over the West*. Princeton: Princeton University Press, 2011.
Angulo, Diana Hutchins. *Peking Sun, Shanghai Moon: Images from a Past Era*. Hong Kong: Old China Hand Press, 2008.
Angus, Marjorie Bird. *Bamboo Connection*. Hong Kong: Heinemann Asia, 1985.
Archer, C. S. *Hankow Return*. London: Collins, 1941.
———. *China Servant*. London: Collins, 1946.
Arnold, Doris 'Missy'. *Missy's China: Letters from Hangchow 1934–1937*. Hong Kong: Old China Hand Press, 2008.
Asakawa, K. *The Russo-Japanese Conflict: Its Causes and Issues*. Boston: Houghton Mifflin, 1904.
Atwell, Pamela. *British Mandarins and Chinese Reformers*. Hong Kong: Oxford University Press, 1985.
Auber, Peter. *China: An Outline*. London: Parbury, Allen, 1834.
Auslin, Michael R. *Negotiating with Imperialism: The Unequal Treaties and the Culture of Japanese Diplomacy*. Cambridge, MA: Harvard University Press, 2004.
Avery, Martha. *The Tea Road: China and Russia Meet across the Steppe*. Beijing: China Intercontinental Press, 2003.
Ball, J. Dyer. *Things Chinese*. Hong Kong: Oxford University Press, 1982 [1892].
Ball, Samuel. 'Observations on the Expediency of opening a Second Port in China, addressed to the President and Select Committee of Supercargoes for the management of the Affairs of the Honourable East India Company in China'. *Journal of the Royal Asiatic Society of Great Britain and Ireland*, vol. 6, no. 1 (London, 1841).
Bard, Solomon. *Traders of Hong Kong: Some Foreign Merchant Houses, 1841–1899*. Hong Kong: Urban Council, 1993.
———. 'Tea and Opium'. *Journal of the Royal Asiatic Society, Hong Kong Branch*, vol. 50 (Hong Kong, 2001).
———. *Light and Shade*. Hong Kong: Hong Kong University Press, 2009.
Bau, Mingchien Joshua. *The Open Door Doctrine in Relation to China*. New York: Macmillan, 1923.
Beardson, Timothy. *Stumbling Giant: The Threats to China's Future*. New Haven: Yale University Press, 2013.
Becker, Bert. *Coastal Shipping in East Asia in the Late Nineteenth Century*. *Journal of the Royal Asiatic Society, Hong Kong Branch*, vol. 50 (Hong Kong, 2010).
Belcher, Sir Edward. *Narrative of a Voyage Round the World*. London: Henry Colburn, 1843.
Benson, Stella. *The Little World*. Project Gutenberg e-book [1925].
Beresford, Lord Charles. *The Break-up of China*. London: Harper Brothers, 1900.
Bernard, W. D. *Narrative of the Voyages and Services of the Nemesis*. London: Henry Colburn, 1844.
Bickers, Robert. *Britain in China*. Manchester: Manchester University Press, 1999.
———. *Empire Made Me*. London: Allen Lane, 2003.
———. *The Scramble for China*. London: Allen Lane, 2011.
Bickers, Robert, Catherine Ladds, Jamie Carstairs, and Yee Wah Foo. *Picturing China 1870–1950: Photographs from British Collections*. Bristol: University of Bristol, 2007a.
Bickers, Robert, and R. G. Tiedemann, eds. *The Boxers, China and the World*. Lanham, Maryland: Rowman and Littlefield, 2007b.
Bingham, J. Elliot. *Narrative of the Expedition to China*. London: Henry Colburn, 1843.
Bird, Isabella L. *The Golden Chersonese and the Way Thither*. London: John Murray, 1883.
———. *The Yangtze Valley and Beyond*. London: Virago, 1985 [1899].
Blake, Robert. *Jardine Matheson*. London: Weidenfeld and Nicolson, 1999.
Bland, J. O. P. *Li Hung-chang*. London: Constable, 1917.

Blue, Archibald Duncan. *The China Coast: A Study of British Shipping in Chinese Waters*. Glasgow: University of Strathclyde, 1982.

Bodde, D. and C. Morris. *Law in Imperial China, Exemplified by 190 Ching Dynasty Cases. With Historical, Social and Juridical Commentaries*. Cambridge, MA: Harvard University Press, 1967.

Boulger, Demetrius C. 'America's Share in a Partition of China'. *The North American Review*, vol. 171, no. 525 (University of Northern Iowa, August 1900).

Bowring, Philip. *Free Trade's First Missionary: Sir John Bowring in Europe and Asia*. Hong Kong: Hong Kong University Press, 2014.

Boxer, C. R., ed. *South China in the Sixteenth Century*. London: The Hakluyt Society, 1953.

———. *The Portuguese Seaborne Empire 1415–1825*. London: Hutchinson, 1977 [1969].

———., ed. *Seventeenth Century Macau in Contemporary Documents and Illustrations*. Hong Kong: Heinemann, 1984.

Braga, J. M. *The Western Pioneers and Their Discovery of Macao*. Macau: Imprensa Nacional, 1949.

———. *China Landfall, 1513: Jorge Alvares' Voyage to China*. Macau: Imprensa Nacional, 1955.

Bray, Denis. *Hong Kong Metamorphosis*. Hong Kong: Hong Kong University Press, 2001.

Bredon, Juliet. *Sir Robert Hart: The Romance of a Great Career*. Project Gutenberg e-book [1910].

Bridge, Robin. 'Chusan's Position in the China Trade'. *Journal of the Royal Asiatic Society, Hong Kong Branch*, vol. 49 (Hong Kong, 2009).

Brodie, Patrick. *Crescent over Cathay: China and I.C.I., 1898 to 1956*. Hong Kong: Oxford University Press, 1990.

Bromfield, A. C. and Rosemary Lee. 'The Life and Times of Captain Samuel Cornel Plant'. *Journal of the Royal Asiatic Society, Hong Kong Branch*, vol. 41 (Hong Kong, 2002).

Brooks, Barbara J. *Japan's Imperial Diplomacy*. Honolulu: University of Hawaii Press, 2000.

Brown, William. *Discover Gulangyu*. Xiamen: Xiamen University Press, 2005.

Browne, G. Waldo. *China: The Country and its People*. Boston: Dana Estes & Co, 1901.

Bruce, Clarence Dalrymple. *The Provinces of China, together with a History of the First Year of H.I.M. Hsuan Tung, and an account of the Government of China*. Shanghai: The National Review Office, 1910.

Bruce, Phillip. *The Story of Old Swatow*. Hong Kong: Ellerbeck, 1988.

Bruce-Mitford, C. E. *The Territory of Wei-Hai-Wei*. Shanghai: Kelly & Walsh, 1902.

Bruner, Katherine Frost, John K. Fairbank and Richard J. Smith. *Entering China's Service: Robert Hart's Journals 1854–1863*. Cambridge, MA: Harvard University Press, 1986.

Brunero, Donna. *Britain's Imperial Cornerstone in China*. London: Routledge, 2006.

Brunnert, H. S. and V. V. Hagelstrom, *Present Day Political Organization of China*. Foochow: Chinese Imperial Maritime Customs, 1911.

Burton St. John, Mrs. *The China Times Guide to Tientsin*. Tientsin: China Times, 1908.

Campbell, Persia Crawford. *Chinese Coolie Emigration to Countries within the British Empire*. London: P. S. King and Son, 1923.

Cannon, Isidore Cyril. *Public Success, Private Sorrow*. Hong Kong: Hong Kong University Press, 2009.

Carlson, Ellsworth C. *The Foochow Missionaries: 1847–1880*. Cambridge, MA: Harvard University Press, 1974.

Carpenter, Francis Ross. *The Old China Trade: Americans in Canton, 1784–1843*. New York: Coward, McCann & Geoghegan, 1976.

Carroll, John M. *Edge of Empires: Chinese Elites and British Colonials in Hong Kong*. Cambridge, MA: Harvard University Press, 2005.

———. *A Concise History of Hong Kong*. Hong Kong: Hong Kong University Press, 2007.

Carter, James H. *Creating a Chinese Harbin: Nationalism in an International City, 1916–1932*. Ithaca, NY: Cornell University Press, 2002.

Chang Hsin-pao. *Commissioner Lin and the Opium War*. Cambridge, MA: Harvard University Press, 1964.

Chang Jung. *Empress Dowager Cixi: The Concubine Who Launched Modern China*. New York: Alfred A. Knopf, 2013.

Chapman, H. Owen. *The Chinese Revolution 1926–27*. London: Constable, 1928.

Chen Yu. 'Land, Title Deed, and Urban Transformation: Foreigners' Acquisition of Real Property in Xiamen (1841–1945)'. Undated Ph.D. thesis.

———. 'The Making of a Bund in China: The British Concession in Xiamen (1852–1930)'. *Journal of Asian Architecture and Building Engineering* (May 2008).

Christman, Margaret C. S. *Adventurous Pursuits: Americans and the China Trade, 1784–1844*. Washington: National Portrait Gallery, 1984.

Chu Chin. 'The Tariff Problem in China'. Ph.D. thesis submitted to Columbia University, 1916.

Chu, Samuel C. and Liu Kwang-ching, eds. *Li Hung-chang and China's Early Modernization*. New York: M. E. Sharpe, 1997.

Clark, Douglas. 'Forgotten Judges of Forgotten Courts'. *Inner Temple Yearbook 2012–2013*. London: Honourable Society of the Inner Temple, 2012.

Clegg, Arthur. *The Birth of New China*. London: Lawrence & Wishart, 1943.

Clift, Lechmere. *Very Far East*. London: Marshall Brothers, 1909.

Cloud, Frederick D. *Hangchow: The City of Heaven, with a Brief Historical Sketch of Soochow*. Shanghai: Presbyterian Mission Press, 1906.

Coates, Austin. *Prelude to Hong Kong*. London: Routledge & Kegan Paul, 1966.

———. *China, India and the Ruins of Washington*. New York: John Day, 1972.

———. *A Macao Narrative*. Hong Kong: Heinemann, 1978.

———. *Whampoa: Ships on the Sore*. Hong Kong: Hong Kong and Whampoa Dock Co., 1980.

———. *China Races*. Hong Kong: Oxford University Press, 1994 [1983].

Coates, P. D. *The China Consuls: British Consular Officers, 1843–1943*. Hong Kong: Oxford University Press, 1988.

Cohen, Paul A. *China and Christianity: The Missionary Movement and the Growth of Chinese Antiforeignism, 1860–1870*. Cambridge, MA: Harvard University Press, 1963.

Collis, Maurice. *Foreign Mud*. New York: Alfred A. Knopf, 1947.

———. *The Great Within*. London: Faber & Faber, 1956.

———. *Wayfoong*. London: Faber & Faber, 1965.

Colquhoun, Archibald R. *China in Transformation*. London: Harper & Brothers, 1912.

Conner, Patrick. *The Hongs of Canton*. London: English Art Books, 2009.

Cook, Christopher. *The Lion and the Dragon: British Voices from the China Coast*. London: Elm Tree, 1985.

Cook's Tourist Handbook of Peking etc. Yokohama: Thomas Cook and Son, 1913.

Cooke, George Wingrove. *China*. London: G. Routledge, 1858.

Costin, W. C. *Great Britain and China 1833–1860*. London: Oxford University Press, 1968 [1937].

Couling, Samuel. *The Encyclopaedia Sinica*. Hong Kong: Oxford University Press, 1983 [1917].

Courtauld, Caroline and May Holdsworth. *The Hong Kong Story*. Hong Kong: Oxford University Press, 1997.

Cox, Kenneth. *The First Hundred Years: The History of the Foochow Lodge*. Hong Kong: Libra Press, 1981.

Coy, Julian. 'The British Occupation of Komundo, 1885–1887'. Undated School of Oriental and African Studies dissertation, www.webcitation.com.

Cribb, Joe. *Money in the Bank*. London: Spink and Son, 1987.

Crow, Carl. *Handbook for China*. Shanghai: Carl Crow, 1921.

———. *Handbook for China*. Hong Kong: Oxford University Press, 1986 [1933].

———. *Four Hundred Million Customers*. New York: Harper & Brothers, 1937.

———. *Foreign Devils in the Flowery Kingdom*. Hong Kong: China Economic Review, 2007 [1940].

Crush, Peter. *Woosung Road: The Story of China's First Railway*. Hong Kong: The Railway Tavern, 1999.

———. *Imperial Railways of North China*. Beijing: Xinhua Publishing House, 2013.

Cunningham, Alfred. *The French in Tonkin and South China*. Hong Kong: Hong Kong Daily Press, 1902.

Cunynghame, Capt. Arthur. *An Aide-de-Camp's Recollections of Service in China etc*. London: Saunders and Otley, 1844.

Danielson, Eric N. 'Revisiting Chongqing'. *Journal of the Royal Asiatic Society, Hong Kong Branch*, vol. 45 (Hong Kong, 2005).

D'Arcy-Brown, Liam. *Chusan: The Forgotten Story of Britain's First Chinese Island*. Kenilworth: Brandram, 2012.

Darroch, Rev J. *China, The Foreign Powers and the 'Unequal' Treaties*. Shanghai: The Presbyterian Mission Press, 1927.

Davidson, James W. *The Island of Formosa: Historical View from 1430 to 1900*. Taipei: Book World, no date [1903].

Davis, John Francis. *Sketches of China*. London: Charles Knight, 1841.

———. *The Chinese*. London: M. A. Nattali, 1846.

———. *China During the War and Since the Peace*. London: Longman, Brown, Green and Longmans, 1852.

Davis, Richard Harding. *Notes of a War Correspondent*. New York: Charles Scribner's Sons, 1910.

De Méritens, Baron. *A Sketch of our Relations within China during Three and a Half Centuries, 1517–1869*. Foochow: Rozario, Marcal & Co., 1871 (Elibron Classics reprint, 2005).

De Moges, Marquis. *Recollections of Baron Gros's Embassy to China and Japan in 1857–58*. London: Griffin, Bohn & Co., 1861.

Dean, Britten. *China and Great Britain: The Diplomacy of Commercial Relations 1860–1864*. Cambridge, MA: Harvard University East Asian Research Center, 1974.

Denby, Jay. *Letters of a Shanghai Griffin*. Shanghai: Kelly & Walsh, 1923.

Dikötter, Frank. 'The Promise of Repentance: The Prison in Modern China'. In *Cultures of Confinement: A History of the Prison in Africa, Asia and Latin America*, edited by Frank Dikötter and Ian Brown. London: C. Hurst & Co., 2007.

———. *The Age of Openness: China before Mao*. Hong Kong: Hong Kong University Press, 2008.

Dong, Stella. *Shanghai 1842–1949: The Rise and Fall of a Decadent City*. New York: Harper Collins, 2000.

Donnelly, Ivon A. *The China Coast*. Tientsin: Tientsin Press, 1931.

Douglas, Robert K. *China*. London: Society for Promoting Christian Knowledge, 1887.

Downing, Charles Toogood. *The Fan-Qui in China in 1836-7*. London: Henry Colburn, 1838.

Drage, Charles. *Taikoo*. London: Constable, 1970.

Dunn, Wie T. *The Opium Traffic in its International Aspects*. Submitted as a Ph.D. thesis to Columbia University, 1920.

Eitel, E. J. *Europe in China*. Hong Kong: Oxford University Press, 1983 [1895].

Elder, Chris, ed. *China's Treaty Ports: Half Love and Half Hate*. Hong Kong: Oxford University Press, 1999.

Ellis, Henry. *Journal of Proceedings of the Late Embassy to China*. London: John Murray, 1818.

Endacott, G. B. *A History of Hong Kong*. Hong Kong: Oxford University Press, 1958.

———. *Government and People in Hong Kong, 1841–1962*. Hong Kong: Hong Kong University Press, 1964.

———. *Hong Kong Eclipse*. Hong Kong: Oxford University Press, 1978.

Events in Hong Kong and the Far East 1875 to 1884. Hong Kong: The Hong Kong Daily Press, 1885.

Extraterritoriality (special supplement). Shanghai: *The China Weekly Review*, 19 June 1926.

Fairbank, John King. *Trade and Diplomacy on the China Coast*. Stanford: Stanford University Press, 1953.

———. *The United States and China*. Cambridge, MA: Harvard University Press, 1958.

———. *Chinabound: A Fifty-Year Memoir*. New York: Harper & Row, 1983 [1982].

Fairbank, John King, Katherine Frost Bruner, and Elizabeth MacLeod Matheson, eds. *The I. G. in Peking*. Cambridge, MA: Harvard University Press, 1975.

Fairbank, John King, Martha Henderson Coolidge, and Richard J. Smith. *H.B. Morse: Customs Commissioner and Historian of China*. Lexington: University of Kentucky, 1995.

Fairbank, John King and Edwin O. Reischauer. *China: Tradition and Transformation*. Sydney: George Allen and Unwin, 1979 [1973].

Fairbank, John King and Teng Ssu-yu. *China's Response to the West*. Cambridge, MA: Harvard University Press, 1954.

Farquharson, Ronald. *Confessions of a China Hand*. London: Hodder and Stoughton, 1950.

Fay, Peter Ward. *The Opium War*. Chapel Hill: University of North Carolina Press, 1997.

Feuerwerker, Albert. *China's Early Industrialization: Sheng Hsuan-huai (1844–1916) and Mandarin Enterprise*. Cambridge, MA: Harvard University Press, 1958.

Field, Andrew David. *Shanghai's Dancing World: Cabaret Culture and Urban Politics, 1919–1954*. Hong Kong: The Chinese University Press, 2010.

Field, Charles et al. *A Visit to China*. San Francisco: The Associated Chambers of Commerce of the Pacific Coast, 1911.

Fieldhouse, D. K. *The Colonial Empires from the Eighteenth Century*. New York: Delta, 1965.

Fisher, Lt.-Col. George Battye, RE. *Personal Narrative of Three Years' Service in China*. London: Richard Bentley, 1863.

Fitch, Robert F. *Hangchow Itineraries*. Shanghai: Kelly & Walsh, 1922.

Fleming, Peter. *One's Company*. London: Jonathan Cape, 1934.

———. *News from Tartary*. London: Macdonald Futura, 1980 [1936].

———. *The Siege at Peking*. New York: Harper and Brothers, 1959.

———. *Bayonets to Lhasa*. London: Rupert Hart-Davis, 1961.

Fortune, Robert. *Three Years' Wanderings in the Northern Provinces of China*. London: John Murray, 1847.
———. *A Journey to the Tea Countries*. London: Midmay, 1987 [1852].
———. *A Residence among the Chinese*. London: John Murray, 1857.
Foster, Mrs Arnold. *In the Valley of the Yangtse*. London: London Missionary Society, 1899.
Foster, Sir William. *England's Quest of Eastern Trade*. London: A. and C. Black, 1933.
Foust, Clifford M. *Muscovite and Mandarin: Russia's Trade with China and its Setting, 1727–1805*. Chapel Hill: University of North Carolina Press, 1969.
French, Paul. *A Tough Old China Hand: The Life, Times and Adventures of an American in Shanghai*. Hong Kong: Hong Kong University Press, 2006.
———. *Through the Looking Glass*. Hong Kong: Hong Kong University Press, 2009.
Gammie, Alexander. *Duncan Main of Hangchow*. London: Pickering and Inglis, 1936.
Garrett, Richard J. *The Defences of Macau: Forts, Ships and Weapons over 450 Years*. Hong Kong: Hong Kong University Press, 2010.
Garrett, Valery. *Heaven is High, the Emperor Far Away*. Hong Kong: Oxford University Press, 2002.
Gerson, Jack J. *Horatio Nelson Lay and Sino-British Relations 1854–1864*. Cambridge, MA: Harvard University Press, 1972.
Gibson, Rowland R. *Forces Mining and Undermining China*. New York: Cosimo, 2005 [1914].
Gilbert, Rodney. *The Unequal Treaties: China and the Foreigner*. London: John Murray, 1929.
Giquel, Prosper. *The Foochow Arsenal and its Results. From the Commencement in 1867 to the End of the Foreign Directorate on the 16th February 1874*. Shanghai: Shanghai Evening Courier, 1874.
Gordon Cumming, Constance. *Wanderings in China*. London: William Blackwood, 1888.
Grantham, A. E. *Hills of Blue*. London: Methuen, 1927.
Greenberg, Michael. *British Trade and the Opening of China: 1800–42*. Cambridge: Cambridge University Press, 1969 [1951].
Greener, William. *A Secret Agent in Port Arthur*. London: Archibald Constable, 1905.
Guide to Tientsin. Tientsin: Astor House Hotel, 1907.
Haan, J. H. 'Origin and Development of the Political System in the Shanghai International Settlement'. *Journal of the Royal Asiatic Society, Hong Kong Branch*, vol. 22 (Hong Kong, 1982).
Haffner, Christopher. *Amoy: The Port and the Lodge*. Hong Kong: The Corinthian Lodge of Amoy, 1978.
Hahn, Emily. *China to Me*. Philadelphia: Blackiston, 1944.
Haines, Gregory. *Gunboats on the Great River*. London: MacDonald and Jane's, 1976.
Halcombe, Charles J. H. *The Mystic Flowery Land*. London: Luzac, 1896.
Hall, B. Foster. *The Chinese Maritime Customs: An International Service*. Greenwich: National Maritime Museum, 1977.
Hammond, Kelly. *The Shanghai Mixed Court 1863–1880 – Colonial Institution Building and the Creation of Legal Knowledge as a Process of Interaction and Mediation between the Chinese and the British*. Master's thesis submitted to Simon Fraser University, Vancouver, 2007.
Hankow Riot of June 11th, 1925, The. Hankow: The Independent Herald, 1925.
Hao Yen-ping. *The Comprador in Nineteenth Century China*. Cambridge, MA: Harvard East Asian Research Center, 1971.
Hase, Patrick. 'In the Beginning: The Development of the Area West of Pottinger Street'. *A Sense of Place*. Hong Kong: Royal Asiatic Society, Hong Kong Branch, 2008a.
———. *The Six-Day War of 1899: Hong Kong in the Age of Imperialism*. Hong Kong: Hong Kong University Press, 2008b.
Hawkins, Horatio B. *Geography of China*. Shanghai: Commercial Press, 1919.
Hayes, James. 'Hong Kong Island before 1841'. *Journal of the Royal Asiatic Society, Hong Kong Branch*, vol. 24 (Hong Kong, 1988).
———. '"That Singular and Hitherto Almost Unknown Country": Opinions on China, the Chinese and the "Opium War" among British Naval and Military Officers who Served During Hostilities There'. *Journal of the Royal Asiatic Society, Hong Kong Branch*, vol. 39 (Hong Kong, 2001).
———. 'Fortunate and Fertile: Shanghai before the Treaty Port Era'. *Journal of the Royal Asiatic Society, Hong Kong Branch*, vol. 48 (Hong Kong, 2008).
Hewlett, Sir Meyrick. *Forty Years in China*. London: Macmillan, 1943.
Hibbard, Peter. *The Bund: Shanghai Faces West*. Hong Kong: Odyssey, 2007.
Hibbert, Christopher. *The Dragon Wakes: China and the West, 1793–1911*. London: Longman, 1970.

Historical View of Qingdao: 1897–1914. Qingdao: Qingdao Publishing, 2005.

Ho Ping-yin. *The Foreign Trade of China.* Shanghai: The Commercial Press, 1935.

Hobart, Alice Tisdale. *By the City of the Long Sand: A Tale of New China.* New York: Grosset & Dunlap, 1926.

———. *Oil for the Lamps of China.* Indianapolis: Bobbs-Merrill, 1933.

Horesh, Niv. *Shanghai's Bund and Beyond.* New Haven: Yale University Press, 2009.

Houghton, Stanley, Edith B. Harman, and Margaret Pyle. *Chefoo.* London: China Inland Mission, 1931.

Hoyt, Edwin. *The Fall of Tsingtao.* London: Arthur Baker, 1975.

Huang Yen-yu. *Viceroy Yeh Ming-chen and the Canton Episode (1856–1861).* Cambridge, MA: Harvard-Yenching Institute, 1941.

Hudson, G. F. *Europe & China: A Survey of their Relations from the Earliest Times to 1800.* London: Edward Arnold, 1931.

Hughes, E. R. *The Invasion of China by the Western World.* London: Adam & Charles Black, 1968 [1937].

Hughes, George. *Amoy and the Surrounding Districts.* Hong Kong: de Souza, 1872.

Humphries, Michael, ed. *Surgeon on the China Seas: The Journal of Charles Courtney, Surgeon RN Recounting Experiences and Observations of the Second Opium War, 1856–1860.* Hong Kong: Atrabates Press, 2012.

Hunter, William C. *An American in Canton (1825–44).* Hong Kong: Derwent, 1994 [*Bits of Old China*, 1855 and *The 'Fan Kwae' at Canton*, 1882].

Hurd, Douglas. *The Arrow War: An Anglo-Chinese Confusion, 1856–60.* London: Collins, 1967.

Hutcheon, Robin. *The Merchants of Shameen: The Story of Deacon & Co.* Hong Kong: Deacon & Co., 1990.

Hyde, Francis E. *Far Eastern Trade: 1860–1914.* Liverpool: University of Liverpool, 1973.

Hyde Lay, A. C. *Four Generations in China, Japan and Korea.* London: Oliver and Boyd, 1952.

Inouye Jukichi. *Japan-China War: The Fall of Wei-hai-wei.* Yokohama: Kelly & Walsh, undated.

Jackson, Stanley. *The Sassoons.* London: Heinemann, 1968.

Jernigan, T. R. *China in Law and Commerce.* New York: Macmillan, 1905.

Jocelyn, Lord. *Six Months with the China Expedition.* London: John Murray, 1841.

Johnson, Linda Cooke. *Shanghai: From Market Town to Treaty Port, 1074–1858.* Stanford: Stanford University Press, 1995.

Johnston, Reginald. *Lion and Dragon in Northern China.* Hong Kong: Oxford University Press, 1986 [1910].

———. 'Weihaiwei'. *Central Asian Society Journal,* vol. 18 (1931).

———. *Twilight in the Forbidden City.* Hong Kong: Oxford University Press, 1985 [1936].

Johnston, Tess, ed. *Treasure Houses: Historic Buildings of the Industrial and Commercial Bank of China.* Hong Kong: Old China Hand Press, 2004.

Johnston, Tess and Deke Erh. *A Last Look: Western Architecture in Old Shanghai.* Hong Kong: Old China Hand Press, 1993.

———. *Near to Heaven: Western Architecture in China's Old Summer Resorts.* Hong Kong: Old China Hand Press, 1994.

———. *Far from Home: Western Architecture in China's Northern Treaty Ports.* Hong Kong: Old China Hand Press, 1996a.

———. *God and Country: Western Religious Architecture in Old China.* Hong Kong: Old China Hand Press, 1996b.

———. *The Last Colonies: Western Architecture in China's Southern Treaty Ports.* Hong Kong: Old China Hand Press, 1997.

———. *Hallowed Halls: Protestant Colleges in Old China.* Hong Kong: Old China Hand Press, 1998.

Karabell, Zachary. *Parting the Desert: The Creation of the Suez Canal.* New York: Alfred A. Knopf, 2003.

Keay, John. *The Honourable Company.* New York: Macmillan, 1991.

Kerr, Dr. John. *The Canton Guide.* Hong Kong: Kelly & Walsh, 1891.

Keswick, Maggie, ed. *The Thistle and the Jade.* London: Frances Lincoln, 2008.

King, Frank H. H. *The History of the Hongkong and Shanghai Banking Corporation.* Cambridge: Cambridge University Press, 1987.

King, Paul. *In the Chinese Customs Service.* London: Heath Cranton, 1924.

Kitto, Mark. *China Cuckoo.* London: Constable & Robinson, 2009.

Knollys, Henry. *English Life in China.* London: Smith, Elder & Co., 1885.

Koffsky, Peter L. *The Consul General's Shanghai Postal Agency, 1867–1907.* Washington: Smithsonian Institute Press, 1972.

Krausse, Alexis. *China in Decay.* London: Chapman and Hall, 1900.

Kwong Chi-man and Tsoi Yiu-Lun. *Eastern Fortress: A Military History of Hong Kong, 1840–1970*. Hong Kong: Hong Kong University Press, 2014.

Kwong, Luke S. K. 'The Chinese Maritime Customs Remembered'. *Journal of the Royal Asiatic Society, Hong Kong Branch*, vol. 19 (Hong Kong, 1979).

Lane-Poole, Stanley. *Sir Harry Parkes in China*. London: Methuen, 1901.

Lanning, G. and S. Couling. *The History of Shanghai*. Shanghai: Kelly & Walsh, 1921.

Latané, John Holladay. 'Our Relations with Japan'. *American Political Science Review*, vol. 8, no. 4 (November 1914).

Le Gendre, General Charles W. *How to Deal with China*. Amoy: Rozario, Marcal, 1871.

Le Pichon, Alain. *China Trade and Empire: Jardine, Matheson & Co and the Origins of British Rule in Hong Kong, 1827–1843*. Oxford: Oxford University Press, 2006.

Lee Chong-sik. *The Politics of Korean Nationalism*. Berkeley: University of California Press, 1963.

Lee En-han. *China's Recovery of the British Hankow and Kiukiang Concessions*. Perth: University of Western Australia, 1980.

Lee, Robert. *France and the Exploitation of China*. Hong Kong: Oxford University Press, 1989.

LeFevour, Edward. *Western Enterprise in Late Ch'ing China*. Cambridge, MA: Harvard University Press, 1970.

Legarda, Benito. *After the Galleons*. Manila: Ateneo de Manila University Press, 1999.

Leibo, Steven A. 'Not so Calm an Administration: The Anglo-French Occupation of Canton, 1858–1861'. *Journal of the Royal Asiatic Society, Hong Kong Branch*, vol. 28 (Hong Kong, 1990).

Lethbridge, Henry James. 'Sir James Haldane Stewart Lockhart: Colonial Civil Servant and Scholar'. *Journal of the Royal Asiatic Society, Hong Kong Branch*, vol. 12 (Hong Kong, 1972).

Levy, Daniel S. *Two-Gun Cohen: A Biography*. New York: St. Martin's, 1997.

Lindsay, Hugh Hamilton. *Report of Proceedings on a Voyage to the Northern Parts of China in the Ship* Lord Amherst. London: B. Fellowes, 1833.

Lindsay, T. J. 'The Hankow Steamer Tea Races'. *Journal of the Royal Asiatic Society, Hong Kong Branch*, vol. 8 (Hong Kong, 1968).

Little, Archibald John. *Through the Yang-tse Gorges*. London: Sampson Low, Marston, 1898 [1887].

———. 'Ex Oriente Lux!' *The North American Review*, vol. 169, no. 514 (Cedar Falls, University of Northern Iowa, 1899).

———. *Gleanings from Fifty Years in China*. London: Sampson Low, Marston, 1910.

Little, Mrs Archibald. *The Land of the Blue Gown*. London: T. Fisher Unwin, 1902.

Little, Edward S. *The Story of Kuling*. Chunkiang Literary Association, 1899.

———. 'The Saddle Islands'. *The East of Asia Magazine*, vol. 4 (Shanghai, 1905).

Liu Kwang-ching. *Anglo-American Steamship Rivalry in China: 1862–1874*. Cambridge, MA: Harvard University Press, 1962.

Ljungstedt, Anders. *An Historical Sketch of the Portuguese Settlements in China*. Hong Kong: Viking, 1992 [1836].

Lo Hui-min and Helen Bryant. *British Diplomatic and Consular Establishments in China: 1793–1949 – II: Consular Establishments 1843–1949*. Taipei: SMC Publishing, 1988.

Loch, Henry Brougham. *Personal Narrative of Occurrences during Lord Elgin's Second Embassy to China, 1860*. London: John Murray, 1870.

Lodwick, Kathleen L. *Educating the Women of Hainan: The Career of Margaret Moninger in China, 1915–1942*. Lexington: University of Kentucky, 1995.

Loureiro, Rui Manuel, ed. 'European Encounters and Clashes in the South China Sea II'. *Macau Review of Culture*, vol. 12 (October 2004). Macau: Instituto Cultural.

Lovell, Julia. *The Opium War: Drugs, Dreams and the Making of China*. London: Picador, 2011.

Lowe, K. J. P. 'Hong Kong, 26 January 1841: Hoisting the Flag Revisited'. *Journal of the Royal Asiatic Society, Hong Kong Branch*, vol. 29 (Hong Kong, 1991).

Lubbock, Basil. *The China Clippers*. Glasgow: Brown, Son and Ferguson, 1914.

———. *The Opium Clippers*. Glasgow: Brown, Son and Ferguson, 1933.

Lunt, Carroll. *Some Builders of Treatyport China*. Los Angeles: privately published, 1965.

Macartney, Lady. *An English Lady in Chinese Turkestan*. London: Ernest Benn, 1931.

Macgowan, Rev. J. *Pictures of Southern China*. London: Religious Tract Society, 1897.

MacGregor, David R. *The China Bird*. London: Chatto & Windus, 1961

Mackerras, Colin. *Modern China: A Chronology from 1842 to the Present*. San Francisco: W. H. Freeman, 1982.

MacMurray, John V. A., ed. *Treaties and Agreements With and Concerning China, 1894–1919*. New York: Oxford University Press, 1921.

Macri, Franco David. *Clash of Empire in South China: The Allied Nations' Proxy War with Japan, 1935–1941*. Lawrence: University Press of Kansas, 2012.

Manchuria: Land of Opportunities. New York: South Manchuria Railway, 1922.

Manchuria: Treaties and Agreements. Washington: Carnegie Endowment for International Peace, 1921.

Marriner, Sheila and Francis E. Hyde. *The Senior*. Liverpool: Liverpool University Press, 1967.

Martin, Gordon. *Chefoo School: 1881–1951*. Braunton: Merlin Books, 1990.

Martin, W. A. P. *The Awakening of China*. New York: Doubleday, 1910.

Mateo, José Eugenio Borao. *The Spanish Experience in Taiwan, 1626–1642*. Hong Kong: Hong Kong University Press, 2009.

Maugham, W. Somerset. *On a Chinese Screen*. New York: George H. Doran, 1922.

Mayers, William Frederick. *Treaties between the Empire of China and Foreign Powers*. Shanghai: North-China Herald, 1906.

Mayers, William Frederick, N. B. Dennys, and Charles King. *The Treaty Ports of China and Japan*. London: Trübner, 1867.

McLeish, William. *Life in a China Outport*. Tientsin: Peking & Tientsin Times, undated.

McPherson, D. *Two Years in China: Narrative of the Chinese Expedition from its formation in April, 1840 till April 1842*. London: Saunders and Otley, 1842.

Meadows, Thomas Taylor. *Desultory Notes on the Government and People of China and on the Chinese Language*. London: Wm. H. Allen and Co., 1847.

Michalk, D. L. 'Hainan Island: A Brief Historical Sketch'. *Journal of the Royal Asiatic Society, Hong Kong Branch*, vol. 26 (Hong Kong, 1988).

Michie, Alexander. *The Englishman in China during the Victorian Era*. Taipei: Cheng Wen Publishing, 1966 [1900].

Miller, Sheila. *Pigtails, Petticoats and the Old School Tie*. Sevenoaks: Overseas Missionary Fellowship, 1981.

Milne, A. A. *The House at Pooh Corner*. London: Methuen, 1928.

Miners, Norman. *Hong Kong under Imperial Rule: 1912–1941*. Hong Kong: Oxford University Press, 1987.

Mitter, Rana. *China's War with Japan 1937–1945: The Struggle for Survival*. London: Allen Lane, 2013.

Molloy, Bob. *Colossus Unsung*. [New Zealand]: Xlibris, 2011.

Montague, Joel. *The Leasehold of Kouang-Tcheou-Wan*. Arlington: Society of Indo-China Philatelists, undated.

Morse, Hosea Ballou. *The International Relations of the Chinese Empire*. Shanghai: Kelly & Walsh, 1910.

———. *The Trade and Administration of China*. London: Longmans, Green, 1920.

———. *The Chronicles of the East India Company Trading to China: 1635–1834*. Taipei: Cheng Wen Publishing, 1975 [1926].

Moseley, Bryan C. *From Swatow to Hong Kong: A History of the Swatow Lodge*. Hong Kong: privately published.

Munn, Christopher. 'The Chusan Episode: Britain's Occupation of a Chinese Island, 1840–46'. *Journal of the Imperial and Commonwealth Society* vol. 25, no. 1 (London, 1997).

———. *Anglo-China: Chinese People and British Rule in Hong Kong, 1841–1880*. Richmond: Curzon, 2001.

Munro-Faure, P. H. 'The Kiukiang Incident of 1927'. *Journal of the Royal Asiatic Society, Hong Kong Branch*, vol. 29 (Hong Kong, 1991).

Murison, William. *Précis-Writing*. Cambridge: Cambridge University Press, 1914.

Murphey, Rhoads. *The Treaty Ports and China's Modernization: What Went Wrong?* Ann Arbor: Michigan University Press, 1970.

———, ed. *Nineteenth Century China: Five Imperialist Perspectives*. Ann Arbor: Michigan University Press, 1972.

Murray, Lt. Alexander. *Doings in China, being the Personal Narrative of an Officer engaged in the late Chinese Expedition, from the Recapture of Chusan in 1841 to the Peace of Nankin in 1842*. London: Richard Bentley, 1843.

Ng Chin-Keong. *The Amoy Riot in 1852: Coolie Emigration and Sino-British Relations from a Labour Perspective*. Pondicherry: Pondicherry University, 1991.

Nield, Robert. 'Bits of Broken China: The RAS Visit to North-east China in Search of Colonial Remnants'. *Journal of the Royal Asiatic Society, Hong Kong Branch*, vol. 38 (Hong Kong, 2000).

———. *The China Coast: Trade and the First Treaty Ports*. Hong Kong: Joint Publishing, 2010a.

———. 'Treaty Ports and Other Foreign Stations in China'. *Journal of the Royal Asiatic Society, Hong Kong Branch*, vol. 50 (Hong Kong, 2010b).

———. 'China's Southernmost Treaty Port'. *Journal of the Royal Asiatic Society, Hong Kong Branch*, vol. 52 (Hong Kong, 2012).

Nolde, John T. 'The "False Edict" of 1849'. *Journal of Asian Studies*, vol. 20, no. 3 (May 1961).

Oakley, David. 'The Foreign Cemetery at Kaohsiung'. *Taiwan Historica*, vol. 56 (2005).

———. *The Story of the British Consulate at Takow, Formosa*. Kaohsiung: Bureau of Cultural Affairs, Kaohsiung City Government, 2013.

Old Fashions [sic] *of Dalian*. Beijing: Beijing People's Fine Arts Publishing House, 2007 [1999].

Old Photos of Harbin. Harbin: Harbin Publishing House, 2000.

Old Photos of Tianjin. Tianjin: People's Fine Arts Publishing House, 1999.

Old Photos of Xiamen. Beijing: People's Fine Arts Publishing House, 1999.

Old Pictures of Chefoo. Yantai: Ling Tian Publishing, 2005.

Old Pictures of Ningbo. Ningbo: Ningbo Publishing House, 2004.

Old Pictures of Port Aruth [sic] *and DaLian* [sic]. Jinan: Shandong Pictorial Publishing House, 2009.

Old Pictures of Weihaiwei. Jinan: Shandong Pictorial Publishing House, 2008.

Oliphant, Laurence. *Lord Elgin's Mission to China*. New York: Harper Brothers, 1860.

O'Regan, John P. 'Foreign Death in China: Symbolism, Ritual and Belief in the Old Protestant Cemetery in Macau'. *Journal of the Royal Asiatic Society, Hong Kong Branch*, vol. 47 (Hong Kong, 2007).

Osborne, Frances. *Lilla's Feast*. London: Doubleday, 2004.

Osterhammel, Jürgen. *The Transformation of the World: A Global History of the Nineteenth Century*. Princeton: Princeton University Press, 2014.

Otness, Harold M. *Toiling and Rowing, and the Wind Contrary: A Hundred Years of Westerners in the Nantai District of Foochow, 1842–1942 – A Guidebook of the Remains*. Ashland: Southern Oregon State College Library, 1994.

Otte, T. G. *The China Question*. Oxford: Oxford University Press, 2007.

Ouchterlony, Lt. John. *The Chinese War: An Account of all the Operations of the British Forces from the Commencement to the Treaty of Nanking*. London: Saunders and Otley, 1844.

Oxford, Emma. *At Least We Lived: The Unlikely Adventures of an English Couple in World War II China*. Charleston: Branksome Books, 2013.

Park, Polly, ed. *To Save their Heathen Souls*. Eugene: Pickwick, 1984.

Parkinson, Jonathan. 'The First Steam-Powered Ascent through the Yangtse Gorges'. *Journal of the Royal Asiatic Society, Hong Kong Branch*, vol. 46 (Hong Kong, 2006).

Pearson, Veronica and Ko Tim-keung, eds. *A Sense of Place: Hong Kong West of Pottinger Street*. Hong Kong: Royal Asiatic Society, Hong Kong Branch, 2008.

Pelissier, Roger. *The Awakening of China*. London: Secker and Warburg, 1967.

Perkins, Dorothy. *The Samurai of Japan: A Chronology from Their Origin in the Heian Era (794–1185) to the Modern Era*. Upland: Diane Publishing, 1998.

Pickering, W. A. *Pioneering in Formosa*. London: Hurst and Blackett, 1898.

Pitcher, Philip W. *In and About Amoy*. Shanghai: Methodist Publishing House in China, 1909.

Platt, Stephen R. *Autumn in the Heavenly Kingdom: China, the West, and the Epic Story of the Taiping Civil War*. New York: Alfred A. Knopf, 2012.

Polo, Marco. *The Travels*. Harmondsworth: Penguin, 1958 [13th century].

Pomerantz-Zhang, Linda. *Wu Tingfang (1842–1922): Reform and Modernization in Modern Chinese History*. Hong Kong: Hong Kong University Press, 1992.

Pong, David. *Shen Pao-chen and China's Modernisation in the Nineteenth Century*. Cambridge: Cambridge University Press, 1994.

Pott, F. L. Hawks, *Shanghai: A Short History*. Shanghai: Kelly & Walsh, 1928.

Pottinger, George. *Sir Henry Pottinger: First Governor of Hong Kong*. Stroud: Sutton, 1997.

Pratt, Sir John T. *China and Britain*. London: Collins, 1945.

Puga, Rogério Miguel. *The British Presence in Macau, 1635–1793*. Hong Kong: Hong Kong University Press, 2013.

Putnam Weale, B. L. *Manchu and Muscovite*. London: Macmillan, 1904.

'Ranger'. *Up and Down the China Coast*. London: Denis Archer, 1936.

Rasmussen, A. H. *China Trader*. New York: Thomas Y. Crowell, 1954.

Rasmussen, O. D. *Tientsin: An Illustrated Outline History*. Tientsin: Tientsin Press, 1925.

Ratepayers and the Crown Leases, The. Tientsin: Peking & Tientsin Times, undated.

Rawlinson, John L. *China's Struggle for Naval Development, 1839–1895*. Cambridge, MA: Harvard University Press, 1967.

Roche, James F. and L. L. Cowen. *The French at Foochow*. Shanghai: The Celestial Press, 1884.

Rose, Sarah. *For All the Tea in China*. London: Hutchinson, 2009.

Ross, Ivan D. 'The Anti-Foreign Movement in China'. *The English Review* (August 1925).

Rowe, William T. *Hankow: Commerce and Society in a Chinese City, 1796–1889*. Stanford: Stanford University Press, 1984.

Rydings, H. A. 'Problems of the China Trade a Century Ago: Two Letters on Transit Passes'. *Journal of the Royal Asiatic Society, Hong Kong Branch*, vol. 22 (Hong Kong, 1983).

Salkeld, Kim. 'Witness to the Revolution: Surgeon Lieutenant Bertram Bickford on the China Station, 1910–12'. *Journal of the Royal Asiatic Society, Hong Kong Branch*, vol. 51 (Hong Kong, 2011).

Sayer, Geoffrey Robley. *Hong Kong 1841–1862: Birth, Adolescence and Coming of Age*. Hong Kong: Hong Kong University Press, 1980 [1937].

———. *Hong Kong 1862–1919: Years of Discretion*. Hong Kong: Hong Kong University Press, 1975.

Schrecker, John E. *Imperialism and Chinese Nationalism: Germany in Shantung*. Cambridge, MA: Harvard University Press, 1971.

Schultheis, Eugenia Barnett. *Hangchow, My Home*. Fort Bragg: Lost Coast, 2000.

Scott, Dorothea. 'The Hankow Collection: Its History and Contents'. *Journal of Oriental Studies*, vol. 2, no. 1 (January 1955).

See Chong-su. *The Foreign Trade of China*. New York: Columbia University Press, 1919.

See Heng Teow. *Japanese Cultural Policy toward China – 1918–1931: A Comparative Perspective*. Cambridge, MA: Harvard University Asia Center, 1999.

Service, John S., ed. *Golden Inches: The China Memoir of Grace Service*. Berkeley: University of California Press, 1991.

Simpson, Peter. 'Hell and High Water'. *South China Morning Post*. Hong Kong, 2 October 2011.

Singer, Aubrey. *The Lion and the Dragon*. London: Barrie and Jenkins, 1992.

Sinn, Elizabeth. *Power and Charity: The Early History of the Tung Wah Hospital, Hong Kong*. Hong Kong: Oxford University Press, 1989.

———. 'Kowloon Walled City: Its Origin and Early History'. *Journal of the Royal Asiatic Society, Hong Kong Branch*, vol. 27 (Hong Kong, 1990).

———. *Pacific Crossing: California Gold, Chinese Migration, and the Making of Hong Kong*. Hong Kong: Hong Kong University Press, 2013.

Sleeman, J. H. C. *White China: An Austral-Asian Sensation*. Sydney: Sleeman, 1933.

Smith, Arthur H. *China in Convulsion*. Edinburgh: Oliphant, Anderson and Ferrier, 1901.

Smith, Carl T. *Chinese Christians: Elites, Middlemen, and the Church in Hong Kong*. Hong Kong: Oxford University Press, 1985.

Smith, Rev. George. *A Narrative of an Exploratory Visit to each of the Consular Cities of China, and to the Islands of Hong Kong and Chusan, in behalf of the Church Missionary Society in the years 1844, 1845, 1846*. London: Seeley, Burnside and Seeley, 1847.

Smith, Richard J., John King Fairbank, and Katherine Frost Bruner, eds. *Robert Hart and China's Early Modernization*. Cambridge, MA: Harvard University Press, 1991.

So, Billy K. L. and Ramon H. Myers. *The Treaty Port Economy in Modern China: Empirical Studies of Institutional Change and Economic Performance*. Berkeley: University of California, 2011.

Spence, Jonathan D. *The Search for Modern China*. New York: W. W. Norton, 1990.

Staples-Smith, Harold. *Diary of Events and the Progress on Shameen: 1859–1938*. Hong Kong: private publication, 1938.

Stevens, Keith. 'A Tale of Sour Grapes: Messrs Little and Mesny and the First Steamship through the Yangzi Gorges'. *Journal of the Royal Asiatic Society, Hong Kong Branch*, vol. 41 (Hong Kong, 2002).

———. 'The Yangzi Port of Zhenjiang down the Centuries'. *Journal of the Royal Asiatic Society, Hong Kong Branch*, vol. 42 (Hong Kong, 2003).

Stevens, Keith and Jennifer Welch. 'Monument to the Westmorland Regiment, the 55th Regiment of Foot, in Dinghai City on Zhoushan Island'. *Journal of the Royal Asiatic Society, Hong Kong Branch*, vol. 38 (Hong Kong, 2000).

Stone, Albert H. and J. Hammond Reed, eds. *Historic Lushan: The Kuling Mountains*. Hankow: Religious Tract Society, 1921.

Stursberg, Peter. *No Foreign Bones in China*. Edmonton: University of Alberta, 2002.

Tai En-sai. *Treaty Ports in China*. New York: Columbia University Press, 1918.

Tan, Carol. *British Rule in China: Law and Justice in Weihaiwei 1898–1930*. London: Wildy, Simmonds and Hill, 2008.

Teichman, Sir Eric. *Affairs of China*. London: Methuen, 1938.

Thomas, Gould H. *An American in China 1936–1939*. New York: Greatrix Press, 2004.

Thomas, R. D. *A Trip on the West River*. Canton: The China Baptist Publication Society, 1903.

Tian Yutang, ed. *Astor Hotel*. Singapore: World Publications Printers, undated.

Tiffen, Mary. *Friends of Sir Robert Hart: Three Generations of Carrall Women in China*. Crewkerne: Tiffania Books, 2012.

Tolley, Kemp. *Yangtze Patrol: The US Navy in China*. Annapolis: Bluejacket Books, 2000 [1971].

Tsai Jung-fang. *Hong Kong in Chinese History: Community and Social Unrest in the British Colony, 1842–1913*. New York: Columbia University Press, 1993.

Tsang, Steve. *A Modern History of Hong Kong*. Hong Kong: Hong Kong University Press, 2004.

Turner, J. A. *Kwang Tung, or Five Years in South China*. London: S. W. Partridge, 1894.

Tyau, Min-ch'ien T. Z. *The Legal Obligations arising out of Treaty Relations between China and Other States*. Shanghai: Commercial Press, 1917.

Uhalley, Stephen Jr. 'The Taipings at Ningpo: The Significance of a Forgotten Event'. *Journal of the Royal Asiatic Society, Hong Kong Branch*, vol. 11 (Hong Kong, 1971).

Utley, Freda. *China at War*. London: Faber & Faber, 1939.

van de Ven, Hans. *Breaking with the Past: The Maritime Customs Service and the Global Origins of Modernity in China*. New York: Columbia University Press, 2014.

van Dyke, Paul A., ed. *Americans and Macao: Trade, Smuggling and Diplomacy on the South China Coast*. Hong Kong: Hong Kong University Press, 2012.

Victoir, Laura and Victor Zatsepine, eds. *Harbin to Hanoi: The Colonial Built Environment in Asia, 1840 to 1940*. Hong Kong: Hong Kong University Press, 2013.

Villiers, Frederic. 'The Truth about Port Arthur'. *The North American Review*, vol. 160, no. 460 (March 1895).

Villiers, John. 'Silk and Silver: Macau, Manila and Trade in the China Seas in the Sixteenth Century'. *Journal of the Royal Asiatic Society, Hong Kong Branch*, vol. 20 (Hong Kong, 1980).

von Gumpach, Johannes. *The Treaty-Rights of the Foreign Merchant, and the Transit-System, in China*. Shanghai: Celestial Empire Office, 1875 (Elibron reprint, 2005).

Wakeman, Frederick. *Strangers at the Gate: Social Disorder in South China, 1839–1861*. Berkeley: University of California Press, 1966.

Waley, Arthur. *The Opium War through Chinese Eyes*. London: George Allen & Unwin, 1960 [1958].

Walton, Joseph. *China and the Present Crisis*. London: Sampson Low, Marston, 1900.

Warner, Torsten. *German Architecture in China*. Berlin: Ernst and Sohn, 1994.

Waters, Dan. 'Hong Kong Hongs with Long Histories and British Connections'. *Journal of the Royal Asiatic Society, Hong Kong Branch*, vol. 30 (Hong Kong, 1993).

Way, Denis and Robert Nield. *Counting House: The History of PricewaterhouseCoopers on the China Coast*. Hong Kong: PricewaterhouseCoopers, 2002.

Wei, Betty Peh-T'i. 'Juan Yüan's Management of Sino-British Relations in Canton, 1817–1826'. *Journal of the Royal Asiatic Society, Hong Kong Branch*, vol. 21 (Hong Kong, 1981).

———. *Shanghai: Crucible of Modern China*. Hong Kong: Oxford University Press, 1987.

Weihaiwei Acts: Compilation of Historical Data regarding the Period of Britain's Leasing of Weihaiwei. Beijing: China International Broadcast Publishing, 2006.

Welsh, Frank. *A History of Hong Kong*. London: Harper Collins, 1993.

Wesley-Smith, Peter. *Unequal Treaty 1898–1997: China, Great Britain, and Hong Kong's New Territories*. Hong Kong: Oxford University Press, 1998.

Williams, E. T. 'The Open Ports of China'. *Geographical Review*, vol. 9, no. 4, American Geographical Society (April–June 1920).

Wilson, Andrew. *England's Policy in China*. Hong Kong: A. Shortrede, 1860.

Wolseley, Lt. Col. G. J. *Narrative of the War with China in 1860*. London: Longman, Green, Longman and Roberts, 1862.

Wong, J. Y. *Anglo-Chinese Relations 1839–1860: A Calendar of Chinese Documents in the British Foreign Office Records*. Oxford: Oxford University Press, 1983.

———. *Deadly Dreams*. Cambridge: Cambridge University Press, 1998.

Bibliography

Wood, Frances. *No Dogs and Not Many Chinese: Treaty Port Life in China, 1843–1943*. London: John Murray, 1998.

Woodhead, H. G. W. *The Truth about the Chinese Republic*. London: Hurst and Blackett, 1925.

———. *Extraterritoriality in China: The Case Against Abolition*. Tientsin: Peking & Tientsin Times, 1929.

———. 'Tientsin's Foreign Concessions'. *Oriental Affairs*, October 1938. Tientsin.

Wright, Arnold, ed. *Twentieth-Century Impressions of Hong Kong, Shanghai and the Other Treaty Ports of China*. London: Lloyd's Greater Britain Publishing, 1908.

Wright, Mary Clabaugh. *The Last Stand of Chinese Conservatism: The Tung-Chih Restoration, 1862–1874*. Stanford: Stanford University Press, 1957.

Wright, Stanley F. *Hart and the Chinese Customs*. Belfast: William Mullan & Son, 1950.

Xiao Xiaoming, ed. *Tianjin: Lustrous Pearl of the Bohai Gulf*. Beijing: Foreign Languages Press, 2006.

Yiu, Elsha. 'Idealizing Space: Americans and the Newly Opened Port of Swatow'. Paper delivered to conference at Hong Kong University, 23–24 May 2011.

Zhang Jianguo. *Weihaiwei under British Rule*. Jinan: Shandong Pictorial Publishing House, 2006.

Zhao Changtian. *An Irishman in China: Robert Hart, Inspector General of the Chinese Imperial Maritime Customs*. New York: Better Link Press, 2014.

Zhe Fu, ed. *Late Qing and Early Republic Wuhan Images*. Shanghai: Shanghai Sanlian Press, 2010.

Zhou Yongming. *Historicizing Online Politics: Telegraphy, the Internet and Political Participation in China*. Stanford: Stanford University Press, 2006.

Index

A-Pak (Pu Hsing-yu), 175–76
Abdoolally Ebrahim & Co., 131
Aberdeen, Lord, xxxvii, 2
Adkins, Thomas, 68
Aigun (Aihun), xvi, xxi, xxiii, 6, 23–24, 289
air travel, 112, 117, 131, 153, 212, 220
Alabaster, Chaloner, 45, 101, 217, 272, 273
Alcock, Sir Rutherford, xvi, xxxvii, 5, 14, 15, 26, 55, 86, 130, 138, 141, 198, 199, 202, 271, 291
Alfred Holt & Co., 112
Algar, Albert, 96
Allen, Clement, 103, 182
Allen, Edward, 72, 184
Allen, Herbert, 72
American Civil War, xvi, 53, 177, 202, 226
American commercial activity, 6, 10, 27, 43, 79, 87, 88, 89, 96, 99, 103, 109, 110, 112, 121, 123, 125, 190, 198, 204, 213, 214, 220, 226, 278
Amherst, Lord, xv, xxxvii, 121, 259
Amoy Canning Co., 35
Amoy Dock Co., 31
Amoy (Xiamen), xix, xxi, xxix, 2, 3, 10, 15, 17, 20, 24–37, 67, 91, 92, 93, 169, 182, 214, 216, 218, 220, 223, 226, 228, 230, 231, 232, 252, 272, 273, 274, 295
Anglo-German Brewery Co., 256
Anking (Anqing), xxvi, 117, 291
Anping, xxix, 20, 226, 228, 295
Anshan, xxv, 290
anti-foreign demonstrations and riots, xvi, xvii, 6, 44, 48, 50, 66, 67, 72, 73, 79, 91, 111, 114, 133, 135, 140, 150, 159, 187, 204, 205, 206, 210, 217, 237, 243, 250, 274, 276, 285, 286, 288
Antung (Dandong), xxv, 9, 37–39, 119, 160, 173
Ariel (British vessel), 89
Arrow (British vessel), xvi, 41
arsenals
   Foochow (Fuzhou), xvi, xvii, 10, 91, 92, 93
   Hanyang (Hankow), 110
   Kiangnan (Shanghai), xvi, 10, 203
   Weihaiwei (Weihai), 259
Arthur, Lieutenant William, 188

Asiatic Petroleum Co., xxxvii, 38, 46, 71, 73, 79, 94, 97, 115, 117, 139, 147, 165, 173, 194, 196, 242, 276, 283
Association of Deli Planters, 219
Astor House hotels, 63, 66, 104, 178, 221, 239, 243, 250, 262
Augustine Heard & Co., 100
Ayrton, William, 275

Baber, Colbourne, 75
Bai Gui, 41
Bailuding (Bailu), xxvi, 67
Baku (Magong), xxix, 39
Balfour, Arthur, 265
Balfour, Captain George, 197, 198
Ball, Samuel, 85
Bank of Taiwan, 140, 223
Banka (Wanhua), xxix, 230, 231, 295
Banker & Co., 166
banking industry, 47, 90, 112, 129, 179, 205, 220, 266
Banque de l'Indo-Chine, 45
Banque de Paris et des Pays-Bas, 108
Bean, William, 72
beans and beancake industry, 29, 35, 38, 53–54, 83, 84, 120, 156, 167, 168, 169, 170, 173, 219, 255
Belcher, Sir Edward, 191
Belgian commercial activity, 74, 106, 108, 109, 248, 249
Bennertz, Henry, 50
Beresford, Lord Charles, xxxvii, 170, 171, 260, 261
Bonham, Sir Samuel, xxxvii, 29, 40, 87, 174
Borodin, Mikhail, 151
Bowra, Eric, 235
Bowring, Sir John, xxxvii, 15, 27, 125, 127, 131
Boxer Rebellion, xviii, 7, 8, 12, 18, 21, 35, 64, 73, 75, 76, 112, 118, 128, 139, 145, 153, 160, 171, 185, 187, 190, 204, 209, 221, 229, 240, 241, 243, 245, 246, 247, 248, 263, 265, 281, 286
boycotts of foreign trade, 36, 48, 59, 64, 65, 67, 100, 101, 128, 132, 135, 140, 180, 195, 205, 208, 222, 258, 259, 283
Bradley & Co., 216, 219, 220, 222

Bradley, C. W., Jr., 216
Bradley, Charles, 175
Brady, Herbert, 192, 193, 194
Bremer, Sir Gordon, 80
brick industry, 33, 211, 212, 258
British & Chinese Corporation, 163
British-American Tobacco Co., 110, 113, 161, 165, 173, 248, 258, 266, 276
British commercial activity, 2, 3, 6, 16, 26, 33, 39, 53, 88, 94, 96, 98, 99, 123, 186, 204, 231, 242
British Consulates, accommodation problems, 26, 30–31, 43, 49, 55, 69, 70, 79, 86, 90, 96, 133, 143–44, 146, 168, 178, 182, 193, 231, 273, 277
British naval vessels
  HMS *Actaeon*, 25
  HMS *Algerine*, 188
  HMS *Capetown*, 117
  HMS *Cockchafer*, 258
  HMS *Daphne*, 64
  HMS *Dwarf*, 217
  HMS *Elk*, 31
  HMS *Encounter*, 176
  HMS *Grasshopper*, 169
  HMS *Isis*, 33
  HMS *Nimrod*, 176
  HMS *Opossum*, 133
  HMS *Rattler*, 29
  HMS *Robin*, 146
  HMS *Sandpiper*, 165
  HMS *Suffolk*, 208
  HMS *Surprise*, 155
  HMS *Terrible*, 209
  HMS *Woodcock*, 166
  HMS *Woodlark*, 108
  HMS *Wyvern*, 140
British North Borneo Co., 179
Bruce, Robert, 32
Bruce, Sir Frederick, xxxvii, 30, 54, 283, 291
Brunner Mond, 59, 60, 79
Bryant, Nelson, 134
bunding schemes, 29, 31, 35, 37, 46, 48, 50, 57, 61, 69, 70, 72, 96, 99, 103, 104, 106, 107, 112, 116, 131, 135, 137, 138, 139, 140, 142, 145, 147, 163, 165, 170, 178, 180, 190, 194, 203, 207, 208, 209, 210, 211, 223, 227, 228, 233, 236, 284, 329
Bush Brothers, 168, 169, 170
Bush, Henry, 168
Butterfield & Swire, xiii, xxxvii, 10, 35, 36, 38, 45, 46, 49, 58, 59, 60, 65, 70, 71, 78, 79, 91, 94, 103, 112, 114, 130, 134, 135, 138, 163, 169, 170, 178, 194, 203, 210, 216, 219, 220, 222, 242, 250, 257, 258, 259, 264, 265, 274, 284, 285, 287

Caine, George, 215, 217
Campbell, Gordon and Mary, 65
Canton (Guangzhou), xv, xvi, xxi, xxviii, 39–49, 122, 124, 132, 141, 146, 155, 157, 165, 194, 238, 277, 295
Capricieuse (French naval vessel), 176
Capsuimoon (Ma Wan), xxviii, 121, 148, 155, 295
Carlowitz & Co., 50, 256
Cass, Francis, 33
Celestial (British vessel), 128
cemeteries, foreign, 34, 63, 88, 177, 192, 198, 229, 232, 269, 277–78
Changchun, xxiii, 119, 160, 290
Changsha, xxvi, 9, 49–51, 279, 287, 289, 295
Chaochow (Chaozhou), 8, 215, 217, 220, 279
Chapei (Zhabei), 208
Chartered Bank of India, Australia and China, 129
Chartered Mercantile Bank of India, London and China, 129
Chater, Sir Paul, 131
Chefoo Agreement, xvi, xvii, 8, 9, 63, 75, 76, 93, 103, 133, 148, 181, 210, 238, 271, 273, 280, 281, 283, 292
Chefoo (Yantai), xxv, 4, 8, 51–66, 82, 157, 168, 170, 237, 238, 242, 255, 260, 261, 262, 263, 265, 266, 267, 295
Chen Yixi, 147
Chen Yujen, Eugene, xxxvii, 115, 140, 151
Chengling, 286
Chengteh (Changde), xxvi
Chengtu (Chengdu), xxi, xxvi, 66–67, 225, 279, 295
Chiang Kai-shek, xi, xxxvii, 48, 114, 115, 116, 120, 132, 140, 151, 160, 164, 206, 251, 259, 279
Chihfeng (Chifeng), xxiii, 290
Chikungshan (Jigongshan), xxvi
Chimmo Bay (Shenhu Wan), xxix, 67–68
China Merchants Steam Navigation Co., xvi, 10, 70, 71, 94, 138, 170, 178, 182, 194, 203, 239, 247, 264, 274, 284, 287
China Navigation Co., 35, 58, 91, 114, 138, 139, 140, 169, 178, 219, 221, 285. *See also* Butterfield & Swire
Chinchew Bay (Quanzhou Wan), xxix, 68
Chinchow (Jinzhou), 290
Chinese commercial activity, 4, 16, 28, 33, 44, 78, 99, 103
Chinese Communist Party, xviii, 186, 205
Chinese Eastern Railway Co., xvii, 83, 118, 119, 171, 189, 289

Index

Chinese emperors
  Daoguang, xv, xxxix, 2, 39, 40
  Guangxu, xxxix
  Hongwu, xxxix
  Jiaqing, xxxix, 174
  Kangxi, xv, xxxix
  Pu Yi (Xuantong), xxxix, 21, 161, 290
  Qianlong, xv, xxxix
  Tongzhi, xxxix, 91
  Xianfeng, xxxix, 87
  Yongle, xxxix, 244
  Yongzheng, xv, xxxix
Chinese Engineering & Mining Co., 74, 240, 242, 247
Chinese Labour Corps, 266–67
Chinese Maritime Customs, xvi, xviii, 8, 9, 18–19, 35, 43, 187, 200, 218, 238, 244, 249
Chinese modernization efforts, 7, 9–12, 108, 164, 168, 188, 203, 239, 243, 259
Chinese nationalism, 21, 35, 44, 48, 49, 128, 205
Chinese navy, modernization of, 1, 10, 48, 91, 92, 188, 238, 259, 279
Chinese Regiment, xviii, 34, 73, 244, 262, 265
Chinghokow (Yidu), xxvi, 291
Chinhai (Zhenhai), 174, 176, 178, 179, 180
Chinkiang (Zhenjiang), xix, xxvi, 4, 68–73, 137, 138, 150, 162, 243, 269, 291, 295
Chinpeng (Jinpeng), xxiii, 290
Chinwangtao (Qinhuangdao), xvii, xxv, 73–75, 185, 209, 240, 295
Choutsun (Zhoucun), xxv, 289
Chuitzuchien (Yanji), xxiii, 290
Chung, Prince, 187
Chungking Agreement, xvii, 76, 78
Chungking (Chongqing), xvii, xix, xxi, xxvi, 16, 67, 75–80, 117, 133, 135, 153, 210, 225, 258, 268, 291, 295
Chusan (Zhoushan), xv, xxvi, xxix, 25, 80–82, 173, 174, 295
Cixi, Empress Dowager, xxxvii, 8, 66, 187, 204
Clark, Duncan, 261–62
Clark, Ernest, 262, 269
Clennell, Walter, 210, 333
Cloud, Frederick, 97
clubs, 19, 32, 45, 49, 51, 58, 62, 63, 64, 65, 66, 72, 73, 90, 100, 102, 113, 117, 118, 120, 134, 138, 145, 159, 173, 177, 191, 198, 203, 207, 209, 220, 221, 228, 233, 236, 239, 243, 247, 249, 250, 261, 262, 268, 282, 288
coal mining industry, 11, 33, 35, 50, 53, 62, 74, 75, 83, 109, 209, 231, 232, 239–40, 252, 255, 258, 266, 290

compradors, 11, 17, 27, 58, 126, 218, 222, 239, 329, 339
concessions and settlements, 3, 7, 8, 11, 103, 107, 108, 151, 245, 329
  American, 6, 198, 201, 235, 247, 272
  Austro-Hungarian, 248–49
  Belgian, 106, 248
  British, xix, 21, 28–29, 31, 34, 36, 42, 43, 44, 47, 52, 54, 68–70, 72, 73, 99, 101, 102, 103, 105–6, 108, 109, 111, 112, 114, 115, 116, 132, 133, 137, 138, 139, 140, 146, 162, 164, 168, 170, 171, 182, 197, 198, 199, 201, 206, 215, 217, 235, 236, 239, 241, 242, 243, 245–46, 250, 272, 283, 284
  foreign (general), 50, 51, 56, 57, 79, 88, 96, 107, 135, 147, 156, 161, 163, 165, 177, 180, 186, 196, 251, 281, 284–85, 286
  French, 15, 42, 45, 54, 55, 104–5, 107, 108, 109, 113, 115, 152, 159, 162, 163, 177, 198, 201, 203, 204, 206, 207, 208, 235, 242, 243, 246–47, 250
  German, 103–4, 107, 108, 109, 110, 247, 254, 281
  international, xvi, xviii, 8, 34, 36, 201, 202, 204–9
  Italian, 15, 248, 250
  Japanese, 33, 37, 79, 96, 97, 106, 108, 110, 115, 116, 117, 161, 171, 210, 211, 247–48, 287
  Russian, 104, 108, 114, 118, 160–61, 171, 190, 248, 289
Conger, Edwin, 187
Conquest (British vessel), 273
consuls and consulates, 4, 8, 14, 17, 27, 186, 329
  American, 9, 14, 31, 37, 41, 55, 56, 64, 71, 72, 79, 88, 96, 102, 119, 134, 160, 164, 169, 175, 177, 180, 198, 200, 215, 216, 221, 250, 272
  Austro-Hungarian, 248
  Belgian, 248
  British, 3, 9, 13, 14, 17, 19, 20, 25, 26, 30, 31, 37, 41, 42, 43, 44, 49, 52, 53, 54, 55, 57, 60, 66, 67, 69, 70, 71, 72, 73, 75, 79, 86, 87, 88, 89, 90, 96, 99, 112, 117, 119, 120, 133, 134, 135, 136, 137, 140, 141, 143, 144, 145, 146, 150, 153, 160, 164, 165, 166, 167, 168, 170, 171, 173, 174, 175, 177, 178, 180, 181, 182, 183, 184, 192, 193, 197, 198, 200, 202, 210, 211, 215, 216, 217, 221, 224, 225, 226, 227, 228, 229, 230, 231, 232, 234, 235, 236, 250, 271, 272, 273, 274, 275, 276, 277, 278, 282, 283, 285, 286, 288
  Danish, 56
  Dutch, 27
  French, 9, 41, 43, 44, 54, 55, 79, 94, 99, 104, 105, 121, 144, 145, 155, 156, 158, 159, 160, 166, 175, 177, 182, 183, 184, 198, 200, 201, 206, 224, 237, 247

Index

consuls and consulates (*continued*)
  German, 32, 55, 56, 104, 160, 183, 214, 218, 219, 247, 250, 251
  Hawaiian, 32
  Italian, 248
  Japanese, 33, 38, 49, 56, 67, 79, 96, 106, 116, 135, 140, 160, 164, 208, 209, 210, 211, 223, 250, 251, 286, 287
  Portuguese, 27, 175, 176
  Russian, 56, 102, 104, 119, 136, 160, 171, 248, 289
  Spanish, 17, 27, 214
Cooke, Major-General James, 177
Cornabé, Eckford & Co., 58
cotton industry, xvi, 10, 11, 12, 16, 21, 106, 110, 163, 180, 197, 202, 203, 204, 206, 210, 212, 249, 256, 258
Couper, John, 278
Courbet, Améedée, 92
Crasemann & Hagen, 58
cricket, 32, 45, 72, 113, 173, 221, 261, 282
Crossman, Major, xxxvii, 31, 168
Cumsingmoon (Jinxingmen), xxviii, 82, 155
currency and coinage, xviii, 12, 31, 128, 129, 131, 205, 223, 249
Curzon, Lord, 225, 288
custom houses, foreign-managed, xvi, xvii, 9, 23, 30, 34, 37, 41, 44, 46, 48, 49, 53, 69, 73, 77, 83, 96, 99, 112, 119, 121, 134, 141, 145, 146, 148, 154, 155, 156, 158, 163, 165, 169, 178, 182, 193, 194, 196, 200, 210, 211, 215, 218, 222, 224, 226, 228, 231, 232, 234, 242, 254, 257, 258, 271, 272, 278, 282, 284, 285, 286, 288
customs arrangements
  cross-border trade, 38, 149
  duty-free status, 122, 147
  in free ports, xvi, 83, 129, 153, 254
  inspection, 70
  prevention of smuggling, 147–48, 149
  responsibility for 'native' customs, 139, 148–49, 172, 244
  tariffs, 132
  transit pass system, xvi, 17–18, 30, 78, 142, 234, 330
Cutty Sark (British vessel), 103

d'Aguilar, Major-General George, xv, 40
d'Aiguebelle, Paul, 91
Dairen (Dalian), xviii, xxv, 15, 16, 22, 58, 61, 82–85, 129, 160, 173, 254, 258, 290, 295
Dalny. *See* Dairen
Danish commercial activity, 31, 93, 241
Danish designs on China, 195

Danish East India Company, 277
Danish missionary activity, 37
Davenport, Arthur, 166, 272, 283
Davis, Sir John, xxxvii, 26, 27, 39–40, 80–81, 86, 87, 125
de Linde, Albert, 241
de St. Croix, W., 170
Deng Tingzhen, xxxvii
Dent & Co., 4, 16, 29, 67, 68, 69, 70, 81, 98, 122, 174, 175, 177, 178, 202, 213, 214, 226, 231, 236
Detring, Gustav, 185, 237–39, 240, 241, 243, 244, 245, 252
Deutsch-Asiatische Bank, 247, 251, 255
Dew, Commander Roderick, 176, 177
Ding Ruchang, Admiral, 238, 259–60
Dircks, Hinrich, 218, 219
Disraeli, Benjamin, 231
docks and shipbuilding, 10, 31, 74, 89, 91, 119, 120, 128, 130, 131, 152, 169, 188, 201, 241, 255, 278
Dodd & Co., 231
Dodd, John, 30, 230
Dolonor (Duolun), xxiii, 290
Dorabjee Naorojee, 131
Dosing (Yunan), xxviii, 292
Double (Mayu) Island, xxix, 214, 215, 295
Douglas Lapraik & Co., 29, 128, 220, 278
Douglas, Robert, 52
Douglas Steamship Co., 94, 220, 233
Doumer, Paul, 48, 152, 292
Drummond, P., 194
Du Yuesheng, 160, 207
Duff, Thomas, 72
Duke of Argyll (British vessel), 27
Dutch commercial activity, 2, 24, 39, 62, 85, 186, 219, 225–26, 228, 230, 232

East India Company, xv, xxxvii, 24, 25, 26, 80, 85, 121, 174, 181, 197, 226
Eckford, Andrew, 58
Edgar, J., 173
Edwards & Co., 166
electricity supply, 46, 83, 104, 108, 131, 145, 223, 242
Elgin, Earl of, xxxvii, 41, 53, 70, 81, 88, 98, 137, 186, 235, 283, 291
Elias, J. R., 268
Elliott, Captain Charles, xxxvii, 80, 121, 127
Emigrant (British vessel), 27
emigration, Chinese, xvi, 11, 17, 27–28, 29, 32, 34–35, 36, 37, 64, 74, 82, 124, 142, 145, 157, 179, 214, 215, 219, 266

350

extraterritoriality, xvi, xvii, xix, 12–15, 22, 33, 37, 108, 187, 201, 202, 205, 207, 289

Fakumen (Faku), xxiii, 289
Feng Zicai, xxxvii
fengshui, 10, 11, 92, 109, 219, 329
Fengwangcheng (Fengcheng), xxv, 289
Fergusson & Co., 53, 58
Fergusson, T. T., 53
First Opium War, xv, 24, 39, 68, 80, 85, 121, 127, 157, 162, 229
First World War, xviii, 21, 38, 47, 104, 111, 119, 130, 156, 161, 205, 256, 257, 266–67, 290
Fisher, Lt. Col. George, 52
Fittock, William, 178
flour industry, 33, 204, 249
Fongchuen (Fengkai), xxviii, 292
Fontanier, Henri, 237
Foochow (Fuzhou), xxix, 3, 10, 20, 26, 29, 30, 31, 85–95, 95, 136, 137, 147, 188, 218, 231, 232, 259, 271, 273, 274, 295
Forbes, Captain Duncan, 25
Ford, Colin, 286
Ford, W. R. C., 173
foreign enclaves as places of refuge, 12, 114, 117, 128, 133, 176, 200, 201, 202, 206, 208, 248
foreign 'spheres of influence', 7, 61, 98, 151, 165, 183, 240, 253, 291
Fortune, Robert, xxxvii, 25, 81, 90
Fox, Harry, 193, 194, 211
fraudulent business arrangements, 100, 142
French commercial activity, 42, 54, 91, 96, 99, 104, 108, 152, 158, 159, 166, 183, 188, 201, 225, 230, 288, 292
French designs on China, 6, 7, 41, 66, 121, 144, 151–52, 155, 158, 164–65, 183, 192, 224, 282, 288, 292
Fuchan (British vessel), 46
Funing (Ningde), xvii, 196
Fushun, xxiii, 290
Fusiyama (British vessel), 98

Gartok (Gar Yasha), xviii, xx, xxiv, 293
gas supply, 46, 232, 242
Gaunt, Lieutenant Ernest, 260
Gérard, Auguste, 92
German commercial activity, xvii, 16, 32, 33, 34, 48, 50, 54, 56, 58, 61, 78, 94, 99, 104, 108, 110, 119, 142, 180, 183, 188, 190, 204, 214, 218–19, 220, 226, 228, 231, 242, 247, 251, 254, 255, 256, 273, 274, 282

German designs on China, 7, 61, 189, 195, 238, 247, 250, 252–53, 260, 281
Gibb, Livingstone & Co., 138
Giles, Herbert, 178, 221
Giquel, Prosper, 91, 92
glass industry, 73, 74, 130
Goffe, Herbert, 115
Gordon, Colonel Charles, xxxvii, 177, 201, 235, 238
Gough, General Sir Henry, 68
Grand Canal, 10, 68, 69, 70, 71, 95, 96, 97, 211, 236
Great Northern Telegraph Co., 31, 93
Great Tea Race, xvi, 89
Gribble, Captain Henry, 25–26
gunboat diplomacy, 16, 21, 29, 31, 33, 40, 48, 50, 64, 67, 91, 103, 111, 114, 115, 116, 117, 132, 140, 144, 151, 164, 169, 171, 185, 205, 237, 259
Guo Songtao, xxxvii
Gutzlaff, Karl, 86
Gyantse (Gyangze), xviii, xxiv, 293, 295

Haichow (Haizhou), xxv, 95
Hailar (Hulunber), xxiii, 289
Hainan (American vessel), 181
Hainan Island, 20, 141, 144, 145, 154, 165, 292
Haiphong, 153, 155, 159, 288
hairnet industry, 58, 60, 267
Hami (Kumul), xxii, 289
Hamilton, Captain William, 191
Hance, Henry, 278
Hangchow (Hangzhou), xxvi, 87, 95–97, 159, 160, 176, 179, 180, 204, 211, 289, 295
Hankow (Hankou), xix, xxvi, 4, 7, 11, 12, 15, 21, 36, 49, 50, 67, 76, 78, 97–118, 133, 134, 135, 137, 138, 139, 140, 150, 151, 164, 200, 206, 210, 212, 242, 254, 275, 279, 284, 287, 288, 291, 295
Harbin, xxiii, 15, 16, 19, 118–21, 160, 190, 289
harbour improvement schemes, 24, 61–62, 71, 73, 83, 84, 95, 143, 145, 156, 188, 228, 252, 255, 261, 267
Hart, Sir Robert, xvi, xxxviii, 19, 30, 43, 44, 63, 70, 76, 78, 83, 99, 148, 149, 158, 169, 172, 181, 185, 187, 217, 218, 231, 232, 238, 240, 253, 254, 278, 279, 286
Harvey, Alexander, 181
Harvey, Frederick, 70
Heinrich, German Prince, 103, 255, 261
Herton, Ebell & Co., 182
Herton, Edward, 142, 183
Hewlett, Meyrick, 36, 173
Hildebrand, Heinrich, 108, 250
Ho Kai, 126

Index

Ho Tung, Sir Robert, 126
Hobson, Customs Commissioner, 77
Hoihow (Haikou), xxvii, 8, 18, 20, 141, 142, 143, 144, 145, 153, 295
Hokow (Hekou) (Red River), xxvii, 121, 158
Hokow (Hekou) (West River), 193–94, 295
Holland, William, 231
Honam (Honan), 40, 41, 42, 43, 44, 45
Hong Kong, xv, xviii, xxi, xxviii, 2, 3, 5, 6, 7, 8, 12, 14, 15, 22, 29, 33, 35, 40, 41, 44, 45, 46, 47, 48, 53, 68, 77, 81, 82, 87, 88, 89, 91, 92, 93, 94, 105, 111, 117, 118, 121–33, 141, 142, 145, 146, 147, 148, 149, 150, 152, 153, 154, 155, 157, 158, 166, 169, 170, 181, 182, 183, 190, 193, 194, 197, 198, 202, 203, 207, 213, 214, 217, 218, 219, 221, 223, 224, 228, 232, 233, 253, 254, 256, 257, 261, 263, 265, 267, 274, 278, 279, 283, 292, 295
Hong Kong & Kowloon Wharf & Godown Co. Ltd., 131
Hong Kong, Canton & Macao Steamboat Co., 194
Hong Xiuquan, xv
Hongkew (Hongkou), 198, 208
Hongkong & Shanghai Bank, 31, 58, 59, 91, 111, 112, 113, 129, 142, 163, 203, 250, 257, 262
Hongkong & Whampoa Dock Co., 278
Hongkong Land Ltd., 131
Hoover, Herbert, 243
Hope, Admiral Sir James, 98, 200
Hopkins, Lionel, 182–83
horse racing, 62, 94, 100, 113, 177, 198, 202, 207, 236, 239, 243
hospitals, foreign, 34, 75, 78, 83, 97, 119, 144, 147, 150, 154, 183, 184, 192, 198, 212, 240, 254, 255, 262, 285, 286, 290
hotels, foreign, 31, 32, 34, 45, 46, 57, 60, 62–63, 64, 65, 84, 104, 119, 120, 140, 150, 151, 159, 160, 161, 163, 178, 185, 187, 198, 207, 209, 212, 218, 221, 239, 242, 250, 253, 256, 258, 262, 265, 268, 271, 279, 288, 290
Howlik (Dinghu), xxviii, 292
Hsiakuan (Xiaguan), 163
Hsiao Kulun (Kulun), xxiii, 290
Hsin Hsu (Xinxu), 194
Hsin King, 290
Hsinho (Xinhu), xxv, 242
Hsinmintun (Xinmin), xxiii, 289
Hsinti (Xindi), xxvi, 291
Hudson Taylor, Rev. Dr. James, 63
Hughes, Patrick, 137
Hukow (Hukou), xxvi, 137, 138, 291
Hulutao (Huludao), xxv, 290
Hunchun, xxiii, 290
Husden, James, 56
Huwei, 230
Hwangchow (Huangzhou), xxvi, 291
Hwangtzekang (Huangshigang), xxvi, 291

Ichang (Yichang), xxvi, 20, 22, 75, 76, 77, 80, 133–35, 211, 258, 291, 295
Iching (Yizheng), xxvi, 291
Ichow (Linyi), xxv, 290
Ili (Yining), xxii, 288
Imperial Chinese Railways, 171
Indian commercial activity, 123, 131
Indo-China Steam Navigation Co., 138. *See also* Jardine, Matheson & Co.
industries. *See respective entries*
   banking
   beans and beancake
   brick
   coal mining
   cotton
   docks and shipbuilding
   flour
   glass
   hairnet
   hotel
   insurance
   iron and steel
   metallurgical
   paper
   porcelain
   shipping
   silk
   straw braid
   sugar
   tea
   telegraph
   timber
   tobacco
   wine-making
Inland Steam Navigation Regulations, xviii, 46, 139, 287, 291, 329. *See also* steam navigation of inland waterways
Innocent, John, 242
insurance industry, 47, 78, 179, 203, 217, 220
iron and steel industry, xvii, 11, 33, 83, 91, 106, 109, 110, 258, 290
Italian designs on China, 195, 248
Izumo (Japanese naval vessel), 208

Index

Jackson, Richard, 87
Japan Cotton Trading Co., 106
Japanese commercial activity, 16, 33, 36, 37, 38, 39, 46, 49, 50, 56, 59, 61, 64, 75, 78, 83, 84, 94, 95, 106, 110, 119, 128, 138, 139, 157, 161, 170, 173, 180, 196, 204, 210, 211, 212, 220, 223, 227, 234, 247–48, 258, 266, 269, 276, 289–90
Japanese piracy, 68, 85, 173, 213, 259
Japanese territorial expansion, xvi, xviii, 6, 7, 9, 21, 22, 24, 33, 36, 37, 49, 51, 66, 67, 75, 80, 82, 85, 97, 117, 120, 133, 135, 145, 147, 153, 156, 157, 158, 160, 161, 164, 170, 172, 188, 191, 195, 196, 205, 207–8, 212, 223, 228, 230, 233, 240, 250, 251, 256–57, 258, 260, 271, 276, 279, 283, 288, 289–90
Japan's 'Twenty-One Demands', xviii, 21, 140, 196, 205, 257, 290
Jardine, Matheson & Co., 4, 16, 24, 25, 36, 38, 46, 49, 67, 68, 71, 78, 80, 81, 94, 100, 103, 122, 126, 129, 130, 135, 138, 139, 155, 163, 166, 168, 170, 173, 174, 177, 182, 185, 194, 197, 203, 213, 218, 219, 220, 222, 226, 230, 231, 236, 238, 239, 250, 272, 273, 278, 280–81, 282, 284, 285, 287
Jardine, William, xv, xxxviii, 24, 174, 252
Jehol (Chengde), xxiii
Johnson, F. Bulkeley, 273
Johnston, Sir Reginald, 267, 270
Jordan, Sir John, 269

Kailan Mining Administration, 74, 240, 250
Kailuhsien (Kailu), xxiii, 290
Kaiping Mining Co., 10, 11, 62, 74, 239–40
Kaiyuan, xxiii, 290
Kakchio (Jiaoshi), 216
Kalgan (Zhangjiakou), xxi, xxiii, 289, 290
Kam Shan Hong, 124
Kashkar (Kashgar), xx, xxii, 136, 191
Kaukong (Jiujiang), xxviii, 292
Keelung (Jilong), xxix, 20, 230, 232, 295
Keswick, Sir William, 208
Kiakhta, xv, xxii, xxiii, 186, 288
Kialat (Jielu), 215–16
Kiangyin (Jiangyin), xxvi, 291
Kiaochow (Jiaozhou), xvii, 7, 189, 250, 252, 256
Kinder, Claude, 184
King, Walter, 133
Kingchow (Jingzhou), 211
Kingtehchen (Jingdezhen), 137
Kirin (Jilin), xxiii, 290

Kiukiang (Jiujiang), xix, xxvi, 4, 21, 36, 76, 115, 137–40, 150, 164, 206, 291, 295
Kiungchow (Qiongzhou), xxvii, 4, 8, 20, 141–45, 146, 184, 271, 295
Kobdo (Khovd), xxii, 289
Kongkun Market (Jianggen), xxviii, 192, 194, 292, 295
Kongmoon (Jiangmen), xxviii, 4, 146–47, 152, 154, 292, 295
Korean Provisional Government, 38
Kowloon-Canton Railway, xviii, 46, 131, 149
Kowloon (Jiulong), xxviii, 121, 122, 125, 127, 131, 147–50, 153, 263, 295
Koxinga, xxxviii, 213, 226, 230, 232
kuan-tu shang-pan, 10, 11, 203
Kucheng (Qitai), xxii, 289
Kueihuacheng (Hohot), xxiii, 290
Kulangsu (Gulangyu), xviii, xxix, 8, 25, 26, 27, 28, 30, 31, 32, 33, 34, 36, 37, 57, 295
Kuliang (Guling), xxix, 92, 295
Kuling (Lushan), xxvi, 92, 150–51, 295
Kuling (river vessel), 76
Kulow (Gulao), xxviii, 292
Kumchuk (Ganzhu), xxviii, 292
Kungchulin (Gongzhuling), xxiii, 290
Kungtung (Kongtong) Islands, 52
Kutzlau, Gustav, 180
Kwangchowwan (Zhanjiang), xviii, xxvii, 7, 15, 144, 151–53, 184, 190, 253, 295
Kwantung (Guandong) Peninsula, 190
Kweilin (Guilin), xxvii, 153, 166

Lady Hughes (British vessel), 13
Lamont, Captain, 128
Lampacao (Langbaigang), xxviii
Lampson, Sir Miles, 115
Lanchow Mining Co., 74
landing stages, 9, 291, 292, 329
Lappa (Hengqin Dao), xxviii, 153–54, 158
Lauts & Haesloop, 219, 222
Lavers & Clark, 262, 270
Lavers, Percy, 56
Lay, George Tradescant, xxxviii, 26, 86
Lay, Horatio Nelson, 215
Layton, Temple, 26, 27
Le Bayard (French naval vessel), 92
Leechuen (river vessel), 76
legal systems, Chinese and foreign compared, 12–15, 126, 127, 202, 264

Index

Li Hongzhang, xvi, xxxviii, 10, 11, 63, 82, 118, 170, 187, 188, 191, 200, 203, 204, 233, 237–39, 240, 241, 242, 243, 252, 253, 259, 280, 289
Li Liejun, xxxviii, 47
Liampo, xxix, 174, 295
Liaodong Peninsula, xvii, 118, 188, 189, 195, 252, 254
Liaoyang, xxv, 289
Lichuan (Fuli), xxiii, 290
Lienyungchiang (Lianyungang), xxv, 95
lighthouses, 19, 82, 145, 169, 178, 192, 215, 222
likin, xvii, xviii, xix, 5, 17–18, 29, 30, 32, 35, 49, 78, 90, 99, 100, 139, 142, 147, 148, 149, 172, 193, 218, 219, 230, 234, 258, 291, 329
Lin Zexu, xxxviii, 86, 87, 91, 289
Lindsay & Co., 52
Lindsay, Hugh Hamilton, xv, xxxviii, 24, 80, 85, 174, 259
Linsi (Linxi), xxiii, 290
Lintin (Neilingding) Island, xxviii, 82, 121, 122, 149, 154–55
Lintsingchow (Linqing), xxv, 290
Little, Archibald, xvii, xxxviii, 76–77, 78, 79, 134
Little, Edward, 150
Little, Henry, 165, 193
Litton, George, 224, 234
Litvinoff, S. W., 102
Liu Mingchuan, xxxviii, 233
Liu Zhennian, 65
Liukungtao (Liugongdao), 259–63
Local Post Office, 57, 60
Lockhart, Sir James Stewart, 263–65
Long Jiguang, 47
Lookong (Ligang), xxix, 81
Lord Amherst (British vessel), xv, 24, 29
Lord, Dr. E. C., 272
Lotinghau (Nandukou), xxviii, 292
Louisa (British vessel), 155
Luchingchiang (Lujinggang), xxvi, 291
Lukikow (Luxi), xxvi, 291
Lukpu (Lubu), xxviii, 292
Lukto (Dahe), xxviii, 292
Lungchingtsun (Longjing), xxiii, 290
Lungchow (Longzhou), xvii, xxvii, 155–56, 158, 166
Lungkow (Longkou), xxv, 64, 156–57, 256, 290, 295

Macao, xvi, xvii, xxi, xxviii, 2, 8, 15, 22, 25, 39, 46, 86, 121, 122, 127, 146, 147, 148, 152, 153, 154, 155, 157–58, 175, 176, 181, 254, 295
Macartney, Lord, xv, xxxviii, 80
MacDonald, Sir Claude, xxxviii, 82, 252, 260, 270, 281

Mackay, Dr. George, 232
Mackellar & Co., 100
Mackenzie, Charles, 174
Maclean, George, 56
Mahning (Maningwei), xxviii, 292
Main, Duncan, 97
Malcampo & Co., 273, 274
Man, Alexander, 284
Manchouli (Manzhouli), xxiii, 289
Manhao, xvii, xxvii, 121, 158, 224
Mannich, Julius, 228
manufacturing, by Chinese, 44, 46, 64, 70, 110, 112, 130, 133, 147, 168, 180, 204, 210, 220
manufacturing, by foreigners, 12, 32, 58, 60, 79, 84, 95, 101–2, 110, 128, 130, 133, 147, 161, 203, 204, 210, 212, 249, 258, 261, 266
Manwyne (Manghuan), xxvii, 234
Mao Zedong, xxxviii, 164
Marco Polo Bridge Incident, xix
Margary, Raymond, xvi, 63, 75, 234, 238, 288
Martin, Montgomery, xxxviii, 81
Matheson, James, xxxviii, 24, 155
May Fourth Movement, xviii, 21, 64, 257
May Thirtieth Movement, 21
McBain, George, 284
McClatchie, Millicent, 275
McMullen, James, 57, 58, 60
Meadows, Thomas Taylor, 166, 170
Medhurst, Walter, 202, 280
Melchers & Co., 104, 108, 110
Mengtse (Mengzi), xvii, xxvii, 158–59, 224
metallurgical industry, 50
Mexico, 24
Meyer & Co., 104
Meyer, H. B., 273
Miao Islands, 52
Michie, Alexander, 52, 239
Middleton, James, 54
Milne, Rev. W. C., 174
missionary activity, 5, 6, 9, 14, 21, 37, 41, 49, 50, 52, 57, 60, 63, 66, 67, 72, 78, 82, 86, 87, 92, 93, 94, 95, 96, 97, 103, 117, 134, 135, 136, 138, 139, 144, 145, 147, 150, 153, 159, 161, 163, 169, 174, 175, 176, 178, 179, 182, 183, 184, 185, 186, 187, 196, 198, 201, 202, 204, 212, 215, 216, 218, 221, 222, 228, 232, 236–37, 242, 243, 251, 252, 254, 258, 264, 268, 274, 275, 276, 283–84, 285, 286
Mitsubishi Corporation, 56, 106, 170, 247
Mitsui Corporation, 50, 56, 83, 223, 247, 276

Index

Mokanshan (Moganshan), xxvi, 92, 159–60, 295
Moller, foreign engineer, 96
Momein, 234
Mongan, James, 236
Moorhead, Customs Commissioner, 103
Morrison, Martin, 52, 53, 54
Morse, Hosea Ballou, 286
Most Favoured Nation principle, xv, 2, 4, 5, 14, 15, 76, 204, 224, 253, 281
Mukden Incident, xix, 21, 161
Mukden (Shenyang), xviii, xxi, xxiii, xxv, 9, 21, 37, 119, 160–61, 248, 268, 289, 295
municipal government arrangements, xvi, 3, 8, 107
   Belgian, 248
   British, 31, 43, 71–72, 99, 114, 116, 138, 197, 239, 250, 260
   Chinese, 165, 196, 284, 286
   Chinese participation in, 9, 34, 58, 114, 116, 117, 120, 185, 202, 205, 206, 249, 264
   French, 45, 104
   German, 103, 247, 254, 255
   international, 34, 56–58, 88, 93, 135, 150, 159, 177, 180, 185, 200, 201–2, 244, 285
   Russian, 104, 119, 172, 190, 248
Muslim rebellions, xvi, 91, 136, 289

Nam Pak Hong, 124
Nam Yeung Hong, 124
Namoa (Nanao), xxix, 213–14, 295
Nanking (Nanjing), xxvi, 2, 4, 22, 68, 73, 151, 162–64, 174, 199, 200, 251, 270, 279, 285, 291, 295
Nanning, xxvii, 153, 155, 164–66, 184, 279, 282, 283
Nantai, 87–88, 90, 94, 295
Nanyang Brothers Tobacco Co., 110
Napier, Lord, xxxviii, 121
National City Bank of New York, 112
navigation improvements, 77, 145, 169
Netherlands Harbour Works Co., 62, 145
Nevius, Rev. Dr. John Livingston, 60
Newchwang (Yingkou), xxv, 4, 8, 35, 61, 64, 83, 166–73, 181, 222, 243, 295
newspapers and the press, 32, 119, 128, 180, 239, 245
Ng Choy (Wu Tingfan), 126
Nichimen Corporation, 106
Ningpo (Ningbo), xxi, xxvi, xxix, 2, 3, 26, 43, 87, 91, 95, 96, 137, 160, 173–81, 197, 198, 230, 271, 272, 273, 274, 276, 295
Ninguta (Ning'an), xxiii, 290
Nipchu, xxi, xxii, 288

Nippon Yusen Kaisha (NYK Line), 56, 94, 264
NKK Line, 46, 49, 139, 210, 287
Norwegian commercial activity, 274

O'Brien-Butler, Pierre, 33, 143
Oliphant, Laurence, 98
O'Malley, Owen, 115
opium trade, xvi, xvii, xviii, 1, 2, 4, 16, 24, 29, 39, 53, 67, 68, 70, 72, 81, 82, 86, 87, 93, 121, 122, 124, 128, 129, 130, 138, 147, 148, 149, 153, 154, 155, 158, 166, 174, 177, 180, 199, 200, 201, 203, 207, 213, 215, 217, 226, 230, 231, 234, 264, 273
Oriental (American vessel), 89–90
Oriental Bank, 129
OSK Line, 196

Pagoda Island (Mawei), xxix, 88–89, 90, 91, 94, 95, 196, 295
Paitsaokou (Baicaogou), xxiii, 290
Pakhoi (Beihai), xxvii, 20, 23, 142, 144, 146, 147, 153, 165, 181–84, 295
Paktauhau (Jiangshui), xxviii, 292
Palmerston, Lord, xxxviii, 40, 41, 87, 174, 252
Panoff, J. K., 102, 112
paper industry, 32, 46, 73, 111, 147, 203
Parker, Admiral Sir William, 68
Parker, Edward, 142, 144, 274
Parkes, Sir Harry, xxxviii, 26, 28, 30, 41, 42, 68–69, 86, 98–99, 137, 168, 176, 191, 235
Parsee commercial activity, 123
Paterson, William, 272
Pedder, William, 30
Peitaiho (Beidaihe), xxv, 9, 74, 184–86, 295
Peking (Beijing), xvi, xxi, 186–87, 243, 260, 295
Pengpu (Bengbu), xix, xxvi
Penhsihu (Benxi), xxv, 290
Peninsular & Oriental Steam Navigation Co. (P&O), 29, 74, 129, 203, 278
Perkins, Commander George, 181
pilots, 77, 89, 169, 192, 215, 241, 274
Pingchuan (Pingquan), xxiii, 290
Pinhingchow (Binxing Zhou), 140
Pioneer (river vessel), 76, 134
Pioneer Wine Co., 59
Pitzuwo (Pikou), xxv, 290
Plant, Cornell, xxxviii, 76–77
Po Leung Kuk, 126
Po Yang (Boyang) Lake, 137, 138, 139
Polo, Marco, 70, 95, 179

Index

Pope Hennessy, Sir John, xxxviii, 126
porcelain industry, 137, 138
Port Adams (Pulandian), xxv, 290
Port Arthur (Lüshun), xvii, xviii, xxv, 7, 22, 61, 82, 84, 118, 160, 172, 188–91, 253, 257, 260, 261, 269, 295
Port Edward (Matou), 264, 270
Port Hamilton (Geomun-do), xxv, 191–92
Port Lazareff (Wonsan), 191–92
ports-of-call, xvi, xviii, 9, 138, 146, 147, 210, 281, 291–92, 329
Portuguese commercial activity, 2, 24, 48, 68, 85, 146, 154, 157, 158, 173, 174, 175–76, 186, 213, 232, 277
Poshan (Boshan), xxv, 290
postal services, 19, 46, 56, 57, 58, 60, 84, 93, 96, 160, 163, 165, 166, 170, 182, 184, 194, 218, 222, 223, 239, 243, 251, 261, 262, 263
Pottinger, Sir Henry, xxxviii, 13, 24, 25, 26, 39–40, 68, 85, 86, 122, 123, 124, 127, 174, 213–14
Pratt, John, 274
public transport, 46, 128, 131, 132, 145, 223, 249, 280
Pukow (Pukou), xxvi, 163
Pulantien (Pulandian), 290

Qishan, xxxviii, 80
Qiying, xv, xxxviii, 26, 39–40, 68, 127, 213
Quemoy (Kinmen), xxix

Railton & Co., H. E., 60
railway development, xvii, xviii, 10, 11, 12, 21, 24, 33, 37, 38, 46, 47, 50, 61, 67, 73, 74, 82, 83, 84, 95, 97, 102, 104, 106, 108–9, 111, 112, 117, 118, 119, 120, 121, 131, 139, 147, 149, 150, 155, 156, 157, 158, 159, 160, 161, 163, 165, 171, 172, 173, 183, 184, 185, 189, 190, 194, 209, 211, 220, 223, 224, 227, 232, 233, 234, 238, 239, 240, 241, 242, 243, 248, 249, 250, 251, 253, 255, 258, 264, 265, 269, 280–81, 287, 288, 289, 290
Rennie, Dr. Thomas, 92
Revive China Society, xvii, 128
river conservation schemes, xviii, 12, 38, 46, 48, 173, 203, 240–41, 244, 281
Robert Bowne (American vessel), 27
Robertson, Daniel, 29, 181
Robinet, W. M., 226
Robinson, Sir Hercules, 131
Rooney, Matthew, 226
Ross, John, 161
Rossich, Antonio, 179
Royal Dutch Petroleum Co., 107

Russell & Co., 4, 10, 16, 87, 103, 138, 178, 180, 181, 203
Russian commercial activity, 24, 83, 90, 101–2, 103, 110, 118, 119, 120, 139, 157, 242, 288
Russian territorial expansion, xvi, xvii, xviii, 6, 23–24, 37, 82, 118, 119, 136, 160, 171, 188–190, 191–92, 196, 209, 240, 252, 260–61, 288–89, 292
Russo-Chinese Bank, 172
Russo-Japanese War, xviii, 23, 37, 49, 64, 83, 119, 160, 172, 189, 190–91, 205, 269, 289, 293

Saddle Islands (Shengsi), xxvi, 192
Sainam, 193
Sakharov, V. V., 83, 84
Salisbury, Lord, xxxviii, 20, 253, 265
Samsah Bay (Sansha Wan), 195, 196
Samshui (Sanshui), xxviii, 146, 192–95, 292, 295
Sanhsing (Yilan), xxiii, 290
Sanmun Bay (Sanmen Wan), xxvi, 195
Santalantu (Langtou), 38
Santuao (Sandu), xvii, xxix, 195–96
Sassoons, 45, 177, 207, 236
Satow, Sir Ernest, 172
Schaar, Bernhard, 218
Schomburg, Augustus, 142, 143, 183
schools and education, foreign, 60, 63, 66, 67, 74, 78, 83, 91, 93, 97, 119, 126, 144, 150, 183, 203, 204, 212, 232, 240, 251, 254, 255, 268, 276, 286, 290
Scott, Benjamin, 184
Sea Witch (American vessel), 214
Second Opium War, xvi, 4, 5, 6, 12, 41, 52, 68, 81, 123, 125, 157, 229, 235, 259, 278
Self-Strengthening Movement, 10, 91, 203, 239, 329
Sengelinqin, 235
Serica (British vessel), 89
Service, Robert, 67
settlements. *See* concessions and settlements
Seymour, Admiral, 41, 187, 188
Shameen (Shamian), 41–49, 42, 91
Shanghai, xxi, xxvi, 3, 6, 8, 9, 10, 11, 12, 14, 15, 19, 20, 21, 22, 29, 31, 34, 36, 38, 44, 48, 50, 52, 53, 57, 58, 63, 65, 66, 70, 73, 76, 78, 80, 85, 87, 88, 91, 93, 94, 95, 96, 97, 99, 100, 101, 103, 110, 112, 113, 116, 117, 120, 123, 129, 132, 133, 138, 142, 150, 160, 163, 174, 175, 176, 177, 178, 179, 180, 186, 187, 192, 196–209, 211, 212, 220, 227, 236, 239, 243, 249, 257, 258, 265, 266, 267, 273, 274, 276, 279, 280, 281, 283, 284, 291, 295
Shanghai (British vessel), 36
Shanghai Cotton Cloth Mill, 10, 203

Shanghai Incident, xix, 21, 132, 140, 206
Shanghai Steam Navigation Co., 103, 203
Shanhaikwan (Shanhaiguan), xxv, 12, 74, 171, 184, 209–10, 244, 295
Shantung Mining Co., 255
Sharp Peak (Chuanshi), xxix, 93
Shasi (Shashi), xxvi, 210–11, 287, 289, 291, 295
Shaw, George, 38
Shell Transport & Trading Co., 107, 110
Shen Baozhen, xxxviii, 91, 93
Sheng Xuanhuai, 11, 204
Sheppard, Eli, 56
shipping industry, 10, 38, 46, 47, 51, 54, 91, 93, 94, 103, 119, 122, 125, 128, 130, 138, 168, 169, 179, 203, 204, 211, 217, 220, 223, 241, 242, 255, 274, 284, 285, 287
Shiuhing (Zhaoqing), xxviii, 292
Shunning-fu (Fengqing), 234
Shutung (river vessel), 77
Siangtan (Xiangtan), 286
silk industry, 33, 39, 44, 45, 47, 58–59, 60, 64, 65, 70, 73, 78, 79, 83, 95, 97, 142, 147, 162, 163, 174, 197, 198, 199, 204, 211, 212, 256, 257, 258, 262, 263, 267
silver, in the Chinese economy, 2, 53, 131, 223
Sino-French War, xvii, 6, 32, 39, 92, 144, 151, 158, 164, 179, 183, 188, 228, 232, 233, 238, 274, 285
Sino-Japanese War, xvii, 1, 12, 13, 33, 39, 64, 76, 82, 95, 103, 108, 112, 118, 127, 160, 170, 184, 188, 189, 204, 209, 210, 234, 238, 247, 252, 259–60
'Small Swords', 29, 199
Song Meiling, 160
Soochow (Suzhou), xxvi, 73, 87, 97, 200, 204, 211–12, 289, 295
Soong, T. V., 140, 151
South Manchuria Railway, 37, 83, 119, 160, 290
Spanish commercial activity, 24, 68, 85, 230, 232, 273
Spence, William, 75
Ssupingkai (Siping), xxiii, 290
Standard Oil Co., 71, 73, 95, 97, 110, 139, 163, 164, 165, 173, 194, 223, 242, 248, 266, 276, 283
Stanley, Lord, xxxix, 81
steam navigation of inland waterways, xvii, 75, 76, 135, 138, 139, 211. *See also* Inland Steam Navigation Regulations; Yangtze River Regulations
stock exchanges, 131
straw braid industry, 57, 58, 59, 61, 180, 255
strike action, 48, 113, 114, 125, 128, 132, 205, 206
Stubbs, Sir Edward, 132
Suchow (Jiuquan), xxii, 289

sugar industry, 26, 28, 29, 35, 54, 130, 142, 152, 155, 166, 167, 169, 173, 181, 183, 219, 226, 227, 228
Suifenho (Suifenhe), xxiii, 289
Sullivan, George, 28
Sun Yat-sen, xi, xvii, xviii, xxxix, 12, 47–48, 128, 132, 164, 279
Swatow (Shantou), xxi, xxix, 4, 8, 11, 20, 28, 29, 30, 91, 92, 130, 142, 169, 213–23, 228, 295
Swedish missionary activity, 136
Swinhoe, Robert, 133, 226, 228, 230
Swiss commercial activity, 110
Syme, Francis, 29
Syme, Muir & Co., 27, 214
Szechuan Steam Navigation Co., 77
Szemao (Simao), xvii, xxvii, 224, 288

Tachienlu (Kangding), xxvi, 225
Taeping (British vessel), 89
Taheiho (Heihe), xxiii, 23
Taiping Rebellion, xv, xvi, 5, 6, 9, 10, 17, 23, 29, 40, 41, 68, 70, 87, 90, 91, 98, 124, 127, 137, 138, 139, 162, 168, 176–77, 199, 200–201, 211, 283
Tait & Co., 28, 31, 214, 228
Tait, James, 17, 27, 29, 30, 31, 214
Taiwan-fu (Tainan), xxix, 4, 225–29, 230, 281, 295
Takhing (Deqing), xxviii, 292
Takow (Kaohsiung), xxi, xxix, 226, 227, 228, 295
Taku (Dagu), xxv, 12, 52, 82, 89, 186, 187, 188, 200, 209, 229, 235, 238, 239, 240, 241, 242, 243, 244, 295
Takutang (Datang), 138, 139
Talai (Dalai Nuori), xxiii, 290
Talbot, R. M., 38
Talienwan (Dalianwan), xvii, 7, 52, 82, 83, 190, 253
Tamsui (Danshui), xxi, xxix, 4, 20, 30, 32, 93, 226, 230–34, 295
Tang Jingxing, xxxix, 239
Tangku (Tanggu), xxv, 239–40, 241–42, 295
Taonan, xxiii, 290
Tarbagatai (Qoqek), xxii, 288
Tashichao (Dashiqiao), xxv, 171, 290
Tatung (Datong), xxvi, 291
Tatungkow (Dadonggou), xxv, 9, 37, 289
tea industry, xvii, 4, 16, 24, 26, 27, 30, 31, 32, 33, 34, 39, 44, 45, 75, 76, 85, 87, 88, 89–90, 93, 97, 100–102, 103, 136, 137, 138, 139, 163, 180, 196, 197, 198, 199, 224, 225, 231, 233, 242, 271, 273, 283, 287, 291, 293
Tehchow (Dezhou), xxv, 290
Teichman, Sir Eric, 268

Index

telegraph industry, 10, 11, 31, 58, 93, 145, 222, 243
telephone services, 35, 46, 58, 75, 108, 119, 145
Tengchow (Penglai), 51, 64
Tengyueh (Tengchong), xxi, xxvii, 234–35
Texas Co., 110
Thom, Robert, 26, 174
Thornton Haven (Haiyang Dao), xxv
Tibet, xviii, 225, 292–93
Tiehling (Tieling), xxiii, 289
Tienhsingchiao (Tianxingqiao), xxvi, 291
Tientsin (Tianjin), xxv, 4, 6, 7, 11, 12, 15, 19, 24, 52, 54, 58, 61, 74, 75, 85, 89, 114, 129, 163, 172, 184, 185, 187, 209, 229, 235–50, 251, 254, 256, 258, 259, 265, 269, 295
timber industry, 37–38, 155, 248, 283, 284, 290
Tinghai (Dinghai), xxix, 80, 295
tobacco industry, 32, 51, 110, 142, 147, 161, 165, 173, 219, 248, 258, 266, 283
Toutaokou (Toudaogou), xxiii, 290
Tower, Sir Reginald, xxxix, 17, 276, 286–87
Trans-Siberian Railway, xvii, xviii, 102, 118, 120, 160, 190
transit passes. *See* customs arrangements
Tratman, John, 76
Tsang Chih-ping, General, 36
Tsinan Incident, 251
Tsinan (Jinan), xxv, 9, 61, 64, 157, 250–52, 255, 258, 289
Tsingtao (Qingdao), xviii, xxv, 58, 61, 65, 95, 156, 157, 195, 249, 250, 251, 252–58, 267, 270, 295
Tsining (Jining), xxv, 290
Tsitsihar (Qiqihar), xxiii, 289
Tsungli Yamen, xviii, 12, 32, 76, 91, 141, 165, 186, 238, 281, 330
Tung Wah Hospital, 126
Tunghing (Dongxing), xxvii
Tungkiangtzu (Tongjiangkou), xxiii, 289
Turfan (Turpan), xxii, 289
Twatutia (Dadaocheng), xxix, 32, 230–31, 233, 295

Uliassutai (Uliastai), xxii, 289
Union Dock Co., 278
Urga (Ulaanbaatar), xxii, xxiii, 289
Urumchi (Urumqi), xxii, 289
USS *Ashuelot* (American naval vessel), 181
USS *Panay* (American naval vessel), 208
USS *Yorktown* (American naval vessel), 64

van Lidth de Jeude, O. C. A., 62
van Straubenzee, General Sir Charles, 41

volunteer militia, foreign, 44, 47, 64, 111, 114, 115, 132, 171, 199, 200, 243
von Babo, Baron, 59
von Diederichs, Admiral Otto, 252, 253
von Hanneken, Major Constantin, 188, 259
von Richthofen, Baron Ferdinand, 252
von Tirpitz, Admiral, 252

Wade, Sir Thomas, xxxix, 63, 82, 178, 280
Wadman, E., 180
Wafangtien (Wafangdian), xxv, 290
Waichow (Weizhou), 183
Walker, James, 87
Walton, Sir Joseph, xxxix, 265
Wanhsien Incident, 258
Wanhsien (Wanxian), xxvi, 258–59
Ward, Frederick Townsend, 200–201
water supply, 32, 35, 57, 64, 75, 83, 121, 122, 190, 219, 240, 244
Watson, Major, 177, 179
Watts, Captain James, 242
Watts, James, Jr., 243
Webster, Lieutenant, 146
Weddell, Captain John, 141
Weihaiwei (Weihai), xviii, xix, xxv, 7, 34, 36, 58, 61, 64, 66, 73, 153, 188, 190, 244, 254, 259–71, 276, 295
Weihsien (Weifang), xxv, 157, 289
Wenchow (Wenzhou), xxvi, 141, 271–76, 295
West River, trade potential, xvii, 6, 9, 46, 47, 146, 154, 155, 165, 183–84, 192, 281, 282, 292
Wetmore, Williams & Co., 198
Whampoa (Huangpu), xxviii, 13, 39, 41, 82, 89, 128, 148, 155, 195, 277–79, 295
Whampoa Military Academy, 48, 279
White, James, 28
Wilkinson, E. S., 268
Williams, C. D., 226
Williams, Franklin Delano, 198
Wilson, Cornabé & Co., 53, 58
wine-making industry, 59
Wingon (Yong'an), xxviii, 292
Wolcott, Henry, 198
Woodhead, H. G. W., 245
Woosung (Wusong), xvii, xxvi, 10, 11, 200, 204, 227, 279–81
Wu Peifu, xxxix
Wuchanghsien (Wuchang), xxiii, 290
Wuchow (Wuzhou), xxi, xxvii, xxviii, 16, 147, 165, 166, 194, 281–83, 292, 295

Wuhu, xxvi, 73, 115, 283–86, 291, 295
Wusueh (Wuxue), xxvi, 291

Xingzhonghui. *See* Revive China Society
Xinhai (1911) Revolution, xviii, 21, 64, 73, 97, 111, 128, 135, 140, 163, 205, 211
Xu Guangjin, 29, 40, 87, 277

Yamato hotels, 84, 85, 161, 290
Yang-tze (British vessel), 98
Yangkiokow (Yangkou), xxv, 290
Yangtze Engineering Works Co., 111
Yangtze River Regulations, xviii, 287, 291. *See also* steam navigation of inland waterways
Yarkand (Yarkant), xxii, 136
Yatung (Yadong), xvii, xxiv, 293
Ye Mingchen, xxxix, 40
Yenchow (Yanzhou), xxv, 290
Yingtze (Yingzi), 166
Yochow (Yueyang), xvii, xxvi, 286–88
Yokohama Specie Bank, 56, 84, 85, 112, 161
Younghusband, Francis, xviii, 293
Yuan Shikai, xviii, xxxix, 47, 64, 140, 240, 244, 245, 249, 290
Yuetsing (Yuecheng), xxviii, 292
Yungki (Suixiang), xxviii, 292
Yunnan-fu (Kunming), xxi, xxvii, 66, 159, 288, 295

Zaiton, 68
Zakow (Zhakou), 97, 295
Zeng Guofan, 11, 200
Zhang Zongchang, 65
Zheng Chenggong. *See* Koxinga
Zhou Enlai, xxxix, 164
Zuo Zongtang, xxxix, 11, 91, 136